The
Historical Atlas
of
Native
Americans

A CARTOGRAPHICA PRESS BOOK

This edition published in 2009 by
Chartwell Books, Inc.
A division of Book Sales, Inc.
114 Northfield Avenue
Edison, New Jersey 08837
USA

ISBN-10: 0-7858-2332-8
ISBN-13: 978-0-7858-2332-2

QUMHANA

This book is produced by
Cartographica Press
6 Blundell Street
London N7 9BH

Production: Rohana Yusof
Editor: Sarah Stubbs

Cartography:
Cartographica Press
Red Lion Media

Printed in Singapore by
Star Standard Industries Pte Ltd.

THE HISTORICAL ATLAS
OF
NATIVE AMERICANS

DR. IAN BARNES

CHARTWELL
BOOKS, INC.

CONTENTS

CHRONOLOGY

c. 50,000–1100 BC	First peoples cross to New World from Siberia.
c. 15,000–8000 BC	Clovis spear point used.
c. 3000 BC	Caral civilization, Peru.
1500–900 BC	Olmec culture.
c. 1200 BC–AD 1450	Hohokam of Sonora.
900–200 BC	Chavin culture.
100 BC–c. 1140	Anasazi.
AD 1–750	Moche civilization, Peru.
AD 300–900	Monte Albán architecture.
AD 300–1550	Classic Maya.
AD 500–1000	Tihuanaco Empire.
AD 650–800	Huari culture.
c. AD 700–1500	Amazon civilizations.
c. AD 700–c. 1550	Mississippian chiefdoms flourish through Southeast—Adena and Hopewell predecessors.
c. AD 800–1550	Mixtec culture.
c. AD 900–1150	Toltec culture.
c. AD 985–1030	Viking contact at L'Anse aux Meadows.
c. 1000–1533	Inca Empire.
c. 1100–1450	Chimú realm.
1300–1521	Aztec Empire.
1492	Columbus arrives in the Americas.
1497–98	John and Sebastian Cabot explore eastern coastline of North America for England.
1497–1503	Amerigo Vespucci explores West Indies and South American coast for Spain.
1504	European commercial fishing begins off Newfoundland and Nova Scotia.
1520s	First epidemics of European diseases hit North America and Caribbean.
1523	Ponce de Léon opens Spanish contact with Florida.
1523–24	Giovanni da Verrazzano sails Atlantic coast from Carolinas to Newfoundland; meets Wampanoag, Narragansett, and Delaware Indians.
1528	Pánfilo de Narváez leads Spanish expedition to Gulf of Mexico.
1534–41	Jacques Cartier travels up the St. Lawrence River.
1539–43	Hernando de Soto invades the Southeast; Battle of Mabila, 1540.
1540–42	Francisco Vásquez de Coronado invades New Mexico.
1578–79	Francis Drake explores Californian coast and meets Miwoks.
1583	Spanish Franciscans establish mission chains in Florida.

1584	British settlement at Roanoke Island.
1598	Juan de Oñate establishes Spanish colony in New Mexico; siezes Acoma, 1599.
1603–15	Samuel de Champlain's voyages in the Northeast; clashes with Iroquois, 1609.
1607	British settle at Jamestown, Virginia.
1616–19	Unknown disease epidemic hits New England.
1622	Opechancanough, chief of the Powhatan Indian confederacy, attacks Virginian towns.
1633–34	Smallpox epidemic affects the Northeast.
1636–37	Pequot War; tribe destroyed by colonists and Narragansett allies.
1639–45	Kieft's War against Munsee Delaware on Manhattan Island.
1644	Powhatan Indians assault Virginia again, killing 500 settlers. Opechancanough captured and murdered while a prisoner in Jamestown.
1649	Iroquois destroy Huron villages.
1655–57	Peach War: Dutch conflict with Delaware.
1659–60	First Esopus War: Dutch-Indian conflict.
1663–64	Second Esopus War: Dutch-Indian conflict.
1675–76	King Philip's War.
1680	Pueblo Revolt.
c. 1680–c. 1750	Indians acquire horses.
1681–82	René Robert Cavelier de La Salle travels down the Mississippi; claims the Mississippi Valley (Louisiana) for Louis XIV of France.
1689–97	King William's War.
1692	Francisco de Vargas reconquers New Mexico.
1700–01	Iroquois make peace with France and Britain at Montréal.
1702–13	Queen Anne's War.
1703–04	Spanish mission system in northern Florida destroyed by British and their Indian allies.
1704	Deerfield, Massachusetts, raided by French and Indians; Connecticut attacked too.
1711–13	Tuscarora War; after defeat, many Tuscaroras flee to the Iroquois.
1711–33	French wars against Fox (Mesquakie) Indians.
1715	Yamasee War; South Carolina severely damaged; start of the Creek threat.
1716–54	Creek-Cherokee Wars.
1729–33	French-Natchez War.
1730–40s	Ojibwa-Dakota Wars.
1736, 1739–40	French-Chickasaw Wars.
1738	Smallpox kills half the Cherokees.
1741	Vitus Bering and Alexei Chirikov open Russian trade with peoples in the Gulf of Alaska.

1744	Treaty of Lancaster between Six Nations and Virginia, Pennsylvania, and Maryland.
1744–48	King George's War.
1755	General Braddock defeated on the Monongahela River by French and Indians, July 9.
1755	Battle of Lake George; Johnson defeats a French, Canadian, and Indian force, and builds Fort William Henry.
1755–63	French and Indian War.
1759–61	War between Cherokees and British colonists.
1763	Treaty of Paris gives Britain Canada and New France east of the Mississippi, except for New Orleans; Indians not consulted.
1763	Pontiac's Revolt and Proclamation of Indian Territory.
1763–76	Creek-Choctaw Wars.
1769	First Franciscan mission established in California.
1774	Lord Dunmore's War between Virginia and the Shawnee.
1776–78	Captain James Cook begins British trade with people of Northwest Pacific Coast.
1776–83	American War of Independence.
1777	Battle of Oriskany, August 6.
1778	Treaty of Fort Pitt, between Delaware and United States; first U.S.-Native American treaty.
1778	Wyoming Valley Massacre, July 3.
1778	Cherry Valley Massacre, November 11.
1779	General John Sullivan, with Clinton and Brodhead, invades Iroquoia, destroying villages and crops.
1779–83	Massive smallpox epidemic from Mexico to Canada.
1780–1800	Smallpox and measles present among Indians in Texas and New Mexico.
1782	Graddenhutten Massacre of Moravian Delaware in Pennsylvania, March.
1783	Treaty of Paris: United States' independence recognized, November 30.
1784	Russians establish settlement on Kodiak Island.
1790	General Harmar enters the Ohio Valley to punish Indians for raiding and is defeated by Miami War Chief Little Turtle, near Fort Wayne, Indiana, October 18–22.
1791	General St. Clair defeated by Little Turtle, who leads a coalition of Wyandots, Iroquois, Shawnee, Miami, Delaware, Ojibwa, and Potawatomi, November 4.
1791–93	George Vancouver trades with Indian people on Pacific Coast.
1794	General Anthony Wayne defeats northwestern tribes at Battle of Fallen Timbers in Ohio, August 20.
1795	Treaty of Greenville; most of Ohio ceded to United States by Indians, August 3.
1799	Handsome Lake religion begins among the Seneca.
1804–06	Lewis and Clark expedition up the Missouri, from St. Louis to the Pacific by way of the Columbia River.
1809	Treaty of Fort Wayne: General William H. Harrison secures 2.5 million acres (1 million hectares) from Indians in Ohio and Indiana.
1811	Battle of Tippecanoe against the Shawnee, November 7.

1813	Battle of the Thames, Ontario; Tecumseh killed, October 5.
1814	Battle of Horseshoe Bend; Jackson defeats the Creeks, March 27.
1814	Treaty of Fort Jackson with Creeks, August 9.
1816–18	First Seminole War.
1819–24	Kickapoo resistance to removal from Illinois country.
1827	Winnebago uprising.
1830	Indian Removal Act.
1832	Black Hawk War.
1835–42	Second Seminole War.
1837	Smallpox epidemic among Mandan, Hidatsa, and Arikara.
1838–39	Cherokee Trail of Tears.
1842	First significant wagon train reaches Oregon.
1847–50	Cayuse Indian war in Oregon
1849	California Gold Rush.
1850–51	Mariposa War in California between miners, Miwoks, and Yokuts.
1855–58	Third Seminole War.
1855–58	Northwestern Wars against Yakama, Rogue, and Coeur d'Alene Indians.
1861–65	American Civil War.
1861–86	Apache Wars.
1862	Santee Sioux uprising.
1864	Sand Creek Massacre.
1864	Navajo Long Walk to Bosque Redondo.
1866–68	Red Cloud's War.
1867	Treaty of Medicine Lodge.
1868	Fort Laramie Treaty.
1869	First Riel uprising in the Red River region, Canada.
1872–73	Modoc War.
1876	Rosebud Campaign.
1876	Battle of the Little Bighorn: Custer's Last Stand, June 25.
1877	Chief Joseph and his Nez Perce band head for Canada.
1879	Second Riel rebellion in Canada.
1887	General Allotment Act (Dawes).
1890	Wounded Knee Massacre, December 29.
1907	Oklahoma State created.
1911	Society of American Indians formed.
1914–18	World War I.
1918	Native American Church incorporated in Oklahoma.
1924	Citizenship Act confers U.S. citizenship on Indians not already citizens.
1934	Indian Reorganization Act.
1939–45	World War II.
1958	3,000 Lumbees in North Carolina drive out Ku Klux Klan rally.
1961	National Indian Youth Council founded.
1968	American Indian Movement created.
1973	Wounded Knee Massacre site seized by Indian activists.
1977	Inuit Circumpolar Conference established.
1978	American Indian Religious Freedom Act.
1990	Native American Graves Protection and Repatriation Act.

MAP LIST

INTRODUCTION

"I beheld too, in that vision
All the secrets of the future
Of the distant days that shall be
I beheld the westward marches
Of the unknown, crowded nations
All the land was full of people,
Restless, struggling, toiling, striving,
Speaking many tongues, yet feeling
But one heart-beat in their bosoms
In the woodlands rain their axes,
Smoking their towns in all the valleys,
Over all the lakes and rivers
Rushed their great canoes of thunder."

Hiawatha,
Henry Wadsworth Longfellow (1807–82)

Hiawatha and Minnehaha, an illustration by Harold Copping for Doris Ashley's book, *Children's Stories from Longfellow*. The poem, and artwork such as this, were instrumental in reinforcing the romantic image of the "noble savage."

Any attempt to understand Native American history is normally bedeviled by images forced upon the public by films and television. Stereotypes abound—the Indian is depicted as a romantic, noble savage or a vicious, blood-soaked, scalping animal, hell-bent on rape and murder. Few people remember that the Japanese samurai and the Celts of Britain collected heads as trophies. Jay Silverheels, a Mohawk, played Tonto, the loyal Indian, in the *The Lone Ranger* TV show (1956). Since then, this classic vision has changed, new film portrayals setting the record straighter or questioning past perceptions. *Soldier Blue* (1970), *A Man Called Horse* (1970), and *Dances with Wolves* (1990) portrayed Native Americans more sympathetically. However, many Indian actors have been cast in the familiar role of the past, such as Chief Dan George (Salish) in *The Outlaw Josie Wales* (1976), or Native Americans have been played by non-natives. A turning point was the film *Smoke Signals* (1998). This was the first ever film written and directed by Indians, the two leading actors being Native American too. Written by Sherman Alexie (Spokane/Coeur d'Alene) and directed by Chris Eyre (Cheyenne/Arapaho), this road movie starred Evan Adams (Coast Salish) and Adam Beach (Saulteaux, or Ojibwa) as two young Indian men traveling from Idaho to Arizona to collect the ashes of Beach's deceased alcoholic father.

Other lesser-known, more accurate images are presented in Christian F. Feest's book, *The Cultures of Native North Americans* (Konemann, 2000). A Tlingit warrior in full wooden armor is shown on a Southeast Alaska Corporation advertising poster. Menesk, a chief of the Tsimshian Nisga'a tribe of British Columbia is depicted wearing a dance blanket, but is remarkable for his full gray beard and mustache. An 1882 photograph shows Chasi, son of Bonito, a Warm Springs Apache, using an Apache fiddle, the only stringed instrument of indigenous America. Senator Ben Nighthorse Campbell (Cheyenne) is pictured riding, in full Indian apparel, at the Tournament of Roses parade in Pasadena, Florida (1993). He was co-leader with a visiting Spanish duke, but insisted on riding ahead because Native Americans were present before the Spaniards. He repeated his ride on January 20, 1993, at the inaugural parade of President Bill Clinton.

Boundaries of consciousness require redefining, and archaeology pushes back the limits of recorded history, both in North and South America. Southern Oregon University's Laboratory of Anthropology, in partnership with Oregon State University and the Southern Oregon Historical Society, has implemented a public archaeology project at the site of Fort Lane in Jackson County. Fort Lane was built in 1853 as one of four posts constructed to protect the Indians in southern Oregon, following the discovery of gold, which led to a large influx of miners and settlers. The whites seemed intent on ethnic cleansing, and the U.S. Army was prepared to use force to stop the genocide. A contemporary report proposed placing the Indians on a reservation to ensure their survival. Captain Andrew Jackson Smith, in command of the fort, actually informed local whites that their plan to attack the reservation would result in conflict with the U.S. Army. Even so, skirmishes broke out between Takelma, Latgawa, Shasta, and Athabaskan peoples, and gold miners and other pioneers. An Indian village was attacked and its inhabitants massacred by a citizen militia led by James Lupton, recently elected southwest Oregon's representative to the territorial legislature. Some Indians moved to the 3,000-square mile (8,000-square kilometer) Table Rock Reservation, trusting in the protection of Fort Lane, where two companies of the U.S. Army's 1st Dragoons were stationed. Other local Indians started the Rogue River War, Chiefs Tecumtum and Cholcultah leading their warriors down the river, torching cabins and killing settlers.

The Army's commitment to Fort Lane was considerable, since its supplies had to be dispatched from Benecia, California, by boat to Crescent City, and then overland by pack train through the Applegate Valley. Brevet Major-General John Wool, commander of the Army of the West, and Oregon Superintendent of Indian Affairs Joel Palmer led a force to round up the insurgent Indians during 1855–56. They were marched or shipped to the Grane Ronde and Siletz Agencies on the Coast Reservation, which eventually became home to the Takelma, Latgawa, Athabaskan, Tatutni, Coos, Coquille, and Umpqua peoples of southwest Oregon. Meanwhile, Wool incurred the anger of the Rogue River settlers by condemning the aggression of citizen militias and promoting the rights of Indians. These events provide a qualification to normal generalizations concerning Native American-U.S. Army relations.

Elsewhere, archaeological evidence shows that the Amazon basin supported more than scattered populations of hunter-gatherers. This flies in the face of arguments that the Amazon had an inadequate soil base for the existence of sophisticated urban communities. Some people managed their crops so successfully that the sites of their settlements are marked by a dark, rich soil, a veritable compost heap, which punctuates the normal, orange, sandy, forest soil. It is thought that there might even have been plazas. However, one century after the arrival of the Portuguese, these stone-age chiefdoms had vanished.

Although firearms were prevalent among the Plains tribes during the second half of the nineteenth century, simpler weapons had not been abandoned. This Sioux war club from Pine Ridge, South Dakota, dates from around 1880 and has a beautifully carved chert head.

Archaeologist Clark L. Erickson, of the University of Pennsylvania, argues that the prehispanic peoples of the Amazon constructed an anthropogenic landscape through building raised fields, large settlement mounds, and causeways. Complexes of fish weirs and ponds could have produced vast quantities of fish and edible snails. An anthropologist, Michael J. Heckenberger, of the University of Florida, has identified nineteen villages in the Upper Xingu River region, all connected by roads and likely to have had populations of between 2,500 and 5,000 people each. Heckenberger cooperated with local native chiefs and a team from the Universidade Federal do Rio de Janeiro in uncovering these sites. He thinks that the settlements date to between 1200 and 1600. He says that all the villages were constructed and laid out in a common fashion, and that the roads were mathematically parallel. In places, some of these roads are 165 feet (50 meters) wide. Heckenberger believes that the roads and village plazas were versions of monuments found elsewhere, the astronomical and mathematical knowledge necessary for their construction being on a par with that needed to build the Mayan pyramids. He said, "Everyone loves the 'lost civilization in the Amazon' story. What the Upper Xingu and middle Amazon stuff shows us is that Amazon people organized in an alternative way to urbanization. We shouldn't be expecting to find lost cities. But that doesn't mean they were primitive tribes, either." Thus, more assumptions about Native Americans are disproved, because sophisticated civilizations did exist in the Amazon basin.

Elsewhere, archaeological finds are pushing back the dates of human occupation. The discovery of Caral, in the Supe Valley of Peru, and its exploration by Ruth Shady uncovered some nineteen pyramid complexes, while there are seventeen other sites in the Supe Valley. Dating back to at least 2627 BC, Caral is thought to be the mother city of the Inca civilization by Shady. The Caral communities probably traded as far as the Amazon. Archaeologist Jonathan Haas pointed out the lack of fortifications and weapons, and he believes, as does Shady, that Caral's existence was based upon trade. Wealth allowed the city of pyramids to be built, and the civilization survived without war. Shady said, "Caral was the first city with the first central government. Caral changes all our current thinking about the origins of civilization." The inhabitants of Caral experienced a thousand years of peace, suggesting that our civilizations were not always created by battle and warfare, as normally thought.

The Native American experience has impacted upon the rest of the world in the fields of agriculture, food, and medicine. Medically speaking, the Amazon rainforest is a cornucopia of delights, and its destruction could limit medical advances, since more exploration for new drugs is required there. The Incas used quinine, which can cure malaria, cramps, chills, and arhythmic problems. Ipecac can be used to treat amebic dysentery and to induce vomiting to remove poisonous foods. Curare, a toxin applied to arrow tips, is a muscle relaxant and can be utilized in abdominal surgery. Coca produces cocaine, which can be synthesized into novocaine, an important anesthetic. Occasionally, Indians employed foxglove (*Digitalis purpurea*) to treat heart conditions. Aztec medical knowledge was so vast that Spain's King Philip II ordered Francisco Hernando to record it.

Herbal remedies soon began to be used by European settlers, and Swedish botanist Peter Kalm traveled to the Middle Atlantic states (1748–50) to document Indian medicinal herbs. Among the most common remedies was witch hazel, used to treat insect bites and cuts. Leaves and roots of wintergreen contain methyl salicylate, which was utilized in various ways to alleviate rheumatic pain and muscular aches. Salicylate acid is the main component of aspirin. Northern Californian and Oregon Native Americans used the bark of cascara, Californian buckthorn, to cure constipation. Today, cascara is the most commonly known laxative, having been introduced commercially in the American pharmaceutical industry in 1878.

The paramount Native American influence lies in the types of food exported to the world. Maize, in all its colors, is now cultivated worldwide. In Africa, it has become a staple food, together with beans, peanuts, and cassava, allowing the population to survive and grow, despite the depredations of slavery. The introduction of the potato from Bolivia and Peru into Ireland and Russia permitted agriculture on really poor soil, but its monoculture in Ireland and four-year potato blight infestation, from 1845, caused mass starvation and around a million deaths. In Asia, *aloo sag* (potato and spinach) is a well-known dish, while maize and sweet potato have allowed marginal land to be brought into cultivation. Where would Mediterranean cuisine be without tomatoes and peppers? Other common Native American foods are pumpkin, squash, chocolate, vanilla, papaya, persimmon, pecan, chilli, sunflower seed, maple syrup, tapioca, avocado, pineapple, turkey, cranberry, cucumber, blueberry, asparagus, and mint.

So, Native Americans provide the historian and cartographer with an ever growing knowledge, while Indian society, with its medicine, agriculture, and food, has stocked world larders. This atlas maps the story of the Native Americans in all its glory, violence, and sadness.

Settling the Hemisphere shows how early peoples crossed into the Americas via Beringia, and gives examples of how some nations saw their own origins, such as the tale of She Who Fell From The Sky. The domestication of plants and agriculture provided the backbone of early civilizations in Central and South America, such as the Maya, Aztec, and Inca. Most Europeans, however, possess scant knowledge of Mississippian society, the Hohokam, and the Anasazi, despite the remarkable edifices and buildings they constructed. Maps show the complex communication and transport systems that developed, while the text explores linguistic diversity, kinship, and societal patterns, especially the importance achieved by women.

First Contacts depicts Native American society on the eve of European contact. Viking encounters are explained, as are the huge industrial fishing enterprises mounted by the Basques, Normans, and Bretons, inveterate explorers and maritime risk takers. Columbus assumes his normal place, while the tales of DeLeon, Narvaez, and Cabeza de Vaca provide an overture to the savage, aggressive, and extreme cruelty of De Soto's *entrada*, and his disgraceful behavior toward Indians. The French efforts to explore the St.

Native American headdress worn by a ceremonial dancer at the Buffalo Nations Event in support of the the American bison.

An example of pictograph rock art, Navajo images show the arrival of Spaniards on horseback.

Lawrence with limited colonization are set against the 1607 British settlement at Jamestown. Whether French, British, or Spanish, the Europeans introduced new diseases that severely depleted indigenous populations. They also brought the horse, which ultimately changed some tribes' cultural and economic patterns.

Allies and Subjects: Indians in the Colonial World demonstrates the result of European-Native American relationships, which often were of a warlike nature. The struggle to control the flow of European trade goods tipped the Iroquois into a war with the Wyandot (Huron), a type of trade war that developed elsewhere between other tribes. Jamestown, with its tobacco-based agriculture, fought the Powhatan Confederacy. This British settlement is also notorious for importing African slaves. The Pequot War and King Philip's War severely damaged Indian population figures, some tribes experiencing mass enslavement. The Dutch and the Spanish experiences were similar, with messy skirmishes around New Amsterdam and the incredibly successful Pueblo Revolt, which rocked the Spanish establishment and ego. The Peace at Montréal in 1701 ended Iroquois depredations and trade wars, the Haudenosaunee promising neutrality in any future Anglo-French colonial wars.

Native Americans in Imperial Wars shows the fate of Indians torn between the policies of the imperial powers, which sometimes incited conflict between tribes when one power attempted to gain allies or prevent another power from winning friends. The civilized tribes—Creek, Choctaw, Chickasaw, and Cherokee—suffered greatly, while the socially interesting Natchez were virtually wiped out by the French. Warfare between the Ojibwa and Lakota is examined, as is the confusion and violence caused by northern Indians—Comanche and Apache—moving south. The Seven Years' War demonstrated the dangers of alliances with whites, admirably shown by the failure of the 1763 Proclamation Line, which colonial governments failed to police. White settlers encroached upon Indian hunting grounds, and land cessions were forced from such tribes as the Shawnee.

Native Americans in an Age of Revolution examines how the Indian nations responded to the American War of Independence. Employed by both the British and Americans, Native Americans made alliances with the combatants in the hope that, as a reward, they would be allowed to keep their lands without fear of further incursions by white settlers. The Treaty of Paris, which ended the conflict, ignored Indian interests, however, and the new republic began expanding rapidly westward into the Ohio Valley. There, various tribal confederations sought to stem the flow, but the efforts of Little Turtle and Tecumseh ended in failure. Matters were not improved when President Jefferson sent Meriwether Lewis and William Clark to explore westward, which helped open up the Northwest to settlement;

previously, the area had been penetrated only by fur hunters and traders, often connected to the Hudson's Bay Company.

American Nations, 1815–65 continues the tale of relentless white pressure. As European economies faced a temporary decline, migrants poured into North America, especially from the British Isles. Removals to reservations took place in the Midwest and Southeast. The civilized nations inhabited villages with European-style farms and dwellings, while the Cherokee Sequoyah had constructed a syllabary used in a Native American newspaper. Nevertheless, the Cherokee were removed, being forced to follow the Trail of Tears, an illegal act, since the Supreme Court had found in favor of the Cherokee. This fact was ignored by President Jackson, an impeachable offense under the Constitution. Black Hawk, a Sauk chief, fought against migrants, but his war was doomed in the face of increasing numbers of Americans moving westward, seeking land, gold, and furs. This relentless migration led to the extinction of several Californian tribes. Resistance by the Apache and Northwestern tribes was in vain.

Conquest, 1865–1900 illustrates the constant fight back by the Native Americans on the Plains, and in the mountains and deserts of the West, which had disastrous results for the Navajo, Nez Perce, Sioux, and Cheyenne. Even the slaughter of Custer and his troops at the Little Bighorn achieved nothing. Forts and reservations confined Native Americans, and eventually even Indian Territory was taken from them by the birth of the state of Oklahoma.

Survival and Renaissance, 1900–2002 portrays the development of tribal economic enterprises, the Native American contribution to America's wars, and the birth of Indian political activism. A growth in the Native American population has coincided with its participation in the professions, politics, the arts, and education. As Native American standards of living rise, there is hope that general poverty and ill health among Indians will decline, and that they will reacquire status in their own land.

The remaining adobe walls of Citadel Pueblo in Wupatki National Monument, Arizona. Built around AD 1100 by the Anasazi, the fortress-like structure stands on a bluff overlooking the surrounding countryside.

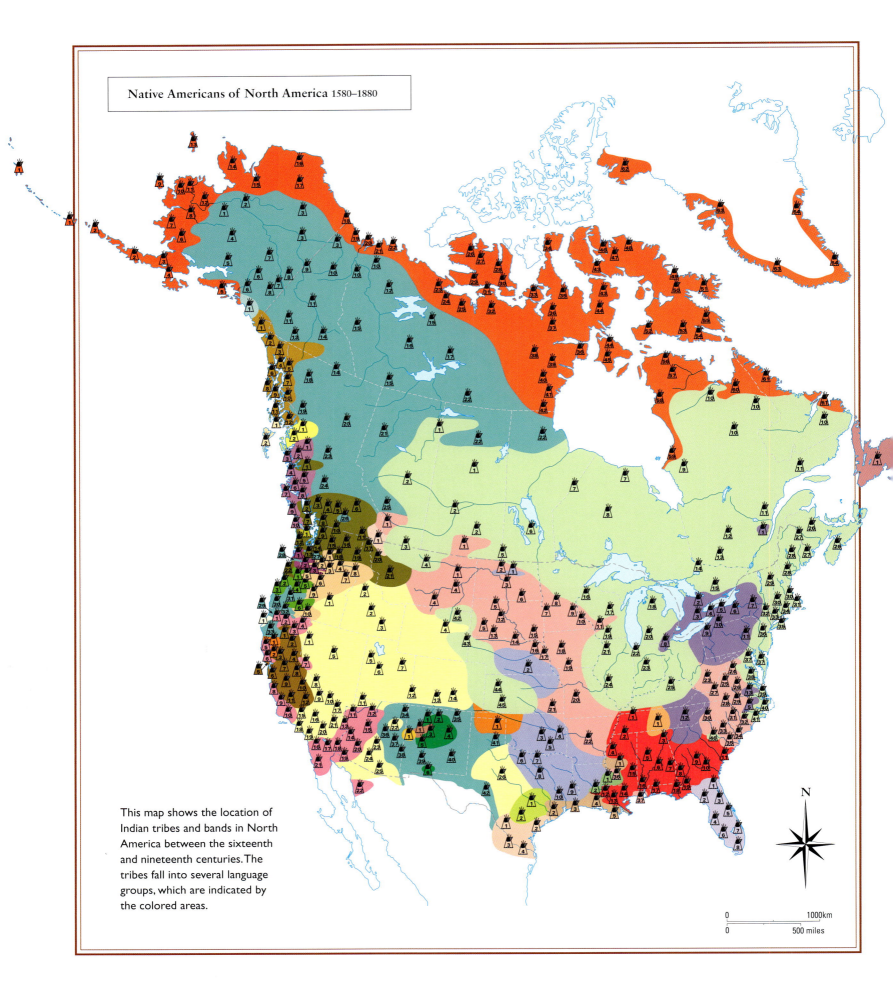

Native Americans of North America 1580–1880

This map shows the location of Indian tribes and bands in North America between the sixteenth and nineteenth centuries. The tribes fall into several language groups, which are indicated by the colored areas.

N

Native Americans of North America 1580–1880

Algonkian

1 Woods Cree
2 Plains Cree
3 Blackfeet
4 Atsina (Gros Ventre)
5 Plains Ojibwa (Bungi)
6 Saulteaux
7 Swampy Cree (Westmain Cree)
8 Northern Ojibwa
9 East Cree (Eastmain Cree)
10 Nascapi
11 Montagnais
12 Tetes du Boule (Attikamek)
13 Algonkin
14 Nipissing
15 Mississauga
16 Chippewa (Southern Ojibwa)
17 Menomini
18 Ottawa
19 Fox
    Sauk
20 Mascouten
21 Kickapoo
22 Potawatomi
23 Miami-Wea
24 Illini-Peoria
25 Shawnee
26 Micmac
27 Malecite-Passamaquoddy
28 Eastern Abenaki-Penobscot
29 Western Abenaki-Sokoki
30 Massachusett-Nipmuc
31 Wampanoag-Nauset
32 Mahican (Mohican) Wapping (Wappinger)
33 Southern New England (Quiripi)-Paugussett,
    Quinnipiac, Tunxis
34 Mohegan-Pequot
    Narraganset-Niantic
35 Eastern Long Island (Unquachog)-Shinnecock,
    Poosepatuck, Montauk
36 Delaware-Munsee, Unami
37 Nanticoke-Conoy
38 Powhatan-Pamunkey, Mattapony, Chickahominy,
    Nansemond, Potomac, Rappahannock
39 Chowanoc, Weapemeoc
40 Hatteras, Machapunga, Pamlico
41 Coree
42 Northern Cheyenne
43 Northern Arapaho
44 Southern Cheyenne
45 Southern Arapaho
46 Saluda

Athabascan

1 Ingalik – Holikachuk
2 Koyukon
3 Kutchin
4 Kolchan
5 Tanaina
6 Ahtena
7 Tanana
8 Nabesna
9 Han
10 Kutchin
11 Tutchone
12 Hare
13 Tagish
14 Kaska – Pelly River
15 Slavey
16 Dogrib
17 Yellowknife
18 Tahltan
19 Tsetsaut
20 Sekani
21 Beaver
22 Chipewyan
23 Carrier
24 Chilcotin
25 Sarsi
26 Nicola
27 Kwalhioqua
28 Clatskanie
29 Tolowa
30 Chetco, Galice Creek, Tututni
31 Umpqua, Upper Coquille
32 Applegate Creek, Chastacosta
33 Chilula, Hupa, Kato, Lassik, Mattole,
    Nongatl, Sinkyone, Wailaki, Whilkut
34 Navajo
35 Jicarilla Apache
36 Tonto – Northern & Southern
37 Cibecue
38 Western Apache, White Mountain
39 Chiricahua Apache
40 Mescalero Apache
41 Kiowa Apache
42 Lipan

Beothuk

1 Beothuk

Caddoan

1 Arikara
2 Pawnee
3 Yscani
4 Tawehash
5 Wichita
6 Kichai or Kitsai
7 Waco
8 Tawakoni
9 Adia, Eyeish, Kadohadacho, Natchitoches
10 Hasinai

California Penutian

1 Nomlaki, Wintu, Wintun
2 Konkow, Maidu
3 Patwin, Plains Miwok
4 Nisenan, Northern Miwok
5 Coast Miwok
6 Costano
7 Central Miwok
8 Southern Miwok
9 Northern Valley Yokuts
10 Chukchansi, Foothills Yokuts, Kings River
11 Southern Valley Yokuts, Tachi
12 Kaweah River, Poso Creek, Tule River

Chimakum

1 Chimakum, Quileute, Hoh

Chinook

1 Cathlamet, Chinook, Clatsop
2 Cathlapotle, Chilluckittequaw, Clackamas
   Clowwewalla, Multnomah, Skilloot, Watlala
3 Wasco, Wishram

Coahuiltecan

1 Coahuilteco
2 Karankawa
3 Borrado
4 Comecrudo, Cotoname

Native Americans of North America 1580–1880

Eskimo Aleut

1 Atka
2 Unalaska
3 Aglemiut
4 Kaniagmiut
5 Chugachigmiut
6 Nushagamiut
7 Togiamiut
8 Kuskwogmiut
9 Nunivagiut
10 Kalaligmiut
11 Magemiut
12 Ikogmiut
13 St. Lawerence Island Eskimo
14 Bering Strait Eskimo
15 Kotzebue Eskimo
16 North Alaskan Eskimo
17 Northern Interior Eskimo
18 Kigirktayuk
19 Kigirktarugmmiut
19 Kupugmiut
20 Novorugmiut
21 Kittegaryumiut
22 Avvagmiut
23 Nuvungmiut
24 Kogluktomuit
24 Agiarmiut
25 Kilsusktormiut
26 Kanghiryuatjagmiut
27 Kanghiryuarmiut
28 Copper Eskimo
29 Nagjuktormiut
   Puivilirmiut
30 Ikaluktukmiut
31 Ahiarmiut
32 Umingmaktormiut
33 Giqiqtarmiut
34 Arviqtuurmiut
35 Netsilingmiut
36 Netsilik Eskimo
37 Utkuhikhalingmiut
38 Caribou Eskimo
39 Qairnirmiut
40 Harvaqtuurmiut
41 Padlimiut
42 Ahiarmiut
43 Iglulik Eskimo
44 Aivilingmiut
45 Sadlermiut
46 Tununirmiut
47 Tununirusirmiut
48 Akudnirmiut
49 Padlimiut
50 Baffin Island Eskimo
51 Oqomuit
52 Sikosuilarmuit
53 Akuliarmiut
54 Qaumauangmiut
55 Nugumiut
56 Tarramiut
57 Eskimo of Quebec
58 Itivimiut
59 Qikirmuit
60 Siqinirmuit
61 Labrador Eskimo
62 Polar Eskimo
63 West Greenland Eskimo
64 East Greenland Eskimo

Eyak

1 Eyak

Keres

1 Keres

Kiowa

1 Kiowa

Kutenai

1 Kutenai

Muskogian

1 Kaskinampo
2 Chickasaw
3 Koasati
4 Chakchiuma, Ibitoupa, Taposa
5 Napochi
6 Alabama
7 Apalachicola, Muklasa, Tuskegee
8 Muskogee, Sawokli
9 Chiaha, Oconee, Okmulgee
10 Hitchiti, Yamasee, Tamathli
11 Cusabo
12 Okelousa, Houma
13 Bayogoula, Quinipissa, Tangipahoa
14 Acolapissa
15 Choctaw
16 Mobile, Pascagoula, Tohome
17 Pensacola
18 Apalachee, Chatot
19 Osochi

Natchez

1 Natchez, Taensa
2 Avoyel

Oregon Penutian

1 Atfalati, Lakmiut, Yamel
2 Alsea, Kuitsh, Siuslaw, Yaquina
3 Coos or Hanis, Miluk
4 Calapodya, Chelamela, Yoncalla
5 Marys River
6 Latgawa, Takelma

Salishan

1 Bellacoola
2 Comox, Puntlatch
3 Seechelt
4 Lillooet, Squawmish
5 Thompson
6 Shuswap
7 Cowichan, Nanaimo, Songish
8 Lummi, Semiahmoo, Stalo
9 Chelan, Nooksack, Samish, Skagit
   Snohomish, Suquamish, Swallah, Swinomish
10 Methow, Okanagan
11 Senijextee (Lakes)
12 Clallam, Copalis, Humptulips, Queets,
Quinault
   Satsop, Skokomish, Twana, Wynoochee
13 Cowlitz, Lower Chehalis, Upper Chehalis
14 Duwamish, Muckleshoot, Nisqually, Puyallup
   Skyomish, Snoqualmie, Squaxon
15 Columbia, Wenatchee
16 Colville, Nespelem, Sanpoil, Sinkakaius, Spokan
17 Lower Kalispel
18 Moses - Columbia
19 Coeur d'Alene
20 Upper Kalispel
21 Flathead

Native Americans of North America 1580–1880

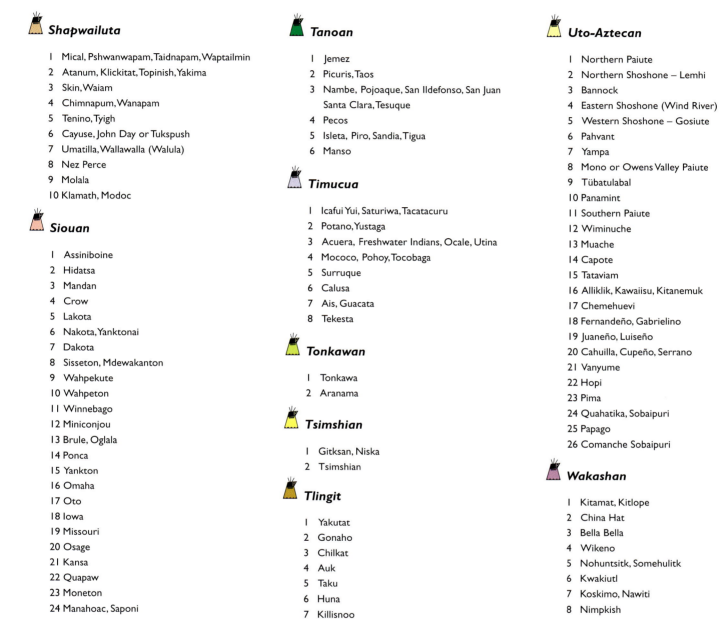

Shapwailuta

1 Mical, Pshwanwapam, Taidnapam, Waptailmin
2 Atanum, Klickitat, Topinish, Yakima
3 Skin, Waiam
4 Chimnapum, Wanapam
5 Tenino, Tyigh
6 Cayuse, John Day or Tukspush
7 Umatilla, Wallawalla (Walula)
8 Nez Perce
9 Molala
10 Klamath, Modoc

Siouan

1 Assiniboine
2 Hidatsa
3 Mandan
4 Crow
5 Lakota
6 Nakota, Yanktonai
7 Dakota
8 Sisseton, Mdewakanton
9 Wahpekute
10 Wahpeton
11 Winnebago
12 Miniconjou
13 Brule, Oglala
14 Ponca
15 Yankton
16 Omaha
17 Oto
18 Iowa
19 Missouri
20 Osage
21 Kansa
22 Quapaw
23 Moneton
24 Manahoac, Saponi
25 Nahyssan
26 Monacan
27 Tutelo
28 Eno - Adshusheer, Occaneechi
29 Shakori, Shoccoree
30 Cheraw - Yadkin
31 Keyauwee, Sissipahaw, Sugaree, Waxhaw, Woccon
32 Cape Fear
33 Catawba, Congaree, Wateree
34 Pedee, Waccamaw, Winyaw
35 Santee, Sewee
36 Ofo
37 Biloxi-Moctobi

Tanoan

1 Jemez
2 Picuris, Taos
3 Nambe, Pojoaque, San Ildefonso, San Juan Santa Clara, Tesuque
4 Pecos
5 Isleta, Piro, Sandia, Tigua
6 Manso

Timucua

1 Icafui Yui, Saturiwa, Tacatacuru
2 Potano, Yustaga
3 Acuera, Freshwater Indians, Ocale, Utina
4 Mococo, Pohoy, Tocobaga
5 Surruque
6 Calusa
7 Ais, Guacata
8 Tekesta

Tonkawan

1 Tonkawa
2 Aranama

Tsimshian

1 Gitksan, Niska
2 Tsimshian

Tlingit

1 Yakutat
2 Gonaho
3 Chilkat
4 Auk
5 Taku
6 Huna
7 Killisnoo
8 Sitka
9 Kake
10 Stikine
11 Henya, Klawak, Kuju
12 Sanya, Tongas

Tunican

1 Grigra, Koroa, Tiou, Tunica, Yazoo
2 Akokisa, Bidai
3 Atakapa
4 Chitimacha, Opelousa
5 Chawasha Washa

Uto-Aztecan

1 Northern Paiute
2 Northern Shoshone – Lemhi
3 Bannock
4 Eastern Shoshone (Wind River)
5 Western Shoshone – Gosiute
6 Pahvant
7 Yampa
8 Mono or Owens Valley Paiute
9 Tübatulabal
10 Panamint
11 Southern Paiute
12 Wiminuche
13 Muache
14 Capote
15 Tataviam
16 Alliklik, Kawaiisu, Kitanemuk
17 Chemehuevi
18 Fernandeño, Gabrielino
19 Juaneño, Luiseño
20 Cahuilla, Cupeño, Serrano
21 Vanyume
22 Hopi
23 Pima
24 Quahatika, Sobaipuri
25 Papago
26 Comanche Sobaipuri

Wakashan

1 Kitamat, Kitlope
2 China Hat
3 Bella Bella
4 Wikeno
5 Nohuntsitk, Somehulitk
6 Kwakiutl
7 Koskimo, Nawiti
8 Nimpkish
9 Nootka
10 Makah, Ozette

Yuchi

1 Yuchi

Yuki

1 Coast Yuki, Huchnom, Yuki
2 Lile'ek, Wappo

Zuni

1 Zuni

SETTLING THE HEMISPHERE

"WHEN WE SAW SO MANY CITIES AND VILLAGES BUILT BOTH ON THE WATER AND DRY LAND ... WE COULD NOT RESIST OUR ADMIRATION ... BECAUSE OF THE HIGH TOWERS, CUES (PYRAMIDS) AND OTHER BUILDINGS, ALL OF MASONRY, WHICH ROSE FROM THE WATER. SOME OF OUR SOLDIERS ASKED IF (IT) WAS A DREAM."
BERNAL DIAZ, WITH CORTES, VIEWING TENOCHTITLAN IN 1519.

Recent archaeological finds have forced historians to reassess the past in South America. The various Mississippian mound civilizations in North America are well known, as are the Hohokam and the Anasazi cultures. Olmec, Maya, Zapotec, Teotihuacan, Toltec, and Aztec cultures of Mesoamerica are likewise well documented. This area, which covered southeast Mexico, Guatemala, Belize, El Salvador, and parts of Honduras, Nicaragua, and Costa Rica, was a region of cultural interaction despite differences in topography that range from volcanic heights to coastal plains, and humid rainforest to dry northern deserts. The ethnic jigsaw of the area borrowed ideas and designs from its several components in complex sequential, and parallel social and political developments. Monumental architecture, building design, and urbanization characterize Mesoamerica. Human sacrifice coexisted with sophisticated astronomical observations and hieroglyphic writing.

Similarly, the various Andean civilizations are well known: Chavin, Moche, Huari, Chimu, and Inca. However, new archaeological finds show that historians still have much to uncover.

New discoveries at Huanca de la Luna, a citadel at the heart of the Moche empire, led Santiago Uceda, director of the Museum of Trujillo, to state, "We believe we have come across the legacy of what can be called the earliest and most sophisticated of the pre-Columbian peoples." However, an

archaeological dig at Caral in the Supe Valley, 120 miles (193 kilometers) north of Lima, uncovered a number of sites dating back to 2670 BC. Other mysteries are unfolding elsewhere according to an exhibition on Amazonian civilization at the British Museum. Furthermore, over 153 square miles (500 square kilometers) of artificial earthworks, identified as fish weirs, have been uncovered by Dr. Clark L. Erickson of the University of Pennsylvania. These are situated at Baures in the eastern lowlands of Bolivia, known as the Llanos de Mojos.

Firstly, Caral. The site occupies a 150–170-acre (60–70-hectare) site comprising six platform mounds surrounding a huge plaza. The largest mound is 500 feet (150 meters) long, 450 feet (140 meters) wide, and 60 feet (20 meters) tall. The architecture has courtyards, rooms, and sunken plazas, suggesting a ritual center. Symmetrical staircases exist, and there is a residential area consisting of 110 acres (45 hectares). Caral is as large as any other world third-millennium site, excluding Sumeria. The carbon dating suggests that Caral arose at the same time as ancient Egypt and Sumer. Caral is so old that it might be called "the mother city," which fed all later Andean civilizations up to the Incas. The buildings show no sign of there being kings, but some class society probably developed to organize the monumental architecture. The mounds and sunken plazas are found frequently in younger South American sites. Caral is important

The ancient city of Caral in the Supe Valley, Peru. In the foreground are the temple and amphitheater, while in the background, several pyramids wait to give up their secrets. This amazing site is providing archaeologists with a new insight into South American peoples.

A mural depicting a Moche decapitator, discovered at Huaca de la Luna, Peru.

because of its size and nearby contemporary sites suggesting a large population in the Supe Valley. Caral itself might have housed as many as 3,000 people.

The Supe Valley is easy to irrigate, which may account for Caral's location. Agriculture produced squash, beans, and cotton. Remains of guava, peppers, avocados, and potatoes have been unearthed too. However, the civilization was pre-ceramic, and neither pottery nor grain have been found, suggesting that Caral was economically different to later civilizations. Instead, anchovy and sardine traces have been discovered in desiccated human feces.

Apparently, cotton was traded with coastal dwellers in exchange for fish and clams. The cotton would be woven into fishing nets. Evidence suggests that Caral was a trading center based upon an early division of labor. Caral supports the theories of archaeologist Michael Moseley, who argued that complex societies evolved first in coastal areas; the orthodox view is that civilizations did not arise until the ceramic period allowed grain cultivation, and seeds to be cooked and stored in pottery vessels. Mollusc shells from the Amazonian rainforests are present, and in one sunken plaza, capable of holding hundreds of people, were found thirty-two flutes made from pelican and condor bones, and thirty-seven cornets carved from deer and llama bones.

Much of Caral is still buried, and some archaeologists think that the Supe culture could be older than 3000 BC. Caral arose at the same time as Middle Eastern civilizations in a parallel development of class societies emerging from tribal ones. Interestingly, no weapons have been found at Caral. Jonathan Haas, curator of anthropology at the Field Museum of Natural History in Chicago, claims, "What we are learning from Caral is going to rewrite the way we think about the development of early Andean civilization."

The desert empire of the Moche flourished on Peru's northern coast from approximately AD 1 to 750. Early Moche developed in the coastal valleys around Trujillo, and by AD 400 reached from Chira Valley in the north to the Huarney Valley in the south. About 15,000 Moche inhabited the civilization, and they built monumental adobe structures, irrigation canals, and terraced fields. The Pyramid of the Sun (Huaca del Sol) is 131 feet (40 meters) high and some 1,148 feet (350 meters) long. Moche artisans wrought fine gold, silver, and copper artifacts, while ceramics often involved stirrup-spout vessels.

Moche religion involved art and iconography, which was painted on walls and illustrated ceremonial sacrifices. Ritual coca leaf chewing is depicted, as are battle scenes and the victims of beheading. The major god of the Moche had feline canines and a belt with snake heads. Moche civilization ended perhaps due to inundations by a sand sheet or an abrupt climatic change, like those associated with El Niño, the warm-water currents from the Pacific that bring raised temperatures and torrential rain. In

1996, the remains of seventy men, women, and children were found in a mass grave; this may have been a ritual killing by priests to appease the rain gods.

Moche finds suggest that Mexican Aztecs, Peruvian Incas, and Guatemalan Mayas were no more advanced than the Moche. Santiago Uceda's archaeologists began digging a new pyramid-citadel at Sipan and, after two years, they unearthed walls decorated with geometric figures, ornate jewelry, gold, and cloaks studded with precious stones. Sixty plates, vases, and jars used in funeral rites were found. Other aspects of moche life were displayed. The tombs of three warriors were opened, and their inhabitants were at least 6 feet (2 meters) tall, whereas the average height of a Moche man was between 4 feet 9 inches and 5 feet 7 inches (1.45 and 1.70 meters). Apparently, elite tall warriors were chosen to fight ritually while being revered as deities. The loser was killed, and the victor given the right to wear a cloak made from puma hides, decorated with feathers, emeralds, other precious stones, and gold shields. The greatest warriors could wear bat masks. The Moche also ate human flesh and drank the victim's blood, mixed with rainwater, to prolong life. Murals display a warrior with the title, "Ai-Apaec" (Strangler), who was always present when priests beheaded and cut up human bodies as offerings to the gods.

The third archaeological development has been the recent assessment of the landscape in the Llanos de Mojos. There, one can find the apparent remains of transportation canals, pyramid-style mounds, elevated causeways, raised agricultural fields, and groups of unusual, zigzag ridges dispersed over the savannah. Several contemporary researchers, among them Clark Erickson, believe these

The Court of the Thousand Columns at Chichén Itzá, in the Yucatan Peninsula, Mexico. These Mayan ruins originally supported a roof for what is thought to have been a great meeting hall.

supported relatively dense populations and elaborate cultures. These earthworks were abandoned by unknown peoples between AD 1400 and 1700. Perhaps European diseases, possibly smallpox, filtered in and destroyed the populations.

The Llanos contains deep alluvial deposits from which a series of mounds were built near Baures and joined by causeways. One forested mound (loma), Ibibaté, is 20 feet (6 meters) higher than the surrounding land. Its soil is filled with pottery fragments; some lomas contain 10–30 feet (3–10 meters) of sherds. Ibibaté is a pair of mounds connected by a short earth wall. Earthen causeways radiate out like roads from the mound toward other mounds. These causeways are about 3 feet (1 meter) high, up to 15 feet (5 meters) wide, are perfectly straight, and are bordered by narrow canals. The lomas were probably small in the beginning, but grew through accumulated garbage and collapsed houses, much like mounds in Palestine.

Erickson claims that these Llanos communities began 3,000–5,000 years ago, and the village cultures built thousands of miles of artificial earth walls and canals, supported by a sophisticated farming system. Around Baures, a series of long, low, zigzag walls were built some 2–2.5 miles (3–5 kilometers) long. Erickson believes these to be fish weirs that were used when the rainy season covered the savannah with up to 2 feet (0.6 meter) of standing water. Narrow channels up to 9 feet (3 meters) long open at angles in the zigzag. Erickson says that woven nets could be used to harvest fish and shellfish at these points. The openings also funneled fish into manmade ponds up to 98 feet (30 meters) across. The weirs are piled high with apple snail shells; the ponds still fill up with fish, which seethe in the dry season.

Erickson's ideas have generated heated debate among archaeologists. Betty Meggers claims that large, complex societies could not exist in Amazonia. Others state that the mounds were made by natural forces, and some claim that the earthworks were probably constructed by a higher culture, likely Andean. Erickson has been criticized because the earthen structures could only be built by a coercive, centralized power with a hierarchical division of labor. He contends that horizontally-linked societies with bonds of kinship, alliances, and informal modes of cooperation could build such earthworks over generations of time. Archaeologist Anna C. Roosevelt believes that fish, and an abundance of fruit, nuts, and edible palm could create a more egalitarian society, such as Native American cultures in the Pacific Northwest and California. Erickson also criticizes Meggers for extrapolating interpretations after fixating on one site at a time, whereas he argues that the entire landscape should be treated as an artifact. In England, long, raised, parallel ridges over miles of lowland can be seen, the result of Anglo-Saxon plowing techniques. Here, the English landscape is indeed an archaeological landscape. As Erickson says about the Llanos, "The raised fields are all aligned in a north–south direction. The landscape is telling us something."

Finally, evidence now exists of a fully operational forest civilization on the Brazilian Amazon. This highly developed Stone Age culture has left few remains except skeletons stored in humanoid ceramic jars. Also evident are decorated tangas, ceramic covers like bikini bottoms, tied on with cords. This civilization lasted some 8,000 years and ended after Europeans arrived in the sixteenth century. Several million people lived here and worked in the rainforest without destroying it; they even managed certain tree varieties according to archaeologists. Stands of the same tree appear around rich, black soil deposits

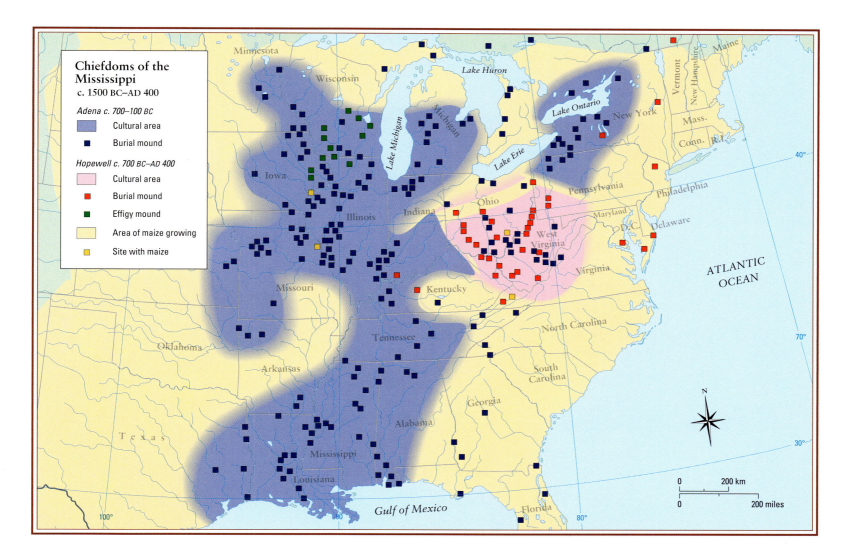

Chiefdoms of the Mississippi
c. 1500 BC–AD 400

Adena c. 700–100 BC

◼ Cultural area

◼ Burial mound

Hopewell c. 700 BC–AD 400

◼ Cultural area

◼ Burial mound

◼ Effigy mound

◼ Area of maize growing

◼ Site with maize

where villages once existed, and where incoming Brazilian farmers like to raise crops.

The population spread thickly along the rivers. Archaeologist Eduardo Neves thinks that towns were often horseshoe-shaped arrangements of thatched wooden dwellings that were aligned north–south to face eastward-flowing rivers. Most villages were located on bluffs, raising them above potential floodwaters and facilitating defense. Roosevelt runs a long-term research project on the region and maintains that Santarém was the center of a great chiefdom in the heart of Amazonia, which acquired power over a large territory between the tenth and sixteenth centuries. Her view is that several chiefs unified and ruled an area of approximately 8,880 square miles (23,000 square kilometers). Riverine chiefdoms were linked together to exchange ideas and trade goods, which might explain the stylistic similarities seen between Santarém pottery and other types from areas of northern South America.

Early European accounts of the Amazon, especially Portuguese, tell of very large and numerous villages, and admit that Amazonian political and territorial power bases with authority over surrounding areas were well constructed. They also admired the sophistication of the pottery. Thus, it seems that from early European encounters, the civilizations were well established, with a developed social order, well-organized leadership, a strong belief system, and an efficient manner of exploiting local resources. So, these Amazonian peoples existed, but possessed no written history save for myth and oral tradition. Then, European diseases struck and the people were wiped out.

Rivers provided early civilizations with "highways" and essential trade routes. In North America, the mighty Mississippi and its tributaries allowed the spread of the Adena and Hopewell.

THE COMPETING THEORIES OF MIGRATION

WHILE MOST EXPERTS BELIEVE THAT HUMANS ARRIVED IN NORTH AMERICA BY LAND BRIDGE FROM ASIA, THERE ARE DIFFERENT OPINIONS AS TO EXACTLY WHEN THIS OCCURRED.

Historians and geologists suggest that a bridge—the Bering Land Bridge—connected Siberia and North America at various times during the Ice Ages. Such a link would have allowed animals and prehistoric peoples to cross from one continent to the other. This thesis applying to people was first mooted by the sixteenth-century Jesuit missionary José de Acosta. Most anthropologists, historical linguists, and archaeologists accept that Native Americans are descended from northeastern Asians, but argue about when the migrations occurred. Some are of the opinion that an initial colonization took place less than 15,000 years ago—that is the main Amerind group, followed by Na-Dene (Athapascan speakers), and then Inuit and Aleut. However, other scholars maintain that human beings arrived earlier in America, but there is no concrete evidence to support this, other than disputed archaeological finds. Biological anthropologists have studied blood groups and dental characteristics, and agree with the three migration waves. These Paleo-Indians were fully modern when they arrived with their Stone-Age toolkits; no evidence has ever been found to support the presence of Neanderthal or other humanoid types. So far, the earliest distinctive American-style artifacts are the Clovis stone blades.

Arguments continue, since campfire remains in

Thor Heyerdahl's Ra II showed that Egyptians could have crossed the Atlantic.

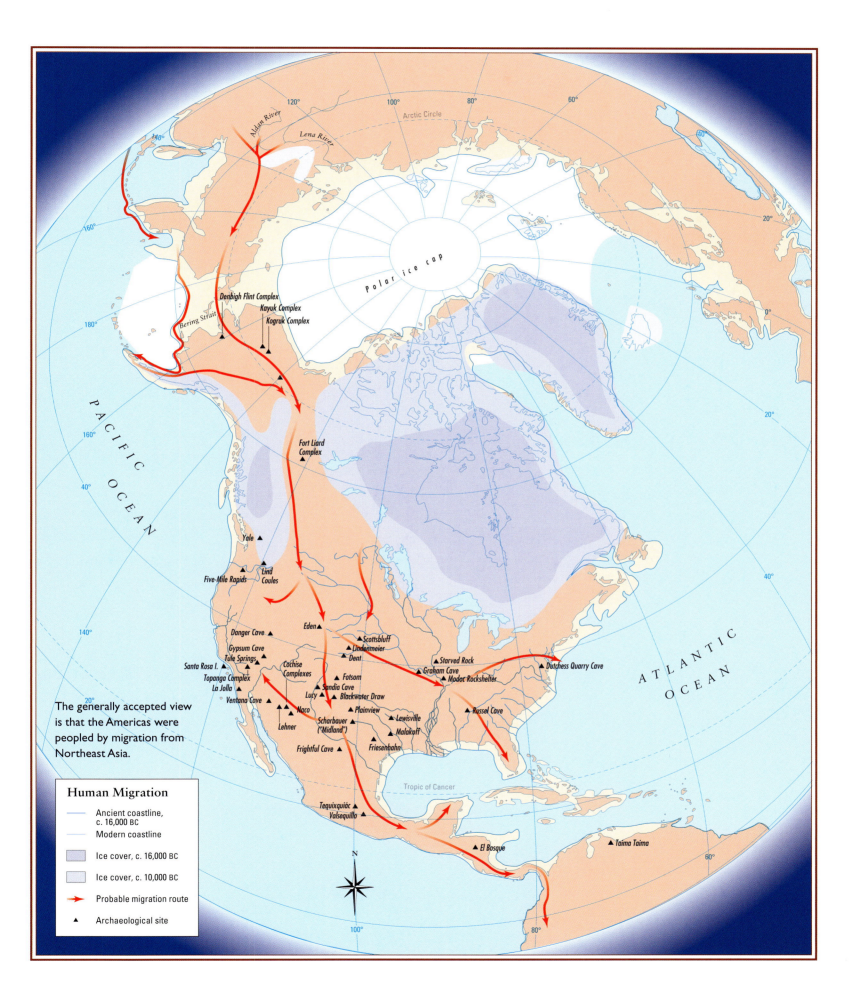

Human Migration

— Ancient coastline, c. 16,000 BC

— Modern coastline

Ice cover, c. 16,000 BC

Ice cover, c. 10,000 BC

➤ Probable migration route

▲ Archaeological site

The generally accepted view is that the Americas were peopled by migration from Northeast Asia.

PACIFIC OCEAN

ATLANTIC OCEAN

Polar ice cap

Arctic Circle

Aldan River

Lena River

Bering Strait

Denbigh Flint Complex

Kayuk Complex

Kogruk Complex

Fort Liard Complex

Yale

Lind Coules

Five-Mile Rapids

Danger Cave

Gypsum Cave

Tule Springs

Santa Rosa I.

Topanga Complex

La Jolla

Ventana Cave

Cochise Complexes

Eden

Scottsbluff

Lindenmeier

Dent

Fotsom

Sandia Cave

Lucy

Blackwater Draw

Naco

Plainview

Lehner

Scharbauer ("Midland")

Lewisville

Malakoff

Frightful Cave

Friesenhahn

Starved Rock

Graham Cave

Modoc Rockshelter

Russel Cave

Dutchess Quarry Cave

Tropic of Cancer

Tequixquiác

Valsequillo

El Bosque

Taima Taima

N

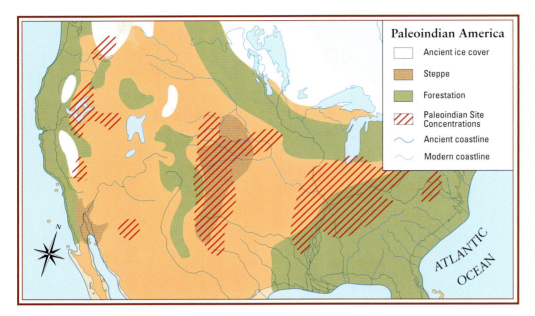

Paleoindian America

☐	Ancient ice cover
▨	Steppe
▨	Forestation
▨	Paleoindian Site Concentrations
∿	Ancient coastline
∿	Modern coastline

Nomadic groups known as paleoindians were the first to populate North America. They spread across the continent.

The various Mississippian cultures are characterized by the mounds they built. These have been found throughout the eastern half of the country.

Adena, Hopewell, and Mississippi Mounds

▲ Major Adena or Hopewell mounds, 1000 BC–AD 1000

▲ Major Mississippian mounds, AD 700–1700

the Valley of Mexico have been radiocarbon dated to 21,000 BC, and bone tools found in the Yukon, Canada, date to 22,000 BC. To confuse matters further, the British Broadcasting Corporation (BBC) showed an archaeological TV documentary that argued that Negroid Australian aborigine types existed in Latin America, especially in Tierra del Fuego, where such genes are to be found, as if an earlier or even later group arriving by sea had been pushed southward to near extinction.

The presence of Vikings at L'Anse aux Meadows, in Newfoundland, demonstrates early transoceanic contact, while Thor Heyerdahl displayed other possibilities in his *Kon-tiki* and *Ra* expeditions. The balsa raft *Kon-tiki* was sailed from Peru to Polynesia, and the *Ra II* was a papyrus vessel that voyaged from North Africa to Barbados in 57 days. The trip was undertaken to support a theory that ancient Egyptians could have reached South America to found Latin American civilizations. The voyage would also please those sceptics who feel that no Native Americans could have developed the Adena and Hopewell Mound cultures.

Other theories of contacts and culture mixes have been suggested. The physical features of Northwest Pacific coast peoples are more Oriental than elsewhere, and notions exist that Japanese could have reached America via the Japanese Current or Hawaii. Also, Tlingit warrior armor has a Japanese appearance. Japanese Jomon pottery resembles Ecuadorean Valdivia pottery. Even the Indus Valley has been linked to Middle America through the similarities between the Asian game Parcheesi and Patolli. The Atlantic, some argue, might have been crossed by Egyptians, Libyans, and Phoenicians, owing to apparent language and inscription similarities. African arrivals in the Olmec culture region could explain the Negroid aspect of Olmec sculpture. Even the Basques are alleged to have reached Pennsylvania and the Gulf of St. Lawrence, because ancient grave markers resemble certain Native American ones.

More unusual contacts are alleged. Clearly, the Lost Tribe of Israel theory is nonsense, but the sixth-century Irish monk St. Brendan was believed to have landed in America. More recently, in 1996, two young men found a human skull and bones at Kennewick in Washington State. The local coroner ordered radiocarbon and DNA analysis of the nearly complete skeleton. The man was 40–55 years old, about 5 feet 9 inches (1.76 meters) tall, and allegedly his skull was of Caucasian style rather than Native American. However, the dental characteristics showed a possible relationship with south Asian peoples. The man had a stone spear point in his hip, and radiocarbon dating of the bone showed its age to be 9,200–9,500 years.

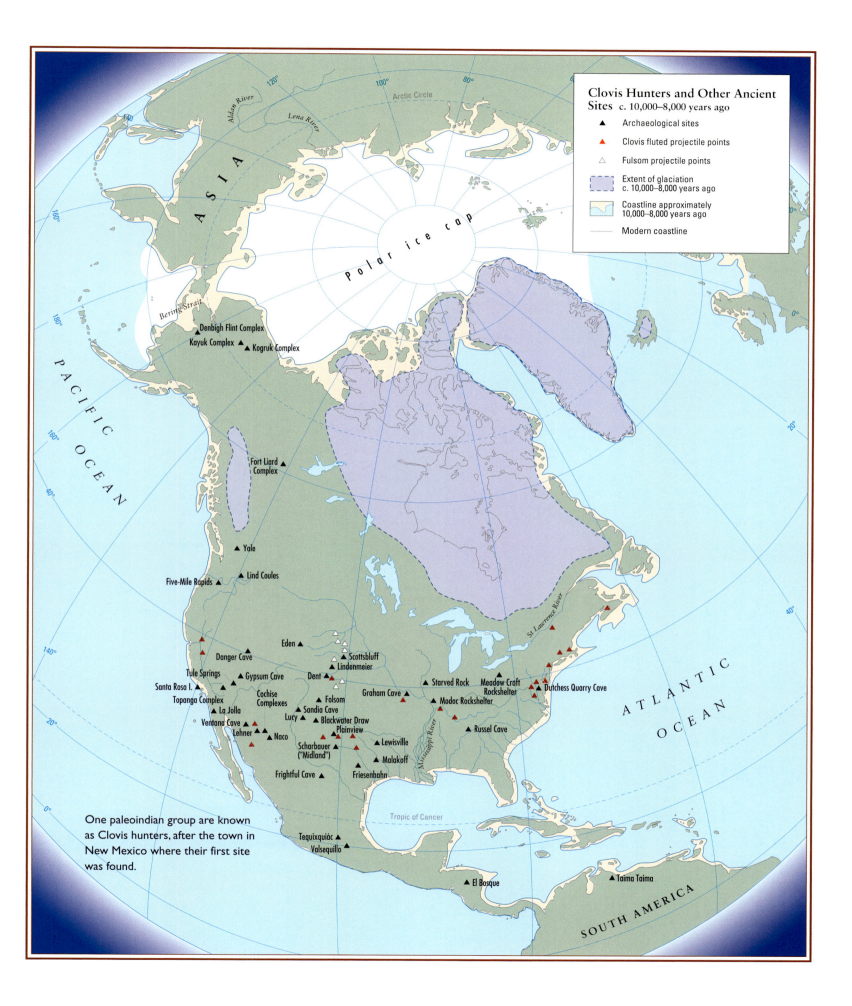

Clovis Hunters and Other Ancient Sites c. 10,000–8,000 years ago

▲ Archaeological sites

▲ Clovis fluted projectile points

△ Fulsom projectile points

Extent of glaciation c. 10,000–8,000 years ago

Coastline approximately 10,000–8,000 years ago

Modern coastline

ASIA

Aldan River

Lena River

Arctic Circle

Polar ice cap

Bering Strait

PACIFIC OCEAN

ATLANTIC OCEAN

SOUTH AMERICA

Tropic of Cancer

St Lawrence River

Mississippi River

▲ Denbigh Flint Complex
Kayuk Complex ▲   ▲ Kogruk Complex

Fort Liard ▲
Complex

▲ Yale

▲ Lind Coules
Five-Mile Rapids ▲

Eden ▲   △ △
        △ ▲ Scottsbluff
        ▲ Lindenmeier
▲ Danger Cave
Tule Springs ▲ ▲
        ▲ Gypsum Cave   Dent ▲ △   △ Starved Rock   Meadow Craft
Santa Rosa I. ▲   ▲ ▲   ▲ Graham Cave   Rockshelter ▲   ▲ Dutchess Quarry Cave
Topanga Complex ▲   Cochise   ▲ Modoc Rockshelter
    ▲ La Jolla   Complexes   ▲ Folsom
Ventana Cave ▲   Lucy ▲ Sandia Cave
Lehner ▲ ▲ ▲   ▲ Blackwater Draw   ▲ Russel Cave
    ▲ ▲ Naco   Plainview
        Scharbauer ▲   ▲ Lewisville
        ("Midland")   ▲ Malakoff
Frightful Cave ▲   Friesenhahn

Tequixquiác ▲
Valsequillo ▲

▲ El Bosque   ▲ Taima Taima

One paleoindian group are known as Clovis hunters, after the town in New Mexico where their first site was found.

CREATION MYTHS

THE MANY DIFFERENT NATIVE AMERICAN PEOPLES HAVE VARYING STORIES THAT EXPLAIN THEIR EXISTENCE. SUCH STORIES HAVE BEEN PASSED DOWN ORALLY THROUGH THE GENERATIONS.

Native American creation myths are as numerous and varied as the different peoples of the Americas. Themes common to nearly all Native American cultures are tales of the great flood, of twins, Mother Earth, and the first men or women. Some stories recount a creator, others that humanity emerged from the womb of Mother Earth. In many cases, ancestors in the spirit world or animal spirits, such as Coyote, are midwives to humanity's origins. Important, too, is the concept of the Sunfather, who inhabits the land above (heaven).

The Miwok people of California tell how Coyote created the world and its creatures. He gathered a council of beasts, birds, and marine life to debate the nature of the Lord of the Animals, whom they had to make to rule over them. Each creature wanted its own special attributes to be incorporated: the strength of the mountain lion, the bear's growl, a deer's eyesight, and a sheep's horns for butting. Coyote criticized them all for wanting replicas of themselves, when he desired all attributes wrapped into one new manifestation. The debate became physical until Coyote ordered the animals to make a clay model of the Lord out of river mud. However, all the mud models disintegrated on the wet river bank while they slept, except for Coyote's, which he had made overnight, giving it life before the others awoke. This Lord, Man, had keen vision and hearing, walked on two legs like a bear, was fleet as a deer, could swim like a fish, and was as cunning as Coyote.

The Zuni maintain that the Sunfather made two twins, who entered Earth Mother's womb to lead them up into the light. The Keresan-speaking Pueblo peoples possess a similar tale about their mother Iyatiku in the underworld. Aided by a woodpecker and a badger, who made holes to let the people out into a new homeland, Iyatiku gave her children her heart, corn to eat, and then returned underground. The Plains Lakota say that they once lived as a people of the bison cows underneath today's world.

The Caddoan-speaking Pawnee of the Nebraskan Platte River areas believed that the creator god Tirawahat ordered the male Morning Star to mate with the female Evening Star. This forced union produced a daughter, the originator of the tribe. Thereafter, periodic ritual sacrifices of a 13-year-old girl were made to appease the gods, ensuring the continued existence of the tribe. The last recorded case of sacrifice occurred in 1838, after a smallpox epidemic had broken out. The epidemic continued its course regardless.

The most familiar myth concerns the natives of the Eastern Woodlands, who say that the present world began in the Sky World. Several Iroquoian groups narrate how a woman living above the Sky-dome was either cast down by her husband or fell through a hole toward earth. She was caught by seabirds or swans, which used their wings to slow her fall until she landed on a turtle's back in the midst of a water world. Animal people were summoned to help this Woman Who Fell from the Sky. Beavers, toads, or a muskrat brought some soil from the sea floor to place on the turtle's back. The soil grew and became the world where this Sky-woman could live with her descendants.

Many oral narratives, normally handed down from mother to daughter over generations, depict active roles of female and male characters among natural forces and animal people, all threads in the same canvas. Iyatiku and Sky-woman are creative forces who provided sustenance for their peoples. The link between people, creatures, and the natural world built a set of relationships around which rules were made concerning government, kinship, marriage, and cultural values.

Like many Native American and non-American peoples, the Iroquoian and Wyandot cultures introduce a Manichaean vision. Sky-woman, Aataentic, gave birth to twins. Tsensta', the good, generous, unselfish Man of Fire was delivered naturally, but evil Taweskare, Man of Flint, tore himself out of his mother's armpit, killing her. Thereafter, the two fought for and against the emergent peoples.

Native Americans tolerantly accept that different peoples have a variety of creation myths and origins, and that human beings were created on American soil. When confronted with Biblical stories, they were annoyed that Christians insisted that the story of Paradise was an exclusive truth, and that a book record should be more valid than hand-me-down tales told by women.

Sky Woman (1936), a painting by E. Smith, a Seneca Iroquois. The Sky-woman features in many creation myths.

The Rise of Agriculture

The development of agriculture among Native Americans gave rise to permanent settlements and the development of important techniques, such as irrigation.

The transition from hunting and gathering plants to growing crops for food took place over thousands of years, and occurred during the Archaic Period, c. 7000–2000 BC. By 7000 BC, Mesoamerican nomadic hunters were growing vegetables like squash and chillis near campsites. Dry cave sites at Tehuacan and Romero's Cave at Tamaulipas provide evidence of cultivated beans, pumpkins, and gourds as far back as 7000 BC, while maize can be dated to around 3000 BC. Gradually, 1-inch (2.5-centimeter) maize cobs were developed into more modern variants, and Mesoamerican civilizations flourished around this food supply.

By 3000 BC, Native Americans in North America were cultivating local plants, such as sunflower, goosefoot, pigweed, knotweed, maygrass, and marsh elder. These provided seeds, starchy flour, and tubers. Gourds and squash, native to the Eastern Woodlands, were grown too. Between 2500 BC and AD 400, Native North Americans seriously began to propagate and produce plants. This was principally a woman's job and probably enhanced female status. Quite when Mesoamerican plants spread into the Southwest is debatable. Bat Cave evidence suggests 3500 BC, but other sites are consistent with 1500 BC. Certainly, the Hohokam tradition may have been established by 300 BC, and the Mogollon by AD 700. The Anasazi were established by 185 BC, so Archaic hunter-gatherers changed into the Pueblo societies of the Southwest.

Southwestern farmers grew maize, squash, and several bean species, all originating in Mexico, as did cotton and amaranth seeds from pigweed. Indians also cultivated agave, little barley grass, tobacco, cholla, dropseed, lamb's quarter, panic grass, and devil's claw cactus, the last being used for basketry. Irrigation was essential for germination and cultivation. Furthermore, effective food storage techniques were developed.

The Eastern Woodlands farmers (2000–1500 BC) had domesticated lamb's quarter, marsh elder, squash, and sunflower before maize was introduced from the Southwest around AD 200. Maize became increasingly important between AD 800 and 1100, and this culture shift was accompanied by the growth of towns, class societies, and fortified civic ceremonial centers, especially among members of the Mississippian culture.

Eventually, maize cultivation was adopted from Florida to the Great Lakes, and the north benefited from a maize variety requiring a shorter growing season. The shift to maize in the northern regions was accepted between AD 1000 and 1500, and varied in time from sub-region to sub-region. These so-called "Oneota" groups, Indian bands involved in the transition, established fortified agricultural villages along lake shores, major waterways, and wetlands. However, agriculture was just one economic strategy. Archaeological evidence indicates the hunting of buffalo, elk, deer, and sometimes raccoon, muskrat, and beaver. Agriculture allowed population increases and resource competition between villages. Thus, pressure existed to confederate to secure zones of influence; the Iroquois are one example. Areas such as Maryland and Virginia developed small economic village units, some of which were organized into the Powhatan paramount state.

Some qualifications should be made about farming. In the East, calories and nutrients came from domesticated plants, while in the Southwest, the most nutritious food was provided by wild plants. Also, the East, with its temperate climate, was easy to farm. The arid Southwest needed constant water management by means of canals, ditches, reservoirs, and dams. These were used to irrigate mulched gardens, terraced gardens, and fields. Also, the differing regions developed various methods of crop protection. The Mohawks and others drenched their seeds with hellebore to poison crows, while the Navajo dribbled squash with a mixture of urine and goat's milk to protect plants from the depredations of clinch bugs and cockroaches. With the domestication of maize came religious rites to secure harvests; here was the Hopi Niman Kachina ceremony, and the Iroquois Green Corn Ceremony.

An early illustration depicting the cultivation of maize (sometimes called Indian corn). In the Southwest, maize became an important ingredient of the Native American diet.

EARLY CIVILIZATIONS IN SOUTH AMERICA

SOPHISTICATED CIVILIZATIONS FLOURISHED IN PARTS OF SOUTH AMERICA LONG BEFORE CONTACT WITH EUROPEANS, AND THEY HAVE LEFT A RICH LEGACY OF ARTIFACTS.

South America has been home to many civilizations, the most famous being the Inca, but earlier cultures existed not only in the Andes, but also in Colombia and the Amazon Basin. The river valleys of Colombia were home to farmers and goldsmiths, who worked gold some 1,000 years before Columbus. Along the Magdalena River in San Augustín, old cultures have left stone statues, relief carvings, burial chambers, and shrines, and have been dated to 500 BC. The rulers of Muisca, near Bogotá, covered themselves in gold dust, sailed onto Lake Guatavita, and threw in offerings of gold and jewels. This gave rise to the myth of El Dorado, the Gilded One. The Amazon has produced evidence of five million people inhabiting its banks in dense villages. Similarly, the middle Orinoco has provided ceramics dating to 3600 BC. Bolivia has hosted an excavation at Ibitaté in the Llanos de Mojos, where evidence was found of a mound culture and raised fields, but archaeological interpretations differ on the find.

Near the Andes, coastal settlements were established as early as 2600 BC at Caral, in the Supe Valley, Peru, with its platform mounds and circular plazas. More well known are such cultures as the Chavín (900–200 BC), the Moche (c. AD 1–750), the Huari (AD 650–800), and the Chimú, whose kingdom reached its height in the fourteenth and fifteenth centuries, before being conquered by the Inca in about 1470.

Temple ruins at Chavín de Huantar on the eastern side of the Andes date, at their earliest, from 1200 BC, but flourished from 900 BC. The ruins are decorated with bas-reliefs showing grotesque human and animal figures. Jaguar motifs have been found on pottery, textiles, and metalwork. The

Chavínoid style spread over much of Peru and can be seen at earlier sites at Huaca de los Reyos, suggesting that the Chavín's precursors emanated from the coast. Other early cultures are apparent on the Paracan Peninsula, with trepanned skulls in its Necropolis, which is full of mummies and grave offerings.

The Moche culture is characterized by its adobe pyramids and rich burials in coastal areas near today's Trujillo. By AD 400, its civilization extended from the Huarmay Valley in the south to Chira Valley in the north. Moche's Temple of the Sun is 1,115 feet (340 meters) long and 131 feet (40 meters) high, and each Moche Valley settlement possessed a ritual site. This fishing and agricultural civilization produced magnificent burials, gold, silver, precious stones, and pottery being found in graves. Evidence also exists of sacrificed servants. Ceramic vessels and adobe wall paintings depict boats, fishermen, birds, shellfish, and animals. The art also shows war and the decapitation of prisoners, and there appears to have been a coca ritual.

Between AD 500 and 1000, the Tihuanaco and Huari empires dominated much of the central and southern Andes, and part of the coast. Tiahuanaco has the Akapana, a large, terraced pyramid, while the Kalasasaya temple enclosure has a famous Gateway of the Sun sculpture. This cosmological model depicts winged figures; other finds have been monolithic sculptures that are 5–24 feet (1.5–7.6 meters) tall with human faces. The Huari city lies near modern Ayacucho and is laid out in a grid pattern. Fields were often terraced and irrigated. The Huari made fine pottery with human, bird, and animal images. Tapestry shirts, hats, and belts have been found.

The Chimú Empire controlled much of northern Peru, and again the agricultural economy depended on irrigation techniques. Also near today's Trujillo was located the capital of Chan Chan, the 2.5-square-mile (6-square-kilometer) site containing ten walled compounds where palaces and storerooms can be found. Some Huari characteristics are in the architecture, while Moche styles can be seen in ceramic vessels. Ultimately, the Chimú controlled territory from Tumbes, on the far north coast, southward to the Chillón Valley, north of Lima. Armed forces and skilful administration had allowed expansion under semi-divine rulers. Organization made possible a 40-mile (65-kilometer) canal, which carried water from the upper Chicama Valley to Chimú fields in the Moche Valley. The Chimú were in conflict with the Inca between 1462 and 1470, the latter including Chimú in their empire.

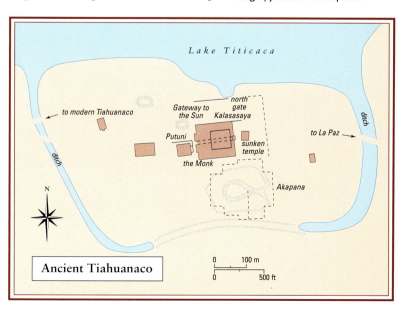

The Tiahuanaco and Huari empires spread thoughout the southern and central Andes.

The site of the ancient city of Tiahuanaco. To the south lies the large pyramid of Akapana.

Tiahuanaco and Wari (Huari)

■ Tiahuanaco state

■ Area under Tiahuanaco influence

• Tiahuanaco site

■ Wari (Huari)

Ancient Tiahuanaco

Early Civilizations in Mesoamerica

Central America has seen several ancient civilizations, which grew as former nomadic peoples embraced agriculture and permanent settlements.

Tula, about 40 miles (64 kilometers) northwest of present-day Mexico City, was the greatest city of the Toltec Empire. It had several pyramids and a ball court.

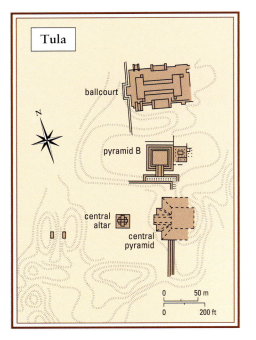

During the Archaic Period, people domesticated maize, moving from nomadic hunting and gathering to agriculture and village settlements. The earliest evidence of maize has been found in cave sites in Tamaulipas and Tehuacan. Farming villages appeared during the Formative period (c. 2000 BC), being concentrated on the Pacific and Gulf lowlands, and the highland valleys of Mexico and Oaxaca.

The first major civilization in Mesoamerica was the Olmec, in the jungles, grasslands, and swamps of the Mexican Gulf coast. Annual flooding left alluvial deposits, making this area agriculturally productive. The Olmec may be the mother culture that influenced other cultures to develop, such as the Maya, Teotihuacan, Totonac, Zapotec, and the later Toltec, Mixtec, and Aztec. Of the known Olmec sites, the most important are San Lorenzo (1200–900 BC), La Venta, where the largest Olmec pyramid stands (800–400 BC), and the Tres Zapotes, which reached its peak around 100 BC. Olmec influence spread along trade routes as they sought basalt, jade, serpentine, and magnetite.

Olmec civilization pursued slash-and-burn agriculture, and comprised a theocratic class society of priests, bureaucrats, merchants, craftsmen, and farmers. Religious objects include snarling and crying, baby-faced figurines, which are thought to be children of the jaguar rain god. The Olmec are most well known for producing huge basalt heads, some weighing 20 tons.

The Mayan city states emerged around 1000 BC, but many cities had been abandoned by AD 869, known because no more dates were carved on buildings and standing stones

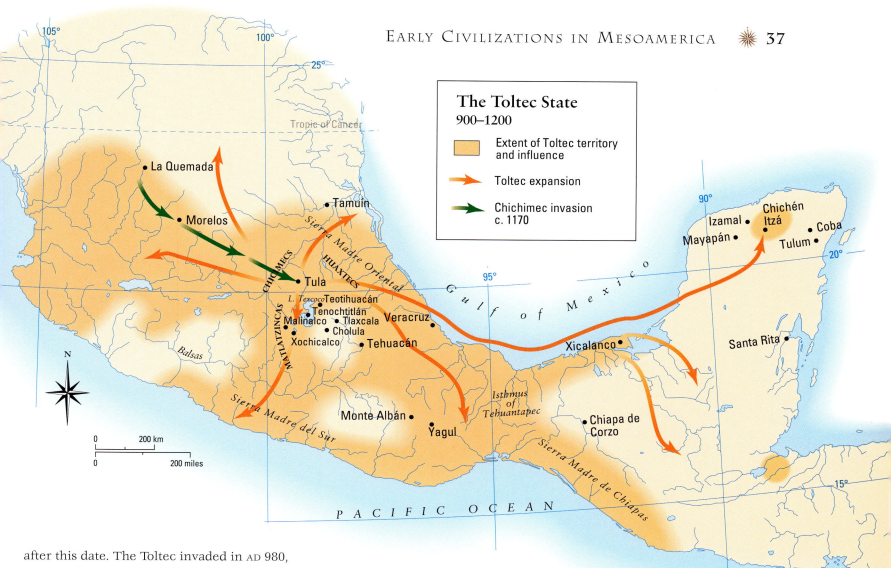

The Toltec State
900–1200

Extent of Toltec territory and influence

Toltec expansion

Chichimec invasion c. 1170

after this date. The Toltec invaded in AD 980, but the civilization continued under Toltec rule, declining in AD 1500. The Spaniards destroyed the remnants between 1517 and 1541.

Each independent city state was ruled by a king, and constant warfare procured prisoners to sacrifice to Mayan gods. The most famous state is Palenque, which sprang to fame under Pacal, whose dead body was interred in a nine-tiered pyramid. Tikal, covering 6 square miles (16 square kilometers), is filled with pyramids and palaces. Copán is another architectural wonder.

The Mayans developed two calendars, one secular and one sacred. The former contained eighteen months of twenty days each, with an extra five days. The calendars were written on two interlocking, cogged wheels so that they could work in concert. In mathematics, the Maya had developed the concept of zero by AD 100. They used hieroglyphic writing, and their records were carved on lintels, funerary vases, and stelae. Also, books were constructed from bark paper.

The Toltec-Chichimeca groups became dominant in the early tenth century, and their greatest city was Tula, the capital of an empire. This polity spread from the Valley of Mexico to Yucatan, Guatemala, and Honduras, and became a model for the Aztecs. Tula had several pyramids, a ball court, and sculpted figures. Several *chacmools* have been discovered. These are reclining warriors with bowls carved on their chests to receive sacrificial offerings. Also, there is an almost life-size clay figure representing Xipe Totec, the god of vegetation and planting. During spring ceremonies, he would be impersonated by a priest wearing the flayed skin of a human sacrificial victim.

Chichen Itzá is another Toltec site with a nine-tier Pyramid of Quetzalcoatl and a huge ball court. Carvings around the court show a winning team decapitating a defeated opponent. The nomadic Toltec, People of the Dog, were themselves conquered by northern nomads, the Chitimecs.

The Toltecs dominated much of Mesoamerica, occupying present-day Mexico and spreading eastward to Yucatan, Guatemala, and Honduras.

The Inca Empire

THE INCAS CREATED A SOPHISTICATED SOCIETY, NOTED FOR ITS WORK ETHIC, ITS ARCHITECTURE, ITS AGRICULTURAL PRACTICES, AND ITS CRAFTSMANSHIP.

Opposite: Huayna Picchu towers above the ruins of the Incas' famed mountain fortress of Machu Picchu.

The Inca Empire spread along the Pacific Coast of South America and was centered on the Andes.

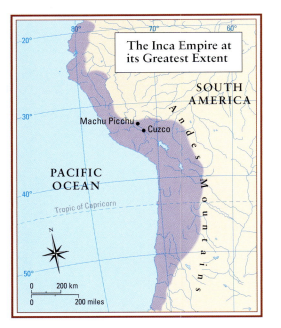

U ntil recently, the world acknowledged the Inca Empire as the most important historical Andean civilization. Interest has focused on the Temple of the Sun at Cuzco, or the mountain fortress of Machu Picchu, with its temple-pyramid, houses, and terraced fields. The Incas, therefore, are the terminal point in a long process, accepted by conventional wisdom, that began about 2500 BC. Apparently, hunter-gatherer groups, who occupied seasonal fishing villages, established permanent settlements along the Peruvian coast and coastal valleys. These isolated communities were unified occasionally by the Chavin culture (900–200 BC), the Moche (c. AD 1–750), the Huari (AD 650–800), the Chimu in the fourteenth and fifteenth centuries, and then the expansionist Inca.

However, an archaeological dig at Caral, in the Supe Valley, 120 miles (190 kilometers) north of Lima, uncovered a number of new sites. Caral dates from 2600 BC and occupies a 200-acre (80-hectare) site comprising six platform mounds surrounding a huge plaza. The architecture has stairs, rooms, and courtyards. Agriculture produced squash, beans, and cotton, all grown with the aid of irrigation. Remains of peppers, avocados, and potatoes were unearthed too. Apparently, cotton was woven into fishing nets and traded with coastal people for sardines, anchovies, and clams. Pottery and grain were not present, suggesting that Caral was a trading center based upon an early division of labor. Mollusc shells from the Amazonian rainforests were also present, as were flutes made from pelican and condor bones. Much of Caral is still buried, and some archaeologists think that the Supe culture could be older than 3000 BC. Dating suggests that Caral arose at the same time as ancient Egypt and Sumeria in a parallel development of class societies emerging from tribal ones. Finally, no weapons have yet been found at Caral.

Caral, then, may be the "mother city" that led to all later Andean civilizations up to the Incas. The latter were a small, aggressive tribe living in central Peru until moving to the Cuzco Valley around AD 1000. They sought to dominate neighboring tribes until the fifteenth century, when they began rapid expansion, conquering and accepting tribute from one valley tribe after another. Pachacuti Inca Yupanqui started the process, which reached its heyday under Huayna Capac (reigned 1493–1525). The multitribal and multilingual empire, using Quechua as a common tongue, stretched from southern Colombia, across Ecuador and Peru, to Bolivia, and northern parts of Argentina and Chile. In 1532, the Spaniard Francisco Pizarro landed in Peru with 180 men during a civil war between contenders for the Inca throne. Pizarro conquered the empire by controlling the Sapa Inca Atahualpa, whom he had strangled in 1533. The Spanish then built Lima as a capital, supplanting Cuzco.

At its height, the Inca Empire was noteworthy for its sophisticated political and administrative system. Its hierarchical society, an agricultural theocracy ruled by the Sapa Inca, the "incarnation" of the sun, placed all subjects under strict control—laziness could be punished by death, because work was being stolen from the Sapa Inca. State records of grain stores, population, troops, and taxes were kept by quipas, a set of color-coded cords with knots tied for accounting divisions. The empire was also characterized by irrigation and aqueducts, monumental stone architecture, and a road network that included suspension bridges, sometimes as long as 330 feet (100 meters).

The Incas grew maize, potatoes, yucca roots, peppers, avocados, peanuts, and lima beans. Notable in Inca society was medicine. Priest-doctors could cure dysentery, ulcers, eye problems, toothache, and lice infestations. Herbal remedies, including quinine, were highly effective. Surgeon-priests could amputate when necessary, after patients were anesthetized by chewing coca leaves, hypnosis, or drinking chicha beer. Even blood transfusions were performed, aided by the fact that all Incas were O rhesus positive.

Inca craftsmen were known for their jewelry—especially large ear-spools—pottery, and metalsmithing in silver and gold. Animals were used for pack transport, wool, and food (llama, alpaca, and the guinea pig). Weavers employed cotton and wool from the llama and alpaca, and from the wild vicuña or guanaco.

The Rise of the Aztecs

RULERS OF AN AREA THAT STRETCHED FROM THE GULF OF MEXICO TO THE PACIFIC, THE AZTECS WORSHIPPED THE SUN, THEIR RELIGION REQUIRING FREQUENT HUMAN SACRIFICES.

The Aztecs claimed to be descendants of a nomadic tribe that arrived in the Valley of Mexico about AD 1300. After paying tribute to nearby city states, the Aztecs settled on swampy islands in Lake Texcoco, where they founded Tenochtitlan and Tlatelolco in 1345. Tenochtitlan, the place of the prickly pear, became the Aztec capital city and eventually incorporated hundreds of buildings, interconnected by canals and linked to land by causeways. An aqueduct was built to bring fresh water to the city, and a big levee was constructed to separate a freshwater part of the lake from a salty, marshy area to improve agriculture.

Initially, the Aztecs paid tribute to the Tepanec rulers of Azcapotzalco, and fought for them to create an empire that extended out of the Valley of Mexico. The Aztecs became so powerful that they overthrew Azcapotzalco and seized its territories. After making an alliance with Tlacopan and Texcoco, dozens of city states were conquered, and evidence for this can be found in the *Codex Mendoza*, a book recounting the history of the Aztecs. By 1500, they controlled an empire that stretched from the Gulf of Mexico to the Pacific and included part of Guatemala. Conquered areas were allowed to retain their governments, but were compelled to pay tribute. Campaigns were not always successful. The people of Oaxaca retained independence, as did the Tlaxcalans, who eventually supported the Spaniards against the Aztecs and fought with great ferocity in the assault on Tenochtitlan. Flower (a euphemism for blood) wars were waged to obtain captives for sacrificing to Aztec gods.

Outside the slave and aristocratic classes, most of the population were commoners who worked land held by usufruct. In the lakes, raised garden beds were constructed out of vegetation and lake-bottom mud. These *chinanpas* produced a rich variety of

Chicomoztoc, the place of the seven caves, the mythical origin of the nahuatlaca tribes, or Aztecs. The illustration comes from the *Historia Toltec chicimeca*, a post-cortesian codex dating from 1550

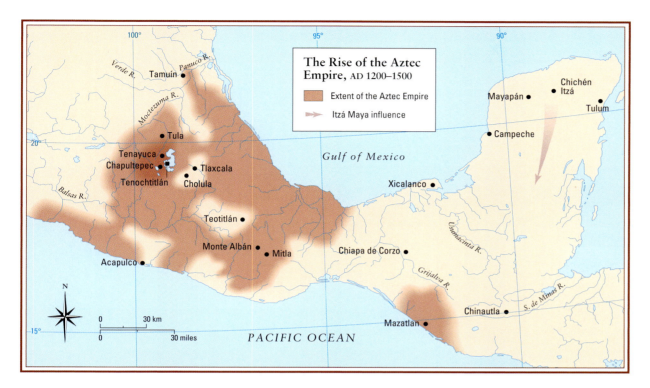

The Aztec Empire stretched across Mesoamerica, from the Gulf of Mexico to the Pacific.

foods, which are well known today. Maize, eaten as cakes or tortillas, was a staple food, as were beans, squash, and amaranth seeds. Cocoa, vanilla, chillis, peppers, avocado, mango, papayas, and tomatoes could be eaten with meat provided by turkeys and domesticated dogs. Food could be demanded as tribute.

A game played by the Aztecs, although not originated by them, is the ballcourt game. The court could be shaped like a capital "I," and set in the walls would be stone rings through which the ball had to pass, being propelled by the players' hips; hands and feet could not be used. The teams of players would wear padding to protect against the hard, solid latex ball. Evidently, the court represented the world, and the ball the sun and moon. Some believed that regular games would improve the harvest.

Aztec religion was concerned with the sun. Their faith believed that the Aztecs lived in the era of the Fifth Sun, and if the sun vanished, their world would end violently. Thus, the Sun had to be propitiated with constant supplies of blood. The Great Temple at Tenochtitlan was a vast pyramid, frequently rebuilt in a more impressive fashion. The temple housed shrines dedicated to Tlaloc, the god of rain, and Huitzilopochtli, the god of war and the Aztec tribal god. At the entrance to the first shrine was a *chacmool*, a reclining figure holding a receptacle for hearts and blood. The priesthood did more than carry out sacrifices. The priests' duty was to keep a calendar and ensure that daily rituals were implemented. The entire religion is represented in a carved stone, the Sun Stone or Calendar Stone, which measures 9 feet 8 inches (2.95 meters) in diameter.

Aztec trade was important, and certain goods were in high demand. Cocoa beans, turquoise, animal skins, gold, silver, copper, pearls, and obsidian were luxury items, as were the green quetzal feathers. Tribute could be traded on, and the Aztec state depended upon this harsh tax. The annual tribute for the province of Cuauhtitlan was 1,200 cotton mantles, sixty-two warriors' costumes with feathered shields, 4,000 reed mats, and one large bin each of maize, beans, sage seeds, and amaranth. The system ended after Hernán Cortés fought his way into the capital in April 1521.

THE HOHOKAM OF SONORA

THE HOHOKAM WERE GREAT TRADERS, BUT THEY ALSO DEVELOPED SOPHISTICATED IRRIGATION SYSTEMS FOR THEIR CROPS, AND ARE NOTED FOR THEIR POTTERY.

Hohokam turquoise mosaics, discovered at Casa Grande, Arizona, in 1925.

Originating from the Archaic Cochise-Desert tradition, the Hohokam people lived in southern Arizona and northern Sonora. This ancient people settled across major continental trade routes probably around 300 BC, but possibly as early as 1200 BC; their culture lasted until AD 1450. Hohokam communities mediated trade from the Californian coast to the Great Plains, and from Mexican civilizations to the Rocky Mountains. Diverse goods passed through them: buffalo and deer skins, marine shells, turquoise, obsidian, rare minerals, textiles (often cotton), salt, exotic feathers, and ceramics.

The early Hohokam period was characterized by pithouses located along the Phoenix Basin river system, and the people developed an extensive irrigation system. This engineering feat utilized diversion dams, woven-mat valves, and a sophisticated grid of wide, shallow canals, sometimes 75 feet (23 meters) across. Some extended 10 miles (16 kilometers), and more than 900 miles (1,450 kilometers) of main canals traversed the Salt River Valley, with many ditches as infillers. Hohokam fields cultivated corn, beans, squash, tobacco, and cotton. Interestingly, the modern city of Phoenix has a canal system that roughly follows the Hohokam one.

Between AD 700 and 1100, the population increased, and the trade system developed to sell artisans' work way beyond the culture's borders. From the south and Mexico, the Hohokam received stone mosaic mirrors, crafted copper bells, brightly colored parrots, shells, and latex balls. The culture is also associated with red-on-buff pottery, often used to hold the ashes of the cremated for burial. Of particular note are their stone paint palettes in human and animal effigy form, and mosaic iron pyrites mirrors. The Hohokam also etched using a process invented after AD 1000. They covered shells with acid-resistant pitch, carved designs in this coating, then soaked the shells in an acidic mixture made from fermented saguaro cactus fruit. The removal of the coating revealed an etched design.

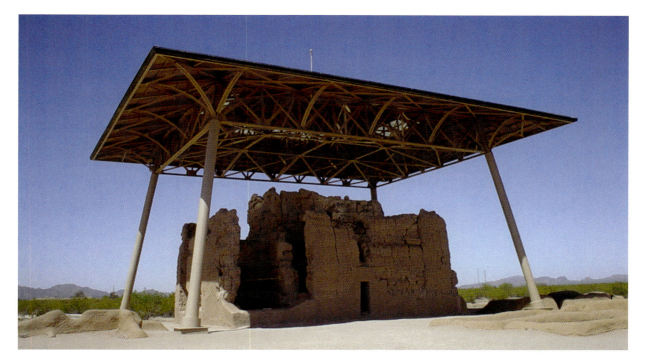

The ruins of Casa Grande Pueblo near Florence, Arizona. The massive central building has four stories. A protective roof was built during the 1930s.

Clearly, Hohokam society was highly organized. Canal maintenance alone took much labor in repairs, removing silt, and the careful management of water. Leadership, organization, and coordination must have been intense. The people normally lived in villages, the largest of which housed more than 500 people; the total population was probably 40–50,000. Archaeologists argue that a Hohokam elite developed, who built homes on the tops of mounds; these can be seen at the Casa Grande Pueblo, which housed 2,000 people. This site, on the Gila River near Florence, Arizona, comprised a large, four-story, multi-room complex with many outbuildings; the central building was a 35-feet (10.5-meter) high tower. The structure has adobe walls 3–5 feet (1–1.5 meters) thick, with five rooms on the ground floor. This site was occupied between AD 1200 and 1450, and incorporated Anasazi influences.

Multiple ballcourts are another key feature of Hohokam culture, but nobody knows anything about the games played, apart from the fact that latex balls were used. The ballcourts began to appear in AD 800, but construction had ceased by 1150. The largest court can be found at Snaketown, Arizona. It stands 16 feet (5 meters) high and was 200 feet (61 meters) along each side; 500 spectators could stand on the raised sidelines. Games probably provided a focus for social interaction within and between communities, and by 1150, 200 courts existed. Games could be meeting points for business, trade, and matchmaking.

By 1450, the flourishing Hohokam culture ended just like the Anasazi. Towns were stripped and burned, or they were abandoned gradually. Perhaps the climate deteriorated, floods destroyed the irrigation system, the soil became salinated, or the ordinary pit-dwellers attacked the mound-inhabiting elite.

Interesting, too, are the Salado people, an Anasazi offshoot who lived among the Hohokam on the Gila River; they vanished about 1400. Possibly Apache raids destroyed the communities, but when the Spanish arrived, the towns, villages, and irrigation systems were abandoned. By the seventeenth century, some 5,000 O'odham (Pima and Papago) people were living in a similar manner to the Hohokam, and they are thought to be their descendants, although O'odham tradition denies this conjecture.

THE ANASAZI

IN THE FOUR CORNERS REGION, WHERE THE STATES OF UTAH, COLORADO, ARIZONA, AND NEW MEXICO MEET, LIVED THE ANASAZI, WHO BECAME VERY INFLUENTIAL IN THE SOUTHWEST.

At about 100 BC, the Anasazi culture became distinct from the Mogollon and Hohokam. Up to AD 750, they lived in pithouses while they developed and refined their agricultural and ceramic skills. Absorbing others' traditions, they produced a startling black-on-white pottery style, making drinking cups with handles, wide-shouldered water jars (*ollas*), animal effigies, and plates. Their baskets were beautifully crafted, and the name Basketmaker Culture was applied to the early Anasazi. Sometimes, Yucca fibers were interwoven with other plant materials to create geometric designs. Some baskets were painted, while others were covered with a layer of pitch or resin to make watertight containers.

After AD 750, the Anasazi began building above-ground structures, but kept the pithouse as a kiva, used by men for ceremonial and social purposes. The pueblo appeared, buildings being constructed from stone and adobe cement, or just adobe bricks. Houses began to have shared walls and were built on top of each other, the inhabitants moving from one level to another by ladders. As levels were stepped back in terraces, the roof of one could be used as the front yard of another. The most well-known Anasazi sites are at Mesa Verde, Canyon de Chelly, and Chaco Canyon.

The Chaco Canyon settlements spread over 53,000 square miles (137,000 square kilometers) of the San Juan water system and comprised 125 known planned towns. Many of these were connected by roads, and all were served by an extensive irrigation system that watered squash, bean, and cornfields. Archaeologists have argued that Chaco Canyon controlled trade in food and turquoise, and that the population gradually accumulated wealth with bought goods and resources. Social distinctions grew, those living in large houses being distinct from those inhabiting scattered, small villages.

An Anasazi "black-on-white" *olla* and redware bowl. This Southwestern culture developed significant ceramic skills.

Communications were provided not only by roads, which sometimes ran 50 miles (80 kilometers) into the interior, but also by signal stations on the mesa tops, using fire, smoke, or reflected light. The Chacoans also built causeways and cut stairways into sheer cliffs. The large Chaco towns were spiritual and ritual centers of pilgrimage, as well as trade centers.

The most impressive town is Pueblo Bonito. Built in a D-shape and covering 2.5 acres (1 hectare), it once contained 800 rooms and thirty kivas. The pueblo, which is linked to seventy-five other settlements, may have been home to 1,200 people. The town comprised four stories within a protective wall, and the different levels could aid defense.

The kiva reflects a belief that people emerged from a former world, which was symbolized by occupants leaving the kiva into full view of the plaza. People descended into this underground world by ladder through the roof smokehole. Set into the floor would be a round, shallow, navel-like *sipapu*, a representation of the place where spiritual access to a deeper world below was possible,

Three major cultures developed in the Southwest: the Anasazi, Hohokam, and Mogollon.

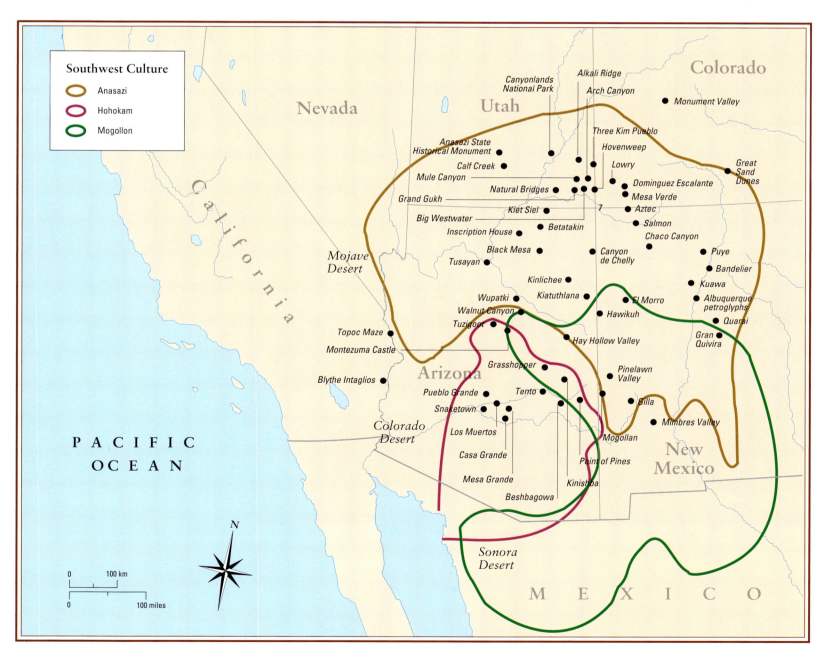

and where Corn Mothers emerged into the world. The Great Kiva at Chetro Ketl, near Pueblo Bonito, is 50 feet (15 meters) across, with an encircling bench, a raised fire container, and masonry vaults.

An Anasazi pueblo in southwestern Colorado, near Cowboy Wash, which dates from the twelfth century, sparked a heated archaeological debate. Seven bodies at the site had been dismembered, the bones being strewn about. Cut marks were found on the bones, suggesting that human flesh had been butchered for cannibal meals. Some bones had burn marks, allegedly from cooking. A coprolite (dried human excrement) contained a protein, myoglobin, apparently from human flesh. No archaeologist has yet provided a totally plausible or acceptable reason for the finds— hunger, site desecration, an isolated incident?

Chaco Canyon had been abandoned by AD 1140, tree-ring tests showing that no new building took place after that date. Severe drought conditions probably drove the people away. A later migration from Mesa Verde to Chaco occurred a century later, but was short-lived; then the Diné (Navajo) moved in during the eighteenth century. The Hopi and Zuni peoples are thought to be descendants of the Anasazi.

Opposite: The ruins of Pueblo Bonito in Chaco Canyon. Spreading over 2.5 acres (1 hectare), the pueblo had around 800 rooms and thirty kivas (pithouses).

Chaco Canyon is thought to have been the political and economic center of the Anasazi culture. It contained a number of settlements spread over an an area of 53,000 square miles (137,00 square kilometers).

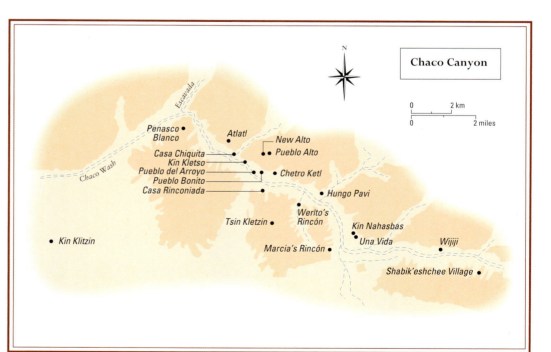

THE MISSISSIPPIANS

CENTERED ON THE GREAT RIVER THAT FLOWS SOUTHWARD
THROUGH THE USA, THE MISSISSIPPIAN CULTURE IS
DISTINGUISHED BY THE FLAT-TOPPED MOUNDS IT ERECTED
WHEN BUILDING ITS TOWNS.

Opposite: Mississippian cultures spread throughout the drainage of the great river.

Black burnish pottery discovered at Moundville.

The Mississippian or Mound Builder Culture flourished between AD 750 and 1500 (or even later) and is characterized by certain distinguishing features. Its pottery was usually tempered with crushed mussel shell, horticulture was maize based, and the major towns comprise series of large, flat-topped mounds, often surrounding a plaza. The organization needed to build the towns was immense, involving a stratified, hierarchical society, probably with hereditary offices. Evidence of this can be found in the records of the Natchez, later destroyed by the French.

The civilization spread along both banks of the Mississippi, from the Gulf of Mexico to Minnesota, and also along such tributaries as the Ohio, Missouri, Tennessee, Arkansas, and Red rivers. The remainder of the region was contained by other river basins along the Gulf and Carolina coasts, from the Neches River in Texas to the Carolina Pee Dee River.

The largest and most interesting Mississippian centers were Cahokia in Illinois; Etowah and Ocmulgee in Georgia; Moundville in Alabama, Spiro in Oklahoma, SunWatch in Ohio; and Nanih Waiya in Mississippi. The entire culture was based on maize production, together with beans and squash. The fields were managed by women, whose main tool was a hoe with a stone, bone, wood, or shell blade.

All of the major settlements have large mounds; Cahokia's Monks Mound covers 16 acres (6.5 hectares) and is 72 feet (22 meters) high.

Mississippian Cultures

- Fort Ancient
- Middle Mississippian
- Caddoan Mississippian
- South Appalachian Mississippian
- Paquemine Mississippian
- • Major archaeological site
- — Modern borders

Lake Superior

Lake Michigan

Lake Huron

Lake Ontario

Lake Erie

Osconto

Reigh

Osceola

Nodwell

London

Maxon-Derby

Sackett

Lamoka Lake

Neville

Boston

Nebo Hill

Koster

Graham Cave

Riverton

Cahokia

St. Louis

Modoc

Rodgers Shelter

Phillips Spring

Kinkaid

Evansville

Carrier Mills

Great Salt Spring

Robin Mound

Adena

Hopewell

Serpent

Mound

Mound

City

FORT

ANCIENT

Grave Creek

Cresap Mound

Marietta

Indian Knoll

MIDDLE MISSISSIPPIAN

Spiro

Stoan

Lace

Brand

Eva

Rose Island

Bacon Farm

Le Croy

Icehouse Bottom

Calloway Island

Hardaway

Doerschuk

**CADDOAN
MISSISSIPPIAN**

Wright

Roden

Coosa

Tunacunhee

Etowah

**SOUTH
APPALACHIAN
MISSISSIPPIAN**

Mississippi

Poverty Point

PLAQUEMINE

Crooks Mounds

Natchez

MISSISSIPPIAN

Moundville

Kolomoki

McKeithen

*ATLANTIC
OCEAN*

Weeden Island

Palmer

Little Salt Spring

Gulf of Mexico

N

0   100 km

0   100 miles

Cahokia in Illinois was one of the largest of the Mississippian centers. It is thought to have been home to 20–40,000 people. A large number of mounds have been discovered there, as has evidence for an enclosed area.

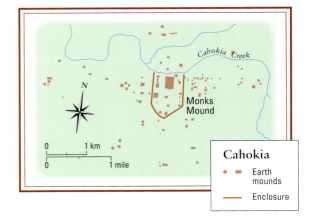

The settlements ranged from under 10 acres (4 hectares) to more than 100 acres (40 hectares), often being surrounded by a fortified palisade and ditch. Encircled by smaller family homes, the wall could separate the social elite from the commoners outside. The mound centers were the focuses of socio-political power; the plazas could encompass feasts, ceremonies, and rituals designed to socially integrate the population. Cahokia is estimated to have held 20–40,000 people. The buildings on mound tops could have been palaces or temples, or have had mortuary functions. Undoubtedly, important leader/priests would have ensured the correct sequences of annual rites to maintain social harmony, respect for the dead, and such forces in the world as the sun and Corn Mothers.

The chief has often been compared with the supreme ruler, the Great Sun of the Natchez, who lived on one mound. Others living on high would have been his mother, the White Woman; his brothers, the Suns, from whom were chosen the war chief and head priests; and his sisters, Woman Suns. Under these select few were the nobles and commoners. When a chief died, his palace would have been razed, more earth added to the mound, and a new building for the next chief constructed. The kinship ties and ritual provided legitimacy and authority over the town, territory, and its people.

The Mississippian culture was also linked by a network of trade routes along the interconnecting river systems. Goods would be readily transported by canoe. Prestige products were important to the elites. Among these were freshwater pearls; Great Lakes and southern Appalachian copper;

The Great Temple Mound at Etowah, Georgia, another major Mississippian site. It was built between AD 1000 and 1500.

hematite; silver from Ontario; chert, a stone capable of producing a sharp edge; galena from the upper Mississippi to make white pigment; Appalachian mica; Ohio flint stones and soapstone pipes; Arkansas quartz; obsidian; bears' teeth; shell beads and shells; shark and alligator teeth; turtle shells; and pottery. Copper was crafted into ritual objects for the elites. Trade in utilitarian tools and everyday objects appears lacking.

Cahokia provides an example of rise and decline between AD 900 and 1400. Covering 5 square miles (13 square kilometers) and incorporating a hundred mounds, the town appears to have one major and several subcommunities. The central enclosed area covers 205 acres (83 hectares) and was fortified. Cahokia was the largest population center north of Mexico.

The people of Cahokia were adept with the bow and arrow, which supplanted the spear and spear thrower, the *atlatl*. The military strength of the culture prevented conquest by Spain, but by the early seventeenth century, Mississippian centers had been abandoned. Overpopulation, climatic deterioration, disease, soil depletion, or warfare might explain the decline; as yet, no archaeologist knows.

Large mounds at Cahokia. There are a hundred in all within an area of 5 square miles (13 square kilometers).

Built by the Hopewell culture on the banks of the Little Miami River, Fort Ancient contains mounds and earth walls.

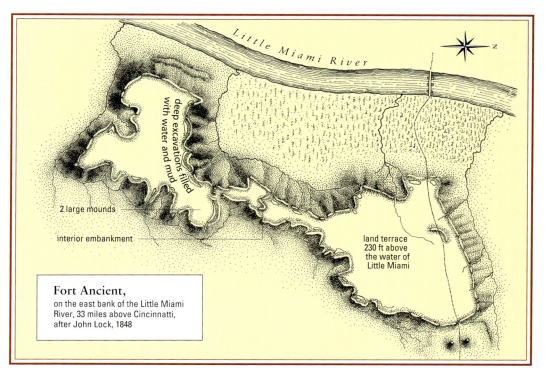

Little Miami River

deep excavations filled with water and mud

2 large mounds

interior embankment

land terrace 230 ft above the water of Little Miami

Fort Ancient,
on the east bank of the Little Miami River, 33 miles above Cincinnatti, after John Lock, 1848

PEOPLE OF THE SALMON

IN THE PACIFIC NORTHWEST, NATIVE PEOPLES UTILIZED WOOD FOR HOUSING AND OTHER ESSENTIAL ITEMS, LIVING ON THE REGION'S RICH DIVERSITY OF FISH, PARTICULARLY SALMON.

The first record of contact between Pacific Northwest Coast Indians and Europeans occurred in 1741, when a Russian explorer, Chirikov, sailed to southeast Alaska. Later, the Spaniard Juan Perez reached the Queen Charlotte Islands in 1774 and traded with Haida Indians. Spaniards arrived in the following year, while James Cook, the British explorer, was there in 1778.

Historians estimate that the Northwest Coast contained a population of at least 130,000 by 1492, making it one of the most populated areas of North America. These Indians were divided into three main groups, but with tremendous linguistic variation between them all. The Tlingit peoples inhabited the far north of the Northwest Coast and its islands. To the south were the Tsimshian Indians along the fjorded coast of British Columbia. Haida-speakers dwelt on the Queen Charlotte Islands and part of Prince of Wales Island. Further south were the various Kwakiutl groups. Elsewhere, Nootkan and other tribes, such as the Makah, hunted whales and seals in the open sea for their meat, using oil rendered from the blubber as a food and food preservative. The Salishan-speakers along the British Columbian coast, and in Washington and western Montana developed twenty-three interlinked languages, split by the Cascade Mountain range into sixteen coastal and seven inland divisions.

All of these tribes benefited from mild winters and large forested areas, which provided wood for board houses and a range of canoe types; by as early as AD 500, wedges and mauls were being used to split boards from red cedars. The large population was supported by runs of Pacific salmon. Five salmon species spawn in upstream rivers, while herring, smelt, and oil-rich candle fish were plentiful, as were shellfish and sea mammals. Society became increasingly stratified, which was marked by material wealth. Some archaeological sites, notably the Makah site at Ozette and that on the Hoko River of the Olympic Peninsula have shown evidence of a rich culture prior to the post-Columbian period.

The Northwest peoples possessed a highly sophisticated knowledge of local woods for house and boat building, weapons, helmets, bowls, canoe paddles, combs, dance helmets, and spirit masks. The Ozette site even shows that the Makah used steel tools before 1492; these probably reached North America by way of Asian vessels that were wrecked after being carried across the Pacific by the Japan current.

The development of a hierarchal society was expressed visually in terms of architectural embellishments and other forms of artwork, such as heraldic totem poles, blankets, basketry hats and containers, and highly-decorated dance capes with mother-of-pearl buttons and cloth appliqué designs, such as whales. Canoes could be painted with heraldic designs; Haida canoe prows bore the images of the Thunderbird, the victor of the heavens and helper of the people, or the Killer Whale, lord of the sea and underworld.

Spirit masks were naturalistic, portraying specific individuals, or were given moving parts for visual impact. Many naturalistic images, such as the raven, eagle, whale, moon, and weather, have been taken as clan or family crests. Winter was the time for dance societies to celebrate theatrical rites and depict myths through transformation masks, which had strings that revealed a mask within a mask when pulled, allowing Wolf to become Man.

The most well-known art form is the totem pole. These include house posts, commemoration works, and poles that show family and clan crests or historical figures; they might also represent family wealth. Another practice was the potlatch, a ceremony of gift giving that involved feats and dances, which conferred status on the givers and redistributed wealth to improve social harmony; the custom probably originated in marriage gifts and death rituals.

The Coast Salish

///// Salish area

SKAGIT Other tribe

Scowlitz site
Vancouver Island
Pacific Ocean
Hoko River site
LUMMI
MAKAH KALLAM
SKAGIT
CHEMAKUM

0 — 150 miles

Salishan speakers occupying the region of southwest coast of British Columbia and Washington around Puget Sound are known as the Coast Salish. They speak many languages and dialects.

Tlingit totem poles. These ornate, carved structures are a visual embodiment of the tribe's hierarchical society.

Trade Routes and Transport

As Native American civilizations flourished, they began to trade with one another, using waterways and other trails to crisscross the continent.

The travois was a popular means of carrying loads. Before the arrival of the horse, Indians used dogs to pull them.

Several long, north–south routes developed in the Mississippi Valley, with links to the regional trade systems of the Pacific, Gulf, and Atlantic coasts. Certain areas, like the western desert and plateau areas, were poor in land routes, while the California mountains largely prevented long journeys. North America was crisscrossed by watercourses, allowing travel by canoes, which were easily portaged around rapids and waterfalls. Land trails followed river valleys or ridges, and it is thought that some were used by animals first.

The Mississippi is the dominant north–south route, and its tributaries provide links between the areas east and west of the river. For example, the Wisconsin, Illinois, and Ohio rivers enter from the east, while the Minnesota, Missouri, and Arkansas rivers flow in from the west. A major east–west route ran down the St. Lawrence, through the Great Lakes to the Grand Portage and onto the Lake of the Woods. Westward from this lake, connections existed via the Yellowstone and Missouri rivers, which eventually reached the Columbia River to the Pacific coast. A nodal point on this route was the Straits of Mackinac, where southward travel was possible across Lakes Huron and Erie. Then, travelers could use the Sandusky and Scioto rivers to reach the Ohio, or could ascend the Maumee, portage to the Wabash, and descend to the Ohio. Moving southward from the Ohio to the Tennessee River, a trader might leave the latter where it bends eastward and follow the trail south to Mobile Bay. Converging north of the bay are the Tombigbee and Alabama rivers, home to many pre-Columbian civilizations, notably the Mobiles at Mauvila, where de Soto slaughtered so many Native Americans.

In the East, a trail ran the length of the Appalachians, from New York to Georgia, while there was a route from the St. Lawrence to New York and the Atlantic via the Richelieu River, Lake Champlain, and the Hudson River. This became an important campaign route during the Anglo-French imperial wars and the American Revolution. Further south, Cuba was linked to Tampa Bay, where a trail ran around Apalachee Bay to Mobile. From there, the Natchez Indians could be reached, also the Arkansas River.

In the Southwest, the Pueblo villages were important focal points near the Rio Grande River. From Texas, a difficult trail followed the Colorado River, then crossed the dry plains. Routes also followed the Red and Arkansas-Canadian rivers to a pass through the Sangria Mountains, which then reached the head of the Rio Grande, with a trail south to Mexico. Trails in today's Idaho and Dakotas were difficult, only becoming really easy with the availability of horses.

Movements into California and the Pacific Coast from the Plains were possible along three routes. In the south, a desert crossing led to the San Diego/Los Angeles region. In the center, passes around Lake Tahoe were used, and in the north, the Klamath River Valley led to the Sacramento River and San Francisco Bay. In the Northwest, the Columbia River was a trading hub; with the Fraser River, it

The canoe was a vital means of transport throughout North America. There were two types: frame and dugout. In the Pacific Northwest, large, seagoing canoes with raised prows were built by the Haida. This painting, Spreading the Canoe, by Bill Holm (1992) depicts a large dugout canoe being shaped by means of steam.

Opposite: By the time that Europeans arrived in North America, there was a network of trade routes that allowed Native Americans to move goods throughout the country.

Native Americans fishing from a frame canoe. These simple vessels could be covered with birch or elder bark, or animal hides. Their light weight made them easy to carry around falls and rapids.

provided access to a huge hinterland. The Willamette River allowed entry into today's Oregon, while Northwest Pacific Coast Indians used large seagoing canoes to reach other coastal areas and islands.

Modes of transport included the travois and canoe. The travois was an A-frame, the point of which was fastened to the shoulders of a dog. Netting spread across the frame held household, hunting, or trade goods. Two basic canoe types are found in North America. Frame canoes were covered by birch or elder bark, or animal hides. These could be designed to carry between three and forty people. The other type is the dugout, used along the Northwest Pacific Coast and in eastern woodlands. These were hollowed out and shaped by steam. Frame canoes were lightweight and relatively easy to portage; after European trade began, they became the preferred form of water transport. The Pacific Coast dugouts are particularly exemplified by the red cedar Haida canoes, which had raised, projecting prows that made them suitable for sea travel and whaling. Swinomish warriors were known to make canoes that were 50 feet (15 meters) long.

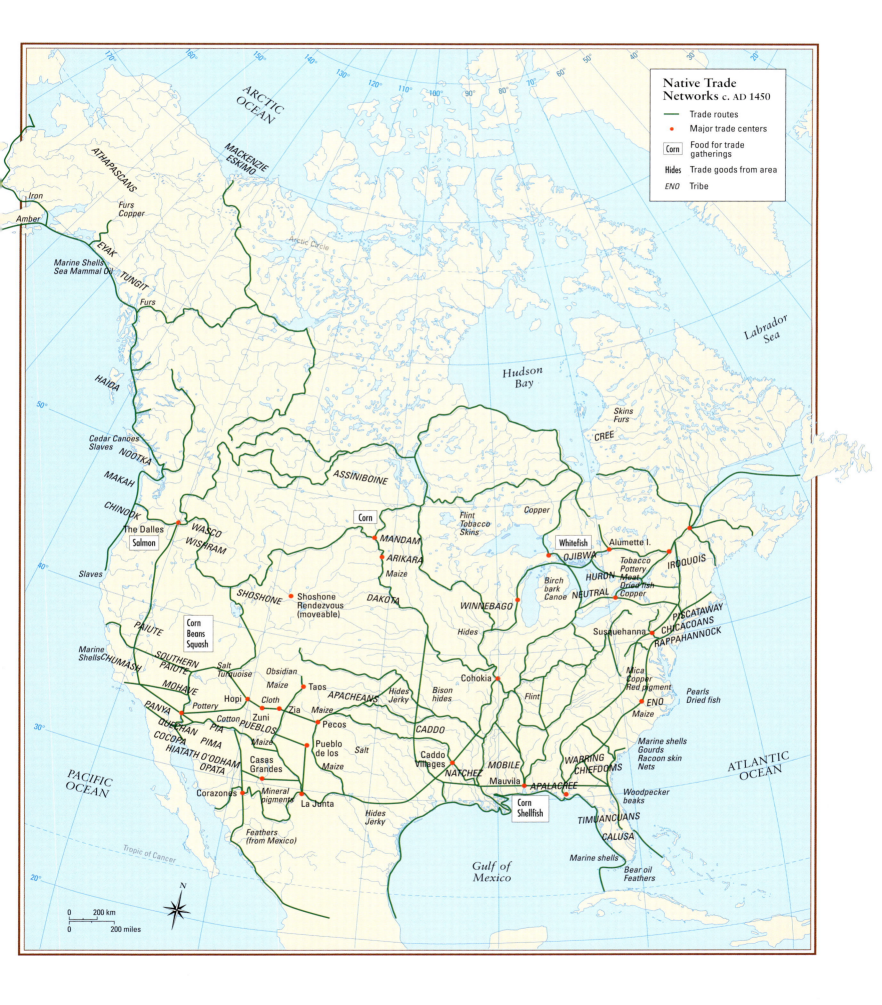

Native Trade Networks c. AD 1450

— Trade routes
• Major trade centers
Corn — Food for trade gatherings
Hides — Trade goods from area
ENO — Tribe

ARCTIC OCEAN

ATHAPASCANS

MACKENZIE ESKIMO

Iron
Amber

Furs
Copper

EYAK

Marine Shells
Sea Mammal Oil

TUNGIT

Furs

HAIDA

MAKAH

CHINOOK

Cedar Canoes
Slaves

NOOTKA

The Dalles
Salmon

WASCO
WISHRAM

Slaves

SHOSHONE

Shoshone
Rendezvous
(moveable)

DAKOTA

ASSINIBOINE

Hudson
Bay

CREE

Labrador
Sea

Skins
Furs

Copper

Corn

MANDAM

ARIKARA

Maize

Flint
Tobacco
Skins

Copper

Whitefish

OJIBWA

Alumette I.

Birch
bark
Canoe

HURON

NEUTRAL

Tobacco
Pottery
Meat
Dried fish
Copper

IROQUOIS

WINNEBAGO

Hides

Marine
Shells

CHUMASH

PAIUTE

Corn
Beans
Squash

SOUTHERN
PAIUTE

MOHAVE

Salt
Turquoise

Obsidian

Maize

Taos

Hopi

Cloth

Zia

Maize

PANYA

Pottery

Zuni

PUEBLOS

APACHEANS

Hides
Jerky

Bison
hides

Cohokia

Flint

PISCATAWAY

CHICACOANS

RAPPAHANNOCK

Susquehanna

Mica
Copper
Red pigment

Pearls
Dried fish

ENO

Maize

QUECHAN

COCOPA

PIMA

PIA

Cotton

Maize

Pecos

Maize

Pueblo
de los

Salt

CADDO

HIATATH O'ODHAM

OPATA

Casas
Grandes

Maize

Caddo
Villages

Natchez

MOBILE

Mauvila

APALACHEE

WABRING
CHIEFDOMS

Marine shells
Gourds
Racoon skin
Nets

Corazones

Mineral
pigments

La Junta

Hides
Jerky

Corn
Shellfish

Woodpecker
beaks

TIMUANCUANS

CALUSA

PACIFIC
OCEAN

Feathers
(from Mexico)

Tropic of Cancer

Gulf of
Mexico

Marine shells

ATLANTIC
OCEAN

Bear oil
Feathers

N

0   200 km
0   200 miles

ART

ALTHOUGH "ART" WAS A FOREIGN CONCEPT TO PRE-CONTACT
NATIVE AMERICANS, THEIR ARTISTIC SKILLS WERE APPARENT IN
THE ADORNMENT OF THE EVERYDAY OBJECTS THEY MADE.

Accepted concepts of art do not apply to pre-contact Native American artifacts. Indian life was motivated by subsistence, and items essential for survival and daily use. Life was circumscribed by ritual, which might have involved collecting materials to make something, or be linked to dance and religion. All aspects came together in a totality that could also embrace religion and shamanism. No Native American language possesses a word meaning "art" in an accepted sense.

Indians used all sorts of symbols from the spiritual and physical worlds to adorn their daily lives and rituals. Symbols could portray power in the world, especially the natural world, demonstrating the interconnection between humanity, animals, and plants. Thus, Native Americans were concerned with

and were aware of the cosmos, which occasionally was represented by a mandala, itself influenced by the shape of a circle, a common image in nature. The circular Aztec calendar was a timekeeping device and a religious symbol. Like Tibetan monks, the Navajo create sand paintings and sand mandalas representing the impermanence of life. Some mandalas are like labyrinths, but with no way out. Medicine wheels and dreamcatchers are two artifacts that exemplify the mandala, linking utensils, religion, and psychology. The hooped willow twig scooping spiders' webs is a form of mandala used by many modern children when out walking on a frosty or dewy morning, when webs are easy to spot. The schematic nature of the patterns in all mandalas depicts the balance of forces within a symbolic universe.

Native Americans, both North and South, have spent thousands of years in relationships with natural forces and life. This understanding

A gold headdress of the
Mochica culture from the North
Coast of Peru.

has generated rituals for specific purposes at important points in time—hunting, cultivating, harvesting, marriage ceremonies, funerary rites, and going to war. The cosmos or world view, however, can be variously depicted by different tribes in differing geographical locations. The Plains and Woodlands societies divided cosmic space into sky, the earth's surface, and places below land and water. Local space was projected as circular, with four quadrant zones representing the cardinal directions of north, south, east, and west in associated colors of red, yellow, white, and black, hues common to many tribes. On the Northwest Pacific Coast, the realms of life were the sea or river, then forests and mountains. All regions of the cosmos were linked to a central vertical axis connecting zones of power and acting as a conduit for prayers. The axis might be represented by a tree of life, especially in modern Navajo blankets or in paintings. The axis could also be a pole, or the space between hearth stones and the overhead smokehole. The cosmic zones were peopled by spirits like the Pueblo kachinas, or the great spirits were represented by etching into stone, pottery, or wood pictures of the Thunderbird, the Underwater Panther, the Eagle, and the Killer Whale. Dreams and vision quests were all part of the all-embracing perceptions in the Native American mind.

A carved Aztec calendar stone, a combination of time keeping device and religious symbol.

How these views are projected into art, perhaps a utensil that is well made and interestingly decorated, can only be seen by observing artifacts that differ according to the cultural region under consideration. The Woodlands communities carved stone and hammered copper with animal symbols. Geometric motifs were common. Porcupine quills were softened and dyed, being used for quilling; shells were another decorative material. Personal adornment could involve tattoos. The Plains tribes employed decorative materials like the Woodland peoples, but increasingly used richly decorated clothing as a way of greeting the gods. Hide paintings might show a tribe's or warrior's history and exploits. The art of the Western Great Basin and Plateau focused on basketry. However, the attempted extermination of the native population by white Americans virtually wiped out their artistic record.

The Navajo are renowned for sand painting. Pictures are made by pouring colored sands onto a surface. They are often used for ritual purposes.

Along the Northwest Pacific Coast, kinship and a hierarchical social system allowed status to be displayed in architecture, totem poles, spirit masks with moving features, and blankets. The masks were important in theater. Southwestern art was also extremely visual, with incredibly beautiful pottery, jewelry, and carefully decorated cotton clothing. Architecturally, the Anasazi were amazing, producing finely wrought pueblos and kivas, while their basketry, textiles, and pottery often depicted animal or astral symbols with an emphasis on contrasting colors.

POPULATION

THE NUMBER OF NATIVE AMERICANS ON THE CONTINENT PRIOR TO EUROPEAN CONTACT IS SUBJECT TO MUCH DEBATE. WHAT IS CLEAR IS THAT AFTER 1492, IT WENT INTO SERIOUS DECLINE.

It has been estimated that there were 75 million Native Americans in both North and South America prior to the arrival of Europeans, the majority living south of the Rio Grande in central Mexico and some of the countries comprising Central and South America. The population north of Mexico, excluding Greenland, has been estimated as being between one and 18 million. Smithsonian Institution anthropologist Douglas Ubelaker states that the generally accepted total for central Mexico, the most densely populated region, is 10–12 million. Peru could have held nine million, while Canada and the United States had two million.

In the early twentieth century, James Mooney concluded that there were only 1.5 million American Indians, Inuit, and Aleuts at the time of the first European contact, but this could vary from the early 1500s to 1845, depending upon the region. In 1966, anthropologist Henry Dobyns argued that European diseases may have wiped out many Native Americans prior to settler contact. For example, illness may have raced down the trade routes from the Labrador fisheries. Also, de Soto found many empty villages during his *entrada*, the result of disease being transported from Spanish Cuba to Florida by local Native American traders. Thus, logically, populations must have been higher than those estimated by Mooney. Dobyns used mortality rates from epidemics and estimates of environmental capabilities for supporting populations in various regions, suggesting that, by 1492, perhaps 18 million lived north of Mesoamerica. Eventually, Ubelaker revised his northern estimate to seven million—five million in the United States' mainland and two million in Alaska, Canada, and Greenland. All scholars agree, however, that 1492 introduced factors that caused population decline for the following 400 years, after which it began to climb.

Whatever the actual population figures, early Americans lived in communities that ranged in size from small villages to cities as large and sophisticated as anywhere else in the world. A minority were nomadic. The densest populations could be found along the coasts and river valleys, around the Great Lakes, in

Mexico, Florida, and the Caribbean Islands, and on the Northwest Pacific Coast. Some 600 languages were spoken, and different communities included bands, chiefdoms, city states, and nations. Native American kings, emperors, prophets, sculptors and poets, scientists, artisans and architects, mathematicians, and doctors could be found. Land, river, and coastal trade routes linked the continent, allowing the spread of ideas and cultural influences among the various peoples. Medicine, surgery, sport, military service, art, diplomatic skills, religion, and dance could all be avenues for social promotion. However, regional distinctions due to climate and environment produced various identities, creating alternative social trajectories, such as the maintenance of tradition, or those of militarization and imperial expansion, as with civilizations in Mesoamerica and the Andes.

Native American cultural areas can be designated in a number of ways. A common system identifies ten regions according to certain characteristics based on climate, land type, and the biological population, and shows how humans adapted to these conditions. The Eastern Woodlands, the Southeast, the Southwest, the Plains, the Californian Inter-mountain region, the Plateau, the Great Basin, the sub-Arctic, the Northwest Pacific Coast, and the Arctic all exist in North America. In addition, to the south were the Mesoamerican and Circum-Caribbean culture areas, and beyond them, the Andean and Amazonian regions. Typical of the various regions were the farmers and fishermen of the woodlands, such as the Iroquoian peoples, who inhabited longhouses, while the Southeast offers the Mound Builders and their civilized tribal heirs. The Southwest is commonly identified with the Pueblos and their Athapascan invaders; the Great Basin was the home of gatherers. California supported a hundred dialects in a food-abundant region, and the Plains were lightly peopled by nomadic hunters. The sub-Arctic peoples comprised small bands of hunters and fishermen, while the Arctic is exemplified by specialized clothing and seal hunting. Mesoamerica and the Andes are commonly represented by the Mayan, Aztec, and Inca civilizations.

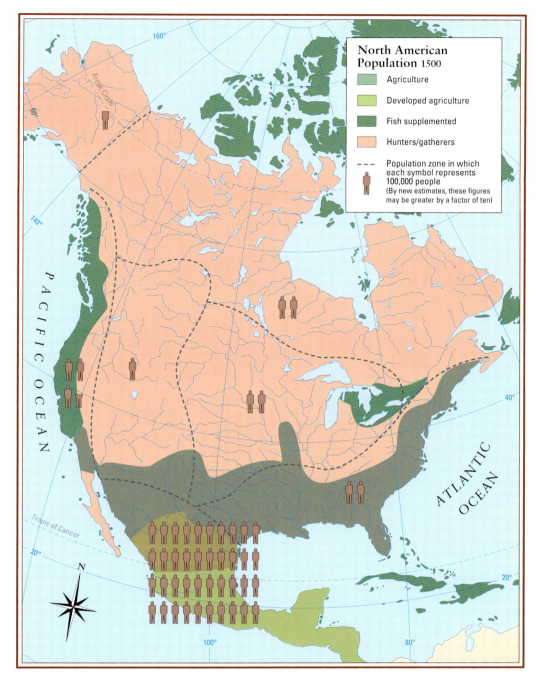

North American Population 1500

- Agriculture
- Developed agriculture
- Fish supplemented
- Hunters/gatherers
- - - - Population zone in which each symbol represents 100,000 people (By new estimates, these figures may be greater by a factor of ten)

At the time of European contact, the majority of Native Americans in North America occupied Mesoamerica.

LANGUAGES

WHEN EUROPEANS FIRST MADE CONTACT WITH NATIVE
AMERICANS, THEY ENCOUNTERED AN ENORMOUS DIVERSITY OF
LANGUAGES AND CULTURES.

An original page from the *Codex Borbonicus* showing the Aztecs' sacred calendar. The Aztecs developed picture writing and produced many books, although few of them have survived.

As many as 2,000 tongues have been estimated in the Americas as a whole. It is not surprising that over thousands of years, languages diversified as people moved, separated, and evolved different cultures. In a few places along the geographically divided Pacific Coast, six mutually unintelligible languages could be spoken in a county-sized area, as in Humboldt County, California.

Students of language development suggest that the first wave of Native American progenitors arriving across Beringia shared a common language or group of closely related languages. This theory argues that a second wave of migrants from northeast Asia settled Alaska and regions of British Columbia; their descendants moved south to become Navajo and Apache, members of the Athabaskan language group, itself belonging to the Na-Dene family. The first wave had moved further south. A third wave became the Aleut/Inuit group. Other theorists argue differently, proffering alternative linguistic classifications. They claim to have identified some sixty-two language families in North America. Some tongues do not fit into a family, however, like the now-extinct Timucuam language of Florida.

Some languages were wiped out by disease and European brutality. Small Indian communities were vulnerable to British linguistic imperialism, as manifested in the Bureau of Indian Affairs boarding schools. Languages likely to survive are Cherokee, Choctaw, Seminole, and some Southwestern tongues, such as Tiwa, Navajo, and Zuni. Algonquian languages are under threat, except perhaps in Canadian Cree and Ojibwa communities. The small groups of Indians in Oregon and California face extinction, such as the Takelma, Yana, Salinan, and Chumash. Efforts to preserve Indian languages result from political and cultural activism, legislation to set up Indian language programs in public schools, tribal-controlled colleges, and through the increasing number of Native Americans entering the broad teaching profession. The national Endowment for the Humanities made a grant to the Makah tribe of Neah Bay, Washington, for the purpose of preserving and teaching their language. Furthermore, written forms of the languages are being used for poetry, narrative, and lexicographic essays on language in Native American tongues, especially in Micmac, Navajo, Winnebago, Miskitu, and Quiché Mayan.

Early European contacts and anthropologists have often regarded

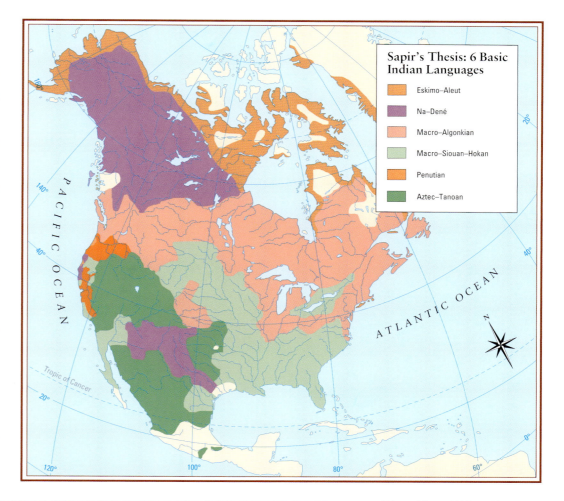

Sapir's Thesis: 6 Basic Indian Languages

- Eskimo–Aleut
- Na–Dené
- Macro–Algonkian
- Macro–Siouan–Hokan
- Penutian
- Aztec–Tanoan

Edward Sapir (1884–1939) was an American anthropologist and linguist. His theory was that there were six basic Native American languages, their spread being shown by this map.

Petroglyphs on Newspaper Rock in southern Utah. This rock has one of the largest known collections of petroglyphs, some of which date to prehistoric times.

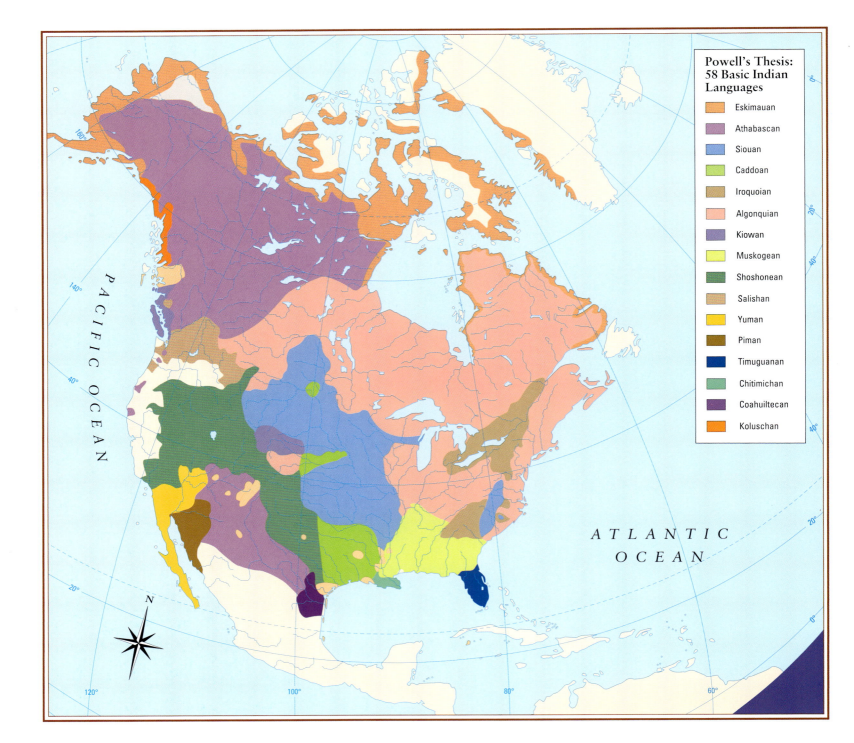

Powell's Thesis:
58 Basic Indian
Languages

- Eskimauan
- Athabascan
- Siouan
- Caddoan
- Iroquoian
- Algonquian
- Kiowan
- Muskogean
- Shoshonean
- Salishan
- Yuman
- Piman
- Timuguanan
- Chitimichan
- Coahuiltecan
- Koluschan

John Wesley Powell (1834–1902) was a soldier, geologist, and explorer of the American West. He became a director of the U.S. Geological Survey and of the Bureau of Ethnology at the Smithsonian Institution. He was responsible for an influential classification of North American Indian languages.

Native Americans as barbaric savages, as witnessed by their lack of written works, despite the fact that most Europeans did not receive an elementary education until the nineteenth century. However, there is evidence for written communication systems. The Olmecs produced plaques and seals marked with glyphs, perhaps a mother culture for the Maya and Aztecs with their similar work. The Iroquois created pictographs in wampum belts to remind oral historians of events, as well as to seal treaties and diplomatic negotiations. The Aztecs and Mayans used picture-writing, but thousands of handwritten Mayan books were burned by fearful Spanish religious zealots; only four remain. Early descriptions of Peruvian languages compiled dictionaries of Incan words, some meaning "to write," "paper," and "letters." A writing system existed with ten consonants. Native American art often recounts stories through images, such as those on rock (petroglyphs) cut by the ancestors of the Pueblo people 600 years ago at Galisteo, New Mexico. They depict an arrow-swallower, a kachina, and a shield.

An early North American written language took the form of hieroglyphics marked on birch bark or animal hides, noticed in the late seventeenth century by a missionary, Father la Clerq, while among the Micmac. He used them to translate holy texts. The Ojibwa etched pictographs into birch-bark scrolls, preserving their sacred songs. The symbols represented sounds, an idea picked up from European contact. A fascinating story recounts how the Cherokee Sequoyah (c. 1770–1843) constructed a syllabary, each Cherokee sound unit being represented by a symbol. Eighty-five symbols represented six vowels, the consonant "s," and seventy-

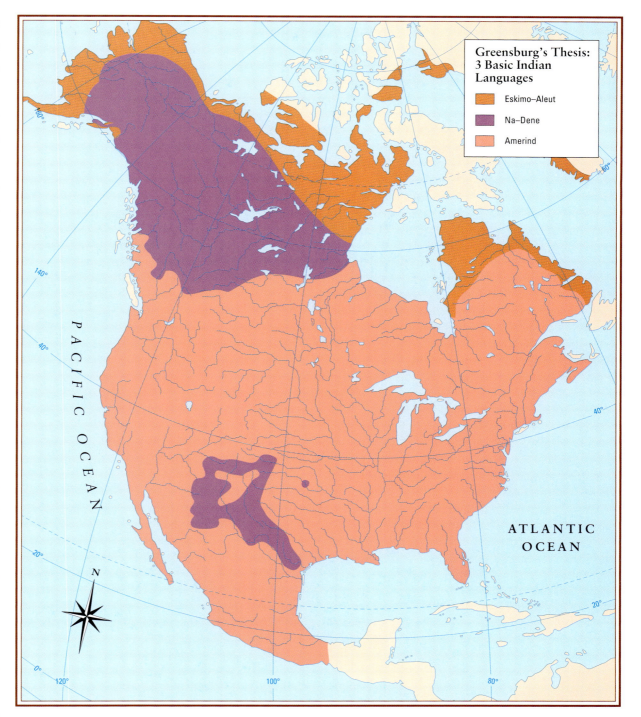

Greensburg's Thesis: 3 Basic Indian Languages
- Eskimo–Aleut
- Na–Dene
- Amerind

eight consonant-vowel units. Capable of being mastered in a few days, the syllabary was typeset to allow the printing of the Bible. Cherokee literacy blossomed; within three years, three-quarters of Cherokee people could read. The *Cherokee Phoenix and Indian Advocate* newspaper was published in bilingual form between 1828 and 1835, when the State of Georgia banned it for advocating Indian rights to their lands in Georgia.

Many words from Indian languages have been absorbed into English, often referring to place names and geographical features. They include the Manhattan cocktail (after a tribe that inhabited the New York region), chocolate, anorak, shark, avocado, and kayak. All have enriched the dominant language's word stock.

Having studied over 1,500 American Indian languages, Joseph Greensburg claimed that all could be placed into one of three groups. His work, plus studies done on blood types and teeth, suggests that there were three separate migrations from Asia into the Americas.

KINSHIP

MATRILINEAL DESCENT IS A COMMON ASPECT OF KINSHIP IN
MANY NATIVE AMERICAN SOCIETIES, AND WOMEN PLAYED A
MUCH MORE IMPORTANT ROLE THAN EUROPEANS REALIZED.

Cherokee Nan'yehi (Nancy Ward), from a drawing by renowned artist George Catlin. Nan'yehi was a famed Native American warrior and diplomat.

Europeans were confused when they first attempted to understand Native American marriage and kinship relations. Women were seen as being exploited by men or were romanticized as being free—the Pocahontas syndrome. Europeans were raised in patrilineal societies and failed to appreciate the role women played in tribal society. Descent through the male line might describe the Ojibwa (Anishinaabe) or Lakota, whose women were not allowed to talk to strangers, but would be inappropriate for the Iroquois, Cherokee, and Pueblo societies. In fact, women were property owners, decision makers, diplomats, and warriors, such as Navajo Annie Wauneka and Chiricahua Apache woman fighter Lozen. Well known is Cherokee Nan'yehi (Nancy Ward, 1738–1824), renowned for her bravery and skill in combat, and her diplomacy. She was called Ghighua, or Beloved Woman (also translates as War Woman), a distinction given to exceptional Cherokee women. In matrilineal Cherokee society, marriages with white traders and diplomats could ratify an alliance or gain commercial advantage. The children of such unions were classed as Cherokee and would blend into tribal life.

Kinship patterns are extremely complex and as diverse as the number of tribes, but the matrilineal societies of the Iroquois (Haudenosaunee) in New York State, and the Arizona Hopi provide clues as to how society was organized. An Iroquois clan mother with her hearth led the system, and all her sons, daughters, and their children for ever were members of the same uterine family and could never inter-marry. The clan mother's husband was the father, but his children were obviously members of his wife's clan by right. Chieftainships (fifty in all) were passed through the female side, and the headwomen chose male representatives to voice clan issues at tribal meetings. If a clan woman moved geographically, she took her clan name with her (Frog, Turtle, Wolf). Her descendants would be related to the mother clan, share its name, and would not inter-marry within it. A collection of such dispersed clans comprised a *phratry*. If a clan member, say Wolf, traveled among the tribes of the

Iroquois League, whether Oneida, Onondaga, Cayuga, or Seneca, he or she would receive hospitality from any constituent Wolf clan. The Iroquois believed that the strength of the nation was built from the collection of individuals from all hearths and clans, and that tribal power was weakened when a member died. Thus, population numbers could be maintained by adoption or by capturing people in war. The whole complex system originated with Onondaga Hiawatha, the legendary figure who assisted the Peacemaker in bringing the tribes together. Also helping the federation to unite was a woman chief, Jikohnsaseh, who crowned the first chairman of the Iroquois League, thereby proclaiming and symbolizing women's power.

The Hopi inhabited the summits of the mesas of the Arizona desert, crowding together into large villages. Previously, when being forced south by Apache bands, natal men, those born of a matrilineal or matrilocal society, moved away to marry. Subsequently, these men would live elsewhere in the village or return to their natal home after a divorce, a fairly common occurrence. Land went with the homes and was owned by women. Men might help with agricultural labor, but the crops remained with the women, to be distributed to household members as the women deemed fit. Another important feature of women was their responsibility for guarding the household fetishes of animals or plants, and to hand their custodianship to a daughter. Interestingly, religious ceremonies were conducted by men, giving a religious basis to a group of descendants through ritual property. The houses were named after natural manifestations—Rabbit, Sun, Corn, Moon. The named houses became the basis for clan development. Like the Iroquois, a daughter might leave the original house, but would take the house name with her. Thus, a number of households would grow, but all would be attached to the same fetish and house/clan name. If a household died out, its lands would be inherited by another related household.

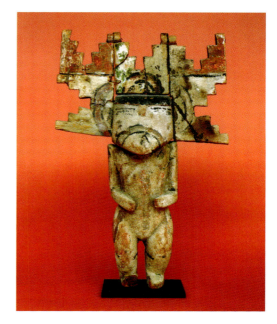

A kachina doll from the late nineteenth century. The dolls play an important role in Hopi and Pueblo cultures, and can represent anything that exists in the natural world. The name itself means "life bringer".

The Hopi community was further strengthened by the Hopi Way, a covenant between their god Masawu and the first Hopi. The community was all, with all relations and clan mothers guiding and inspiring the tribal membership in a spirit of discipline, cooperation, and reciprocity. The kivas, kachina dolls, and religious leaders provided a social cement. The lifestyle of this peaceful people, self-designated as the Hopitou, with its corn-based economy, continues with a yearly cycle of rites and ceremonies.

Annie Wauneka, Navajo leader and chairwoman of the Navajo Tribal Fair, presents a blanket as prize in a fry bread making contest in 1963.

FIRST CONTACTS

"... WHEN THE SKRAELINGS SAW THE MILK THEY WANTED TO BUY NOTHING ELSE. AND SO THE OUTCOME OF THEIR TRADING ... WAS THAT THE SKRAELINGS CARRIED THEIR PURCHASES AWAY IN THEIR BELLIES, AND LEFT THEIR PACKS AND FURS ..."

GRAENLENDINGA SAGA (1382–95), ABOUT VOYAGES TO AMERICA.

Native Americans made their first long-term contacts with Europeans on lands near the Newfoundland and Labrador fishing banks. The earlier Norse/Viking contact was probably short-lived and minimal. Apart from meetings with fishermen, various other types of encounter took place. Firstly, accidental contacts occurred along the American coastline, involving explorers, traders, pirates, shipwrecked sailors, and the crews of ships seeking shelter from storms. Secondly, European explorers and potential colonists wintered among Indians and met nations in the interior. Thirdly, Native Americans in the North met Mesoamericans and Caribbean peoples accompanying de Soto's and Coronado's entradas. Fourthly, there was the missionary experience. Fifthly, trading relationships were made through the early fur business. Finally, contacts were made with colonists from Portugal, France, Spain, and England.

The various early contacts occurred at a time when Native American society was undergoing considerable change. The Iroquoian groups had increased their population owing to the development of a corn-based economy to such an extent that they probably began to develop small alliances, later to become the Iroquois Confederacy, the Five Nations of the Long House (Haudenosaunee). Further south, the late Mississippian society was disintegrating, and tribes were coalescing into new units or confederacies, such as the Creek, Cherokee, Choctaw, and Catawba. On the Atlantic coasts, new "states," based upon overbearing chiefdoms, were being created, like the Virginian-based Powhatans and the Georgia Coosas. In the Southeast, large-scale societies developed in Florida—Calusa and Timucuan— and they bore the brunt of early Spanish incursions. Into this range of societies came a number of different European groups, each with a separate, inchoate agenda. Initially, the St. Lawrence and Labrador tribes met Basque and Breton fishermen, many of whom dried fish on land and established amicable minor trading relations with the Micmac and Montagnais, although the Beothuk were fairly hostile. Added to these encounters were occasional meetings with pirates, traders, and the crews of ships seeking secure harbors. Among these was Giovanni da Verrazzano (1524), an Italian navigator employed by France, who found New York and Narragansett bays. Other examples were Cartier (1534), Diaz (1539), and Cabrillo (1542–43), who eventually explored the Californian coast.

The second manner of contact occurred when the Spanish pushed into Florida and the Southeast, spending winters among Native Americans. Here, Pánfilo de Narváez landed in Tampa Bay in 1528; his expedition was recounted in 1542 by survivor Alvar Núñez Cabeza de Vaca, which stimulated the de Soto (1539–43) and Coronado (1540–42) entradas. These leaders arrived with servants of Caribbean, African, and mestizo origin. De Soto entered the Mississippi region, while Coronado explored the Southwest.

The French impact did not involve large-scale "invasion" forces, but was a bid for mastery of parts of North America to counterbalance Spain. King Francis I sent the Sieur de Roberval (1540–43) to follow up Cartier's earlier exploration of the St. Lawrence. The failure of these expeditions ended French interest in the Americas until Champlain established a presence on the river after his 1604 expedition to the Bay of Fundy.

A most significant series of contacts were those implemented by missionaries, often Franciscan or Dominican friars, who accompanied early Spanish incursions. Such missionary activity began in

A contemporary illustration depicting Samuel de Champlain aiding a war party of Montagnais, Algonkin, and Huron warriors in an attack on the Iroquois. Champlain's activities in this respect would eventually lead to a Franco-British war.

the Caribbean and spread to Mexico after its conquest. Then Franciscans moved into Florida, and Dominicans into New Mexico in 1549 and 1581 respectively. Missionary settlements often ran foul of Indians, who resented their presence. The motives behind missionary penetration were not merely the attempt to "Christianize" Native American souls, but also to push ever onward in the search for lost cities replete with gold and jewels.

The fur trade became a vital ingredient in Native American-European relations. This business contact became linked into the complex Indian trade routes that stretched along the St. Lawrence deep into the Great Lakes region. Rare furs were transported through North America, and some ended up in western Europe. However, early trade in animal products was mainly in hides for leather, known as "deerskins." By 1580, beaver pelts had become an important trade item, exchanged for all manner of metal trinkets and tools. Although French privateers plied their trade along the Atlantic seaboard, genuine businessmen used the St. Lawrence River as a conduit for goods.

The major and lasting incursions into Native American lands were colonies established by Azorean, French, Spanish, and British settlers. Cape Breton Island hosted an Azorean community that pursued fishing, soap making, and farming activities. The first significant European settlements were set up in 1565 at St. Augustine, Florida, and at Santa Elena (1564) in South Carolina. The Spanish treatment meted out to Native Americans resulted in resistance and eventual bloody subjugation, local populations becoming virtual chattels. In 1597, the Guales fought back and ousted the Spanish for several years. The latter retreated to St. Augustine, abandoning Parris Island and its Santa Elena settlement. Elsewhere, the Spanish spread north from Mexico into the Southwest, after discovering silver in Nueva Galicia and Nueva Vizcaya in the mid-1500s. The new settlements became the outer bastions of Mexico and would be used as staging posts for new northward incursions into North America.

Meanwhile, the British established a colony under Raleigh on Roanoke Island, which ultimately failed. However, a second colony was founded in 1607 at Jamestown on the Chesapeake Bay, which grew stronger and wealthier as tobacco cropping grew into a commercial activity. The search for labor led to the acquisition of African slaves, who were introduced into Jamestown in 1619. New diseases joined those brought in by Basque and Breton fishermen in the early 1500s, and by the Spanish in the South. Indians in Spanish territories suffered more than those around the Great Lakes and on the Atlantic seaboard.

By the early 1600s, Native Americans had suffered severe losses through disease, hunger, Spanish violence, and general European greed. However, the European colonial venture had achieved very little in population terms. New settlements were white islands and enclaves in a sea of Native Americans. Jamestown (1607), Québec (1608), and Santa Fé (1610) were surrounded, and all settlers were seriously outnumbered, but Indians were seldom united in resistance to these aliens. Possibly, during this early colonial period, the Indians and Europeans achieved a symbiotic relationship, whereby food and skins were exchanged for metal tools and other trade goods.

Opposite: When Europeans first arrived in North America, the native population was spread throughout the continent and pursuing a number of lifeways.

The appearance of Europeans was a shock to many Native Americans, who responded in a variety of ways. In 1633, a Montagnais Indian, from eastern Canada, told a French Jesuit priest a tale recounted to him by his grandmother of the Indian reaction to seeing the first French ship in their world. The vessel was described as a floating island, its masts being trees, and the sail spars branches. Climbing in this

Lifeways at the Moment of European Contact c. AD 1515

- Arctic hunter-gatherers
- Sub-Arctic hunter-fisher-gatherers
- NW coast marine economy
- Plains hunter-gatherers
- Farming people of the plains
- Animal herding, non-farming people
- Animal herding people with low-intensity farming
- Animal herding people with extensive farming
- Pueblos with intensive farming
- Seacoast foragers
- Hunters with limited farming
- Farming chiefdoms on river settlements
- Orchard-growing alligator hunters
- Tidewater farmers
- Fishers and wild rice gatherers

PACIFIC OCEAN

ATLANTIC OCEAN

Tropic of Cancer

N

forest were bears who turned out to be men. The French offered the Montagnais wine and ship's biscuit, but from these, the Indians gained the impression that the newcomers drank blood and ate wood. Thus, the Indians appeared to attribute certain mystical and magical properties to the Europeans, and this was not an uncommon perception. Despite awe, Indians traded with Cartier, but kept their women out of sight in the forest. Later, however, the Iroquois of Hochelaga would take their sick to him to heal. Survivors of the Narváez expedition only managed to cross Texas because the local peoples thought Cabeza de Vaca was a shaman/healer who had extracted an arrowhead from a man's chest.

Another response was immediate armed resistance. Whereas some Indians gave the invaders food and women, rather than have them forcefully seized, others waited to attack de Soto en route. The antagonism was fueled by knowledge of the massacres at Tiguex and Mabila. Native Americans rapidly realized that armored Europeans were not immune from arrows. Despite superiority in weapons technology, horses, and fierce dogs, all Spanish entradas left a trail of dead Spaniards and their Native American allies.

Indians were interested in European goods, just as Europeans studied Indian agricultural methods and needed their aid. Native Americans acquired European products from shipwrecks, as gifts from explorers, from abandoned fishing stations and settlements, and by theft, but mostly from trade. Many items emanated from the Canadian fishing grounds and Florida, and occasionally from Europeans in the Chesapeake Bay. Indians desired these goods for a variety of reasons. Some were considered exotic and could be used as grave goods. One historian, Hamell, suggested that this process revitalized burial ceremonials and rituals, with a renaissance of tribal interchanges of luxury items. Additionally, Native

Americans appreciated the durability of metal knives, hatchets, and other ironware

A largely ignored Native American-European cultural exchange lay in foods and diet. Europeans introduced chickens, pigs, sheep, cows, and horses, which eventually revolutionized diet and transportation. Pigs or hogs were lost on the entradas and became significant food sources, while the Navajo eventually herded sheep. The horse was exchanged all over the Plains and Great Plateau in advance of further European exploration and expansion. Corn, beans, and squash remained more important than European cereals, yet European vegetables, such as cabbages, lettuces, peas, carrots, turnips, onions, garlic, and cucumbers, were introduced into Indian gardens by the Spanish. By 1690, the Hopi were growing peaches, plums, cherries, chillis, and onions; the deconstruction of adobe bricks from the Abo and Awatabi missions revealed the seeds and pips of wheat, apricot, and wine grapes. The introduction of chillis from the Spanish-held South made these peppers essential cultural ingredients for Pueblo inhabitants.

The lessons of early contacts, before the colonial venture was thoroughly under way, showed that strongly fortified European settlements could be overcome by Native American resistance. In European terms, ultimate survival meant expansion and conquest, a lesson from the European homeland political and economic experience. In the short term, Indians and Europeans accepted each other, although in a tense fashion, but generally maintained cultural boundaries. Yet, as increasing quantities of European metal goods were obtained and circulated among the tribes, Native Americans wanted more to gain an advantage over tribal neighbors. European contacts and goods were not just a potential threat to Native Americans, but also a means of exacerbating existing inter-tribal conflicts.

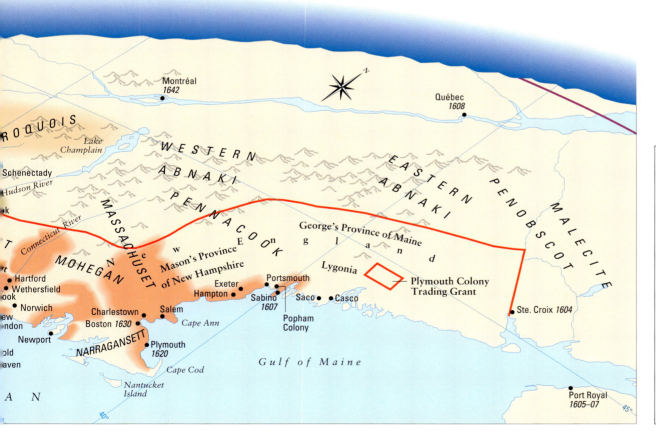

By 1660, a number of European settlements had been established on the Atlantic coast. The British had a substantial presence, as did the Dutch; Sweden had a small colony too.

European Settlement along the Atlantic Coast
c. 1660

HURON Indian tribe

█ British settlement

█ Dutch settlement

█ Swedish settlement

1634 Date of settlement

◯ Grant to Virginia Company of London

◯ Grant to Virginia Company of Plymouth

◯ Grant to Council for New England

‐‐‐ Treaty of Hartford boundary between English and Dutch, 1650

Nations and Tribes, c. 1450

Native American history before major European contact is difficult to ascertain, but archaeological research gives an idea of their distribution.

Native American history before major European contact is difficult to ascertain. European records begin in the late fifteenth and early sixteenth centuries, and tend to be maps or lists of place names. Only a small body of written documents provides eyewitness accounts of European-Indian contacts. Whalers and fishermen who frequented the Canadian coast provide no evidence, although commercial fisheries were large-scale ventures. When records do emerge of Spanish entradas, Francis Drake on the Pacific Coast, and French penetration of the St. Lawrence, together with their meetings with Indians, they merely provide snapshots of immediate locales, rather than the interior. However, information and supposition allow some estimate to be made of where various nations lived; the first map of North America was compiled in 1500 by Juan de la Cosa, a colleague of Columbus. The history of Central America can be judged from rich archaeological evidence, early Spanish records of the Aztecs, and from Mayan books, such as the *Codex Tro-Cortesianus*.

Elsewhere, in the Northeast, two language groups existed, the Algonquian and the Iroquoian. The former inhabited Nova Scotia to New England, through the Hudson Valley, Long Island, and the Delaware Valley, and included Micmac, Abenaki, Pequot, Narragansett, and Wampanoag. A further group lived around the Great Lakes, exemplified by the Algonkin, Menominee, Ottowa, and Potawatomi. A third branch were the Prairie Algonkin, the Illinois, Kickapoo, Miami, Sauk, and Shawnee. The Iroquoian dwelt in New York State, Québec, and Ontario; some of them formed the League of Five Nations. Some evidence of the area can be discovered in the records left by the explorers Verrazzano, Gomez, and Cartier.

The distribution of Indian nations in the early sixteenth century.

Indian Culture Areas, North America c. 1500

- Arctic
- Subarctic
- Northwest Coast
- Plateau
- Great Basin
- California
- Southwest
- Plains
- Eastern Woodlands Northeast
- Eastern Woodlands Southeast

ESKIMOS

ALIKS

KUTCHINS

NAS

Victoria Island

Great Bear Lake

DOGRIBS

Great Slave Lake

SLAVEYS

CHIPPEWYANS

Baffin Island

ESKIMOS

Hudson Bay

NASKAPIS

CREES

CREES

BEAVERS

MONTAGNAIS

BEOTHUKS
Newfoundland

NGITS

TAIMSHIAN

SARAIS

ST. Lawrence R.

MICMACS

ABENAKIS

KWAKIUTIS

SHUSWAPS

BLACKFEET

ASSINIBOINS

OOTKAS

THOMPSONS

SALISHS

SANPOILS

GROS VENTRE

OJIBWAS

OTTAWAS

HURONS

Lake Superior

CHINOOKS

YAKIMAS

NEZ PERCÉS

FLATHEADS

SIOUX

SACS

WINNEBAGOS

Lake Michigan

Lake Huron

L. Ontario

IROQUOIS

MASSACHUSETTS

WAMPANOAGS

NARRAGANSETTS

CROWS

MANDANS

FOXES

Lake Erie

SUSQUEHANNOCKS

PEQUOTS

OKAS

MOS

WASHOS

SHOSHONES

CHEYENNES

ARIKARAS

MIAMIS

ERIES

DELAWARES

OKUTS

PAIUTES

PAWNEES

ILLINOIS

SHAWNEES

MASH

Colorado R.

UTES

ARAPAHOS

Arkansas R.

Missouri R.

OSAGES

POWHATANS

LUISEÑOS

WALAPAIS

MOHAVES

HOPIS

NAVAJOS

ZUNIS

KIOWAS

WICHITAS

TUSCARORAS

YUMAS

PAPAGOS

RIO GRANDE PUEBLOS

APACHES

Mississippi R.

CHEROKEES

CHICKASAWS

CATAWBAS

CREEKS

PIMAS

CADDOS

CHOCTAWS

GUALES (YAMASEES)

NATCHEZ

MOBILES

ATLANTIC OCEAN

N

Rio Grande

COAHULTECS

Gulf of Mexico

CALUSAS

0   400 km

0   400 miles

Tropic of Cancer

The concept of Indian "nations" stems largely from the desire of European governments to negotiate with other governments. In fact, the tribes were mainly language groups comprising a number of largely independent bands with little or no centralized control. This map shows the location of the "nations" at the beginning of the seventeenth century.

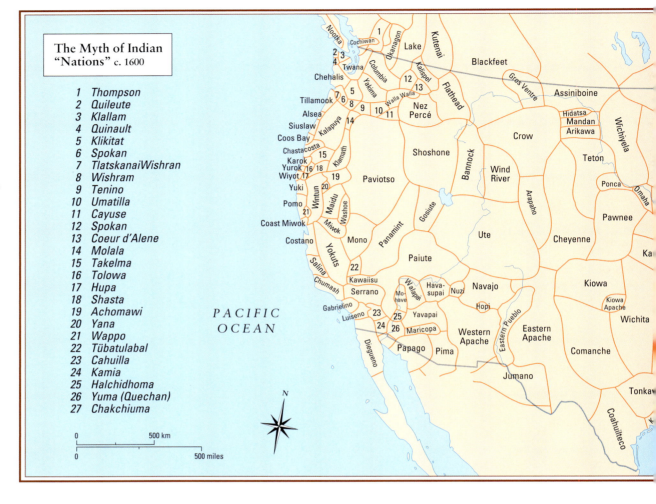

The Myth of Indian "Nations" c. 1600

1 Thompson
2 Quileute
3 Klallam
4 Quinault
5 Klikitat
6 Spokan
7 TlatskanaiWishran
8 Wishram
9 Tenino
10 Umatilla
11 Cayuse
12 Spokan
13 Coeur d'Alene
14 Molala
15 Takelma
16 Tolowa
17 Hupa
18 Shasta
19 Achomawi
20 Yana
21 Wappo
22 Tübatulabal
23 Cahuilla
24 Kamia
25 Halchidhoma
26 Yuma (Quechan)
27 Chakchiuma

In the Southwest, populations began collecting around the Zuni and Pecos Pueblos, evidenced by the spreading Kachina cult, and the region became a nodal trade point. The Southeast comprised a number of farming, fishing, and hunting communities: from north to south, there were Iroquoians (Meherrin, Nottaway, and Tuscarora); Algonquian sharing the same lands (Powhatan, Secotan, and Weapemeoc), and some of these were merging into larger units, such as the so-called Powhatan Confederacy. Next were Muskogean speakers, who included Apalachee, Choctaw, Chickasaw, and Creek. The Cherokee were related more to the Iroquois, but were distinct. These peoples, with the unrelated Natchez, Caddo, and Atakapa, were restructuring after the erosion of the Mound Culture and the impact of European disease. Although these civilizations were robust, they felt the impact of Spanish entradas. The Florida tribes of the Calusa, Tekesta, and Timucua are clearly described in Spanish records, and they suffered the devastating impact of European sickness and warfare before other nations.

The vast Great Plains area was sparsely inhabited. The Blackfeet and Shoshone hunted buffalo, but the Siouan Mandan and Hidatsa, and the Caddoan Caddo, Wichita, Pawnee, and Arikara settled in farming villages in river valleys. Brief contacts were made with Europeans via the Cabeza de Vaca and Coronado incursions.

California was occupied by diverse tribes with many differing tongues, each relating to a particular environment. Bands such as the Miwok met Drake in 1579, while the Spanish expeditions of Unamuno (1587) and Cirmenho (1590) had little impact. The Plateau was sparsely populated along river valleys

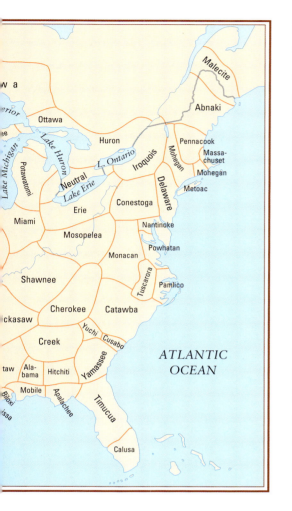

by such tribes as the Klamath, Modoc, Nez Perce, Cayuse, and Walla Walla to the South, and by the Salish and Spokane to the North. The Great Basin is a desert characterized by the Great Salt Lake. There, tribes lived by gathering and hunting small game, the main tribal groups being Paiute, Shoshone, and Ute.

The Northwest might be a narrow strip of land, but it contains many isolated microenvironments, the rich conditions of which allowed up to 200,000 inhabitants— such as the Tlingit, Haida, and Chinook—to develop many cultures and languages. These tribes probably encountered Europeans centuries after those in Florida. The Arctic was inhabited by Inuit and Aleut; British Captain Frobisher was shot at with an iron-headed arrow during his 1576–78 expedition. The Subarctic incorporated the vast territory from Alaska to Newfoundland, and was home to Athabaskan and Algonquian tribes. The former included the Ahtena, Beaver, Hare, Ingalik, and Tagish, while the latter comprised Cree, Montagnais, Naskapi, and northern Ojibwa among others. The Newfoundland Beothuk appear unrelated to these two groups

Fort Yukon, established in Alaska in 1847 by Alexander Murray. It acted as a trading post among the Kutchin people, an Athabaskan tribal group.

Food and Nutrition, 1450

BEFORE CONTACT WITH EUROPEANS, NATIVE AMERICANS THROUGHOUT THE CONTINENT HAD ACCESS TO A WIDE VARIETY OF FOODS, MANY OF WHICH ARE STILL EATEN TODAY.

Native Americans used a vast range of domesticated and wild plants. The New York and Ohio valley regions provided many fruits, such as grapes, plums, thorn apples, cherries, strawberries, bear berries, blackberries, blueberries, elderberries, and sumac berries. Nuts included acorns, butternuts, hickory nuts, walnuts, hazelnuts, and beechnuts. The Northeast witnessed the domestication of sunflowers for seed and tubers (Jerusalem artichokes), sumpweed, goosefoot, maygrass, and giant ragweed. Throughout the area, as elsewhere, corn, beans, and squash became staple foods.

The Great Lakes provided wild rice in shallow waters, and the Ojibwa fought hard to hold and increase control of these rice lands. A common food for hunting expeditions and traveling was pemmican, pounded dried meat mixed with fat and berries. Spring greens were commonly grown, and the Delaware are reported to have harvested young dandelion, milkweed, pokeweed, lamb's quarters, mustard, dock, and watercress, mixing them with cooked meat.

Corn was immensely important, and many varieties were developed to suit diverse growing conditions. Originally the small seeds of a wild grass, teosinte, the 1450 varieties could produce a crop in the short northern growing season or have deep roots to suit Southwest conditions. Through selected breeding, the Navajo developed white, red, black and white, and the usual yellow corn. The botanical treasure store of Central and South America also produced pineapples, avocado, papaya, cocoa, beans, tomatoes, chillis, potatoes, sweet potatoes, peanuts, cashews, vanilla, and manioc, but many of these never traveled north.

The Southwest provided corn, squash, and bean varieties, including the protein-rich tepary. Wild foods included seeds—amaranth, lamb's quarter, saguaro, mustard and pigweed; fruits—cholla and prickly pear; and nuts—black walnuts and piñon. Interestingly, corn provides 348 calories per 3.5 ounces (100 grams), whereas the same weight of piñon nuts gives 635 calories.

Over time, beans, squash, and corn became the most important crops; when beans and corn are cooked together, by virtue of their amino acids, they produce complete protein. Added to these were sweeteners in the form of wild honey, dried and fresh fruit, and maple syrup. The last was commonly used by the Great Lakes nations. Indian cuisine tended to comprise a soup or stew accompanied by some type of bread, or roasted meat or fish. Boiling food was achieved with the aid of ceramic vessels in the Southwest and East; on the Plains, a cleaned buffalo paunch could be held by sticks and filled with water, into which hot stones were dropped.

Protein was readily available. Eastern coastal regions provided deer, wild geese, lobsters, clams, mussels, bass, cod, and squid. Wild turkeys and, occasionally, dogs were also eaten. The Plains provided buffalo in vast herds. The Northwest gave up salmon, halibut, and whales. Flesh could be dried, smoked, or preserved in rendered whale and seal oil. In fact, fats were important for all Native Americans, and bears provided a sustainable source. California and the Great Basin were rich in plants and small game.

Native Americans also employed wild and cultivated plants for social and religious purposes. South Americans had the coca leaf, the origin of cocaine, while tobacco was used throughout North America, with the exception of the extreme north. Tobacco was a feature of social rituals and could be smoked, eaten, used as snuff, or burned for incense. Alcohol was widely imbibed in certain areas before Europeans arrived. Mexicans produced forty different beverages, ranging from corn beer to fermented honey. The Southwest had a cactus wine, and the Southeast persimmon wine. The Aztecs used intoxication for meditation and to aid prophecy. Papagos and Pimas believed drinking alcohol would bring rain. In Northern Mexico and along the Rio Grande, the people valued the hallucinogenic properties of peyote buttons. Certain Mexican tribes and Apaches took them to suppress hunger and thirst or for religious purposes to induce psychedelic experiences, which later might be expressed in art. Comanche raids spread peyote to the Kiowa, Cheyenne, and Arapaho. Other drugs used were mescal and certain mushrooms, such as the teonanacatl.

A Pima woman grinding corn. Although this photograph was taken in 1913, the technique used is ancient. The kernels of corn are placed on a flat rock known as a *matate* and then a smaller rock, a *mano*, is rolled over them. Years of use would gradually create a depression in the *matate*.

L'Anse aux Meadows: The Vikings

Although short-lived, Norsemen established a presence in present-day Newfoundland. Their contacts with Native Americans were not always amicable.

Two Viking sagas, *The Greenlanders' Saga* and *The Saga of Erik the Red*, agree that in approximately AD 985, Erik the Red sailed from Iceland to settle in Greenland. In that year, Bjarni Herjolfsson attempted the same voyage, but bad weather drove him west, past Greenland to a low, wooded shore, which he briefly explored before returning eastward. Later, Erik's son, Leif, sailed to the newly discovered lands and came across salmon and grapes; hence, he called the country Vinland (Wineland). Other places mentioned in the sagas are Helluland (Flat Stone Land—Baffin Island) and Markland (Forest Land—Labrador). Vinland is now known to be the northern peninsula of Newfoundland. Or, to be more precise, that is the entry point into Vinland.

Between AD 1000 and 1030, the Vikings made at least four voyages to Vinland. Houses were constructed, as was a smelting works. The site of this settlement was discovered in 1960 at L'Anse aux Meadows, and excavations began under Helge and Anne Stine Ingstad; Parks Canada continued the dig between 1973 and 1976. The settlement was large, due to the fact that Thorfinn Karlsefni, an Icelandic trader, reached Newfoundland with 135 men, fifteen women, livestock, and at least three ships. The archaeological site comprises eight Norse buildings, dwelling places, workshops, a furnace, and a smithy. The area has provided some 2,000 pieces of worked wood, basically debris from smoothing and trimming lumber, which later was transported to Greenland, as the sagas describe.

The site has three complexes, each used as winter quarters, but probably housing specialist workers.

It is likely that the smiths lived near the brook, where a workshop was used to heat bog iron ore; they also had a forge to smelt iron in a furnace. The operation was inefficient, and the slag heaps show that 80 percent of the iron remained in the slag. About 6.5 pounds (3 kilograms) of iron were made, which was used mainly to make nails and rivets. These would have been used to repair and refurbish the Vikings' ships.

Among the ruins of the settlement, archaeologists found a bronze, ring-headed pin, a stone oil lamp, and a spindle whorl. A bone needle and small whetstone were also discovered. The large, multiroomed buildings were constructed of sod over wooden frames, while workshops were small, square huts sunk into the ground; all are in Icelandic styles. Since the buildings appear permanent and seem similar to Viking trading centers elsewhere, the settlement was probably used as a collection point for shipping lumber to treeless Greenland, along with other useful products, such as grapes. Evidence that the Norsemen explored further south can be seen in the find of three butternuts, a Northern American type of walnut, and a knot of butternut wood. These nuts have never grown north of the St. Lawrence Valley and northeastern New Brunswick.

No one knows why the settlement was short-lived. Karlsefni's group met Native Americans, possibly ancestors of the Montagnais and Beothuks, or possibly Inuit. The Norsemen called them Skraelings, and relationships were often violent. Being outnumbered by the Indians could be the reason for the settlement's abandonment, or perhaps the constant voyages were too costly. Whatever the case, the Norsemen retrenched to Greenland. There, they had arrived simultaneously with the Inuit of the Thule culture, who had reached northwestern Greenland.

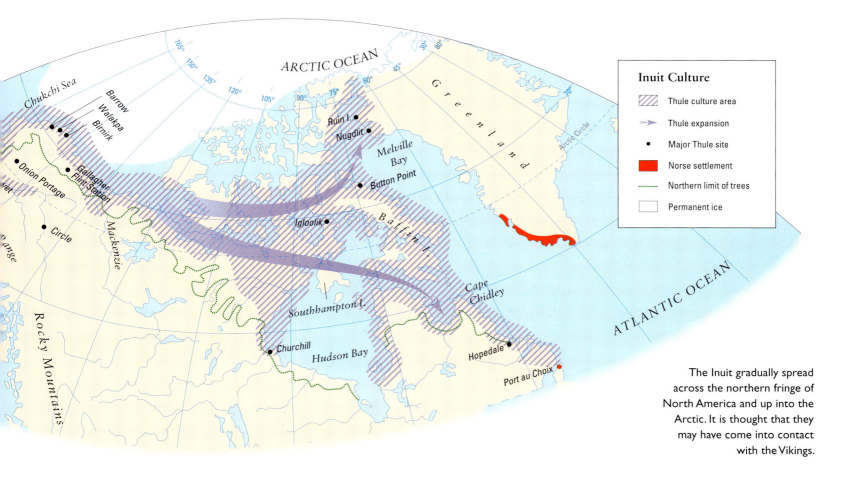

Inuit Culture

⬚ Thule culture area

➤ Thule expansion

● Major Thule site

▮ Norse settlement

⋯ Northern limit of trees

☐ Permanent ice

The Inuit gradually spread across the northern fringe of North America and up into the Arctic. It is thought that they may have come into contact with the Vikings.

Opposite: Vikings voyaged to North America from Greenland, establishing at least one settlement, at L'Anse aux Meadows on the coast of present-day Newfoundland. It is possible that they journeyed further south.

Inuit-Norse contact has resulted in Norse objects being found in Inuit archaeological sites; much would have been stripped out of Norse farms when their inhabitants left. Chain mail, woolen cloth, metal clinch nails, and a comb have been discovered in northwestern Greenland and on Ellesmere Island. The relations between the Inuit and the Norsemen probably ranged from trade to warfare. Greenlanders were dependent on Iceland and Europe for grain, lumber, and luxury goods; they would have been purchased with walrus, polar bear, and other skins. Also useful was walrus and narwhal ivory, and records show that vast quantities of this material were sold. However, it could only be obtained 300 miles (500 kilometers) north of the Greenland settlements. Logic suggests that the Norsemen would have traded with the Inuit for ivory to ensure a ready and continuous supply.

Dating from 1741, this etching by J.M. Fosie depicts Inuit dwellings in Greenland. They would have employed similar structures elsewhere.

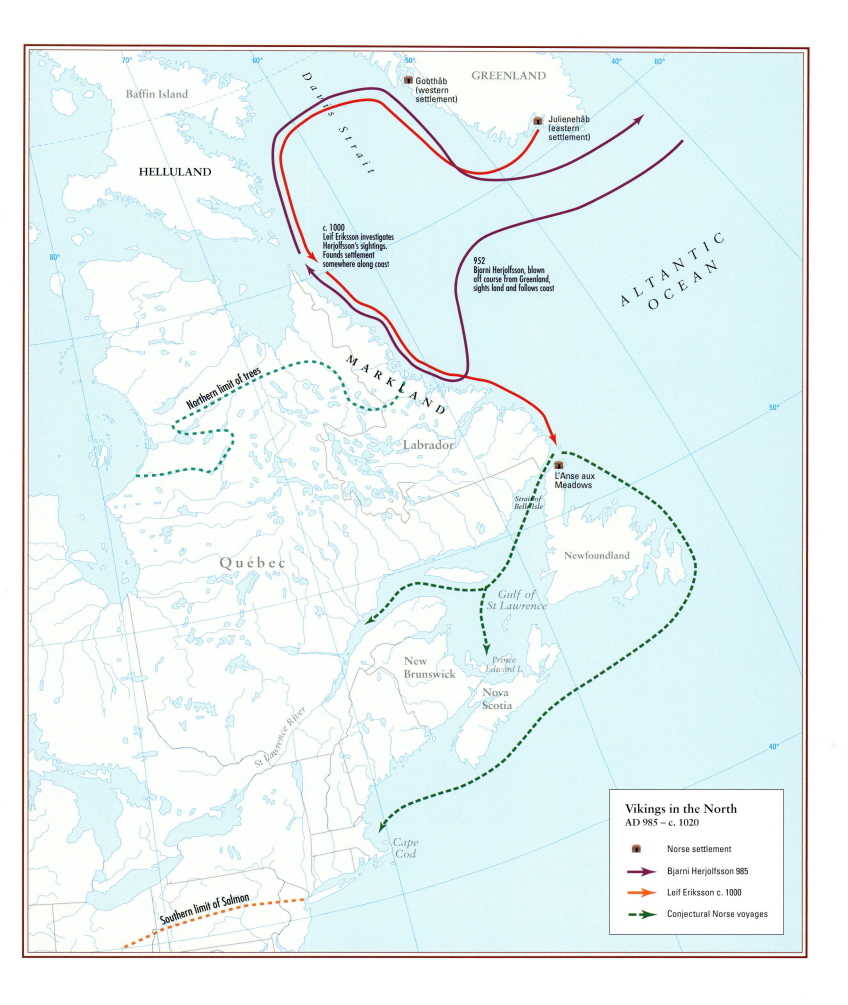

Baffin Island

Davis Strait

Gobthåb (western settlement)

GREENLAND

Julienehåb (eastern settlement)

HELLULAND

c. 1000
Leif Eriksson investigates
Herjolfsson's sightings.
Founds settlement
somewhere along coast

952
Bjarni Herjolfsson, blown
off course from Greenland,
sights land and follows coast

ATLANTIC OCEAN

Northern limit of trees

MARKLAND

Labrador

L'Anse aux Meadows

Strait of Belle Isle

Newfoundland

Québec

Gulf of St Lawrence

Prince Edward I.

New Brunswick

Nova Scotia

St Lawrence River

Cape Cod

Southern limit of Salmon

Vikings in the North
AD 985 – c. 1020

Norse settlement

Bjarni Herjolfsson 985

Leif Eriksson c. 1000

Conjectural Norse voyages

COMMERCIAL FISHERIES:
THE BASQUES AND FRENCH

ATTRACTED TO THE NORTH AMERICAN COAST BY THE PROMISE
OF GOOD FISHING, THE BASQUES AND FRENCH DEVELOPED
SUBSTANTIAL FISHERIES IN THE REGION, AND PAVED THE WAY
FOR COLONIZATION.

Newfoundland fish are recorded as having been landed in England in 1504, and in 1506, Portugal was levying customs duties on American cod. Normans were fishing in American waters in 1504, and Bretons in 1511, followed by the Basques in 1512. Ships crossed the Atlantic each summer and engaged in one of two practices. Wet fishing involved salting a catch and returning to Europe immediately, whereas dry fishing involved landing the catch in North America, where it was gutted, salted, washed, and dried on racks, before sailing back to Europe to sell the product.

The Portuguese and Spanish Basques fished off the south and east coasts of Newfoundland, while the Bretons sailed into the Belle Isle Straits, fishing off Cape Breton and the nearby Nova Scotian coasts. By 1540, Spanish and French Basques controlled the Belle Isle Straits, and hunted bowhead and right whales off the coast of Newfoundland. Dead whales were towed to rendering stations established around the edge of Red Bay, Labrador. The flukes and flippers were removed, then strips of skin and blubber were cut into chunks and boiled down in large copper cauldrons, the oil being stored in wooden casks before being shipped to Europe. Bones of whales killed by Basques still litter the beaches of Red Bay Harbor. As many as 1,000 Basques were engaged in the whaling industry at one time, sailing ships of up to 600 tons.

By the 1570s, British fishermen had taken control of the eastern Avalon Peninsula of Newfoundland, while Spanish and French Basques fished waters in the Gulf of St. Lawrence and off the rest of Newfoundland. By 1578, between 300 and 350 ships were engaged in these fisheries. Those operating the dry fisheries and whaling landed thousands of Europeans on the northeastern coasts of North America, perhaps as many as 20,000 by 1580. These fishermen met Beothuks, Montagnais, and Micmac Indians. Conflict could occur over competition for fishing sites and because the Europeans felled timber to produce flakes for drying fires. When Europeans returned home, the Indians would dismantle the fishing installations to reuse iron nails and other goods. In general, though, the Indians would accept gifts, help in processing fish, and occasionally engage in treading animal skins. Basque-Montagnais relations were amicable, such that small boats could be left in Labrador over the winter and remain untouched for the following season. The Beothuks were recorded as being cruel, however, and boats and gear needed guarding against attack.

The European fishermen were a valuable asset to be exploited by the Indians—a source of new technologies and metal. Thus, Indians would compete among themselves violently to control the flow of goods. Moreover, inter-European rivalries could cause competition and aggression over the control of the fishing waters.

Much evidence for the fisheries was discovered by historical geographer Selma Barkham in Spanish Basque archives. Thousands of documents established the importance of the Red Bay whaling settlement. Papers showed that a Basque whaler, the *San Juan*, had sunk with 1,000 barrels of newly processed whale oil. Underwater archaeologists found this ship in 24 feet (7 meters) of water, together with the remains of other sunken ships. Adzes, axes, knives, harpoons, and pitchers were recovered from the *San Juan*. Graves of European seamen were also discovered in the area, men presumably killed in the whale hunt.

A detail from a 1721 map of North America by Herman Moll, showing cod being dressed and dried in Newfoundland. There were extensive fishing grounds off the northeast coast of North America, which drew boats from France, Spain, and England.

The result of such commercial fisheries was the virtual eradication of right and bowhead whales; archaeologists have estimated that Basque hunting was responsible for a global decline in whales, which began in European waters. Another outcome was the impact on Native Americans. New trade routes were developed to channel the annual influx of European goods. European metal and hardwoods were crafted into knives, drills, engraving tools, and axes. Indian settlements moved nearer to the Basque fisheries to exploit prestige goods, and an Indian entrepreneurial class developed to trade in European products. Probably the most significant result of the commercial fisheries was the importation of European diseases, soon to be spread along the new trade routes into the interior.

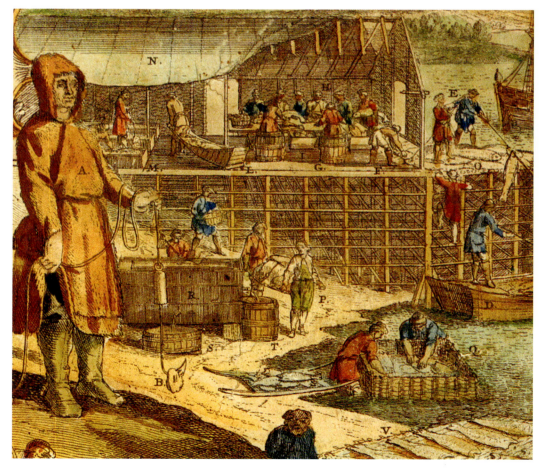

Caribbean Encounters

DISCOVERED BY COLUMBUS, THE ISLANDS OF THE CARIBBEAN WERE SOON STRIPPED OF THEIR POPULATIONS AS THE SPANISH ENSLAVED THEIR INHABITANTS.

On August 3, 1492, Christopher Columbus sailed west from Palos, Spain, intending to find a way to the Orient. On October 12, his expedition reached the Bahamas, and Columbus claimed the islands for Spain in front of dismayed and uncomprehending Arawakan Lucayos Indians. Further landings were made, including those at Cuba and Hispaniola. Then he returned home, leaving several men at a small fort, La Navidad, Hispaniola. These men were killed by the Arawak after acting brutally toward the Indians. A second expedition left Spain in September 1493, with seventeen ships and 1,500 men. Calling at Dominica, Guadeloupe, and Antigua, Columbus reached Hispaniola and established the colony of Isabella.

During these travels, Columbus met the Arawak, whose elite were the Tainos; they inhabited the Greater Antilles, Cuba, Hispaniola, Jamaica, and Puerto Rico. The Guanahatabeys (Ciboneys) lived in extreme western Cuba, and the Caribs in the Lesser Antilles. The former originated from the north, probably Florida, while the latter and the Arawak sailed to the islands from northern South America. The more aggressive Carib had forced the Arawak out of the Lesser Antilles.

Historians have estimated an island population of over four million people. By 1492, the Arawak were the most culturally advanced islanders, and their canoe traders brought influences from Mesoamerica, Mayan links being obvious, especially the ballcourt. Families of Taino rank inhabited houses facing an open plaza, used for rituals and meetings. Surrounding these would be the dwellings of commoners. Each village was ruled by a cacique, and sometimes several villages were united in a cicazgos ruled by a supreme chief. Some towns housed up to 3,000 people. Arawak agriculture was sophisticated, with cultivated fields producing many fruits and vegetables. Cassava cakes made from yucca roots, iguana meat, fish, and maize were eaten. Other foods were maguez, pawpaw, mammee apple, edible cactus, and guaicum. The Arawak traded feathers, gold, wood, pottery, cotton, parrots, and foodstuffs.

A late-nineteenth century, romantic depiction of Columbus taking possession of the New World in the name of Spain in 1492. The arrival of the Europeans would have a disastrous outcome for all Native American populations.

Although the Arawak are now extinct, some of their words were adopted by Spaniards and other western settlers. Hammock came from *hamaca*, while maize, manatee, caymen, savanna, and hurricane are well known. The great wind, the divine Huracán, was taken by Arawak traders to the mainland and became a god of the Maya.

Initially friendly, Spanish-Arawak relations soon became tainted. Columbus thought that the Arawak possessed no religion and that this situation demanded Christianization, part of a European superiority complex. The Dominican missionary Father Bartolomé de las Casas entered the West Indies in 1502, noting that the Indians were natural, kind, and humble, whereas the Spaniards were insolent and dealt "with them in any way they wish … without regard to sex, age, status, or dignity." The Arawak had given gifts of gold to Columbus, which spelled danger for them, since King Ferdinand and Queen Isabella had promised Columbus 10 percent of all precious metals found, while they would receive the remainder as recompense for funding his expeditions.

Columbus's second expedition began the real Spanish conquest of the Caribbean. Indians were forced to pan gold, and rebellions were crushed with cavalry and fierce dogs. In 1495 and 1496, European epidemics swept through the islands, as did famine. Some Indians killed their own children, then hung themselves rather than live under Spanish cruelty. Columbus introduced the encomienda system into the islands. Individual Spaniards would be given Arawak and Carib lands, together with the labor of the Indians dwelling on them; thus, the Indians were enslaved.

The slave trade helped destroy the Indians. The Bahamas had been depopulated by 1514. In 1509, Indian slaves fetched 150 pesos each, compared with 5 pesos in 1508. The population of the Lesser Antilles had left by 1520 to work in Hispaniola's mines or on its plantations. Puerto Rico had been emptied of Arawak by 1508, Jamaica by 1509, Cuba by 1511; by 1552, the Hispaniola Indians were extinct.

FLORIDA AND THE SOUTHEAST

THE SPANISH THOUGHT FLORIDA TO BE A LAND OF GREAT WEALTH, BUT EXPEDITIONS SENT TO PLUNDER ITS RESOURCES RECEIVED A HOSTILE RECEPTION FROM LOCAL TRIBES.

Juan Ponce de Léon, the governor of Puerto Rico who sought to establish a Spanish presence in Florida, but was fatally wounded when local Indians repelled the invasion.

In 1512, Juan Ponce de Léon, governor of Puerto Rico, sailed north in an attempt to find and conquer Bimini, an island where, reputedly, there existed a spring whose waters restored youth. He reached Florida in 1513, naming it Pascua Florida (Flowery Easter). His landings were resisted by the Timucuan and Ais Indians. An attempt to reach shore in San Carlos Bay, on the west coast in Calusa territory, was prevented by war canoes, but a few Indians were captured.

Although driven away, Ponce de Léon returned in 1521, arriving with some 200 Spanish settlers, again in Calusa lands. The Indians fought with poisoned darts and arrows, repulsed the Spaniards, and fatally wounded Ponce de Léon. The Spaniards were still keen to acquire Florida territory, however, seeing it as a source of loot, land, and souls to convert. Moreover, Spanish ships had been wrecked on the coasts, and their goods and crews seized. These men needed rescue.

The next adventurer to invade Florida was Pánfilo de Narváez, who landed at Tampa Bay with 400 followers and eighty horses in April 1528. Having acquired a patent from Spain's King Charles V to settle Florida, he landed and then sent his five ships on to Mexico. Narváez adopted violent tactics, attacking Indians. He sliced off the nose of a Timucuan chief, afterward tossing the man's mother to mastiffs, which ripped her apart. After such aggression, Narváez faced constant Timucuan onslaughts while chasing the rainbow dream of gold. Bogged down in swamplands, he lost 150 men to disease and ambush. Eventually, the expedition managed to reach an Apalachee village, now known as Tallahassee. Finding nothing but forty thatched huts, the Spaniards pressed on to the sea at Apalachee Bay. Having lost contact with the ships, Narváez and his men built five crude boats to transport the 242 survivors to Mexico. In September 1528, these craft hit the boiling mouth of the Mississippi, which swamped three of them. Eighty survivors managed to land on an island in Galveston Bay; Narváez was lost.

Local Indians nursed the remnants of the party, but by spring 1529, only fifteen were alive. These

Juan Ponce de Léon being greeted by Chief Agueybana of the Taino people in Hispaniola. The unsuspecting Taino were soon subjugated by the Spaniards. For his part in their destruction, Ponce de Léon was awarded the governorship of Puerto Rico.

few wandered among the Charruas, Abaraes, Malicones, Cibolas, Tagos, and other tribes. The group dwindled, but one, Álvar Núñez Cabeza de Vaca, built a reputation as a healer and medicine man. Eventually, he left the one remaining survivor and traveled along the Texan coast, happening upon three other Spaniards and Andres Dorantes, otherwise known as Estevan the Black, a Moroccan-born slave. Cabeza de Vaca led the group until they reached a Spanish settlement on the Sinalo River in Mexico, from where they finally reached Mexico City in April 1536.

Cabeza de Vaca recounted his adventures to the authorities, mentioning that he had not seen any cities, gold or silver. Instead, he told of poor Indians living on roots, insects, and the occasional deer. The local Spaniards had picked up on Indian tales, however, and imagined that there were towns full of gold to be found. Cabeza de Vaca finally decided to jump on the bandwagon, telling the Spaniards what they wanted to hear. His adventures were printed in *Los Naufragios*, which kept alive Spanish interest in the Southeast. He visited Spain in 1537 and persuaded the Spanish nobility that he had seen the richest country in the world.

Cabeza de Vaca's accounts interested adventurers such as de Soto and Coronado. Andres Dorantes eventually traveled with Friar Marcos de Niza and reached the Zuni town of Hawikuh, later mentioned incorrectly as a constituent member of the Seven Cities of Cibola.

A result of Spanish incursions into the Southeast was disease. Some Texan Indian groups described by Cabeza de Vaca had vanished or amalgamated into different ethnic groups by the early eighteenth century. Cabeza de Vaca noted that the Karankawa lost half their population, and that influenza spread with him, but did not infect the entire area he crossed.

Álvar Núñez Cabeza de Vaca, one of the few survivors of the expedition led by Pánfilo de Narváez in 1528. Cabeza de Vaca's subsequent, untrue, tales of having seen the richest country in the world led to more Spanish incursions into the Southeast with devastating results for local populations.

DE SOTO'S ENTRADA

FOOLED BY TALES OF CITIES FULL OF GOLD, HERNANDO DE SOTO TRAVELED THROUGH THE SOUTHEAST, DEVASTATING INDIAN COMMUNITIES WITH BRUTALITY AND DISEASE.

Hernando de Soto led a fateful expedition to Florida in search of the riches said to exist there, but failed to find the fabled wealth. Instead, he met his death far from home, his final resting place being the depths of the Mississippi River.

Fascinated by Cabeza de Vaca's stories, Hernando de Soto acquired a grant from Charles V of Spain and sailed for Florida with a large expedition. He established a base in Cuba, and accumulated nine ships, 600 men, some 200 horses, sundry women, and slaves. In May 1539, he landed at Tampa Bay and set about conquering the local inhabitants in brutal fashion. De Soto would capture a chief or village headman, then ransom him for food, women, and slaves. If their demands were met, the Spaniards would move on to the next village.

The land entered by de Soto comprised rich, agricultural chiefdoms, mound building societies that were heirs of the Mississippian civilization. The towns were profuse, with state buildings, plazas, ritual areas, and ballcourts. Over four years, this region was devastated by de Soto's expedition as it traversed parts of South Carolina, North Carolina, Tennessee, Alabama, Arkansas, and Texas.

De Soto began by marching through Timucuan territory, stealing, and enslaving large numbers of men and women. Timucuan chiefs moved their people out of the Spaniard's path and engaged in guerrilla warfare. At another village, the conquistadores attacked with cavalry and seized hundreds of prisoners. After a chief punched de Soto, the Timucuans were slaughtered, being literally hacked apart or shot at the stake; the Indians suffered this violence while in chains.

The Spaniards left Timucuan territory and entered Kasihta land, where they learned that the Indian town of Cofitachequi, near today's Augusta, Georgia, possessed quantities of river pearls; these were seized. Then de Soto crossed into Coosa lands, which extended through parts of Tennessee, Georgia, and Alabama. He marched into the Mississippian chiefdom of Mabila in south-central Alabama. Its Mobile fighters engaged the Spaniards, and a bloody battle was fought from house to house in Mauvila while the town was torched. Some seventy-two Spaniards died, but at least 2,500 Mobiles were slain.

De Soto's men licked their wounds and renewed their journey. The conquistadores wintered in a

De Soto and his conquistadores wreaked havoc throughout Florida and the Southeast, but in the process many died. After de Soto's death, command of the expedition fell to Luis de Moscoso, but the Spaniards were driven down the Mississippi by the Natchez. After floundering through Texas, they returned to the Mississippi and finally retreated to Mexico.

De Soto's Refutation

⟋ De Soto's expedition (probable route)

⟋ Moscoso's route

⬭ Major mound sites

☠ Death of De Soto

Chickasaw town. This nation refused to give de Soto bearers and attacked him in March 1541, then chased the Spaniards as they fled the town. The Chickasaw became respected as fierce and skilful fighters after their four-month guerrilla campaign against the Spaniards.

Next, de Soto marched to the Mississippi, spending the remainder of 1541 among east-bank chiefdoms. Eventually, the Spaniards approached the temple pyramids of the Natchez, where the paramount chief, the Great Sun, refused to meet de Soto. On May 21, 1542, de Soto died, and his body was weighted and sunk into the Mississippi. His soldiers built boats either to cross or row down the river, but a fleet of Natchez canoes drove them downriver out of their lands. Subsequently, one tribe after another pursued the Spaniards to the sea. On July 18, 1543, the Spanish remnants of the expedition reached the Gulf of Mexico, 311 survivors achieving safety at Panuco in Mexico.

Spanish adventures changed the population profile of the Southeast. De Soto found that disease had preceded him in Florida, where smallpox seemed to have struck, perhaps carried there by Calusas trading with Cuba. Many towns in the Carolinas were found abandoned. De Soto's venture itself devastated populations, and much of northwestern Georgia and eastern Tennessee became depopulated, allowing Cherokee peoples to spread into the vacuum. Few Florida Timucuans, Guales, and Apalachee survived, and they soon congregated around the St. Augustine mission, established in 1565. In 1559, Tristan du Luna sailed along the west Florida coast to establish a colony. He found the formerly rich and populous Coosa towns totally ruined, with decaying temples, abandoned fields, and empty settlements. A sick Spanish slave, left with the Coosas, had spread a deadly epidemic. Old chiefdoms had lost their chiefs, knowledge, and politico-religious structures. Centuries-old civilizations had been blotted out. The damaged peoples would eventually amalgamate as the Creeks in Florida and the Choctaw, who probably included the Mobile survivors.

CORONADO

STILL LOOKING FOR FABLED CITIES MADE OF GOLD, THE
SPANISH SENT THEIR CONQUISTADORES INTO THE AMERICAN
SOUTHWEST, WHERE, AS ELSEWHERE, THEY WROUGHT HAVOC.

In 1540, Francisco Vázquez de Coronado was selected by New Spain's first viceroy, Antonio de Mendoza, to lead an expedition to find the fabled Seven Cities of Cibola. Reports of these cities had been given by Friar Marcos de Niza and Cabeza de Vaca. The Incan and Aztec conquests had produced vast quantities of gold, so why not this potentially new province? According to myth, it had been founded by seven refugee bishops, fleeing the Moors in Spain. It was said that they had crossed the Atlantic in the eighth century to found a new Christian realm.

Coronado collected together some 230 mounted troops, 62 infantry, 800 Mexican Indians, 1,000 African and native slaves, a group of priests, and vast herds of horses, oxen, cows, sheep, pigs, and mules. They left Compostela, guided by Friar Marcos, while three supply ships followed the coast and entered the Colorado River. The expedition eventually covered several thousand miles, from the Gulf of California to south-central Kansas, and from Compostela to the Pueblos at Zuni, Hopi, Acoma, Tiguez, Taos, and Pecos, in today's Arizona and New Mexico.

First, Coronado's conquistadores reached Hawikuh, a Pueblo that appeared golden in the sunlight, but in reality was a collection of stone buildings. There, they acquired quantities of corn and beans. Still hoping to find Cibola, Coronado sent out scouting parties. Pedro de Tovar found the mesa towns of the Hopi, while García López de Cárdenas reached the Colorado Grand Canyon. Meanwhile, Hernando de Alvardo discovered the Rio Grande Pueblos inhabited by descendants of the Anasazi. Despite a lack of gold and jewels, the Pueblos possessed fields and food stocks, which could supply the Spanish over winter. Coronado moved from Zuni territory to the Tiwa Pueblo town of Alcanfor.

The onset of winter led the Spanish to empty the town for their own quarters, after which they made demands for food and clothes from all the Tiwa towns. Tiwa resentment occasioned a revolt,

the Tiguex War. Spanish retaliation was harsh, and the towns were burned. Women and children were seized, people enslaved, and men burned at the stake.

In spring 1541, Coronado responded to tales of new cities to the northeast at Quivira. A Pawnee, named Turk by the Spanish, regaled the invaders with stories of gold bells, plates, jugs, and bowls. Coronado crossed the panhandles of Texas and Oklahoma, and entered Kansas. He encountered the vast high plains and the huge herds of buffalo. The expedition followed the Pecos and Brazos Rivers, then headed northward for forty-two days, until they reached Quivira. This Wichita Indian encampment on the Kansas River was a collection of grass huts; there was no gold. Turk was strangled, and the frustrated Spaniards returned to the Tiwa Pueblos for another winter. Totally discouraged, Coronado returned to Mexico City in 1542.

However, Viceroy Mendoza still hoped that the north would be bountiful. Two vessels under Juan Rodriguez Cabrillo sailed along the coast of California, but missed the harbors of San Francisco and Monterey. He did find San Diego Bay, eventually an important Spanish outpost.

The next attempt on the Pueblos was made by Juan de Oñate, who, in 1598, led an expedition of 500, with 7,000 head of livestock, northward along the Rio Grande. He crossed the center of New Mexico and arrived at Okhe Pueblo in the Española Valley. The Indians were ordered out, and Oñate named the town San Juan, choosing it as the capital of the new Spanish colony. Oñate began conquering the surrounding Pueblos, and in 1599, a major conflict occurred at Acoma Pueblo, on a high mesa. The Spaniards forced their way in, but the battle lasted three days and resulted in more than 800 of the 6,000 inhabitants being killed; 500 women and children, and eighty men became indentured for twenty years. In addition, the men were mutilated in the Rio Grande towns, each losing a foot.

A depiction of Francisco Vázquez de Coronado's expedition in the Southwest by the noted American artist Frederick Remington. Like many before him, Coronado endured many hardships only to discover that there were no cities of gold.

Overleaf: Throughout the sixteenth century, Spanish expeditions ranged through the southern half of the North American continent seeking fabled riches. They found none, but had a devastating effect on the Native Americans they encountered.

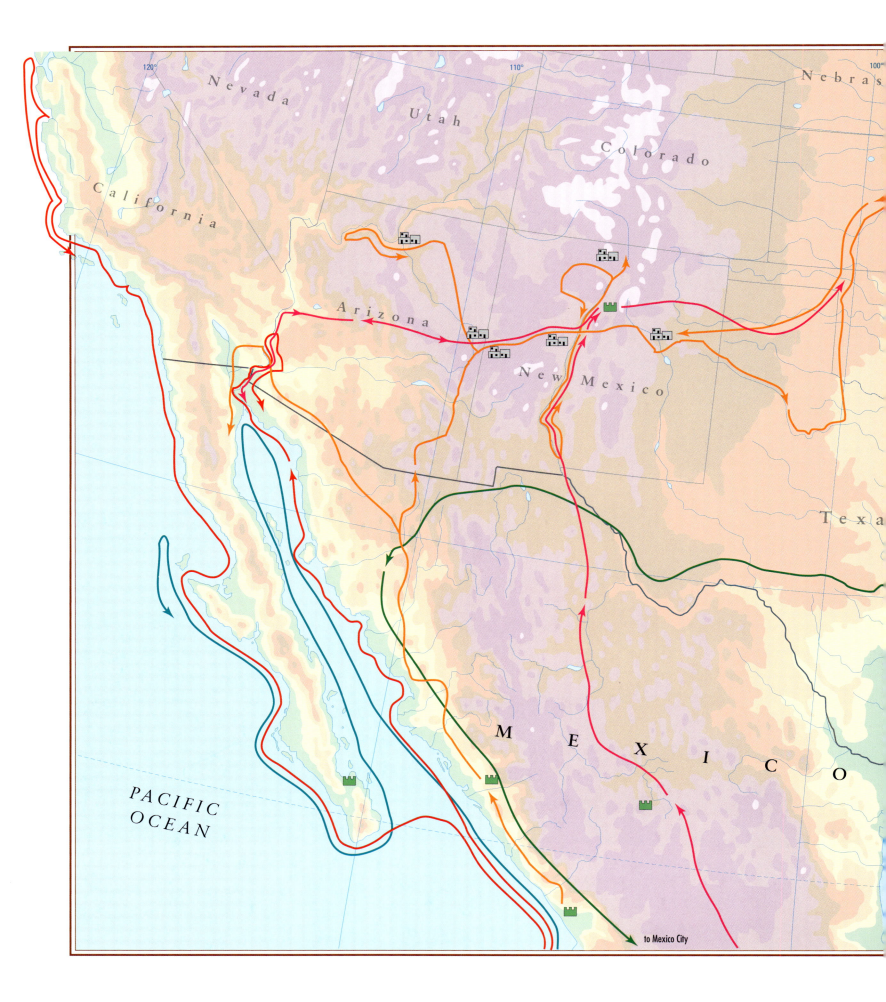

to Mexico City

Iowa
90°
Pennsylvania
80°
New Jersey
40°
Illinois   Indiana   Ohio
Maryland
Delaware
D.C.
West Virginia
Virginia
ma
Missouri
Kentucky
North Carolina
Tennessee
Arkansas
oma
South Carolina
Alabama
Mississippi
Georgia
ATLANTIC OCEAN
30°
Louisiana
Gulf of Mexico
Flórida
C U B A
Tropic of Cancer

Spanish Explorations
1513–1605

⟶ Ponce de León 1513
⟶ Pineda 1519
⟶ Gordillo and Quexos 1521
⟶ Ayllón 1526
⟶ Narváez 1526
⟶ Cabeza de Vaca 1528–36
⟶ de Ulloa 1539–40

⟶ de Soto 1539–44
⟶ Alarcón 1540
⟶ de Coronado 1540–42
⟶ Oñate 1598–1605
Modern borders
△ Native American settlements
▣ Spanish forts/settlements
▦ Pueblos

CARTIER AND CHAMPLAIN

INSPIRED INITIALLY BY IDEAS OF A PASSAGE TO THE ORIENT,
AND THEN BY THE POTENTIAL PROFITS OF THE FUR TRADE, THE
FRENCH SENT EXPLORERS AND COLONISTS TO NORTH AMERICA.

A representation of Jacques Cartier dating from c. 1844 by Théophile Hamel. No portraits painted in his own time are known to exist of the sixteenth-century navigator. Cartier landed on Newfoundland while attempting to discover a Northwest Passage to China and thus inspired French interest in the region.

King Francis I (1494–1547) of France, short of money after waging war in Europe, was interested in finding a Northwest Passage through North America to China in order to trade and repair his finances. Accordingly, in 1534, he sent Jacques Cartier with two ships that made landfall on Newfoundland. They sailed through the Belle Isle Straits into the Gulf of St. Lawrence, and saw Prince Edward Island and New Brunswick. Cartier named Chaleur Bay and landed on the Gaspé Peninsula. In the following year, he explored the St. Lawrence River, meeting Beothuks, Micmacs, Montagnais, and Hurons, wintering near today's Québec. Later, he reached the point where Montréal would stand, then known as Hochelaga. A third voyage with a backer, Sieur de Roberval, and colonists ended in failure in 1543. A severe winter, scurvy among the settlers, squabbling, and hostility from the Iroquois had combined to end the venture.

This abortive attempt at empire building ended official French interest in North America. However, the fishing grounds of the Newfoundland Banks acted as a magnet to fishermen from Rouen, St. Malo, and Dieppe, as well as to the Portuguese and the British. By 1578, 150 French ships were engaged in this trade. The crews traded with the Indians, and the fur business was born, culminating in traders sailing up the St. Lawrence River. French King Henry IV quickly realized the value of Canada and the establishment of a taxable fur-trade monopoly in a royal province, if it could be secured.

In 1603, Samuel de Champlain, with Sieur du Pontgravé, crossed the Atlantic, landing at Tadoussac. Conversations with Indians made Champlain realize that a river and portage route along the Sagueney and Mistassini rivers led to Hudson Bay, while a passage headed south through lakes and rivers south of the Richelieu River (Lake Champlain and the Hudson River). Also, a portage route existed to the Great Lakes along the Ottowa River, across Lake Nipissing, and down the French River. The Indians told him of Lakes Superior, Erie, and Huron, giving the impression that there might be a route to the Pacific.

Champlain was an accomplished geographer and cartographer, and he went on to explore the Bay of Fundy in 1604, and the New England coast as far south as Massachusetts. In 1605, colonists established a settlement at Port Royal, adapted to the environment, and enjoyed friendly relations with the Indians. Québec was founded in 1608 and became a haven for French-Indian trade. Champlain's explorations led to the discovery of Lake Champlain, and he traveled along the inland waterways of southern Ontario and northern New York State. Lakes Huron and Ontario were also investigated.

Relationships with the Native Americans became complex. North of the St. Lawrence were three mutually hostile tribes who sought control of the waterway. The Montagnais roamed the headwaters of the Saguenay, the Algonkin resided in the Ottowa

THE "DAUPHIN MAP" OF CANADA, *CIRCA* 1543, SHOWING CARTIER'S DISCOVERIES

River Valley, and the Huron lived between the Ottowa River and Lake Huron. South of Lake Huron were the five tribes of the Iroquois Confederation. When Europeans first arrived in the St. Lawrence Valley, the Iroquois controlled Lake Ontario and the valley up to Québec, and were expanding eastward. The French opened trade with the Montagnais, and a few years later, the Algonkin and

A contemporary map of the North American Atlantic coast, illustrating Cartier's discoveries on the continent. This map was known as the Dauphin Map.

Samuel de Champlain's arrival off the site of the future city of Québec, from a painting by George Agnew Reid. Champlain explored much of the Northeast of the North American continent, leading the way for the establishment of the colony of New France.

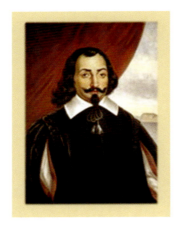

Théophile Hamel's impression of Samuel de Champlain, painted in 1870. No contemporary portrait of the French explorer is known to exist.

Huron traded at Tadoussac. The three northern tribes were determined to push the Iroquois from the St. Lawrence Valley so that they could gain a monopoly over French trade. By 1608, the Iroquois had been driven south of the St. Lawrence.

In 1609, Champlain joined an Algonkin war party, helping them defeat some Iroquois at the site of Ticonderoga. In 1615, he aided the Huron against the Onondaga, leading some French musketeers up the Ottowa Valley and across Lake Nipissing to Georgian Bay. The French joined 500 Huron and attacked an Iroquois village near Lake Oneida. The assault was repulsed and Champlain was wounded. This fight was pivotal; the defensive Iroquois turned on the Huron and pressurized New France. Champlain had instigated a long-lasting conflict that would become a French-British war, during which the latter were bolstered by Iroquois allies.

In 1629, British raiders captured Québec and imprisoned Champlain. Three years later, the Treaty of Saint German-en-Laye freed him and returned Québec to the French. By the time of Champlain's death, in 1635, New France had grown along both banks of the St. Lawrence, but was vulnerable to Iroquois attack, particularly when they acquired guns from the Dutch in the 1640s.

A depiction of French musketeers led by Samuel de Champlain aiding Algonkins to defeat an Iroquois war party at Ticonderoga in 1609.

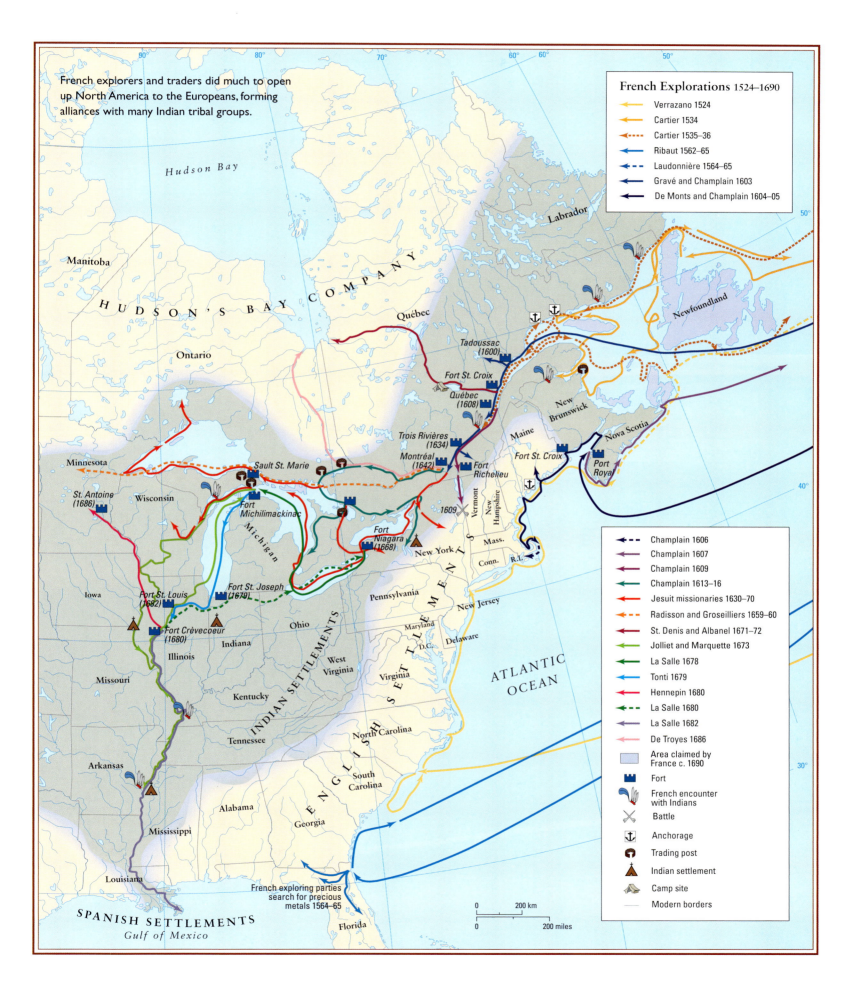

French explorers and traders did much to open up North America to the Europeans, forming alliances with many Indian tribal groups.

French Explorations 1524–1690

- Verrazano 1524
- Cartier 1534
- Cartier 1535–36
- Ribaut 1562–65
- Laudonnière 1564–65
- Gravé and Champlain 1603
- De Monts and Champlain 1604–05

- Champlain 1606
- Champlain 1607
- Champlain 1609
- Champlain 1613–16
- Jesuit missionaries 1630–70
- Radisson and Groseilliers 1659–60
- St. Denis and Albanel 1671–72
- Jolliet and Marquette 1673
- La Salle 1678
- Tonti 1679
- Hennepin 1680
- La Salle 1680
- La Salle 1682
- De Troyes 1686
- Area claimed by France c. 1690
- Fort
- French encounter with Indians
- Battle
- Anchorage
- Trading post
- Indian settlement
- Camp site
- Modern borders

Hudson Bay

Manitoba

HUDSON'S BAY COMPANY

Ontario

Labrador

Québec

Newfoundland

Tadoussac (1600)

Fort St. Croix

Québec (1608)

New Brunswick

Nova Scotia

Minnesota

Trois Rivières (1634)

Montréal (1642)

Fort Richelieu

Maine

Fort St. Croix

Port Royal

Sault St. Marie

Wisconsin

St. Antoine (1686)

Fort Michilimackinac

Michigan

Fort Niagara (1668)

1609

Vermont

New Hampshire

New York

Mass.

Conn.

R.I.

Iowa

Fort St. Louis (1682)

Fort St. Joseph (1679)

Pennsylvania

New Jersey

Fort Crèvecoeur (1680)

Illinois

Indiana

Ohio

Maryland

Delaware

D.C.

West Virginia

Missouri

Kentucky

Virginia

ATLANTIC OCEAN

Arkansas

Tennessee

North Carolina

INDIAN SETTLEMENTS

ENGLISH SETTLEMENTS

Mississippi

Alabama

Georgia

South Carolina

Louisiana

French exploring parties search for precious metals 1564–65

SPANISH SETTLEMENTS

Gulf of Mexico

Florida

0   200 km
0   200 miles

ROANOKE AND JAMESTOWN

LOCKED IN A POWER STRUGGLE WITH THE SPANISH, THE BRITISH SAW COLONIES IN THE "NEW WORLD" AS A MEANS OF COMBATING THEIR EUROPEAN ENEMY.

Opposite: Britain's first North American colony was established on Roanoke Island, off the coast of present-day North Carolina.

Before British colonists attempted to establish a presence in today's North Carolina, the coastal areas were inhabited by a variety of small Indian tribes. Among these were the Algonquian-speaking Poteskeet, Pasquotank, Yeopim, Chowanok, Moratoc, Roanoc, Machapunga, Hatteras, Pamlico, and Secotan. Unfortunately for these Native Americans, there was a sudden British interest in the Americas during Queen Elizabeth I's confrontation with Spain. Courtier Walter Raleigh thought that Spain's power could be destroyed by establishing British colonies in the Americas as bases for actions against Spanish interests. Raw materials could be extracted, markets established, and the New World exploited to finance a European power struggle.

In 1578, Raleigh sailed for America to reconnoiter the coast. This expedition stimulated his desire to found colonies, and in 1584 he sponsored another voyage, which reached Roanoke Island, where the party met the local Secotan Indians. Reports made by Barlowe, the captain of one ship, praised the Secotan's farming, food production, and variety of crops. Queen Elizabeth enthused over the news and knighted Raleigh. A second expedition was dispatched in 1585 to Roanoke Island, where 107 men were left under Ralph Lane to build a fort and explore the region. The expedition had arrived too late to plant crops, however, and food ran short. Lane's attitude toward the Indians became violent as he appropriated their surplus corn. He upset the Secotan and the Chowanoac; then an epidemic raged through the Indian population, and Lane's community was blamed. The Indians planned war, but Lane struck preemptively, killing the Secotan chief, Pemisapan, and slaughtering the settlement of Dasemunkapeac. In 1586, Sir Francis Drake evacuated Lane's colony, but Raleigh sent a third expedition in 1587.

Sir Walter Raleigh, instigator of the Roanoke colony.

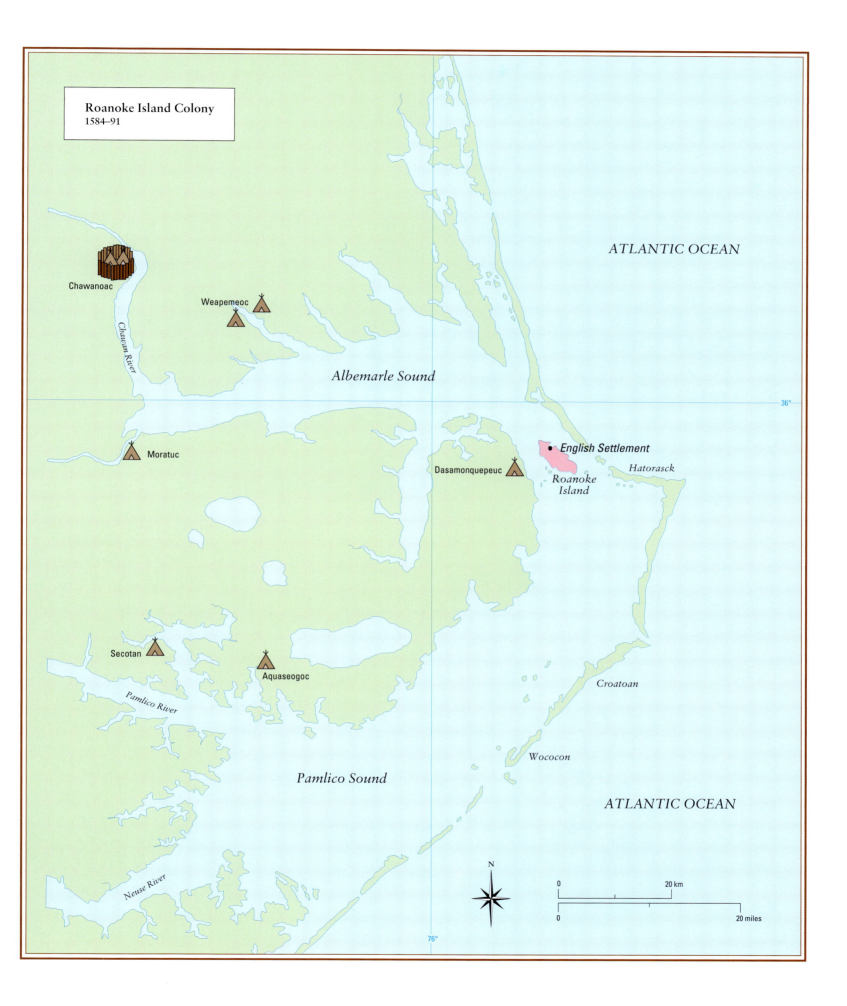

Roanoke Island Colony
1584–91

Chawanoac

Chawan River

Weapemeoc

ATLANTIC OCEAN

Albemarle Sound

36°

Moratuc

Dasamonquepeuc

English Settlement

Hatorasck

Roanoke Island

Secotan

Aquaseogoc

Pamlico River

Croatan

Wococon

Pamlico Sound

ATLANTIC OCEAN

Neuse River

N

0   20 km

0   20 miles

76°

A watercolor by John White, leader of the Roanoke colonists, depicting a Secotan village. White's return to Britain to seek help for the settlement saved his life.

INDIAN VILLAGE OF SECOTON (no. xxx of pl. i.ix)

Raleigh intended that the latest venture would establish a permanent colony of 118 men, women, and children. Again, the settlers arrived too late to plant crops, and the Secotan seemed unfriendly. Governor John White, who had been with Lane, was persuaded to return to England to obtain supplies. He left behind his daughter and granddaughter, Virginia Dare, the first British child to be born in North America. White was prevented from returning to Roanoke until 1590, because England was too busy combating the Spanish Armada to worry about the colony.

On his return, White found the colony deserted, the houses pulled down, and goods scattered about. The only clue to the colonists' fate was the word "CROATAN" carved into a gatepost. Historians have sought to explain where the colonists went, and one day archaeologists may find the answer. Perhaps the colonists sought Croatan Indian help on the

Despite the setback at Roanoke Island, the British persisted in their attempts to establish a colony in North America. The Virginia Company created the settlement of Jamestown on the Chesapeake Bay, and others soon followed in the region.

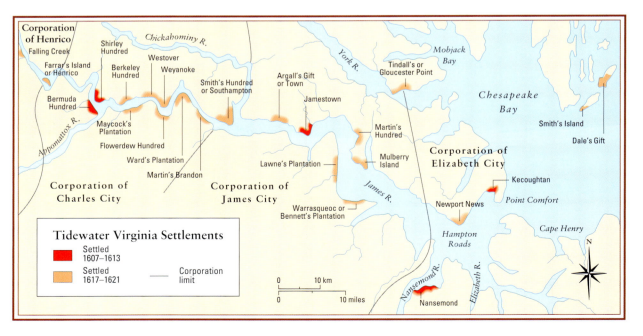

Chesapeake. However, Indians told Captain John Smith that they had been massacred during an Indian war.

Despite the failure of Raleigh's ventures, these early attempts to establish colonies did produce some interesting outcomes. Written reports by Thomas Harriot, a scientist, were published in *A Brief and True Report of the New Found Land of Virginia* (1588). John White produced many watercolors of wildlife and Indians, depicting the latter's clothing, dancing, tattoos, ornaments, ceremonies, cooking styles, and methods of fishing and farming. Noteworthy was his portrait of a woman and baby in Pomeicooc, a Pamlico Sound village.

Raleigh was persistent in his attempts to establish colonies. Although he fell from favor under King James I, the latter was persuaded that further efforts were necessary. Accordingly, the Virginia Company was chartered and authorized to colonize the Americas from latitude 34°N to 45°N, from southern Cape Fear to northern contemporary Bangor, Maine. The company established a colony at Jamestown (1607) on the Chesapeake Bay, where Raleigh had wanted his 1587 colony to be built.

The colonists were regarded with suspicion by Indians, given knowledge of white attacks on the Secotan; the local Powhatan Imperium prepared for trouble. Jamestown was located close to malarial swamps and subject to Indian attack. Even so, the settlement flourished, beginning commercial tobacco production in 1612 and introducing the first African slaves into British North America in 1619.

A recreation of a Powhatan village at the Jamestown Settlement, a living history center on the coast of Virginia.

Spanish Missions, from 1565

FOR THE SPANISH, MISSIONS HAD A TWOFOLD PURPOSE: TO CONVERT "HEATHEN" NATIVE AMERICANS TO CHRISTIANITY, AND TO ACT AS A DEFENSE AGAINST OTHER COLONIAL POWERS.

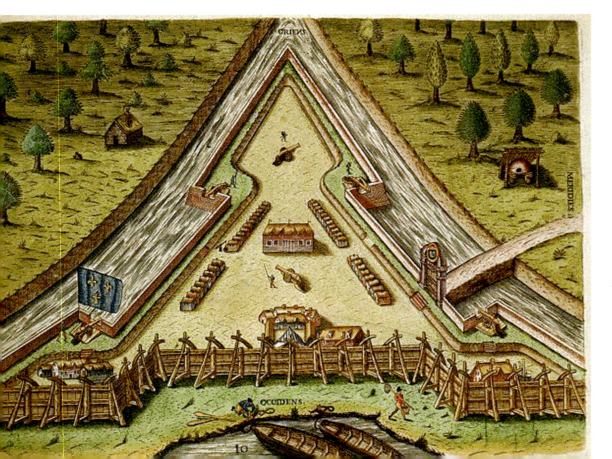

A hand-colored engraving by Théodor de Bry depicting the French-built Fort Caroline in northern Florida. The fort lasted no more than a year before the Spanish destroyed it.

Spain took real interest in Florida when French Huguenots built Fort Caroline at the mouth of the St. John's River. This potential threat to Spanish shipping was countered by a Spanish attempt to colonize Florida, beginning with the construction of the San Augustine presidio. Missions and garrisons soon dotted the coast, from Tampa Bay to the Carolinas. The first missions were established by Jesuits, but these succumbed to revolts by the Guales and Orista tribes. By 1583, the Franciscans had reopened them and established two mission chains, one along the Atlantic coast, the other spreading westward across the Florida peninsula. Indians were required to pay tribute to the missions in maize, skins, and other goods, and eventually labor too, yet the Spaniards were a small minority. The Franciscans converted large numbers of Guale, Apalachee, and Timucuan Indians, but they began to interfere in Indian domestic politics, and in 1597, the Guale rebelled. Later, the Christian Apalachee revolted, in 1638 and 1647, followed by the Timucuans in 1656.

By 1650, the friars controlled about 26,000 Indians, but the congested mission settlements incubated killer diseases, decimating many coastal tribes. This occurred shortly after the original

A statue of Juan de Oñate by Reynaldo Rivera at the Oñate Monument Visitors Center, New Mexico. Oñate is honored by some Anglo-, Spanish-, and Mexican-Americans for his explorations of the Southwest, but is vilified by others for his cruelty to the Indians, particularly the Acoma tribe in 1599. Following a skirmish with the tribe during which thirteen Spaniards were killed, his conquistadores murdered 800 of the villagers, enslaved the women and children, and cut off the left foot of every surviving man over the age of twenty-five. In 1998, during New Mexico's celebrations of the 400th anniversary of Oñate's arrival in the region, a group opposed to the statue cut off its right foot, leaving a note saying, "Fair is fair." Although the statue was repaired, some suggested that it should have been left damaged as a symbolic reminder of the foot mutilating incident.

depopulation by disease in the late sixteenth century. The mission system was too weak to resist British slave raids, and by 1710, all missions north of St. Augustine had been destroyed. The Spanish experience left Florida devastated. The Tekesta Indians became extinct, as did the Calusa. The Ais had died out by the 1720s, while the Apalachee were almost annihilated by British and Creek raids.

A second missionary thrust from Mexico was led by Juan de Oñate (1598), accompanied by soldier-settlers, slaves, and Franciscans. Heading from Santa Barbara to San Juan, de Oñate realized that

Florida to Mexico
1685–1721

- • Town
- • Modern town
- ☦ Mission
- ▪ Garrison town
- ▪ French fort
- ▪ Spanish fort
- ▪ British fort
- *CADDO* Indian tribe
- — Modern border

N

0   400 km
0   400 miles

Missouri

Kentucky

Tennessee

Oklahoma

Arkansas River

Arkansas

Mississippi River

CHICKASAW

Arkansas Post
1721

Mississippi

Tennessee River

Tombigbee River

Alabama

Fort Toulouse
1717

Red River

CADDO

CHOCTAW

LIPÁN APACHE

Brazos River

Trinity River

• Dallas

Purísima
Concepción
1716

San José de
los Nazones
1716

Natchitoches

Los Adaes
1716

Natchez
1714 Fort Rosalie

Alabama River

ALA

Texas

San Francisco
de los Tejas
1690

San Francisco
de los Dolores
1716

HASINAI

MIDDL

Santísimo Nombre
de María
1690

Nuestra Señora
de los Nacogches
1716

Mobile
1702 Fort Conde

Fort Maurepas
1699

San Carlos de
1699

Colorado River

New Orleans
1718

Fort Mississippi
1700

San Antonio de Valero
1718
San Antonio de Béjar
1718

Houston •

San José
1720

Fort St. Louis 1685
Nuestra Señora de la
Bahía de Espíritu Santo
1721

Alabama

Georgia

• Eagle Pass
San Juan Bautista
1700

• Laredo

Rio Grande

Cadereyta

• Monterrey
• Saltillo

Gulf of Mexico

Missions in Spanish Florida c. 1674–1675

MEXICO

95°

90°

sheep farming would suit New Mexico. Eventually, the missionary border moved north, pushing into Texas and Arizona. Missions were established in every Pueblo on the Rio Grande, but 1680 saw a Pueblo Revolt, which drove out the Spaniards for twelve years.

Further impetus to Spanish expansion was the fear of French influence on the Mississippi. Thus, Father Damian Massenet, seeking to counter the feared La Salle, had established two missions in Texas by 1690; Texas became a province in the following year. In addition, a Spanish fort was built at Pensacola in West Florida to block French westward expansion. The Texan missions failed in the face of the hostile Tejas tribe, but when the French built a fort at Natchitoches in 1714, the Spanish returned. Then, in 1716, Captain Domingo Ramón constructed a mission station on the Neches River, Nuestre Padre san Francisco de los tejas, followed by five others. By 1718, San Antonio and a fort at Los Adaes had been established in western Texas as extra frontier outposts.

Franco-Spanish border skirmishing continued after 1719, but by 1720, the Spanish missions were secure. At the end of Spanish rule in 1821, about 4,000 Spaniards occupied Texas, mainly at San Antonio, Goliad, and Nacogdoches. Behind the Spanish border defenses, towns and villages were settled by Spaniards, mestizos, and Indians, sometimes forcibly relocated. The 1763 Treaty of Paris granted Louisiana to Spain, but Florida was lost to Great Britain.

Meanwhile, missionary activity continued among the Pima tribe, descendants of the Hohokam people, of northern Sonora and southern Arizona, and known as Spanish Pimeria Alta. Father Eusebio Francisco Kino built a mission at Dolores, then he moved along the Altar and Magdalena rivers. Next, he traveled into Arizona along the Santa Cruz and San Pedro valleys. After his death in 1711, missionary activity declined in the face of Apache raids. The Pima traded with the Tucson presidio, and helped the Spanish against the Yavapai and Apache, but rebelled in 1751. In 1752, the Tubac presidio was built in Arizona to reestablish Spanish control in the area.

Fear of French expansion and influence in the Mississippi region caused Spain to step up the establishment of forts and settlements from Florida to Texas. Jesuit and Franciscan missions played a major role in Spain's colonization plan.

THE SPREAD OF EPIDEMIC DISEASES

APART FROM DISPOSSESSING NATIVE AMERICANS OF THEIR LAND, EUROPEANS CARRIED WITH THEM DISEASES THAT WOULD DECIMATE LOCAL POPULATIONS.

The spread of European and African killer diseases in the Americas after 1492 was speedy, wreaking untold damage among the civilizations of Mexico, Peru, and Central America. Trade routes helped diseases and germs to spread inland to regions that had never seen a European. The main illnesses were smallpox, measles, influenza, bubonic plague, diptheria, typhus, cholera, scarlet fever, trachoma, whooping cough, chicken pox, and tropical malaria.

Hispaniola was devastated by the first smallpox outbreak in 1513, and the disease quickly reached the Greater Antilles, then hit the Aztec capital in 1520. Apparently, Florida traded with Cuba, and the disease had arrived before even de Soto started his entrada in 1539. He found numerous abandoned villages choked with vegetation. Apparently, disease had swept the Southeast, and de Soto exacerbated the situation, chiefdoms, customs, and rituals being destroyed. The remnants of the different surviving refugee populations coalesced into federations, such as the Creeks, Choctaw, and Catawba. The population of Florida collapsed under smallpox, measles, and typhus. The Timucuans are thought to have numbered 150,000 before European contact, but by the end of the seventeenth century, 98 percent had died. The Apalachee of northern Florida have been estimated at 25,000–30,000 in the early seventeenth century, but only 8,000 remained at the end of it. Some 250 years after the Spaniards reached Florida, all the original population had vanished. In 1559, influenza swept Europe; two years later, it was an epidemic in the Caribbean and Mesoamerica, before being carried to North America.

In 1585, the Roanoke colony in Virginia transmitted an unknown disease to local villages, killing scores. Even the Pueblo Indians are thought to have suffered smallpox between 1519 and 1524. In 1539, there were 130,000 inhabitants in 150 Pueblos. By 1706, the population had dropped to 6,440 in eighteen Pueblos. De Soto found Arkansas thriving with large towns and cornfields, but when the French arrived in the mid-seventeenth century, the area was empty, with Quapaws, Osage, and Caddoes on the margins.

Survivors of the first smallpox epidemic became immune, but the disease returned in 1562. Whole families were wiped out; sometimes, the young were left with no one to hunt or prepare food. Elders, teachers, and medicine men died, and social bonds were broken as societies were ripped apart. In 1645, a Wampanoag Indian saw a smallpox epidemic tear through Martha's Vineyard. He said, "A long time ago they had wise men which in a grave manner taught the people knowledge, but they are dead and their wisdom is buried with them."

In 1619, the Massachusetts were slaughtered by bubonic plague. In response, the Pilgrims proclaimed that God had killed the natives to free the land

for them. Measles, and possibly smallpox, hit New England and the Great Lakes in 1633. Four years later, another pathogen, probably scarlet fever, hammered the same regions, then smallpox returned in 1639. The swathes of death meant that Indian military power could not combat the westward advance of European colonists. Other dangers were measles in 1658 and 1693; influenza in 1647 and 1675; and diptheria in 1659. Malaria spread through southern North America in the 1690s. Altogether, thirteen known epidemics occurred during the seventeenth century.

Later, smallpox traveled from Texas to New England (1715–21), to the Hudson Bay (1738–39), and to New England again in 1746. Other waves spread to the Great Lakes in 1750–52, 1755–60, and 1762–66; all over North America in 1779–83; to Alaska and Canada in 1785–87; and to the Pueblos in 1788. Measles swept through in 1713–15, and probably across the continent again in 1727–28, followed by the Southwest in 1768–70. Influenza struck in 1761, and diptheria took hold in New England in 1735–36.

Not only did multiple deaths prevent Indians from defending themselves adequately against Europeans, but also disease impacted upon relations between nations. In 1781, smallpox so weakened the Shoshone that by the 1790s, they and their Flathead and Kutenais allies had been pushed out of Montana. In 1778, the Arikara lost 80 percent of their populations and could no longer fight the Sioux. The remnants combined their thirty-two villages into two and retreated north to the Cheyenne River.

The traditional method used by some Indians to cure diseases such as smallpox was the sweat lodge. The lodge was built near a creek and rocks were heated in a fire nearby. The hot rocks were placed inside the lodge and the sick Indian would enter, having removed all clothing. The covers would be pulled over the lodge to seal in the heat and the Indian would remain inside until completely drenched in sweat. Then he would run to the creek and plunge into the cold water. Not surprisingly, such treatment proved more detrimental than beneficial.

THE SPREAD OF TRADE

BEFORE EUROPEANS ARRIVED IN NORTH AMERICA, NATIVE
AMERICANS HAD DEVELOPED AN EXTENSIVE TRADE NETWORK
THAT CRISSCROSSED THE CONTINENT.

N ative Americans traded extensively among themselves before 1492. The Hopewell civilization created networks for moving goods from the Atlantic coast to the Rocky Mountains, and from the Gulf of Mexico to the Great Lakes. Artifacts made from copper, bone, antler, stone, and shell have been found. Further south, the Arawak employed large ocean-going canoes to allow them to trade in Florida and Mesoamerica.

A contemporary illustration (1634) of Europeans trading with Native Americans, by Théodor de Bry.

Prior to major European contact, the Pecos and Zuni Pueblos in the Southwest acted as trade centers to link the Plains, Great Basin, California, and northern Mexico. Middlemen traders moved goods across vast distances; Comanche and Apache traded with Caddo, Wichita, and Pawnee. Utes, Paiutes, and then Shoshone carried products into the Great Basin. Trading hubs in California were the Owens Valley Paiutes and the Great Basin Washoes. Certainly, shells from southern California were traded with the Great Basin, the Southwest, and beyond. Trade feasts were held by the Pomos and Chumash.

Northern Californian tribes traded with Oregon, the products being transported by Klamath, Molalan, Kalapuyan, and Modoc middlemen. Ultimately, goods tended to reach the Dalles on the Columbia River, the largest emporium in the Northwest, perhaps all of America. There, thousands of local Wasco-Wishrans caught and processed vast quantities of salmon, exchanging the Celilo Falls harvest for goods from all parts of the continent. Animal pelts, dentalia, shells, dried plant food, and slaves were on offer. The Dalles was not discovered by Europeans until after 1800. Dalles trade patterns were dominant until the Hudson's Bay Company penetrated the area; Dalles-style seasonal exchanges were prevalent in the Arctic too.

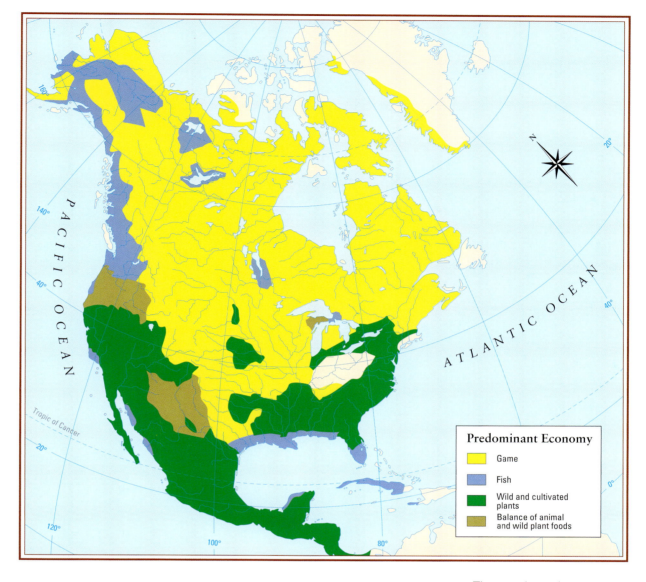

Predominant Economy

- Game
- Fish
- Wild and cultivated plants
- Balance of animal and wild plant foods

This map shows the predominant economies of the Native American populations c.1500. Geographical location was the determining factor.

The East possessed its cobweb of trade routes. The Huron exchanged corn with the Nipissings for pelts and dried fish. Luxury items were marine shells, copper, rare furs (such as black squirrel and racoon), and quartz. Lake Superior copper reached the St. Lawrence, then was transported south. Gulf of Mexico marine shells traveled to the Chesapeake and Long Island. Incised Gulf conch artifacts are strewn through the Mississippi region. Also, catlinite pipestone, mica, galena lead, flint, and buffalo hides passed from the Plains eastward.

Into this well-established system came European trade goods. Some trade in furs was being carried out by Basque fishermen by the 1580s, European knives being prized by the Indians. Before 1600, Spanish products spread through the Southeast and included knives, chisels, wedges, brass bells, gorgets, pendants, and beads. In addition, the de Soto expedition left most of its weapons and tools behind, while dozens of iron nails were lost.

The demand for leather and fur in Europe led to Spanish ranching, and in 1537, ironware was taken to the Belle Isle Straits. By 1541, furs and skins were being traded for iron axes and knives. Also, the Basques sold copper kettles, which the Indians preferred to ceramics for cooking. In 1565, reports state that 6,000 hides arrived each year at La Rochelle in France. In 1610, John Smith maintained that the

Iroquois were obtaining European goods from the St. Lawrence Valley, and that the Susquehannocks were supplying Algonquian groups with iron hatchets, knives, and pieces of iron and brass.

As disease struck, the trade links became more tenuous, so the French stepped in as middlemen traders; to secure good relations, they often married Native American women. The Indians appreciated the benefits of European technology, and became increasingly reliant and dependent upon it. Iron knives and fishhooks were exchanged by the British with the Narragansetts, while the Micmacs wanted metalware from Cartier in Chaleur Bay, especially axes, knives, awls, and trinkets.

More archaeological excavations will be necessary to ascertain the extent of the spread of European goods, but it seems that only small quantities arrived before 1580. Evidence suggests that trade routes spread from Tadoussac along the Ottowa Valley to Lakes Huron and Superior. The St. Lawrence was another route, and goods flowed down to New England. In the late sixteenth century, European goods tended to move from east to west, rather than north to south..

Opposite: A detail from
The Zapotec Civilization by
Diego Rivera, showing Zapotec
Indians at work at a number of
crafts.

A number of major trading
centers were established by the
western Indians. The tribes in
these areas acted as middlemen,
facilitating the exchange of
trade goods, which thus were
transported throughout the
regions they served.

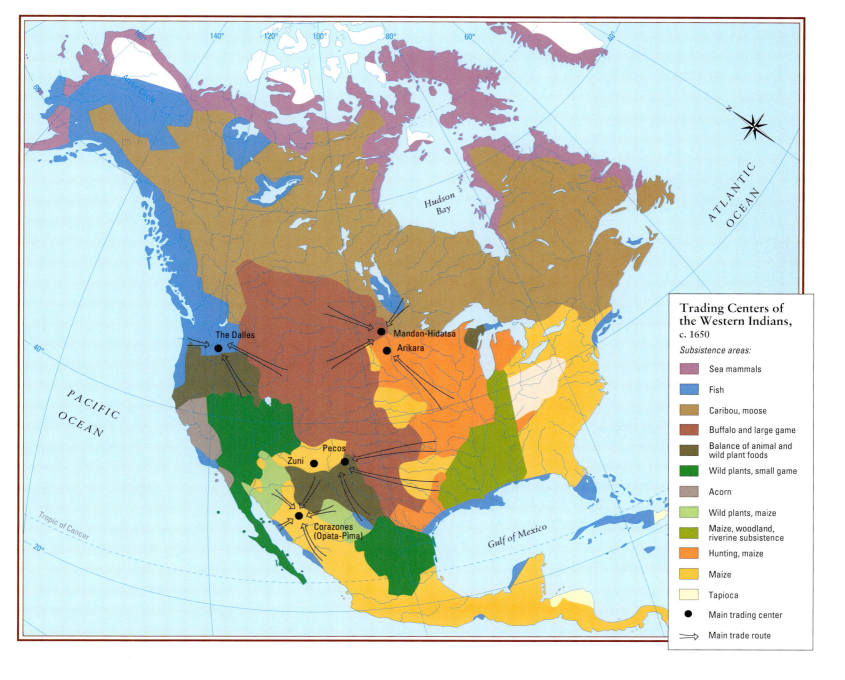

Trading Centers of the Western Indians, c. 1650

Subsistence areas:

- Sea mammals
- Fish
- Caribou, moose
- Buffalo and large game
- Balance of animal and wild plant foods
- Wild plants, small game
- Acorn
- Wild plants, maize
- Maize, woodland, riverine subsistence
- Hunting, maize
- Maize
- Tapioca
- ● Main trading center
- ⟶ Main trade route

THE HORSE

TRANSPORTED TO NORTH AMERICA BY THE SPANISH, THE HORSE WOULD COMPLETELY TRANSFORM THE LIVES OF MANY NATIVE AMERICAN TRIBES, BECOMING A VALUABLE POSSESSION.

Hernán Cortés demonstrates the value of the horse in combat with a Native American.

The Spanish introduced the horse into the Plains, and the animal was traded northward. During the seventeenth and eighteenth centuries, Spanish traders exchanged their goods, horses, and mules for war captives, hides, and skins, especially at Taos, Picos, and Pecos Pueblos, and at Santa Fé. Apache raids ensured that they became the first mounted Indians and, in turn, they sold horses. The 1680 Pueblo Revolt drove the Spanish from New Mexico for several years, and horses left behind were acquired by the Indians. In 1659, Navajos were seen riding horses, and by the 1680s and 1690s, Kiowas and Kiowa-Apaches were selling horses to southern Caddoans, such as the Hasinai villages; the Wichita and Pawnee supplied to the Osage.

In the early eighteenth century, the Comanche raided the Apache and Spanish for horses, trading their booty to the northern Shoshone, on the upper Missouri and during gatherings in the Black Hills. The Shoshone traveled in the Plateau area, following the Green and Colorado rivers; they bartered with the Flatheads and Nez Perce. By the 1740s, Blackfeet and Gros Ventre were mounted, buying their horses from Plateau peoples, the Arapaho, or both. Then, Blackfeet and Gros Ventre sold stock to the western Assiniboines. Simultaneously, the Crow bought from the Shoshone and the Flatheads, then traded in the Mandan and Hidatsa villages, as did other Plains nomads, such as the Kiowa,

A Shoshone man in traditional warrior dress. He wears a war bonnet of eagle feathers and carries a coup stick, while his horse is painted with war symbols.

Looking Glass, a Nez Perce chief. The Nez Perce became major horse traders.

The horse was introduced to the North American continent by the Spanish, and from around 1600 began reaching the hands of the Indians. Some of these had escaped to the wild and been captured, while others were seized during raids. Gradually, the use of the horse by Native Americans spread from tribe to tribe across the Great Plains.

The Great Plains

Vegetation

- Forest and woodland
- Short / tall grass
- Grass and scrubland
- Desert and scrub
- Mountain vegetation
- → Spread of horses, with date of arrival
- CROW Indian nation

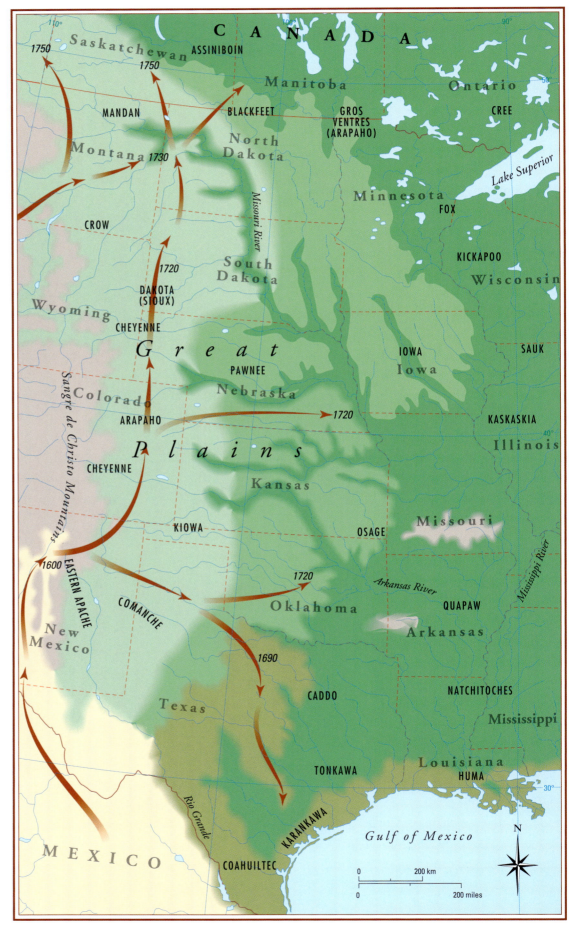

Kiowa-Apache, Arapaho, and Cheyenne. They sold in Arikara villages where Assiniboines and Plains Cree exchanged British and French guns for horses, also at the Mandan and Hidatsa settlements. The Arikara villages distributed to the Teton Sioux, who traveled to the James River trade gathering in South Dakota to sell to Yankton, Yanktonnais, and Santee Sioux in the 1750s.

Some Indians became virtual horse merchants, and others horse breeders, such as the Cayuse; the Palouses gave their name to the Appaloosa breed, famous for its spotted coat. Estimates suggest that horses moved north and northwest from Santa Fé at the rate of ten miles (16 kilometers) annually. In addition, herds of wild horses became established in southern Texas and in California after the Spanish settled these areas in 1769. So large were the Californian herds that they became a nuisance to the rancheros.

Horses changed the lives of the Indians. Some previously horticultural bands moved from the Missouri River bluff settlements onto the Plains. Hunting buffalo from horseback transformed Indian food supplies by allowing a surplus to be preserved. This led to a growth in populations. Thus, many sedentary bands left their farms for a nomadic hunting lifestyle.

Apart from being ridden, horses could be used as pack animals and travois pullers, allowing tribes to travel further and faster. Goods could be accumulated, then transported by horse, which was a far easier method than relying on dogs or women for pulling power. Tribes became increasingly mobile in the constant search for fresh horse pastures. Camps were moved frequently, and Indians acquired the skill of burning the ground to encourage early spring growth of grass.

The easier acquisition of food by the hunt liberated young men, who could now engage in horse raiding, since horses had become an economic necessity. Raiding could also lead to the capture of children, who would be adopted, and women for marriage or other liaisons. The personal acquisition of horses could raise a man's status and increase wealth. The more horses owned, the greater the quantity of property that could be carried. Wealthy elites emerged, especially among the Blackfeet and Kiowa.

The Appaloosa horse, with its distinctive spotted coat, came about through the efforts of Palouse breeders in the Pacific Northwest.

Owning many horses could mean that a man could marry several women. Moreover, individuals of low status could improve their social standing by capturing horses, which could be kept or traded with Europeans.

As a consequence, warfare escalated for economic and social reasons, and it changed from pitched battles to small raids relying on surprise. Weapons became shorter to allow mounted combat. Battle achievements were based upon the seizure of an enemy's horse or gun, while casualties could lead to revenge raids. Two tribes that became especially dominant were the Comanche below the Platte River, and the Osage to the east of the Comanche.

Allies and Subjects: Indians in the Colonial World

"WHAT CAN YOU GET BY WARRE, WHEN WE CAN HIDE OUR PROVISIONS AND FLY TO THE WOODS? AND WHY ARE YOU JEALOUS OF OUR LOVES SEEING US UNARMED AND BOTH DOE, AND ARE WILLING STILL TO FEEDE YOU, WITH THAT YOU CANNOT GET BUT BY OUR LABOURS? ... LET THIS THEREFORE ASSURE YOU OF OUR LOVES, AND EVERY YEARE OUR FRIENDLY TRADE SHALL FURNISH YOU WITH CORNE ..."

POWHATAN TO CAPTAIN JOHN SMITH, 1609.

The advent of European settlement in North America caused a drop in the population of Native Americans, and many migrated out of the way of white settlers and their diseases. Some tribal bands became partially dependent on European goods, however, which affected regional tribal alliances and rivalries. The years after 1600 saw an incredible increase in the numbers of Europeans on the Atlantic seaboard, a response to the rise of mercantile nation-states in western Europe. These new political formations regarded colonies as makeweights in the European balance of power, and supply depots of raw materials and wealth that could be transported back to the mother country. Parallel to this idea was the notion that the seizure or destruction of enemy colonies would weaken them and strengthen the victor. Thus, colonial outposts became increasingly significant to western European monarchical governments. Part of the European view was that Native Americans

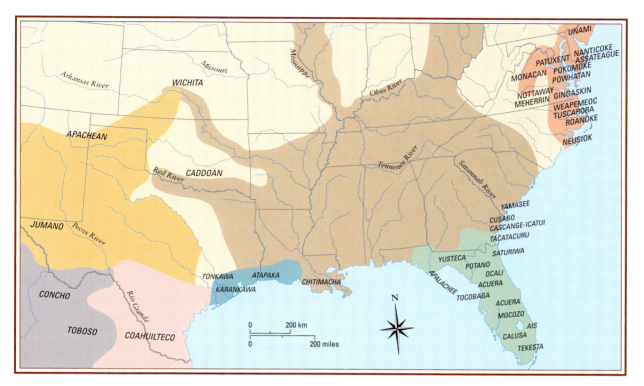

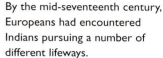

By the mid-seventeenth century, Europeans had encountered Indians pursuing a number of different lifeways.

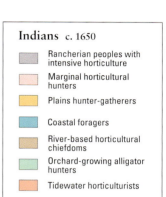

Indians c. 1650

▨	Rancherian peoples with intensive horticulture
▨	Marginal horticultural hunters
▨	Plains hunter-gatherers
▨	Coastal foragers
▨	River-based horticultural chiefdoms
▨	Orchard-growing alligator hunters
▨	Tidewater horticulturists

were peoples to be exploited, peoples who were culturally inferior and "other" than European. This "otherness" caused Europeans to misunderstand Indian society and its cultural values. Two examples of this attitude are the failure to understand the role of Native American women in New England and Virginia; and the European attack on Pueblo religion before the 1680 Pueblo Revolt.

Evidence of inter-European hostility can be found in the competition between the Québec French and their Huron allies, and the Dutch and Mohawks. In this case, European rivalries depended upon Native American alliances and Huron-Mohawk enmity. As far as the Plymouth colony was concerned, the British entered the arena after 1620, when they supported the Wampanoags against the Narragansetts, Pequots, and Micmac. Outside this mercantilist theater, the Virginian region of the Chesapeake saw no inter-European competition, but a conflict surfaced between Jamestown and the Powhatans, despite the "diplomatic" activity of Pocahontas. Further south, the Spanish recovered from the 1597–1601 revolt, but the renewal of contact and missionary work among the Guale and Timucuans led to epidemics in 1613 and 1617, which killed 50 percent of Indians associated with the missions, some 8,000 people.

The flow of European trade goods became a target for control, and eventually the Iroquoian Mohawk defeated the Mahicans to command access to the Dutch at Fort Orange. The acquisition of guns from this source armed the other Iroquois, enabling them to engage in the Beaver Wars against French-allied Indians. Mohawk strength and the rapid influx of British settlers weakened the tribes in southern New England. The British overpowered the Massachusetts and Pawtuckets near Massachusetts Bay, taking most of their land while protecting the remnant against Micmac attacks in return for corn supplies. Another tribe, the Pequots, was surrounded by the Dutch, Narragansett, and Mohegan enemies. An alliance with the Massachusetts Bay colony and the newer Connecticut (1636) colony provided protection in return for land and tribute. The failure to pay the latter caused the outbreak of the Pequot

C. Smith taketh the King of Pamavnkee prifoner. -1608.

A contemporary engraving showing Captain John Smith capturing Opechancanough, a tribal chief of the Powhatan Confederacy, in 1608.

Opposite: As the seventeenth century progressed, European settlements in the North expanded rapidly, encroaching continually on Indian lands.

War and the Mystic village massacre.

The regional hegemony of the Europeans, and their territorial expansion, ousted the Delaware from their lands in New England, while attacks on Jamestown and its outposts by Opechancanough's Powhatans in 1622 and 1644 resulted in a British attempt to exterminate these confederated tribes. The destruction of the Powhatan political entity allowed British expansion throughout the Virginian Tidewater region and into the Piedmont, where the tribes suffered from European violence. In southern New England, vulnerable Indians facing European territorial expansion were overcome by debt (to be redeemed by land cessions), were cheated by land speculators, faced missionary attacks on their culture, were subjected forcibly to British law, and fell under the influence of alcohol. The erosion of territory and the destructiveness of the capitalist economy goaded the Pokanet Wampanoags, Narragansetts, Nipmucs, and Pocumtuckets into defensive aggression in King Philip's War (1675–76). Male and female Indian chiefs resisted strongly, but were defeated. The encounter with female "Amazons" probably forced the British into reassessing their prejudicial views of Native American women, at least in the short term.

Most historical records and accounts of Native American life in the seventeenth century were written by white men, be they traders, missionaries, soldiers, or government envoys and agents. Their writings concentrated upon male activities, displaying a remarkable lack of understanding of the position and power of important Indian women. Little realization was shown that women played major roles and exercised considerable authority in the social, political, economic, religious, and military aspects of tribal life. The only woman to receive significant attention, and far more than she warranted, was Pocahontas. The daughter of Powhatan, allegedly she saved Captain John Smith's life. Accounts failed to explore the accepted powers of leading women to save prisoners, often for adoption; the white men had completely misunderstood the Indian culture. It is possible that Powhatan spared Smith's life as an act of diplomacy, fearing that his death would provoke a massive retaliation.

In New England, Algonquian speaking people lived in a matrilineal society, tracing their descent through the female line. The confederated Wampanoag tribes of Massachusetts and Rhode Island were also matrilocal, meaning that husbands moved into their wives' households. Chieftainship was hereditary, but a post went to the individual with the most ability among those eligible to hold it, including women. Chiefs had the power of persuasion, and legitimacy was gained by exercising wisdom, not force.

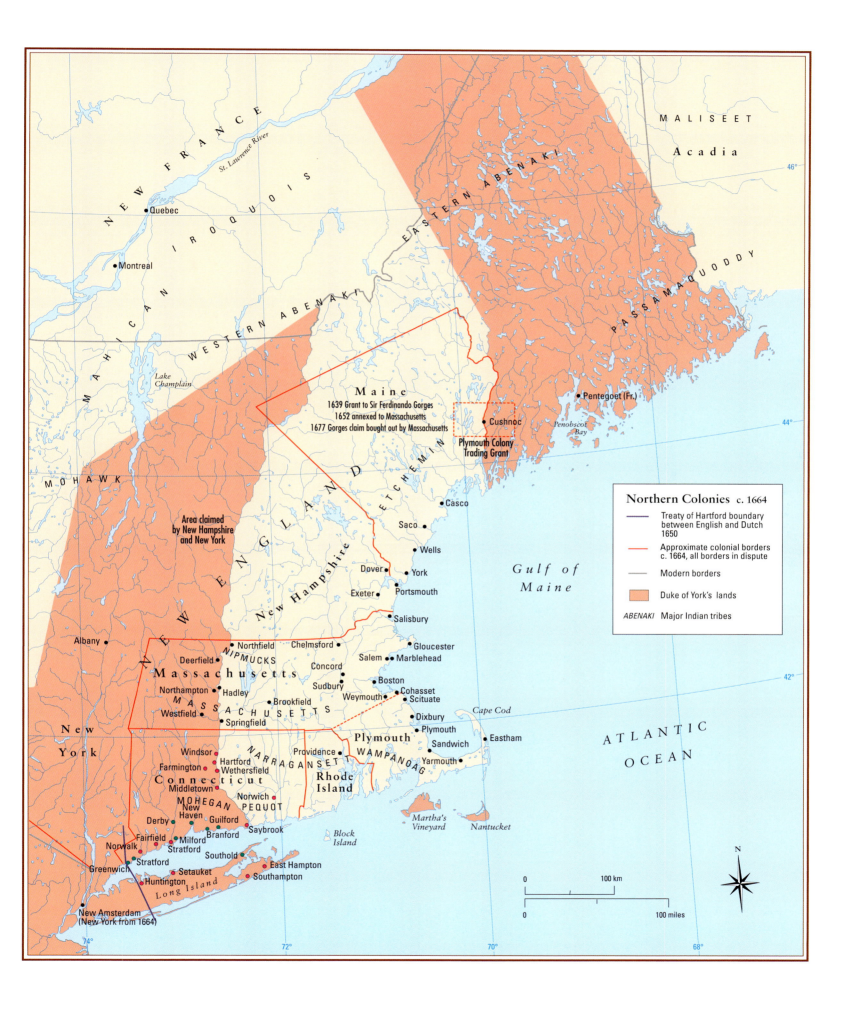

NEW FRANCE

St. Lawrence River

MAHICAN IROQUOIS

• Quebec

• Montreal

WESTERN ABENAKI

Lake
Champlain

MOHAWK

EASTERN ABENAKI

MALISEET

Acadia

PASSAMAQUODDY

• Pentegoet (Fr.)

Penobscot
Bay

Maine
1639 Grant to Sir Ferdinando Gorges
1652 annexed to Massachusetts
1677 Gorges claim bought out by Massachusetts

Plymouth Colony
Trading Grant

• Cushnoc

Area claimed
by New Hampshire
and New York

ETCHEMIN

• Casco

N E W   E N G L A N D

• Saco

New Hampshire

Dover •   • York
• Wells

Exeter •   • Portsmouth

• Salisbury

Gulf of
Maine

• Albany

NIPMUCKS

• Northfield   • Chelmsford

• Gloucester

• Deerfield

Massachusetts

• Concord   Salem • • Marblehead

• Northampton   • Hadley

M A S S -

• Boston

• Westfield

A C H U S E T T S

Sudbury •

Weymouth •   • Cohasset
            • Scituate

• Springfield

• Brookfield

• Dixbury

Cape Cod

**New
York**

N E W

Windsor •

NARRAGANSETT

• Plymouth
• Sandwich

• Eastham

Farmington •   • Hartford
           • Wethersfield

• Providence

Plymouth

WAMPANOAG

• Yarmouth

ATLANTIC

OCEAN

Middletown •

Connecticut

MOHEGAN

Norwich •

**Rhode
Island**

PEQUOT

Derby •   New
        Haven •   • Guilford

Fairfield •   • Branford

• Saybrook

Martha's
Vineyard

Nantucket

Norwalk •   • Milford
          • Stratford

• Southold

Block
Island

Greenwich •   • Stratford
          Setauket •   • East Hampton
          • Huntington   • Southampton

Long Island

New Amsterdam
(New York from 1664)

Northern Colonies c. 1664

— Treaty of Hartford boundary
   between English and Dutch
   1650

— Approximate colonial borders
   c. 1664, all borders in dispute

— Modern borders

▨ Duke of York's lands

ABENAKI Major Indian tribes

0   100 km

0   100 miles

N

74°   72°   70°   68°
46°   44°   42°

Middle Colonies c. 1632–82

- —— Maryland border according to Baltimore's interpretation of the 1632 Charter
- —— New Netherland c. 1654
- —— Granted to William Penn 1681
- —— New Jersey Quintipartite Deed division line 1676
- —— New Sweden c. 1654
- ▢ Grant to the Duke of York in 1664
- ▨ Grant by the Duke of York to Lord Berkeley and Sir George Carteret in 1664
- ▨ Grant to William Penn by the Duke of York in 1682
- • Quaker towns

Lake Ontario

Lake Erie

HURON

ONEIDA

ONONDAGA

SENECA

CAYUGA

ERIE

MAHIGAN

MOHAWK

MUNSEE

Pennsylvania 1681

During the seventeenth century, the colonies spread northward along the Atlantic coast and then began pressing inland, absorbing ever larger amounts of territory.

SUSQUEHANNA

ONAMI

Schenectady •
Albany •
Kinderhook •
Coxsackle •

New York (New Netherland) to 1664

Kingston •
Pokeepsie •

Sint Sings •

East Jersey

Yonkers •

Hackensack •

Newark •
Elizabethtown • New York (New Amsterdam)

Spotswood • Middletown •
Cranbury • Shrewsbury •

Bordentown •

Burlington •
• Mount Holly
Bridgeton •

Philadelphia • • Gloucester
Paulsboro • • Woodbury

Lancaster •

New Castle •

West Jersey

Little Egg Harbor

Salem •

Maryland

Joppa •

Baltimore •

• Bohemia Manor
Greenwich •
• Bridgeton

Dover •

Delaware Bay

CONOY

Arundelton •
D.C.

Chesapeake Bay

Cape Island •

• Lewes

Delaware

ATLANTIC OCEAN

CHICKAHOMINY

NANTICOKE

Virginia

N

0   100 km
0   100 miles

• St. Marys

Maryland

Delaware

● St. Marys

Fairfax Propriety

V i r g i n i a

James River

● Williamsburg ● Jamestown

*Albemarle
(Durant's Neck)*

● Norfolk

Northern boundary of Carolina
according to the Charter of 1665

C H E R O K E E

Roanoke River

Northern boundary of Carolina
according to the Charter of 1663

North Carolina
Royal Province from 1729

Neuse River

● New Berne

C A T A W B A

T U S C A R O R A

Separation 1712

Cape Fear River

Cape Lookout

South Carolina
Royal Province from 1729

G e o r g i a

● Brunswick

Cape Fear

Santee River

● Augusta

● Jamestown

Savannah River

In the Southeast, the British
colonists encountered the Spanish,
who claimed Florida and beyond.

Ogeechee River

Y A M A S E E

● Goose Creek

● Charles Town

Limit of Spanish claim
Treaty of Madrid 1670

Beaufort ●

C R E E K

● Stuart's Town
Port Royal

Ocmulgee River

● Savannah

Altamaha River

A T L A N T I C   O C E A N

Fort George

Southern boundary of Carolina
according to the Charter of 1663

A P A L A C H E

St Mary's River

F l o r i d a

● St Augustine

N

S E M I N O L E

Southern boundary of Carolina
according to the Charter of 1665

Southern Colonies c. 1664–1735

— Extent of the Carolina Charter 1663

— Extent of the Carolina Charter 1665

— Northern limit of the Spanish claim
  Treaty of Madrid 1670

☐ Grant to James Oglethorpe in 1732

— Modern borders

▨ Maximum extent of Spanish claim

0   100 km

0   100 miles

84   83   82   81   80   79°   78°   77°   76°

38°
37°
36°
35°
34°
33°
32°
31°
30°

A souvenir postcard from the 1907 Jamestown Exposition, depicting Pocahontas, daughter of Powhatan, saving the life of Captain John Smith.

Opposite: The British increasingly became the dominant European nation in the East and far North of the North American continent. They dispatched many expeditions to explore the New World.

Weetamoo was wife to Wamsutta, who succeeded his father, Massasoit, in 1662, becoming principal chief of the Wampanoag. Weetamoo was a chief in her own right of the Pocasset tribe in the confederacy. When Wamsutta died, she married Quinnapin, the son of Ninigret, chief of the Niantic tribe of the Wampanoag. She retained her status in the Pocasset tribe, despite her new husband already having two other wives. Ninigret's sister, Quaiapan, married the son of a Narragansett tribal chief and headed Queen's North village in Rhode Island. Ninigret had another sister, Awashonks, who was chief of the Sakonnet Wampanoag. Metacomet (Philip) succeeded Wamsutta, and he was married to Weetamoo's sister. Thus, the region was home to several powerful women.

During King Philip's War, Weetamoo supported Metacomet, whereas Awashonks joined the British. Weetamoo commanded 300 warriors, but only thirty survived the fighting. After Philip was killed on August 12, 1676, Weetamoo fled from the British, but drowned in the Taunton River during her flight. Her head and Philip's were displayed on poles in Plymouth to deter any Native American chief who might be considering further resistance against the colony. The British had learned the importance of female power.

Elsewhere, the Spanish faced their own difficulties. Renewed missionary activity in Florida, with consequent epidemics, was accompanied by an influx of soldiers, which led to further conflict with the Guales, Timicuans, and Apalachees. Forced labor on plantations owned by soldiers contributed to Apalachee resistance in 1647, and more self-defense by the Apalachee and Timicuans in 1656.

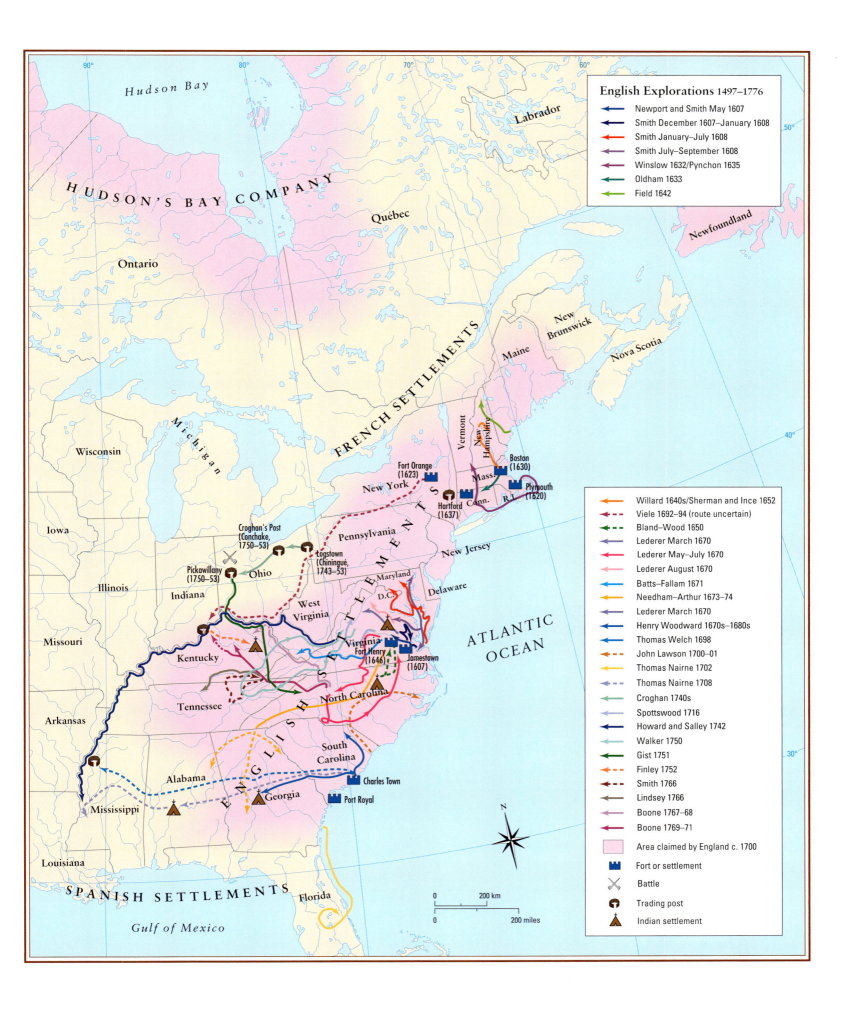

Hudson Bay

Labrador

HUDSON'S BAY COMPANY

Québec

Newfoundland

Ontario

English Explorations 1497–1776
- Newport and Smith May 1607
- Smith December 1607–January 1608
- Smith January–July 1608
- Smith July–September 1608
- Winslow 1632/Pynchon 1635
- Oldham 1633
- Field 1642

Maine

New Brunswick

Nova Scotia

FRENCH SETTLEMENTS

Wisconsin

Michigan

Vermont

New Hampshire

Boston (1630)

Fort Orange (1623)

New York

Mass.

Conn.

R.I.

Plymouth (1620)

Iowa

Hartford (1637)

Pennsylvania

Croghan's Post (Conchake, 1750–53)

Logstown (Chiningué, 1743–53)

Pickawillany (1750–53)

Ohio

Indiana

New Jersey

Delaware

Maryland

D.C.

West Virginia

Virginia

Fort Henry (1646)

Jamestown (1607)

ATLANTIC OCEAN

Illinois

Missouri

Kentucky

- Willard 1640s/Sherman and Ince 1652
- Viele 1692–94 (route uncertain)
- Bland–Wood 1650
- Lederer March 1670
- Lederer May–July 1670
- Lederer August 1670
- Batts–Fallam 1671
- Needham–Arthur 1673–74
- Lederer March 1670
- Henry Woodward 1670s–1680s
- Thomas Welch 1698
- John Lawson 1700–01
- Thomas Nairne 1702
- Thomas Nairne 1708
- Croghan 1740s
- Spottswood 1716
- Howard and Salley 1742
- Walker 1750
- Gist 1751
- Finley 1752
- Smith 1766
- Lindsey 1766
- Boone 1767–68
- Boone 1769–71

Tennessee

North Carolina

Arkansas

ENGLISH SETTLEMENTS

South Carolina

Alabama

Mississippi

Georgia

Charles Town

Port Royal

Louisiana

SPANISH SETTLEMENTS

Florida

Gulf of Mexico

- Area claimed by England c. 1700
- Fort or settlement
- Battle
- Trading post
- Indian settlement

0   200 km

0   200 miles

N

The Indians destroyed all the missions, suggesting that they were resisting the cultural attacks of the Franciscan version of Christianity. One consequence was the movement of Indian refugees to the Carolinas and westward. The Guales in the Carolinas became known as Yamasees. Other Guales, who might have spoken a Hitchiti dialect, were probably absorbed into the Muskogee Creek. The Apalachee were crushed, becoming loyal converts and allies of Spain. The northward move of Spanish missions and their Appalachee followers into South Carolina led to conflict with the British and Creeks. The latter attacked the Appalachee missions and, by 1704, they had been destroyed; the Spanish retreated from South Carolina.

The 1680 Pueblo Revolt is largely attributed to Popé, a shaman from the Tewa San Juan Pueblo. His victory turned sour, however, when he became a despot. He traveled between the Pueblos in ceremonial dress, acted like a Spanish governor, killed dissidents, and seized beautiful women for himself and his military leaders. Eventually, he was deposed for his dictatorial manner.

Many accounts of the revolt fail to consider the intense religious conflict that occurred as Indians resisted involuntary conversion to Roman Catholicism. When analyzing the Pueblo Revolt, it is essential to consider political, economic and personal factors, but any cultural hostility between the Spanish and Pueblos had basically religious roots. The Indians attempted to preserve their lifeways, which had been ordained by their gods, in the face of a cultural holocaust applied by aliens.

The cultural clash began when Spanish control was exerted over the Pueblos in 1598 by Oñate, but real Indian bitterness began in 1675. Pueblo missions were seen by the Spanish as forming a defensive barrier against European competitors, and aggressive Apache and Navajo raiders. Superficially, there were similarities between the two cultures: both used altars and religious calendars, and while priests baptized, the Pueblos practiced head washing. At a spiritual level, however, there were extremely deep, basic differences. The Pueblo view was that the underworld was the source of life, rather than heaven. The Indians considered the earth to be sacred, unlike Europeans, and ran their lives according to natural cycles of nature and the seasons, instead of bowing to a creator.

Another point of contention was the significance of the individual. Europeans stressed the role of the individual and the value of personal talent, heroism, and sacrifice. The Pueblos abhorred personal distinction, however, and considered that a harmonious society could only exist when the individual became submerged in the identity of the community. The final distinguishing feature of the two cultures was the idea of moral obligation. The Pueblos considered good to be exhibited by a sense of duty toward the community, whereas the European church defined good and evil in its own terms, stating that evil actions would be punished both on earth and in the afterlife. The Pueblos thought that bad conduct would be punished in the here-and-now, and that the punished person could return to the underworld with everyone else. Thus, the Pueblo Revolt was the act of a people intent on rejecting Christian culture and civilization because it threatened their own socially integrated culture and religion.

After Diego de Vargas reconquered the Pueblos in 1692, Roman Catholicism became more pragmatic. The Pueblo inhabitants adopted the outward trappings of Spanish Christianity, but kept the friars away from clan rituals, the kiva, and kachina. Thus, many Pueblo people became notionally Roman Catholic, but also they practiced their own faith, thereby retaining their world view and identity.

Opposite: Pressed continuously to give up land to meet the demands of the European colonists, the Indians reacted by waging war on the invaders.

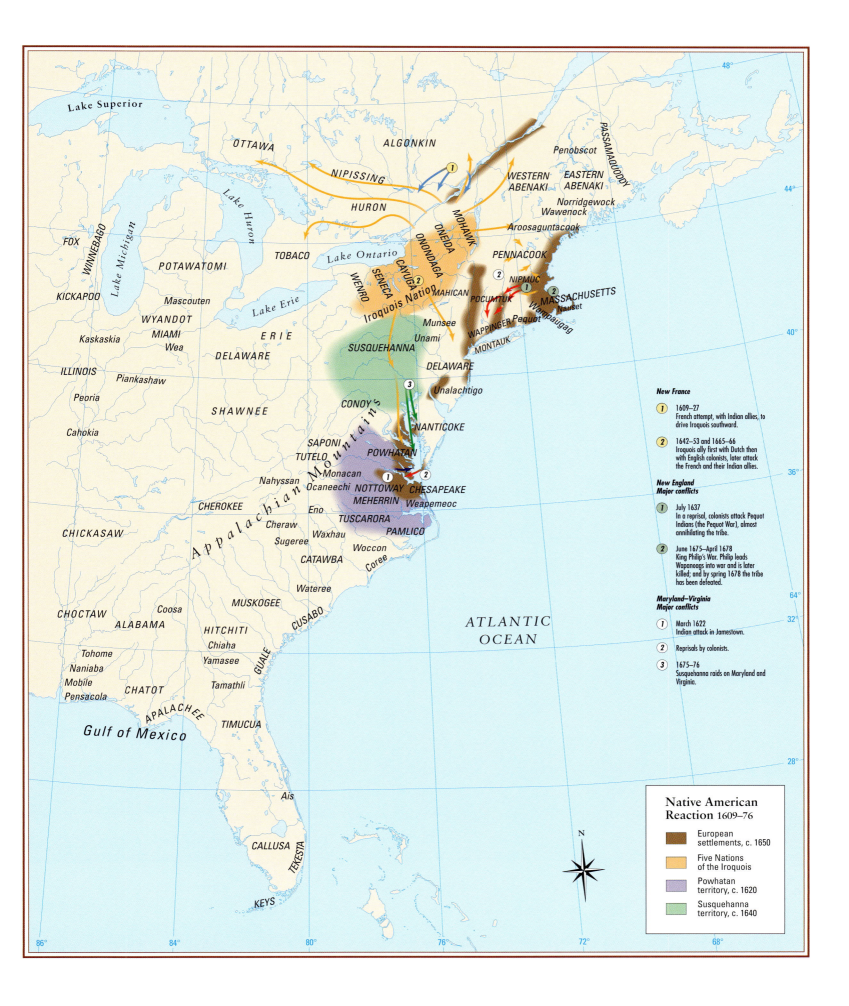

Lake Superior

OTTAWA

ALGONKIN

Penobscot

PASSAMAQUODDY

NIPISSING

WESTERN ABENAKI

EASTERN ABENAKI

HURON

MOHAWK

Norridgewock
Wawenock

Aroosaguntacook

FOX

WINNEBAGO

Lake Michigan

Lake Huron

TOBACO

ONEIDA

PENNACOOK

POTAWATOMI

Lake Ontario

CAYUGA
ONONDAGA

NIPMUC

MASSACHUSETTS

KICKAPOO

Mascouten

Lake Erie

WENRO
SENECA

Iroquois Nation

MAHICAN

POCUMTUK

Nauset

WYANDOT

Kaskaskia

MIAMI

Wea

ERIE

DELAWARE

Munsee

Unami

WAPPINGER Pequot

Wappaugag

MONTAUK

SUSQUEHANNA

ILLINOIS

Piankashaw

DELAWARE

Peoria

SHAWNEE

Unalachtigo

Cahokia

CONOY

NANTICOKE

SAPONI
TUTELO

POWHATAN

Nahyssan

Monacan

CHEROKEE

Ocaneechi

NOTTOWAY
MEHERRIN

CHESAPEAKE

Weapemeoc

Eno

TUSCARORA

CHICKASAW

Cheraw

Sugeree

Waxhaw

PAMLICO

Woccon

CATAWBA

Coree

Wateree

MUSKOGEE

CHOCTAW

Coosa

ALABAMA

HITCHITI

CUSABO

ATLANTIC
OCEAN

Tohome

Chiaha

Naniaba

Yamasee

Mobile

Tamathli

Pensacola

CHATOT

APALACHEE

TIMUCUA

Gulf of Mexico

Ais

CALLUSA

TEKESTA

KEYS

Appalachian Mountains

New France

① 1609–27
French attempt, with Indian allies, to drive Iroquois southward.

② 1642–53 and 1665–66
Iroquois ally first with Dutch then with English colonists, later attack the French and their Indian allies.

**New England
Major conflicts**

① July 1637
In a reprisal, colonists attack Pequot Indians (the Pequot War), almost annihilating the tribe.

② June 1675–April 1678
King Philip's War. Philip leads Wapanoags into war and is later killed; and by spring 1678 the tribe has been defeated.

**Maryland–Virginia
Major conflicts**

① March 1622
Indian attack in Jamestown.

② Reprisals by colonists.

③ 1675–76
Susquehanna raids on Maryland and Virginia.

N

Native American Reaction 1609–76

- European settlements, c. 1650
- Five Nations of the Iroquois
- Powhatan territory, c. 1620
- Susquehanna territory, c. 1640

Iroquois Imperium, from 1142

A POWERFUL ALLIANCE OF FIVE, AND LATER SIX, TRIBES IN THE NORTHEAST, THE IROQUOIS WAGED A DEADLY WAR AGAINST THE FRENCH AND THEIR HURON ALLIES.

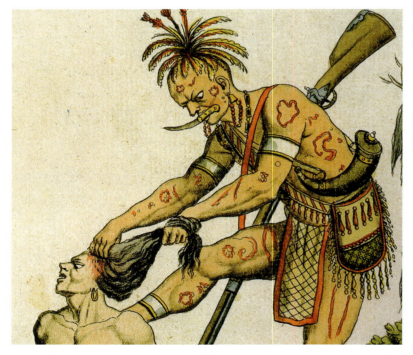

A late-eighteenth-century, French depiction of an Iroquois taking a scalp.

The Northern Iroquoian peoples lived in woodlands to the northeast of the tribes of the Mississippi. By AD 1000, they were dispersed over broad territories around the eastern Great Lakes and along the St. Lawrence River. Among the various Iroquoian tribes were the Seneca, Cayuga, Onondaga, Oneida, and Mohawk—the Five Nations of the Long House (Haudenosaunee), which were joined in the mid-1720s by the Tuscaroras to become the Six Nations. This confederacy's homelands spread through upstate New York, between the Mohawk and Genesee river valleys.

The Five Nations existed as a political entity to suppress internal warfare, but not as a single political unit for diplomatic purposes. Apparently, the legendary Hiawatha, a Mohawk, founded the confederacy. The village, sometimes inhabited by 2,000 people, was the major expression of sovereignty, with power emanating upward from the women of matrilineal kin groups. League councils contained chiefly delegates who could be expelled by the clan women if they lost their confidence. The Long House comprised some 20,000 people prior to European contact, but by the mid-seventeenth century, foreign diseases had halved the population.

Having penetrated the St. Lawrence River, the French supported the Hurons, who not only supplied their own beaver pelts and furs, but also those from such tribes as the Petun, Neutrals, Nipissings, and Ottawas. In return, they received metal and cloth goods, plus protection against the Five Nations.

In 1624, the Dutch established a trading post at Fort Orange, on the Hudson River, which became a center for the fur trade, but the route to the fort crossed Mahican territory. Consequently, the Mohawks attacked the Mahicans, defeating them by 1630; thereafter, the Mohawks controlled access to the Dutch. They soon acquired European goods and guns, which became spread among the other tribes of the Long House. Meanwhile, the Hurons, like the Iroquois, were exhausting supplies of furs in their own lands, becoming dependent on other tribes to the north and west for pelts to feed the growing European demand. Despite such economic resources, the Hurons were forced to confront two problems. Firstly, smallpox killed half their populations between 1639 and 1640; secondly, the tribes of the Long House had become well armed with Dutch guns.

The increase in epidemic-induced death had also affected the Mohawks and their Iroquois confederates. Initially, the Mohawks had acquired furs by raiding the St. Lawrence trade, the results of this piracy paying for trade goods and guns at Fort Orange. However, when disease struck the Five Nations, destroying 75 percent of the Mohawks, the tribes of the Long House were forced to rethink their policies and strategies. The normal mourning warfare to acquire captives to replace the dead was transformed into carefully coordinated, spiralling, large-scale warfare, initially directed against the Hurons. In 1642, a major attack was carried out against an exposed Huron village; between 1643 and 1644, Senecas, Cayugas, and Onondagas battled the Hurons, while Mohawks and Oneidas blockaded the St. Lawrence. The spoils of this warfare included large quantities of furs, captives, and trade goods. Huron villages were subjected to intense assaults, any survivors fleeing to their neighbors, who also faced the wrath of the Long House. Other tribes were scattered—the Petuns (1650), the Neutrals (1651), and the Eries (1657)—as the Five Nations fought nearly all the northeastern tribes, benefiting from a superior supply of guns. These "Beaver Wars" eventually resulted in the Long House expelling Ottowas, Shawnees, and other Algonquian-speakers into Wisconsin and the Ohio Valley. The Iroquois blitzkrieg was halted by Green Bay Potowatomis in 1653. The Iroquois Imperium, with its subject tribes, now faced the increasing power of New France in Canada. In reply, the Long House sought to preserve an independent balancing role between French and Dutch-British interests.

To the south of Lake Ontario lived the Seneca, Cayuga, Onondaga, Oneida, and Mohawk, Iroquoian tribes that made up the Five Nations of the Long House (Haudenosaunee).

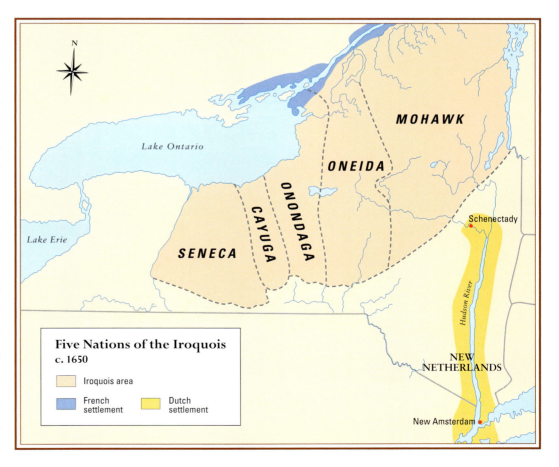

Five Nations of the Iroquois
c. 1650

Iroquois area

French settlement

Dutch settlement

POWHATAN'S CONFEDERACY

ANGERED BY CONTINUAL LAND SEIZURES BY BRITISH SETTLERS, POWHATAN LED HIS CHIEFDOM OF OVER THIRTY TRIBES IN A BITTER WAR AGAINST THE COLONISTS.

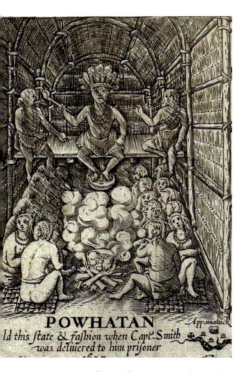

Detail from a map drawn by Captain John Smith, dating from 1612. It shows Powhatan holding court in a longhouse at Werowocomoco.

The Powhatan (also known as Wahunsunacock) Confederacy comprised some thirty-two tribes and 200 villages, which controlled eastern Virginia, dominating the James, York, and Rappahannock River valleys. It also projected power into the Virginia Delamarva Peninsula and the south bank of the Potomac River. Powhatan's lands were bordered by the friendly Nottaways and Meherrins, but also by Monacan and Mannahoac enemies in the Virginia Piedmont; other foes were probably the Iroquoian Susquehannocks, and certainly the Massawomocks and Pecoughtaonacks from the upper Potomac.

Powhatan's rule was not based upon a confederation, but can be identified as a paramount chiefdom. As a rule, chiefs of subordinate tribes were left in peace, but Powhatan's relatives were often district chiefs. His sons, Pochins and Parahunt, ruled strategic towns at the mouth and falls of the James River respectively, while his brother, Opechancanough, lived near the Piedmont to observe the Monacan enemy. Powhatan's rule was further cemented by marrying women from all districts under his authority. The women would be returned to their original home after childbirth. He is alleged to have married over a hundred women by his sixtieth birthday in 1607. His power was further strengthened by his political and military harshness. The Chesapeake tribe, living near contemporary Virginia Beach, refused to join his chiefdom and were exterminated. Thus, intimidation was a weapon in his armory, to which the conquered Kecoughtans, at the mouth of the James River, could attest after being defeated in 1596 and 1597.

Powhatan was extremely powerful and could have smashed the British colony established at Jamestown in 1607. Moreover, by 1610, only 150 of the original 900 settlers remained alive, the dead being victims of disease and starvation. Sporadic violence turned into open warfare between 1610 and 1614, as a response to British seizures of land. The settlers captured Powhatan's daughter, Pocahontas,

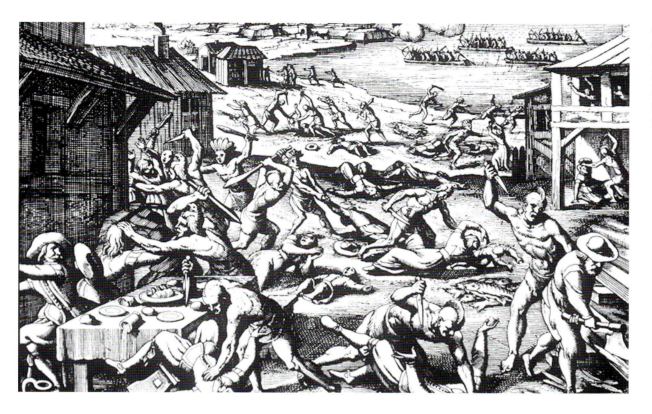

A contemporary woodcut depicting the attack on the British in March 1622 by Indians led by Opechancanough. Some 347 colonists were killed during the attack, and many tobacco plantations torched.

whose marriage to John Rolfe helped smooth matters until 1618, when Powhatan died. Meanwhile, the colonists had discovered that tobacco was an excellent cash crop, and their demands for more land antagonized the Indians, especially on the James River. In addition, the British undermined the chiefdom by winning over Indians in the Delmarva Peninsula, making them allies in 1621.

Powhatan's successor, Opechancanough, realized that increasing British numbers would mean even greater demands for agricultural land. Consequently, on March 22, 1622, his warriors attacked the British, killing some 347 men, women, and children, and burning every outlying plantation. The remaining settlers fled to Henrico, Shirley Hundred, Jamestown, and Keocoughton. The British then sent their militias into Indian villages to destroy buildings and crops, with the intention of clearing the Tidewater of Indians by pushing them inland. The war carried on, 11,000 Pamunkey Indians being killed in 1625; minor clashes continued until 1632, when a peace treaty was agreed.

Commercial tobacco planting continued apace, with more settlers arriving, while disease took its toll of the Indians. In retaliation, Opechancanough planned another attack on the settlers, who were spreading into the Rappahannock and Potomac valleys. On April 18, 1644, the Indians struck, killing between 400 and 500 British out of some 8,000. Most assaults occurred against outlying villages on the York and Pamunkey rivers. Governor William Berkeley organized a British militia, which entered Indian territory, killing the inhabitants, and burning their villages and produce. Eventually, Opechancanough was captured and shot dead by a guard. Peace was concluded in 1646 with his successor, Necotowance.

Despite Indian lands being protected by treaty, the British spread north of the York River and had acquired the rest of the Virginia coastal plain by the 1670s; the Powhatan chiefdom had disintegrated by 1649. The Pamunkey and Mattaponi peoples absorbed the tribal remnants, but the 10,000 surviving Powhatans were quickly reduced to a few hundred.

THE DIVIDED SOUTHEAST

THE SOUTHEAST BECAME A PLACE OF TURMOIL, THE BRITISH, FRENCH, AND SPANISH ALL SEEKING TO GAIN TERRITORY WITH THE AID OF NATIVE AMERICAN ALLIES.

Pierre Le Moyne d'Iberville, founder of the colony of French Louisiana. In 1690, he instigated the construction of Fort Maurepas at Biloxi in a bid to counter British expansion in the Southeast.

Opposite: As Spanish power in the Southeast diminished, the British pushed steadily southward. By 1665, the Charter of Carolina set the southern border of Carolina at 29 degrees North latitude in northern Florida.

Eventually, the Southeast was split under the spheres of influence of Britain, France, and Spain. Britain established a presence in the Carolinas after 1670 by founding Charles Town. The Weapemeoc nation sold its coastal lands and moved away from the European settlers. Erie refugees, known as Westos, became a target for Virginia traders entering the Carolinas, as did the Tuscarora and the Catawba nation. The Westos were adept at hunting for deerskins and capturing slaves by attacking Yuchis, Cherokees, and others; they managed to force the Spanish to close two missions among the Guale in Florida. Traders allied themselves with Shawnee refugees (Savannahs) and slaughtered Westos, driving them from the colony and into confederation with the Creeks.

Many Guales, potential victims of slavers, fled to St. Augustine and Spanish protection, while those remaining in the Carolinas became known as Yamasees. In the late 1680s, Anglo-Creek trade began in earnest. Heavily armed by the British, Yamasees and Creeks attacked Apalachee and Timucuan mission stations for slaves and horses. So badly did they damage the Spanish that their influence north of St. Augustine was severely restricted. The British then began trade with Upper Creeks, who raided the Cherokee and Choctaw for slaves; the Chickasaw also mounted slave raids against the Choctaw and the Illinois on the Mississippi River. Some commerce took place with the Cherokee, but they were less important to the British than the Creek, so the colonists ignored Cherokee complaints about Creek slave raids. By 1700, the region had become so destabilized by slave wars that conflict broke out between the Tuscarora and the Yamasees.

Spanish settlements in Florida were subjected to constant attack, and missions were established in today's Georgia in an attempt to provide a buffer for St. Augustine against encroaching Carolinians. Also, the Spanish employed naval power to prevent the French from entering Pensacola in 1698, and Biloxi in 1699. However, the 26,000 Guale, Apalachee, and Timucua were becoming less loyal to

The Divided Southeast

CREEK

Coosa River

Tallapoosa River

Coweta Town

Ocmulgee River

Oconee River

Savannah River

Ogeechee River

Georgia

Carolina

CUSABO

Santa Elena

Port Royal

Fort Toulouse (French)

Northern line of Spanish claim

Savacola

Spanish Fort

Savannah

Altamaha River

MIDDLE CREEK

Tombigbee River

Alabama River

Pearl River

Escambia River

Perdido River

Choctawhatchee River

Apalachicola River

Chattahoochee River

Pedernales (Flint) River

Ochlockonee River

LOWER CREEK

Santa Cruz de Savacola

Southern boundary of Carolina under Charter of 1663

Santa Catalina

Frederica

San Pedro

ATLANTIC OCEAN

Mobile (French)

Pensacola (San Carlos de Austria)

APALACHE

San Pedro

San Luis

Conception

Ayubale

Massacre

San Marcos

Aucilla River

Suwannee River

St. Marys River

St. Johns River

TIMUCUA

Santa Fe

Fort Picolata

Fort St. Francis

Fort San Mateo

Fort Diego

Santa Cruz

Port Mooas

St. Augustine

Fort San Marco

Fort Matanzas

Matanzan Inlet

Southern limit of English claim (Carolina Charter of 1665)

30°

FLORIDA

Gulf of Mexico

Cape Canaveral

ACUERA

AIS

MOCOZO

San Carlos

Ponce de Leon Bay

Caloosahatchee River

Lake Okeechobee

CALOOSA

San Ignacio

TEKESTA

25°

Spanish Florida c. 1660

- Spanish claims
- English claims
- Disputed territory
- Fort
- Mission

0   10 km

0   10 miles

N

85°   80°

the Spanish, since the missions could not protect them. In 1676, only forty men were available for seventy missions, and by 1681, only thirty-four. Crumbling Spanish power allowed British influence to penetrate the Creeks completely. The Santa Catalina and San Buenoventura missions were destroyed by the Carolina militia in the 1680s, and Spain's Indian allies deserted to make accords with the British. Creek trade with the British was so great that the Spaniards were forced to build a fort in Creek territory. This so angered the Indians that in 1690, the entire Creek population of Coweta and Kashita moved to the Oconee and Ocmulgee rivers to be nearer British trading centers. Eventually, the Creek learned to play the European powers against each other to maintain three lines of trade.

The French sought to counter British expansion in the Southeast and to stabilize the area as Spanish influence declined. Fort Maurepas was constructed at Biloxi in 1699 by Pierre Le Moyne d'Iberville, and Fort Mobile by his brother in 1702. A later reinforcement was the founding of New Orleans in 1718, at the mouth of the Tombigbee River. The new colony of Louisiana was formed; French interest in the region is evidenced by Delisle's map making. Also, La Salle had descended the Illinois and Mississippi rivers to the Gulf of Mexico in 1682. The French then began trading with Choctaws, Chickasaws, the Natchez, and other groups. When Queen Anne's War began in 1702, trade and imperial war became intertwined. The Apalachee fought for Spain, the Chickasaw and Creeks for the British, and the recently formed Choctaw Confederacy for the French. Anglo-Creek forces killed and enslaved Spanish Indians, destroying all remaining Guale, Apalachee, and Timucuan mission stations, which left the Spanish St. Augustine and Pensacola. The Chickasaw successfully attacked Fort Mobile and hammered the Choctaw with slave raids. By 1712, the Creek had become the most powerful Native American force in the Southeast.

A fanciful illustration of René-Robert Cavelier, Sieur de La Salle leading his expedition to explore the Mississippi in 1682, taken from the 1920 book, *The Story of Our Country*, by E. Boyd Smith. As a result of his journey, La Salle claimed the Mississippi basin region for France. Previously, he had explored the Great Lakes and Gulf of Mexico.

Queen Anne's War 1702–13

→ French movement

→ British movement

→ French–Spanish movement

→ Native American movement (allied with the French)

✳ Raid

French fort

British fort

THE PEQUOT WAR, 1636–38

BLAMED FOR THE MURDER OF A BRITISH SETTLER, THE PEQUOT WERE SUBJECTED TO MILITARY ATTACKS THAT CAME TO A HEAD IN A BLOODY MASSACRE.

Lion Gardiner, founder of the first British colony in what became the State of New York, battles with Indians during the Pequot War (from a watercolor by Stanley Reinhart). Gardiner later wrote of his exploits in *Relation of the Pequot Warres*.

The Pequot tribe had settled in the area of Connecticut, and its influence spread from New Haven to Rhode Island, and from Hartford to eastern Long Island. By 1636, the nation had European neighbors in the form of British settlements, such as Warwick, Portsmouth, and Providence in the Rhode Island region; Fort Saybrook at the mouth of the Connecticut; and Hartford and Wethersfield on the upper Connecticut. Two nearby major Indian nations were the Mohegan and Narragansett.

Relations with the British had deteriorated in 1633, when settlers bought land on the Connecticut River from chiefdoms subordinate to the Pequot, instead of from the Pequot leadership. Simultaneously, Dutch traders had murdered a chief, so relations with Europeans were fraught. Allegedly, the Pequot retaliated by killing Captain John Stone, a Virginia merchant. In addition, the Pequot and Narragansett were at war, and the British feared that the latter might align themselves with the Dutch and threaten British interests. They brokered a peace, which opened up both nations to lucrative trade.

In July 1636, John Oldham, a trader, was murdered. The Pequot were blamed, and their failure to hand over Stone's killers was used as a reason for punitive action. A ninety-strong Massachusetts force, led by John Endecott, invaded Block Island, supposedly where Oldham's

murderers were located. The
Indians had vanished, however, and
the force moved to Fort Saybrook,
which was subjected to a desultory
Pequot siege for a year.

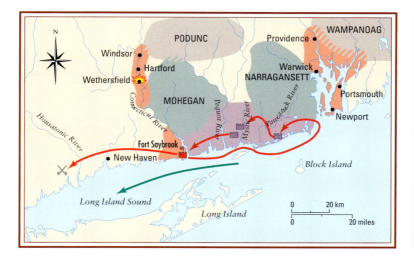

The Pequot mounted a guerrilla
campaign against the Connecticut
British, killing four soldiers in
February 1637, and nine settlers at
Wethersfield, capturing two girls.
The settlers were under serious
threat, since they numbered only 250, other than those at Fort Saybrook, while they faced many
hundreds of Pequot warriors. By April, thirty settlers were dead. The Connecticut leaders dispatched
about ninety men under Captain John Mason to attack the Pequot forts, being joined by several
hundred Mohegan, Narragansett, and Niantic warriors. They advanced on the major fort at Groton, but
instead decided to assault the Pequot village on the Mystic River.

On May 26, 1637, the village was surrounded, the entrances and its palisade forced, and the buildings
torched. The Pequot were slaughtered as they fled the flames, some estimates suggesting that 700 died.
About eighteen were captured and eight escaped. The British losses were two dead and twenty-five
wounded, while the allied Indian casualties reached forty. As the British withdrew, they were attacked
by 300 Pequot from the Groton fort, but they escaped and spent the summer hunting small bands of
Pequot. They killed some and gave others to the Narragansett as rewards for their friendship.

Governor Bradford of Massachusetts, after reading an eyewitness report of the Mystic River
massacre, said that the Indians were "frying in the fire, streams of blood quenching the same, and
horrible was the stink and scent thereof: but the victory was a sweet sacrifice, and they (the victors)
gave prayer thereof to God."

The Mystic River massacre totally disorientated the Pequot, and many left their leader, Sassacus,
to join other tribes, such as the Manhattance on Long Island. Sassacus appealed to other tribes for aid
and alliances, but the Mohawk killed him and gave his scalp to the Massachusetts leaders. The Pequot
refugees, encumbered by many children, reached safety in a swamp near New Haven. On July 13,
1637, the British surrounded the area, and the two sides engaged in an inconsequential firefight. In the
evening, Thomas Stanton, a Pequot speaker, entered the swamp and negotiated with the refugees, and
some 200 old men, women, and children were evacuated to become slaves. By the terms of the 1638
Treaty of Hartford, Uncas' Mohegans received eighty slaves, the Niantics twenty, and Miantonomo,
chief of the Narragansett, eighty; the remainder were sold into Caribbean slavery.

The Treaty ensured short-term peace between the British, Mohegans, and Narragansett. One clause
stated that the Pequot were no longer entitled to their traditional lands, nor their tribal name. A
handful of Pequot warriors escaped; ironically, small groups allied themselves with the British during
King Philip's War (1675–76). Meanwhile, the British gained control of a fertile region, having initiated
the process of clearing New England of Indians.

The Pequot War saw the British
mount a murderous campaign
against the Pequot tribe,
effectively wiping them out. It
was the first step in a move to
clear New England of Indians.

THE DUTCH-INDIAN WARS, 1655–64

THREE DUTCH-INDIAN WARS TOOK PLACE IN NEW NETHERLAND, A COLONY FOUNDED ON THE NORTHEAST COAST BY THE DUTCH WEST INDIA COMPANY IN 1624.

Peter Stuyvesant, Director General of the Dutch colony of New Netherland during the Peach and Esopus wars.

Opposite: The Dutch colony of New Netherland stretched along the banks of the Hudson River and became a province of the Dutch Republic in 1624.

The first clash, known as Kieft's War, took place between 1639 and 1645, then the Peach War ran from 1655 to 1657; the final conflict, the Esopus Wars, encompassed two major outbreaks of violence, 1659–60 and 1663–64.

During the fall of 1639, Director General Kieft, of Fort Amsterdam on Manhatten Island, decided to tax the Munsee-speaking Delaware groups and Mantinecocks on Long Island. Confrontations broke out between the Dutch and Delaware bands, especially the Wacquaesgeak and Hackensack, and settlers were murdered. In 1643, Dutch soldiers killed a hundred Indians in their camp near New Amsterdam; full-scale war erupted, all the Munsee Delawares being involved. Eventually, peace was made, but it lasted only two months, after which the Wappinger Delaware began attacking Dutch vessels on the Hudson River.

Kieft felt that all local Indians should be exterminated, and he recruited an army of Dutch and British mercenaries. Among the latter was John Underhill of the Mystic River Pequot massacre. He led troops against a village near today's Poundridge. Over 500 Indians died from gunfire or were burned to death in the torched village. In August 1645, the Dutch and Delaware signed a peace treaty, both sides being exhausted by the conflict. A thousand Delaware had died, and New Netherland was a landscape of burned farms and houses; many of the Dutch had migrated through fear. Then Kieft was replaced by Petrus (Peter) Stuyvesant.

The Peach War began when an Indian woman was murdered for stealing peaches from a Dutch orchard. While Stuyvesant was leading troops against Swedish settlements, hundreds of Delaware overran New Amsterdam, ostensibly seeking Indian enemies. Hendrick van Dyck, the orchard owner,

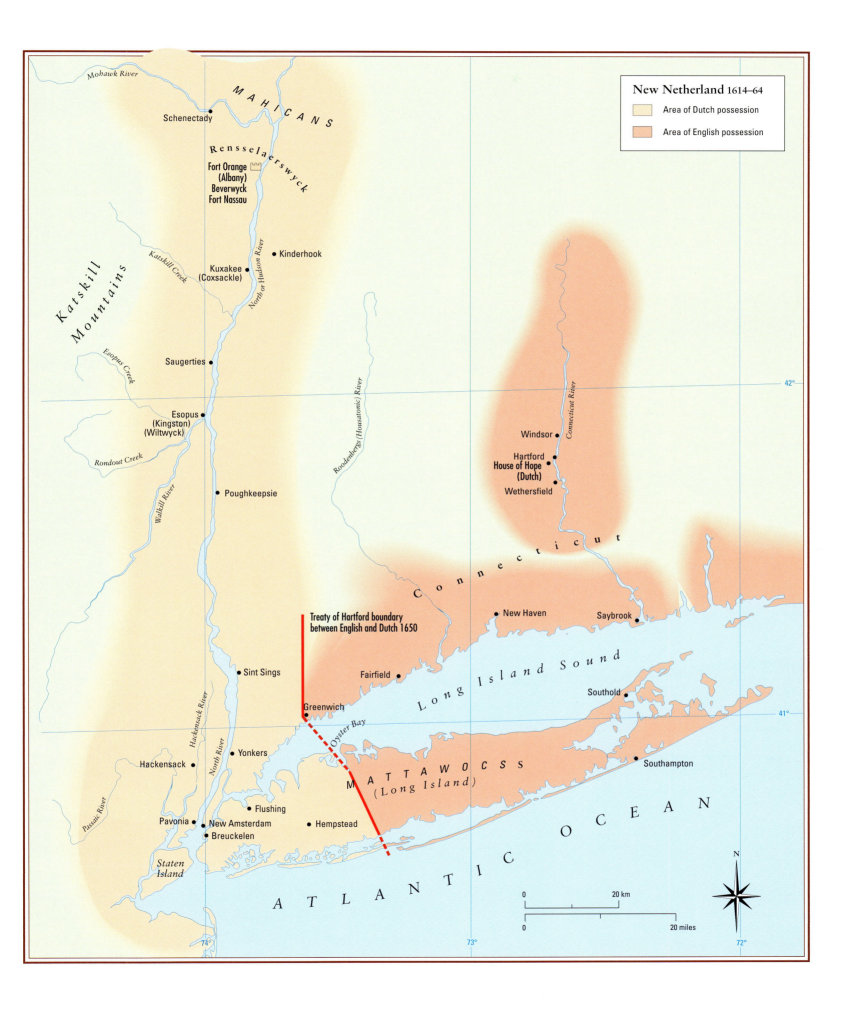

Mohawk River

MAHICANS

Schenectady

Rensselaerswyck

Fort Orange
(Albany)
Beverwyck
Fort Nassau

Katskill Creek

Kinderhook

North or Hudson River

Katskill
Mountains

Kuxakee
(Coxsackle)

New Netherland 1614–64
Area of Dutch possession
Area of English possession

Saugerties

Esopus Creek

Roodenberg (Housatonic) River

42°

Windsor

Connecticut River

Esopus
(Kingston)
(Wiltwyck)

Hartford
House of Hope
(Dutch)
Wethersfield

Rondout Creek

Walkill River

Poughkeepsie

Connecticut

Treaty of Hartford boundary
between English and Dutch 1650

New Haven

Saybrook

Sint Sings

Fairfield

Long Island Sound

Southold

Greenwich

Oyster Bay

41°

Hackensack River

Yonkers

Hackensack

North River

MATTAWOCSS
(Long Island)

Southampton

Passaic River

Flushing

Pavonia   New Amsterdam
Breuckelen

Hempstead

ATLANTIC OCEAN

Staten
Island

0   20 km

0   20 miles

N

74°   73°   72°

A contemporary woodcut showing the Dutch negotiating a treaty with the Manahatta band of the Lenape tribe for the purchase of Manhattan Island in 1626. The backdrop is of Fort Amsterdam, which was built on the island in 1625. The town of New Amsterdam grew around the fort and eventually became the City of New York.

Opposite: Dutch territorial claims stretched as far west as the Delaware River, where they met those of the British in Maryland. In the middle was the small Scandinavian colony of New Sweden, on the banks of the Delaware. Conflict arose between the Swedes and Dutch, the latter seizing the Swedish colony, although the settlers there were allowed a degree of autonomy.

was shot, and the Indians began to leave. Undisciplined Dutch militia pursued the Indians, opening fire as the Delaware withdrew to Staten Island and Pavonia. Then they moved to New Jersey, where they destroyed twenty-eight farms, killed fifty Dutch settlers, and took a hundred prisoners.

Eventually, Stuyvesant negotiated the return of seventy hostages. Records fail to mention the remainder, except five children, who were found with the Delaware two years later. Perhaps the Indians felt that hostages would be a surety against Dutch military action, or planned to adopt them. Whatever the case, the Delaware remained peaceful during the remainder of Stuyvesant's administration.

The Esopus Wars were occasioned by Dutch settlers building Wittwyck village and farms along the Rondout and Esopus creeks. Indian-Dutch relations became tense as young warriors became dependent on alcohol from illegal liquor sales. Violence broke out, but Stuyvesant managed to damp it down. The settlers were persuaded to concentrate their numbers for security, and a fort was built at Wittwyck. Bad relations made the settlers attack a group of drunken Indians; some Dutch were killed in retaliation, and the fort was besieged for a short while. Johannes La Montagne, in charge of Fort Orange, employed Mohawks, Mahicans, and Catskill Indians to secure a cease fire. Nevertheless, hostilities continued until Montagne's Indian diplomats were joined by Susquehannas and Delaware, who arranged a peace in 1660.

War broke out again when another village, Nieuwdorp, was built near Wittwyck. The Esopus Indians were incensed and assaulted both villages in 1663. Nieuwdorp was incinerated, but Indians who had infiltrated Wittwyck were driven out. Twenty Dutch were killed and forty-five captured, leaving sixty-nine to defend Wittwyck. The Dutch retaliated, sending troops, led by Martin Crieger, to attack an Esopus village as it was being fortified. The Indians were defeated, thirty being killed or captured, while twenty-three Dutch prisoners were recovered. Peace was secured, but the Esopus were forced to cede more land and compelled to trade at one spot under a flag of truce. New Indian-Dutch disputes would be settled in Dutch courts

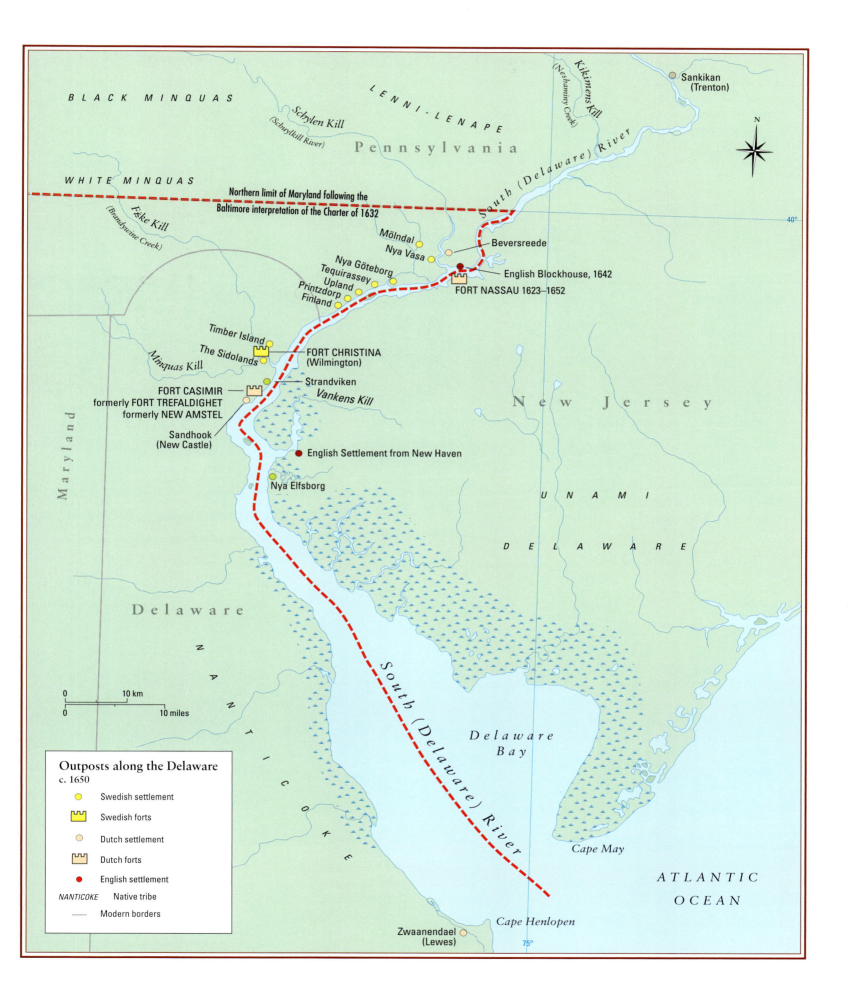

BLACK MINQUAS

LENNI-LENAPE

Schylen Kill
(Schuylkill River)

Pennsylvania

(Neshaminy Creek)

Kikimens Kill

● Sankikan
(Trenton)

N

WHITE MINQUAS

Fiske Kill
(Brandywine Creek)

Northern limit of Maryland following the
Baltimore interpretation of the Charter of 1632

South (Delaware) River

40°

Mölndal ○
Nya Vasa ○

━ Beversreede

Nya Göteborg ○
Tequirassey ○
Upland ○
Printzdorp ○
Finland ○

▪ English Blockhouse, 1642

FORT NASSAU 1623–1652

Timber Island ▥
The Sidolands ○

FORT CHRISTINA
(Wilmington)

Minquas Kill

FORT CASIMIR
formerly FORT TREFALDIGHET
formerly NEW AMSTEL

▥
○ ━ Strandviken
Vankens Kill

New Jersey

Sandhook
(New Castle)

● English Settlement from New Haven

Maryland

Nya Elfsborg ○

U N A M I

D E L A W A R E

Delaware

N
A
N
T
I
C
O
K
E

South (Delaware) River

Outposts along the Delaware
c. 1650

○ Swedish settlement

▥ Swedish forts

○ Dutch settlement

▥ Dutch forts

● English settlement

NANTICOKE Native tribe

— Modern borders

0   10 km
0   10 miles

*Delaware
Bay*

Cape May

ATLANTIC
OCEAN

Cape Henlopen

Zwaanendael ○
(Lewes)

75°

KING PHILIP'S WAR, 1675–76

OVERWHELMED BY THE STEADILY RISING POPULATION OF BRITISH SETTLERS, AND DEVASTATED BY DISEASE, THE WAMPANOAG, UNDER METACOMET (PHILIP), MADE WAR ON THE COLONISTS.

Puritan missionary John Eliot established a number of missions in New England, converting Indians to Christianity, which angered local tribes.

T he British population in southern New England grew steadily, and they acquired increasingly large tracts of land. Dubious business practices by the Pettiquamscutt, Misquamicut, and Atherton Companies concluded with a claim over all Narragansett territory. Not only were the Indians angry, but also they felt overwhelmed as their numbers dwindled through disease. By 1675, some 35,000 British in Plymouth, Massachusetts, Connecticut, and Rhode Island outnumbered the region's Indians. In the west, the local tribes were being squeezed by Iroquois power. In addition, the nations were becoming increasingly dependent on European trade goods, with consequent indebtedness. Furthermore, their culture was threatened by missionary activity, which was creating Christian "Praying Indians." Being subject to colonial justice caused resentment too. The region was a powder keg waiting to be ignited.

By 1675, Metacomet (Philip), chief of the diminished Wampanoag (also called Pokanoket), a people who had helped the Pilgrim Fathers on their arrival, had attempted to end inter-tribal rivalries and build an alliance against the British.

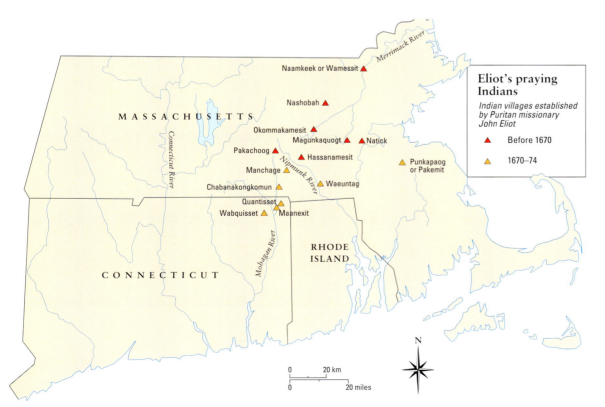

Eliot's praying Indians

Indian villages established by Puritan missionary John Eliot

▲ Before 1670

▲ 1670–74

Wampanoag warriors waged war with an attack on Swansea, having previously killed some cattle. Unrestrained violence spread throughout the outlying settlements, and Metacomet was joined by related bands (Pocasset and Sakonnet), the Narragansetts, and Nipmucs of western Massachusetts.

The colonial governments of New England gathered their trained militias in July to battle with the 300 Wampanoag warriors. A desultory fight occurred in Pocasset Swamp, and several British patrols were ambushed. On September 3, Captain Beers and twenty men were killed at Squakeag, and on September 18, Captain Lathrop and sixty-three men died while evacuating Deerfield. Eventually, the British learned to counterattack and to employ Pequot, Mohegan, Niantic, and Massachusetts warriors as scouts and intelligence gatherers. On December 19, a British and Indian army found the Narragansett's main village and destroyed it in the Great Swamp Fight. Hundreds of Narragansett braves were killed, as were women and children when their bark shelters were torched. Probably a third of the nation were killed; others died from wounds and starvation. The British suffered twenty dead and 200 wounded.

Indian raids continued, and 800–1,000 British were killed during the war. Villages were evacuated, and many attacked and burned, including Deerfield, Groton, Mendon, Warwik, and Wrentham. Fleeing Narragansett warriors entered Nipmuc land and exhausted that nation's food supplies. Thus, foraging raids lasted for another eight months; the village of Lancaster was completely destroyed, and one garrison house was captured, its men being killed and women taken captive. Mary Rowlandson, seized at Lancaster, remarked upon the Indians' hunger and their scavenging in British fields.

In May 1676, a Massachusetts British army marched north from Hadley and attacked the Indian village of Peskeompskut, killing many and destroying Indian food supplies in the upper Connecticut Valley. Indian resistance collapsed and, in June, Connecticut troops and Mohegan allies swept north to push their starving enemies into the wilds of New Hampshire.

Meanwhile, Philip and his few followers, having lain low near Albany, were driven back into New England by the Iroquois; he was killed shortly after a fight near Bridgewater Swamp in August 1676. Colonial forces hunted down and killed many remaining bands of Indians, selling hundreds into slavery in the Caribbean and even Spain. Metacomet's wife and son fetched 30 shillings each.

The war saw the near extermination of the Wampanaoag, Nipmuc, and Narragansett nations. Survivors fled their homelands to join other tribes. Initial Indian success had caused intense fear, since twenty-five towns were destroyed; in Maine, where fighting against the Abenaki continued until 1678, only six British villages withstood attack. However, British firepower and the destruction of Indian food supplies ensured final victory. Elsewhere, the Susquehannock people were being massacred by Maryland and Virginia troops; survivors merged with the Delaware and Iroquois.

King Philip's War
1675–76

➤ English attacks

✕ Battles

• English settlements

✳ English settlement attacked by Indians

⬚ Indian tribes

King Philip's war threw New England into turmoil.

Metacomet, known as King Philip, waged war on the British.

The Embattled Delaware

The fate of the Delaware is a prime example of the vagaries of Indian existence when under pressure from colonial settlers and other Indian tribes.

The history of the Delaware includes land losses, relocation, and changes in identity and tribal designation. Their ancestors were a number of small Indian bands who inhabited today's Delaware, New Jersey, southwestern Pennsylvania, and southeastern New York. Three bands, among other independent groups, were Munsee-speakers at the headwaters of the Delaware River, the Unami-speakers to the south, and the Unalachtigo on the coast. These groups suffered from white incursions in 1626, when part of Manhattan was sold to the Dutch, through the bullock-hide scam, and further land was lost through William Penn's sons' fraudulent Walking Purchase Treaty of 1737. In addition, the Delaware faced incursions from northern Iroquoian neighbors, the Mingos (Minquas), who were raiding as early as 1633, while the Five Nations were also spreading south. Squeezed from all sides between 1630 and 1767, the Delaware, or Lenni Lenape, agreed some 800 land cessions and sales to Dutch, Swedish, and British colonists. By 1737, they had lost all their lands in the Upper Delaware and Lehigh valleys in Pennsylvania.

The Delaware also suffered epidemics of measles and smallpox, while alcohol consumption increased. By 1660, these factors, coupled with increased Iroquois attacks, had forced many of the Delaware toward the Susquehanna River and Mingo territory. There, they were joined by retreating Shawnee, Conoy, Nanticoke, Mahican, Tutelo, and Twightwee. All these peoples came under the tutelage of the Iroquois, who gained the right to represent the Delaware when dealing with the British. Some youthful Delaware became so resentful that they moved to the Allegheny River and founded Kittanning village; others moved on to Logtown on the Ohio. The Iroquois Confederacy claimed suzerainty over them there.

The Mingo gradually absorbed some Seneca, Wyandot, Shawnee, Costenoga, and Delaware refugees, moving to western Pennsylvania; by 1740, they were independent of the Iroquois. The Delaware in

Ohio gradually found themselves being pressured by the encroaching British and French empires, each colonial power trying to win their allegiance. Meanwhile, Moravian missionaries moved on to the Susquehanna; one chief, Teedyuscung, uprooted a Delaware band and settled in the Wyoming Valley.

By 1754, underhand white dealings had deprived the Delaware of lands in the Wyoming Valley and at Shamokin on the Susquehanna. The Delaware on the Ohio, and the Shawnee, were alienated from the British after their General Braddock was defeated in July 1755 on the Monongahela by the French, during the French-Indian War.

Meanwhile, the Susquehanna Delaware had been summoned by the Oneida to aid an attack on the French. The Shamokin and Wyoming bands refused, since famine affected their lands, and their families could not be left unprotected. Shingas, chief of the Ohio Delaware, went to help his Susquehanna kin after allying himself with the French. Eventually, both groups attacked settlers in Pennsylvania, Virginia, and Maryland. In retaliation, Colonel John Armstrong attacked Kittanning in 1756. Thirty houses were destroyed, French munitions exploded, and a chief and his family were killed. The Susquehanna band made peace, but not the Ohio group. Eventually, Shingas abdicated his chieftainship; his successor, Beaver, signed a peace treaty. Intended to stabilize and pacify the area, this Treaty of Easton required that the Ohio and Pennsylvania Delaware accepted Iroquois suzerainty and renounced their friendship with the French.

In 1763, the end of the French-British wars triggered Pontiac's Rebellion, which was inspired partially by Neolin, the Delaware Prophet. He preached against white ways and urged that the British be driven from Indian lands. Delaware warriors were involved in the defeat at Bushy Run in August 1763, and a 1765 peace treaty eradicated all their rights to land. During the American Revolution, the Delaware were divided, some groups moving to Ontario, Canada, others retreating to Indiana, then Missouri, Alabama, and Texas. Subsequently, some Delaware moved to Kansas in 1829, and then Oklahoma in 1867.

William Penn, founder of Pennsylvania, concluding a peace treaty with the Delaware Indians in 1682 (a postcard reproduction from a painting by Benjamin West). Penn was said to be always fair in his dealings with the Indians; others, among them his sons, were less fair.

THE PUEBLO REVOLT, 1680

EXPLOITED BY A BRUTAL SPANISH REGIME AND FORCED TO RENOUNCE THEIR RELIGION, THE PUEBLO INDIANS FINALLY ROSE UP TO DRIVE THE OPPRESSORS FROM THEIR LANDS.

The Spaniards faced only one serious Indian uprising in New Spain. Juan de Oñate led settlers into the Rio Grande Valley in 1598, making the region the most northern part of Spain's colonial endeavor. Situated thousands of miles from Mexico City, the area was inhabited by the Pueblo Indians, including the Piro, Keres, southern and northern Tiwa, Tano, Towa, Tewa, Hopi, and Zuni nations. The Spanish settlers—small farmers, cattle ranchers, and missionaries—had moved to a potentially hostile environment; the Indians had not forgotten the Acoma massacre.

The agricultural Indian communities were subjected to Spanish economic and religious pressures. The *encomienda* and *repartimiento* systems forced tribute from the people in the forms of food and labor. The governor and priests required corn, wheat, wood, water, and personal servants. Furthermore, the priests were determined to eradicate Native American religious practices and to impose their particularly cruel form of Christianity. Thus, the Indians were the targets of competing religious and secular jurisdictions, each of which accused the other of economic exploitation. Bernardo López, governor from 1659 to 1662, demanded that certain Pueblos gave him hides, salt, and piñon nuts for resale. Furthermore, the priests invaded sacred kivas and flogged Indians who continued their own religious observances, such as dancing in costumes and masks as part of the Kachina Spirit cult.

By the late seventeenth century, there were approximately 2,350 Europeans in New Mexico, comprising Spaniards, mestizos, and mulattoes, mostly living in or near Santa Fé. About thirty-three missionaries dwelt in the Pueblos, whose native inhabitants numbered between 25,000 and 30,000. The 1660s brought drought and food

A depiction of the Pueblo Revolt by George Chacón, painted as part of the Taos Mural Project.

shortages, which caused the Utes, Navajos, and Apaches to raid the Pueblos. A Spanish feudal promise had been always to protect their Indians from raids, but by 1675, six Pueblos had been destroyed. As religious repression increased, the Pueblos managed to overcome their mutual hostility and cooperate in conspiring to rebel against the Spaniards. Two shamans from San Juan and San Ildefonso Pueblos, Popé, and Catiti, came to prominence. Popé was a visionary who preached resistance to Spanish rule and religion; he attributed the Indians' misfortunes to the anger of neglected gods. With other leaders, he was accused of witchcraft and idolatry, and was whipped. The two shamans and the San Ildefonso war chief, El Ollita, conspired to expel the Spaniards. Interestingly, the Indians had learned to speak Spanish to deal with the colonials, and this language became the medium to foment revolt, since it was the only common tongue among the linguistically-diverse Pueblos.

Eventually, most Pueblos agreed to rebel, and despite Governor Antonio de Otermin being forewarned, the revolt exploded on August 10, 1680, when the priest at Tesuque was murdered. The fury of the Indians spread like wildfire, and twenty-one missionaries and 375 settlers were butchered. Survivors fled to Santa Fé, but the Indians diverted the town's water supply, and the remaining Spaniards were forced to retreat to El Paso in Mexico.

Popé occupied the governor's palace and established despotic rule. Churches were burned, and vestments and icons desecrated. People using Spanish tools were punished, even executed. Meanwhile, Popé used the governor's carriage to travel around Santa Fé; his reign became as onerous as the Spanish. In 1688, Popé died and Indian unity dissolved rapidly. Continued droughts and Apache raids

At the beginning of the seventeenth century, Spain controlled the Southwest, but the Spaniards' harsh rule and religious repression caused a rebellion among the Pueblo Indians that made them retreat to Mexico.

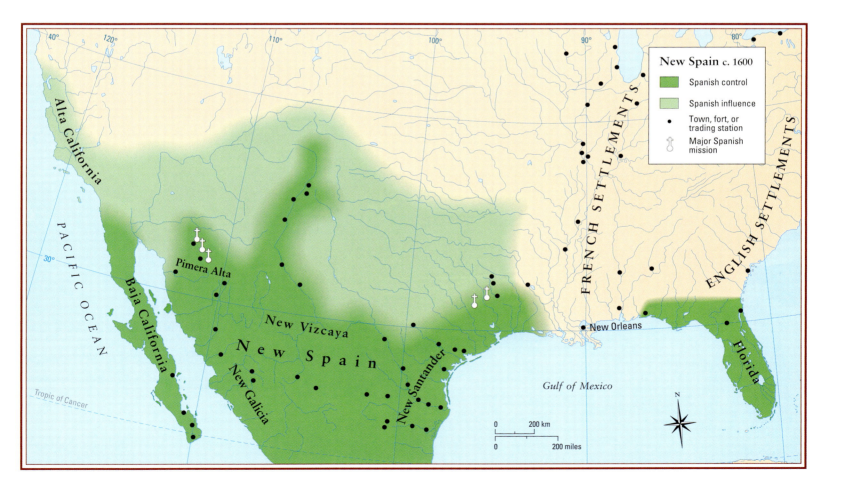

further weakened the Pueblo resolve. Moreover, some Pueblos recognized the benefits accruing from Spanish agricultural methods, and the introduction of cattle, horses, and olive trees.

Eventually, Spanish troops returned, Zia Pueblo being captured in 1689. The new governor, Diego de Vargas, regained Santa Fé in 1692, symbolizing the reconquest of New Mexico. When de Vargas met the leader of all the Pueblos, Luis Tupatu of Picuris Pueblo, he saw irony in a man dressed in skins, wearing a rosary around his neck, and carrying a silver cross, an Agnus Dei, and a cloth depicting Our Lady of Guadeloupe. Henceforth, Spanish rule was more lenient, bringing an end to cultural warfare.

Don Diego de Vargas became governor of New Spain following the recapture of Santa Fé in 1692. His tenure saw a less harsh form of rule.

Opposite: Angered by the Spaniards' failure to protect them from being raided by Utes, Navajos, and Apaches, and by the missionaries' repressive religious regime, the Pueblo peoples united under the shaman Popé and rose up against their European overlords. They drove the Spanish back to Mexico, where they remained for nine years.

Pueblo ruins at Wupatki National Monument.

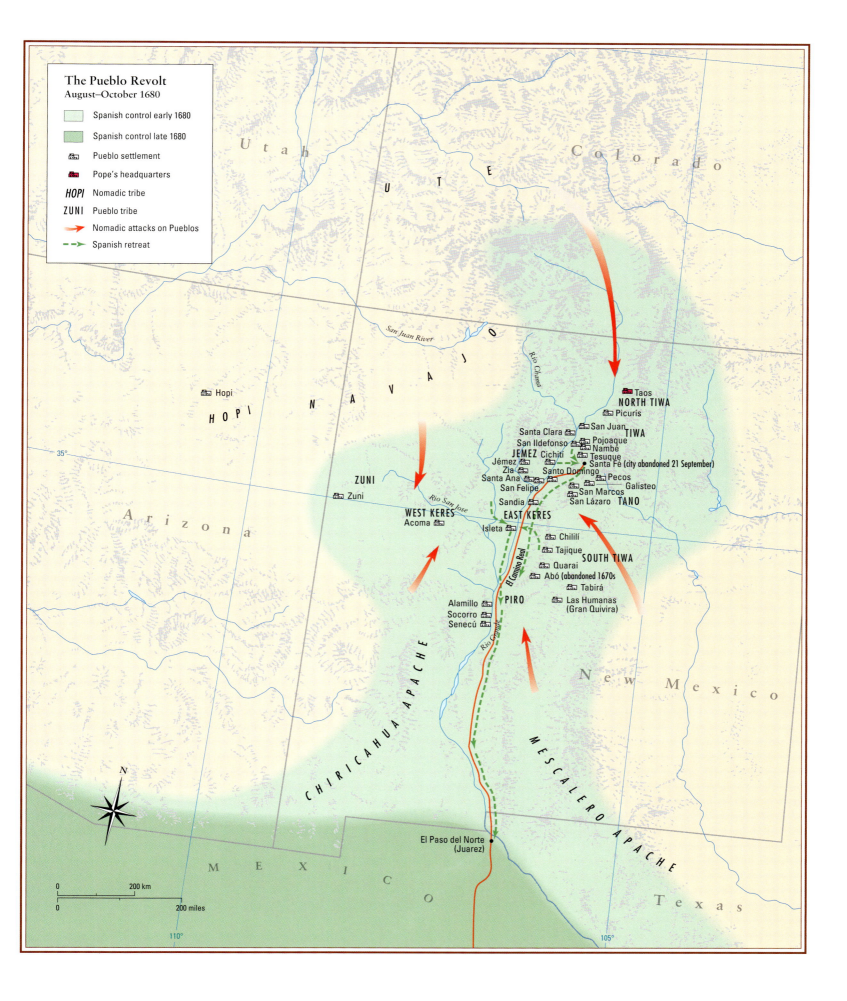

The Pueblo Revolt
August–October 1680

- Spanish control early 1680
- Spanish control late 1680
- 🏠 Pueblo settlement
- 🏠 Pope's headquarters
- *HOPI* Nomadic tribe
- ZUNI Pueblo tribe
- → Nomadic attacks on Pueblos
- → Spanish retreat

Utah

Colorado

U T E

San Juan River

Rio Chama

🏠 Hopi

H O P I

N A V A J O

Taos 🏠
NORTH TIWA
Picurís 🏠
Santa Clara 🏠 🏠 San Juan **TIWA**
San Ildefonso 🏠 🏠 Pojoaque
JEMEZ Cichití 🏠 🏠 Nambé
Jémez 🏠 🏠 Tesuque
Zía 🏠 Santo Domingo ● Santa Fé (city abandoned 21 September)
Santa Ana 🏠
San Felipe 🏠 🏠 Pecos
🏠 San Marcos
Sandia 🏠 San Lázaro 🏠 Galisteo
TANO

ZUNI
🏠 Zuni

A r i z o n a

Rio San Jose

WEST KERES
Acoma 🏠

EAST KERES

Isleta 🏠

🏠 Chililí
🏠 Tajique
🏠 Quarai **SOUTH TIWA**
🏠 Abó (abandoned 1670s)
🏠 Tabirá

Alamillo 🏠
Socorro 🏠 **PIRO**
Senecú 🏠

El Camino Real

Rio Grande

🏠 Las Humanas
(Gran Quivira)

N e w   M e x i c o

C H I R I C A H U A   A P A C H E

M E S C A L E R O   A P A C H E

N

El Paso del Norte ●
(Juarez)

M   E   X   I   C   O

T e x a s

0   200 km
0   200 miles

110°   105°

Peace at Montréal, 1701

Decimated by European disease, and defeated by the French and their Native American allies, the Five Nations of the Iroquois were forced to sue for peace.

The Five Nations of the Iroquois Confederacy faced constant threats to their existence during the seventeenth century. European diseases hammered population figures, and the Iroquois attempted to maintain their numbers by capturing people in mourning wars, after which they could be adopted. The Iroquois waged war against their neighbors to gain access to the fur trade, and acquire goods and guns from the Dutch at New Amsterdam.

The Iroquois were located away from the Richelieu and St. Lawrence rivers, along which most trade goods flowed from French sources. Thus, the Mohawk often attacked Huron and Algonkin traders returning from Québec. During the second decade of the seventeenth century, some pressure was lifted when the Dutch began trading along the Hudson River. To acquire a monopoly of trade, the Mohawks fought the Mahicans for four years, eventually driving them from the west bank of the Hudson and, thereby, gaining unrestricted access to Fort Orange.

During the 1630s, the Five Nations constantly blockaded the St. Lawrence to hijack furs from northern tribes traveling to Québec. In this fashion, the Iroquois could compensate for the fact that their own hunting grounds had been trapped out. The 1630s also witnessed smallpox epidemics among the Mohawk and Seneca, and by the 1640s, the population of the Five Nations had been halved; the Mohawk may have lost three-quarters of their numbers. Thus, the pressure was on to grab more prisoners as adoptees. The acquisition of guns from the Dutch allowed the Confederacy to destroy the Hurons, then overrun the Petuns by 1650, the Neutrals by 1651, and the Eries by 1657. These conflicts were called "Beaver Wars," since they were aimed primarily at acquiring furs and captives. Thousands of Eries went to live among the Iroquois, but this barely kept pace with losses.

In 1664, the British captured New Netherland, thereby disrupting the flow of goods. The Iroquois were forced to approach the French until such time as the British in New York courted the Iroquois. This

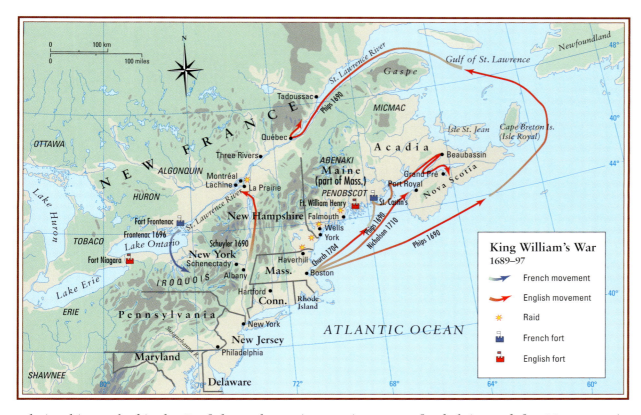

King William's War was yet another tussle for power in North America between the British and French. The Iroquois became involved as allies of the British, but suffered severely from attacks by the French and their Indian allies.

relationship resulted in the Confederacy becoming a major power after helping to defeat Metacomet in King Philip's War, and then turning on the Mahicans and Susquehannocks. In the 1670s and 1680s, the Iroquois were attacking Miamis, Illinois, Ojibwa, Fox, Wyandots, and Ottowa. In addition, they roamed further afield, raiding Conoys, Piscataways, and Catawbas in Maryland, Virginia, and the Carolinas. Despite increases in captives, disease and mourning-war losses still reduced the Iroquois numbers.

During King William's War (1689–97), the Iroquois sided mainly with the British, while their enemies supported the French. Between 1693 and 1696, French regulars, Canadians, and Native American allies attacked and burned Mohawk, Onondaga, and Oneida towns. Losses forced the Iroquois to seek peace with the French and their Indian allies. Survival was the key issue, and a treaty was signed with the French at Montréal. The French agreed to reopen their trading posts to the Iroquois so that they could access Great Lakes trade networks. The Iroquois maintained that nations living in western hunting regions would have grievances against them redressed. In August 1701, Iroquois leaders met several hundred chiefs of the French allies from the Ottowa, Wyandots, Miamis, Sauk, Potawatomi, Fox, Mascoutens, Menominees, Ojibwa, Winnebagos, Nipissings, Eastern and Western Abenaki, and Canadian mission Iroquois. In return for access to the Great Lakes trade, the Five Nations agreed to be neutral in future imperial wars between Britain and France.

In reality, the French had readjusted the power relationships in lands surrounding the Great Lakes and St. Lawrence. Also, the Missisauga Ojibwa and allies had expanded into the eastern Lake Ontario area recently acquired by the Iroquois during the Beaver Wars. Montréal ratified this Confederacy defeat. To secure their position, the Iroquois ceded to the British the use of hunting lands stretching from today's Erie, Pennsylvania, to Chicago and Michilimackinac. In fact, this area was controlled by the French and their allies, but the Iroquois hoped, to no avail, that the British would use the agreement in border disputes with the French. Thus, the Iroquois planned to play off France and Britain against each other.

Native Americans in Imperial Wars

"WE HAVE NOT YET SOLD THE LANDS WE INHABIT, WE WISH TO
KEEP POSSESSION OF THEM ... WE ACKNOWLEDGE NO OTHER
BOUNDARIES OF YOURS THAN YOUR SETTLEMENTS WHEREON
YOU HAVE BUILT ... WE ARE ALLIES OF THE KING OF FRANCE, FROM
WHOM WE HAVE RECEIVED THE FAITH ..."

ABENAKI SPEAKER ATIWANTO AT MONTRÉAL, JULY 1752.

Opposite: By the beginning of the eighteenth century, large parts of North America were under the control of European nations. The Indian nations were being squeezed inexorably by the insatiable demands for land by the newcomers.

The Native American experience between 1701 and 1763 was characterized by five major trends, all involving intense bouts of conflict. First, the acquisition of the horse and gun led to a southward move of some tribes, who displaced others, creating a ripple effect that impacted upon peoples as far south as New Mexico and Texas. Second, tribes in the South were fighting each other intermittently: for example, there was conflict between the Creek and Choctaw, and the Creek and Cherokee. Eventually, these inter-tribal hostilities became enmeshed in the colonial rivalries between the French and British. Third, bitter Native American war occurred around the Great Lakes. There, the Iroquois enmity toward French-allied Canadian Indian nations remained latent, ready to boil over when triggered by an appropriate incident. Furthermore, the Ojibwa were expanding out of Michigan into Alberta, Minnesota, and North Dakota at the expense of the Lakota. Fourth, the French and British engaged in a series of violent clashes that were intended to crush certain tribes and sell them into slavery. The victims were the Tuscarora, Yamasee, Natchez, and Chickasaw. Fifth, and most importantly, internal Native American rivalries became linked inextricably with the colonial competition pursued by France, Britain, and Spain. Thus, Native Americans were sucked into King William's War (1689–97),

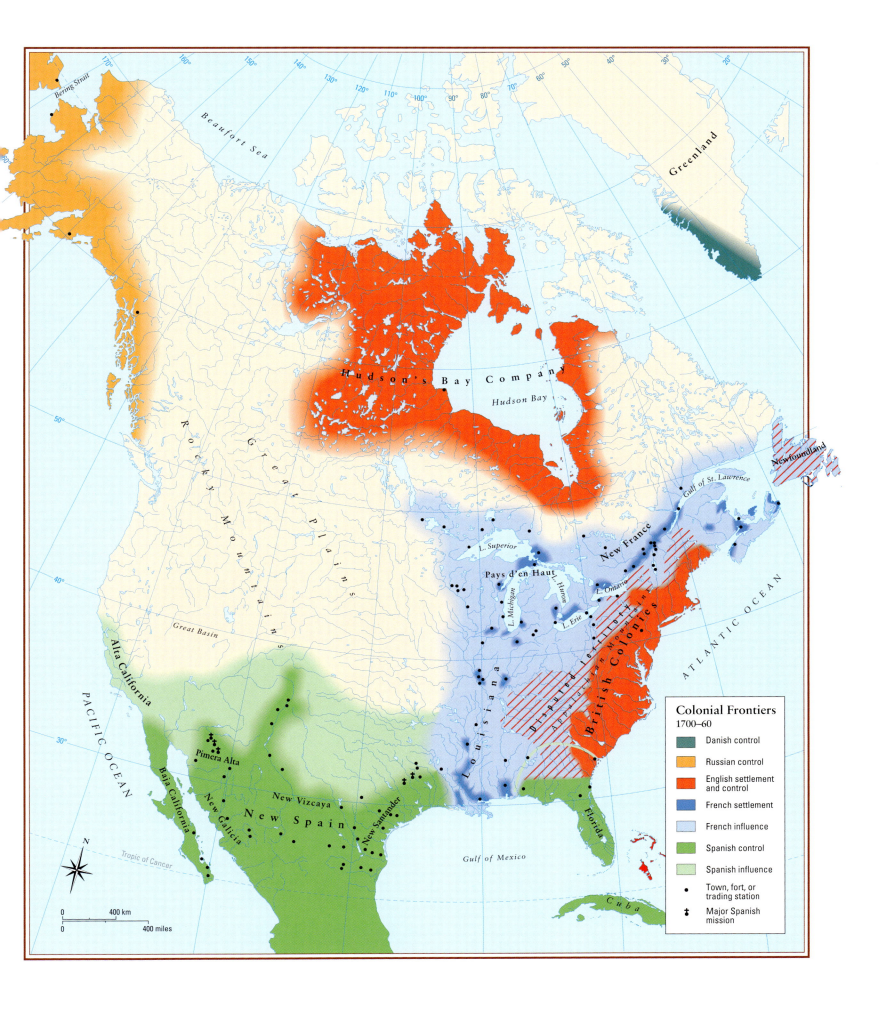

Bering Strait

Beaufort Sea

Greenland

Hudson's Bay Company

Hudson Bay

Gulf of St. Lawrence

Newfoundland

New France

L. Superior

Pays d'en Haut

L. Michigan

L. Huron

L. Ontario

L. Erie

British Colonies

Disputed territory

Appalachian Mountains

Rocky Mountains

Great Plains

Great Basin

PACIFIC OCEAN

ATLANTIC OCEAN

Alta California

Baja California

New Galicia

New Spain

New Vizcaya

New Santander

Louisiana

Pimera Alta

Florida

Tropic of Cancer

Gulf of Mexico

Cuba

Colonial Frontiers
1700–60

- Danish control
- Russian control
- English settlement and control
- French settlement
- French influence
- Spanish control
- Spanish influence
- • Town, fort, or trading station
- ‡ Major Spanish mission

N

400 km

400 miles

A contemporary engraving depicting the destruction of the French Fort Frontenac by the British in 1758 during the French and Indian War. The fort occupied a strategic position at the mouth of the Cataraqui River, overlooking the point where the St. Lawrence River leaves Lake Ontario.

Queen Anne's War (1702–13), King George's War (1743–48), and the French and Indian War, also known as the Seven Years' War (1754–61), which finally led to the 1763 Treaty of Paris.

The Comanche were originally Shoshone, but in 1500, they left their homeland near the Great Salt Lake and in present-day Nevada, traveling through the South Pass onto the western part of the northern Plains, where they made a home on the Upper Platte River and in eastern Wyoming. Then they pushed north and east to the Alberta and Saskatchewan plains. The Comanche economy was based upon hunting buffalo on foot, in competition with the Blackfeet, Crow, and Plains Apache. After the 1680 Pueblo Revolt, which forced the Spanish to abandon their New Mexico outposts and leave their horses behind, the Comanche began to acquire these animals from either the Apache or Ute. Since the Comanche were divided into several bands, who seldom cooperated,

Hudson Bay

Fort Albany

Fort Rupert

Fort St Charles

Fort St Pierre

Fort Michipicton

Lake Superior

Plains of Abraham
1759

1759

Montreal

Québec

Fort Beauséjour

1744

1745
Louisbourg
1748 returned
to France

Halifax

1758
Louisbourg
captured

Fort Edward
Augustus

1756

1757

Raids
1703–7

1755

Port
Royal

Fort Frontenac

1755

1758

1710

Fort
Ticonderoga

Lake Huron

Lake Michigan

Fort
Beauharnais

1759

Fort
Oswego

1758

Fort
St Joseph

Fort
Niagara

Fort
Pontchartrain

Fort Presqu'isle

Lake Erie

1759

1746–8

Boston

Fort
William Henry

New York

Fort Duquesne

1758

Philadelphia

Fort
Pickawillany

1755

1755

Baltimore

Fort Orléans

Fort Necessity

Mississippi

Fort Vincennes

Richmond

Fort Chartres

Appalachian Mountains

New Bern

Wilmington

Fort Arkansas

Georgetown

Fort Augusta

Charleston

Fort Natchitoches

1742

Savannah

Fort King George

Fort Rosalie

Fort Condé

New Orleans

Fort Mauvepas

1740, 1743

St Augustine

Fort Mississippi

ATLANTIC OCEAN

Gulf of Mexico

0   200 km
0   200 miles

Anglo-French Struggle for North America
1700–63

→	British campaign
→	French campaign
→	Spanish campaign
✕	Battle
♜	British fort
♜	French fort

European territorial claims 1750

▨	British
▨	French
▨	Spanish

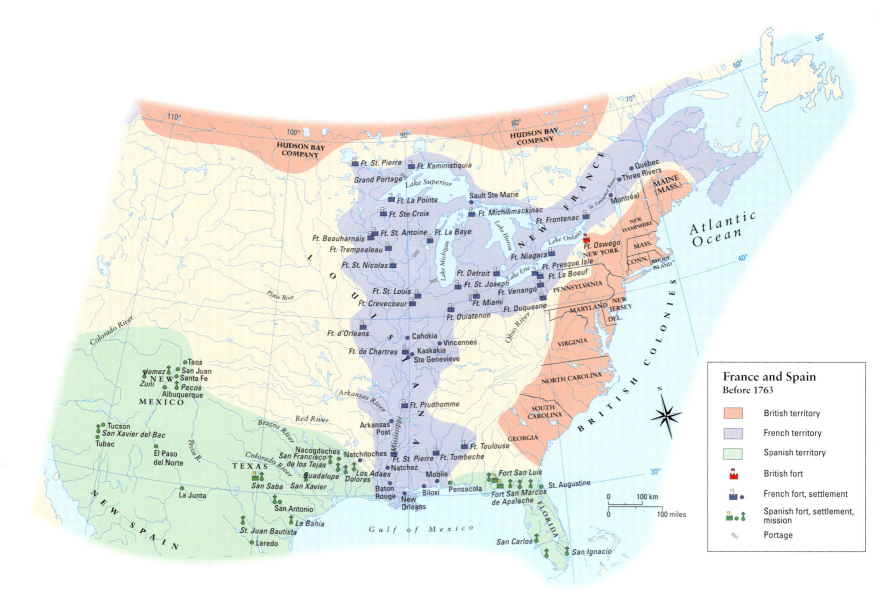

France and Spain
Before 1763

British territory

French territory

Spanish territory

British fort

French fort, settlement

Spanish fort, settlement, mission

Portage

While conflict between Britain and France took place in the Northeast, further south French incursions brought them up against the Spanish, who were well established, particularly in the Southwest.

some would trade with the Apache while others fought them—a chaos that made perfect sense to the Comanche. Subsequently, the tribe migrated south, not to hunt buffalo, which were plentiful in the north, but probably to gain access to the supply of horses in New Mexico. These could be captured and traded to increase tribal wealth. Forming an alliance with the Ute, the Comanche moved from their roaming grounds between the Rocky Mountains and Black Hills, entering the central Plains of eastern Colorado and western Kansas, between the Platte and Arkansas rivers. They displaced the Plains Apache, and by 1706, both the Comanche and Ute were trading in Taos, New Mexico.

The Apache suffered from constant attacks, the Jicarilla and Plains Apache (Lipan and Mescalero) being forced into southern Texas and New Mexico, where they began raiding Spanish settlements. Other Apache bands crossed into Arizona and virtually cut off Santa Fé from El Paso in north Mexico. By 1730, the Comanche controlled the Texas Panhandle, central Texas, and northeastern New Mexico, despite living north of the Arkansas River. Simultaneously, the Ute-Comanche alliance collapsed, the Ute being pushed from the Plains into the western mountains. There, they became allied with the

Spanish and Jicarilla Apache against their common foe, but the Comanche were strong enough to cross the Arkansas, moving into northeastern New Mexico and onto the edges of the Staked Plains of the Texas Panhandle.

The Comanche became notorious horse thieves, supplying former Spanish horses to other tribes, and trading buffalo robes and slaves with New Mexico. French traders penetrated Kansas and moved up the Red River, making contact with the Wichita tribe; they sold guns to the Comanche. In return, they received stolen horses and mules from the Spanish territories. The Comanche became so strong that some bands raided Pecos in 1746, 1750, 1773, and 1775, and Taos in 1760. The Comanche were fighting most tribes of the Central Plains, as well as Spanish expeditions sent against them. Even in 1775, the Yamparika division was fighting the Lakota and Cheyenne near the Black Hills, and attacking the Arikara on the Missouri River. Other tribes were interested in stealing Comanche horses, and war broke out with the Osage and Pawnee in 1746, but the Wichita arranged peace in 1750, which allowed a combined Pawnee-Comanche attack against the Osage in 1751, the latter being defeated. Then the Pawnee moved to the Platte River in Nebraska, but they still mounted raids into Texas and New Mexico to steal Comanche horses; alliances were soon forgotten. The Comanche also fought the Crow, Pueblo, Lakota, Kansa, Navajo, Wichita, Waco, Tonkawa, Sauk, Fox, Creek, Choctaw, Seminole, and Chickasaw.

Elsewhere in Texas, the Spanish felt threatened by French expansion from Louisiana and incursions by their traders from Illinois. Thus, in 1716, a mission-presidio was built at Nacogdoches, soon being followed by additional missions and outposts in eastern Texas. Eventually, this area came under threat from the Plains Apache, pushed south by the Comanche until squeezed into southern Texas along the Rio Grande (1728). When the Apache encountered local tribes, they either wiped them out or assimilated them. Thus were destroyed the Coahuiltec, Cisos, Jano, and Manso nations. These Lipan Apache attacked and traded with the Tonkawa and Caddo tribes of eastern Texas, while still being attacked themselves by the Comanche, who also fought the Spanish. Comanche raids into Texas were only curtailed when the tribe was devastated by a smallpox epidemic between 1780 and 1781.

Warfare in the eastern woodlands differed from the turmoil on the Plains. Whereas an Apache warrior's status would depend upon the food or horses he brought back from a raid, the eastern tribes often took scalps as proof of a warrior's involvement in combat. The Indians were not driven to acquire material possessions, but would seek vengeance. Others would engage in mourning wars, in which the aim was to seize captives who could be adopted and assimilated into the tribe to replace those killed in battle or by disease. Thus, women and children would be prime targets (and allegedly easier to socialize), and the number of captives taken would symbolize one tribe's strength and dominance over another. Adoption after capture was prevalent among Indians in the region between the Atlantic seaboard and Mississippi, from the Iroquois and Huron in the northeast to the Cherokee in the southeast, and among the Great Lakes Ojibwa (Chippewa) and Santee Sioux. However, adoption was not always successful—Huron women were known to commit suicide rather than become Iroquois. On the other hand, white female captives sometimes preferred to stay with their captors rather than return to their own society.

COLONIAL CAPTIVES

THERE WERE MANY INDIAN RAIDS AND PRISONERS CAPTURED ON THE FRONTIERS OF NEW ENGLAND, ESPECIALLY DURING THE COLONIAL WARS BETWEEN FRANCE AND BRITAIN.

Opposite: A monument in honor of Hannah Dustin in Boscawen, New Hampshire. Seized by Indians with another woman and a boy in 1697, Dustin and her fellow prisoners eventually managed to escape by killing and scalping the Indians.

B etween 1675 and 1763, some 1,641 white captives were seized in Indian raids and battles. As a rule, the French and their Abenaki allies fought the British with their Iroquois friends. The French allies, from Maine, New Brunswick, and Québec, poured through New England's Iroquois shield to attack settlements in New York, Massachusetts, and New Hampshire.

Indians waged war for many reasons. During the Beaver Wars, the Iroquois fought the Huron, Petun, Neutrals, Erie, and Nipissing to gain control of the fur trade with England. However, there were reasons other than economics and vengeance that prompted war. Taking captives offered the possibility of obtaining a ransom, or a family might adopt a captive to compensate for the loss of one of its members. Women, but more often children, were adopted, since they were easier to socialize and they could maintain tribal numbers; captives were also symbols of victory.

Many captives were ransomed, escaped, or were freed through negotiation. Upon returning to the settlements, many victims published their experiences. Mary Rowlandson's account convinced many that capture was God's punishment for past sins, while others recounted Indian customs, becoming material for anthropological and ethnographical study. Some captives actually preferred the Indian lifestyle, or valued escape from Puritan strictures, even refusing to return to European society. Of these, a few became "white Indians" and fought the colonists.

Mary Rowlandson's account was the first major witness record. It described a raid on Lancaster, Massachusetts, where she was captured in February 1675. Later, she was sold to Quinnapin, a Narragansett chief, but was ransomed in May 1676 at Redemption Rock in Princeton, Massachusetts. Another captive was John Gyles, taken at the age of nine years from Maine in August 1689, during King William's War. He spent six years with Indians, and three years with a Frenchman. In 1698, he was granted his freedom and later wrote an account, published 1736, of his time among the Maliseet Indians along the St. John River Valley.

Map opposite: By 1750, New France surrounded the British colonies along the Atlantic coast. Constant aggression between the two European powers and their Indian allies saw many settlers kidnapped.

A well-known captive is Hannah Dustin, who was seized on March 15, 1697, at Haverhill, Massachusetts, while lying in bed recuperating from the birth of her twelfth child. Taken with Mary Neff, her midwife, and a teenage boy, she was marched some 120 miles (190 kilometers) by two warriors, their wives, seven children, and an older woman. On March 30, they camped on an island at the juncture of the Contoocook and Merrimack rivers, near contemporary Boscawen, New Hampshire. During the night, Dustin, Neff, and the boy killed all but two of the Indians with an axe, scalped them, and returned to Massachusetts. Dustin was granted a £25 scalp bounty; the other two shared a similar sum.

The most memorable captive incident occurred in February 1704, at Deerfield, Massachusetts. Fifty-six settlers were killed and 109 captured, being marched to Canada. Only eighty-eight survived the trek. Eventually, fifty-nine were returned, but the young, mainly those under fourteen years, remained. The Reverend John Williams' daughter, Eunice, married an Indian and refused to return.

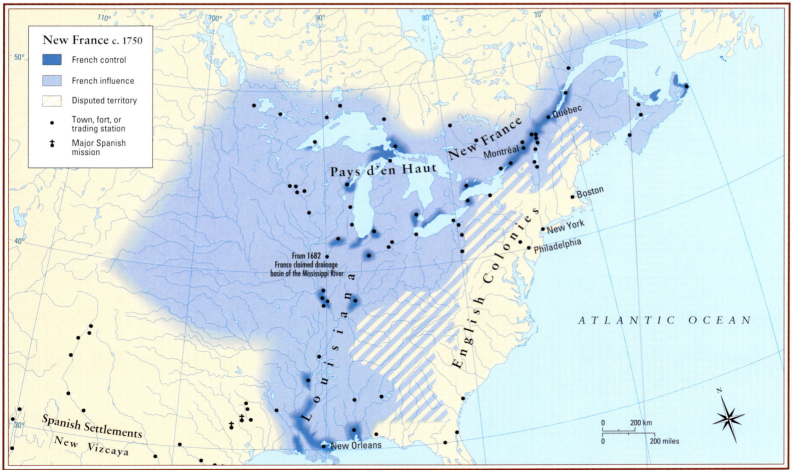

New France c. 1750

- French control
- French influence
- Disputed territory
- Town, fort, or trading station
- Major Spanish mission

Pays d'en Haut

New France

Québec

Montréal

From 1682 France claimed drainage basin of the Mississippi River

Louisiana

English Colonies

Boston

New York

Philadelphia

ATLANTIC OCEAN

Spanish Settlements

New Vizcaya

New Orleans

0   200 km
0   200 miles

A contemporary illustration showing British colonists being taken prisoner by Indians during the French and Indian Wars.

Apparently, the onslaught against the British colonies had been an attempt by the French to show the Abenakis that they were reliable allies, and to warn the British that war would be fought in New England, not New France.

Mary Jemison, aged fifteen years, was captured in western Pennsylvania in April 1758 by Shawnee warriors. She was taken to the Seneca near the Sciota River, had two Indian husbands, eight children, thirty-nine grandchildren, and fourteen great grandchildren. She suffered with her adoptive tribe during the American Revolution and eventually died aged nintey years. She is claimed by both whites and Iroquois as a folk heroine.

In 1763, after Indians had been defeated at Bushy Run, Colonel Bouquet demanded the return of captives held by the Shawnee and Delaware. Most of them wished to remain with the Indians, however, and some had to be bound before their return, for fear that they would abscond. Some women fled back to Indian villages rather than remain in white society.

Opposite: Throughout the first half of the eighteenth century, the French and British vied for control of North America. Numerous battles took place, involving Indian allies on both sides. After 1763 almost all the French territory was ceded to Britain or Spain, their sole remaining possession being the tiny islands of St. Pierre et Miquelon, off the coast of southern Newfoundland.

The charge of the Highlanders at the Battle of Bushy Run in 1763, from a painting by C.W. Jeffreys. The action routed a combined force of Delaware, Shawnee, Wyandot, and Mingo warriors.

Hudson Bay

Hudson's Bay Company

Labrador

Fort Winnipeg
Fort Albany
Moose Factory
Fort Rupert

Fort St. Charles
Fort Nippigon
Fort William
Newfoundland

Lake Superior
St. Pierre et Miquelon

Sault Ste. Marie

I N D I A N   R E S E R V E

Québec
QUÉBEC
Montréal
Nova Scotia
Halifax

Lake Huron
Lake Michigan
Lake Ontario

Fort Pontchartrain
Lake Erie

St. Lawrence River

Boston

SPANISH-
LOUISIANA

Fort Vincennes
New York
Philadelphia

Fort Kaskaskia

I N D I A N   R E S E R V E

T H E   T H I R T E E N   C O L O N I E S

ATLANTIC OCEAN

Norfolk

Bermuda

West Florida
Charles Town
Savannah

New Orleans
St. Augustine

Gulf of Mexico

East
Florida

Bahamas

1762–63
British occupied

British North America
1764–76

☐ Original Thirteen Colonies

☐ Other British territories

▨ Spanish Louisiana, secretly
ceded by France in 1763

🏳 Only French possession
after Treaty of Paris, 1763

🏰 Fort

0   300 km

0   300 miles

TUSCARORA AND YAMASEE WARS, 1711–17

FOR 200 YEARS, THE TUSCARORA LIVED PEACEFULLY WITH THEIR EUROPEAN NEIGHBORS, BUT THE SEIZURE OF THEIR LANDS AND ENSLAVEMENT PUSHED THEM TO VIOLENCE.

Incursions by settlers into their lands were resented by the Indians, while the European sale of alcohol damaged their society, as did European slave raids. The Tuscarora retaliated by attacking European settlements, killing whole families and capturing women. A Carolinas military expedition, aided by Indian allies, devastated some Tuscarora villages in response.

In 1711, Swiss colonists, led by Baron Christoph von Graffenreid, drove some Tuscarora from their land without offering payment. This prompted the Tuscarora, in company with Meherrin and Nottaway allies, to raid villages between the Neuse River and Pamlico Sound, where they killed 200 settlers, including eighty children. The baron was captured and promised to make peace, but other settlers seized a local chief and roasted him alive. Subsequently, several smaller tribes, including the Corees, joined the Tuscarora in further raiding.

In 1712, the first of two expeditions by South Carolinan John Barnwell, with several hundred Indian allies, notably the Yamasee, attacked the main Tuscarora village without success. During negotiations with Barnwell at Core Town for the return of captives, some Tuscarora were attacked, losing 40–50 dead, while 200 women and children were captured for the slave market.

In 1713, a second colonial force, under the command of Colonel James Moore and including 1,000 Indian allies, attacked the Tuscarora and defeated them. Hundreds were sold into slavery, while others settled on a reservation on the lower Roanoke River. Over the following ninety years, family groups and small bands moved north into New York State, joining their cultural relatives in the Iroquois League as early as 1722 to become the sixth member nation. This was the result of a policy aimed at exterminating the Tuscarora or driving them out of North Carolina, an early example of ethnic cleansing.

Two years after the Tuscarora War, the Yamasee rebelled against the European settlers, despite having supported them against the Tuscarora. They were being exploited by traders, especially in the sale of deerskins, while other grievances included forced labor in the wilderness and the accumulation of debts in excess £50,000, a substantial portion of which was for the purchase of rum. Often, their women and children were seized for sale into slavery to settle such debts. On April 15, 1715, the Yamasee, with Catawba, Creek, Saraw, Apalachee, and Creek allies, carried out an attack on all European traders in Indian towns. Over 100 were killed, while others were driven into Charles Town.

Carolina Governor Charles Crown sent a force against the southern Yamasee and defeated them, shipping women and child captives to Caribbean slave markets. Other noncombatants fled to St. Augustine in Spanish Florida, where they were joined by warrior fugitives and Lower Creek allies. These began raiding across the border, torching twenty plantations. After this, the war was pursued largely by the Creek, but a Creek and Apalachee onslaught upon Charles Town failed, bringing an end to the major battles; occasional raiding was the only form of warfare left open to the Indians.

The British convinced the Cherokee not to become involved, causing decades of enmity between the Creek and Cherokee. Isolated from British trade, the Creek nation sought trade goods from other European powers. The Lower Creek returned their villages to the Chattahoochee and turned to the Spanish, while the Upper Creek made overtures toward the French. Peace was finally brokered between the Creek and Carolinians in November 1717. Thus, the Creek became an important weight in the Southern European colonial balance of power.

Now, nearly all of Carolina west of the Appalachians was opened to white settlement, especially after the Waxhaw, Sugaree, Wateree, Eno, and Santee were absorbed into the Catawba after being decimated by disease and conflict. In this way, the Catawba were able to survive.

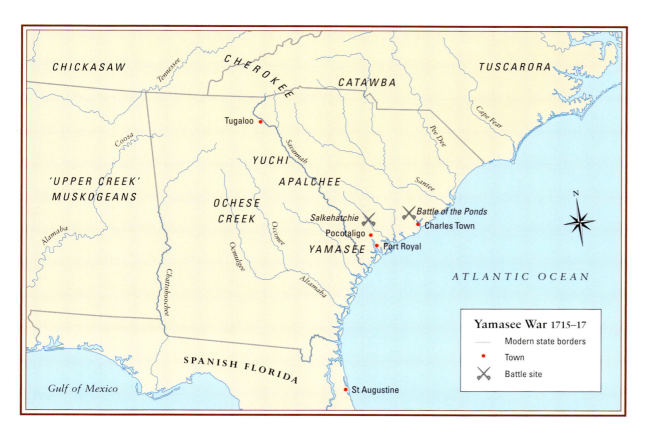

The Yamasee War was fought between a variety of Indian tribes and colonists in South Carolina. Hundreds of the latter were killed and many small settlements were abandoned; the survival of South Carolina itself was threatened. The tide turned, however, when the Cherokee sided with the colonists. During the war, South Carolina militia enjoyed significant successes over the Indians at the Indian town of Salkehatchie and at the Battle of the Ponds, to the north of Charles Town.

The Destruction of the Natchez, 1729–33

Descendants of the Mississippian mound builders, the Natchez maintained a socially stratified society, in which their leader, the Great Sun, had authority over life and death.

In 1542, the Natchez had helped drive de Soto's Spanish troops from the south. They occupied four villages on the first bluffs overlooking the Mississippi. This nation's major European encounter was with the French, who built Fort Rosalie overlooking the major Natchez village.

Initially, French-Natchez relations had been intermittently violent, but eventually the Tattered Serpent, the Great Sun's brother, brought about cordial relations. On his death, however, the French commander of Fort Rosalie, Sieur de Chépart, with the support of Louisiana Governor Étienne Périer de Salvert, began to confront the Natchez. In August 1729, de Chépart demanded that the Natchez leave their main village, which contained their most sacred sites and objects, so that he could establish a tobacco plantation. Such plantations were becoming common in the area, being operated with imported African slave labor.

The Natchez decided to attack all Frenchmen in their lands, persuading the plantation slaves to join them in return for their freedom. On November 29, 1729, the Natchez struck at Fort Rosalie and the French plantations. Approximately 145 men, thirty-six women, and fifty-six children were killed, while 300 African slaves and fifty French women were captured; only twelve Natchez died. Elsewhere, Yazoo allies stormed Fort St. Pierre in their territory. De Chépart was captured, but warriors would not defile their weapons by killing him. Instead, a Stinkard, a member of the lowest Natchez caste, clubbed him to death.

In retaliation, the French sent an expedition, which included 700 Choctaw allies, against the Natchez. On January 27, 1730, the Natchez were attacked, and French women and slaves were recovered, but the Natchez slipped out of their forts at St. Catherine's Creek and eventually reached the Ouachita Indians near contemporary Sicily Island, Louisiana. The French strength was boosted by the arrival of 350 reinforcements from the Company of the Indies and Ministry of Marine. Their commander, the governor's brother, decided to destroy the Natchez by killing or enslaving them.

French forces concentrated on the Red River in early January 1731, assaulting the Natchez forts with cannons and mortars on January 20. After four days, negotiations were opened and some slaves were returned. Around 500 Natchez agreed to surrender and were taken captive, but some Natchez managed to escape. The summer of 1713 saw the construction of a new Natchez village with the Chickasaw, while some 150 Natchez lived in four other villages among the Yazoo, and three on the Mississippi's west side. The Natchez asked neighboring Tunica Indians to treat with the French on their behalf, but fearing a deception, turned on the Tunica with Chickasaw and Koroa allies. Elsewhere, some forty Natchez surrendered, but were all killed after attempting to escape.

Other Natchez, under Flour Chief, attacked, captured, and refortified the French fort of Natchitoches on the Red River. The French retaliated by laying siege for several weeks, being aided by Attakapas, Caddo, and Natchitoches Indians. Many Natchez were killed, but around fifty escaped and waged guerrilla war from the Ouiachita River, attacking the French settlement at Point Coupee during 1732, and also the Chacchiuma Indians. Lack of total success occasioned Périer de Salvert's recall in September 1732, to be replaced by Bienville. During the summer of 1733, Bienville drove the remaining bands of Natchez from their villages on the Yazoo, but a remnant established a refugee village in 1733 with the Chickasaw. Together, war and disease in 1731 virtually wiped out the Natchez. Captives were sold into slavery in Santo Domingo, Haiti. As a tribal entity, the Natchez were destroyed. However, the refugees eventually spread from the Chickasaw to the Creek and Cherokee, where they continued their mystical, sun-oriented religious ceremonies.

A mural from the Natchez Visitor Center, Mississippi, depicting Natchez warriors attacking French troops.

THE CREEK-CHOCKTAW WARS, 1730–36

SUPPORTED BY THE BRITISH, THE CREEK CARRIED ON A WAR AGAINST THE CHOCTAW, WHO TURNED TO THE FRENCH FOR SUPPORT. THESE ALLIANCES CONTINUED FOR MANY YEARS.

The hostility between the Choctaw and Creek probably existed before the arrival of European settlers. However, the groups are distantly related, and they existed as multilingual confederations, the coalescing remnants of peoples decimated by disease following de Soto's *entrada*. The Choctaw shared closely related languages and gathered in east-central Mississippi. The Noxubee and Sucarnochee, called the Pafalya by de Soto, had been connected to earlier civilizations. The Noxubee were linked to Moundville chiefdoms, and the Sucarnochee came from a satellite, semi-independent chiefdom, such as the Lubbub Creek community. Additional members were remnants from the Mobile delta and the prairie people of the Nanih Waiya.

The Creek encompassed groups who came together to confront the raids of northern Native Americans and European slave traders. Muskogee-speakers were joined by Hitchiti, Tuchebatchee, Alabama, and Yuchi; Natchez, Yamasee, Apalachee, Apalachicola, Chiaha, Guale, Icafui, Kasihta, Oconee, Osochi, Okmukgee, Tacatacuru, and Tamathli were also assimilated. These peoples were descended from inhabitants of the Etowah Mounds.

The European presence pushed the two confederations into hostility and frequent violence. British-armed Creek fighters with South Carolina traders carried out slave raids against the Choctaw. The last were forced to rely on the French in the new colony of Louisiana for guns and supplies to defend themselves. The Choctaw fed the French when their crops failed, but the friendship killed 5,000 Choctaw through disease. Nevertheless, the nation helped the French in the Natchez War (1730–31), and Chief Red Shoe fought on the French side in the Chickasaw Wars. One slave raid occurred in 1711, when over 1,000 Creeks marched against the Choctaw during Queen Anne's War. The slave trade ended after 1715, but hostility continued as each nation supported France or Britain until the end of the Seven Years' War (the French and Indian War). The Choctaw were not the only victims of slave raids. Many nations disappeared—the Cusabo, Wimbee, Edisto, Stono, Kiawa, Coosa, Isaw, Wanniah, Sampa, Ashepoo, and Elasie. These remnants were assimilated by nations of the interior. When the Creek could not supply slaves, they themselves would be taken and sold by white slavers.

A particularly damaging war began in 1763, after the French withdrew from America. The British summoned leaders of the southern tribes to a conference at Augusta, Georgia, where the colonials sought to establish better relations with all the tribes. The Creek feared that their enemies would now be supplied from Mobile or Georgia. Consequently, they stated that any Choctaw diplomat traveling to Augusta through Creek lands would be killed. One Choctaw chief, Red Shoe, did manage to reach Georgia, however, because he went with a Chickasaw delegation. After the conference, he was returned to his lands via Mobile, sailing on a British naval vessel.

Obviously, the British planned peace and trade with the Choctaw, so the Creeks went to war to block the relationship and to protect hunting lands on the eastern bank of the Tombigbee River. The resultant violence was exploited by the British, who supplied both sides. Georgia and West Florida settlers encouraged the hostility so that the nations would wear each other out and pose less danger to the colonies. The war lasted from 1763 to 1776, both Creek and Choctaw sustaining numerous casualties. Winter hunts were disrupted, which meant that there were fewer deerskins for sale. The Creek ceded land to Georgia to pay for accumulated debts when obtaining munitions, whereas the Choctaw were supplied by the British. One outcome of such partial treatment was the promotion of Anglo-Choctaw friendship. When the American Revolution erupted, Britain brokered a peace with the Indians, the war being ended at Pensacola by the British Indian Superintendent John Stuart.

During the revolution, the Creek, Choctaw, and Chickasaw wanted the rebellion crushed to protect their interests. In 1780, the Choctaw aided Loyalists in an attack on Mobile, but Loyalist cowardice prevented success. Later, British regulars failed to support Choctaw warriors after they had breached Spanish lines encircling Pensacola. The Creek aided the British at Savannah and Pensacola, but failed to benefit from the war.

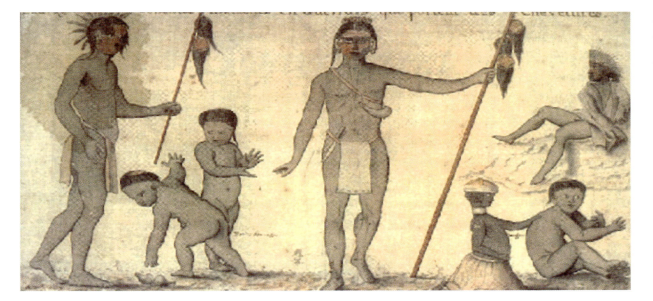

An early watercolor by Alexander de Batz, depicting Chocktaw Indians, some of whom display scalps on poles.

THE CHICKASAW-FRENCH WAR, 1735–40

THE CONFLICT BETWEEN THE FRENCH AND CHICKASAWS DEMONSTRATES HOW AN INDIAN NATION COULD RESIST ONE EUROPEAN POWER BY CONCLUDING A FRIENDSHIP WITH ANOTHER.

A contemporary map showing the area affected by the Chickasaw Wars of 1720–60. The French campaigns started from Mobile and New Orleans in the south, and Forts Chartres and Vincennes in the north.

The Chickasaw occupied a strategic area centered on Chikasahha, near today's Memphis, Tennessee. Therefore, they could pose a threat to the French domination of the Mississippi by interdicting the route between the French settlements in Illinois, and the southern posts at Mobile and New Orleans. Between the 1690s and 1729, the Chickasaw maintained a balance in their relations with the French and British. In November 1729, however, the Natchez attacked the French forts at Rosalie and St. Pierre, killing or capturing most of the inhabitants. The Chickasaw refused a French request to help punish the Natchez; indeed, fleeing Natchez found sanctuary with the Chickasaw.

Next, the French decided to ally themselves with the Choctaw and hound the Chickasaw, both policies designed to block the British influence in the Mississippi Valley. By 1730, though, some Choctaw had approached the British for support, and this decline in French influence persuaded the French to strike at the Chickasaw. One advantage lay with France's enemy, however, since the Chickasaw had been trained by the British to build fortifications. Nevertheless, the French pressed ahead, planning attacks that employed Choctaw forces to drag them into French affairs.

In 1735, Jean-Baptiste Le Moyne de Bienville, Louisiana's governor, organized an army to assault Chikasahha. In 1736, French and Indian troops advanced up the Tombigbee River to meet forces under d'Artaguette from Illinois. The latter's units attacked Ogoula Tchetoka village, but half of the 137 French soldiers were killed. Bienville fought the Chickasaw at the Battle of Ackia on May 26, 1736. His force comprised 500 troops, settlers, Indians, and armed Africans commanded by free African officers. They were easily defeated, however, and were fortunate that the Choctaw rescued the wounded.

Bienville became determined to thrash the Chickasaw and began organizing troops from Canada, Illinois, and Louisiana; also, he asked for regulars from France. He mobilized 1,200 French soldiers and 2,400 Native American allies in Arkansas, then marched up the Mississippi rather than the Tombigbee River. Lack of geographic knowledge, poor logistics, disease, and delays turned the advance into a shambles, and Bienville was forced to retreat after a provincial council of war. In 1740, he descended the Mississippi just as 100

A section of a map drawn by Edward Crisp, showing the Mississippi River and the disposition of the tribes along it. These include the Chickasaw.

French colonials and 500 Indians, led by Pierre-Joseph Céloron de Blainville, approached Chikasahha. The Chickasaw thought the French force was the vanguard of an entire army. Rather than attack, they sued for peace. Bienville agreed to their terms, but the Choctaw continued to raid the Chickasaw and sell their scalps to the French. Obviously, Bienville was still attempting to weaken the British allies, and he encouraged the Choctaw to avenge French deaths as well as their own.

After the Chickasaw were weakened by a smallpox attack in 1749, the new Louisiana governor, Pierre de Rigaud de Vaudreuil, urged the Choctaw to reengage them. Two forces were dispatched against the Chickasaw in 1752 and 1753. On both occasions, the Chickasaw forts beat off the invaders with enough success not to be involved in the 1754–63 French and Indian War. Nevertheless, the Chickasaw still felt threatened, and on April 5, 1756, one of their leaders addressed the governor of South Carolina: "This is to let you know we are daily cut oft (sic) by our enemies the French and their Indians who seems to be resolved to drive us from this land."

Later, the Chickasaw felt that the 1763 Proclamation Line would protect them, and peace was made with the Choctaw. Support for Britain continued during the American Revolution, the Chickasaw raiding Virginia and the Carolinas. In 1783, Chickasaw representatives signed peace treaties with Virginia at French Licks, and agreed to expel British refugees from their lands, while the Americans promised to keep white settlers out of Chickasaw territory.

THE CREEK-CHEROKEE WARS, 1740–54

HOSTILITY BETWEEN NATIVE AMERICAN TRIBES, SUCH AS
THE CREEK AND CHEROKEE, WAS OFTEN EXPLOITED BY THE
EUROPEANS, WHO WOULD BACK ONE SIDE AGAINST THE OTHER.

The Creek-Cherokee Wars are one more example of unstable Native American relationships during a time of competing imperial influences. The initial Creek-Cherokee conflict occurred during the 1716 Yamasee War. Cherokees murdered some Creek delegates who were visiting the Lower Cherokee towns to win support for war against South Carolina. Cherokees and Carolinians then attacked a Creek war party awaiting their delegates' return. A long war ensued, with South Carolina backing the Cherokee against the Creek. In 1726, large numbers of Cherokee and Chickasaw were killed; in January 1727, Charles Town brokered a peace between the antagonists.

In 1740, Creeks attacked some Cherokee who were about to assault Choctaws allied to the French during the 1739–44 War of Jenkins's Ear. Governor Glen of South Carolina negotiated peace, but the Southeast was destabilized further by long-distance raids by the Seneca and Iroquois. Using Cherokee territory as a base, they attacked the Creek and Choctaw in what appear to be new mourning wars. The Creek-Cherokee War was renewed, but ended again in 1749, when Glen's good offices secured another peace agreement. The Cherokee agreed to prevent northern warriors from using their lands, and South Carolina said it would levy a trade embargo on any nations that broke the treaty.

This new agreement was quickly disrupted, but peace between the Cherokee and Upper Creek towns was preserved. However, the Lower Creek towns, especially Coweta and Cussita, decided to wrest their hunting grounds from the Lower Cherokee. In spring 1750, 500 Creek warriors, led by Malatchi of Coweta, attacked the Lower Cherokee towns of Echoi and Estatoe. The Cherokee incurred great losses and their towns were torched, while South Carolina imposed a trade embargo on them, leaving them short of guns and ammunition. Taking advantage of this opportunity, the Creek attacked and burned more Lower Cherokee towns, including Hiwassee, Keowee, and Tugaloo. Cherokee survivors fled to the Overhill and Middle Cherokee towns.

Again, Governor Glen in Charles Town brought together representatives of the nations, and in April 1754, the fourteen-year-old conflict was finally ended. The Carolinians had supported the belligerent Creek as a buffer against other tribes. South Carolina possessed a small population, whereas in 1685, the Creek and Cherokee together numbered some 50,000. By 1754, the slave population on the plantations had grown sufficiently large to be policed by South Carolina militia, leaving fewer soldiers to defend the frontier. Thus, Indian alliances were essential; they could be profitable as well. The last war had led to seizure by the Lower Creek of Lower Cherokee hunting grounds. This territory was located between the Little and Broad Rivers on the south side of the Savannah River, near Augusta, Georgia. The Cherokee and British recognized the Creek ownership of the land by right of conquest.

British tactics became apparent when Glen visited the Overhill Cherokee and had Fort Prince George built (1753) near Keowee, on the eastern side of the Appalachians. In 1755, he made a treaty with the Cherokee, by which the Indians sold 40 million acres (16 million hectares) of land to the colonials. By 1773, the Cherokee and Creek were so indebted to Georgia through trade that a New Purchase agreement handed over recently acquired Creek conquests as part of the debt repayment. Meanwhile, Fort Prince George defended not only the Cherokee and Creek from northern Indian raids, but also the increasing numbers of colonial villages being built.

Despite British support for the Creek, that nation posed a military threat to Georgia, but the only way the Creek could be controlled was to threaten a trade embargo. To help keep peace, the Georgia government did try to prevent illegal white settlements and encouraged Creek hostilities against the Choctaw. Ultimately, colonial governments could not prevent settlers from moving in, and the Creek attacked them in 1761. The Cherokee also waged war against them between 1759 and 1761.

The War of Jenkins's Ear was fought between Britain and Spain, mainly in the Caribbean, but hostilities spread to their colonies in North America, the British attacking St. Augustine in Florida without success. The Spanish counterattacked against Georgia, but were repulsed at the Battle of Bloody Marsh. The war gained its name because Spanish coastguards had caused outrage in the British parliament by severing the ear of a British sea captain, Robert Jenkins. Eventually, it became part of the War of the Austrian Succession. During the later stages of the war, the British began attacking French merchantmen, which prompted retaliation by the French and their Indian allies.

The Ojibwa-Lakota Wars, 1740–1858

The Ojibwa, Armed by the French, Waged a War of Expansion Against Many Tribes, Among Them the Lakota, Who Were Pushed On To the Plains, Far From Their Original Homeland.

The Ojibwa-Lakota wars can be regarded as one stage in an Ojibwa expansion, which proved that the nation was one of the most powerful forces in North American history, a largely unrecognized fact. The early Ojibwa are thought to have split from the Ottawa and Potawatomi; their home territory was around Sault Ste. Marie, Michigan. Geopolitically, the nation inhabited part of a major transcontinental waterway and, thus, was involved in the fur trade, and inter-tribal rivalries and conflicts. Tribal unity demonstrated itself when faced by direct threat, whereupon the loose confederation with the Ottawa and Potawatomi—The Three Fires—could be mobilized.

Ojibwa military expertise was aided by a French supply of guns, which allowed territorial aggrandizement over a long period of time. In 1662, a large Iroquois war party was pursuing its retreating enemies, but was wiped out at Lake Superior by the Ojibwa and their allies. Then the Iroquois were pushed out of the lands north of Lakes Erie and Ontario, and by the end of the Iroquois war, the Ojibwa had expanded into the area around Georgian Bay and Lake Huron. Eastern Michigan was in the hands of the Ojibwa, while the friendly Ottawa occupied West Michigan. In the 1660s, the Ojibwa spread out southwestward from their heartland, the southern Ojibwa, or Chippewa, reaching La Pointe (1680) on Chequamegon Bay in southwestern Lake Superior, Wisconsin. Their expansion occasioned much hostility from the Lakota and their Fox allies. The former were located around the headwaters of the Mississippi, the latter around the headwaters of the St. Clair River in Wisconsin.

The Ojibwa enjoyed good relations with the French, aiding them in their war with the Fox (1729–30).

This opened up avenues into Lakota hunting territory. Then, aided by Cree and Assiniboine allies, the Ojibwa moved west into Minnesota, while some fought northwest along the river from Lake Superior's northwest Grand Portage to the Winnipeg region, via the Lake of the Woods. In 1736, the Lakota killed a party of French on Massacre Island, near Fort St. Charles on the Lake of the Woods. This area was strategic. Fort St. Charles could control the southern parts of the Hudson Bay river-basin system and the headwaters of the Mississippi, and was an entrance onto the Plains. The Ojibwa retaliated in the 1740s, seizing control of the upper areas of the Mississippi, and moving toward the Red River and the Plains. Then the Lakota were forced out of the Mille Lacs area in Minnesota. By 1770, the Ojibwa occupied all of northern Minnesota and the northern branches of the Mississippi; no Lakota lived east of this river.

Despite military setbacks and disease, the Ojibwa sustained their westward and southwestward advances, pushing the Lakota further afield. In 1782, the Cree, northwest of Lake Superior, were ravaged by smallpox and invited the Ojibwa into their lands. By 1790, Ojibwa villages had spread along the Rainy River, around Lake of the Woods and Red Lake, and along the lower Red River districts, south of Lake Winnipeg. The Ojibwa moved onto the Plains, and their final battle with the Lakota occurred in 1858. The nation spread to the area of today's Edmonton, Alberta, displacing the Hidatsa, later raiding the latter's displaced villages on the Missouri. They attacked the Mandan and Arikara, and pushed the Cheyenne out of North Dakota, before spreading into Montana and Saskatchewan. The Ojibwa also took part in colonial wars when their hunting grounds and trade were threatened.

A mid-nineteenth-century illustration of Ojibwa warriors performing a war dance. The tribe's original homeland was in Michigan, but they moved steadily westward onto the Plains, clashing with other tribes as they went.

Turmoil on the Plains

In various ways, the arrival of the Europeans created movement among the Indian nations, which often brought them into conflict with each other.

Demographic disruption and dispersion were common in America during the European expansion. De Soto's travels through Arkansas devastated the local population—the land was so depopulated that survivors from Iroquois aggression crossed the Mississippi to hunt. Miami, Delaware, Shawnee, Piankashaw, Peoria, Chickasaw, and Choctaw tribes moved into east Arkansas, confronting settled Caddoes and Quapaw. Further west, along the Line of Semiaridity, lived the "prairie" Indians—the Mandan, Iowa, Kansa, Missouri, Omaha, Osage, Pawnee, Oto, and Ponca. These tribes grew maize and built permanent villages, which provided homes after the annual summer buffalo hunt.

Into this scenario was introduced the horse, originally brought to the continent by the Spanish in the Southwest. This animal set in train a second cycle of migrations as eastern tribes, armed with European guns, pushed the "prairie" Indians onto the Plains. The Cheyenne were encountered by the French on the upper Mississippi in the 1660s, but they migrated from Minnesota to become Plains buffalo hunters, having been expelled by the Lakota. Ojibwa and Cree fought the Teton Lakota, who moved west to begin a nomadic life. Similarly, the Yankton Lakota traveled west from the Red Lake area of Minnesota into North Dakota. The Lakota waged war on the Mandan, Hidatsa, and Arikara, aided by a supply of guns from the Santee Lakota, who lived near British and Canadian traders in Minnesota. The Teton and Yankton Lakota became the dominant power on the Missouri. Their quest for power was helped by an 80-percent reduction in the Arikara population through smallpox. In 1782, the Mandan and Hidatsa were also devastated by epidemics, followed by the Omaha. In North Dakota, the Hidatsa split, one group moving onto the northern Plains and into Yellowstone Valley—they became the Crow tribe. The Shoshone, originally from the Great Basin and the Rocky Mountains, became mounted and also spread onto the Plains, but they were pushed back to the mountains by other tribes.

The Plains Apache, who originated in Canada, had reached the Texas Panhandle by 1515 and split into the Eastern and Western Apache. The former comprised the Mescalero, Jicarilla, Chiricahua, Lipan, and Kiowa; the latter, the Cibecue, Mimbreño, and Coyotero. During the eighteenth century, Kiowa, Comanche, and Wichita horse soldiers, armed with guns, pushed the lance carrying Apache southward into the Spanish border territories of contemporary Arizona and New Mexico.

The Apache tribes generated population movements in the Southwest. In the 1670s, raids by the Apache, Navajo, and Utes, combined with the effects of drought, pushed many Pueblo dwellers to the Rio Grande. When the Pueblos rebelled against the Spanish in 1680, not only did the Europeans flee, but also their Christian Indian followers. The Spanish concentrated their missionary zeal upon the Apache, and eventually mixed marriages detribalized many Indians, who helped New Mexican colonists construct new towns, missions, and forts, such as Albuquerque (1706). A mission was established on the San Sabá tributary of the Colorado River in 1757, but it was destroyed by an Indian alliance led by the Caddoan Hasinai, who thought the Apache might obtain guns there. However, missions were built among the Lipan, on the Nueces River, between 1762 and 1771.

East of the Comanche, the Osage played off the Spanish and French against each other, using French guns to attack Caddoan and Wichita enemies to the southwest, and Pawnee to the northwest. Seizing horses and captives for slavery, the Osage forced the Caddoan down the Red River, while the Pawnee moved back toward the Platte River. The Wichita were pushed south of the Arkansas Valley, and the Osage dominated the area between the Red and Missouri rivers. The small Kansa tribe allied themselves with the Osage for survival. The Osage raided as far as Santa Fé and into Louisiana, while the Lipan Apache reached the Gulf of Mexico in 1796. Such was the turmoil accentuated by the horse and firearms.

A painting by famed American artist George Catlin showing Indians on a winter buffalo hunt on the Plains around the upper Missouri River (c. 1830).

THE CALIFORNIA MISSIONS

FEARING THE INCURSION OF RUSSIAN TRADERS FROM THE NORTH, THE SPANISH SET OUT TO SEIZE THE CALIFORNIA REGION BY ESTABLISHING A STRING OF MISSION COMMUNITIES.

José de Gálvez, Visitor-General of New Spain, sent expeditions northward to counter Russian moves off the Oregon Country.

Opposite: In the late eighteenth century, the Spanish established settlements and missions throughout California.

Spanish colonization in North America made a last "defensive expansion" in the late eighteenth century. Imperial northward movement in Texas had ended in 1763, when the French danger was removed by the cession of Louisiana to Spain. Subsequently, the region became home to 2,000 Spaniards in a dispersed collection of missions, presidios, and villages.

A new perceived threat to Spanish interests was a southward Russian thrust from Alaska by Cossack traders, whose ships were sailing in Oregon Country waters, and who could have threatened Mexico and outflanked possessions in Texas. Thus, the Spanish sought to forestall the Russians by the preemptive seizure of California. Visitor-General of New Spain, José de Gálvez, dispatched two parties from sparsely populated Baja California, one by land, the other by sea. In 1769, two ships reached San Diego Bay from La Paz, being joined later by Gaspar de Portola and the priest Father Serra, who journeyed through 400 miles (640 kilometers) of unexplored desert after leaving Loreto. In July 1769, Portola and 126 survivors of the land party formally took possession of California in the name of Spain. Portola sent a small expedition north to acquire the landlocked harbor of Monterey, where a new settlement became the Californian capital, next to the new mission of San Carlos. Three further missions were established—San Antonio, San Gabriel, and San Luis Obispo. In 1773, sixty-one soldiers and eleven friars maintained five stations and two presidios in California. In 1774, Juan Batista Anza and Father Garcés, with a few servants and muleteers, pioneered an overland route from Tubac to San Gabriel, through the San Jacinto Mountains. In 1775, Anza and Father Pedro led 240 colonists from Sonora to San Francisco harbor. Before long, twenty-one missions dotted the 650 miles (1,050 kilometers) through California between San Diego and Solano,

PACIFIC
OCEAN

Fort Ross

San Francisco
Solano 1823

San Rafael
1817

San Francisco   San Francisco
de Asis 1776

San José
1797

Santa Clara
1777   San José

Santa Cruz
1791

San Juan Bautista
1797

San Carlos   Monterey
Borromeo 1770   Seat of provincial
government
from 1777

Saledad
1791

San Antonio
de Padua
1771

San Miguel Arcángel
1797

San Luis Obispo
1772

La Purisima
1787   Santa Inés
1804

Santa Barbara   Santa Barbara
1786

San Buenaventura
1782

San Fernando
1797

San Gabriel
Los Angeles   1771

Cajon Pass

San Juan Capistrano
1776

San Luis Rey
1798

San Diego de Alcala   San Diego
1769

Sacramento River

Lake
Tahoe

Sierra Nevada Mountains

Walker
Lake

Utah
Territory

Mono Lake

San Joaquin River

Province of the Californias

Mohave Desert

Channel Islands

N

35°

120°

Spanish Colonial California

Settled from 1769 to 1823

Spanish Trail

El Camino Real

• Settlement

† Mission

Fort

0   200 km

0   200 miles

A contemporary illustration of Franciscan missionaries. The Spanish dispensed Christianity to the Indians with the lash and the branding iron.

being served by ports at San Francisco, Monterey, Los Angeles, and San Diego, which were defended by four presidios.

Colonists of mixed Spanish, Indian, and African descent drifted in and helped establish the mission system. Indian neophytes from dozens of tribes congregated in new communities, some 20,000 being converted to Christianity. Cattle herds grew on mission ranches, and Indians trained in new farming methods produced crops in irrigated fields. Hides, tallow, wine, brandy, grain, olive oil, and leather goods were exchanged for manufactured products brought around Cape Horn by American trading vessels, thereby establishing an American interest in the region.

The Spanish regarded the Indians as a valuable economic workforce in the controlled southern and coastal areas. Thus, the imperial presence was sustained by a virtual slave system. No one is entirely certain why Indians joined the missions. Perhaps they enjoyed the rituals, rites, and festivals of the new religious system, assuming that it would coexist with their own traditions. Whatever the reason, the Spanish

Founded in 1772, halfway between present-day Santa Barbara and Monterey, on the Californian coast, Mission San Luis Obispo de Tolosa was one of a chain of Spanish missions that ran throughout California. The mission remains a fully functional Catholic church.

segregated unmarried men and women into separate dormitories at night, using the lash, branding, chains, stocks, and solitary confinement to enforce discipline—"civilization and salvation."

The packed mission communities became breeding grounds for new diseases; between 1769 and 1848, the coastal regions of California witnessed a drop in Native American population of 90 percent. Epidemics such as measles, cholera, and smallpox caused devastation, particularly among the vulnerable young, old, and pregnant women. The Esselen people were the first to become extinct, while the neighboring Salinan suffered great losses, as did the Diegueño in the southernmost region of California. Indian resistance took two forms—escape and violence—as when several hundred Indians made an unsuccessful attack on the San Diego mission in 1775. All this servitude and misery helped provide a home for some 4,000–5,000 Hispanic settlers by 1821.

Even as Spanish California developed, the newly independent United States (1776) became a potential enemy to Hispanics and surviving Indians alike. By 1821, The Spanish empire had crumbled under the impact of the Napoleonic Wars in Spain, the return of Louisiana to France, and the independence of Mexico, which ruled California until 1848.

Mission San Luis Rey de Francia was founded in 1798. It was the eighteenth of the twenty-one missions established by the Spanish in California.

THE SEVEN YEARS' WAR

FROM 1756 TO 1763, ALL OF THE MAJOR EUROPEAN POWERS WERE AT WAR, AND THAT WAR SPREAD TO THEIR COLONIES AROUND THE WORLD, INCLUDING THOSE IN NORTH AMERICA.

After King George's War, the third of four French and Indian Wars, Virginians and Pennsylvanians pushed westward into the Ohio Valley and reached the Mississippi River. In 1749, the Ohio Company was organized and granted half a million acres (200,000 hectares) on the Upper Ohio, where it established a trading center at Cumberland, Maryland. The British claimed Ohio by the Treaty of Lancaster (1744) with the Iroquois, and the Treaty of Logtown (1748) with the Shawnee, Delaware, and Wyandot. The French response was to send a force of Ottawa and Ojibwa warriors, led by Charles Langlade, to attack a British trading post at Pickawillany (1752), where they killed Demoiselle, a Miami chief, and thirteen of his men. Next, the French refurbished some old forts and built new ones: Gaspereau (Nova Scotia), St. Fréderic and Niagara (New York), Toulouse (Alabama), and Presque Isle, Le Boeuf, Venango, and Duquesne (western Pennsylvania). The French planned to construct a complete chain of forts along the Mississippi to link their Canadian and Louisiana territories.

This show of French strength, and the surrender of Fort Necessity (built to mask Fort Duquesne at the fork of the Ohio and Monongahela rivers) by George Washington impressed the Indians. Ottawa, Algonkin, Wyandot, Nipissing, Ojibwa, Potawatomi, Sauk, Shawnee, and Seneca reinforced their dealings with the French. Also, the Delaware, who had been dispossessed by the British and Iroquois, moved into the French camp. On the other side, the British tried to enlist Iroquois support. However, only Chief Hendrick of the Mohawk was willing to be an ally; the remainder of the Confederacy remained neutral.

War formally began in 1755. Major General Braddock decided to attack the French with four columns. One force sailed into the Bay of Fundy, in Acadia, capturing Forts St. John and Beauséjour in June. The second column, led by Braddock, and comprising some 2,500 regulars and provincial militia, advanced on Fort Duquesne. However, the French threw 250 regulars and 600 Indians against the column as it passed through forested country. In the confused fighting, the British were shot down

A late nineteenth-century engraving depicting General Montcalm attempting to stop some of his Indian allies from attacking British soldiers and civilians as they leave Fort William Henry following its surrender to the French in August 1757.

by unseen enemies, and they broke. Washington and his Virginia militia were left to cover the rout. The British force suffered over 800 casualties, whereas the combined French and Indian force had thirty-nine. Braddock died of his wounds, while Washington marched the survivors to Pennsylvania after this disastrous Battle of the Monongahela River.

The third of Braddock's columns, under William Johnson, comprised 3,500 colonials and 300 Indians led by Chief Hendrick. This force advanced from Albany to Crown Point. Johnson's orders were to capture Forts Carillon and St. Fréderic. He was attacked by some 1,600 French, Canadians, and Indians, under the command of Baron Jean-Armand de Dieskau, on September 8, 1755. At Lake George, the French hit a reconnaissance force of 500 Americans and Indians, whose panicky retreat spread confusion among the rest of the column. Colonel Phineas Lyman, of Connecticut, rallied and inspired the Americans and Indians to fight back, and the French retreated after suffering 230 casualties; Johnson lost 262. Johnson then built Fort William Henry, but left his target forts untouched.

The final column, under Massachusetts Governor Shirley, comprised 1,500 men. They marched up the Mohawk Valley to Oswego, intending to attack Niagara, but retreated without attempting anything. Elsewhere, the border regions from Maine to Virginia were raided by Indians, and by mid-1756, they had killed 376 people and captured 276, for the loss of fewer than 100. Many white farmers in Pennsylvania and Virginia abandoned their homes. Attempts to fend off Indian attacks began in 1756. Major Andrew Lewis led 236 Virginia militia to burn Shawnee villages, but his badly organized force deserted him. Delaware from Kittaning village captured Fort Granville, and in retaliation, Lieutenant Armstrong attacked the village and burned it.

In 1756, the French General Montcalm arrived in Canada, as did Loudon to command the British. July saw Captain John Bradstreet, Oswego's commissary, beating off a French and Indian ambush while he was resupplying the settlement. Montcalm harassed British outposts and disrupted Oswego's supply line by seizing Fort Bull and its garrison. Then he assaulted the exposed Oswego and captured four armed ships, seventy cannon, and 1,606 soldiers and sailors, including two regular regiments.

Between June and September 1757, the British mounted an expedition against Louisbourg, but found a French fleet in the harbor and abandoned the attempt after a storm scattered the British fleet. Meanwhile, Montcalm marched into New York State with 6,200 French and 1,200 Indians, laying siege to Fort William Henry. Lieutenant Colonel Munro's 2,100 defenders resisted for a week, but with French artillery within 100 yards (90 meters) of the walls, they were forced to surrender. The British were allowed to march away, having given their parole that they would not fight for eighteen months, but the Indians killed about thirty wounded and seized 529 soldiers to sell to Canadians as forced labor. Montcalm paid for the release of every soldier he could find, but some prisoners were infected with smallpox, which spread among the nations of the Ohio Valley and the Plains.

In 1757, after so many British misfortunes, William Pitt was appointed with the ineffectual Duke of Newcastle to act in coalition and head the British government. The dominant Pitt devised fresh, aggressive plans for the conflict in North America. He encouraged the colonies to raise 21,000 provincial soldiers because he needed to keep regulars in Europe and the Caribbean. Pitt appointed General James Abercrombie as commander-in-chief of British forces; Carillon and Duquesne were Pitt's targets. Abercrombie had 42,000 troops to combat 7,000 French regulars, 12,000 militia, and some 2,000 Indians.

Abercrombie launched an amphibious assault across Lake Champlain against Fort Carillon (later Ticonderoga), but his 15,000-man force was defeated by Montcalm's 3,600, suffering 1,600 casualties. Abercrombie retreated. Next, he dispatched Captain Bradstreet with 3,700 provincial militia and 150 regulars to take Fort Frontenac on Lake Ontario. Bradstreet marched 430 miles, and on August 25, 1758, captured the fort with its 110 troops, nine warships, and seventy-six artillery pieces.

Another major British campaign of 1758 was mounted against Louisbourg. New commander-in-chief Jeffrey Amherst's 14,000 men stormed beaches on Nova Scotia and besieged the fort for six weeks. Governor Augustin de Drucour surrendered on July 25, costing France 3,000 soldiers, 2,600 marines and sailors, and five ships of the line. The final offensive of 1758 was General John Forbes' campaign against Fort Duquesne. All 270 Highlanders and militia of the advanced scouting force were killed or captured. Then, Forbes' main force was attacked by 570 French and Indians, and the British lost all their cattle and packhorses. Forbes was stopped in his tracks, only 40 miles (65 kilometers) from Duquesne. Intelligence persuaded him that the fort was weak, however, so he marched for nine days, only to discover its burnt-out ruins, the French having abandoned it. The British rebuilt it as Fort Pitt.

Elsewhere, Amherst ordered General Prideaux to reoccupy Oswego, then capture Fort Niagara. By early July, Niagara was besieged, and a 2,000-strong French and Indian relief column was driven off by Sir William Johnson's troops, among whom were 900 Mohawks. However, Prideaux died of wounds. Niagara surrendered on July 25, the British taking 600 prisoners, while the French abandoned and burned Fort Toronto before the British arrived. Amherst himself attacked Ticonderoga, capturing its ruins, which had been blown up by the French. Then he advanced to Fort St. Frédéric, which the French had also destroyed, and built Fort Crown Point upon the site. The war then became bogged down, but was enlivened by Major Robert Rogers and his Rangers, who burned the Abenaki village of St. Francis on October 6.

A late campaign against Québec was launched by General Wolfe, who died defeating Montcalm at the

Battle of the Heights of Abraham on September 13, 1759. Montcalm was also killed. Subsequently, the British defeated a French force that attempted to retake Québec. Then British forces were concentrated against Montréal, which was seized, leading to the surrender of all the remaining French garrisons.

The collapse of French Canada coincided with a volcanic outburst of violence in South Carolina. The British had profited from Chickasaw disruption of French trade, aided by some Cherokee and Catawba support. Ill treatment of Indians by the garrison of Fort Prince George caused the Cherokee to attack frontier settlements. Indian aggression ended after a force of 2,500 Highlanders and militia burned fifteen Cherokee towns.

General Montcalm and his French troops celebrate victory over the British at the Battle of Carillon, July 7–8, 1758. They had routed a numerically superior force commanded by General Abercrombie. Painting by Henry Alexander Ogden.

PONTIAC'S WAR, 1763–64

AFTER BRITAIN ASSUMED CONTROL OF NEW FRANCE, THE BRITISH BEGAN TO TREAT THE INDIANS OF THE REGION HARSHLY. THERE WAS AN UPRISING, LED BY THE OTTAWA CHIEF PONTIAC.

A nineteenth-century, imagined likeness of Pontiac by John Mix Stanley. No authentic portraits of the Ottawa chief exist.

After the French signed the Treaty of Paris in 1763, which ceded New France to Britain, relations between the British and Native Americans deteriorated. During the colonial wars, the western tribes had received gifts and alcohol, and had been paid higher fur prices by the British than the French. After Britain assumed control of the newly acquired lands, General Amherst rescinded this policy, depriving the Indians of a source of goods upon which they had become reliant. Now these products could only be bought from fur traders. Amherst also ordered severe restrictions upon the sale of alcohol, and stated that if the Indians misbehaved, they would be punished.

The abolition of French trade led to the Indians being cheated and charged high prices by the British. Indians were also compelled to sell their furs at forts where sometimes they were abused. Furthermore, the Indians were confronted by settlers from the east moving into Kentucky, western Pennsylvania, and Tennessee. Rumors spread that war belts were passing among the Ottawa, Huron, Potawatami, and Chippewa nations in the Lake Superior region. Also, there were reports of a link between the Delaware and Shawnee. Perhaps encouraged by French inhabitants on the St. Lawrence, war belts were passed from the Seneca, via the Delaware, to the Shawnee and the Miami, and from the Seneca to the Detroit Indians.

An engraving by Alfred Bobbet, depicting Pontiac urging tribal leaders to rise up against the British on April 27, 1753. Pontiac was aided in his task by the teachings of Neolin, known as the Delaware Prophet, who preached that all white men were enemies of the Indians.

Accordingly, Pontiac, an Ottowa chief, felt obliged to confront the British, and aired his concerns to other tribes. He was helped by the teachings of a Delaware, Neolin, who taught that all white men were enemies, and that Indians should return to their ancient traditions. Pontiac played on these sentiments, but said that French colonials were exempt from blame.

Pontiac realized that Britain's tenuous control of its western lands hinged upon Forts Pitt and Detroit, together with a few smaller forts. Failing to take Detroit by a ruse, Pontiac laid siege to the fort. Other Indian forces took forts Sandusky, St. Joseph, and Miami (near Fort Wayne). A ninety-six-man unit using boats to run supplies on Lake Erie, from Niagara to Detroit, was attacked at Point Pelee on May 28, 1763, and fifty-six of the men were killed. A Fort Michilimackinac detachment was annihilated. A the end of July, Captain James Dalyell led a sortie out of a reinforced Detroit; twenty of the 247-man force died in a defeat at Bloody Run. However, the British gained a victory at Bushy Run, south of Lake Erie, where a relief force of 460 men from Fort Pitt, under Colonel Henry Bouquet, was attacked by Delaware, Shawnee, Wyandot, and Mingo warriors. The Indians were outfought, but Bouquet lost some fifty men, along with the supplies he was carrying.

Elsewhere, Indians rallied to Pontiac's call—Chippewa, Ottowa, Potawatomi, Menominee, Huron, Seneca, Fox, Kickapoo, Mascouten, Wea, Sauk, and Miami warriors acted in concert. On June 1, Fort Ouiatenon fell, followed soon by Michilimackinac, Venango, Le Boeuf, and Presque Isle. By June's end, saving Detroit, all British military installations west of Fort Pitt had been taken. Furthermore, settlements had been destroyed and some 2,000 settlers killed.

By September, Pontiac still had not captured Detroit, and he realized that a stalemate had been reached. Also, the schooner *Huron* had beaten off a canoe attack and broken through Indian lines to deliver fresh supplies and reinforcements. On October 20, Pontiac received a letter from Major

Opposite: Pontiac's War threw the region south of the Great Lakes into turmoil. Several British forts were overrun by Indians incensed by their treatment following withdrawal of the French.

de Villiers, who commanded the French Fort de Chartres on the Mississippi River in Louisiana. He advised Pontiac to make peace. Winter was approaching, quarrels broke out among the tribes, and some bands were negotiating peace with Major Henry Gladwin, Detroit's commander.

Amherst suggested that blankets infected with smallpox should be given to the Indians. Some Shawnee and Delaware received these at Fort Pitt in 1764; the disease spread rapidly and with

A contemporary engraving showing a British fort being attacked by Indians during Pontiac's War. Although the British eventually regained control of the region, they suffered several defeats in the early stages of the war.

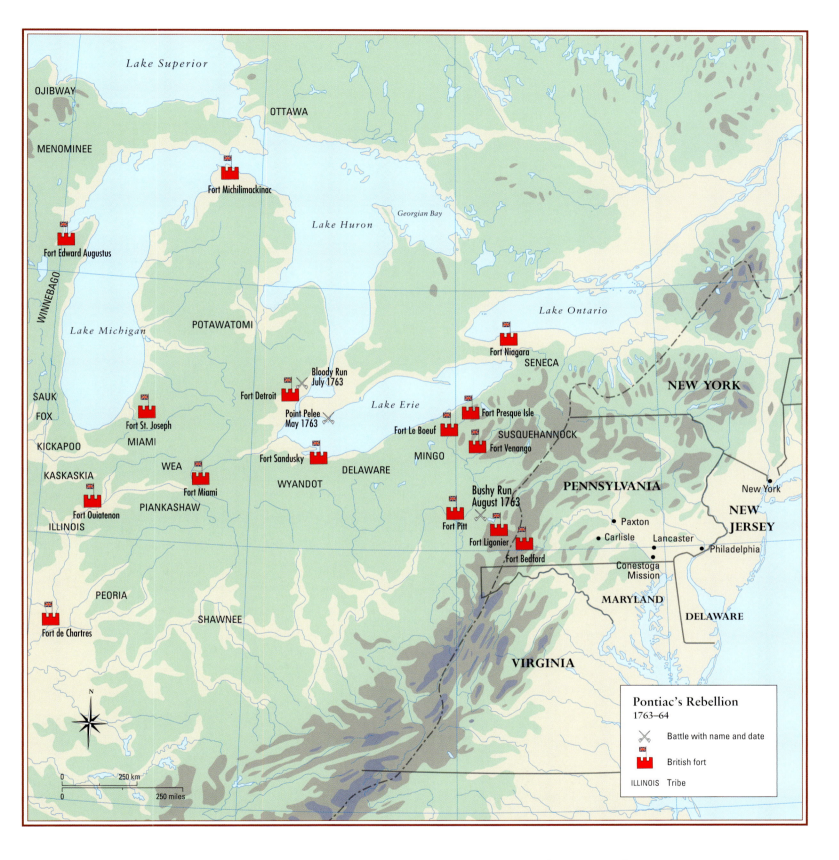

Pontiac's Rebellion
1763–64

⚔ Battle with name and date

🏰 British fort

ILLINOIS Tribe

devastating effects, weakening the tribes to such an extent that they were forced to make peace with the British. However, Pontiac did achieve one success. Although the British knew that Indians could be defeated, they realized that the tribes would never submit. Consequently, redress was made with the Proclamation Line of 1763.

THE PROCLAMATION OF 1763

REALIZING THE NEED TO APPEASE THE INDIANS, IN 1763,
THE BRITISH ISSUED A PROCLAMATION THAT DETAILED AN
INVIOLABLE BOUNDARY LINE BETWEEN THE COLONIES AND
INDIAN LAND.

The Proclamation Line of 1763 came about because of the British government's desire to appease the Indians, who resented the incursions of white settlers onto their lands. The line was drawn along the Appalachian watershed, from New York to northern Florida, and colonial settlement was excluded from the interior west of the line. However, the Crown could acquire Indian lands by cession, or could purchase them, but only after a public meeting of the Indians and the governor or commander-in-chief of the colonies. Such a meeting was held with the Creek, Choctaw, Cherokee, and Catawba.

The Indian boundary line finally stretched from the Mississippi, near the mouth of the Yazoo River, eastward across the Gulf coastal plain, around the coastal area of the Florida peninsula, and then north across Georgia and the Carolinas. It progressed westward across Virginia and Kentucky. From the mouth of the Kentucky River, the line followed the Ohio River upstream, crossed Pennsylvania from southwest to northeast, and traversed central New York State to the Mohawk River, near contemporary Rome. From there, it ran north to meet the St. Lawrence River.

In addition, a system of licensing traders was created, and the British administration was responsible for preventing criminals and fugitives from entering Indian land. Superintendents of Indian Affairs in northern and southern areas were to implement these conditions.

The Proclamation was a short-term success. In November 1763, Superintendent John Stuart met most of the southern chiefs at Augusta with governors of the four southern colonies, and boundaries between Indians and settlers were agreed, but not formalized. In spring 1765, Stuart persuaded the Choctaws and Chickasaws to accept British authority and trade. They also agreed to cede land along the coast, and lower Mobile and Tombigbee rivers. These bands helped the British to establish themselves in the Mississippi region to help counteract Pontiac's campaigns in Illinois. In May 1765, the Upper Creek agreed to peace and to regulated trade from Pensacola to Mobile, and to the cession of a ten-mile (16-kilometer) wide parcel of land between the two posts.

In the long term, white demographic growth prompted a flow of settlers, traders, speculators, and hunters onto Indian land, while the colonial authorities had insufficient funds to finance the work of the superintendents, to garrison forts, or to provide gifts for Indian allies. In 1768, Britain's Board of Trade returned control of British-Indian trade to colonial governments, following colonial resistance to further taxation deemed necessary to finance commitments agreed in the Proclamation. The Indians

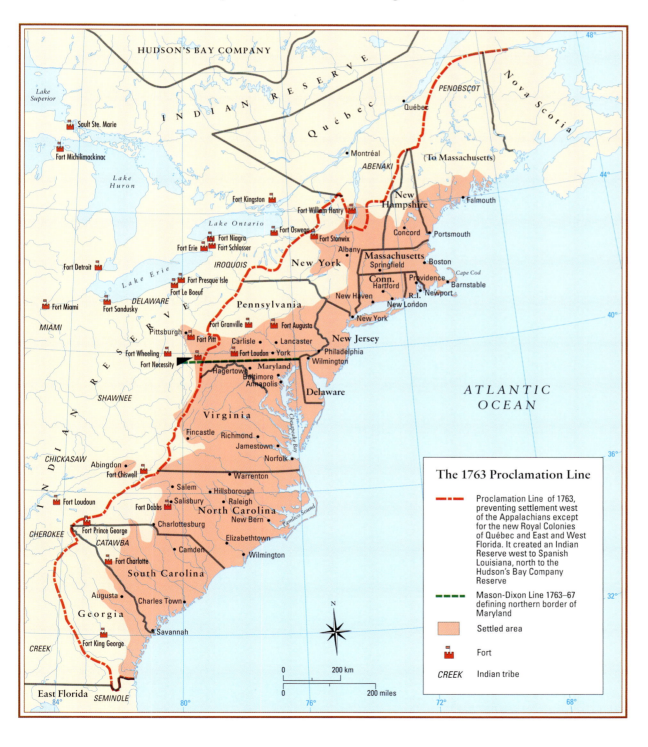

The 1763 Proclamation Line, devised by the British, ran from Nova Scotia to northern Florida and was supposed to provide an inviolable boundary between the colonies and Indian lands. Before long, however, settlers began pushing further westward.

Opposite: After victory over France in the Seven Years' War, Britain gained all the French territory east of the Mississippi River—New France. This new territory was named the Province of Québec under the terms of an Act of Parliament, known as the Québec Act. The province was several times larger than the old French province of Québec. The Act also included a number of provisions to appease the resident French Canadians in a bid to encourage them not to join the growing unrest in the colonies to the south, which ultimately would result in the American War of Independence. In this respect it succeeded, but in the process it angered the American colonists, who saw it as promoting papism and restricting traditional freedoms.

became more resentful. Matters were not helped immediately after Pontiac's resistance came to an end, when Britain was left with forts and garrisons occupying Indian land. White investors were also disgruntled, especially the Virginians, whose ancient charter claimed sea-to-sea rights. They were demanding jurisdiction over much of the Ohio Country. During a treaty conference in 1768, at Fort Stanwix, New York, in response to colonial pressure, northern Indian Superintendent William Johnson induced the Iroquois to cede huge tracts of hunting land on the Ohio, belonging to the Shawnee, Delaware, and Cherokee, territories that the Iroquois had never controlled, nor even occupied. In return, the Confederation was confirmed in its ancestral lands around the Finger Lakes, a situation that would be terminated by the American Revolution.

The Fort Stanwix Treaty, together with other land cessions, instigated a rush of speculators and settlers along the frontiers. By 1774, Virginians were killing Ohio Indians; a Cayuga-Mingo chief, Tachnechdorus (also known as Logan), had all thirteen members of his family murdered at Yellow Creek on the Ohio, 50 miles (80 kilometers) from Fort Pitt and the new settler town of Pittsburg. With Shawnees and Mingos, Logan retaliated, killing several white families and thus unleashing Lord Dunmore's War.

A watercolor depicting a Potawatomi camp at Crooked Creek, just before the tribe was ousted to make way for white settlers.

Hudson Bay

60°

56°

HUDSON BAY COMPANY

LABRADOR

52°

Lake Superior

48°

NEWFOUNDLAND

PROVINCE OF QUÉBEC

52°

St. Pierre
et Miquelon

Québec

QUÉBEC

NOVA SCOTIA

44°

Lake Michigan

Lake Huron

Montréal

Lake Ontario

Lake Erie

Boston

40°

SPANISH-
LOUISIANA

VANDALIA

THE THIRTEEN COLONIES

New York

Philadelphia

ATLANTIC OCEAN

36°

TRANSYLVANIA

56°

Norfolk

INDIAN RESERVE

32°

Bermuda

Charleston

Savannah

WEST FLORIDA
(formerly Spanish)

St. Augustine

92°

28°

EAST
FLORIDA

Gulf of Mexico

Bahamas

24°

88°   84°   80°   76°   72°   68°   64°   60°

The Québec Act
1774

Original province
of Québec

Province of Québec
after 1774

The Thirteen Colonies and
British possessions

Indian Reservation open for
settlers for the Thirteen
Colonies 1767–71

Spanish Louisiana, secretly
ceded by France in 1763

Only French possession
after Treaty of Paris, 1763

Native Americans in an Age of Revolution

"A part of our corn they burnt, and threw the remainder into the river. They burnt our houses, killed what few cattle and horses they could find, and destroyed our fruit trees, and left nothing but our bare soil and timber ..."

LONGTIME CAPTIVE AND ADOPTEE MARY JEMISON'S RECOLLECTIONS OF SULLIVAN'S TORCHING OF HER SENECA HOMELAND, 1799.

The two decades prior to American Independence were characterized by perpetual conflict on the borderlands. When Britain eradicated the French empire in North America and acquired Spanish colonies, the hegemonic imperial power proved incapable of imposing its authority over such a huge land mass, in which Native Americans, speculative land companies, settlers, aggressive colonial governors, and Indian agents were in constant mutual opposition. Setting the boundary of the 1763 Proclamation with the Indians had been difficult, and only confirmed by the Treaty of Stanwix (1784). Meanwhile, the Paxton Riots (1763) and Lord Dunmore's War (1773) set the scene for events in the later War of Independence. In fact, the American campaigns against the Iroquois, Ohio tribes, and the Cherokee, together with the movement of settlers into the Ohio lands and Kentucky, were a climax of dislocation, land cession, ethnic cleansing, cultural destruction, and internecine Native American strife. In addition, the war triggered the fragmentation of formerly powerful leagues, like the Iroquois Haudenosaunee, and the introduction of conflict between tribal elders and young warriors. The whole

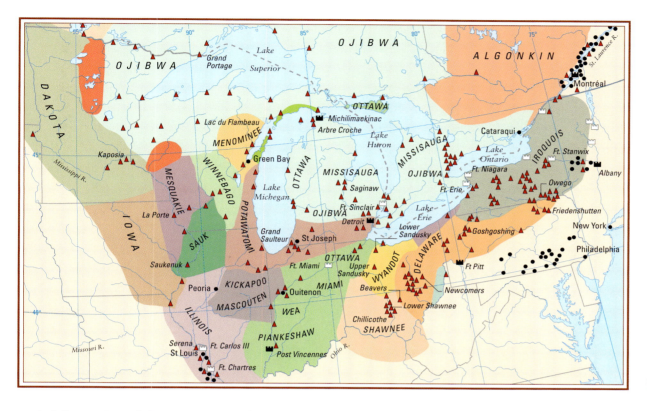

Indian Territory in the Great Lakes Region 1768

▲	Indian village
⌂	British fort
♜	Fort
●	White settlement
▮	Zone contested between tribes
—	Modern borders

By 1768, the Ojibwa occupied much of the Great Lakes region and were pushing westward against the Lakota (Dakota). Many of the tribes to the south of the lakes would be drawn into the conflict between Britain and the American colonies, particularly the Iroquois, who would suffer badly at the hands of Major General John Sullivan.

period from King Philip's War onward was a time when Native Americans fought to preserve their hunting grounds, traditions, religions, and values. The border warfare culminated in the American Revolution, an unmitigated disaster for Indians east of the Mississippi.

After Pontiac's War, anti-Indian hysteria surged through colonial frontier communities. At Conestoga, Pennsylvania, twenty Christian Susquehannock Indians, the remnants of their tribe, half being aged and small children, lived under the protection of the territory. On December 14, 1763, some border thugs, known as the Paxton Boys and led by a Presbyterian Church elder, butchered six of the Indians. The survivors were moved to a safe blockhouse, but the mob broke in and killed them all: "... they divided into their little families, the children clinging to their parents; they fell on their knees, protested their innocence, declared their love to the English, and that, in their whole lives, they had never done them injury; and in this posture they all received the hatchet! Men, women, and little children were every one inhumanely murdered!—in cold blood." John Penn, eyewitness.

The slaughter inspired 500 rioters to march on Philadelphia to kill 140 Christian Indians living there, but they were dispersed by the militia. Later, fifty-six Indians died from smallpox contracted in the army barracks where they were living—a bleak postscript.

The memories of the riots festered among the Indians, causing resentment and continued hatred of the settlers. This witches brew boiled over in Lord Dunmore's War. Dunmore, the governor of Virginia, fomented the war with the aim of grabbing Indian land, and after his victory, he victimized the Indians. The Ohio River basin was home to Delaware, Miami, Mingo, Shawnee, and Wyandot, whose territory had been guaranteed by the 1763 Proclamation, but Dunmore claimed the upper Ohio Valley for Virginia. Meanwhile, some hunters had murdered a group of Indians at Yellow Creek, including Shawnee and Mingo (refugee Seneca and Cayuga). Dunmore targeted the Shawnee, and his diplomacy isolated them from potential Ohio allies. The perceived threat of Indian attack occasioned a Virginian

Opposite: After removing the French threat to Britain's North American colonies in 1763, the British government sought to impose unpopular taxes and laws upon the colonists. The latter considered that these were a violation of their rights, since they were not represented in the British parliament. The colonists set up their own form of government in the colonies, effectively sidelining British rule. The British sent in troops, causing the colonists to mobilize their militia, and fighting broke out in 1775. By that time, only a few small pockets within the Thirteen Colonies remained loyal to Britain. In the following year, 1776, delegates from the Thirteen Colonies issued a Declaration of Independence, giving birth to the United States.

invasion of Shawnee country, during which the tribe lost the Battle of Mount Pleasant. Dunmore's peace treaty demanded that the Shawnee end their hunting south and west of the Ohio River, thereby leaving contemporary West Virginia and Kentucky to land speculators and illegal settlers.

The beginning of the American Revolution took Native Americans by surprise. Initially, the Indians regarded the conflict as a family affair and attempted to remain neutral, but gradually they realized that they had to choose sides, since they needed a guaranteed source of trade goods.

"A modern Indian cannot subsist without Europeans; and would handle a flint ax or any other rude utensil used by his ancestors very awkwardly: so what was only conveniency at first is now become necessity and the original tie is strengthened." John Stuart, Southern Indian Superintendent, 1764.

John Stuart enjoyed good relations with the Cherokee, and British General Gage exhorted him to persuade the Indians to war. The Choctaw, Chickasaw, Cherokee, and Creek could field 11,750 warriors, much needed by the British. However, Stuart knew that conflict would lead to total war, which would devastate civilians and have an adverse political outcome. He preferred combined Indian and regular British Army operations, rather than unleashing terror against the American border regions. The Cherokee ignored Stuart, however, by attacking the South Carolina frontier and villages along the Tennessee River, near North Carolina and Virginia, isolating Kentucky settlements. Other Cherokees poured into North Carolina. The remaining southern tribes raided settlers in the Tennessee and Kentucky regions, and along the Mississippi. This aggressive defense of their lands generated harsh American retaliation. Villages were burned and food stores destroyed, most Cherokees being forced to flee down the Tennessee Valley, abandoning their homes, fields, and livestock.

Subsequent treaties forced the Lower, Middle, and Valley Cherokee to cede all their land in South Carolina. The Overhill Cherokee surrendered all land east of the Blue Ridge Mountains, which effectively kicked them out of Virginia while halving their possessions in Tennessee and North Carolina. In sum, 10,000 square miles (26,000 square kilometers) were lost. The Cherokee War occasioned an internal tribal gender conflict, and American victory intimidated the tribes into quiescence. During the treaty talks in 1777, Chief Corn Tassel carefully defined the differences between Native American and white lifestyles: *"I am sensible that if we give up these lands they will bring you a great deal more than hundreds of pounds. It spoils our hunting grounds; but always remains good to you to raise families and stocks on, when the goods we receive of you are rotten and gone to nothing your stocks are tame and marked; but we don't know ours they are wild. Hunting is our principle way of living."*

On the lower Mississippi, Choctaws held Mobile for Britain until the Spanish attacked and overwhelmed them. The pro-British Choctaw faction then gradually disengaged from the British, finding a home in Spanish Florida after the 1783 Treaty of Paris. Many Creeks joined the British, which eventually triggered a Creek civil war. By 1782, they had been defeated, and many fled to Florida. When peace was sealed, the Creek ceded 800 square miles (2,100 square kilometers) to Georgia, although mixed-blood leader McGillivray held out.

In comparison to the British, the Americans were short of supplies and, thus, were less able to bribe Indians to support their cause. Also, the leaders of the revolution failed to prevent the continued encroachment by settlers on tribal lands. In addition, American troops could be ill-disciplined; they murdered neutral Delaware Chief White Eyes and Shawnee Chief Cornstalk. In 1778, White Eyes had

Loyalists and Patriots
c. 1775

- Loyalist or neutral Native Americans
- Rebel area
- Strongly neutralist
- Loyalist area
- Spanish possession
- Site of major demonstrations against the Stamp Act
- Passive aid to rebels

The Shawnee chief Tecumseh, a visionary who dreamed of creating a Native American state in the Great Lakes and Ohio Valley region, sided with the British during the War of 1812, but died during the Battle of the Thames in 1813. His death is recorded in this contemporary lithograph.

Opposite: After the War of Independence, the Mississippi River became the border between the United States and Spanish territory, but before long, American traders and explorers were probing across the great river.

helped lead an American expedition across tribal lands against Detroit. The Delaware turned on the Americans, supporting the pro-British Chief Pipe. Some Delaware sought sanctuary at Fort Pitt, while Pipe moved his people to the upper Sandusky River, leaving Moravian Christian Delaware isolated. In March 1782, ninety Moravian Indians were clubbed to death at Gnadenhutten by American militia. Later, when American Colonel Crawford attacked the Wyandot and Delaware on the Sandusky in June, his force was defeated; Crawford was captured and tortured to death for two hours in retaliation for the Moravian slaughter. "*Crawford died like a hero; never changed his countenance, tho' they scalped him alive, and then laid hot ashes on his head; after which they roasted him by a slow firer.*" Captain Caldwell, June 1782.

The killing of Chief Cornstalk inflamed the Shawnee. Previously, in the face of constant American westward expansion, some had joined the Creek, while others had moved west across the Mississippi into Spanish territory. Most Shawnee joined the British after the murder, but Cornstalk's Maquachakes journeyed to the Delaware capital at Coshocton, hoping to retain their neutrality. Later, the Shawnee were thoroughly hammered by Bowman and Clark's expeditions, but many continued to resist until the 1795 Treaty of Greenville. Shawnee anguish caused some to join Tecumseh at the Battle of the Thames (1813) during the War of 1812.

The experiences of the Shawnee and Delaware demonstrate the destruction of traditional Indian society and tribal relationships, while the Americans appeared to be callous, untrustworthy murderers. Thomas Jefferson, Governor of Virginia at the time, saw the conflict with the Shawnee as a war of extermination. Indian society was further shattered when Massachusetts Christian Stockbridge Indians served as Minutemen, while Micmacs, Passamaquoddies, and Penobscots from Maine and Nova Scotia supported the Americans, as did the South Carolina Catawba. After the war, Stockbridge Mahicans returned home to find that their Indian town had been taken over by white neighbors, but they received no recompense. They moved to New York and later Wisconsin. Elsewhere, factionalism split the Iroquois: Mohawks, Onondagas, Cayugas, and Senecas fought Oneidas and Tuscaroras.

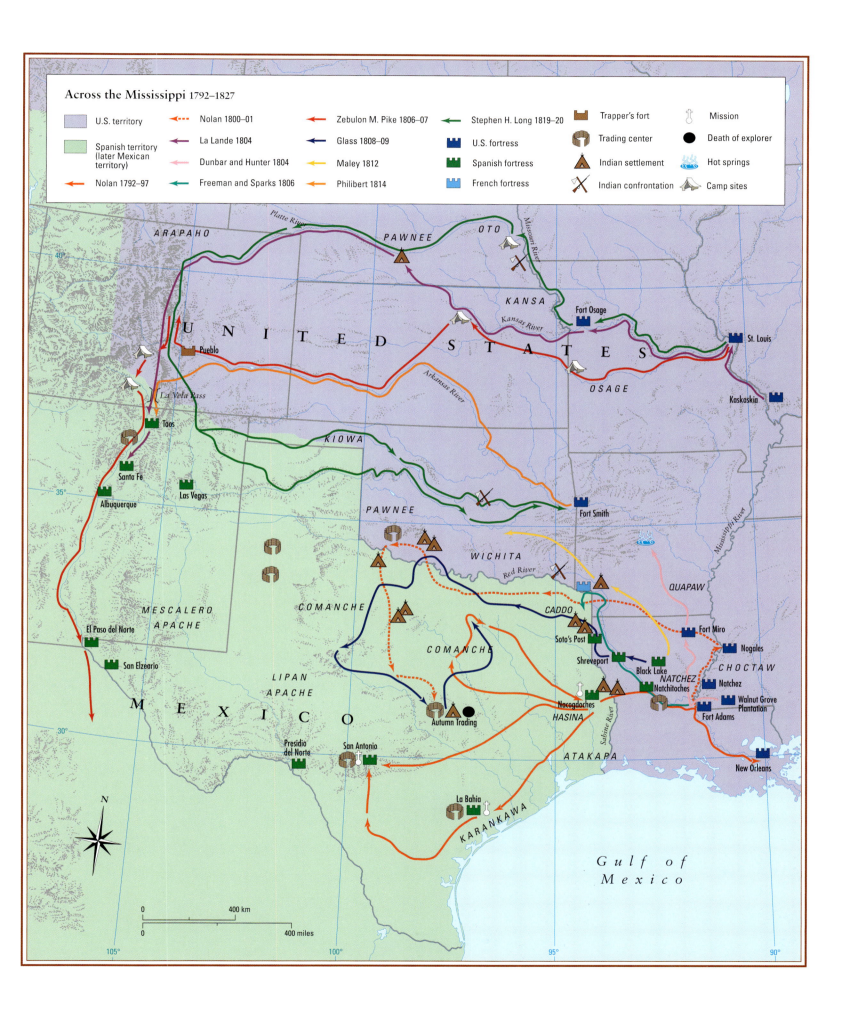

Across the Mississippi 1792–1827

- U.S. territory
- Spanish territory (later Mexican territory)
- Nolan 1792–97
- Nolan 1800–01
- La Lande 1804
- Dunbar and Hunter 1804
- Freeman and Sparks 1806
- Zebulon M. Pike 1806–07
- Glass 1808–09
- Maley 1812
- Philibert 1814
- Stephen H. Long 1819–20
- Trapper's fort
- Trading center
- Indian settlement
- Indian confrontation
- U.S. fortress
- Spanish fortress
- French fortress
- Mission
- Death of explorer
- Hot springs
- Camp sites

Opposite: The War of 1812, between Britain and the United States, was caused by the former applying trade embargoes against the latter.

George Washington, from a painting by Gilbert Stuart (1796). Incensed by raids against New York and Pennsylvania, Washington ordered the destruction of the Iroquois.

The War of Independence saw Indian warriors assaulting the American frontier, from New York south to Georgia. Some cooperated with British regulars and Loyalist forces, such as Butler's Rangers. Constant raiding tied up American resources that were needed to combat the British Redcoats in New Jersey and the South. Americans were terrified of raids, expecting capture, torture, rape, and death. So-called Indian massacres became Native American propaganda victories, such as the Cherry Valley Massacre (November 1778), during which only forty-six people were killed, a mere bagatelle compared to any other fight. Many Americans fled the border, having been scared by the incident, which pushed the border toward the Atlantic—a Native American and Loyalist strategic victory. The earlier Wyoming Valley Massacre, in Pennsylvania, had resulted from settlers from Pennsylvania, Connecticut, and New York entering the Susquehanna Valley, which the Iroquois regarded as their own. The 3,000 whites had built eight forts and blockhouses, legitimate military targets for Butler's Rangers, the Royal Greens, and Indian allies. This campaign was very successful, some 227 American scalps being taken. Mohawk Chief Brant and his Loyalist allies virtually destroyed the New York and Pennsylvania backcountry, which had been an important grain and cattle region for supplying the American Continental Army.

George Washington was incensed, demanding the destruction of the Iroquois and the burning of their settlements, crops, orchards, and food stores. General Sullivan's forces captured the Iroquois settlement of Chemung in what became known as the Battle of Newtown, and Captain James Norris stated that the *"Genl. Gave orders for the Town to be illuminated, and accordingly we had a glorious Bonfire of upwards of 30 buildings at once…"*

After the Battle of Newtown, Nathan Davies stated that a party counting dead Indians *"found them and skinned two of them from their hips down for boot legs; one for the Major the other for myself."*

The devastation of Haudenosaunee country may have involved jealousy too. One of Sullivan's men noted, *"The Indians live much better than most of the Mohawk River farmers their Houses very well furnished with all necessary Household utensils, great plenty of grain, several Horses, cows and wagons…"* Another wrote, *"The town which consisted of one hundred and twenty-eight houses, mostly very large and elegant…encircled with a clear flat which extends for a number of miles, where the most extensive fields of corn were and every kind of vegetable that can be conceived…"*

The winter following Sullivan's campaign (1779–80) was

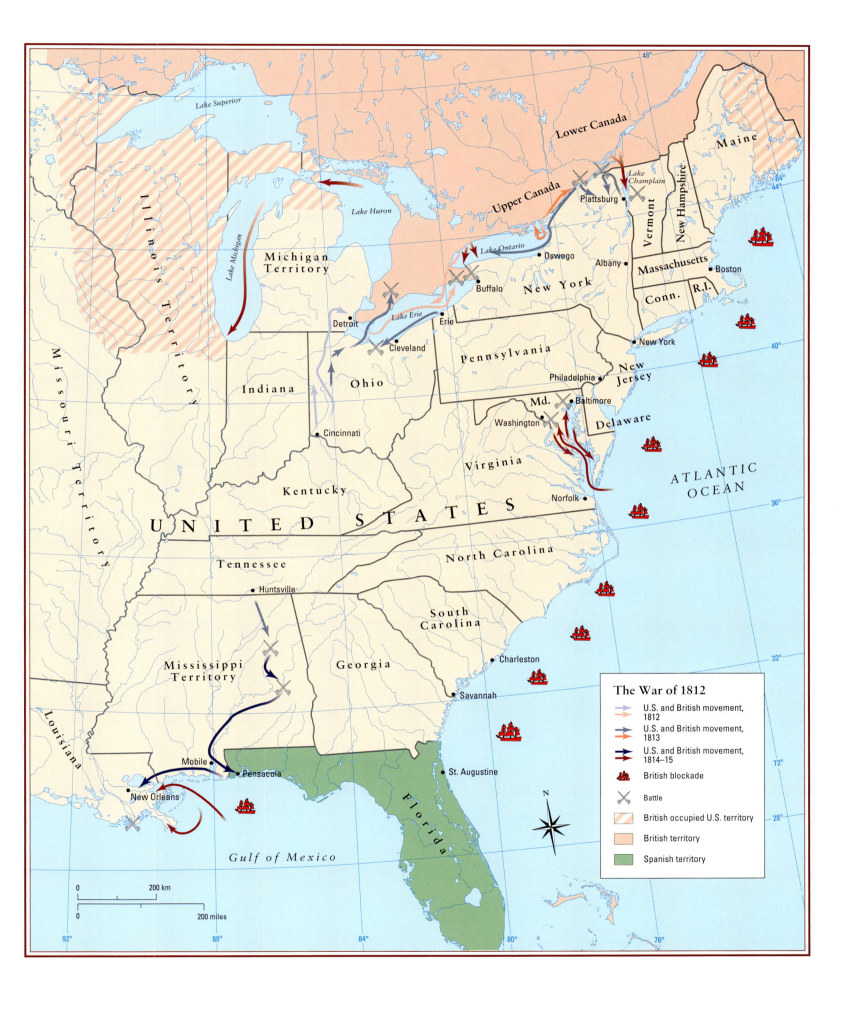

The War of 1812

→ U.S. and British movement, 1812

→ U.S. and British movement, 1813

→ U.S. and British movement, 1814–15

🚢 British blockade

✗ Battle

▨ British occupied U.S. territory

▧ British territory

▨ Spanish territory

The U.S. Army's "Old Guard" in a historical reenactment to celebrate George Washington's assumption of command of the Continental Army in 1775.

one of the worst on record. Starving Iroquois fled to Fort Niagara, imposing a burden on British logistics. Even before Sullivan's invasion, the Iroquois lifeway had been disrupted, since warriors away fighting could neither hunt nor clear fields. Endemic warfare increased the dependency of the Iroquois on their allies for supplies. Sullivan's victories did not prevent some Iroquois from continuing to raid. One of Sullivan's officers said, "*The nests are destroyed but the birds are still on the wing.*"

Chief Brant led raids against the Oneida and Tuscarora in revenge. The Oneida sought sanctuary under American protection near Schenectady, but suffered from the cold, hunger, and inadequate clothing and housing. The Iroquois hegemony over smaller tribes and their united military strength were sundered. After the Treaty of Paris, the British government established reserves in Canada, and many Mohawks followed Brant to the Grand River in Ontario; others went to the Bay of Quinte. Those Iroquois who remained south of the Canadian border saw their reservations shrink, and they became increasingly dependent on the American government. Despair led to alcoholism.

During the war, encroaching settlers led to continual border skirmishes. Even in 1776, Shawnee Cornstalk traveled south from western Pennsylvania to visit the Cherokee, remarking that the old buffalo and deer hunting grounds were inhabited by armed Americans, with forts everywhere. He

Opposite: Spanish explorers continued to lead expeditions into California and the Southwest toward the end of the eighteenth century and beginning of the nineteenth. France had ceded the Louisiana Territory to Spain at the end of the Seven Years' War in 1762.

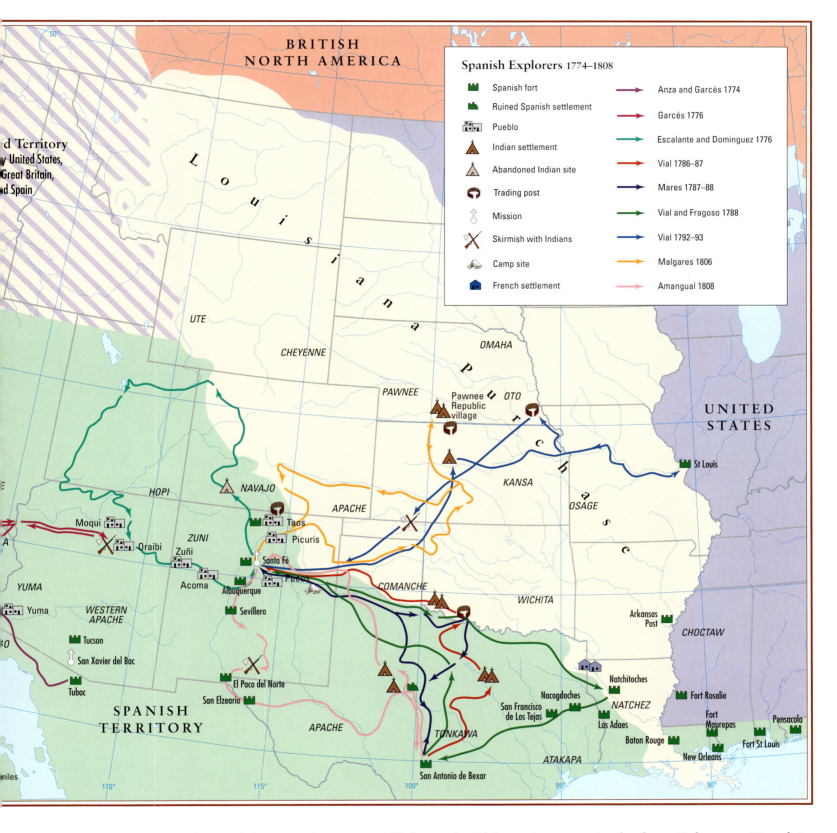

BRITISH
NORTH AMERICA

Spanish Explorers 1774–1808

🏰	Spanish fort	→ Anza and Garcés 1774
🏰	Ruined Spanish settlement	→ Garcés 1776
🏘	Pueblo	→ Escalante and Dominguez 1776
⛺	Indian settlement	→ Vial 1786–87
⛺	Abandoned Indian site	→ Mares 1787–88
⬤	Trading post	→ Vial and Fragoso 1788
✝	Mission	→ Vial 1792–93
⚔	Skirmish with Indians	→ Malgares 1806
⛺	Camp site	→ Amangual 1808
🏠	French settlement	

d Territory
y United States,
Great Britain,
d Spain

UTE

CHEYENNE

OMAHA

PAWNEE

Pawnee
Republic
village

OTO

L o u i s i a n a   P u r c h a s e

UNITED
STATES

St Louis

HOPI

Moqui

Oraibi

ZUNI

Zuñi

Acoma

NAVAJO

Taos
Picuris

Santa Fé

Pecos

APACHE

KANSA

OSAGE

WICHITA

CHOCTAW

Arkansas
Post

YUMA

Yuma

WESTERN
APACHE

Tucson

San Xavier del Bac

Tubac

Albuquerque

Sevillera

COMANCHE

SPANISH
TERRITORY

El Paco del Norte

San Elzeario

APACHE

TONKAWA

San Francisco
de Los Tejas

Nacogdoches

Los Adaes

NATCHEZ

Natchitoches

ATAKAPA

San Antonio de Bexar

Baton Rouge

New Orleans

Fort
Maurepas

Fort St Louis

Fort Rosalie

Pensacola

Fort St Louis

miles

was forced to make a 300-mile (480-kilometer) detour to avoid them. The Ohio territory contained refugee Delawares, Wyandots,
Ottowas, Chippewas, Shawnees, Miamis, Potowatomies, and Kickapoos. All were awaiting their fate, since the victorious,
independent Americans and the British had ignored the Indians in the Treaty of Paris. All land east of the Mississippi was regarded
as conquered territory and owned by the Americans, irrespective of its inhabitants. Indian lands, customs, values, and religions
would soon come under siege.

New York and the Ohio Country, 1763

FROM 1763, COMPETITION BETWEEN WHITE SETTLERS AND INDIANS INCREASED AS THE LATTER MOVED INTO THE OHIO COUNTRY, ATTRACTED BY THE PROSPECT OF GOOD HUNTING AND TRADING CENTERS.

A lithograph depicting the Paxton Boys' massacre of Indians at Lancaster, by John Wimer (1841).

Originally, the Indians had played off the French and the British against each other, but the French defeat in 1763 destroyed this delicate balance; the colonials of New York, Pennsylvania, and Virginia regarded the Ohio as ripe for settlement and commercial exploitation. The Ohio Country was a vast area. Located between the Ohio and Wabash rivers, its lands spread into the Great Lakes region. Thus, Ohio comprised parts of contemporary Indiana, Ohio, Michigan, and Pennsylvania, and anyone who controlled the strategic confluence of the Allegheny and Monongahela rivers would dominate the Ohio Valley.

Colonial desire for the region and fear of the Indian inhabitants generated a conflict that ran from the end of 1763 to 1774, one year before the American Revolution began. On December 14, 1763, a group of seventy-five Pennsylvanians from Paxton, Lancaster County, assailed a village of Conestoga Mission Indians, mainly Susquehannocks. The Paxton Boys, as they became known, butchered and scalped three men, two women, and a boy. The survivors were placed in the Lancaster jailhouse for safety, but their attackers broke in and murdered them all, including the children. The unruly mob then traveled toward Philadelphia with the intention of killing another 140 Indians, who were under government protection. Local Quakers mobilized against the Paxton Boys, who complained about Moravian missionaries among the Indians. Benjamin Franklin defused the situation, and the Paxton Boys agreed to disperse, provided they received a cash bounty for any scalp brought in from members of warring tribes. This agreement would be abused.

More formal attacks occurred after Lord John Dunmore, colonial governor of Virginia, sent surveyors into Kentucky and the Ohio. These lands had been guaranteed to the Shawnee by a treaty signed in 1768 at Fort Stanwix, on the site of present-day Rome, New York. The surveyors were ambushed in May 1773, the Shawnee having threatened to kill any white man who crossed the Ohio River. All but one surveyor died. In 1774, Dunmore seized parts of western Pennsylvania and Kentucky for Virginia, and settlements began to be built in the region, among them Harrodsburg. Violent incidents took place such as the Logan Affair, when the entire family of Mingo Chief Tachnechdorus (also known as John Logan) was murdered by white settlers. Logan had been a good friend of the colonials up to that point, but not surprisingly this action turned him against them. Chief Cornstalk, with other Shawnee chiefs, traveled to Pittsburgh to negotiate peace, but his brother, Silverheels, was murdered, further enraging the Shawnee, who stepped up attacks against the settlers.

Dunmore responded by sending two forces against the Shawnee. One column of 1,500 men moved down the Ohio against the Shawnee villages; the other approached from the south. The Iroquois refused to help Cornstalk, as did the Delaware and Cherokee. The Shawnee crossed the Ohio and launched a surprise attack on the second column on October 6, 1774, at Point Pleasant. The Virginians suffered 150 casualties, but the Indians lost far more. Eventually, the Treaty of Camp Charlotte ended Lord Dunmore's War, and it forced Cornstalk to give up Indian hunting grounds in Kentucky. This opened up the Ohio Country, which paved the way for further Indian resistance.

By the outbreak of the American War of Independence, tensions existed not just between Native Americans and settlers, but also between Britain and the colonies, and between American patriots and potential British loyalists. The British forces in North America comprised about 8,000 men, spread from Canada southward, with naval bases and anchorages at Halifax, Nova Scotia, Boston, and Philadelphia. Other northern cities of importance were New York and Newport. Hovering to the north, around the Finger Lakes region of New York State, were the Iroquois, always loyal to the British. The Six Nations could launch potential raids down the Wyoming and Hudson river valleys, where there was little to prevent them. To the west, a line of forts guarded the border with the Ohio Country, where Shawnee, Delaware, and Miami would resist settler incursions. In the north, the border was studded with British-held forts, such as Detroit and, especially, Niagara, which could be used to influence Native Americans with trade goods and weapons.

THE SOUTHEAST, 1763

NOT ONLY DID THE YEAR 1763 SEE THE END OF WAR BETWEEN FRANCE AND BRITAIN, BUT ALSO THE ADVENT OF MEETINGS BETWEEN COLONIALS AND INDIANS IN AN ATTEMPT TO ENSURE PEACE THROUGHOUT THE SOUTHEAST.

The Cherokee were particularly resentful after General James Grant's expedition against them at the end of the Seven Years' War, when fifteen of their towns and 15,000 acres (6,000 hectares) of crops had been destroyed. Despite the defeat, the settlers still feared the Indians, who remained a potential threat. John Stuart, Superintendent of Indian Affairs south of the Ohio, estimated that the Cherokee could muster 2,750 warriors, the Creek could field 3,600, the Choctaw 5,000, and the Chickasaw 450. Moreover, the Cherokee, Creek, and Catawba had all been involved in anti-British campaigns from Virginia to Georgia. Stuart was instrumental in securing the southern frontiers, and he sought to ensure that a "southern Pontiac" did not emerge. Thus, he held a congress at Augusta in November 1763, which was attended by four southern governors plus representatives of the Cherokee, Lower Creek, Choctaw, and Chickasaw. Some Upper Creeks and Catawbas also attended, but members of the militant and hostile Nativist Creek group, led by Yahatastanage (known as the Mortar), were absent. The Mortar wanted improved trading terms, and by 1767, the prices for Creek goods had been renegotiated; at Pensacola, he was designated one of the five Great Medal Chiefs of the Upper Creek.

The Creek rapidly agreed borders and ceded some land in return for being forgiven for past offences. Stuart told the Chickasaw to prevent unwelcome traders from entering their lands, since officials in the southern colonies could not do so. After the treaty had been signed, Stuart played an important role in persuading the Upper Creek to agree terms. However, the land ceded by the Creek was soon filled by settlers and unscrupulous traders. Intermittent violence followed, and some backcountry farmers turned against Britain during the War of Independence, because they felt that George III's government was more interested in supporting traders and their Indian customers, than in giving the settlers extra land at the Indians' expense.

The Augusta treaty exposed factionalism within the Creek nation, but tensions also existed between the Creek and Choctaw, who were able to gain weapons from unscrupulous British traders. They had already threatened to prevent any Choctaw from crossing their land on the way to Augusta. One Choctaw chief, Red Shoe, had managed the journey, but he had to be returned to Mobile by a British naval ship. The Creek waged war on the Choctaw to disrupt British trade and to hold disputed hunting grounds east of the Tombigbee River. Each side suffered many casualties, while the conflict disrupted winter hunting, which meant that fewer deerskins were available for trade. Britain distributed free ammunition to the Choctaw, but the Creek depended on credit and accumulated huge debts, which were only cleared by the cession of land to Georgia in 1773. During this conflict, in 1774, the Mortar and a Creek band journeyed toward New Orleans to buy ammunition from the Spanish, but they were attacked by Choctaw warriors, and the Mortar died from wounds to his chest, stomach, and thigh. Eventually, John Stuart brokered peace at the Indians' request, and the war ended in October 1776 at Pensacola.

Elsewhere, the Cherokee were under pressure from settler incursions. Some 2,000 had moved into Cherokee lands by 1775, when the Cherokee went to war against settlements in Georgia, the Carolinas, and Virginia.

Before the War of Independence began in 1775, Britain was finding it difficult and costly to garrison all of its forts, particularly those acquired in the former French territories and Spanish Florida. Main garrisons were maintained at Mobile, Pensacola, and St. Augustine, while Charleston's port could service naval vessels. Britain's new possessions were also vulnerable to the threat of Spanish invasions from New Orleans and Havana in Cuba.

This detail from John Mitchell's 1755 map of the Southeast clearly shows the large area dominated by the Creek.

BURGOYNE'S CAMPAIGN

IN THE SPRING OF 1777, MAJOR GENERAL JOHN BURGOYNE IMPLEMENTED HIS PART OF A BRITISH CAMPAIGN THAT WAS INTENDED TO CUT OFF NEW ENGLAND FROM THE REST OF THE UNITED STATES.

Burgoyne thought that New England was the center of rebellion, and thus a prime target. His complicated plan envisaged a major southward advance from Canada via the Lake Champlain-Lake George route to Albany. A second force (800 men), commanded by Colonel Barry St. Leger, would be augmented by 800 Mohawk and other Iroquois Indians under Joseph Brant. This detachment would travel up the St. Lawrence to Lake Ontario, then move via Oswego to take Fort Stanwix, before proceeding down the Mohawk River valley in the hope that the Iroquois would be suitably impressed. The final aspect of the plan envisaged General Howe advancing from New York up the Hudson Valley to Albany, in a diversionary attack.

Burgoyne advanced with British troops and German mercenaries, together with some 1,000 largely uncontrollable Indians. He took Fort Ticonderoga, his advance being screened by the Indians. However, these auxiliaries started murdering and scalping women and children, including the locally popular Jane MacRae. The regional militia and remnants of the rearguard who had protected the American retreat from Ticonderoga were so incensed that they attacked some Hessian forage columns at nearby Bennington, the mercenaries suffering some 200 dead and 700 missing or captured. Burgoyne's criticism of Indian behavior was so harsh that they left his main advance.

Meanwhile, St. Leger had reached Fort Stanwix (on August 2), which was placed under siege, since its garrison numbered 700 men. Oneida Indians informed Brigadier General of Militia Nicholas Herkimer of events. He summoned 800 militia from Tryon County, New York, and, aided by sixty Oneida warriors, marched to relieve Stanwix.

When St. Leger was informed of this militia column, he hastily assembled an ambush force, concealing it in a defile that seemed suitable for his purpose. Situated 6 miles (10 kilometers) from the fort, and 2 miles (3 kilometers) northwest of Oriskany village, the marshy ravine's road followed a log causeway, which was hemmed in by undergrowth and brush. The ambush involved placing Loyalist Royal Greens and John Butler's Tory Rangers across the western end of the ravine, with Brant's Indians hidden along the flanks. Herkimer's mile-long (1.6-kilometer) column comprised an advance guard of 600 militia, followed by 400 oxcarts, with a 200-man rearguard.

The Indians sprang the trap early, cutting off the rearguard, who fled with some Indians in hot pursuit. Other Mohawk completed an encirclement of Herkimer's main force, which was attacked by Tories and flanking Indians. These used the ploy of charging at an American after he had fired, killing him before he could reload. Herkimer ordered his men to fight in pairs, one man guarding the other while he was reloading. This Battle of Oriskany was immensely bloody, with vicious hand-to-hand fighting between not only Indians and militia, but also the Tryon force and Tories. Knives and bayonets were used, while muskets were swung as clubs. After Tory reinforcements arrived, Butler ordered some of the Royal Greens to turn their coats inside-out and advance, pretending to be a Patriot relief detachment from Fort

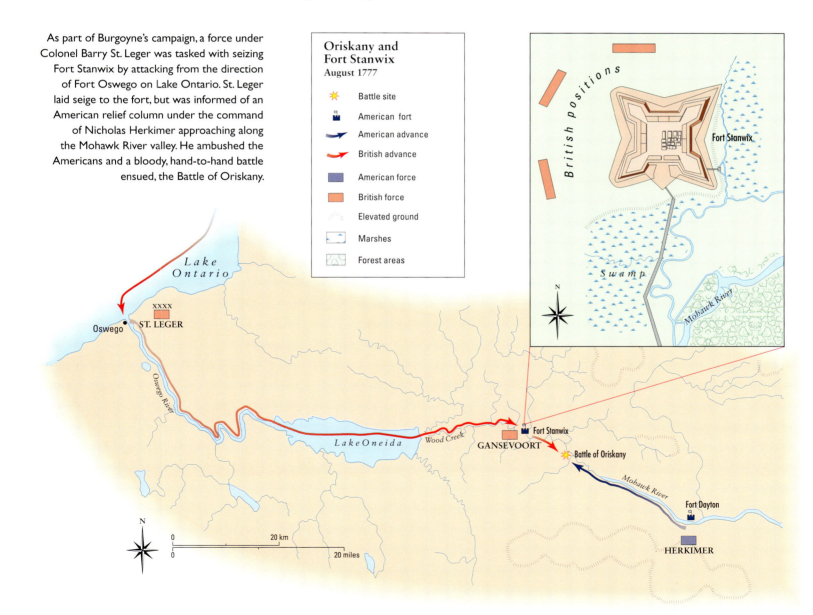

As part of Burgoyne's campaign, a force under Colonel Barry St. Leger was tasked with seizing Fort Stanwix by attacking from the direction of Fort Oswego on Lake Ontario. St. Leger laid seige to the fort, but was informed of an American relief column under the command of Nicholas Herkimer approaching along the Mohawk River valley. He ambushed the Americans and a bloody, hand-to-hand battle ensued, the Battle of Oriskany.

Oriskany and Fort Stanwix
August 1777

✴ Battle site
American fort
American advance
British advance
American force
British force
Elevated ground
Marshes
Forest areas

Opposite: Burgoyne's campaign envisioned a thrust southward from Canada to attack Albany, together with a diversionary attack by Colonel St. Leger on Fort Stanwix and then Albany via the Mohawk River valley. A third force, under General Howe, would approach Albany up the Hudson River valley. The last did not materialize, however, and St. Leger was forced to turn back by Benedict Arnold. Burgoyne, meanwhile, had fought his way to Saratoga, but by then was short of supplies and manpower, while American forces were overwhelming. Two major battles took place, the Battle of Freeman's Farm, in which Arnold stopped the British advance, and the Battle of Bemis Heights. In the latter, Arnold drove the British back to their starting positions, precipitating their surrender.

Stanwix. The ruse was foiled when one of the Patriots recognized a former neighbor, now a Tory, and the Americans opened fire upon the force. The fight raged for hours, but the American militia routed the Indians, and the Tories retreated after them.

The losses were high. The Indians probably lost 150, including some Seneca chiefs, which damaged and dismayed that nation, reported later by a white adoptee, Mary Jemison. The Americans suffered between 150 and 200 dead, some fifty wounded, and about 200 captured. St. Leger's Indians, who had suffered so heavily in combat, found that their encampment at Stanwix had been destroyed by a sortie from the fort. They became disgruntled, abandoning St. Leger when they thought Benedict Arnold was advancing with a 623-strong relief column, a rumor that had been planted by Indian spies.

The surrender of General Burgoyne at Saratoga, October 17, 1777. Some 5,800 British troops laid down their arms, the greatest success enjoyed by the Patriots up to that point in the war, and a turning point in the conflict in the North.

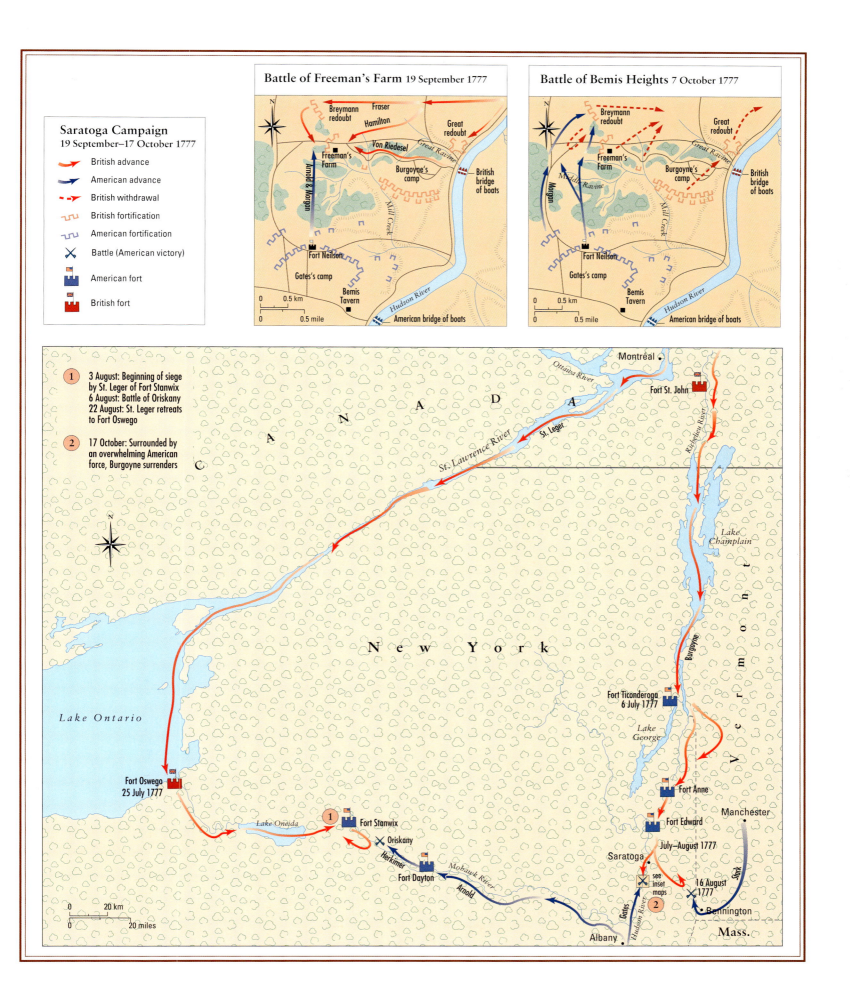

Battle of Freeman's Farm 19 September 1777

Breymann redoubt
Fraser
Hamilton
Freeman's Farm
Von Riedesel
Great Ravine
Great redoubt
British bridge of boats
Arnold & Morgan
Burgoyne's camp
Mill Creek
Fort Neilson
Gates's camp
Bemis Tavern
Hudson River
American bridge of boats

0   0.5 km
0   0.5 mile

Battle of Bemis Heights 7 October 1777

Breymann redoubt
Freeman's Farm
Great redoubt
Great Ravine
British bridge of boats
Morgan
Middle Ravine
Burgoyne's camp
Mill Creek
Fort Neilson
Gates's camp
Bemis Tavern
Hudson River
American bridge of boats

0   0.5 km
0   0.5 mile

Saratoga Campaign
19 September–17 October 1777

➔ British advance

➔ American advance

⇢ British withdrawal

British fortification

American fortification

✕ Battle (American victory)

🏰 American fort

🏰 British fort

1. 3 August: Beginning of siege by St. Leger of Fort Stanwix
6 August: Battle of Oriskany
22 August: St. Leger retreats to Fort Oswego

2. 17 October: Surrounded by an overwhelming American force, Burgoyne surrenders

C A N A D A

Montréal
Ottawa River
Fort St. John
St. Lawrence River
St. Leger
Richelieu River
Lake Champlain

N E W   Y O R K

Lake Ontario

Fort Oswego
25 July 1777

Lake Oneida

Fort Stanwix
Oriskany
Herkimer
Fort Dayton
Mohawk River
Arnold

Fort Ticonderoga
6 July 1777

Lake George

Burgoyne

V e r m o n t

Fort Anne

Fort Edward
July–August 1777

Manchester

Saratoga
see inset maps
16 August 1777
Bennington

Stark

Gates
Hudson River

Albany

Mass.

0   20 km
0   20 miles

THE OHIO CAMPAIGNS

IN THE EARLY 1780s, THE OHIO COUNTRY WAS AFLAME AS THE
BRITISH AND THEIR INDIAN ALLIES ATTACKED AMERICAN FORTS
AND SETTLEMENTS, PROMPTING RETALIATORY RAIDS BY MILITIA.

Opposite: To stop Indian raids on Kentucky sponsored by the British, Clark led a force to capture Kaskaskia, Cahokia, and Vincennes in 1778. The British, under Henry Hamilton, retook Vincennes, but Clark seized it again in 1779 during a daring winter campaign.

A depiction of George Rogers Clark leading the march on Vincennes in 1779. Two years later, he destroyed Chillicothe, home of the Shawnee.

An essential center of the Shawnee people was Chillicothe, on the Little Miami River, near present-day Xenia, Ohio, which was attacked on July 10, 1779, by an American force under Colonel Bowman, while most of the Shawnee warriors were out raiding. In retaliation, the Shawnee assaulted American border settlements, applying particular pressure to new Kentucky outposts and stations. In 1780, a British force was sent in support of the Indians. Commanded by Emanuel Hesse, it comprised some Redcoats, but mainly Great Lakes Indians. They attacked St. Louis and Cahokia, but were beaten back, and Hesse withdrew. One British group retreated up the Illinois River, but was pursued by a combined American, Spanish, and French force. Although the latter failed to catch Hesse, it destroyed a Sauk and Fox village.

Elsewhere, Lieutenant Governor de Peyster at Detroit sent Loyalist Captain Byrd, with a mixed force of Wyandot and Shawnee, to attack American posts on the Maumee and Miami rivers. This group grew to 1,000 men, having been joined by Indian volunteers on the march. Byrd struck at Ruddle's and Martin's stations. At the former, 200 men, women, and children were massacred by uncontrollable Indians, after surrendering to the notorious renegade Simon Girty, because they realized that they could not withstand artillery fire and had opened the gates. Byrd prevented a similar occurrence at Martin's, and managed to protect extra prisoners. Then he defeated a unit of Kentucky militia.

Clark's Operations in the West
1778–79

KICKAPOO   Native American tribes

→ Hamilton's movements

→ Clark's movements

→ Spanish movements

MISSOURI
TERRITORY

MISSOURI

St. Lo

ARKANSAS
TERRITORY

French missionaries visited many northeastern tribes and made many converts, benefiting from their willingness to accept local traditions and cultures. British missionaries were less successful, however, since they considered native beliefs as barbaric.

In 1781, a combined Chickasaw and Tory force captured Fort Jefferson in southwest Kentucky. In retaliation, George Rogers Clark, captor of Kaskaskia, Cahokia, and Vincennes in 1778, led 1,000 men to abandoned Chillicothe, destroying the village and its crops. Then he marched to Piqua Town, near present-day Springfield, Ohio. His force was supported by a single cannon, which was instrumental in defeating the Indians, but an enveloping movement failed. Clark's force suffered sixty casualties, although the Indian losses are unknown. Nevertheless, Indian raids on Kentucky diminished, so they must have been severely defeated in the short term.

In 1782, Tories, under Captain William Caldwell attempted to take Bryan's Station, near Lexington, but failed. While retreating, Caldwell was chased by 200 militia, among whom was Daniel Boone, who had advised against the pursuit. This force, from Harrodsburg, Boonesboro, and Lexington, was ambushed by Girty and some Indians at the Battle of Blue Licks, and the Americans lost seventy men. Clark responded by mobilizing another 1,000 men and marched up the Miami from Louisville, destroying Indian villages and their supplies in his path. The destruction was so great that the winter of 1782–3 saw a reduction in raids.

Opposite: Thrust and counter thrust characterized the fighting between British and American forces, and their Indian allies, in the Ohio Country during the early 1780s.

Elsewhere in the north, Brant was raiding after Sullivan's victory, and his activities led to the violent Gnaddenhutten Massacre. Some Delawares, who had been converted to Moravian Christianity, were ordered north by British Major Peyster for their own safety. However, some returned to their village

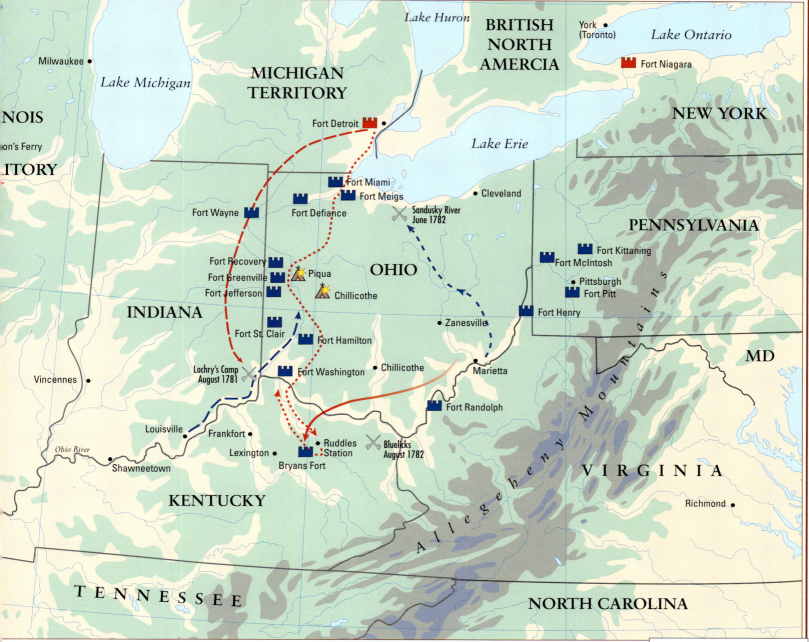

to collect food. Arriving in the aftermath of Brant's raid, they were captured by militia commanded by Colonel David Williamson. Ninety captives (twenty-nine men, twenty-seven women, and thirty-four children) were clubbed to death with mallets. Despite the Pennsylvania legislature's condemnation of the slaughter, no action was ever taken against Colonel Williamson.

The Delaware began retaliatory raids, and another campaign against the Indians was launched by Colonel William Crawford, a personal friend of George Washington. His column was ambushed and surrounded by Loyalists, Shawnees, and Delawares at the Sandusky River. Some 250 Americans died; Crawford was captured, mutilated, and roasted to death, taking two hours to die. Such was the vengeance for Gnaddenhutten.

Fighting against the Delaware and their Wyandot allies continued sporadically until 1817, part of an Indian-white conflict as the new American state expanded westward.

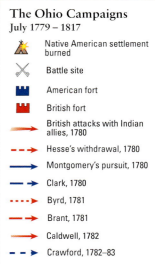

The Ohio Campaigns
July 1779 – 1817

🔥	Native American settlement burned
✕	Battle site
🏰	American fort
🏰	British fort
➤	British attacks with Indian allies, 1780
---➤	Hesse's withdrawal, 1780
➤	Montgomery's pursuit, 1780
- -➤	Clark, 1780
·····➤	Byrd, 1781
—➤	Brant, 1781
➤	Caldwell, 1782
- -➤	Crawford, 1782–83

Wyoming Valley Fighting

A friend of the British, Joseph Brant, a Mohawk, led Indian forces against the Americans over a wide front, leaving a trail of destruction among the settlements.

George Romney's painting of Joseph Brant (1776). Brant was around thirty-three years of age when this portrait was painted while he was visiting London. He was a major asset to the British during the American War of Independence.

Joseph Brant was the most important Mohawk participant in the American War of Independence. Born as Thayendanegea in 1742 or 1743, he was educated at Eleazor Wheelock's Indian Charity School in Lebanon, Connecticut, having been sent there by William Johnson, the British Indian Superintendant and lover of Brant's sister, Molly. Brant owed his influence among the Iroquois not only to his own abilities, but also to Molly's support, and his marriage to the daughter of a Mohawk chief.

In 1776, Brant was sent to London, where he met King George III, Lord George Germain, and James Boswell; he was painted by Romney and given a commission in the British Army. He complained to Germain about encroachments on Mohawk land by settlers in Albany, and appealed for redress.

Brant's earliest military exploits were fighting for Britain against Pontiac, and at the Battle of Long Island. In July 1777, British and Iroquois representatives met at Oswego, New York, where Brant persuaded four of the six nations to support the British; eventually, the Oneida and Tuscarora chose the American cause, an act that caused civil war in Iroquoia.

In August 1777, during the Saratoga Campaign, Brant and 800 Iroquois joined Colonel St. Leger in the failed attack on Fort Stanwix. Then they fought an American relief force under General Herkimer at the Battle of Oriskany. Herkimer was stopped by a vicious engagement, although eventually his men routed the Indians, 150 of whom became casualties. Brant then burned the Oneida village of Oriska, while Americans assaulted Mohawk settlements, forcing Mary Brant to flee to the Onondaga.

In the spring and summer of 1778, Brant's warriors, supported by Loyalists, raided several American settlements, including Sacandaga, Cobleskill, Springfield, and German Flats. Brant always insisted that no settlers should be attacked unless they fought the Indians. In July 1778, Loyalist John Butler led his Rangers and Indians, mainly Seneca and Cayuga, into the Wyoming Valley in Pennsylvania, where they captured eight forts. At Forty Fort, Colonel Zebulon Butler led his 300 militia outside the

The Wyoming Valley Massacre, as portrayed in the nineteenth century. A force of Rangers and Indians under Loyalist John Butler fell on the American militia from Fort Forty after they had surrendered, killing 227 of them.

walls, where they were overwhelmed; 227 militia were killed, and many were wounded. This became known as the Wyoming Valley Massacre. A thousand homes were burned and a thousand cows seized, together with pigs and sheep. Many of the settlers who fled died from hunger and exhaustion in the Pocono great swamp.

On November 11, 1778, Brant and Captain Walter (Hell Hound) Butler, son of John Butler, launched some 700 Rangers and Indians against an American fort in the Cherry Valley, near Lake Otsego in the upper Susquehanna Valley. The fort was ably defended by the 7th Massachusetts Regiment under Colonel Ichabod Alden. However, since Alden had not posted pickets on the Indians' approach trail, many settlers failed to reach the stockade, and thirty-two were killed. Brant managed to restrain some Indians and Loyalists, however, saving many innocent women and children.

Although General John Sullivan was sent against the Iroquois and Brant in retaliation, Brant continued his raids. In 1780, he attacked Minisink, New York, where his forces caused forty-five casualties among the militia. In 1781, he foiled an American expedition against Detroit.

In 1782, Brant planned a campaign against American villages in the Ohio Valley. His Indians turned the border regions into a war zone after the end of the Saratoga campaign. A reign of fear spread throughout the northeastern frontier, and the occasional wanton cruelty of the Indians caused many settlers to move east, while the barbarous war between Loyalist and Patriot increased in viciousness. In Tryon County, New York, during the War of Independence, 12,000 farms were abandoned, 380 women were widowed, and 2,000 children lost their fathers.

A brilliant military leader, Brant ranged over a wide front, paralyzing militia units, destroying provisions and settlements, and diverting the Continentals from their eastern war zones.

SULLIVAN'S INVASION OF IROQUOIA

IN RESPONSE TO BRITISH INSPIRED ATTACKS IN THE WYOMING VALLEY, AND OTHER RAIDS, DURING 1778, WASHINGTON WAS ORDERED BY CONGRESS TO DESTROY THE IROQUOIS.

A contemporary portrait of Major General John Sullivan, who was ordered to destroy the Iroquois by George Washington.

Washington gave Major General John Sullivan the job of crushing Iroquois power, but he never achieved that goal, because he was unable to force a final battle against the Haudenosaunee. Before the campaign began, Washington outlined Sullivan's tasks: *"The immediate objects are the total destruction and devastation of their [Iroquois] settlements and the capture of as many persons of every age and sex as possible. It will be essential to ruin their crops now in the ground and prevent their planting more."*

Sullivan's force comprised some 2,300 Continentals, 1,000 men under General Clinton, and 1,100 volunteers, an army so great that the Iroquois felt unable to confront it and withdrew. Sullivan's strategy involved an advance from Easton, Pennsylvania, up the Wyoming and Susquehanna valleys to the New York Finger Lakes. At the same time, Clinton's force would depart from Canajoharie, near Fort Dayton, and join Sullivan via the Mohawk or Susquehanna valleys. A supporting diversionary attack into the Alleghenies was implemented by Colonel Daniel Brodhead out of Fort Pitt.

As Sullivan advanced, Loyalist Colonel Butler's Tories and Joseph Brant's Iroquois moved toward him, thereby denuding Iroquois territory of its defenses. Accordingly, Brodhead entered the Alleghenies with 600 men, burning eight villages and 500 acres (200 hectares) of crops before returning to Fort Pitt. Butler and Brant decided to confront Sullivan at Chemung, assembling a force of 200 Redcoats, 200 Loyalists, and 600 Indians. Their ambush was spotted by Sullivan's advance guard, however, and the general attempted an enveloping maneuver, aided by artillery. The tactic failed because the British force retreated rather

than face the artillery and Continentals. This Battle of Newtown (August 29, 1779) allowed Sullivan into Iroquois territory, where his force burned Indian villages, stripped fields of corn, and removed the bark from fruit trees to kill them. Butler and Brant could not prevent this carnage. One Indian success, however, was the destruction of a twenty-three-man American patrol near Chenesee; its commander, Captain Boyd, was tortured to death.

In retaliation, Sullivan burned Chenesee, before withdrawing to Easton. At the same time, he sent

British General John Burgoyne negotiates with the Haudenosaunee, hoping to gain their support for his 1777 campaign. In 1778, American revolutionary forces, under John Sullivan, took the field against Britain's Indian allies.

a Colonel Butler east of Lake Cayuga to incinerate more Indian townships, before proceeding to Fort Stanwix. In total, Sullivan torched forty Iroquois settlements and their food supplies, which forced the Iroquois to seek sanctuary and aid at Fort Niagara, rendering them even more dependent upon British resources. Mary Jemison, a captive and later adoptee of the Seneca, a woman who refused to return to American society when given the chance, remarked upon the devastation: *"They ... left nothing but our bare soil and timber ... There was not a mouthful of any kind of sustenance left, not even enough to keep a child one day from perishing with hunger."*

Indian raids continued, however, so Sullivan's actions could be deemed a failure. Nevertheless, he weakened Iroquois influence and projected American power into the western lands, south of the Great

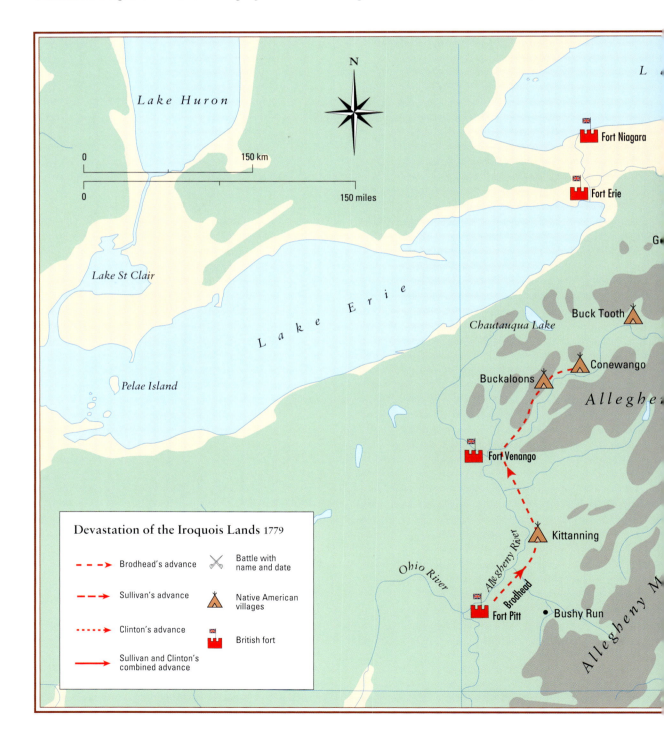

Lakes, a basis for later territorial claims. Yet he failed to capture Indian women and children to use as hostages and a lever against further raiding. The Iroquois were also weakened, the Confederation becoming split along religious lines. Many Mohawks were members of the Church of England, while a number of Oneida fighters had converted to the puritanism of Bostonian Reverend Kirkland. The Oneida had helped Sullivan, and soon a civil war broke out among the Iroquois, the Tuscarora and Oneida being attacked by Brant's Mohawks. The Oneida sought refuge with Americans around Schenectady, suffering the same cold and hunger as other Iroquois at Niagara. In the meantime, the Onondaga had suffered a disastrous plague in 1777. No longer could the Confederation mount large attacks like those at Cherry Valley, Wyoming Valley, and the German Flats.

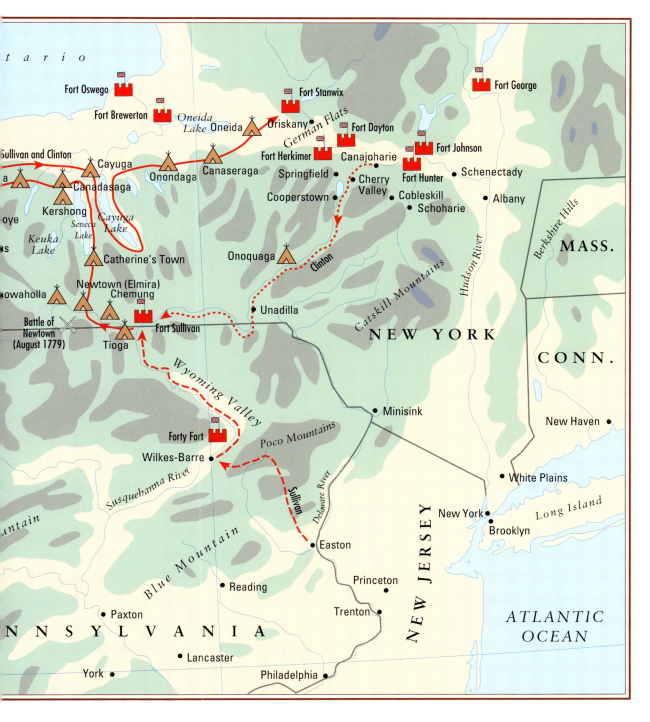

Sullivan's campaign against the Iroquois was based on a three-pronged assault on their homeland to the south of the Great Lakes. Although he severely weakened the tribal alliance, he was unable to force a final, decisive battle.

CHEROKEES AND THE REVOLUTION

PUSHED INTO WAR BY CONTINUAL ENCROACHMENTS ON THEIR LAND BY COLONIAL SETTLERS, THE CHEROKEE FOUND THEMSELVES FACING A DEVASTATING RETALIATION.

Between 1768 and 1775, the Cherokee ceded about 50,000 square miles (130,000 square kilometers) of territory to colonial governments to ensure peaceful relations. Nevertheless, by 1776, settlers were squatting on Cherokee land on the Tennessee/North Carolina border, along the Holston, Nolichuky, and Watauga rivers. Not surprisingly, the Cherokee responded favorably to the incitement to war by Shawnee, Delaware, and Mohawk emissaries.

A campaign was to be waged on three fronts. Abram of Chilhowee would attack Watauga and Nolichuky settlements; Raven of Chota would wipe out Carter's Valley settlers; and Dragging Canoe, the most hostile Cherokee, would assault settlers on the Holston. Furthermore, warriors from the Cherokee Middle Towns would attack North Carolina, while South Carolina and Georgia would receive attention from the Lower Towns. However, the settlers were forwarned, and surprise was lost. The war began with attacks on Georgia and South Carolina; in July, thirty-seven settlers were killed along the Catawba River. Dragging Canoe was wounded during an assault on Eaton's Station and forced to retreat, leaving fourteen dead. Abram's fighters laid siege to Fort Caswell on the Watauga River for two weeks, but withdrew when American reinforcements arrived.

The Americans retaliated by torching Lower Town villages. In late July, 200 Georgia militia attacked two towns on the Upper Chattahoochie and Tugaloo rivers. In August, 1,800 men advanced on the Lower Towns, but were ambushed by 1,000 Cherokee warriors at Black Hole. The Americans routed the Indians, however, and moved to contemporary Topton, burning six towns. In September, thirty-six Cherokee villages were burned in the Middle Towns and Valley Towns on the Valley and Highwassee rivers. Later, Sticoe and another village on the Oconaluftee River were burned.

A fresh onslaught occurred in October, when William Christian and 1,700 men crossed the Holston, advancing across the French Broad and Little Tennessee rivers to Dragging Canoe's village, Island Town. The Indians had fled, but his men destroyed 50,000 bushels of corn and 15,000 bushels of potatoes. By late October, the Cherokee had been forced to sue for peace, aghast at the destruction just as winter was approaching. They signed two humiliating treaties, at Delwitt's Corner (May 20, 1777) and Long Island (July 20, 1777). The first forced the cession of all remaining Lower, Middle, and Valley Cherokee territory in South Carolina, with the exception of a small strip along the western border. By the second treaty, the Overhill Cherokee ceded all lands east of the Blue Ridge Mountains, which expelled them from Virginia, and halved their lands in Tennessee and North Carolina. Later, in 1783, Georgia made the Cherokee part with lands near the Chattahoochie River. In total, the Cherokee lost 10,000 square miles (26,000 square kilometers).

A later flare-up occurred in 1779, in the Chickamauga Cherokee villages on the Tennessee. A thousand warriors under Dragging Canoe, supplied by the British, attacked settlers, but a 600-man North Carolina/Virginia force, under Colonel Evan Shelby, invaded the Chickamauga territory and destroyed eleven villages. In the fall, a South Carolina column eradicated six more towns.

In 1780, backcountry Patriots left their villages to engage Loyalists in the Battle of King's Mountain, which took place in the upper Piedmont, near the border between North and South Carolina. The Cherokee were encouraged by their absence and began raiding again. In the fall, Colonels Campbell and Sevier assaulted the Overhill Cherokee, destroying towns and crops, and leaving the Indians to starve through the winter. In the spring of the following year, Campbell and Sevier moved against the Middle Cherokee, along the upper French Broad, wiping out more villages and food. This forced the Cherokee chiefs to sign the second Treaty of Long Island (July 26, 1781), by which they ceded another slice of territory. Thus, Cherokee power was broken. Finally, in 1785, by the Treaty of Hopewell, the Americans purchased a further strip of Cherokee land in North Carolina.

The Battle of King's Mountain in 1780, between Loyalists and Patriots in the upper Piedmont, stripped the settlements of their protection, encouraging the Cherokee to raid them. This provoked a vicious backlash.

THE TREATY OF PARIS, 1783

THE AMERICAN WAR OF INDEPENDENCE WAS ENDED BY THE TREATY OF PARIS IN 1783, BUT FOR NATIVE AMERICANS, IT SIMPLY MEANT THE LOSS OF EVEN MORE LAND.

Daniel Boone leading settlers through the Cumberland Gap, by George Caleb Bingham (1851).

Opposite: The United States came into being with the Treaty of Paris, but no one consulted the Indians about the massive land grant.

The Treaty of Paris ended the American Revolution, and its first article granted American independence, giving the new country the lands between the Great Lakes and the 31st Parallel to the northern border of Spanish Florida, and westward to the Mississippi River. Britain retained Canada.

One group of participants in the recent war who were the real losers were the Native Americans, who were not consulted over the expansion of the United States into their lands. Control of the new territories depended upon military forts at Niagara, Detroit, and Michilimackinac. Britain refused to evacuate these posts, using them to distribute aid and arms to its former Indian allies.

The organization of the new lands was accomplished by the Northwest Ordinances of 1784, 1785, and 1787. The first established the national American domain, while that of 1785 required that land be surveyed by a rectangular system, providing a map and plan in advance of land sales to private citizens. Townships of 6 square miles (15.5 square kilometers) were divided into 640-acre (260-hectare) sections. Monies received from land sales were to be retained, in part, for establishing public schools; other proceeds became revenue for the national government. Indeed, such funds were the main form of state revenue until 1830. When a designated area contained 20,000 people,

Boundary not defined

Lake of the Woods

BRITISH NORTH AMERICA

Lake Superior

CANADA

St. Lawrence River

District of Maine

Fort Michilimackinac

Fort Oswegarchie

Pte-au-Fer

Lake Huron

Lake Michigan

VERMONT
NEW HAMPSHIRE

MASSACHUSETTS

SPANISH–LOUISIANA

Detroit

Fort Miami

Lake Ontario

Fort Oswego

Fort Niagara

Lake Erie

NEW YORK

CONN.

R.I.

UNITED STATES

Pennsylvania

NEW JERSEY

MARYLAND

DELAWARE

Ohio River

VIRGINIA

Mississippi River

NORTH CAROLINA

ATLANTIC OCEAN

SOUTH CAROLINA

GEORGIA

FLORIDA

Gulf of Mexico

N

Treaty of Paris 1783

— Proclamation Line of 1763 and extent of original Thirteen Colonies

--- U.S. demanded boundary of 1779

Spanish–Louisiana

British territory, 1783

U.S. territory defined by the Treaty of Paris, 1783

disputed with Spain and its Native American allies until the Treaty of San Lorenzo, 1795

disputed with Britain until 1842

British posts in U.S. territory, held until the Treaty of 1794, evacuated by June 1795

The Mitchell Map. Drawn by John Mitchell, this map is the most comprehensive map of the eastern portion of North America created during the Colonial era. It was used to define the borders of the United States during the negotiations for the Treaty of Paris, and subsequently to resolve border disputes between the United States and Canada, and between individual states. This huge map measures around 6.5 feet (2 meters) wide by 4.5 feet (1.4 meters) high.

Opposite: Following the Treaty of Paris, many colonists who had remained loyal to Britain continued to live in the United States. A significant number (between 60,000 and 70,000), however, migrated to Canada, Florida, and the West Indies.

After the war, Britain rewarded its Iroquois allies and the members of Butler's Rangers with land grants.

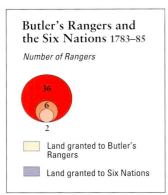

Butler's Rangers and the Six Nations 1783–85

Number of Rangers

36
6
2

Land granted to Butler's Rangers

Land granted to Six Nations

a convention could be held, a constitution adopted, and the area would become a Territory with its own legislature and a non-voting delegate to Congress. When the population of the Territory equaled the free population of the smallest state (about 60,000), it became a State of the Union.

Obviously, the peace treaty and the ordinances envisaged demographic movements into the new lands, and the state had a vested interest in land sales for revenue generation. However, the 1787 ordinance stated that the utmost good faith would be observed toward the Indians, and that their lands and property would never be taken from them. The earlier Royal Proclamation of 1763 forbade colonial settlement west of the Appalachians, while the 1784 Stanwix treaty had established some sort of Indian-American border, albeit constantly disputed.

Irrespective of good intentions, settlers flooded into Indian lands. By 1790, Kentucky had a white population of 74,000, while Tennessee and other frontier regions had 36,000. By 1800, 300,000 people had passed through the Cumberland Gap; avoiding populous Kentucky, many settled in present-day Missouri. Between 1784 and 1789, government officials pressured Indian leaders into land cession treaties, forcing Native Americans into small reservations. The means of acquiring land were decidedly dubious, and most Indians denounced the agreements.

The Iroquois suffered especially, being treated as inferiors and losing much territory to land companies and speculators. Some of their land was granted to war veterans in lieu of cash. Eventually, the Iroquois lost all their lands west of New York and Pennsylvania, as did some of their dependent tribes; instead, they were given small reservations in New York. Alcohol was often used as a bribe, as were threats. Pressure was also applied to the Delaware, Wyandot, Ottowa, Chippewa, Shawnee, and other smaller tribes.

George Washington had been a land speculator, which may have colored his administration's attitude toward Indians. The legal title to Indian land would be held by Indians until it was acquired by the government through fair negotiation or a "just" war, which would terminate the title. Many settlers squatted illegally on non-ceded lands, which provoked the Indians into driving them away. In response, the government would send in military forces to protect the squatters and seize land from the Indians by coercive treaties after the conflict.

Indian culture and identity were under threat from drunkenness and being forced to live on tiny reservations surrounded by a sea of new, hostile settlers. Eventually, these conditions prompted the emergence of visionaries and leaders who sought to reverse the decline, men such as Handsome Lake with his Good Word (gaiwiio), Little Turtle, Tecumseh, and Tenskwatawa.

Grand River Tract, purchased by Britain from the Mississauga Indians to make land grants to Mohawks and other of the Six nations who allied with the British fought to prevent American Independence

Land set aside for Butler's Rangers. The Rangers commanded by Col. John Butler were composed of Loyalists from New York and Pennsylvania; their headquarters had been at Niagara

NICHOL
WOOLWICH
WATERLOO GUELPH
PUSHLINCH
DUMFRIES
BEVERLY
FLAMBORO'S
ANCASTER
BARTON
GLANFORD SALTFLEET
PINBROOK

SIX NATIONS
Grand River

Western areas

Lake Ontario

Kingston areas

Butler's Rangers

Lake Erie

NEW YORK

0   15 miles

Empire Loyalists 1776–92

Spanish–Louisiana

British territory

United States, 1783

8,000 — approximate number of Loyalist settlements

Migration routes of Loyalists, 1776–83

Area of Loyalist settlement

Lake Superior

BRITISH NORTH AMERICA

10,000

Québec

Lake Huron

Montréal

1,000

Lake Michigan

St. Lawrence R.

1783

Lake Ontario

1783

Lake Erie

NEW YORK

District of Maine

Gulf of St. Lawrence

Isle St. John

1,000

Cape Breton I.

Nova Scotia

Moncton

13,500

St. John

Halifax

20,000

Shelbourne

To England

9000

1776

1792

1783

NEW HAMPSHIRE

Boston

MASSACHUSETTS

CONN

R.I.

New York

PENNSYLVANIA

NEW JERSEY

MARYLAND

DELAWARE

U N I T E D

S T A T E S

VIRGINIA

Norfolk

NORTH CAROLINA

1782–83

To Sierra Leone

1,200

Spanish–Louisiana

1781

SOUTH CAROLINA

Charleston

GEORGIA

Savannah

Mobile

1782–83

St. Augustine

1782–83

1783

1783

FLORIDA

Gulf of Mexico

A T L A N T I C

O C E A N

N

Bahamas

7,000

1783

To St. Lucia 400

To Antigua 400

To Jamaica

8,000

To Jamaica

War for the Ohio Country

ALTHOUGH THE TREATY OF PARIS ENDED THE BRITISH-AMERICAN CONFLICT, TRIBES FORMERLY ALLIED TO THE BRITISH CONTINUED TO RESIST INCURSIONS INTO LANDS NORTH OF THE OHIO RIVER.

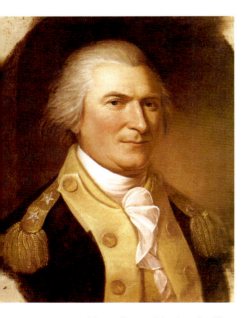

Major General Arthur St. Clair mounted two expeditions against the Indians north of the Ohio, but was soundly defeated.

Opposite: Throughout the late eighteenth and early nineteenth centuries, the Indians of the East resisted the westward push, but in the end had to give ground.

After the Treaty of Paris had been signed, Congress had begun land-cession talks with the Indians to clarify ownership. The northern tribes met American officials at Fort Stanwix in 1784, while southern tribes met them at Hopewell, South Carolina, in 1785. The United States took the resultant treaties as evidence that the land belonged to America, and settlers were allowed in; however, the Indians denied the veracity of the treaties. The Shawnee, Miami, Chippewa, and Potawatomi continued to receive encouragement, food, and arms from the British at Detroit and other forts that should have been evacuated.

The Indians attempted to create a confederacy that could make peace, and establish a boundary between them and the Americans. The tribes themselves differed over possible boundaries, but these tensions ceased when two expeditions invaded their lands. George Rogers Clark led 1,000 Kentuckians up the Wabash River, but failed to engage the Indians; his drunken and disorderly force went home. A second Kentuckian raid led to the torching of Shawnee villages on the Miami River, during which Indians were murdered, tortured, and scalped. The construction of Fort Washington (1789) on the north bank of the Ohio in Miami lands, together with American settlements—the origins of Cincinnati—totally enraged the Shawnee and Miami.

Commanded by Little Turtle and Blue Jacket, the tribes struck settlements repeatedly, killing whole families. Indeed, between 1783 and 1790, the Indians killed, wounded, or enslaved 1,500 people. In the meantime, incidents involving Chickasaws and other western tribes painted a picture of a potential pan-Indian war. Major General Arthur St. Clair tried to negotiate peace with the Indians, who insisted that all Americans should withdraw from north of the Ohio.

Native American Resistance
1785–1842

Area ceded 1768–74

✷ Center of insurrection

✕ Battle site

Native American settlement

Fort

Borders c. 1840

A depiction of Major General Anthony Wayne, creator of the Legion of the United States.

Opposite: With the Treaty of Paris, land to the north of the Ohio River became part of the United States. It was designated the Northwest Territory, but eventually would form the State of Ohio. The first settlement was Marietta, founded by the Ohio Company of Associates in 1788. Two areas, the Western Reserve and Virginia Military District, were used by Connecticut and Virginia to provide land grants to Revolutionary War veterans.

Subsequently, St. Clair mobilized some 1,500 men, comprising regulars and Kentucky and Pennsylvania volunteers, placing them under the command of Brigadier General Josiah Harmer. This force lumbered from Fort Washington through forested country and burned the evacuated Indian town of Kekionga on the Maumee River. Several engagements followed, during which 183 Americans were killed and some militiamen ran away; Harmer withdrew. The exultant Indians continued raiding settlements and Ohio River boats, but also moved their villages down the Maumee to its confluence with the Auglaize River.

After this shambles, St. Clair was ordered to mount a second expedition. In August 1791, he advanced from Fort Washington to Fort Recovery, Ohio, with the entire regular army (600 men) and 1,500 militia, plus 200 camp followers, both women and children. By mid-October, St. Clair had begun construction of Fort Hamilton on the Miami, which was followed by Fort Jefferson, about 5 miles (8 kilometers) south of present-day Greenville, after 300 Kentucky reinforcements arrived. By early November, St. Clair had reached the banks of the Wabash, but had been spotted by Indian scouting parties, among them the young Shawnee warrior Tecumseh. On November 4, Little Turtle and Blue Jacket led a force of warriors from fourteen tribes against the Americans. The latter were crushed, with 623 killed, 258 wounded, and 197 camp followers scalped. Indian losses were twenty-one killed and forty wounded.

Next, Congress ordered Major General Anthony Wayne to build a larger army, which he started in 1792, stamping out drunkenness, malingering, and poor discipline. His command, known as the Legion of the United States and comprising between 3,000 and 4,000 men, advanced from Pittsburgh to Greenville, and then to what is now Toledo, Ohio. Opposing Wayne were some 1,500 Indians. They were located a few miles from the British post of Fort Miami in an area known as Fallen Timbers, because of the many trees that had been toppled by a tornado. The region was full of brush and swamp, and the Indians made effective use of the landscape to harrass the Americans as they passed through. However, there was no American attack for several days, and many Indians gave up waiting and withdrew. When the attack did come, repeated bayonet charges broke the remaining Indians, who fled to Fort Miami, where the gates were shut. Subsequently, the Americans torched the Indian villages and thousands of acres of crops. For 133 casualties, Wayne managed to subdue the local tribes for decades, the conflict being ended by the Treaty of Greenville in 1795.

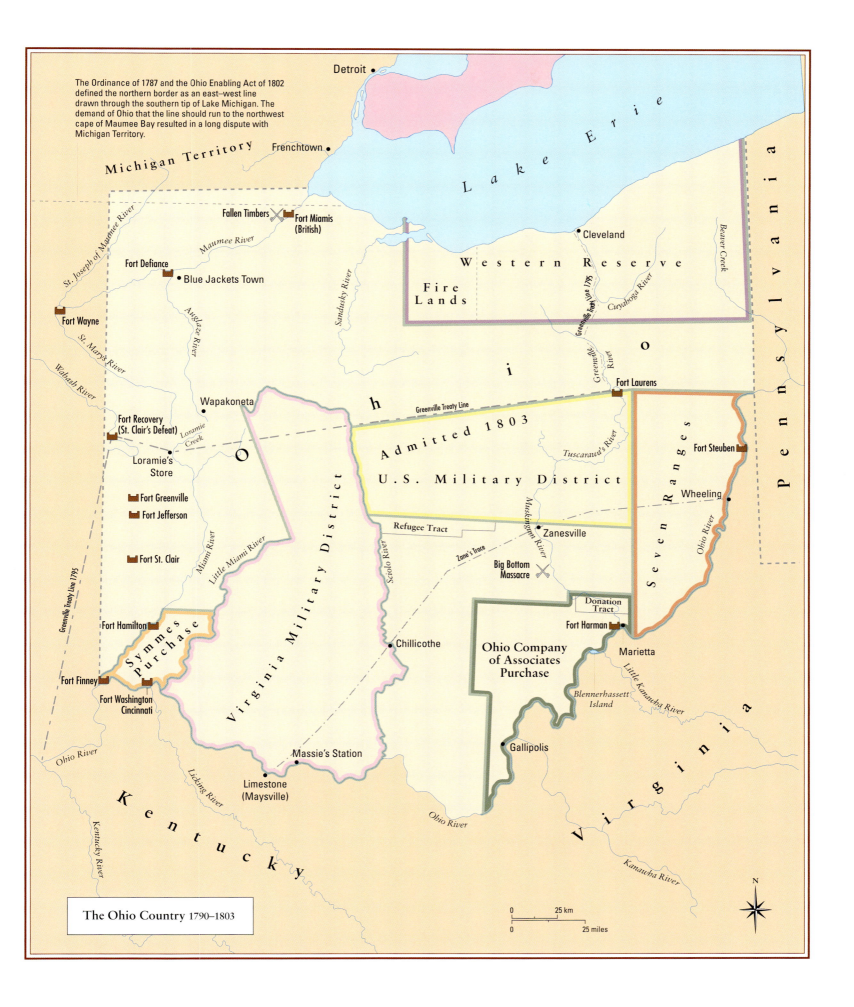

The Ordinance of 1787 and the Ohio Enabling Act of 1802 defined the northern border as an east–west line drawn through the southern tip of Lake Michigan. The demand of Ohio that the line should run to the northwest cape of Maumee Bay resulted in a long dispute with Michigan Territory.

Detroit

Michigan Territory

Frenchtown

Lake Erie

Fallen Timbers
Fort Miamis (British)

Maumee River

St. Joseph of Maumee River

Fort Defiance
Blue Jackets Town

Cleveland

Western Reserve

Fire Lands

Greenville Treaty Line 1795

Beaver Creek

Cuyahoga River

Fort Wayne

St. Marys River

Wabash River

Sandusky River

Anglaize River

o

h

i

Pennsylvania

Wapakoneta

Fort Recovery (St. Clair's Defeat)

Loramie Creek

O

Loramie's Store

Fort Greenville

Fort Jefferson

Fort St. Clair

Greenville River

Fort Laurens

Greenville Treaty Line

Admitted 1803

U.S. Military District

Tuscarawas River

Seven Ranges

Fort Steuben

Refugee Tract

Muskingum River

Zanesville

Wheeling

Ohio River

Virginia Military District

Miami River

Little Miami River

Scioto River

Zane's Trace

Big Bottom Massacre

Donation Tract

Fort Hamilton

Symmes Purchase

Greenville Treaty Line 1795

Fort Finney

Fort Washington
Cincinnati

Chillicothe

Ohio Company of Associates Purchase

Fort Harman

Marietta

Blennerhassett Island

Little Kanawha River

Ohio River

Massie's Station

Limestone (Maysville)

Licking River

Gallipolis

Ohio River

Kentucky

Kentucky River

Virginia

Kanawha River

0   25 km
0   25 miles

N

The Ohio Country 1790–1803

THE TREATY OF GREENVILLE, 1795

MAJOR GENERAL WAYNE'S VICTORY AT THE BATTLE OF FALLEN
TIMBERS FORCED THE NORTHWESTERN INDIANS TO A PEACE
COUNCIL LEST EVEN MORE VILLAGES AND CROPS BE DESTROYED.

Totally disoriented and broken militarily, bereft of aid from their British supporters, and tormented by raids across the Ohio by Kentucky settlers, the Indians met Major General Wayne at Fort Greenville, Ohio. The meeting, which took place in the summer of 1795, drew in many tribes, including Shawnee, Potawatomi, Kickapoo, Delaware, Ottowa, Wyandot, Ojibwa, and Miami, as well as other smaller tribes. On August 3, a treaty was signed by which the Indian nations ceded 25,000 square miles (65,000 square kilometers) north of the Ohio, more than half of contemporary Ohio. The boundary began opposite the mouth of the Kentucky River, on the north shore of the Ohio, and ran to Fort Recovery, then to Loramie's Creek and Fort Laurens on the Tuscarawas tributary of the Muskingum River, crossing the portage to the Cuyahoga River and along it to Lake Erie. The Indians retained a strip along Lake Erie, a triangle of land in Indiana, and sixteen small patches for trading posts and strategic waterways. In return, Wayne stated that the United States would renounce claims *"to all other Indian lands, northward of the river Ohio, eastward of the Mississippi, and westward and southward of the Great Lakes, and the waters uniting them, according to the boundary line agreed on by the United States and the King of Great Britain."*

The agreement was remarkably precise: *"The Indian tribes who have a right to these lands, are … to enjoy them, so long as they please, without any molestation from the United States; but when those tribes … shall be disposed to sell their lands, or any part of them, they are to be sold only to the United States; and until such sale, the United States will protect all the said Indian tribes … against all citizens of the United States, and against all other white persons who intrude upon the same. And the said Indian tribes again acknowledge themselves to be under the protection of the said United States, and no other power whatsoever."*

The United States benefited from the peace because the British were compelled to quit the forts south of the Great Lakes, which they had been occupying against the terms of the 1783 Treaty of Paris. However, the British were still allowed to trade with the Indians, according to the terms of the 1795 Jay treaty. Settlers flooded into the Ohio Country, totaling some 45,000 by 1800, and 250,000 by 1812. By that date, roads were passable, small cities abustle, and the countryside covered by cultivated fields.

In 1803, the United States purchased Louisiana from the French, who had recently regained control of the region from Spain. At the same time, President Thomas Jefferson sought to grab as much Indian territory as possible that fronted the Mississippi. Governor Harrison of the Indiana Territory bought large tracts of land, promising future annuities to the Indians. By 1809, the United States had gained title to lands along the Ohio River to the Mississippi, and up that river to the Wisconsin River. Jefferson thought that when hunting lands were purchased, the Indians would become "civilized" and turn to farming instead. Moreover, the acquisition of lands hundreds of miles from the nearest settlement demonstrated the possibility for eventual future white expansion.

The Battle of Fallen Timbers, an illustration from *Harper's* magazine, 1896. The decisive defeat in this battle of the Indians of the Western Lakes Confederacy by "Mad Anthony" Wayne's Legion of the United States forced the tribes to the negotiating table and led to the Treaty of Greenville.

Howard Chandler Christy's painting depicting the signing of the Treaty of Greenville.

Although the Treaty of Greenville was signed by almost all of the Indian leadership, many of the young warriors, including Tecumseh, refused to recognize its legality and resisted all incursions upon their lands with violence. Historians have called Tecumseh and similar thinkers Nativist, because of their refusal to reach an accommodation with the white man; as such, they were inclined to bind Native American nations into a pan-Indian force based on prophecy, spiritualism, and combined military might.

The Frontier in 1800

Area of settlement

Fort

BRITISH NORTH AMERICA

Disputed with Britain

To Mass.

Lake Superior

Lake Huron

Lake Michigan

Fort Detroit

Lake Ontario

Lake Erie

Portland

N.H.

Vermont

Salem
Boston

New York

Albany

Mass.
Worcester
Providence
Conn.   R.I.
New Bedford

Territory
Northwest
of Ohio River

Pennsylvania

New York ● Brooklyn

Lancaster

New Jersey

Philadelphia

Wilmington

Indiana
Territory

Chillicothe

Cincinnati

Louisville
Lexington

Cumberland
Baltimore
Maryland Delaware
Washington

Fort Orleans

St. Louis

Staunton

Richmond

Virginia

Williamsburg

Kentucky

Tennessee

North
Carolina

Raleigh

Charlotte

Louisiana

Ceded by Spain to France in secret treaty, 1800
Possession not taken by France until 1803

Memphis

South
Carlonia

Augusta

Charleston

Arkansas Post

Territory
South of
Ohio River

Georgia

Savannah

Mississippi Territory

Natchitoches
Nacogdoches

Natchez

West Florida

Pensacola

St. Augustine

New Orleans

East
Florida

By 1800, the settlements
were pushing steadily
westward with disastrous
consequences for the
Indians.

ATLANTIC OCEAN

N

Gulf of Mexico

Bahamas

400 km

400 miles

A late-nineteenth-century depiction of Tecumseh, chief of the Shawnee.

Opposite: The cession of Indian lands that would form Michigan, Indiana, and Illinois prompted Tecumseh to urge resistance.

TECUMSEH AND THE PROPHET

DISPUTES OVER THE TREATY OF GREENVILLE AND SUBSEQUENT LAND CESSIONS CAUSED MUCH INDIAN DISQUIET. FROM THIS EMERGED TWO CHARACTERS WHO WOULD INSPIRE RESISTANCE.

In 1803 and 1804, through treaties signed at Vincennes, Indiana, the Kaskaskia had given up a large part of Illinois territory, while the Sauk and Fox had surrendered some 15 million acres (6 million hectares) south of the Wisconsin River. By the end of 1807, the United States had acquired eastern Michigan, southern Indiana, and nearly all of Illinois. This was the work of Governor William Henry Harrison of Indiana Territory.

In response, two Shawnees, Tecumseh and his brother, Tenskwatawa, set out to inspire a united Indian resistance. Tecumseh was unusual in that he had studied American and world history, and literature under the guidance of Rebecca Galloway, a white friend. He began to consider himself as a Native American first and Shawnee second; he believed that the Indian nations should confederate and create their own state in the Great Lakes and Ohio Valley region. He also felt that no Indian individual nor nation had the right to sell land to white people.

Tenskwatawa became known as the Prophet, because he had predicted an eclipse that occurred in 1805, although he might have known about the event anyway. He preached the virtues of old Indian traditions and the need for Native Americans to cast from their lives any vestiges of the white man's world, especially alcohol. The brothers traveled among the tribes spreading their word, and in 1808, they founded the village of Prophetstown at the confluence of the Wabash River and Tippecanoe Creek. Indians from many tribes in the Northeast—Shawnee, Delaware, Wyandot, and Ottawa—

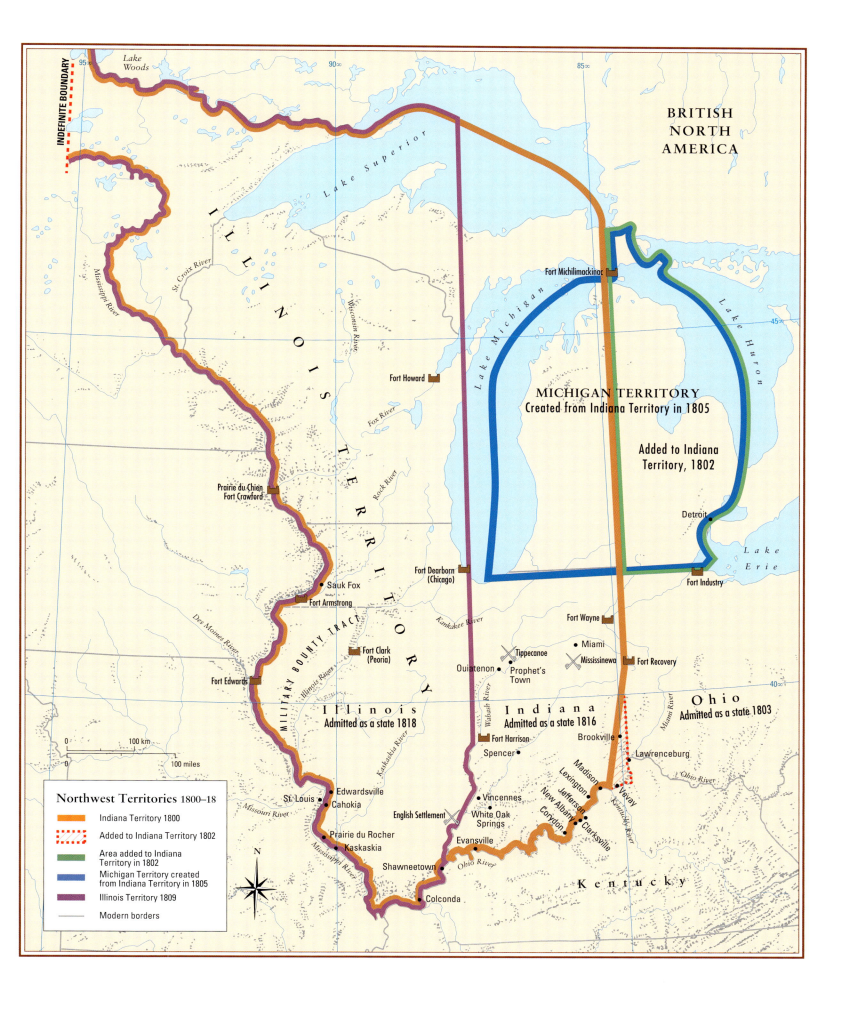

BRITISH
NORTH
AMERICA

Lake Woods

INDEFINITE BOUNDARY

Lake Superior

Mississippi River

St. Croix River

Wisconsin River

Fort Howard

Fox River

ILLINOIS TERRITORY

Lake Michigan

Lake Huron

Fort Michilimackinac

MICHIGAN TERRITORY
Created from Indiana Territory in 1805

Added to Indiana
Territory, 1802

Detroit

Lake Erie

Rock River

Prairie du Chien
Fort Crawford

Des Moines River

Sauk Fox

Fort Armstrong

MILITARY BOUNTY TRACT

Illinois River

Fort Clark
(Peoria)

Fort Dearborn
(Chicago)

Kankakee River

Fort Industry

Fort Wayne

Miami

Tippecanoe

Mississinewa

Fort Recovery

Miami River

Fort Edwards

I l l i n o i s
Admitted as a state 1818

Ouiatenon

Prophet's
Town

O h i o
Admitted as a state 1803

Wabash River

I n d i a n a
Admitted as a state 1816

Fort Harrison

Spencer

Brookville

Lawrenceburg

Kaskaskia River

Ohio River

St. Louis

Edwardsville

Cahokia

Madison

Lexington

Jefferson

Vevay

Missouri River

English Settlement

Vincennes

White Oak
Springs

New Albany

Corydon

Clarksville

Kentucky River

Prairie du Rocher

Kaskaskia

Evansville

Mississippi River

Shawneetown

Ohio River

K e n t u c k y

N

Colconda

0   100 km
0   100 miles

Northwest Territories 1800–18

— Indiana Territory 1800

▨ Added to Indiana Territory 1802

— Area added to Indiana
Territory in 1802

— Michigan Territory created
from Indiana Territory in 1805

— Illinois Territory 1809

— Modern borders

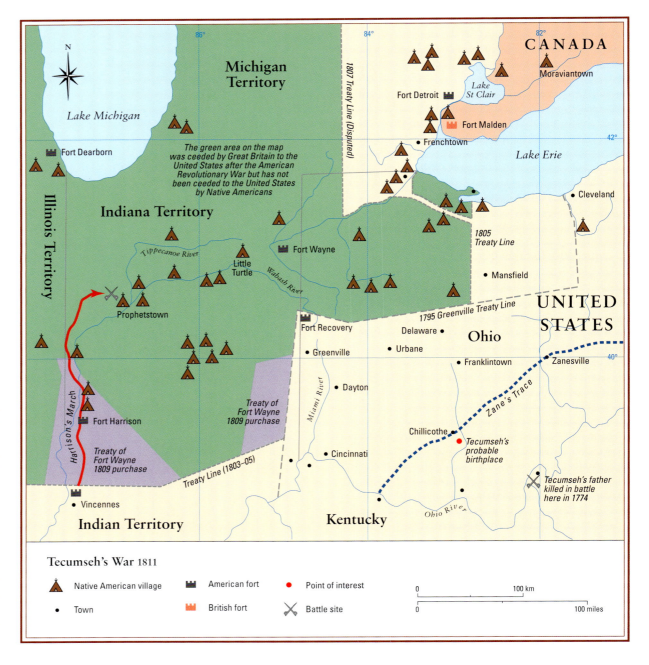

In 1811, encouraged by Tecumseh's absence (he was attempting to subdue the more hot-blooded among his followers), William Henry Harrison, governor of the Indiana Territory, marched on Prophetstown with a 1,000-strong force. Forewarned, the Indians made a preemptive attack on the Americans on the morning of November 7. The resulting Battle of Tippecanoe was a bloody fight, each side losing around 200 killed. It was only ended when Harrison's cavalry managed to drive the Indians from the field.

Tecumseh's War 1811

🏕 Native American village   🏰 American fort   ● Point of interest

● Town   🏰 British fort   ✕ Battle site

journeyed to Prophetstown to listen to the brothers expound their political and religious ideas.

The year 1808 is also significant for the Treaty of Fort Wayne. It was through this treaty that Harrison persuaded the Delaware and Potawatomi to sell 3 million acres (1.2 million hectares) of Indiana land to the United States. Tecumseh told Harrison that no one tribe had title to the land, and that any attempt to occupy it would be resisted. Younger warriors started to pass war belts around the region during 1810–11, and Tecumseh had difficulty in restraining his fighters. In 1811, at a conference in the South, on the Tallapoosa River, he talked with Creek, Cherokee, and Choctaw representatives. He won over the Creeks, but the other tribes were prepared to resist only if their lands were invaded again.

Harrison used Tecumseh's absence to goad the Prophet and his warriors into war. He advanced on Prophetstown with 1,000 regulars and militia, but the Indians left the village and attacked the American camp at dawn on November 7, 1811. The subsequent Battle of Tippecanoe was violent, each side suffering some 190 casualties; only cavalry charges drove the Indians from the battlefield. This indecisive encounter caused the Indians to flee from Prophetstown, which the Americans burned. Subsequently, the Indian survivors launched raids along the frontier during 1812.

The Americans thought that the British in Canada, especially at Fort Malden, were supplying and encouraging the Indians. This belief was one of the factors that led to the War of 1812 between the United States and Great Britain. The American view was that capturing Canada would remove the Indian threat. Tecumseh saw the war as a chance to build an Indian state, and he sided with the British in declaring war upon the United States. Many Indians joined him, and he was ranked a brigadier general in the British Army. Meanwhile, other Indians were continuing their raids against settlers.

Tecumseh aided British Major General Brock in capturing Detroit, and some of his warriors helped take Fort Dearborn, on the site of present-day Chicago. After Brock was killed at the Battle of Queenstown, Tecumseh was forced to cooperate with his successor, General Henry Proctor. The latter was partially responsible for the River Raisin Massacre, when a small party of Kentucky militia, who had surrendered, were slaughtered and scalped by Indians with the British force. Tecumseh, elsewhere at the time, stopped the violence upon his return and berated the British officers for allowing it to happen. Proctor retreated after a force under Commodore Oliver Perry beat the British at the Battle of Put-in-Bay on Lake Erie. Eventually, he stood his ground and was defeated at the Battle of the Thames on October 3, 1813, when Tecumseh was killed—his pan-Indian dream died with him. The Prophet died in obscurity in Canada in 1826.

One of the reasons for the War of 1812 was that the United States believed that Britain was arming Indians, who were attacking American settlers. To prevent this, an invasion of Canada was launched in August 1812, but it was repulsed and the British seized Fort Detroit. A second invasion of the Niagara peninsula was also defeated in October that year. Tecumseh, who saw the war as an opportunity to establish an Indian state, threw in his lot with the British, but was killed in 1813 at the Battle of the Thames. Eventually, the Americans gained naval superiority on the Great Lakes, taking control of Lake Erie and Lake Champlain, but no further invasion of Canada was attempted.

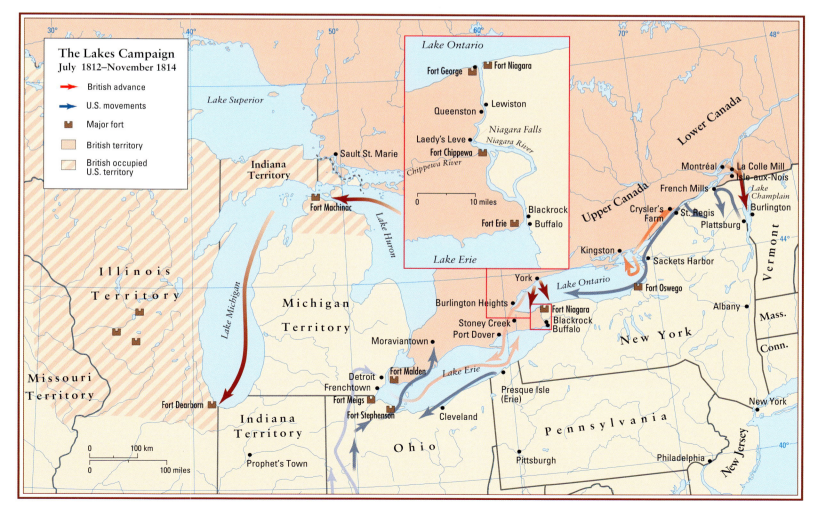

The Lakes Campaign
July 1812–November 1814

→ British advance

→ U.S. movements

🏰 Major fort

British territory

British occupied U.S. territory

Lewis, Clark, and the Indians

FOLLOWING THE LOUISIANA PURCHASE, PRESIDENT JEFFERSON SENT THE CORPS OF DISCOVERY TO MAP THE REGION AND MAKE A STUDY OF THE INDIAN TRIBES THEY MET.

Fearful of an aggressive French presence in Louisiana after Napoleon had forced Spain to cede him the region, in 1803, President Jefferson sent James Monroe to France to negotiate the purchase of New Orleans. In Paris, Monroe learned that Napoleon was losing interest in the Americas. The Emperor offered the United States not only New Orleans, but also some 828,000 square miles (2,150,000 square kilometers) of territory, all of Louisiana, for $15 million. This new territorial acquisition ensured Jefferson's reelection as president in 1804.

The American government required maps of the region, and Jefferson persuaded Congress to finance a scientific and cartographic expedition. His private secretary, Meriwether Lewis, William Clark, and some forty-five men were formed into the Corps of Discovery to explore the Missouri River. Jefferson hoped that the river could be used for commerce and communication with the Pacific, and to provide a link with the China trade. He also instructed the men to collect ethnographic information on the various Indian tribes they encountered, and to determine to what extent trade, especially in furs, might be entertained.

In preparation for the task, Lewis studied celestial navigation, botany, and zoology in Philadelphia. The expedition left from St. Louis in May 1804, the party traveling in keelboats along the Missouri. The passage was relatively smooth, and Lewis remarked that the Indians were friendly, generous, and welcoming. The men overwintered near a Mandan village, in present-day North Dakota, and built Fort Mandan. There, Lewis and Clark hired Toussaint Charbonneau as an interpreter, and he was accompanied by his Shoshone wife, Sacagawea (Bird Woman). She proved a useful interpreter and probably made the expedition appear less threatening to the Indians they met.

So far, the corps had overcome all obstacles successfully, feeding itself while collecting botanical and geological specimens, together with data on climate and terrain. In February 1805, however, a brush occurred with a Sioux raiding party. Five members of the expedition were returning to camp with game on sleds when the Sioux attacked, seizing two of three horses, but they were driven off by gunfire.

In the course of exploration, the corps held a council with the Teton Sioux at the site of Fort Pierre, in an attempt to gain their allegiance from Britain. In the spring of 1805, the expedition reached the Falls of the Missouri, and then progressed to its source. Next, Lewis and Clark crossed the Continental Divide in the Rocky Mountains, traveling down the Snake and Columbia rivers to reach the Pacific. They built Fort Clatsop, near a Clatsop village; this tribe belonged to the Chinook.

Winter was spent on the Columbia, and the return began in 1806, the party splitting into two to cover more ground. Lewis's group met and made camp with eight Blackfeet, but the Indians tried to steal their guns and horses. One Indian was stabbed, and Lewis shot another in the stomach. The Indians fled, and the Americans found they had captured four Indian mounts and sundry weaponry. They rode fast for 80 miles (130 kilometers) in case the Indians were joined by a war party.

In September 1806, the Corps of Discovery returned to St. Louis, having covered 8,000 miles (13,000 kilometers) in twenty-eight months. The expedition warned Britain that U.S. power had been projected to the Pacific and enhanced claims to the Oregon territory. Most importantly, Lewis and Clark's collections and diaries added much to the sum of knowledge about the region, its peoples, and a potential peltry trade.

Sacagawea, Shoshone wife of Toussaint Charbonneau, guides members of the Lewis and Clark expedition through the Rocky Mountains. From a painting by Alfred Russell (1904).

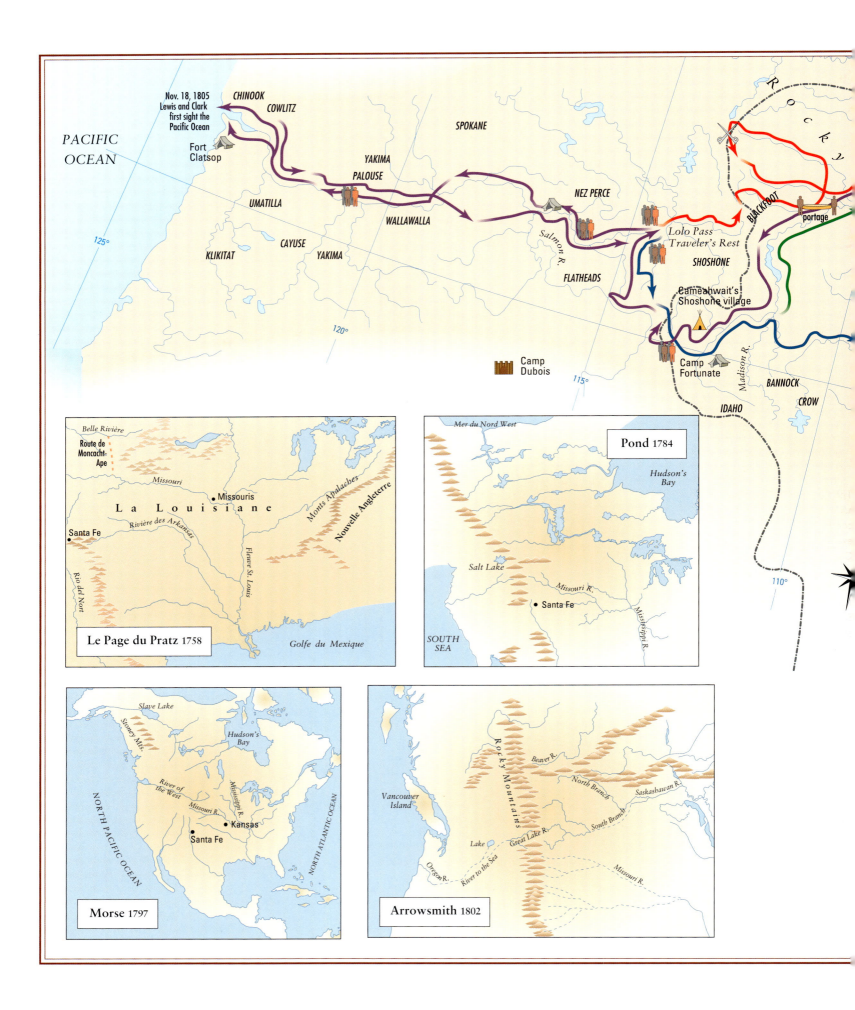

PACIFIC OCEAN

Nov. 18, 1805
Lewis and Clark
first sight the
Pacific Ocean

CHINOOK
COWLITZ
SPOKANE

Fort Clatsop

YAKIMA
PALOUSE

UMATILLA
WALLAWALLA

NEZ PERCE

Salmon R.

Lolo Pass
Traveler's Rest

ROCKY

BLACKFOOT

portage

125°

KLIKITAT
CAYUSE
YAKIMA

120°

SHOSHONE

FLATHEADS

Cameahwait's
Shoshone village

Camp
Fortunate

Madison R.

BANNOCK

Camp
Dubois

115°

IDAHO

CROW

Belle Rivière

Route de
Moncacht-
Ape

Missouri

Missouris

La Louisiane

Rivière des Arkansas

Santa Fe

Monts Apalaches

Nouvelle Angleterre

Rio del Nort

Fleuve St. Louis

Le Page du Pratz 1758

Golfe du Mexique

Mer du Nord West

Pond 1784

Hudson's Bay

Salt Lake

Missouri R.

Santa Fe

Mississippi R.

SOUTH SEA

Slave Lake

Stoney Mts.

Hudson's Bay

River of the West

Missouri R.

Mississippi R.

Kansas

Santa Fe

NORTH PACIFIC OCEAN

NORTH ATLANTIC OCEAN

Morse 1797

Rocky Mountains

Beaver R.

North Branch

Saskashawan R.

Vancouver Island

South Branch

Lake

Great Lake R.

Oregon R.

River to the Sea

Missouri R.

Arrowsmith 1802

110°

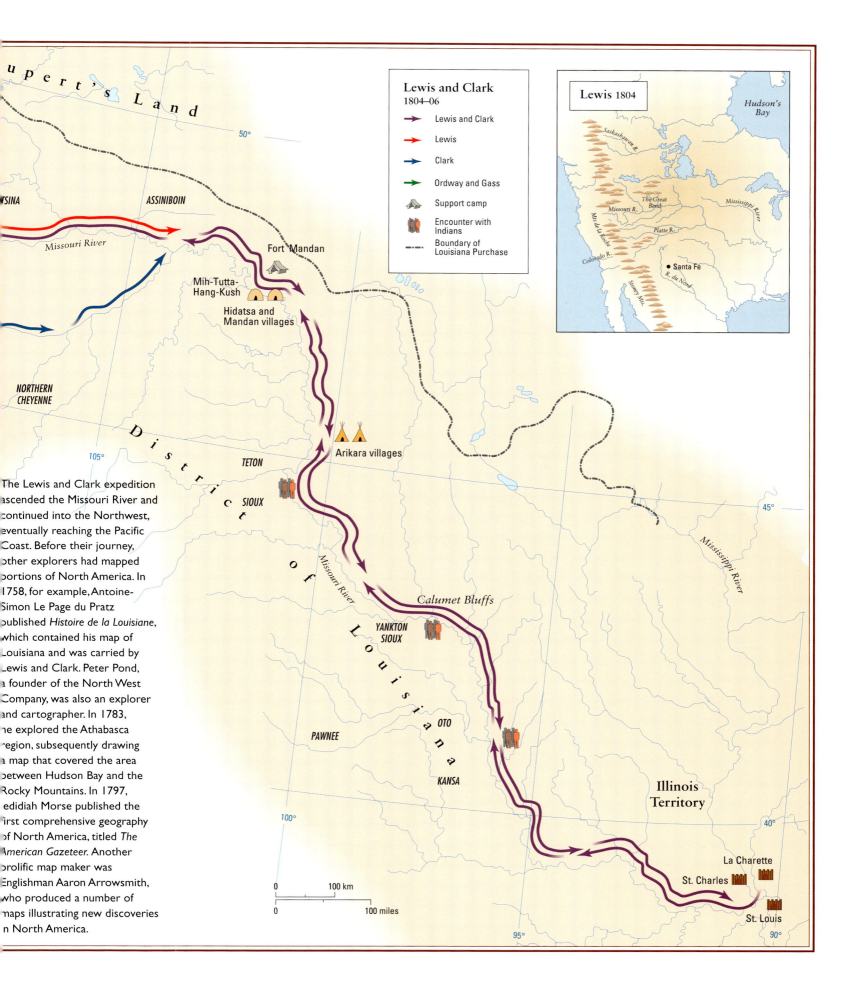

The Lewis and Clark expedition ascended the Missouri River and continued into the Northwest, eventually reaching the Pacific Coast. Before their journey, other explorers had mapped portions of North America. In 1758, for example, Antoine-Simon Le Page du Pratz published *Histoire de la Louisiane*, which contained his map of Louisiana and was carried by Lewis and Clark. Peter Pond, a founder of the North West Company, was also an explorer and cartographer. In 1783, he explored the Athabasca region, subsequently drawing a map that covered the area between Hudson Bay and the Rocky Mountains. In 1797, Jedidiah Morse published the first comprehensive geography of North America, titled *The American Gazeteer*. Another prolific map maker was Englishman Aaron Arrowsmith, who produced a number of maps illustrating new discoveries in North America.

Lewis and Clark
1804–06

→ Lewis and Clark
→ Lewis
→ Clark
→ Ordway and Gass
⛺ Support camp
Encounter with Indians
–·– Boundary of Louisiana Purchase

Lewis 1804

The Opening of the Northwest

THE EUROPEANS AND, LATER, AMERICANS FOUND THE PACIFIC NORTHWEST TO BE A LUCRATIVE REGION FOR FUR TRADING WITH LOCAL NATIVE AMERICAN TRIBES.

Although Russian and Spanish traders had made sporadic forays into the Northwest from 1741, the first major European contact occurred in the spring of 1778, when James Cook arrived in Nootka Sound, off Vancouver Island. Instigated by the Hudson Bay Company, this voyage was made in the hope of finding a Northwest Passage to the Pacific, together with new markets and routes for the company. Cook's crew traded with the Yuquot Indians, acquiring sea otter furs that fetched high prices when the expedition reached Canton in China. News of this fur trade galvanized others, and by the late 1790s, twenty-one vessels were trading in Nootka Sound annually.

In 1792, Captain George Vancouver, a former midshipman on Cook's *Resolution*, arrived and surveyed the American West Coast, from Baja California to Cook Inlet, discovering the insularity of Vancouver Island. At Nootka Sound, he negotiated with Juan Bodega y Quadra for the cession to Britain of all Spanish claims to the Pacific coast north of California. Six weeks after Vancouver left Elcho Harbour in Dean Channel, in the summer of 1793,

Alexander Mackenzie reached the same spot. He had been employed by the North West Company, a rival of the Hudson Bay Company, and had left Fort Chippewa in Athabasca Country in October 1792. Mackenzie had wintered at the confluence of the Peace and Smoky rivers, and reached Elcho Harbor on July 22, 1793. Another notable expedition of the time was that led by Robert Gray, who discovered the mouth of the Columbia River in 1792.

The travels of Vancouver and Mackenzie had a momentous impact, leading to the triangular maritime fur trade. British and, later, Boston vessels sailed to the Northwest to trade goods with the Indians for sea otter pelts, then traveled on to China, where they were exchanged for tea, spices, and silk. This trade had peaked by 1800, however, being overtaken by land-based trade.

A notable trader was the German-American John Jacob Astor, who entered the fur trade in 1786. He formed the American Fur Company in 1808, constructed trading posts along the Missouri and Columbia rivers, and founded the settlement of Fort Astoria, at the mouth of the Columbia River, which became his trade terminus. The fort was taken over by the North West Company during the War of 1812.

The relationship between the early traders and the Indians of the Northwest demonstrates that the latter knew how to drive a hard bargain; they rapidly realized the value of sea otters. Prices were fixed by supply and demand, and competition. Native American requirements had to be met before

Alexander Mackenzie also carried out a major exploration of the Northwest for the North West Company. He left his mark on a rock at Elcho Harbor in 1793. Remarkably, it remains there to this day.

Opposite: A portrait of James Cook by Nathaniel Dance, c. 1775. The British Royal Naval officer helped open up the Northwest to fur traders through his voyage of 1778 in search of the fabled Northwest Passage to Asia.

trade began. Ceremonies were performed and gifts given, and trade took place at the Indians' pace. They exercised great control over the fur trade, which was concentrated at Vancouver Island and the Queen Charlotte Islands. By the 1790s, more traders having entered the business, the Indians were

demanding higher prices; they could choose between traders to get the best profit. Initially, payment for furs was made by giving metal tools, but as the number of tools in Indian hands increased, their value dropped; instead, cloth, clothing, and heavy blankets were demanded, and eventually rum, tobacco, molasses, and guns.

The Chinook were important traders, providing a connection for goods to the Dalles trade center. To cement good relations, traders often entered long lasting marriages with Native American women. For example, Fort Simpson trader John Kennedy wed the daughter of Legaic, a Tsimshian leader who controlled trade on the Upper Skeena River.

Trade brought a variety of problems in the early years of European contact, although most relations between traders and Indians were amicable, except in the far north, where Russians virtually enslaved the Aleuts. After the Russians moved to the Alaskan Panhandle, they confronted the more warlike Tlingits, who destroyed Fort New Archangel, Sitka, in 1802, killing twenty Russians and 130 Aleuts, and seizing 3,000 furs. In 1805, Yakutat was destroyed, but antagonism declined after 1820. The only other major attack on Europeans was the 1803 assault at Vancouver Island on a merchant vessel, the *Boston*, which nearly lost its entire crew.

The other major problem was disease; there were smallpox outbreaks in the 1770s and 1801. Venereal disease hit women of childbearing age, affecting fertility rates. Other dangers were malaria, respiratory illnesses, influenza, dysentery, measles,

whooping cough, and tuberculosis. Death rates were high, and by 1840, the Chinooks and other Indians on the lower Columbia River had lost 70–80 percent of their population. The evidence for the impact of disease is patchy, however, and in many cases, figures are little more than guesswork.

Traders and Trappers
1822–30

- U.S. territory 1818
- Joint U.S.–British territory 1818–46
- British territory 1818
- Mexican territory 1818
- → Ashley, Henry, and Smith 1822–23
- → Smith 1823–24
- → Weber and Bridger 1823–24
- → Ashley 1824–25
- → Provost 1824–25
- → Sylvester and James Pattie 1825
- → James Pattie, Robidoux, and Young 1826–27
- → Pattie's claimed route 1827
- → Sylvester and James Pattie 1829–30
- 🏰 Fort
- ⛺ Indian settlement
- ⚙ Trading post
- ⚚ Mission
- ⚔ Confrontation with Indians
- ⊗ Meeting place
- CROW Indian tribe
- ‿ Mountain pass
- — Modern borders

After Lewis and Clark, many fur trappers and traders entered the Northwest and West during the early nineteenth century. Their wanderings and expeditions created a bank of knowledge about the country that later would help guide settlers into the wilderness, leading to confrontations with the Indians. Among those whose explorations contributed to the opening up of the country was famed mountain man Jedidiah Smith, the first white man to enter California by the overland route and the first to scale the High Sierras among many other accomplishments. William Henry Ashley and his partner, Andrew Henry, set up the Rocky Mountain Fur Company in competition with the Hudson Bay Company, and financed a number of major expeditions, employing, among others, Jim Bridger and John Henry Weber. The first man of European descent to see the Great Salt Lake was Étienne Provost, a French Canadian trapper and trader. Other well-known trappers were Miguel Robidoux, Ewing Young, and Sylvester Pattie and his son, James. The Patties were the first Americans to set foot on Arizona soil.

AMERICAN NATIONS, 1815–65

"THE GEORGIANS HAVE SHOWN A GRASPING SPIRIT LATELY; ... THEY ARE STRONG AND WE ARE WEAK. WE ARE FEW, THEY ARE MANY. WE CANNOT REMAIN HERE IN SAFETY AND COMFORT. ... THERE IS BUT ONE PATH OF SAFETY, ONE ROAD TO FUTURE EXISTENCE AS A NATION. THAT PATH IS OPEN BEFORE YOU. MAKE A TREATY OF CESSION. GIVE UP THESE LANDS, AND GO OVER BEYOND THE GREAT FATHER OF WATERS."

MAJOR RIDGE OF THE CHEROKEE TREATY PARTY.

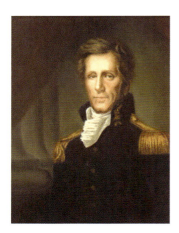

Andrew Jackson, seventh president of the United States.

The birth of the American Republic brought a variety of problems to the new nation. How could the state survive when surrounded by British Canada, Spanish Florida, and, at one point, Napoleonic Louisiana? In addition, the new political leaders wondered how the enclaves of Indian territory, surrounded by white westward expansion, could be accommodated. In Georgia, the Cherokee did their level best to fit in with white society, but aggressive Georgians wanted their removal, despite their attempts to mirror the republic in political, social, and educational terms. The removal of the Indians became an issue eventually confronted by President Andrew Jackson, who had learned much fighting the Creek in 1812. Removal led to the Cherokee Trail of Tears and bursts of warfare, exemplified by the Black Hawk War (1832) and the Seminole Wars (between 1835 and 1842). Moreover, U.S. Indian policy forced eastern tribes to confront western nations, which caused violence over access to hunting grounds. Removal also meant extermination, as seen in California after the Gold Rush. Once tribes had been pushed onto reservations, they had to be contained, which gave rise to further conflict, such as the Apache and Northwestern wars.

By 1790, the Indians had lost a lot of land.

BRITISH NORTH AMERICA

Lake Superior

Lake Michigan

Lake Huron

Lake Ontario

Lake Erie

Fort Poutchartrain (Detroit)

Claimed by Connecticut

Territory Northwest of Ohio River

Harman's Battle September 1790
St. Clair's Battle November 1791

Cincinnati

St. Louis • Cahokia

Kaskaskia

Ohio River

Louisville

Ceded by Virginia 1789

Nashville

Territory South of Ohio River

Arkansas Post

Claimed by Georgia

Disputed with Spain

New Orleans

Mobile • • Pensacola

Gulf of Mexico

Florida

• St. Augustine

Savannah

Charleston

Georgia

Augusta

South Carolina

North Carolina

Richmond

V i r g i n i a

Washington • Md.

Baltimore

Delaware

New Jersey

Pennsylvania

Brooklyn

New York

New York

Albany

Vt.

N.H.

Mass.

Salem
Boston

Haverhill

Providence
Conn. R.I. New Bedford
Taunton

Maine (Massachusetts)

Portland

Lake Ontario

ATLANTIC OCEAN

Land Held by Native Americans c. 1790

— Border of United States 1790

Largely occupied or controlled by Native Americans

Ceded by Native Americans 1768–74

Ceded by Native Americans 1790

Settled by or controlled by Europeans/descendants

52°

48°

44°

40°

36°

32°

88° 84° 80° 76° 72° 68°

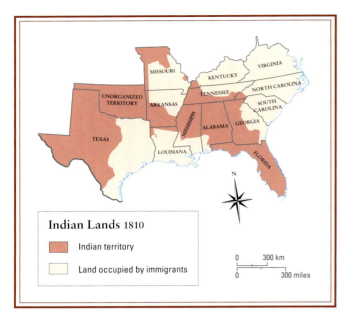

Indian Lands 1810

- Indian territory
- Land occupied by immigrants

0   300 km

0   300 miles

The early nineteenth century saw a steady movement westward by American settlers, squeezing the Indians into an ever-smaller area of land.

Opposite: Mississippi Territory came into being in 1798 from land ceded to the United States by Spain through the 1795 Treaty of Madrid. In 1804, the territory was enlarged northward to include land originally claimed by Georgia. Then in 1812, the Mobile district of West Florida was added, the United States claiming that this had been part of the Louisiana Purchase, although this was disputed by Spain until it was occupied by U.S. troops. Eventually, the territory was divided, the eastern portion forming Alabama. The formation of Mississippi Territory, and later Alabama, required substantial land cessions by the Indians, notably the Creek, Chickasaw, and Choctaw nations. They were also subjected to Jackson's removal policy.

In 1812, a band of Creeks under Little Warrior joined Tecumseh in Canada. They were involved in the Raisin River Massacre, then killed two white families at the mouth of the Ohio while returning. The Lower Creek on the lower Chattahoochee and Apalachiola rivers feared white retaliation when the U.S. Government demanded that the murderers be handed over. These moderate Creeks, led by Big Warrior, executed the murderers, which caused the Upper Creek to seek vengeance for Little Warrior. The majority of the Upper Creek towns declared war, taking up their red war clubs, from which they were known as the Red Sticks. They attacked Fort Mims, which was held by mixed-blood Creeks and some white men who had ambushed an ammunition train belonging to the Red Sticks. The defenders were slaughtered, and the incident pushed the United States to intervene in this Creek civil war.

Three U.S. columns advanced on the Red Stick strongholds, two achieving limited success. However, a 2,500-strong Tennessee militia force, led by Andrew Jackson, secured two victories at Tallasahatchee and Talladega. Jackson was reinforced by the 39th U.S. Infantry and, with White Stick Creek and Cherokee allies, advanced on a Red Stick fortification at Horseshoe Bend, on the Tallapoosa River. Battle ensued, during which a certain Ensign Sam Houston was wounded; the Indians lost about 800 dead and wounded, some being drowned in the river. Jackson then enforced the Treaty of Fort Jackson on both Red Stick and White Stick Creeks, gaining a cession of 23 million acres (9.4 million hectares) for the USA, about 60 percent of Alabama and 20 percent of Georgia.

Was this Creek War a forcing ground for Jackson's later removal policy? Certainly, he was concerned with national security in the West. He thought that if white settlers could replace Indians in the Chickasaw and Choctaw regions, the lower Mississippi would be defensible. When he fought the Creek, and the Seminole in the First Seminole War, he was hard on the enemy, but, when commander of the Division of the South, he ordered soldiers to remove white squatters from Cherokee lands. Jackson believed that Native Americans had no concrete title to all the lands they claimed, but were entitled to retain sufficient for their needs. Also, the idea that Indians were sovereign nations, especially when surrounded by U.S. territory, was anathema to him. He thought that these "islands" should be subjected to U.S. laws. He also felt that Indians would adopt the ways of white society and become farmers. After Horseshoe Bend, in April 1814, he pronounced that, *"The weapons of warefare will be exchanged for the utensils of husbandry, and the wilderness which now withers in sterility and seems to mourn the desolation which overspreads it, will blossom as the rose, and become the nursery of the arts."*

Jackson envisaged removal as a means of protecting U.S. civilization, providing land for white settlers, gaining security and buffer lands against foreign invaders, appeasing the Georgia legislature against the federal government, and probably winning votes to boot. He thought that conversion of the Indians to an agricultural way of life could only be achieved if they were not pressured by surrounding white settlements. Thus, removal west of the Mississippi would allow time for them to become

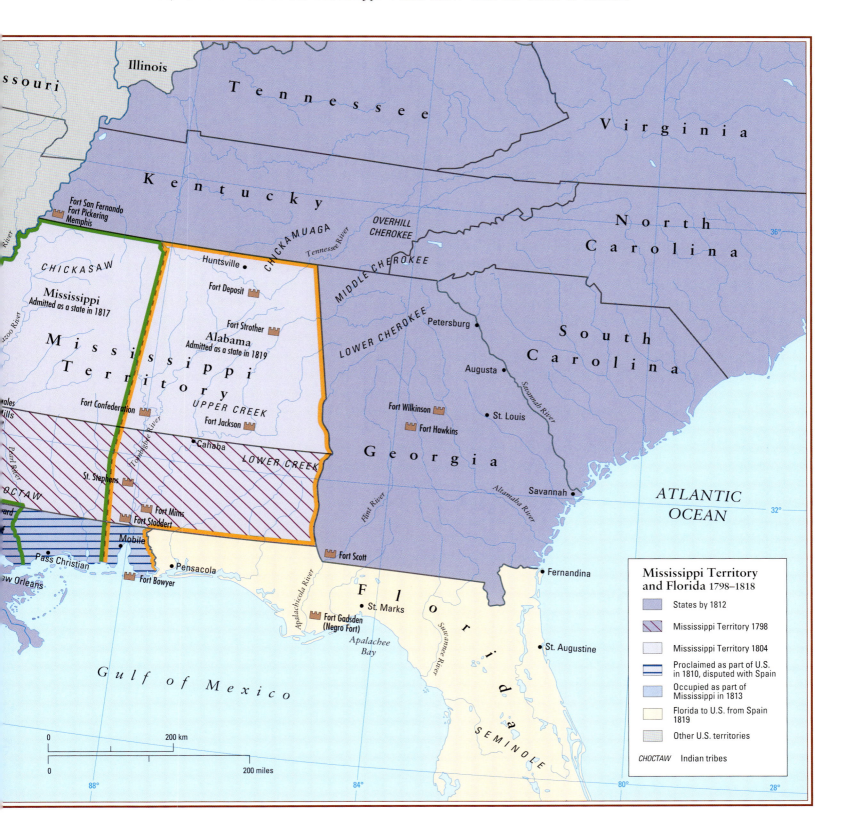

Mississippi Territory and Florida 1798–1818

- States by 1812
- Mississippi Territory 1798
- Mississippi Territory 1804
- Proclaimed as part of U.S. in 1810, disputed with Spain
- Occupied as part of Mississippi in 1813
- Florida to U.S. from Spain 1819
- Other U.S. territories

CHOCTAW Indian tribes

Expansion and Settlement
to 1820

- United States, 1783
- Louisiana Purchase, 1803 (natural boundary)
- Joint occupation with Great Britain
- Ceded by the United States to Great Britain, 1818
- Ceded by Great Britain to the United States, 1818
- Ceded by Spain to the United States, 1819
- Spanish Empire after 1819
- Spanish Treaty Line of 1819
- 1812 New state admitted with date

By 1820, the steady growth of the United States was apparent. Settlers were moving westward, although a substantial portion of the West was in Spanish hands.

agriculturalists. What could Jackson actually achieve in terms of Indian policy? Firstly, he could protect Indian enclaves in the East by treaty agreements and military force. However, the U.S. standing army was too small to achieve this task, and it would be costly. Again, such a policy would allow the Cherokee to be a nation within a nation, and U.S. politics would not let this happen. Secondly, the Indians could be encouraged to assimilate into white society, losing their own culture and identity. However, Indian resilience was too intractable for this to occur. Finally, the Native Americans could have been obliterated and hounded into oblivion by military force, disease, and starvation. Such an extermination policy was actually followed in California, but it was not a policy that Jackson could pursue. Thus, when president, he took over existing removal policies as the only viable alternative to allow survival of culture, to avoid white incursions, and to distance the Indians from federal and state jurisdictions. Removal would rescue Indians from the evils of white civilization, and then they would

"share in the blessings of civilization and be saved from that degradation and destruction to which they were rapidly hastening while they remained in the States…"

The removal policy suffered many problems. Eastern Native Americans found difficulty in adapting to a new, alien, Plains environment in Indian Territory. Ottowa, Shawnee, Potawatomi, Sauk and Fox, Miami, and Kickapoo from the North, and the Five Civilized Tribes from the South, were all used to a sedentary, agricultural lifestyle among the eastern woodlands. Now they faced vast grasslands, which needed different agricultural methods. Furthermore, Native Americans already inhabiting the West were not consulted about this forced invasion of their traditional hunting grounds. The Eastern interlopers, as they were regarded, thought the nomadic Plains Indians to be primitive barbarians. The Osage were furious when the newcomers moved onto their land, while the Kiowa, Wichita, and Comanche claimed that half the lands settled by the Five Civilized Tribes were their own. When the newcomers spread west in search of buffalo, the Kiowa and Comanche attacked them, and federal troops were called in to settle disputes and keep the peace. Clearly, the removal policy had not ended federal involvement in Indian affairs. Also, when the Arapaho and Cheyenne attempted to drive away the Potawatomi, the latter, having been trained by the British during the War of 1812, formed ranks and used volley fire to inflict serious casualties on their attackers, gaining command of the battlefields. Eventually, the

Seminole chiefs are captured by U.S. troops in Florida during the First Seminole War (1816–18). The war had been prompted when settlers attacked the Florida Indians, who then retaliated by raiding settlements in Georgia. At the time, Florida was under Spanish control.

mutually-hostile groups kept out of each other's way, the peace being policed by troops from Forts Leavenworth, Gibson, and Towson.

When the Five Civilized Tribes journeyed to Indian Territory, they took their slaves with them. Mixed-blood Indians tended to be the slave owners, but not entirely. Certainly, by 1860, the Cherokee owned 4,600 slaves, the Choctaw 2,344, the Creek 1,532, the Chickasaw 975, and the Seminole 500. The Seminole treated their black "slaves" differently to the other four tribes, however, which led to unexpected trouble. Traditionally, the Seminole did not practice chattel slavery, but called fugitive slaves their "property" to protect them from slave-catchers, whether Chickasaw hunters or white patrollers. The Black Seminoles lived in separate villages in Seminole territory and paid food tribute to the Indians, but also they were allied militarily and fought in the Seminole Wars. When removed to Indian Territory, the Black Seminoles rode in on their own horses and carried their own personal rifles. The Seminole were relocated to Cherokee lands around Fort Gibson, where Creek and Cherokee slave owners feared the influence of free Black Seminoles upon their slave populations. The Black Seminoles settled in the Illinois River bottoms, near Webbers Falls, where the Cherokee slaves socialized with them.

The demand for land from the Indians was continuous, as this map shows. Westward expansion of the United States put unrelenting pressure on Native Americans as the nineteenth century progressed.

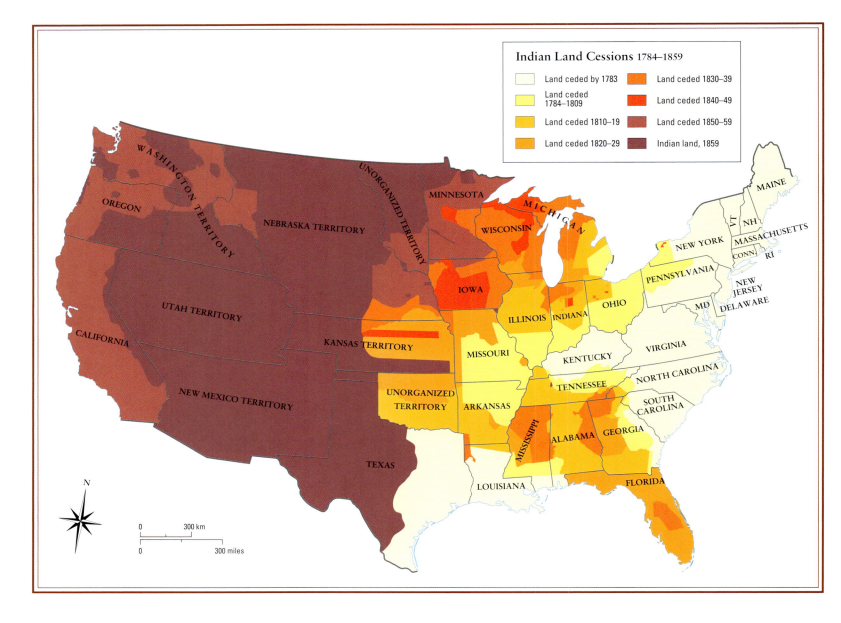

Indian Land Cessions 1784–1859

- Land ceded by 1783
- Land ceded 1784–1809
- Land ceded 1810–19
- Land ceded 1820–29
- Land ceded 1830–39
- Land ceded 1840–49
- Land ceded 1850–59
- Indian land, 1859

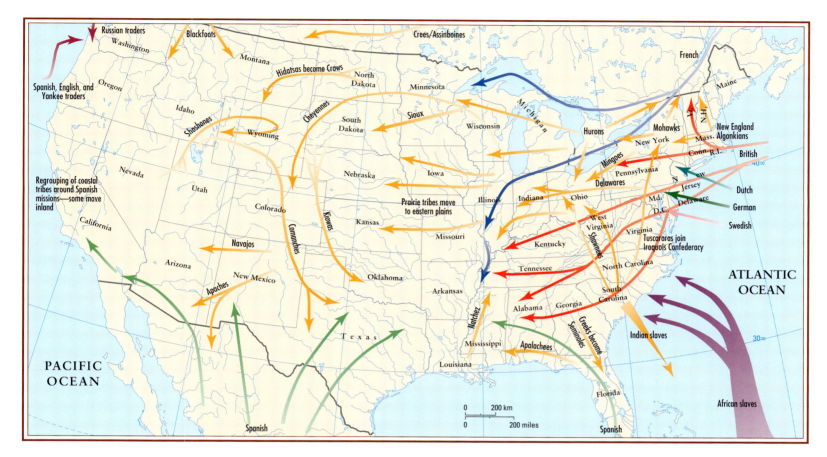

American Migrations
18th and 19th Centuries

- Native tribes
- Spanish
- British
- French
- Dutch
- German
- Swedish
- Native slaves
- African slaves
- Traders
- Modern borders

On November 15, 1842, some twenty-five slaves, mainly from a plantation belonging to Joseph Vann, a steamboat owner, locked up their owners and overseers, stole guns, horses, and mules, and set off toward Mexico, where slavery was illegal. Eventually, more than thirty-five men, women, and children were chased by Cherokees and Creeks, who caught up with them near the Canadian River in the Choctaw Nation. A two-day fight began, and two slaves were killed, while twelve were captured. The Cherokees and Creeks went home to summon reinforcements, while the slaves encountered slave-catcher James Edwards with his Delaware companion, Billy Wilson. The slaves killed them and released eight Africans who were being returned to their owner in the Choctaw Nation.

Meanwhile, the Cherokee leader, John Ross, had ordered a well-armed group to chase the slaves. They were discovered north of the Red River, approximately 280 miles (450 kilometers) from Fort Gibson, and surrendered.

The Cherokee attitude toward Black Seminoles became increasingly antagonistic, and by 1843, they were demanding that the group leave the Cherokee Nation. In 1849, some Black Seminoles, under Chief John Horse, left Indian Territory, joining Chief Wildcat and his band; together, they reached Mexico. By 1851, some 300 African slaves had attempted to escape from Indian Territory, heading for Texas or Mexico, while an "underground railroad" route left Washington County, Oklahoma, for Kansas.

Despite the U.S. federal policy that Indian Territory should be inviolate, increasing numbers of miners and settlers were crossing the land en route to Oregon and California. In 1845 alone, some 3,000 people reached Oregon by the overland route. The result was a foregone conclusion.

In the West, missionary doctor Marcus Whitman and his family had settled near Walla Walla, Washington. In 1847, Cayuse Indians were hit by a measles epidemic; shamans blamed the disease on

The eighteenth and nineteenth centuries saw a steady westward movement of populations in North America. As emigrants poured into the East, the Indians fell back or were pushed back. Eventually, however, the Eastern tribes came into conflict with those in the West, who resented the incursion into their territory.

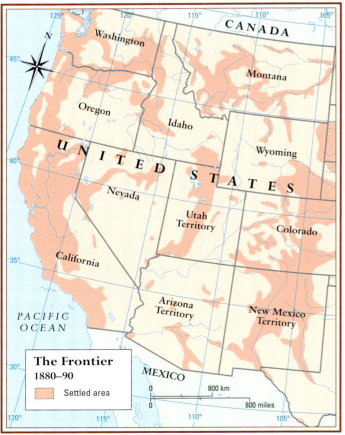

The Frontier
1880–90

Settled area

0   800 km

0   800 miles

the doctor and incited the murder of whites. The Whitmans and twelve others were killed, while forty-seven whites were captured, although later released. The Whitman Massacre instigated the events that led to the creation of Oregon Territory in 1848. The Indians were now in a vise, being pressured by settlers on both sides of the continent.

In California, the sudden invasion of white miners devastated some 150,000 local Indians. Having survived Spanish exploitation, now the Indians watched their game being driven away or killed, while the rivers were polluted or rerouted by mine workings. Indian subsistence patterns were destroyed, so they raided mine settlements, stealing cattle and horses. They were decimated by disease, then slaughtered deliberately, until their number had been reduced to below 30,000 by 1870. Marysvllle and Honey Lake townships paid bounties for Indian scalps; Shasta City gave five dollars for each Indian head presented at the city hall. At Roffs Ranch, in 1860, whites killed nine men, then butchered forty women and children, splitting open the latters' heads with hatchets.

A strange occurrence took place in Utah. Democrat President James Buchanan sent an army to eradicate polygamy among the Mormons of Salt Lake City and Utah, and while the federal units advanced west,

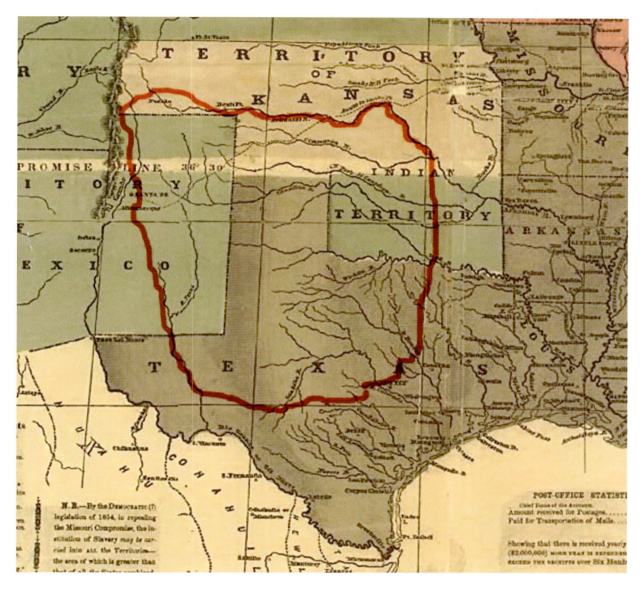

The Comancheria, the historical homeland of the Comanche. This region spanned parts of New Mexico, Texas, Kansas, and Indian Territory (subsequently Oklahoma). For many years, the Comanche maintained their independence, but a peace treaty with the Republic of Texas was thwarted when the Texas legislature refused to guarantee the boundary of the Comancheria. Subsequently, the tribe was decimated by disease through contact with settlers. The remnants were forced to move to a reservation near Fort Sill, Oklahoma, in the 1870s.

the Mormons made an alliance with the Paiutes. Meanwhile, a wagon train, not connected with the federal force, had reached southern Mormon territory at Mountain Meadows on September 7, 1857. About 200 Paiutes attacked, believing that the Missouri train was poisoning the local watering holes. The Indians were driven off, but one escaping Missourian, who sought help for the besieged train, was shot by young Mormons. Their elders realized that if this event was reported by any survivor of the wagon train, the federal troops would punish them. They resolved to wipe out the members of the train and blame the massacre on the Paiutes. On September 11, Mormon John D. Lee approached the wagons under a flag of truce, telling the migrants that if they lay down their arms, he could lead them to safety, and the Indians would not attack. The deceived Missourians followed him, whereupon the Mormons gunned down the men while the Paiutes attacked the women and children. They killed 120 people; Lee murdered all the sick and wounded. Seventeen small children survived and were adopted by Mormon families.

Eventually, the Mormons negotiated peace with President Buchanan. However, their southern Paiute allies were subjected to Navajo and Ute slave raids. They also suffered from white diseases and lost their best lands to their white allies.

Opposite, top: A contemporary engraving depicting the U.S. military expedition sent by President Buchanan to quell the Mormons in Utah.

Opposite: This map shows how white settlement in the West grew rapidly throughout the nineteenth century. This increase put overwhelming pressure on Native Americans.

REMOVALS IN THE MIDWEST

THE GROWING NUMBER OF WHITE SETTLERS, AND THEIR CONSTANT WESTWARD MOVEMENT, PROMPTED THE U.S. GOVERNMENT TO CONSIDER THE IDEA OF A "PERMANENT INDIAN FRONTIER."

John C. Calhoun, Secretary of War under President Monroe, was responsible for drawing up a plan to remove all Indians east of the Mississippi in 1824.

To clear the land for settlement, it was proposed that all Indians should be moved from east of the Mississippi to lands between the 95th and the 101st meridians. A removal plan was formulated in 1824 by John C. Calhoun, President Monroe's Secretary of War, and eastern tribes were "persuaded to accept new western lands." Often, government agents would bribe a corrupt or unthinking chief into signing a removal treaty, which meant an enforced move west.

In reality, the westward migration of Indians from the southern Great Lakes area had begun after the 1780s. In cooperation with Spanish authorities at St. Louis, Delaware, Shawnee, and Cherokee survivors of border warfare in the Ohio territory led a movement into Upper Louisiana. Other Delawares, Kickapoos, and Shawnees entered contemporary Missouri, but when that area became a state in 1821, the white population wanted to expel these Indians. Shawnees from Ohio moved into a 20-mile (32-kilometer) wide strip south of the Kansas River, where they were joined by the Delaware. In the 1830s, Ohio and Illinois also urged the removal of Indian inhabitants. Rapidly, more Kickapoo, Sauk, Fox (Mesquakie), Chippewa, Iowa, Potawatomi, Ottowa, Peoria, and Miami were crowded into reservations just west of the 95th meridian, and a few into western Iowa.

The Potawatomi had numbered some 9,000 and had lived around the base of Lake Michigan and in the Indiana-Michigan border region; they resisted migration. Around 2,000 from northwestern Indiana endured forced removal, while about half of the rest moved to allocated land in western Iowa. The Miami, weakened by the Ohio wars, were slow in leaving their Indiana home by the Wabash River; an 1838 treaty allowed some to remain. The last northwestern tribes to surrender their territories were the Wyandots of Ohio and northwest Michigan, originally Petuns and Hurons retreating from Iroquois expansion. An 1842 treaty removed them, but not to Kansas. Instead, the Wyandots bought a tract from the Delaware at the confluence of the Missouri and Kansas rivers. Eventually, some of the Wyandots were resettled in Wyandot County, Kansas.

The Seneca provide an interesting example of removal. Much of their land had been seized through the 1784 Fort Stanwix treaty and by land speculators, while they lost the remainder on the Genessee River through the 1797 Treaty of Big Tree. Final efforts to remove the Seneca occurred at the 1838 Treaty of Buffalo Creek, by which the four surviving Seneca reservations—Buffalo Creek, Tonawanda, Cattaraugus, and Allegany—were sold, provision being made to relocate the tribe to Kansas. The proceedings were deemed to be corrupt, and the contested treaty was rewritten in 1842. The new terms agreed the sale of Buffalo Creek and

The Seneca Chief Sagoyewatha, also known as Red Jacket for the coat given him by the British during the Revolutionary War, attempted to stop the sale of Seneca land west of the Genesee River by the Treaty of Big Tree in 1797, but without success. The Indians had been supplied with copious quantities of liquor during the treaty talks, while the Seneca women had received plenty of gifts.

Tonawanda, but the Seneca retained Cattaraugus and Allegany. Even so, some Seneca migrated to Kansas, but all bar two returned. The Tonawanda Seneca were not present at the signing of the 1842 treaty and protested. In 1857, another treaty returned most of their reservation, which was purchased with Kansas removal funds. In 1848, the Allegany and Cattaraugus reservations formed the Seneca Nation, which had a written constitution and a democratically elected government.

The Kickapoo were subjected to many removals. Some bands moved to Mexico, while the Prairie band relocated to southwestern Missouri in the 1820s. Treaties of 1832 led to the resettlement of the Prairie and Vermillion bands near Fort Leavenworth in Kansas. However, by the 1860s, many Prairie Kickapoo had moved to Mexico. These southern Kickapoo gained notoriety for raiding American ranches and settlements along the Rio Grande. The U.S. Army attacked them in Mexico, and in 1874, many left Mexico for Oklahoma.

Eventually, it was considered that many northern Indian bands were blocking Missouri River traffic, so they were concentrated gradually in Oklahoma. Even so, many thousands of Indians remained east of the Mississippi.

REMOVALS IN THE SOUTHEAST

THE REMOVAL OF TRIBES FROM THE SOUTHEAST WAS YET ANOTHER SHAMEFUL, BLOODY EPISODE IN THE UNITED STATES' DEALINGS WITH NATIVE AMERICANS.

U.S. Secretary of War John Eaton was charged with implementing President Jackson's removal policy.

On May 28, 1830, President Andrew Jackson signed into law the Indian Removal Act. This bill was aimed primarily at the Chickasaw, Choctaw, Creek, Seminole, and Cherokee nations. Orthodox wisdom has it that Jackson was courting southern voters for the 1832 election, but he was also interested in national security and wanted the borderlands peopled with whites.

The Secretary of War, John Eaton, invited delegates from all tribes to negotiate removal treaties at his home in Franklin, Tennessee. Only the Chickasaw turned up. They agreed that their lands would be surveyed into individual tracts held in free simple title. Each family could then sell their tract of land and use the proceeds to move west. The Chickasaw also won the right to choose their own land. Eventually, in January 1837, the Chickasaw leaders purchased the right to settle among the Choctaw. Some 4,900 people enrolled for removal, marched to Memphis, and crossed the Mississippi with their 1,100 slaves and 4–5,000 horses. The Chickasaw never really relished being engulfed by the Choctaw, and in 1855, the nations separated peacefully, a new independent Chickasaw Nation being created.

The Choctaw were treated similarly. Under the terms of the 1820 Treaty of Doak's Stand, the nation already owned some western land, between the Canadian and Red rivers. Eaton wanted to acquire the Choctaw's eastern landholding of 10,000,000 acres (4,000,000 hectares). Negotiations were bitter, but the newly elected Choctaw Chief Greenwood LeFlore, son of a French father and a mixed-blood Choctaw mother, finalized a deal. In return for ceding the land, the Choctaw wanted annuity payments, finance for the construction of churches and schools, removal expenses, and subsistence for one

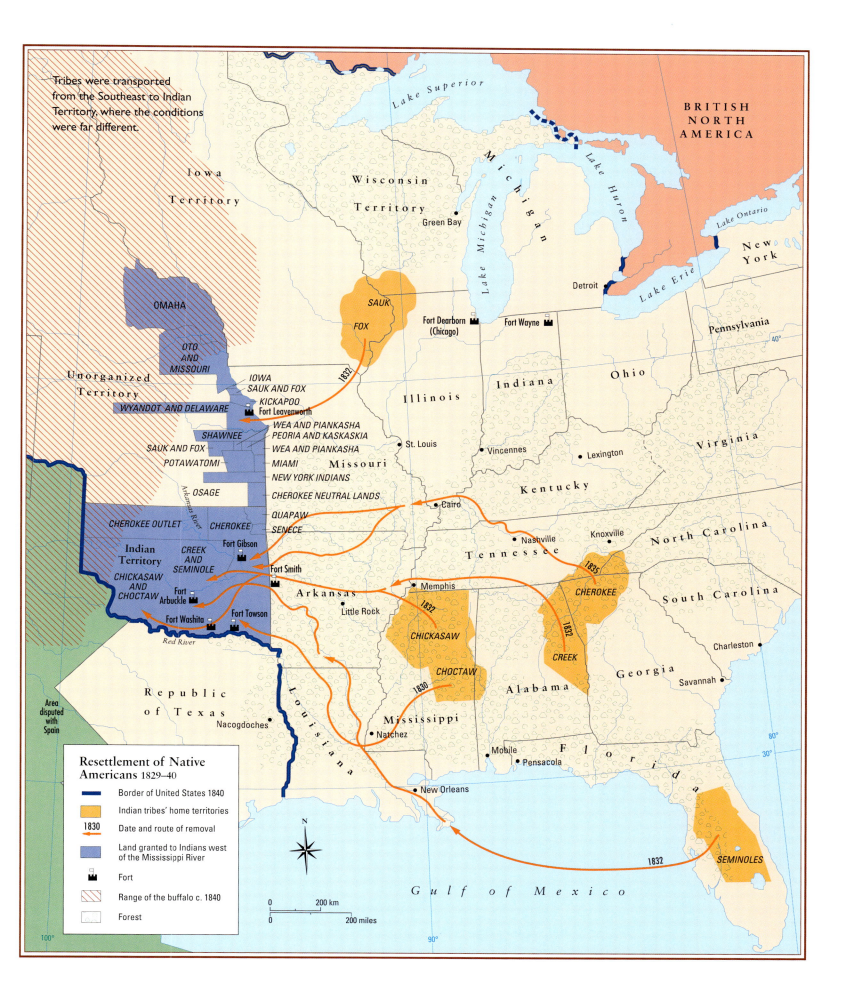

Tribes were transported from the Southeast to Indian Territory, where the conditions were far different.

BRITISH NORTH AMERICA

Lake Superior

Iowa Territory

Wisconsin Territory

Green Bay

Lake Michigan

Lake Huron

Lake Ontario

New York

Detroit

Lake Erie

OMAHA

OTO AND MISSOURI

Unorganized Territory

WYANDOT AND DELAWARE

IOWA
SAUK AND FOX
KICKAPOO
Fort Leavenworth

SAUK
FOX

Fort Dearborn (Chicago)

Fort Wayne

Pennsylvania

Illinois

Indiana

Ohio

40°

SHAWNEE

SAUK AND FOX

POTAWATOMI

Arkansas River

OSAGE

WEA AND PIANKASHA
PEORIA AND KASKASKIA
WEA AND PIANKASHA
MIAMI
NEW YORK INDIANS
CHEROKEE NEUTRAL LANDS
QUAPAW
SENECE

St. Louis

Vincennes

Lexington

Missouri

Virginia

Cairo

Kentucky

Nashville

Knoxville

North Carolina

CHEROKEE OUTLET

CHEROKEE

Fort Gibson

Indian Territory

CREEK AND SEMINOLE

CHICKASAW AND CHOCTAW

Fort Arbuckle

Fort Smith

Fort Washita   Fort Towson

Red River

Republic of Texas

Nacogdoches

Louisiana

1832

1830

Memphis

CHICKASAW

CHOCTAW

Arkansas

Little Rock

Tennessee

1835

CHEROKEE

1832

CREEK

South Carolina

Charleston

Savannah

Georgia

Alabama

Mississippi

Natchez

Mobile

Pensacola

Florida

30°

80°

New Orleans

Gulf of Mexico

SEMINOLES

1832

N

Area disputed with Spain

100°

90°

Resettlement of Native Americans 1829–40

▬▬ Border of United States 1840

⬛ Indian tribes' home territories

→ **1830** Date and route of removal

⬛ Land granted to Indians west of the Mississippi River

🏰 Fort

▨ Range of the buffalo c. 1840

▨ Forest

0   200 km

0   200 miles

Osceola, who led the Seminole in a war against the Americans in Florida that cost the lives of 1,500 United States citizens.

year. The Treaty of Dancing Rabbit Creek encouraged thousands of Choctaw to travel 550 miles (890 kilometers) to their new home. Most journeyed in the bitter cold winter of 1831–32, and some 2,500 out of 13–14,000 died from exposure and cholera. They settled on the western banks of the Arkansas River without adequate supplies, and in the following spring, floods destroyed their newly planted crops. Around 2,000 Choctaw refused to go and remained in Mississippi, becoming sharecroppers and wage laborers. The descendants of this group remained on tribal owned land in and near Neshola County.

Under the terms of the 1826 Treaty of Washington, the Creek or Muskogee Nation possessed western lands north of the Choctaw, between the Arkansas and Canadian rivers. Initially, substantial numbers of Creeks left Georgia and Alabama, encouraging President Jackson to assume that the remainder would follow. Chief Opothle Yoholo negotiated the adoption of allotment terms, as in the Chickasaw and Choctaw treaties, but individual reserves would be clustered to continue old township relationships. However, land grabbers and squatters evicted Creeks from their allotments before the migration began. In response, young warriors retaliated in a "war," during which they burned a steamboat on the Chattahoochee. The incidents caused the U.S. Army to round up the Creeks and force them to move. Some 14,500 reached the west, their number having been cut by one of the coldest and snowiest winters on record, and by the sinking of a steamship while crossing a river.

The Seminole were more difficult to remove. This nation of migrant Lower Creeks included the remnants of tribes from earlier confrontations with Europeans, such as the Hichite, Apalachee, and Yamasee. Large numbers of African slaves had escaped to the isolation of Florida, and had intermarried, been enslaved, or built their

own communities in alliance with the Seminole. Under an 1832 treaty, the nation was allowed to choose its western lands in Oklahoma., but the Seminole land scouts signed an agreement stating that they had found desirable land before discussing it with the nation. Resentful Seminole waged war, led by Osceola, (1836–42), which cost the United States 1,500 lives and $20 million. Some towns moved voluntarily, and by 1842, some 4,000 Seminole and their allies had been relocated to New Orleans, and along the Mississippi and Arkansas rivers as far as the Creek Nation. Approximately 500 remained in Florida, in Big Cyprus swamp and the Everglades. Another war occurred between 1855 and 1858, and 200 more Seminole were dispatched west, but the remainder stayed.

Resentful at being forcibly removed from their lands in Central Florida, the Seminole rebelled, leading to the Second Seminole War with the United States. The war lasted for six years, the resistance movement being led by Osceola.

THE TRAIL OF TEARS

FORCED TO LEAVE THEIR HOMES AND FARMS IN THE TENNESSEE VALLEY, THE CHEROKEE WERE SENT ON A 1,200-MILE (1,900-KILOMETER) MARCH TO THE WEST AND INDIAN TERRITORY.

After American independence, the Cherokee Nation kept its traditions, but also rapidly acquired skills that it hoped would aid its survival. In addition to converting them to Christianity, missionaries taught the people white agricultural techniques, and how to read and write English. Dissemination of ideas was helped by Sequoyah, a Cherokee silversmith who developed a syllabary, in which each symbol reflected a sound in the Cherokee language. The symbols allowed the nation to read its own language in record time. The American Board of Foreign Missions had the syllabary typeset and sent it to the Cherokee with a white printer. In developing politically, the nation wrote a constitution (1826), with a principal chief, a two-chambered council, and a court system.

The Cherokee owned 40,000 acres (16,000 hectares) of Tennessee Valley farmland, 22,000 cattle, 7,200 horses, wagons, sawmills, and large numbers of African slaves; log and frame houses were their normal habitations. All this was anathema to the white inhabitants of Georgia, however, who wanted Cherokee land and the removal of the nation west of the Mississippi. Some Cherokees, the Treaty Party, not one of whom was an elected chief, signed the Treaty of New Echota in 1835, by which they sold all eastern lands for $5 million and 7 million acres (2.8 million hectares) in the west, with an option to buy a further 8 million acres (3.2 million hectares) for $500,000. Under the terms of the treaty, the Cherokee were to leave by the spring of 1838. The Treaty Party and some 7,000 Cherokees moved west, but the majority protested against the treaty and made no attempt to prepare for removal.

In response, some 7,000 troops rounded up 18,000 Cherokees, holding them in stockades during the summer, when dysentery and fever killed many. During the winter of 1838–39, the Cherokees were allowed to organize their own westward march. Thirteen separate parties set out on the six-month trip, but some 4,000 died, either in the stockades or on what became known as the Trail of Tears. Among the dead was the wife of Chief John Ross. In Oklahoma, Ross' group sought to dominate the Cherokee, killing the leaders of the Treaty Party. Civil disturbances lasted until 1846, when disputing groups made peace.

Initially, problems faced all the southern Indian tribes in Oklahoma. Different farming techniques were required in the semi-arid grasslands to which they had been sent, while the Comanche, Kiowa, and Wichita insisted that 50 percent of the lands occupied by the Five Civilized Tribes—the Chickasaw, Choctaw, Creek, Seminole, and Cherokee—was still theirs. Violence broke out, especially when the easterners began hunting buffalo. Fortunately, a 30-mile (50-kilometer) wide belt of hardwood forest, Cross Timbers, divided the eastern and western Indians. Eventually, a treaty was signed between the two parties at Camp Holmes, on the South Canadian River, although it was not always followed. However, the continual skirmishes convinced the tribes that Cross Timbers would be a practical frontier.

Once in Oklahoma, the Cherokee adopted a new constitution, and schools, churches, newspapers, and businesses flourished. The *Cherokee Advocate* and *Cherokee Messenger* became the first bilingual newspaper and periodical respectively. The education system included 144 elementary schools, and Cherokee male and female seminaries, institutions of higher education. In addition, the land proved fertile; all the southern tribes sold surplus corn in American markets, and developed horse and cattle herds, which drew purchasers from all over the Midwest. Slave owners developed cotton fields and sold produce at Little Rock, Arkansas, and New Orleans. Cherokee John Vann bought a steamboat, and plied for trade on the Mississippi and Arkansas rivers.

Despite the enforced removal, about 1,000 Cherokees remained behind. The Oconaluftee Citizen Cherokee Indians lived outside the Cherokee Nation and were untouched. Villagers at Cheoih, in North Carolina, were allied with the local white population, while other families were headed by white males. Others lived in Turtle Town and Ducks Town in Tennessee, Fighting Town in Georgia, and Shooting Creek Town and Hanging Dog Town in North Carolina. In 1848, all of these Cherokees were given state rights as permanent residents, and during the Civil War, many served with the Confederate 69th North Carolina Infantry. The Oklahoma Cherokee had divided loyalties during this war, however, and a third died or moved away as a result of its devastation.

John Ross, a Cherokee chief whose wife died on the Trail of Tears. In Indian Territory, Ross led a group who attempted to dominate the tribe. They were responsible for killing the original Treaty Party who had agreed that the Cherokee should be moved from their home in the Tennessee Valley.

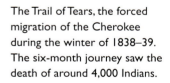

The Trail of Tears, the forced migration of the Cherokee during the winter of 1838–39. The six-month journey saw the death of around 4,000 Indians.

The Trail of Tears

···· Land and water routes to the west

▢ Area ceded by the Treaty of New Echota

THE BLACK HAWK WAR

WHEN PEACEFUL PROTEST OVER THE SEIZURE OF HIS LAND
FAILED, SAUK CHIEF BLACK HAWK SOUGHT AN ALLIANCE WITH
OTHER TRIBES AND DECLARED WAR ON THE AMERICANS.

An 1837 painting of the Sauk
war chief Black Hawk by Charles
Bird King. The chief suffered
humiliation after his defeat.

The Black Hawk War was the last violent Indian episode in the old Northwest Territory. After the War of 1812, southwest Wisconsin and northeast Illinois were opened to white settlement. Black Hawk, a Sauk chief of the allied Sauk (Sac) and Mesquakie (Fox) became increasingly angry at the encroachment of white settlements. In the spring of 1829, he had returned to his village, Saukenuk, after a winter hunt, to find white squatters in some of the Sauk lodges.

Unrest grew, and the U.S. government decided to remove all Indians from Illinois. The General Land Office put up Black Hawk's property for sale. Nevertheless, the chief said that he would return to farm his land after the next winter hunt. In 1832, he returned with 300 warriors and their families, and General Edmund Gaines was given the task of moving the Saukenuk band across the Mississippi. However, Black Hawk vanished across the river, although he returned in June to capitulate. One condition was that he had to submit his authority to Keokuk, a rival chief favored by the Americans.

Black Hawk tried to construct an alliance against the Americans. In this, he was helped by White Cloud, a Winnebago medicine man, who preached conflict with the whites, and sought support for the Sauk Mesquakie from the Winnebago, Potawatomi, and Kickapoo. Black Hawk's force grew to 600 men, and he decided to return to Saukenuk to plant his fields. This peaceful protest was met by Brigadier General Henry Atkinson with over 2,000 men, and supported by Colonel Zachary Taylor, Lieutenant Jefferson Davis, Captain Abraham Lincoln, and Daniel Boone's son, Nat. Black Hawk sent a truce party forward, but some Indians were killed by the Americans. Fighting broke out, Black Hawk's advance guard of forty men repelling 275 militia, who fled 25 miles (40 kilometers) to their camp. This Battle of Stillman's Run encouraged other tribes to raid settlers and miners in southern Wisconsin. As Black Hawk's group moved further into Wisconsin, pursued by U.S. troops, he realized that survival meant crossing to the west bank of the Mississippi.

The Sauk refugees reached the Mississippi at its confluence with the Bad Axe River on August 1, 1832. While they were preparing rafts and canoes, the armed steamboat *Warrior* arrived, whereupon Black Hawk tried to negotiate with its troops under a flag of truce. The Americans opened fire, killing twenty-three warriors. Thwarted in his attempt to cross the river, Black Hawk decided to travel north to Ojibwa territory, but only fifty Indians would join him; the

Chief Keokuk, from an 1834 painting. Keokuk collaborated with the Americans, which brought him into conflict with Black Hawk.

remainder preferred to attempt another crossing. While they were doing this, Atkinson and a force of 1,300 federal troops caught up with them. The Indians tried to surrender, but to no avail. An eight-hour massacre followed, during which the women and children were clubbed to death. Thirty warriors were taken prisoner, while other Sauk and Mesquakie continued the crossing, being shelled by a six-pounder cannon aboard the *Warrior*. Those who made the west bank were attacked by Lakotas, being scalped or enslaved.

Black Hawk moved on to Winnebago territory, but he and White Cloud were interned at Prairie du Chien, near the confluence of the Wisconsin and Mississippi rivers, allegedly for a reward of $100 and twenty horses. Keokuk, the pro-American chief, and other Mesquakie leaders ceded all their Iowa land, the tribes being granted a reservation in Kansas. In 1869, all but Mokohoko's band moved to Oklahoma, but this band eventually joined the Oklahoma reservation in 1886.

Black Hawk was sent to President Jackson, who had him paraded through eastern cities like booty from a war. He died in 1838, but ghoulish thieves robbed his grave and stole his head. Keokuk died a wealthy man in Kansas in 1848, being succeeded by his son, Moses, who remained chief until he died in 1903.

Some Mesquakie wanted to return to Iowa, and in 1856, the Iowa State Legislature approved their plea to remain in the state. The group pooled their money from the sale of horses, annuity payments, and the sale of personal possessions. They purchased 4,000 acres (1,600 hectares) on the banks of the Iowa River, in Tama County, where they remain today, having bought more land since.

INDIAN TERRITORY

THE REMOVAL POLICIES OF THE U.S. GOVERNMENT CRAMMED MANY INDIAN NATIONS INTO A LARGE AREA WEST OF THE MISSISSIPPI, WHICH WAS KNOWN AS INDIAN TERRITORY.

Opposite: The Louisiana Purchase suggested that the Indian nations could be settled beyond the Mississippi.

By 1850, the Indian tribes were being pushed into the Unorganized Territory in the center of the country.

Indian Territory never had a territorial government nor a federally appointed territorial governor. Instead, the Indian nations inhabiting the regions had their own individual governments. Thus, Indian Territory was the Indian inhabited area of the United States, which was not a part of any state or organized territory. Indian Territory was the result of U.S. Indian removal policies. After the 1803 Louisiana Purchase, the notion occurred that the various Indian nations of the eastern United States could be settled west of the Mississippi. Government policies resulted in 1804 legislation that authorized removal treaties with the eastern tribes, preferably on a voluntary basis. Unfortunately for

the Indians, white settlers were also moving west of the Mississippi—in 1819 Arkansas Territory was established, and its western border was fixed in 1824, while Missouri had been admitted to the Union in 1821. By 1825, the lands west of Arkansas, Missouri, and Iowa, and east of Mexican sovereignty, became Indian Territory. At its fullest extent, before 1854, it reached the 100th meridian.

In 1830, Congress passed the Indian Removal Act, and in 1834, the Secretary of War established the Bureau of Indian Affairs to implement U.S. policy toward Indians. In March 1849, the Bureau became part of the Department of the Interior, passing Indians from military to civilian control.

Settled Areas
1850

Area settled by non-Indians

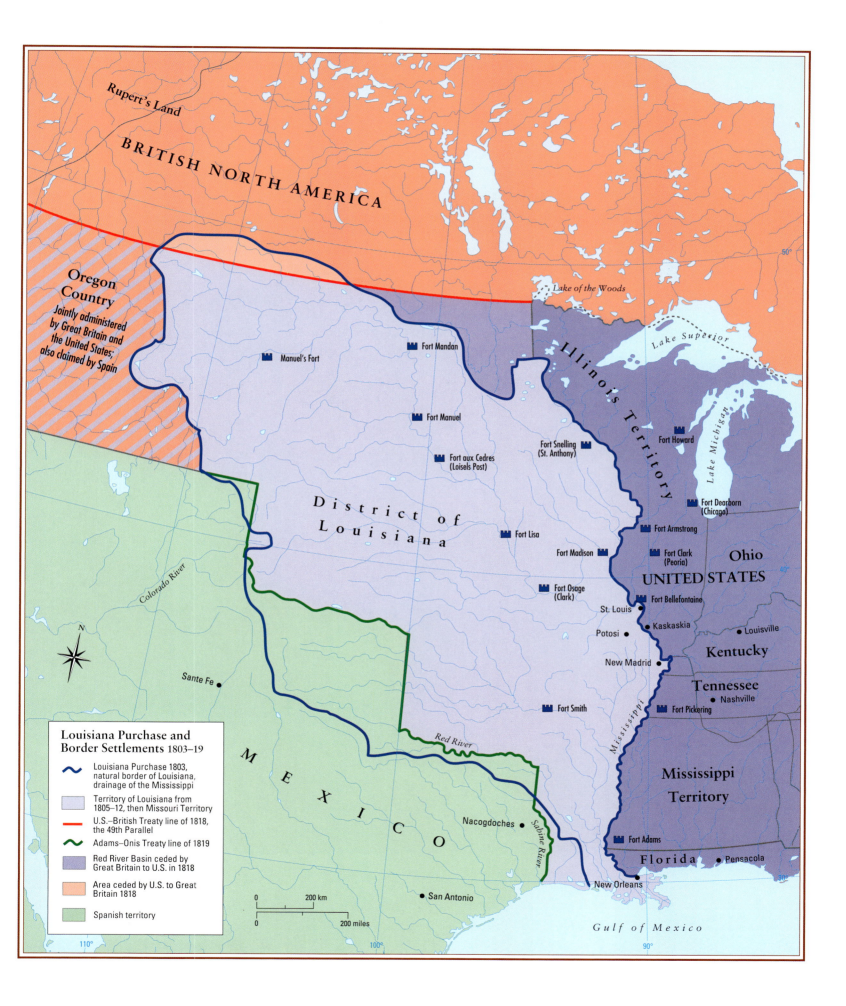

Rupert's Land

BRITISH NORTH AMERICA

Oregon
Country
Jointly administered
by Great Britain and
the United States;
also claimed by Spain

Lake of the Woods

Lake Superior

Illinois Territory

Manuel's Fort

Fort Mandan

Fort Manuel

Fort Howard

Lake Michigan

Fort Snelling
(St. Anthony)

Fort aux Cedres
(Loisels Post)

Fort Dearborn
(Chicago)

District of
Louisiana

Fort Lisa

Fort Armstrong

Ohio

Fort Madison

Fort Clark
(Peoria)

UNITED STATES

Colorado River

Fort Osage
(Clark)

Fort Bellefontaine

St. Louis

Kaskaskia

Louisville

Potosi

Kentucky

Sante Fe

New Madrid

Tennessee

Nashville

M E X I C O

Fort Smith

Red River

Fort Pickering

Mississippi
Territory

Mississippi

Nacogdoches

Sabine River

Florida

Pensacola

Fort Adams

San Antonio

New Orleans

Gulf of Mexico

**Louisiana Purchase and
Border Settlements 1803–19**

〜 Louisiana Purchase 1803,
natural border of Louisiana,
drainage of the Mississippi

Territory of Louisiana from
1805–12, then Missouri Territory

— U.S.–British Treaty line of 1818,
the 49th Parallel

〜 Adams–Onis Treaty line of 1819

Red River Basin ceded by
Great Britain to U.S. in 1818

Area ceded by U.S. to Great
Britain 1818

Spanish territory

N

0   200 km

0   200 miles

110°   100°   90°

50°

40°

30°

During the fifteen years after 1830, nearly 100,000 eastern Indians were resettled in a chain of Indian nations and reservations. President Andrew Jackson wanted to go further, however, and argued for a Western Territory Bill, which would have proclaimed Indian Territory as being bordered in the north by the Platte and Missouri rivers, in the south by the Red River, in the east by the states of Arkansas and Missouri, and in the west by the Mexican border. In today's terms, the region included all of Kansas, most of Oklahoma, southern Nebraska, and eastern Colorado. The scheme failed. Into the territory were poured the eastern Great Plains Pawnee, Missouri, Iowa, Omaha, and Oto. These were located near the old northeast tribes, such as the Potawatomi, Miami, Ottowa, Kickapoo, Shawnee, and Sauk and Fox. To their south were the Five Civilized Tribes—the Cherokee, Choctaw, Chickasaw, Creek, and Seminole. Roaming nearby were the western Plains tribes, such as the Comanche, Arapaho, Cheyenne, and Lakota. Conflict arose between the tribes as the newcomers attempted to hunt on the Plains Indians' hunting grounds.

Moreover, Indian Territory soon began to be crossed by white settlers traveling along the Santa Fé, Oregon, and Mormon trails, especially during the period of the California Gold Rush, which began in 1848. Pressure from railroad interests mounted too, as they sought transcontinental routes. Soon, the many small tribes in the north of the territory, being poor and disorganized, were persuaded by federal agents to cede their rights to the land. In 1854, the northern sections of Indian Territory were organized

By 1860, the Unorganized Territory had shrunk considerably because of the steady encroachment of white settlers on Indian land.

Settled Areas 1860

Settled area

Unsettled area

into Kansas and Nebraska Territories. By 1862, the Homestead Act had opened up Indian lands in the territories to white settlers, who were granted 160-acre (65-hectare) plots after living on them for five years. A similar bill, which would have led to the southern portion of Indian Territory being nibbled away, was defeated. So, by this time, the Indian Territory had been reduced to the approximate size of present-day Oklahoma.

Another wave of removals occurred as the U.S. government started clearing the remaining tribes from Texas, Kansas, and Nebraska into the territory. Further shrinkage of the territory occurred in 1866, after the Civil War. Owing to their involvement with the Confederacy, especially through the activities of Cherokee leader Stand Watie, the Five Civilized Tribes were forced to accept reconstruction, which gave the federal government the right to sequester Indian lands. Between 1866 and 1885, new reservations in Indian Territory were given to the Cheyenne, Arapaho, Comanche, Kiowa-Apache, Wichita, Caddo, Potawatomi, Shawnee, Kickapoo, Iowa, Sauk and Fox, Pawnee, Oto, Missouri, Ponca, Tonkawa, Kaw, Osage, Peoria, Wyandot, Eastern Shawnee, Modoc, and Ottowa. By 1885, all the lands available in Indian Territory—except a 2-million-acre (810,000-hectare) region in the center, the Unassigned Lands and the Cherokee Outlet—had been granted to Indian peoples.

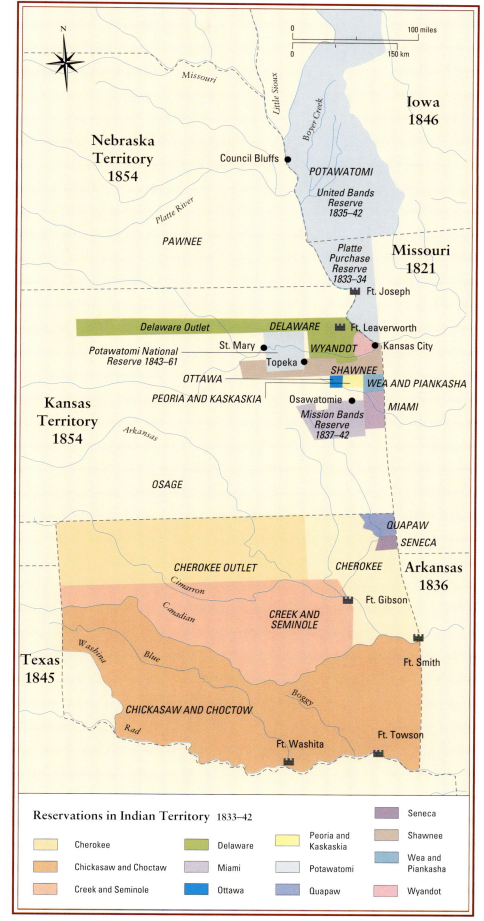

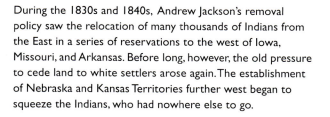

During the 1830s and 1840s, Andrew Jackson's removal policy saw the relocation of many thousands of Indians from the East in a series of reservations to the west of Iowa, Missouri, and Arkansas. Before long, however, the old pressure to cede land to white settlers arose again. The establishment of Nebraska and Kansas Territories further west began to squeeze the Indians, who had nowhere else to go.

Overland Trails and the Indians

A CONSTANT STREAM OF MIGRANTS, HEADING WEST TO FIND NEW LIVES, FOLLOWED ESTABLISHED TRAILS THROUGH INDIAN TERRITORY, SOMETIMES WITH DISASTROUS RESULTS.

Jim Bridger was a trapper, scout, and guide who traveled throughout the western United States between 1820 and 1840.

Many routes to the West had their starting points at Independence, Missouri, or Omaha, Nebraska. The oldest was the Santa Fé Trail, but more important was the Oregon Trail, with its various branches and cutoffs. The route followed the Platte River to Fort Laramie in present-day Goshen County, Wyoming. From there, it followed the North Platte and Sweetwater rivers to South Pass in the Wind River Range, and on to Fort Bridger, constructed by famed mountain man Jim Bridger. The trail ran through the Bear River valley and north to Fort Hall, in Idaho, then followed the Snake River to Salmon Falls. Fort Boise, a Hudson Bay Company post on the Snake was another stopping point. The route traversed the Grand Ronde River valley and the Blue Mountains, before reaching the Columbia River. A branch left the Oregon Trail at Fort Laramie to become the Bozeman Trail, which ran into Montana and the Yellowstone River country. Another branch left at Fort Hall to form the Mormon Trail into Utah, but the most important branch was the California Trail, from Fort Hall to Sacramento, which fueled the 1849 California Gold Rush.

The first significant wagon train, led by Elijah White, reached Oregon in 1842. Most of the trains stopped at Oregon City, but many others continued south to the bountiful Willamette Valley. The entire journey transported people some 2,020 miles (3,250 kilometers), and arrivals wrote home inspiring others to follow. In 1845, some 3,000 people arrived in Oregon, doubling its population. Migration was an instrument of U.S. government policy, providing an American presence in Oregon to counter any threat from the British or Russians. Oregon fever transferred eastern lifestyles to the Pacific Coast, despite the discomfort of travel and the fear of Indian raids.

Wagon trains encountered huge herds of buffalo west of the Platte River. Sometimes, the trains would wait for hours when herds blocked their way. The migrants hunted the animals for sport, but failed to use the buffalo like the Native Americans, who were astounded at the wasteful, rotting carcasses. One emigrant, Isaac Foster, wrote, *"The valley of the Platte for 200 miles* [320 kilometers]; *dotted with skeletons of buffaloes; such a waste of the creatures God had for man seems wicked, but every emigrant seems to wish to signalise himself by killing a buffalo."* Thus, the migrants contributed to the near extinction of the buffalo and damaged Native American food supplies.

Initially, the Oregon Trail passed through Cheyenne and Pawnee territory, then that of the Shoshone. Expected attacks were infrequent; Native Americans are known to have helped free stuck wagons, rescued drowning migrants, and also rounded up straying cattle. Most meetings with Indians led to the trade of clothes, tobacco, or rifles in exchange for horses or food. However, the Oregon

A hand-colored print depicting an Indian chief forbidding a party of settlers from passing through his land. In the early days of migration, such meetings were rare; in fact, the Indians were often of help to migrant trains experiencing difficulty.

The first wagon train to use the Oregon Trail was not a party of emigrants, but a caravan of trade goods headed for the 1830 trappers' rendezvous at Wind River. It was led by Jedediah Smith, David Jackson, and William Sublette, and comprised ten wagons and eighty-one men.

Opposite: Eventually, several trails were established to allow settlers to head westward in pursuit of the United States' cultural goal of Manifest Destiny—to expand the nation from the Atlantic to the Pacific Ocean.

Trail did not follow one track only, but many, all of which concentrated at river crossings and passes. The many routes and cutoffs meant that the migrants overgrazed the prairie grasses, burned all the available firewood, and severely damaged the Indians' environment.

From time to time, violence did occur. In 1854, a migrant cow strayed into a Sioux village, or was stolen, and it was killed and eaten. A Lieutenant Grattan and twenty-seven men left Fort Laramie to punish the Indians for the "theft." The Sioux offered a horse in exchange, but Grattan and his men opened fire, killing Chief Conquering Bear. In retaliation, the Indians slayed every soldier but one.

The Hudson Bay Company had policed the area around the Snake River, but when the company left in the 1850s, attacks on migrants increased. One such incident took place on August 9, 1862, at Massacre Rocks in southern Idaho, where five migrants were killed. After that, many migrants avoided the area by taking the Goodale Cutoff. In Utah, an increase in attacks on wagon trains prompted the Army to send a force from Fort Douglas, under Colonel Patrick Connor, to attack the Bannocks and Shoshone. Connor struck Chief Bear Hunter's village with 300 cavalry, killing 200–400 Shoshone men, women, and children.

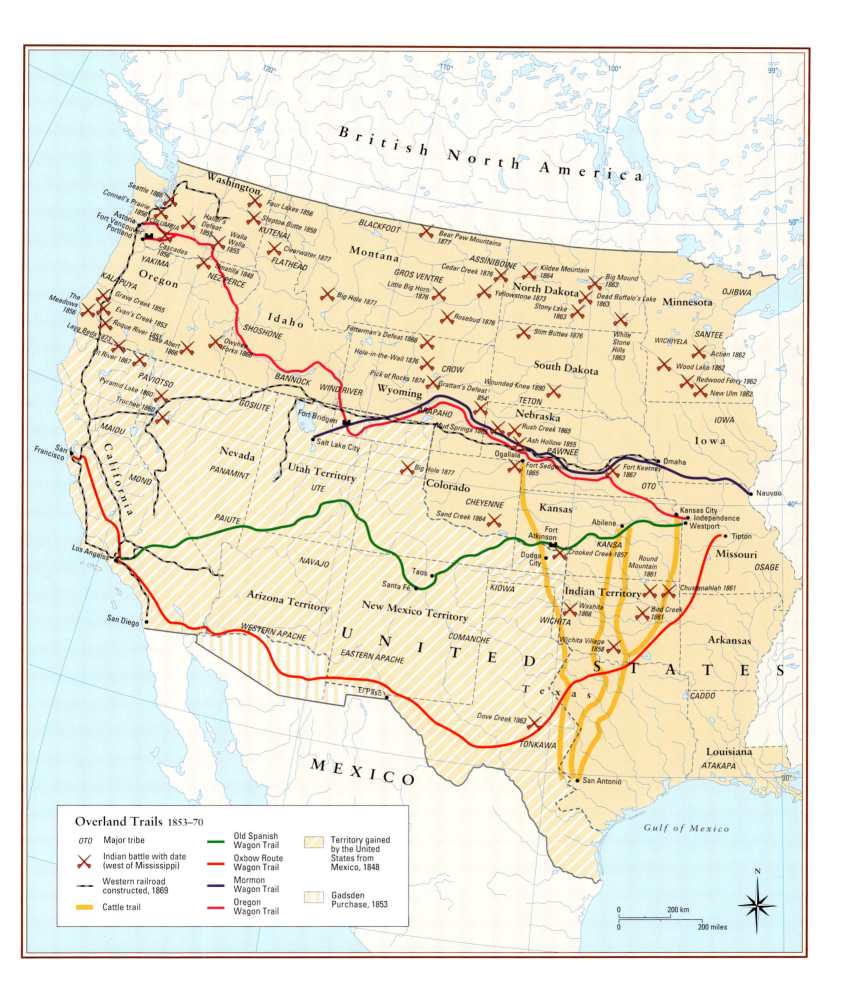

Overland Trails 1853–70

OTO — Major tribe

✗ — Indian battle with date (west of Mississippi)

⌗ — Western railroad constructed, 1869

▬ — Cattle trail

▬ — Old Spanish Wagon Trail

▬ — Oxbow Route Wagon Trail

▬ — Mormon Wagon Trail

▬ — Oregon Wagon Trail

▨ — Territory gained by the United States from Mexico, 1848

▨ — Gadsden Purchase, 1853

THE GOLD RUSH AND THE CALIFORNIAN INDIANS

THE DISCOVERY OF GOLD IN CALIFORNIA LED TO A MASSIVE INFLUX OF FORTUNE SEEKERS, AND CONFLICT WITH LOCAL TRIBES WAS INEVITABLE. THE OUTCOME WAS ETHNIC CLEANSING.

In 1848, the United States acquired California from Mexico by the Treaty of Guadalupe Hidalgo. Subsequently, the discovery of gold at Sutter's Mill, Coloma, on the American River, prompted thousands of fortune seekers to travel to the region. The prospectors damaged the environmental balance by catching large amounts of salmon, and importing pigs and cattle, which damaged Indian food supplies. The Indians retaliated by stealing livestock. The Californian legislature passed the 1850 Government and Protection of the Indians Act, which allowed the indenture of loitering, drunk, or orphaned Indians.

The state government paid for military campaigns that led to the indiscriminate slaughter of Indian women and children as a means of protecting settlers against the perceived Indian threat. Entire villages were eliminated, and young women and children were sold to unmarried farmers. Slavery ensued. In addition, a program of genocide was implemented by the California Volunteer Militia, and by bands of roaming miners and ranchers. Between 1845 and 1870, the Californian Native American population declined by 80 percent, from 150,000 to 30,000; some 40 percent of the losses were caused by murder. Seven military reservations were planned to protect the survivors, and eventually three were created in the Hoopa Valley, Tule River, and Round Valley Reserves. The first of these was formed only after the Hoopa (Hupa) had defended themselves fiercely; they retained the major part of their territories in the reservations. Their neighbors, the Karok and Yurok, were helped by influential settlers, some of whom had married Yurok women. Consequently, they escaped much persecution and terror. Elsewhere, the Miwoks and Yokuts of the Sierra Nevada foothills and San Joaquin Valley attacked miners and trading posts. Chief Tenaya and his warriors burned the post of James D. Savage on the Fresno River. In retaliation, Savage led a force of state militia, the Mariposa Battalion, into the Sierra Nevada in 1851, leading to the Mariposa War, in which the Indians were gradually defeated.

The Bureau of Indian Affairs was responsible for the Native Americans, but its agents were often incompetent and corrupt. Herds of cattle destined to feed the hungry tribes vanished onto the black market, while the reservations were usually the poorest land, and Indian fields often had cattle driven over them. The Indian experience was perilous, and they were "bestialized" by journalists, politicians, and businessmen. Referred to as "diggers," after the foraging tool they used to gather edible roots, they faced ethnic cleansing.

A Hoopa man with a long spear used for catching salmon. The Hoopa fought fiercely to defend their homeland from invasion by prospectors and settlers.

Opposite: A "forty-niner" panning for gold on the American River in California. The influx of fortune seekers to the region brought conflict with the Indians.

Hundreds of Pomo were forced to work at a cattle ranch run by Charles Stone and Andrew Kelsey, in northern California. In 1850, the Pomos killed these slavers, and the group fled into the hills. They were hunted by a U.S. Army detachment under Captain Nathaniel Lyon, who came upon a Pomo village on an island in Clear Lake. Although these Indians had had nothing to do with the killing of the ranchers, the troops slaughtered 130 men, women, and children. In 1860, 188 Indians of both sexes and all ages were hacked to death with hatchets and axes in villages on Humboldt Bay.

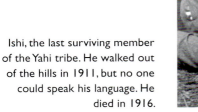

A contemporary image of goldmining in California during the mid-nineteenth century. Gold fever saw thousands flock to the West Coast, where the Indians got in the way.

Ishi, the last surviving member of the Yahi tribe. He walked out of the hills in 1911, but no one could speak his language. He died in 1916.

The Yuma controlled the Yuma crossing of the Colorado River, near the mouth of the Gila River, and could keep the Southern Overland Trail to California closed. The U.S. Army built a fort there in 1850, which was attacked by the Yuma and subsequently abandoned at the end of 1851. In early 1852, the fort was reoccupied and, later that year, used as a base for raids against the Yuma. On one of these, a detachment of twenty-five soldiers entered Baja California, destroying villages and crops, and capturing 150 people.

Ultimately, the Indian population in California was reduced by 90 percent. Fortunately, some people recognized the imminent demise of the Indians, and anthropologists began recording their traditions, helped by survivors, such as the Chumash Fernandi Librado, who had reached the age of 111 years at his death in 1916.

By the late nineteenth century, Indian slave labor was no longer needed, but Indians often worked as domestic servants and fruit growers. The Miwok survived in the lumber, fishing, mining, ranching, and farming industries. The saddest tale is that of Ishi, the last surviving Yahi, who walked out of the hills near Oroville, California, in 1911 to discover that there was no one alive who could speak his language.

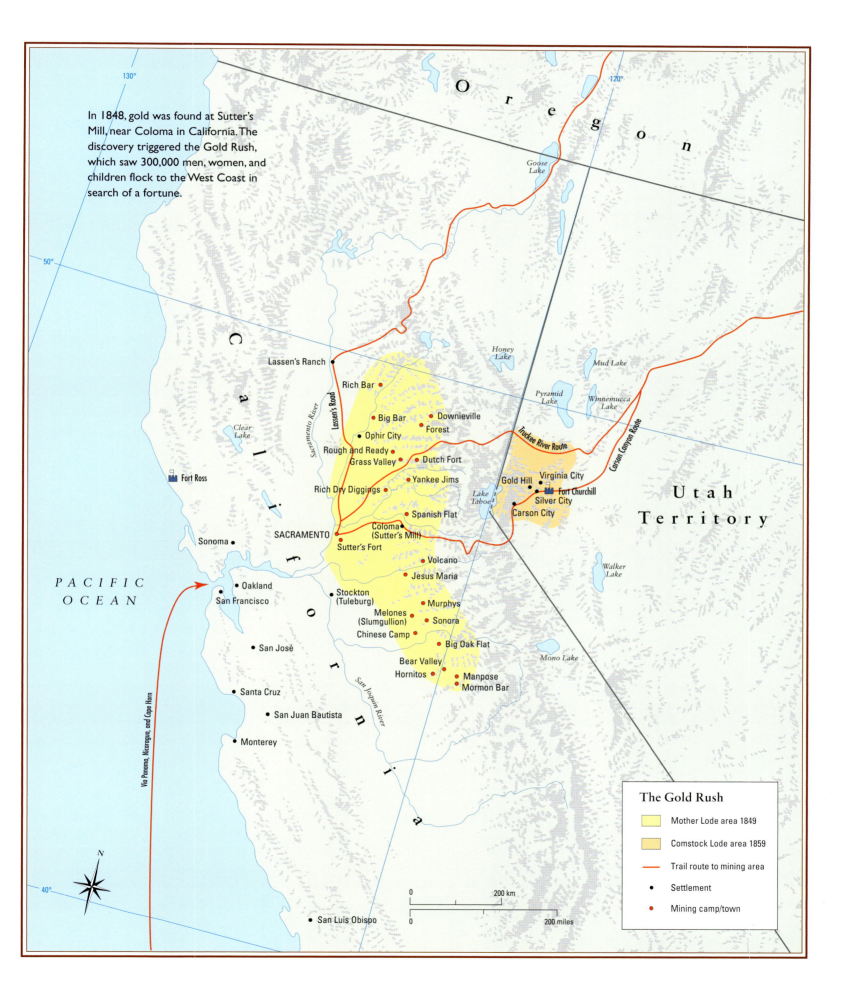

In 1848, gold was found at Sutter's Mill, near Coloma in California. The discovery triggered the Gold Rush, which saw 300,000 men, women, and children flock to the West Coast in search of a fortune.

O r e g o n

Goose Lake

130°

120°

50°

C a l i f o r n i a

Sacramento River

Lassen's Road

Lassen's Ranch

Rich Bar

Big Bar   Downieville

Forest

Ophir City

Rough and Ready

Grass Valley   Dutch Fort

Yankee Jims

Rich Dry Diggings

Spanish Flat

SACRAMENTO

Coloma (Sutter's Mill)

Sutter's Fort

Clear Lake

Fort Ross

Sonoma

PACIFIC OCEAN

Oakland

San Francisco

San José

Santa Cruz

San Juan Bautista

Monterey

Via Panama, Nicaragua, and Cape Horn

Volcano

Jesus Maria

Stockton (Tuleburg)

Murphys

Melones (Slumgullion)

Sonora

Chinese Camp

Big Oak Flat

Bear Valley

Hornitos   Manpose

Mormon Bar

San Joaquin River

Honey Lake

Pyramid Lake

Mud Lake

Winnemucca Lake

Truckee River Route

Carson Canyon Route

Gold Hill   Virginia City

Lake Tahoe   Fort Churchill

Silver City

Carson City

Walker Lake

Mono Lake

U t a h T e r r i t o r y

40°

N

The Gold Rush

Mother Lode area 1849

Comstock Lode area 1859

Trail route to mining area

● Settlement

● Mining camp/town

0   200 km

0   200 miles

San Luis Obispo

THE HUDSON'S BAY COMPANY EMPIRE

HOLDING SWAY OVER A VAST AREA OF TERRITORY IN CANADA AND THE NORTHERN UNITED STATES, THE HUDSON'S BAY COMPANY CAME TO MONOPOLIZE THE FUR TRADE.

The Hudson's Bay Company was founded in 1670, when Britain's King Charles II issued a charter to his cousin, Prince Rupert, and seventeen other aristocrats. The charter granted them a monopoly over trade in the entire area watered by streams and rivers flowing into Hudson Bay. This huge territory became known as Rupert's Land, and although its boundaries were never clearly defined, it was understood to have extended from Labrador to the Rocky Mountains, and from the headwaters of the Red River to Chesterfield Inlet on Hudson Bay. In this empire, the charter holders could make laws and punish those who broke them, build forts, keep warships, and make peace or war with Native Americans.

In the company's early years, posts were established on the shores of James and Hudson bays, but eventually they spread like a rash over all Canada. Most of the posts were captured by the French and remained in their hands until 1713, when they were returned by the Treaty of Utrecht. The company traded knives, axes, guns, and blankets to Indian trappers for hundreds of thousands of beaver pelts annually. That trade was pushed steadily westward.

The Hudson's Bay Company based its operations on making the Native American leaders of small hunting groups reliant upon its stores and supplies. In comparison, the Russian-American Company used military forces and diplomacy to ensure that Aleut and Koniag families engaged in an annual sea otter hunt, or at least until 1867, when the United States purchased Alaska from Russia. Historians stress the downside for Native Americans of specializing in fur hunting rather than searching for food, since this led to a growing dependence on goods supplied by the Hudson's Bay Company. In 1781/82, a smallpox epidemic killed up to 90 percent of the population of some Chippewyan and Western Woods Cree bands, thereby allowing other tribes to encroach on the depopulated areas. This fueled existing tribal enmities in the scrabble to control hunting grounds and access to the fur trade.

While Cree and Assiniboine peoples engaged in trapping for furs, they also profited from selling buffalo meat to the Hudson's Bay Company. At the same time, their women made warm clothes, snow shoes, and canoes for white traders, demonstrating a reciprocity of needs. Some families lived by the trading posts for most of the year, acting as a Native American "home guard" for company agents. Beyond the direct reach of the company, the Chippewyan acted as middlemen for their northwestern Athapascan neighbors, such as the Yellowknives, Beavers, Slaveys, and Dogribs.

Thus, a complex Native American trading system melded with the Hudson's Bay Company activities in a reciprocal economic relationship.

Trading in a typical Hudson's Bay Company post. The company provided the Indians with knives, axes, guns, and blankets in return for beaver pelts. Later, luxury trade goods like lace, flannel, beads, and looking glasses were made available.

By 1783, competitors had organized the Montréal-backed North West Company, and the two organizations engaged in fierce competition, which sometimes escalated to violence. The desired prize was the Columbia River drainage basin.

In 1816, some sixty Métis, mixed French-Indian stock, under Cuthbert Grant, attempted to transport provisions, mainly pemmican, past the Hudson's Bay Red River colony—near present-day Winnipeg, Manitoba—to a meeting with North West Company traders further along the river. They had looted outlying Hudson's Bay posts on the Assiniboine River, and they stopped near the Hudson's Bay Fort Douglas, at Seven Oaks. Robert Semple, governor of the colony, led a group of about twenty-five soldiers and settlers to confront the Métis. A fight occurred, and Semple was killed, along with nineteen of his men.

In 1821, the British government brokered a merger of the two competing companies, under the name of the Hudson Bay Company. This was given a monopoly over even more lands, including the Northwest Territories beyond Rupert's Land; the company acquired control of the fur trade in the Oregon Territory, which comprised today's Oregon, Washington, Idaho, British Columbia, and parts of Montana and Wyoming. It had 173 posts in nearly 3 million square miles (8 million square kilometers) of territory. A new fort was built at Vancouver, which was a nodal point on three fur trade routes through the Columbia basin, the Willamette, and the Cowlitz.

The company suffered when American settlers started to pour into the Oregon Territory, which was disputed by Britain and the United States. Matters were not helped by the fact that the area contained only 750 British compared with nearly 6,000 Americans. Since the Americans seemed aggressive and unruly in the Willamette Valley, the company felt that Fort Vancouver was endangered. Consequently, in 1845, its headquarters were moved to Fort Victoria, on Vancouver Island. In 1846, the Oregon Treaty delineated the British-American border at the 49th parallel.

In 1869, the company's monopoly was ended, and it sold its territories to Canada for £300,000, although it retained territorial blocks immediately surrounding its posts and title to one twentieth of lands in the fertile belt of western Canada.

THE FUR TRADE

ALTHOUGH THERE WERE MANY WHITE TRAPPERS WHO BENEFITED FROM THE FUR TRADE, IT BROUGHT MUCH WEALTH AND ADVANCEMENT TO NATIVE AMERICAN COMMUNITIES.

Opposite: In the early nineteenth century, Canadian fur trappers and traders carried out many explorations of the Oregon Country and even penetrated further south. Leading figures were Donald Mackenzie (North West Company), Archibald McDonald (Hudson's Bay Company), and Peter Skene Ogden (Hudson's Bay).

The American Fur Company was chartered by Jacob Astor in 1808 to compete with the Hudson's Bay Company and the Canadian North West Company. The venture managed to crush or absorb its rivals in the Great Lakes region, the Missouri River valley, the Rocky Mountains, and Oregon.

Astor sent two expeditions to the Columbia River, one by sea and the other overland. The former established Fort Astoria at the mouth of the Columbia River in April 1811. Meanwhile, the overland party had left St. Louis in March of that year, reaching Astoria in early 1812. When Astoria was seized by the British during the War of 1812, Astor's major competitors were able to entrench themselves in the Pacific Northwest fur trade.

Hundreds of trappers and a thousand or so Indians would turn up at a rendezvous to meet the St. Louis caravan, exchanging furs for goods and alcohol. Business concluded, the trappers and Indians would entertain themselves with horse races, wrestling, shooting matches, and debauchery. This could lead to violent repercussions.

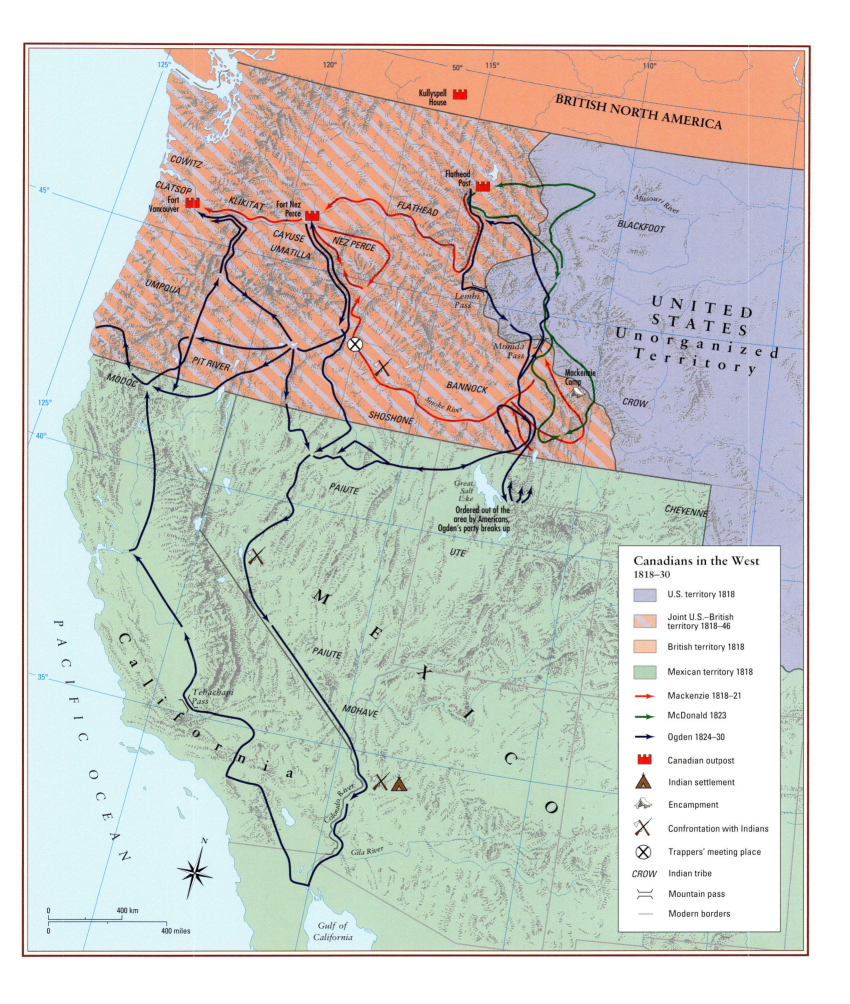

Canadians in the West
1818–30

- U.S. territory 1818
- Joint U.S.–British territory 1818–46
- British territory 1818
- Mexican territory 1818
- → Mackenzie 1818–21
- → McDonald 1823
- → Ogden 1824–30
- Canadian outpost
- Indian settlement
- Encampment
- Confrontation with Indians
- ⊗ Trappers' meeting place
- *CROW* Indian tribe
- Mountain pass
- Modern borders

A drawing of Jedidiah Smith created by a friend from memory around four years after the mountain man's death. Smith, who traveled more extensively in unknown territory than any other mountain man, blazed many of the trails that helped settlers cross the Rocky Mountains. This tough explorer once survived a run-in with a grizzly bear that left him with a lacerated side, broken ribs, and severe head wounds. He became involved in the Rocky Mountain Fur Company later in life and, in May 1831, was leading a party of traders along the Santa Fé trail when he left them to scout for water. He was never seen again, and it is thought that he was killed by a group of Comanches.

Opposite: This map shows the most significant expeditions carried out by Jedidiah Smith. He once wrote, "*I wanted to be the first to view a country on which the eyes of a white man had never gazed and to follow the course of rivers that run through a new land.*"

The North West and Hudson's Bay companies engaged in a trade war, the latter being victorious in 1821, when the two companies merged. That year, the American Fur Company became prominent again by entering an alliance with Chouteau business interests in St. Louis, thereby gaining a trade monopoly in the Missouri River region and eventually the Rockies.

Before Astor's company penetrated the Northwest in 1827, however, other traders had been busy. In 1824, Peter Skene Ogden, with seventy-five trappers, moved into the Snake River country. This expedition, on behalf of the Hudson's Bay Company, opened up the area to that company for twelve years. Another entrepreneur was William Henry Ashley, from St. Louis. Although his initial trapping expedition was turned back in the Dakotas by hostile Arikara, he went on to target the central Rockies. The region was rich in beaver, and Ashley worked out a novel method of exploiting the area. Normally, Indians and trappers would take their pelts to fortified trading posts, but these angered the Indians, being seen as symbols of white occupation. Also, there were no navigable rivers in the region for transporting furs and merchandise, so Ashley developed the rendezvous system. Trappers would live permanently in the mountains, and in early summer, they would meet at an annual rendevous at a site where game, water, and grazing were plentiful. The mountain men, known for their toughness and survival skills, often married Indian women.

Competition between the Rocky Mountain Fur Company, run by Jim Bridger and Milton Sublette, and small groups from Arkansas and Texas could be accommodated. In 1832, however, the American Fur Company moved into the area. Astor had acquired the Columbia Fur Company in 1827, and in 1831 had established Fort Mackenzie on the Marias River. That year, a steamer had reached Fort Union, built by the company in 1828 at the confluence of the Upper Missouri and Yellowstone rivers, on the edge of Blackfeet territory.

In 1834, the American Fur Company split after Astor's withdrawal. Then the Hudson's Bay Company penetrated the Snake River and gradually monopolized trade. As beaver hats became unfashionable and silk took over, however, beaver pelts began to fetch lower prices. Moreover, many rivers had been trapped out. The mountain men declined in numbers and were forced to seek other occupations, such as guiding expeditions and wagon trains.

The fur trade was extremely important for Native Americans, since it allowed them to join the consumer revolution of the eighteenth century. The introduction of European goods changed the manner in which Native Americans achieved subsistence, while profits bought luxury goods beyond the requirements of subsistence. Hudson's Bay Company records show such luxuries as lace, baize, duffel, flannel, gartering, beads, combs, looking glasses, rings, shirts, and vermillion.

Native Americans along the Northwestern Pacific Coast certainly benefited from the fur trade, although wealth did not reach all tribes. The Chinook around Fort Astoria became middlemen between coastal trade and the interior. Native Americans were canny, tough-minded negotiators, who manipulated competition between white traders.

Newly acquired wealth encouraged art to flourish, along with ceremonial life. Metal

45°

P A C I F I C   O C E A N

40°

35°

N

tools facilitated woodcarving, and Haida totem poles increased in number and innovative design. Haida carvers made curios, which they sold to seamen as a precursor to a tourist trade. The Tlingits grew potatoes and sold them to Russian settlers, as well as exporting them, thus developing an alternative income, like the Haida, to compensate for the eventual decline in the fur trade. Thus, Native Americans entered the capitalist system, seeing and responding to economic change.

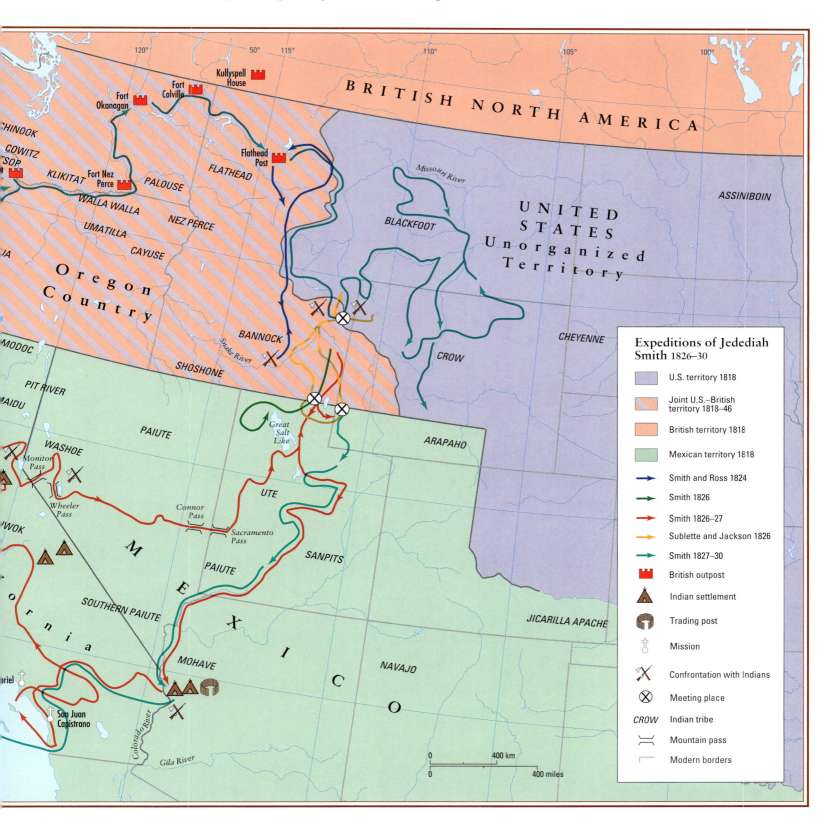

Expeditions of Jedediah Smith 1826–30

- U.S. territory 1818
- Joint U.S.–British territory 1818–46
- British territory 1818
- Mexican territory 1818
- Smith and Ross 1824
- Smith 1826
- Smith 1826–27
- Sublette and Jackson 1826
- Smith 1827–30
- British outpost
- Indian settlement
- Trading post
- Mission
- Confrontation with Indians
- Meeting place
- CROW Indian tribe
- Mountain pass
- Modern borders

THE APACHE WARS

THE MEXICAN CESSION OF SOUTHWESTERN LANDS TO THE UNITED STATES LED TO CONFLICT WITH THE APACHE, WHICH SPREAD ON BOTH SIDES OF THE BORDER.

General George Crook, named by the Apache Nantan Lupan (Gray Wolf), employed Apache scouts to hunt down their own tribe. In the field, he favored mule trains for carrying supplies rather than wagons, allowing his troops to traverse rough country with relative ease.

The Apache bands, who had arrived in the Southwest about AD 850, developed a reputation as nomadic raiders, targeting Spaniards, Mexicans, Pueblo Indians, and, later, Americans. After checking Spanish-Mexican advances northward, they confronted American troops when the United States acquired their homelands from Mexico in 1848. After this date, while attempting to assess U.S. power, the Apache attacked Mexicans south of the border and, occasionally, travelers on the Santa Fé Trail and southern Butterfield Stage route.

In 1854, the Gadsden Treaty led to the cession of Arizona and New Mexico from Mexico to the United States, which led to further U.S. encroachment into the Southwest. An incident in 1861 inflamed relations between the Apache and the United States. Cochise of the Chiricahua Apache had been accused (incorrectly) of stealing a rancher's children and cattle. Unaware of this, he agreed to meet Lieutenant Bascom of Fort Buchanan, near present-day Sonoita, Arizona. Cochise and members of his family were arrested, but he escaped and began raiding along the Butterfield route, being joined by White Mountain Apache and Mimbrenos, led by Mangas Coloradas, Cochise's father-in-law. In retaliation, Bascom seized more hostages, hanging all the males, among them Cochise's brother. In revenge, the Apache killed 150 Americans and Mexicans over the following two months; thirty-five years of unrest followed.

To secure peace, General Joseph West, commander of the Department of New Mexico's southern region, invited Mangas Coloradas to negotiations at Pinos Altos in January 1863. When he arrived, he was imprisoned, then shot dead while allegedly escaping. Elsewhere, General James Carleton sent Kit Carson against Mescalero Apaches who were raiding the Butterfield Stage route near El Paso,

Texas. Carson's forces wore down the Apache and forced them onto a reservation at Bosque Redondo, in southeastern New Mexico.

Ten years later, the Apache erupted again. At Camp Grant, north of Tucson, Eskiminzin's Aravaipa (Western) Apache had made camp and surrendered their weapons. Fearful Tucson citizens organized a vigilante force that attacked the Aravaipa on April 30, 1871; 90–150 innocents, mainly women and children, were slaughtered. President Grant was so angered that he sent a peace commission to Arizona, and a reservation system was established for the Apache, with four agencies in Arizona and one in New Mexico. The Chiricahua came in under Cochise, remaining peacefully at Apache Pass until his death in 1874.

Other Apaches continued raiding, however, while drawing reservation agency rations. To end their depredations, the U.S. Army pursued the Tonto Basin Campaign in central Arizona, near the Mogollon Rim. General George Crook engaged the Apaches at Salt River Canyon (December 28, 1872), and their friends, the Yavapais, at the Battle of Skull Cave and Turret Peak in March 1873. Some 6,000 exhausted Apaches and Yavapais surrendered and entered the reservations. In 1875, however, all Apaches west of the Rio Grande were ordered to the San Carlos Reservation in Arizona.

Two warriors resisted reservation life. Victorio led Mimbreno Apaches in a war that lasted from 1877 to 1880; Geronimo led Chiricahuas and others in a final stand between 1881 and 1886. From San Carlos, Victorio led 300 men into the mountains, and in September 1879, he killed eight buffalo soldiers (African-Americans in the U.S. Army). Joined by Mimbrenos, his group ranged from Mexico to Texas, through New Mexico, and back to Arizona. They were hunted by American and Mexican troops on their respective sides of the border. Eventually, Victorio was cornered by Mexican forces in the fall of 1880 at the Battle of Tres Castillos, in northeastern Chihuahua, where he and half his warriors died. Most of the survivors were captured.

Geronimo had wanted to remain at Apache Pass, but was interned at San Carlos. After an Apache mystic, Nakaidoklini, was killed at Cibecue Creek in August 1881, Geronimo and another Apache chief, Chato, together with seventy-four men, quit the reservation, attacked its police chief, and persuaded Mimbrenos to join them. Elsewhere, on July 17, 1882, White Mountain Apaches fought the U.S. Army at the Battle of the Big Dry Wash, on the Mogollon Rim. In May 1883, General Crook led troops into the Sierra Madre and wore down Apache resistance. Warriors trickled back onto the reservation, among them Geronimo, but he broke loose again, was returned, and then escaped with twenty-four Apaches and Nachise, Cochise's son. Some 5,000 U.S. troops were mobilized, and finally Geronimo was captured at Skeleton Canyon, in the Peloncillo Mountains, on September 4, 1886. The Apache were relocated to San Carlos, but the Chiricahua were offered a home with the Comanche and Kiowa in Indian Territory. Geronimo died from pneumonia, a prisoner-of-war at Fort Sill, Oklahoma, in 1909.

Geronimo, probably the most famous of the Apache leaders. He broke out from the reservation with Chiricahua and Mibreno warriors in 1881, and over the next five years led a bloody resistance to the Army's attempts to return them.

NORTHWESTERN WARS

AT FIRST PEACEFUL TOWARD SETTLERS IN THE NORTHWEST, LOCAL TRIBES WENT TO WAR WHEN DECEIVED OVER LAND DEALS AND ATTACKED BY CIVILIAN MILITIA.

Isaac Stevens, the first governor of Washington Territory, promised several tribes that they could stay put for two years if they ceded most of their land, but he had lied. During the Civil War, he served as a Major General in the Union Army and was killed at the Battle of Chantilly in 1862.

Native Americans in the Northwest had been peaceful ever since white settlers had entered the Columbia Basin, although the presence of the latter had caused the depletion of salmon stocks, a staple Indian food. In 1853, Lieutenant George McClellan arrived at Fort Vancouver to explore the Cascades for a pass for the Northern Pacific Railroad. To facilitate the railroad's construction, and in the hope of opening up the region for further white settlement, Governor Isaac Stevens of Washington Territory held a conference with local Indians in the Walla Walla Valley, between May and June 1855. Stevens wanted the Nez Perce, Cayuse, Umatilla, Walla Walla, and Yakama to hand over most of their lands in exchange for reservations, homes, schools, horses, cattle, and annuities. Most tribal leaders signed because they were promised that they could stay put for two years. The Yakama were asked to give up 29,000 square miles (75,000 square kilometers) in return for 1.2 million acres (490,000 hectares). Stevens had lied, however, and settlers were allowed to enter the region before the two years were up.

As settlers moved in and miners headed to the Colville mines, Kamiakin of the Yakama readied for war, persuading the Puget Sound tribes to act likewise. Several prospectors were killed, as was A.J. Bolon, a respected Indian agent; he had been investigating the murders, but the Indians thought that he was about to call in the Army. Other tribes also rose in rebellion, among them the Takelma and Tututni (Rogue Indians), and the Coeur d'Alene (Schitsu' Umish). On October 6, 1855, a U.S. Army detachment under Major Granville Haller, from Fort Dalles, was on patrol in the Cascades, but was beaten back by 500 Yakama, suffering twenty-two dead and wounded. A November expedition also achieved nothing, but a group of volunteer militia from Oregon City, under Colonel James Kelly, killed the chief of the Walla Walla, thereby bringing them, the Umatilla, and Cayuse into the war. Raid and counterraid ensued, and innocent settlers and peaceful Indians died, while the Army failed to protect anyone. By the summer of 1856, the Indians had scattered, but in July, 300 of them were defeated in the Grande Ronde Valley, forty warriors being killed and a village burned, at a cost of seven white casualties. The responsibility for policing the region was given to Colonel George Wright of the regular U.S. Army, and the volunteers pulled out. Although the Indians honored the treaties, the region was dominated by two new forts, Simcoe and Walla Walla.

Elsewhere, war erupted on the Rogue River, in southern Oregon. Captain Andrew Jackson Smith of Fort Lane took in some peaceful Indians, but before they were joined by their women and children, some volunteer militia attacked their camp, killing twenty-three. In revenge, the Indians slaughtered twenty-seven innocent settlers. In the spring of 1856, Smith was on patrol with eighty soldiers when he was assailed by Rogues. He held out until rescued by reinforcements under Captain Augur. The combined U.S. force suffered thirty-one casualties. A month later, the Rogues surrendered and were herded onto the coastal Siletz Reservation, but their leader, Old John, was imprisoned at Fort Alcatraz.

The Yakamas were not prepared to be full reservation Indians like the Rogues, and some militants killed settlers and Colville miners, while Kamiakin sought alliances with the Palouse, Coeur d'Alene, and Spokane against the whites. In 1858, the Army decided to intervene, and Lieutenant Colonel Edward J. Steptoe, from Fort Walla Walla, moved against the hostile Indians in what became known as the Coeur d'Alene or Spokane War. Steptoe was leading a force of 164 men and Nez Perce scouts, equipped with two howitzers, when they encountered 1,200 mounted Indians of the alliance. He was formally warned off and he retreated, but the Indians fell upon his rearguard. Steptoe defended Steptoe Butte throughout May 17, 1858, but retreated during darkness. Later, Colonel Wright confronted the Indians at the Battle of Four Lakes (September 1, 1858). His howitzers drove the Indians from their cover among the trees, then his troops' new rifled muskets, which had increased range, tore into them. Finally, the Indians were charged by dragoons and they fled, leaving behind sixty dead, while more were wounded; the Americans were unscathed.

On September 5, 1858, Wright again encountered war parties on the Spokane Plain. His 680 men faced around 1,000 Indians from several tribes, using artillery, the new rifles, and dragoon charges to scatter them. Wright demanded unconditional surrender from the beaten tribes, and the ringleaders were hanged. In addition, 900 Palouse ponies were shot to immobilize the tribe; Indian cattle and grain were also destroyed. Subsequently, forts were built at Boise and Colville to protect settlers and subdue the tribes.

This painting by John Mix Stanley, dating from the 1870s, shows an Indian war band traveling through a pass in the Rocky Mountains.

CONQUEST, 1865–1900

"AT SAN CARLOS ARE THE APACHES, WHO ARE REGARDED AS THE MOST VICIOUS OF THE INDIANS WITH WHO WE HAVE TO DEAL … I HAVE WITHIN THE LAST TWELVE MONTHS TAKEN FROM THAT RESERVATION ABOUT TWO HUNDRED [CHILDREN]. THEY ARE TODAY WELL FED AND PROPERLY CLOTHED, ARE HAPPY AND CONTENTED, AND MAKING GOOD PROGRESS. DID I DO RIGHT?"

THOMAS JEFFERSON MORGAN,
COMMISSIONER OF INDIAN AFFAIRS, 1889.

The 1860s and 1870s saw an increase in conflict between white Americans and nomadic Native Americans. Whether against the Comanche and Apache of the Southwest, or the Sioux in the North, the U.S. Army faced a difficult task in confronting fast moving guerrilla horsemen. The 1851 Fort Laramie treaty and the 1867 Medicine Lodge Creek Treaty attempted to fix boundaries and reservations, but a major problem was convincing Native Americans to honor treaty provisions and remain on reservations while settlers and miners made incursions into Indian lands. Events like the 1864 Sand Creek Massacre served to harden Indian resolve to resist white hypocrisy, especially after the Cheyenne and Arapaho were forced to concede lands agreed by the Fort Laramie treaty in 1861. The Red Cloud War and the 1874 campaign against the Southern Cheyenne, Kiowa, and Comanche exacerbated tensions. The failure of the U.S. government to prevent miners from entering the Black Hills, sacred to the Sioux, brought matters to a head in 1876, when Custer's command was annihilated in the valley of the Little Bighorn. The subsequent Great Sioux War saw the Sioux and Cheyenne bands being systematically defeated and forced back onto the reservations. In the South, the

Indian Wars
1860–90

Land seccessions:

- ■ Ceded before 1850
- ■ Ceded before 1850–70
- ■ Ceded before 1871–90
- ■ Never formerly ceded

NAVAJO Indian tribe

✗ Indian battles with dates (west of Mississippi)

Railroads in the West
1869–93

- ⟋ Railroads
- ① Central Pacific Railroads-Union Pacific Railroads 1869
- ② Northern Pacific Railroads 1883
- ③ Atchison, Topeka and Santa Fe Railroads 1883
- ④ Southern Pacific Railroads 1883
- ⑤ Great Northern Railroads 1893

Apache were defeated by 1886. Thus, the American military conquest of the West was complete and, according to Hollywood, that goal had been achieved exclusively by white cavalrymen.

In reality, the defeat of the Native Americans had been brought about through internecine strife between tribes, the substantial employment of African-American (buffalo) soldiers by the U.S. Army, and the slaughter of the buffalo, a major life resource of the Plains Indians. However, the last was partially caused by the Indians themselves, who never matched the patronising and mythological

During the second half of the nineteenth century, the West was engulfed in several Indian Wars as Native Americans fought to keep their way of life. The flood of settlers, aided by the railroads, however, would change their lives forever.

A corporal of the 9th Cavalry, one of the all-African-American regiments raised by Congress after the American Civil War and known to the Indians as "buffalo soldiers." These regiments, both cavalry and infantry, played a major part in subduing Native American resistance during the late nineteenth century.

image of the "ecological Indian" applied to them by European observers.

The U.S. Army's activities on the Great Plains became enmeshed in inter-tribal conflicts. In Montana, Teton Sioux contested buffalo hunting grounds with Crow, Blackfeet, Gros Ventre, and Assiniboine groups. These tribes considered the Teton to be more dangerous than the United States, and Crow warriors began scouting for the Army against the Sioux in the hope that their last hunting grounds would be preserved. In 1868, the Crow ceded most of their land and were given a reservation on the remainder. The Gros Ventre comprised one third of the Blackfeet confederacy, and were pressured by Teton, Yankton, Yanktonais, and Santee Sioux flooding into Montana to hunt buffalo. They needed U.S. and Crow allies to survive.

This state of tribal movement coincided with U.S. military actions in the area. The Army realized the merits of Native American scouts, who served in nearly every area of western conflict. Scouts were given a uniform and repeating rifle, but they supplied their own mounts. These Indian soldiers would find and reconnoiter enemy trails, then ascertain the enemy's tribal name and numbers. The Army needed the Indians to keep pace with their mobile enemies, to aid concealment, and to help execute surprise attacks. In many ways, the Army was forced to adopt its scouts' methods, tactics, and use of terrain. Sometimes, when patrols were attacked, rescue occurred at the hands of Indian scouts.

Native Americans joined or helped the Army for many reasons. Pamnee, Arikara, and Hidatsa bands needed Army assistance against the Sioux during the 1860s and 1870s. Osage scouts aided the Army against the Cheyenne, who competed with them for buffalo on the Arkansas. Elsewhere, Pavmee, Caddo, and Wichita sought help against tribes like the Comanche, who persistently raided for horses. Scouting had other advantages. Food and ammunition were of personal benefit to the Indian soldier, but families left on reservations were fed, too. Also, any enemy horses and property captured could be retained. The monthly pay of $13 was an absolute necessity for some Indian families.

Scouts were essential in locating Comanche and Kiowa bands who attacked buffalo hunters. During the 1870s, winter campaigns destroyed their camps and provisions, driving the hungry Indians back to their reservations. By that time, the Arapaho had been reduced to fewer than 1,000 souls, and in this weakened state were dependent upon reservation supplies. When war broke out over white incursions into the Black Hills, the Northern Arapaho abandoned their Cheyenne and Sioux allies, and some became Army scouts in 1876 and 1877. As a reward, they negotiated a permanent settlement on the large Shoshone reservation in Wyoming—an irony, since the tribes were traditional enemies. After the Little Bighorn battle, the Northern Cheyenne were hit hard by Army attacks on their winter camps. One group surrendered at Fort Keogh in Montana, some enlisting as scouts.

Particularly effective were the Seminole Scouts. Of mixed Indian and African-American slave parentage, these thirty men were employed by the Army in Florida, then moved west in 1870, when the Army needed more scouts in that region. They operated for nine years, fought in twelve major engagements, and finally fled to Mexico to escape racial discrimination and in anger against the government's refusal to grant them land as promised.

African-American troops also played a vital part in conquering the West. Two regiments of African-

American cavalry were formed, the 9th and 10th, as were two infantry regiments, the 24th and 25th. The 9th Cavalry first saw service in Texas in June 1867. It was ordered to protect stage and mail routes, build and maintain forts, and police the area from the Staked Plains to Brownsville. Its enemies were Mexican revolutionaries, and Comanche, Cheyenne, Kiowa, and Apache raiders. By 1876, the 9th had been transferred to New Mexico, where it fought the Apache led by Nana, Victorio, and Geronimo. In 1881, the regiment moved to various forts in Kansas and Indian Territory, and was charged with evicting illegal white settlers from Indian lands. During 1885, the regiment operated from Forts Robinson and Niobrara in Nebraska, and Fort Duchesne, Utah. The 9th's last action on the frontier was the 1891 Ghost Dance Campaign, although it was not involved in the massacre at Wounded Knee.

The 10th Cavalry, formed at Fort Leavenworth in 1866, moved to Fort Riley, Kansas, and for the next eight years was stationed at various forts throughout Kansas and Indian Territory. The regiment guarded work parties on the Kansas and Pacific Railroad, strung telegraph lines, and built much of Fort

The African-American regiments acquitted themselves well in a number of battles during the Indian Wars.

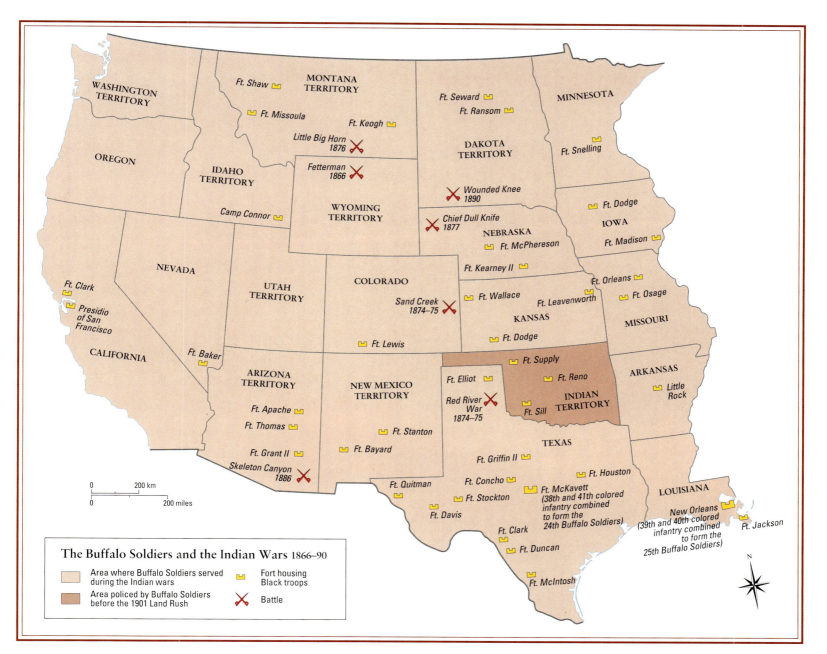

The Buffalo Soldiers and the Indian Wars 1866–90

- Area where Buffalo Soldiers served during the Indian wars
- Area policed by Buffalo Soldiers before the 1901 Land Rush
- Fort housing Black troops
- Battle

x2574-07

Oglala warriors, from the Pine Ridge Indian Reservation in South Dakota, stage the planning of a raid for photographer Edward S. Curtis. The picture appeared in the third volume of Curtis's work, *The North American Indian* (1908).

Sill. During the winter of 1867/68, the 10th joined General Sherman's campaign against the Comanche, Cheyenne, and Arapaho, and was instrumental in driving the Cheyenne toward Custer, whose 7th Cavalry gained a decisive victory over them on the Washita, near Fort Cobb. In 1875, the 10th moved to Fort Concho in west Texas, where it scouted nearly 35,000 square miles (90,000 square kilometers) of unmapped terrain, built 300 miles (500 kilometers) of road, and strung 200 miles (300 kilometers) of telegraph line. During 1879–80, the 10th campaigned against Victorio and his Chiricahua Apache band. They had broken out of their New Mexico reservation and raided settlements on their way to Mexico. The 10th engaged the Apaches at Tinaja de las Palmas, a waterhole south of Sierra Blanca, and at Rattlesnake Springs, north of Van Horn. Victorio was prevented from returning to New Mexico and was forced back into Mexico, where he and many of his men were killed by Mexican soldiers on October 14, 1880, at the Battle of Tres Castillos. In 1885, the regiment was transferred to Arizona, where it became involved in campaigns against the Apaches under Geronimo.

The 24th Infantry Regiment occupied posts in the Southwest, fought Indians, built roads, guarded stage stations, and strung telegraph lines. In addition, it guarded waterholes, escorted supply wagons, survey parties and mail coaches, and scouted the region. The 25th had been organized in Louisiana in 1868, but after 1870, its units were scattered among many posts in west Texas. Those at Fort Davis protected nearby stage stations, and built and operated a lumber camp and saw mill. Off-post activities included constructing new roads through Wild Rose Pass and Musquiz Canyon, guarding government lumber trains, and protecting U.S. citizens at Presidio del Norte from Mexican bandits. In 1880, the regiment was transferred to the Dakotas, Minnesota, and Montana; some units took part in the Pine Ridge Campaign of 1890–91.

The conquest of the West was not achieved purely by the Army and Indian auxiliaries, but mainly by the destruction of the Indians' primary food source, the buffalo, which historians claim began in 1867, when the Union Pacific Railroad was built. The vast numbers of buffalo (estimated at approximately 13,000,000) provided the Plains Indians with food, and skins for tepees, robes, and other clothing. Glue could be made from boiled horns, bones, and hooves, and paunches could be formed into buckets, while the guts could be made into bow strings. In 1846, before white hunters moved onto the Plains, Southern Cheyenne Chief Yellow Wolf observed that the buffalo were decreasing. At that time, increasing numbers of tribes were moving onto the Plains, and pressure on the herds was growing. Occasional droughts cut the grazing capacity, while competition from Indian horses and cattle belonging to settlers exacerbated the situation. Bovine diseases also struck down buffalo. Indian hunting methods could be wasteful, too, such as when vast numbers of animals were driven over a cliff and not all were butchered. Furthermore, Indians realized that there was a European market for buffalo robes and began killing for trade reasons.

However, the severest damage occurred when commercial buffalo hunting began in 1870. The hunters and European sportsmen began killing the animals in large numbers. The Army, in concert with the hunters, set out to destroy the buffalo to make way for railroads, ranchers, and settlers. Destruction of their natural food source would break Native American resistance by causing starvation and dependence on reservation agency food supplies. Although the end of the buffalo-robe trade occurred in the 1870s, it gave way to a demand in the eastern United States for hides that could be made into leather and machinery belts for factories. By 1878, the southern herd had been exterminated, and by 1883, the buffalo had become almost extinct on the Northern Plains. By 1903, the number had declined to thirty-four. One hunter claimed that if he could shoot a hundred buffalo a day, he would earn $6,000 a month. The construction of railroads meant that buffalo meat and hides could be shipped rapidly to eastern markets, making the trade even more attractive.

The winter campaign was an effective method of destroying Indian food supplies. After the Battle of the Little Bighorn, troops hit Dull Knife's Northern Cheyenne village on the Powder River in Wyoming. Two hundred tepees were burned, tons of buffalo meat destroyed, and 1,000 buffalo robes and 750 ponies seized. Such campaigns led to the death of many Indians through starvation, among them more than a quarter of the Blackfeet in 1883.

The destruction of the buffalo turned the Indians into starving dependents. Crow woman Pretty Shield said, "*We believed for a long time that the buffalo would again come to us; but they did not. We grew hungry and sick and afraid, all in one. Not believing their own eyes our hunters rode very far looking for buffalo, so far away that even if they had found a herd we could not have reached it in half a moon.*" Crow Chief Plenty Coups was even sadder: "*When the buffalo went away the hearts of my people fell to the ground, and they could not lift them up again. After this nothing happened. There was little singing anymore.*"

The westward movement of Indians from the East, displaced by white settlers, brought the tribes into conflict with Native Americans on the Plains. The Assiniboine, for example, were faced with competition for buffalo from the Ojibwa. This increased pressure on the Plains Indians' primary food source contributed to the animal's near extinction.

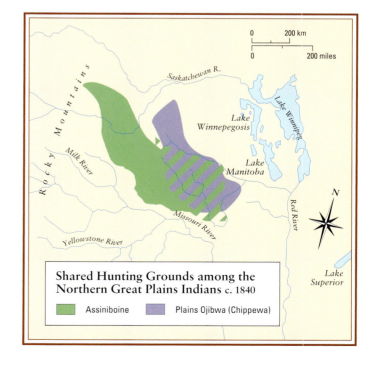

Shared Hunting Grounds among the Northern Great Plains Indians c. 1840

🟩 Assiniboine   🟪 Plains Ojibwa (Chippewa)

THE SANTEE SIOUX AND THE 1862 UPRISING

FURIOUS AT BEING DEPRIVED OF PROMISED, AND VITAL, ANNUITY PAYMENTS AND RATIONS, THE SANTEE SIOUX WERE TIPPED INTO A WAR THAT HAD DREADFUL CONSEQUENCES.

Little Crow, who was the reluctant leader of the Santee Sioux in the 1862 Uprising.

The Santee, or Eastern Lakota, of Minnesota, were the most peaceful of the Lakota, although they disliked their prairie reservation and longed to return to their former woodland home. In addition, they were making the transition from hunting to a sedentary farming economy. By 1862, cutworm had devastated their spring corn crop, and hunger was increasing. Moreover, the 1851 Traverse des Sioux treaty with the United States had taken 24 million acres (10 million hectares) from them in return for annuity payments. Another million acres (400,000 hectares) were sold, but the return barely covered their debts. The steady encroachment of German, Swedish, and British settlers was fueling anger, too.

The American Civil War caused difficulties, since annuity payments, essential during a period of starvation, were slow in arriving. The Upper Indian Agency provided emergency rations for 5,000 Santee, but the Lower Agency traders refused credit. On August 17, 1862, four incensed young warriors killed five settlers. Simmering resentment roused the Indians onto the warpath, led by a reluctant Little Crow. Trading posts and settlers were attacked, and some 400 whites, including twenty-three soldiers, were killed on the first day of rebellion. Survivors fled to Fort Ridgely in southwest Minnesota.

On August 20 and 22, Little Crow assaulted the fort with 800 warriors, but was driven off by howitzer fire. On the 23rd, more Santees stormed the village of New Ulm, but the inhabitants drove off the Indians after a day's fighting, each side sustaining heavy casualties. The next day, New Ulm was abandoned. The first week of the uprising saw the deaths of 800 settlers, but the Santee were not joined by other Lakotas.

The U.S. response was to send Colonel Henry Sibley of the Minnesota militia to the area with 1,500

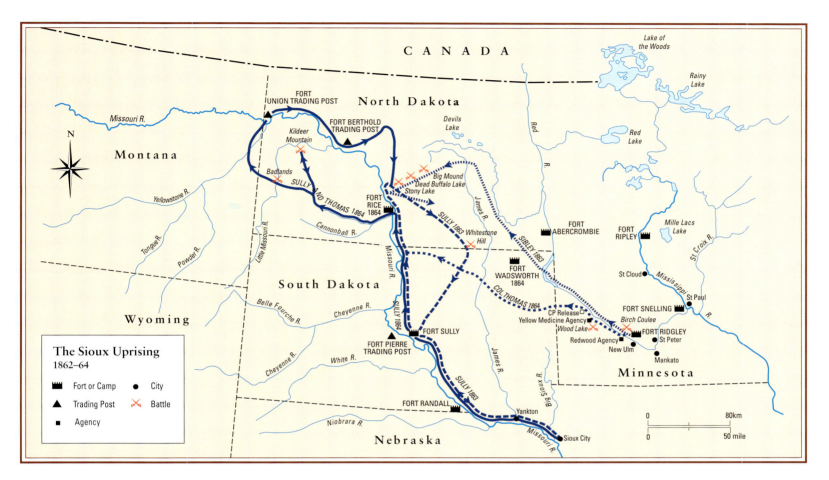

The Sioux Uprising
1862–64

▉ Fort or Camp   ● City
▲ Trading Post   ✕ Battle
■ Agency

men. A burial detail was attacked at Birch Coulee on September 2, but was relieved next day after losing twenty-three men. On September 23, the Santee, now arguing among themselves as to whether they should surrender or fight, attacked Sibley at Wood Lake, but were dispersed by artillery. The Santee began surrendering; many had never wanted war and many were of mixed blood after generations of intermarriage. Some of the latter had tried to protect friends and family in the attacked settlements.

After the surrender, interned Santees were marched from Fort Snelling, at the confluence of the Minnesota and Mississippi rivers, 60 miles (95 kilometers) southwest to Mankato. On the way, some had to run a gauntlet of settlers, where a baby was torn from its mother's arms and smashed to death on the ground.

In November 1862, a military commission sentenced 303 Santee to public execution, a figure reduced to thirty-eight by President Abraham Lincoln. A further group of 326 were imprisoned for three years at Davenport, Iowa, where over 30 percent died. Little Crow fled to Dakota, but returned to Minnesota in 1863; he and his son were shot dead by farmers while picking raspberries.

Next, Sibley embarked on a punitive expedition, defeating Santee remnants with their Teton relations at Big Mound, Dead Buffalo Creek, and Stoney Lake in present-day North Dakota. Another column under Brigadier Alfred Sully found 4,000 Indians encamped at today's Ellendale, North Dakota. Battle ensued, resulting in the surrender of some Lakota, and the destruction of the camp and large supplies of dried buffalo meat. On July 28, 1864, the Brigadier's force of 2,000 troops discovered a Lakota encampment at Killdeer Mountain. A temporary peace followed the Army's victory, the Yankton Lakota being placed on the Crow reservation, while the Santee were confined elsewhere.

Following the Santee Sioux uprising in Minnesota in 1862, the U.S. army campaigned against the tribe for a period of two years. Columns under Colonel Henry Sibley and Brigadier Alfred Sully gained major victories in 1863, while a combined forced under Sully and Colonel Minor Thomas inflicted a final defeat at Killdeer Mountain in 1864.

SAND CREEK, 1864

HAVING OPTED FOR PEACE AND GIVEN THEMSELVES UP, BANDS
OF ARAPAHO AND CHEYENNE DID NOT EXPECT THE ONSLAUGHT
THAT WAS ABOUT TO FALL UPON THEM AT SAND CREEK.

A contemporary illustration showing the relative positions of the Cheyenne village and troops of the 3rd Colorado Cavalry at the beginning of the massacre at Sand Creek.

In 1859, the Cheyenne and Arapaho were pushed from some of their lands as 100,000 miners crossed the Plains to Pike's Peak in Colorado, where gold had been discovered. Tribal unrest spilled over in 1864, the warriors cutting a swathe of destruction from the North Platte to Arkansas, where settlers were killed, and overland mail stations and homes burned. By the fall of that year, the Colorado countryside had been ruined and Denver isolated.

During the American Civil War, settler protection was provided by volunteer units, allowing regular troops to be sent east to the main theaters of war. A brigade of the 1st Nebraska, 7th Iowa, and 16th Kansas Cavalries was organized, which set out from Fort Kearny, in Nebraska, in a search-and-destroy mission. No opposition was found, but some Cheyenne leaders decided that to continue raids was pointless and ultimately would be suicidal. In Colorado, Colonel John Chivington, who commanded the 1st Colorado Cavalry, thought that all Cheyenne villages should be burned, and all Cheyennes exterminated.

In September, Black Kettle and other

Cheyenne leaders went to meet Colorado Governor John Evans at Denver. Evans had stated that any Indian bands who ended hostilities, and left their militant comrades, could make camp near selected army posts and be given military protection. However, Evans made another contradictory proclamation in response to a public outcry over the murder in June of the Hungate family, whose mutilated bodies had been displayed in Denver. He gave citizens a free hand with any hostile Indians they encountered. Nevertheless, some Indians did come in. In early October, a large band of Arapaho, led by Left Hand, surrendered to Major Edward Wynkoop at Fort Lyon, near present-day Lamar, Colorado. The Indians were disarmed and ordered to establish camp 40 miles (65 kilometers) away at the mouth of Sand Creek. In early November, Black Kettle arrived at Fort Lyon to report that his band had also camped at Sand Creek. He was told to remain there and hunt buffalo until the Army was able to issue rations.

A powder flask decorated with the image of an elk and tree. It was found at the site of the Sand Creek Massacre.

Major Scott J. Anthony of the 1st Colorado Cavalry, who commanded Fort Lyon. He told Black Kettle to remain at Sand Creek and later guided Chivington's force to the Indians' camp.

Meanwhile, Chivington's superior officer, General Samuel Curtis, said that peace must be ignored until the Indians were made to suffer more. Chivington was given command of the 3rd Colorado Cavalry, raised for 100 days and comprising the sweepings of frontier bars. They joined part of the 1st Colorado at Fort Lyon, before moving off toward Sand Creek. The 700-man force was supported by four mountain howitzers. On arrival at Sand Creek, some soldiers were ordered to capture the Indian pony herds, while the rest attacked the Indian encampment. Despite Black Kettle's tepee flying an American flag and a flag of truce from the lodge poles, the Americans opened fire with rifles and artillery.

Chivington had surrounded the Indians and intended that no mercy be shown. His troops moved into the camp firing and tomahawking. Some warriors managed to dig gunpits in the bed and banks of a dry creek, and fought a rearguard action, killing eight and wounding thirty-eight of their attackers. Meanwhile, Cheyenne Chief White Antelope was killed in front of his tepee, arms folded and singing his death song. Black Kettle and others managed to escape, but his wife was shot nine times, although she survived. The butchery was indiscriminate, the troops carrying out atrocities, including the mutilation of sexual organs. Allegedly, one lieutenant killed and scalped three women and five children who were all screaming for mercy. Pregnant women were ripped open, and children and babies slaughtered. Most victims were not warriors. Estimates of those killed vary from 200 to 300. The survivors, over half of them wounded, found sanctuary at the camp of the Cheyenne Dog Soldiers at Smoky Hill River, where they obtained food and horses. Black Kettle's village was destroyed, as were the band's winter food supplies. Blankets and horses were stolen. Black Kettle said, *"I once thought that I was the only man that persevered to be the friend of the white man. But since they have come and cleaned out our lodges, horses, and everything else, it is hard for me to believe white men anymore."*

The Cheyenne and Arapaho increased their raiding, and on January 7 and February 18, 1865, they stormed and closed down the town of Julesburg and its freight station on the South Platte River, just south of the Nebraska border. In November 1868, Lieutenant Colonel George Armstrong Custer led his 7th Cavalry to Black Kettle's encampment on the Washita River in Indian Territory. There, the Cheyenne leader and his wife were gunned down as they tried to escape.

RED CLOUD'S WAR, 1866–68

ANGERED BY REPORTS OF MASSACRES, THE SIOUX WAGED WAR AGAINST THE BOZEMAN TRAIL AND THE FORTS BUILT TO PROTECT IT, EVENTUALLY FORCING THEIR CLOSURE.

Red Cloud led the Sioux in a guerrilla campaign against the forts along the Bozeman Trail, which provided a route to the mining settlements of Montana. Despite the Army's superior firepower, the Indians still managed to virtually close the trail.

Mackenzie's 1865 Powder River expedition, the Chivington Massacre, and tales of the recent Cheyenne-Arapaho War had angered the Sioux. Moreover, the defeated Minnesota Sioux, who had found sanctuary among the Plains Indians, were demanding revenge. Other Indians were fearful of the American advance into Montana, since, by 1865, thriving mining settlements existed at Virginia City, Bozeman, and Helena. The government planned to build a road, the Bozeman Trail, from Fort Laramie to Bozeman so that the miners could be better supplied.

The proposed trail would cut through hunting grounds in the foothills of the Bighorn Mountains, and the Sioux became more apprehensive when three Army outposts were constructed: Fort Reno on the Powder River; Fort Philip Kearny, south of Sheridan, Wyoming; and, Fort C.F. Smith, at the junction of the Bighorn and the Powder River road. The Sioux hindered the building of Fort Philip Kearny by sniping at sentries, and ambushing hay and wood cutting parties; when shelled by howitzers, they retreated, only to return at night to shoot at sentries. Wagon trains were harassed, and the forts were virtually under siege. Led by Red Cloud, the Sioux were waging a successful guerrilla campaign. He was joined by Arapahoes under Black Bear; Hunkpapa Sioux led by Sitting Bull and Gall; Oglalas with Crazy Horse; and Miniconjous commanded by Hump.

On December 21, 1866, the Indians struck hard. Crazy Horse and Hump led two small parties of warriors against a wood train. Captain William Fetterman led a mixed force of cavalry and infantry from the fort to rescue the wood train, but the eighty-one-man detachment was ambushed, and all died. Fetterman and another officer, Captain Brown, probably committed suicide to avoid torture. The bodies of the Americans were mutilated, and even a pet dog was killed. However, the wood train made it back to the fort.

The weather worsened, with appalling snowy conditions, and before Red Cloud could attack the fort itself, infantry reinforcements arrived from Fort Laramie, 235 miles (380 kilometers) to the south. These had been summoned following an epic four-day ride through blizzards by a miner named John Phillips.

Red Cloud had hoped to prevent all traffic to and between the forts, but the garrison at Fort Philip Kearny, under Colonel Henry Carrington, had been rearmed with breech-loading Springfield rifles. Although single-shot, they could be reloaded much quicker and were more effective than the previous muzzle-loaders. On August 1 and 2, 1867, the Indians

A contemporary illustration depicting the Fetterman Fight close to Fort Philip Kearny on December 21, 1866. A clever ambush by the Sioux led to a detachment of eighty-one men, under Captain William Fetterman, being wiped out.

attacked again. Thirty civilian hay cutters plus nineteen guards were working 2 miles (3 kilometers) from Fort C.F. Smith. When attacked by 500 Cheyennes, the Americans sheltered in a log corral and stopped the Indians in their tracks with the new rifles. The Indians set the grass on fire to use the smoke for cover, and although this failed, they did manage to retrieve their wounded. Subsequently, this battle became known as the Hayfield Fight.

Next day, Red Cloud, Crazy Horse, and another Sioux chief, American Horse, led a force against Fort Philip Kearny. They stampeded the mule and horse herds, then attacked a wood cutting party. The Americans withdrew to a makeshift fortification assembled from fourteen wagon beds. The thirty-two-man party, led by Major J.W. Powell, fought 500 Sioux. Six Americans died and two were wounded, while Red Cloud's force lost an estimated sixty dead, with 120 wounded.

Fetterman's defeat and the virtual closure of the Bozeman Trail made it clear that the besieged soldiers could not protect travelers. This forced the U.S. government to face the fact that its Indian policy was failing. One reason was that two of its institutions were employing contradictory policies. The Department of the Interior's Indian Office appeased the nations with gifts, reservations, and annuities, while the War Department attacked them whenever they broke any white rules. Moreover, settlers and miners, under federal protection, were constantly encroaching on Indian lands. The Army was attacked for the Chivington Massacre, and Congress created a Peace Commission of four civilians and three generals. Their purpose was to end Red Cloud's War and remove the causes for conflict. A prevailing view was that the Indians should be isolated and reeducated as sedentary farmers to help their transition into the white world. Treaties were necessary to contain the 54,000 Plains Indians and 86,000 southern Indians. The 1867 Medicine Lodge Creek Treaty gave the Cheyenne and Arapaho a reservation in Indian Territory; the Comanche, Kiowa, and Kiowa-Apache were treated similarly. However, the Sioux had to wait another year for a treaty, which was signed at Fort Laramie.

The 1868 Fort Laramie Treaty

TO SECURE PEACE ON THE NORTHERN PLAINS, THE U.S. GOVERNMENT ESTABLISHED A PEACE COMMISSION IN JULY 1867, HEADED BY FAMED GENERAL WILLIAM TECUMSEH SHERMAN.

Friendly Indian leaders were invited to a conference at Fort Laramie, in southeastern Wyoming, in the spring of 1868. By the end of the year, a series of negotiations had taken place. In April and May, Spotted Tail, of the Brulé Sioux, and American Horse, of the Oglalas, had signed agreements. In July, the commission entertained Hunkpapa, Blackfeet, Two Kettles, Sans Arc, and Miniconjou chiefs on board the steamboat *Agnes* on the Missouri. Finally, in November, Red Cloud signed the treaty, which was ratified by Congress on February 16, 1869.

General William Tecumseh Sherman, who led the 1867 peace commission. This photograph, taken earlier in his career, clearly shows his uncompromising personality.

The treaty incorporated important provisions that guaranteed peace between the Sioux and the United States, and fixed the boundaries of the Great Sioux Nation Reservation, which would be free from white incursions. Sioux lands would comprise western South Dakota, and parts of present-day Wyoming, Montana, North Dakota, and Nebraska. This land, between the Rockies in the west and the Missouri River in the east, was there for the "absolute and undisturbed use and occupation" by the Sioux. The Treaty recognized the Bozeman Trail area as "unceded Indian territory," where whites would not be allowed to settle; the forts along the trail would be abandoned. Other provisions of the treaty set out mechanisms by which the government would aid the Indians.

A key element of the treaty was contained in Article 12, which stated that *"no treaty for the cession of any portion or part of the reservation herein described which may be held in common shall be of any validity or force as against said Indians, unless executed and signed by at least three-fourths of all adult male Indians, occupying or interested in the same."* The provisions of the treaty, combined with the supremacy clause of the United States Constitution recognizing treaties as the supreme law of the land, established a legally binding agreement between two sovereign nations.

Two major points arise from the Laramie Treaty. One is that the Sioux, or Lakota, were really sovereign. They considered themselves to be a nation and were prepared to fight to the death against the United States. They possessed thousands of warriors and vast potential destructive power. In addition, Lakota society had not been infiltrated by notions of U.S. law and politics. The Lakota and the United States were two separate entities, and honor could ensure continued peace.

The second point was the Lakota vision of the treaty. The U.S. government regarded a treaty as something that could be altered by further treaties to make it fit changing circumstances: for example, if white settlers and miners wanted to use Indian lands. On the other hand, the Lakota had sealed the Fort Laramie treaty by smoking the pipe, thus making it sacred and its terms inviolate.

The U.S. government abandoned Forts Reno, Philip Kearny, and C.F. Smith, and the Sioux promptly burned them. The political capitulation of the government and its appeasement policy signaled weakness to Red Cloud, who now thought that fighting would secure all. The warlike Tall Bull, of the Cheyenne, thought likewise. Meanwhile, General Philip Sheridan, commanding officer of the Army's Department of the West, believed that a firm hand should be used to force the Indians onto the reservations and keep them there.

Trouble was being stored up for the future, too. The "unceded lands," between the Black Hills and the Big Horn Mountains, were attractive to white settlers in Montana, Wyoming, and South Dakota. In addition, the government felt obliged to clear all Indians from the Platte River valley so that the Union Pacific Railroad could be built through it. Causing further unease was a scientific expedition, led by George Armstrong Custer, into the Black Hills, where gold was found. This discovery triggered an invasion of the region by miners

The Peace Commission led by General William Tecumseh Sherman negotiates the details of the Fort Laramie Treaty with representatives of the Sioux at Fort Laramie, Wyoming, 1868.

THE NAVAJO WAR AND THE LONG WALK

BEATEN INTO SUBMISSION BY KIT CARSON, THE NAVAJO WERE FORCED TO WALK 300 MILES (480 KILOMETERS) TO THE HELL OF THE BOSQUE REDONDO RESERVATION.

Manuelito of the Navajo. When the Indian leader refused to move his people to Bosque Redondo in 1864, he provoked the wrath of Colonel Kit Carson, who led a force of volunteers against the Navajo homeland. Manuelito held out until 1866, but eventually all his people were sent on the Long Walk.

The Navajo, or Diné (the People), arrived in the Southwest about AD 1050, occupying lands between the Rio Grande, San Juan, and Colorado rivers. This area, known as Dinéteh, placed the Navajo close to the Pueblo peoples, from whom they learned agriculture and architecture. They acquired sheep through raiding, and their flocks soon multiplied. They also acquired slaves in the same manner. During the 1846–48 Mexican War, U.S. troops entered the area and threatened punishment if the Navajo continued their slave raiding habits.

Treaties with the Americans were broken several times, and tensions increased because the Navajo continued raiding. The Americans built Fort Defiance near Canyon Bonito, in present-day northeast Arizona, and pastureland at the mouth of the canyon became disputed territory. The Navajo wanted the land for sheep grazing, but the Army needed it as horse pasture. Soldiers shot Navajo animals, and on April 30, 1860, Navajo warriors, led by Manuelito and Barboncito, attacked the fort, coming close to capturing it. The Americans responded by sending a force under Colonel Edward Canby into the Chuska Mountains to pursue the Navajo. Skirmishes took place, but a truce was agreed in January 1861, since the fleeing Navajo needed to tend their sheep and fields, and obtain food.

During the American Civil War, the U.S. government wanted to keep the Arizona and New Mexico territories within the Union, and to maintain transport links with California. To achieve this, Mescalero Apache and Navajo raids had to be prevented. A five-month campaign by Colonel Kit Carson placed the Mescalero on a reservation at Bosque Redondo, an arid, barren area near Fort Sumner on the Pecos River.

When Manuelito refused to move his people, Carson turned on the Navajo. His New Mexican volunteers together with some Utes, devastated Dinéteh, destroying fields and peach orchards, and seizing livestock. Then Carson moved against the Navajos' sacred stronghold in the Canyon de Chelly. He blocked one end and sent in troops at the other. The Navajo were flushed from their hiding places, and by the summer of 1864, Carson had sent 8,000 of them on the Long Walk to Bosque Redondo. A further 4,000, under Manuelito, fled west, but eventually surrendered at Fort Wingate on September 1, 1866. The Long Walk was a journey of some 300 miles (480 kilometers), and people were shot if they complained.

Bosque Redondo was a hideous place, and the Army had made inadequate arrangements for the Indians sent there. Disease and a lack of food, blankets, and good shelter killed many. Drought conditions and poor agricultural land made the reservation useless. Disputes with hostile Mescalero Apaches were a further problem, as was homesickness and general misery. A delegation was permitted to visit Washington in 1868 to ask the government to allow the Navajo to return to Dinéteh. General Sheridan was shocked by conditions at Bosque Redondo and approved a return to the homeland, provided the Navajo remained peaceful; if they did not, they would be sent to Oklahoma Indian Territory. This undertaking was enshrined in an 1868 treaty.

The Navajo reestablished themselves as farmers and herders, as well as turning to new economic ventures; they became famous as weavers and silversmiths, and are well known for sand painting. They grew more prosperous after they were given sheep by the U.S. government. The railroad arrived in the region in 1880, and the Navajo began to trade maize, wool, mutton, hides, livestock, and crafts in return for food and manufactured products. Eventually, leases were negotiated with them to exploit the oil, gas, timber, coal, and uranium found on their reservation.

Kit Carson, trapper, guide, Indian agent, and soldier. When the American Civil War began, Carson joined the New Mexico Volunteer Infantry, which was part of the Union Army. He was given the task of subduing the Apache and Navajo to prevent their raiding.

The Long Walk, an arduous trek through the harsh desert lands to the hell of Bosque Redondo.

The Long Walk 1864

0 — 150 km
0 — 150 miles

THE CIVIL WAR IN INDIAN TERRITORY

THE CIVIL WAR ENCAPSULATED TWO CONFLICTS IN INDIAN TERRITORY: BETWEEN THE OPPOSING ARMIES, AND BETWEEN PRO-UNION AND PRO-CONFEDERATE FACTIONS AMONG THE TRIBES.

Stand Watie, a Cherokee leader, raised his own regiment of Cherokees to fight for the Confederacy during the American Civil War.

In May 1861, Captain Albert Pike traveled to Indian Territory to negotiate treaties of alliance for the Confederacy; these were signed by most Creeks, the Choctaw, Chickasaw, Seminole, Quapaw, Seneca, Caddo, Wichita, Osage, and Shawnee. Even Chief Ross of the Cherokee ended his neutrality and signed for the Confederacy. Immediately, three Native American regiments were raised for the South: a Choctaw-Chickasaw, a Creek-Seminole, and a Cherokee unit under Colonel Drew, a Ross supporter. Elsewhere, Stand Watie of the old Treaty Party raised his own anti-Ross regiment.

Some 6,000 Creeks and Seminoles, under Chief Opothle Yoholo, sought Union protection and were urged to head for Kansas. Confederate Indians and Texan cavalry attacked them at the battles of Round Mountain and Chusto-Talasah, finally inflicting a crushing defeat at Chustenahlah, in the north of present-day Oklahoma (December 26, 1861). Opothleyahola retreated to Kansas, where his Creeks and Seminoles remained quiescent for the rest of the war.

In March 1862, a Confederate attack into Arkansas was defeated at the three-day Battle of Pea Ridge, where 800 Cherokee troops fought. After this, Drew's 2nd Indian Mounted Rifles defected to the Union, followed by many more when Ross was captured at Tahlequah. The Union raised two Indian regiments from Creek, Seminole, and Cherokee refugees and deserters.

In the summer of 1862, a Union expedition of nine regiments, including the Indians, attacked and defeated the Confederates at Cowskin Prairie and Locust Grove. In July 1863, a Union supply train from Fort Scott, Kansas, to Fort Gibson, Indian Territory, was attacked by Stand Watie and driven back. In the fall, a Union victory at Old Fort Wayne, in Indian Territory, near the border with Arkansas, together with eastern victories at Gettysburg and Vicksburg, encouraged a second Union invasion of the territory under General James Blunt. He captured Fort Gibson (October 22) and met the Confederates at the Battle of Honey Springs (July 17, 1863). His 8,000 men defeated General Douglas Cooper's 6,000 Indians and Texans, the 1st Kansas Colored Regiment fighting with utmost distinction.

When Chief Ross was captured, Stand Watie took over the Cherokee Nation, being chosen Principal Chief in March 1863. Watie conscripted Cherokee men, between the ages of eighteen and fifty, and led raids against the Fort Scott–Fort Gibson military trails. He also attacked Ross' remaining Cherokee supporters, looting and burning their property, and sometimes killing full-bloods, known as Pins, after the crossed pins worn by the 5,000-strong Keetowah society.

In August, 4,500 Union soldiers raided and destroyed the Confederate arms depot at Perryville, in the Choctaw Nation, and caused widespread destruction before retreating across the Canadian River. In September 1863, Fort Smith, Arkansas, was captured, cutting off Confederate supplies from the East. In February 1864, a Union force of 1,500 troops struck down the Texas road from Missouri, destroying all it could as it passed through the Choctaw Nation.

The final stage of the war in Indian Territory began with pro-Union Indians in Union controlled areas attacking Confederate sympathizers. Refugees fled south, and by 1864, some 11,000 were living along the Red River in disease-ridden camps; others had traveled to Texas. Stand Watie refused to give up, however, and in June 1864, he captured a Union steamboat, the *J.R. Williams*, on the Arkansas as it made its way from Fort Smith to Fort Gibson. Its provisions were looted and burned by Watie's Indian Cavalry Brigade, which comprised Cherokee, Creek, Osage, and Seminole soldiers. Next, this group rode 400 miles (640 kilometers) to engage the largest wagon train ever to leave Fort Smith (September 19). Known as the Second Battle of Cabin Creek, the action caused 300 Union casualties, and led to the seizure and destruction of $1.5 million of food and supplies intended for 16,000 Indian Union sympathizers around Fort Gibson. Finally, on June 23, 1865, Watie surrendered, long after Robert E. Lee's capitulation on April 9.

The cost of the war to Native Americans was immense. Disease and fighting had wiped out one sixth of the population of the Five Civilized Tribes, and Indian Territory was totally devastated. To make matters worse, Federal authorities blamed the entire Cherokee Nation for disloyalty. In 1866, a new Cherokee-Federal treaty, and treaties negotiated with other nations, gave the western part of Indian Territory to the United States. This land was to be settled by other tribes or sold to friendly nations, especially those from Kansas. In addition, restrictive reconstruction edicts were imposed on the inhabitants of the territory.

Billy Bowlegs, a Seminole chief who took part in the Seminole Wars in Florida. Eventually, he settled in Indian Territory and when the Civil War broke out joined the Union forces. He was commissioned as a captain in the First Indian Home Guards and won praise for his actions at the Battle of Cane Hill in 1862.

Other Native Americans in the Civil War

MANY NATIVE AMERICANS FROM OUTSIDE INDIAN TERRITORY
SERVED IN BOTH CONFEDERATE AND UNION FORCES DURING
THE AMERICAN CIVIL WAR, AND FOR A VARIETY OF REASONS.

Native Americans were present at the Second Battle of Bull Run and the Battle of Antietam in 1862; at Chattanooga in 1863; at the Wilderness, Spotsylvania, and Cold Harbor in 1864; in Union attacks on Petersburg in 1864 and 1865; and during Sherman's Carolina campaign toward the end of the war. While some 20,000 Indians were actively involved in the war, other tribes waged their own campaigns against the Union and whites generally. During the war years, Cochise was at large; the Great Sioux Uprising occurred in Minnesota; the Navajo were being chased by Kit Carson; and the Sand Creek Massacre was overseen by Chivington.

Indians possessed contrasting allegiances, and a wide range of motives persuaded them to join the white man's war. Ottowa and Ojibwa from Michigan served the Union as sharpshooters, in the hope that they would be rewarded with a larger, consolidated land base. Company K of the First Michigan Sharpshooters became a famous Indian unit, which fought in adverse conditions from Spotsylvania to the Crater at Petersburg and the Appotomax. Fewer than two-thirds of their original number were mustered out of service at the war's end.

One aspect of the Civil War in southern New England was the characterization of Native Americans as colored, thereby writing them out of history in the U.S. Colored Infantry. The surviving Pequots and Mohegans from the early colonial wars were deprived both economically and politically. Some had found work on whaling ships, but that industry was declining, and the military offered some economic salvation. By 1864, the state of Connecticut was offering a $600 bounty to any recruit who signed up.

The most famous Native American in the Union forces was Brigadier General Ely S. Parker, a Seneca, who became General Grant's adjutant. Later, he became the first Native American to serve as the United States Commissioner of Indian Affairs (1869–71). Parker had been born Hasanoanda at Indian Falls, New York, on what was then the Tonawanda Reservation. He became a translator to the Seneca chiefs in their dealings with the government, then sought a law career, but was prevented from taking the bar exam because he was an Indian. Then he studied engineering and became a civil engineer. After an abortive attempt to raise a regiment of Iroquois for the Union, he joined the Union Army following Grant's intervention. He was commissioned a captain in 1863.

Other Senecas from the Tonawanda band supported the Union because they regarded the Federal government as an ally against those whites who wanted to acquire their lands in western New York State.

There were other reasons for joining the Union. The Kansas Delaware had fought for the United States before in many campaigns, yet they had been pushed progressively westward. They thought that fighting for the Union cause might result in a settled homeland. Eventually, the Delaware were allowed to buy land from the Cherokee, and 985 Delaware registered themselves as citizens of the Cherokee Nation. The Pamunkey tribe, the last of the old Powhatan Empire, served as river pilots for George B. McClellan's Army of the Potomac in 1862. One Pamunkey, Terrill Bradley of Chickahominy ancestry, became a land guide, then a spy for Allan Pinkerton's Secret Service, and finally a pilot on the USS *Schockon*, where he was wounded in action.

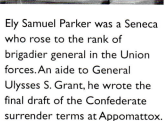

Ely Samuel Parker was a Seneca who rose to the rank of brigadier general in the Union forces. An aide to General Ulysses S. Grant, he wrote the final draft of the Confederate surrender terms at Appomattox.

In North Carolina, the Lumbee Indians were classed as non-white and were not allowed to fight for the South. Instead, many were sent into virtual slavery at Fort Fisher on the North Carolina coast, being employed to build fortifications. Their lot was starvation and disease. Many escaped, while other Lumbees hid in the swamps to avoid conscription. When William Tecumseh Sherman marched from Savannah to Goldsboro in fifty days, he was aided by Lumbee swamp guerrillas, who attacked Confederate Home Guard white-supremacist units. After the war, between 1865 and 1874, one guerrilla band, the Lowries, continued their campaign against racists. In contrast, the tiny Catawba tribe sent nineteen men to serve the Confederacy; reputedly, only three made it back home in one piece. Another notable Native American contribution to the Civil War was the North Carolina Thomas Legion, based on the Eastern band of the Cherokee. Employed for local defense, it saw varied service and surrendered one month after Lee.

Other tribes earned respect during the summer of 1863 at Vicksburg, where Indians of the 14th Wisconsin Sharpshooters silenced cannonfire by sniping at Confederate gun crews. A year later, Seneca of the 14th New York Heavy Artillery captured snipers at Spotsylvania. Oneida in the 14th Wisconsin were noteworthy hunters, who made squirrel soup as a break from normal rations.

While African-Americans were emancipated at the end of the war, Native Americans remained "domestic dependent nations," and their communities had to contend with amputees and cases of shell shock among returning warriors. Indians had a dubious status. The 1868 Fourteenth Amendment excluded "Indians not taxed" from the number of people in each state, which was used to apportion the number of congressmen.

COMANCHES AND KIOWAS

FOR DECADES, THE COMANCHE AND KIOWA RAIDED SETTLEMENTS IN TEXAS AND MEXICO, AND CAUSED DISRUPTION ON THE SANTA FÉ TRAIL.

A Comanche or Kiowa shield adorned with feathers together with a bow, arrows, tomahawk, pipe, and knife.

The Comanche first felt threatened by Americans when eastern tribes were relocated west of the Mississippi. The migrants came into conflict with the Osage and Comanche when they began hunting on the Plains. To keep the peace, the Comanche signed the 1835 Camp Holmes Treaty, promising not to fight their new neighbors, the Quapaw, Seneca, Cherokee, Choctaw, and Creek.

After the USA annexed Texas in 1846, its government inherited problems involving the Comanche. The tribe had fought Mexicans and Texans, and saw the latter as being different from Americans, so continued raiding Texas. This marauding activity was ended by the Butler-Lewis Treaty of May 1846, signed on the upper Brazos River. However, German settlers in Texas, near Fredericksburg and New Braunfeld, signed their own treaty with the Comanche, by which they gained land in exchange for a trading post and gifts. The failure of the Germans to pay resulted in Comanche raids. The Indians were also aggrieved because the Texas Rangers failed to prevent new white settlements, and were ready to retaliate if these new settlements were attacked.

When Mexico was defeated by the USA in 1848, the discovery of gold in California led to the Comanche selling horses to miners. When demand outstripped supply, they raided for horses in Texas, although their main targets were in Mexico.

When the tribes met to sign the 1851 Fort Laramie Treaty, the Comanche and Kiowa were absent. In 1853, however, the Yamparika Comanche and Kiowa signed their own treaty at Fort Atkinson, in Kansas, by which they agreed to refrain from raiding Mexico and the Santa Fé Trail in return for a $10,000 annuity for ten years.

However, the Comanche and Kiowa were in a dangerous mood. The gold rush brought epidemics of smallpox and cholera (1848 and 1849); the estimated 20,000 Comanche had been reduced to 12,000 by 1851. White encroachments on their territory continued, the Texas Rangers were hostile, and the Army built Fort Stockton at Comanche Springs, in North Texas, to block the war trail into Mexico. The U.S. government also pursued peaceful policies, establishing three reservations for Texan tribes. Some Comanches moved in, but in 1859 they were attacked by Texan civilians, so they were moved to Indian Territory.

The Comanche used Indian Territory as a base for raiding Texas, but the Rangers retaliated. In response, the Comanche began raiding the Santa Fé Trail. During the American Civil War, the Penateka, Nokoni, Yamparika, Tenawa, and Kotsoteka Comanche signed treaties with the Confederacy, but they never received the goods they had been promised in return. As Texas sent its men to fight the Union, the defenseless frontier was pushed back 100 miles (160 kilometers) by marauding Comanches.

By 1861, the Comanche, Kiowa, Cheyenne, and Arapaho had almost closed the Santa Fé Trail. These Indians formed an alliance with the Lakota and Kiowa-Apache against the irregular militias sent against them. On November 25, 1864, they fought a battle against Kit Carson and 300 New Mexican volunteers at Adobe Walls, a ruined trading post in the Texas Panhandle. Carson and his men only escaped by using howitzers against the Indians. By the end of the Civil War, the Union was at war with nearly all the Plains tribes. In an attempt to secure peace, the Little Arkansas Treaty (October 1865) gave the Comanche and Kiowa western Oklahoma, the entire Texas Panhandle, and an annuity of $15 per person for forty years.

Unfortunately, General Sheridan was made responsible for ensuring that the treaty provisions were carried out, and in 1868, he ordered all tribes to report to Fort Cobb or be considered hostile. After Custer's massacre of Cheyennes in Black Kettle's village on the Washita River, and an attack on a Comanche village at Soldiers Spring, most Comanches returned to the agencies.

By 1869, small Comanche and Kiowa bands were raiding Texas, while Texans had stolen some 1,900 horses from tribes at Fort Sill. The Comanche were slowed down by Mackenzie's buffalo soldiers capturing women and children, but the slaughter of buffalo led to further Indian raids in the 1874 Buffalo/Red River War. Eventually, the Army located the Kiowa and Comanche camp in Palo Duro Canyon, in the Texas Panhandle, and killed 2,000 ponies. By 1875, the immobilized Indians had surrendered, and the war was over.

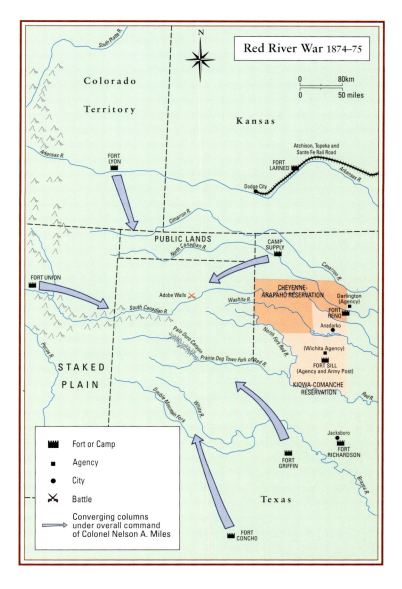

The Army brought an end to the Red River War by cornering the Kiowa and Comanche at their retreat in the Texas Panhandle.

A contemporary illustration of the Battle of Adobe Walls.

THE MODOCS

EJECTED FROM THEIR HOMELAND AND FORCED ONTO A
RESERVATION, THE MODOCS ESCAPED, BUT SOON FOUND
THEMSELVES CAUGHT UP IN A SIX-MONTH WAR.

Captain Jack led some of his
people back to their home on
Lost River after suffering on the
Klamath reservation. After some
years, an attempt was made to
round them up, but they fled,
leading to the Modoc War.

The few Modocs who lived at Lost River in California were under pressure from white farmers and miners encroaching on their rich lands. The government supported white interests and forced the Modocs to cede their land, placing them on the Klamath reservation in southern Oregon. However., there had been a long history of enmity between the two tribes, as a result of which the more numerous Klamath harassed the Modocs. In 1872, some Modocs left the reservation under a leader known as Captain Jack, returning to Lost River, where they remained unmolested for several years. Eventually, their presence caused concern among settlers, and a force of cavalry, under Captain James Jackson, was sent from Fort Klamath to round up the Modocs and return them to the reservation. While Jackson was negotiating with the Indians, a fight broke out, causing a fatality on each side. Captain Jack extricated his people from their village and they retreated to an area of lava beds near Tule Lake. This region, known as the Land of the Burnt Out Fires by Indians, and measuring 8 miles (13 kilometers) long by 4 miles (6 kilometers) wide, formed a natural fortress.

Another dissident Modoc band, under Hooker Jim, resisted being rounded up by civilians and went on the rampage, killing fifteen ranchers. Subsequently, this group joined Captain Jack, who found himself with 50–70 warriors, and 150 women and children. The slaughter of civilians made war inevitable, and the normally peaceful Jack realized that they would not be left alone. Before long, 400 soldiers from the 1st Cavalry, 21st Infantry, and militia companies from Oregon and California were concentrated near the lava beds under Colonel Frank Wheaton.

On January 17, 1873, the soldiers attacked the Modoc position, supported by artillery. The majority of the Modoc warriors voted to fight, following Hooker Jim's wish, but going against Captain Jack. They camouflaged themselves with sagebrush and counterattacked, using cover and constantly changing position. By nightfall, nine Americans had been killed, while thirty had been wounded. A standoff occurred, lasting

until early April, when Jack's female cousin, Winema, who was married to a white settler, helped arrange peace talks between Jack and Wheaton's replacement, General Edward Canby. During the negotiations, Jack killed Canby, thus dashing all hopes of peace and prolonging the conflict.

On April 15, Colonel Alvan Gillem launched another attack. The result was similar to the previous Battle of the Lava Beds. Artillery shelled the Modocs, and on April 17, the troops stormed the Indian positions, only to find them empty. The battle had killed eleven Modocs, but the soldiers suffered some twenty-five dead and wounded.

An eighty-five-man detachment was sent to locate the escaping Indians, but it was ambushed by a group of twenty-one Modocs under war leader Scarfaced Charley. Five officers were among the twenty-five dead and eighteen wounded. None of the Modocs was hurt. Nevertheless, their situation was parlous, since they had no food or water and little ammunition, while disagreements were breaking out among them.

Captain Jack decided to break the encirclement, but was repulsed, and he lost twenty-four pack animals carrying most of the Modocs' remaining ammunition. Internal dissension came to a head, and the Indians split into two groups. On May 22, 100 Indians were captured; then Hooker Jim turned himself in with a small group. He offered information about the remaining escapees to Brigadier General Jefferson Davis, yet another new American commander. Small groups of Indians were captured, and on June 1, Captain Jack was seized at Willow Creek Canyon, where he had been discovered with his three remaining warriors. On October 3, Captain Jack and three other Modocs were hung at Fort Klamath. President Grant sentenced two others to imprisonment on Alcatraz Island in San Francisco Bay. The bodies of the executed Indians were preserved and put on public display in the East, later being decapitated; the skulls were sent to the Army Medical Museum, then to the Smithsonian Institution.

Hooker Jim escaped death, despite having killed civilians. He was sent with the other 155 Modocs to the Quapaw reservation in Indian Territory, where he died six years later, Scarfaced Charley becoming tribal leader. In 1909, the remaining fifty-one Modocs were allowed to return to the Klamath reservation. The six-month conflict cost the U.S. taxpayer around half a million dollars, while there were about 130 Army and civilian casualties.

Modoc Princess Winema, Captain Jack's cousin, stands between her husband, Frank Riddle (to her left), and an Indian agent. Seated are four Modoc women. The Riddles acted as go-betweens during the conflict.

During the Modoc War, groups of Modocs led by Captain Jack and Hooker Jim retreated to a stronghold among the lava beds south of Tule Lake.

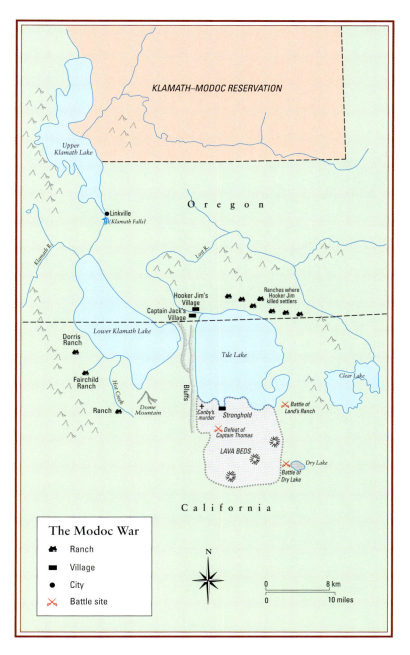

The Modoc War

Ranch
Village
City
Battle site

The Rosebud Campaign

Determined to wrest control of the Black Hills from the Sioux, the U.S. Army moved against them at Rosebud Creek, but with disastrous results.

Despite the 1868 Fort Laramie Treaty, which protected the Great Sioux Reservation from white incursions, Colonel George Armstrong Custer led an expedition into the tribe's sacred Black Hills in 1874, and some of his party found gold. Immediately, miners crowded into the area, and by 1875, there were some 15,000 of them. Before long, the two towns of Custer City and Deadwood were booming. To prevent a violent Lakota reaction, the U.S. government offered to pay the the tribe $6 million for the Black Hills. Several chiefs objected during negotiations; Red Cloud stated that he wanted enough money to feed seven generations. His words demonstrated an appreciation of white ways: "*I want to put the money that we get for the Black Hills at interest among the whites, to buy with the interest wagons and cattle.*"

To pressurize the Indians, Congress threatened to withhold food supplies until the Lakota caved in. By 1876, 50,000 Indians were in rebellion The Department of the Interior demanded that unceded hunting grounds be abandoned and that the Lakota should return to their reservation by January 31, 1876. If they did not, they would be considered hostile. Sitting Bull, Crazy Horse, and others refused, preferring to remain where the buffalo were plentiful during the winter.

In Chicago, General Sheridan had planned a campaign that would dispatch three military columns to drive the Lakota onto the reservations. One, led by General George Crook, was to leave Fort Fetterman in eastern Wyoming; another, under Colonel John Gibbon, would march east from western Montana, leaving Fort Shaw and moving to Helena, Fort Ellis, and beyond. Finally, Lieutenant Colonel Custer and his 7th Cavalry would move west from Fort Abraham Lincoln in North Dakota. Custer was eager for action.

When Crook quit Fort Fetterman (March 1, 1876), he left behind some eighty wagons and a mule train, forging on through freezing winds. Meanwhile, Custer had been delayed by snow. Colonel J.J. Reynolds rode point for Crook, and on March 17, his detachment discovered a mixed Cheyenne-Oglala

A contemporary illustration from Frank Leslie's *Illustrated Newspaper* showing Sioux warriors attacking a detachment of cavalry under Colonel Royall during the Battle of Rosebud Creek. The action was a near disaster for General Crook.

Lakota encampment. An attack was mounted by the 2nd Cavalry to capture the pony herd, while dismounted soldiers approached the village. In this Battle of Powder River, the troops faced intense opposition for five hours, and Reynolds ordered a retreat. Even so, the Americans suffered only seven casualties, while the Indians recaptured most of their ponies. One wounded soldier was left behind and was tortured to death. Nevertheless, the battle had destroyed Indian shelter, winter food, and equipment. Crook returned to Fort Fetterman to reequip, but his apparent failure increased Crazy Horse's recruiting power.

In May, Crook left the fort again with 1,000 cavalry and infantry, plus more than 250 Crow and Shoshone scouts. He wanted to disperse any Indian concentration and defeat each band separately. Two other columns were in the field: one led by Gibbon from Montana, the other by General Alfred Terry, with Custer, from Fort Abraham Lincoln. By mid-June, Crook had followed the Bozeman Trail until he had encountered Sitting Bull and Crazy Horse with their Lakota warriors.

On June 17, Captain Anson Mills led a squadron of 3rd Cavalry against an Indian village on Rosebud Creek, but was ambushed and had to be rescued by the 9th Infantry. The Americans retreated to Crook's main force, eventually pursued by 4,000–6,000 warriors. The six-hour Battle of Rosebud Creek ensued, almost becoming a disaster for Crook. Throughout, though, his Indian scouts acquitted themselves well, displaying superior fighting spirit. The Indians withdrew from the battlefield, since they knew of the other converging columns and needed to regroup to face them. Later, Crook tried to minimize his casualties, claiming only thirty-one, but another estimate gave twenty-eight dead and fifty-six wounded. Crazy Horse suffered 100 losses. Crook's resultant military paralysis meant that he could not support the other columns under Gibbon and Terry. The Lakota victory drew in more recruits for Crazy Horse and Sitting Bull.

LITTLE BIGHORN

BLOODIED BY THE BATTLE OF THE ROSEBUD, THE ARMY
ATTACKED THE SIOUX AND THEIR ALLIES AT THEIR ENCAMPMENT
ON THE LITTLE BIGHORN RIVER, LEADING TO THE MOST FAMOUS
ACTION OF THE INDIAN WARS.

George Armstrong Custer,
headstrong leader of the U.S.
Army's 7th Cavalry.

After the Rosebud battle, the Native Americans gathered by the Little Bighorn River. Northern Cheyenne and various Lakota divisions (Brulé, Oglala, Yankton, Santee, Miniconjou, Sans Arc, and Hunkpapa) were encamped and numbered some 15,000, among them 4,000 warriors. Major chiefs included Sitting Bull, Crazy Horse, Gall, Hump, and Two Moons. Four days after the Battle of the Rosebud, Terry's and Gibbon's columns met on the Yellowstone River. A scouting party under Major Marcus Reno found the general location of the Indian camp, and Terry dispatched Custer's 7th Cavalry to cut them off from the south, while the rest of the force moved in from the north. Terry wanted Custer to attack and drive the Indians toward Gibbon's infantry, who would pin down the warriors. Thus, the Lakota and Cheyenne would be bottled up in the Little Bighorn Valley.

Custer moved off with between 600 and 700 cavalry, but refused the offer of four troops from the 2nd Cavalry and a Gatling-gun platoon. None of the Americans knew the size of the Indian concentration, or that some warriors were armed with Winchester repeating rifles—the soldiers were equipped with single-shot Springfield carbines. The Indians were prepared to stand and die, which meant that Custer's method of dashing in, as he had done at Black Kettle's camp on the Washita, would not work this time.

At around noon on June 25, 1876, Custer divided his command. Captain Frederick Benteen was sent with three companies to scout on his left; three hours later, he found the upper end of the Indian camp. Next, Custer sent Reno with three companies to cross the river and charge the camp between the river and Shoulderblade Creek, on the extreme left of the 7th Cavalry's thrust. Custer personally led four companies into a fold in the ground where he could not see the size of the camp.

Reno began the battle at 3pm, his force advancing against the southern end of the camp, where it met a counteradvance by the Hunkpapa, who wanted to gain time for their women and children to escape. Reno's 112 men were vastly outnumbered, and with no support from Benteen or Custer, they retreated into a cottonwood grove. Finding his force being infiltrated, Reno retreated further, digging in on a bluff across the river, but he left some men among the trees. Many of these were lost as they tried to withdraw. In forty-five minutes, Reno had lost half his command as casualties or missing.

Meanwhile, Custer charged the first northern village, but was counterattacked by Northern

Gall, a Hunkpapa Lakota, who fought with utter determination at the Battle of Little Big Horn armed only with a hatchet, driven by the desire to avenge the loss of two of his wives and three of his children killed by the U.S. army.

During the Bighorn campaign, the U.S. Army sent three converging columns against the Cheyenne and Sioux, leading to battles at the Powder River (Reynolds), Rosebud Creek (Crook), and the Little Bighorn (Custer), but all three saw intense Indian opposition.

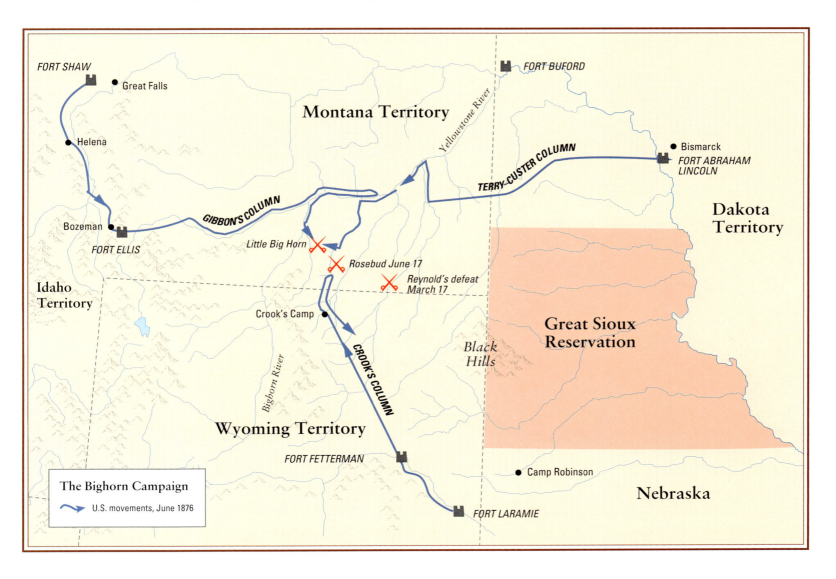

FORT SHAW
• Great Falls

FORT BUFORD

Montana Territory

Yellowstone River

• Helena

TERRY-CUSTER COLUMN

• Bismarck
FORT ABRAHAM LINCOLN

Dakota Territory

GIBBON'S COLUMN

Bozeman

FORT ELLIS

Little Big Horn ✕

Rosebud June 17 ✕

Reynold's defeat ✕
March 17

Idaho Territory

Crook's Camp •

CROOK'S COLUMN

Bighorn River

Great Sioux Reservation

Black Hills

Wyoming Territory

FORT FETTERMAN

• Camp Robinson

Nebraska

FORT LARAMIE

The Bighorn Campaign

〜 U.S. movements, June 1876

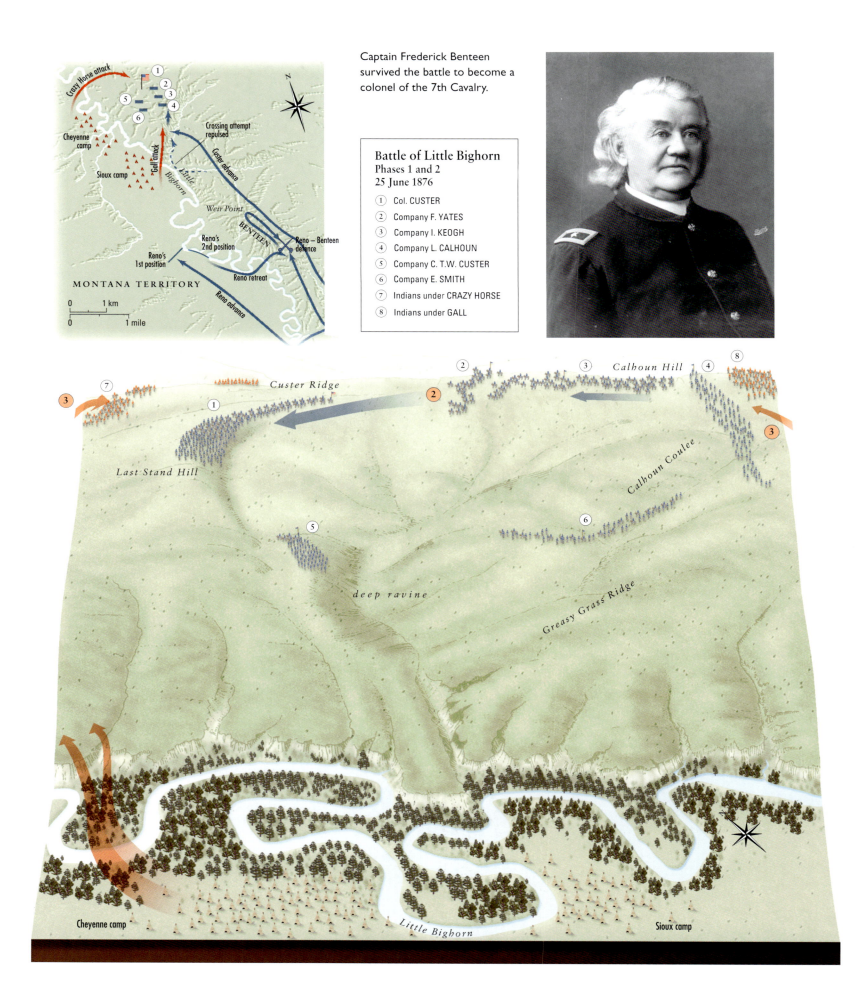

Captain Frederick Benteen survived the battle to become a colonel of the 7th Cavalry.

Battle of Little Bighorn
Phases 1 and 2
25 June 1876

1. Col. CUSTER
2. Company F. YATES
3. Company I. KEOGH
4. Company L. CALHOUN
5. Company C. T.W. CUSTER
6. Company E. SMITH
7. Indians under CRAZY HORSE
8. Indians under GALL

Crazy Horse attack

Cheyenne camp

Sioux camp

Little Bighorn

Gall attack

Crossing attempt repulsed

Custer advance

Weir Point

BENTEEN

Reno's 2nd position

Reno's 1st position

Reno – Benteen defence

Reno retreat

MONTANA TERRITORY

Reno advance

0   1 km
0   1 mile

Custer Ridge

Last Stand Hill

Calhoun Hill

Calhoun Coulee

deep ravine

Greasy Grass Ridge

Cheyenne camp

Little Bighorn

Sioux camp

Custer Ridge

Calhoun Hill

Last Stand Hill

Calhoun Coulee

deep ravine

Greasy Grass Ridge

Cheyenne camp

Little Bighorn

Sioux camp

Battle of Little Bighorn
Phase 3
25 June 1876

1. Custer divides his command of 600 men into 3 groups, he then leads his own group northwest along the ridges above the Little Bighorn River. Meanwhile the other 2 groups are beaten off by Indian forces isolating Custer and his men

2. Custer's force moves in loose company formations along the ridge deep in Indian controlled territory, contact with Reno and Beufeau is lost. Large Indian forces move across the Little Bighorn River

3. Indian forces under Crazy Horse and Gall move to surround Custers 212 cavalry men, and begin their attack

4. The Indian attack rapidly overwhelms the companies to the east and south of Custer's position, the few survivors collect around Custer for a last stand

The progression of the Battle of the Little Bighorn. Custer's troops were completely overwhelmed by the Cheyenne and Sioux warriors.

A fanciful vision of "Custer's Last Stand" at the Battle of the Little Bighorn.

Major Marcus Reno set the battle in motion with his attack on the southern end of the Indians' camp.

Cheyennes, and Brulés and Oglalas under Crazy Horse. Then Gall arrived with Hunkpapa, and Sans Arc warriors. Custer was surrounded on a high, grassy ridge. By 5pm, his 215 men had been wiped out, among them his brother, Tom. Rain In The Face, a Hunkpapa previously captured by Tom Custer, cut out his heart and ate it.

Meanwhile, Benteen saw Reno's predicament and rode to his relief. Hearing gunshots from downstream, the two officers realized that Custer was engaged. Against orders, Captain Thomas Weir led his company toward Custer. He was followed by Reno, but they were pinned down while Custer and his command were destroyed. Reno's men retreated to the bluff, where they lost eighteen more killed and forty-three wounded. Fending off several assaults, Reno was eventually rescued by Terry and Gibbon on June 27; he was lucky not to have been overrun like Custer.

In the aftermath of the Battle of the Little Bighorn, U.S. forces regrouped and began harassing and pursuing Indians, resulting in several engagements. On July 17, a group of Cheyennes were defeated at Warbonnet Creek, and a fight at Slim Buttes in September led to the capture of some Tetons. The Battle of Dull Knife (November 25) routed the Northern Cheyenne, while in January 1877, Crazy Horse was beaten at Wolf Mountain; in May, Lame Deer's Lakota were defeated in Montana. The war ended officially on July 16, 1877, and sick, cold, and hungry warriors gradually surrendered. Sitting Bull fled to Canada, but returned in 1881; in 1885, he joined Buffalo Bill's Wild West Show.

Sitting Bull, holy man and war chief of the Sioux, with his adopted son, One Bull. They went into exile together to Canada after the victory at the Battle of Little Big Horn.

CHIEF JOSEPH

DRAWN INTO A WAR
THAT WAS NOT OF THEIR
CHOOSING, THE NEZ PERCE
WERE HARRIED BY THE
U.S. ARMY AS THEY MADE A
DESPERATE FLIGHT TOWARD
THE CANADIAN BORDER.

Chief Joseph was one of the chiefs who led the Nez Perce in a desperate bid to reach Canada, where they hoped to join Sitting Bull. They never made the border and were sent to Kansas, then Oklahoma. Thanks to Joseph's campaigning, the people were eventually allowed to return to Washington Territory, where the old chief died suddenly in 1904, some said of a broken heart.

The Nez Perce lands in Washington Territory were increasingly affected by incursions of settlers and miners. During the 1860s gold rush, they entered the Wallowa Valley, which was supposed to be an inviolable reservation. Its size was reduced substantially, however, and in 1877, the Lower Nez Perce in Wallowa were ordered to relocate to the Lapwai reservation in Idaho Territory. While preparations were being made, some drunken warriors went on the rampage, killing four white men who were hostile to the Indians. Within two days, sixteen settlers were dead.

With war inevitable, the Nez Perce moved to White Bird Canyon where they could make a stand. On June 17, 1877, a cavalry detachment entered the canyon, but were driven off. The Nez Perce, led by Joseph, White Bird, Looking Glass, and others, fled down the Salmon River, killing a U.S. scouting party. The Indians numbered some 700, but at least 550 were women, children, and the aged. On July 11, General Howard, with 600 regulars, caught up and attacked the Indians at Clearwater Creek. A two-day battle ensued, but the Nez Perce escaped. The tribe decided to seek refuge with the Crow, which meant crossing the Bitterroot Mountains. They traveled to Big Hole Valley, but failed to realize that the U.S. Army was using the telegraph to position blocking forces. On August 9, 200 soldiers made a surprise attack on the Indian camp, killing eighty-nine.

The Nez Perce escaped again. One group raided Howard's camp at Camas Creek (August 20), allowing the others to use the Targhee Pass into Wyoming Territory. East of Yellowstone Park, they encountered the Crow, who would not accept them; indeed, some were scouting for the Army. Consequently, the Nez Perce decided to head for Canada. Meanwhile, a 350-strong force of 7th Cavalry, under Colonel Samuel Sturgis, had set out westward from Fort Keogh, while General Nelson Miles, with another large force of cavalry, was moving northwest of the fort.

Sturgis attacked on September 13 at Canyon Creek, but the bands moved on in a fighting retreat. With the old and wounded falling behind, they traveled through Montana, being harassed by Crow scouts. They crossed the Bear Paw Mountains, but then were caught by Miles; battle began on September 30. The initial cavalry charge was repulsed, but then the soldiers took cover and brought up artillery. The Indians had no reply to howitzers and Gatling guns, finally surrendering on October 5. Some warriors had escaped, however, under the war chief White Bird. Chief Joseph had stayed behind with the remaining eighty men, and 350 women and children.

The Nez Perce ended up in Oklahoma, where a quarter of them died from malaria. Joseph continued to plead for their return to their homeland, however, and eventually they were allowed back to Washington State, to reside on the Colville reservation.

Joseph was not a war chief during the 1,700-mile (2,700-kilometer) flight of the Nez Perce, but his words of surrender make him a Native American icon: *"I am tired of fighting ... It is cold and we have no blankets ... The little children are freezing to death ... My heart is sick and sad. From where the sun now stands, I will fight no more forever."*

The Nez Perce fled their home in the Wallowa Valley and trekked through the Bitterroot Mountains, hoping to find refuge with the Crow. They were harried by the Army all the way. Turned away by the Crow, they headed for Canada, but were finally caught by Nelson Miles in the Bear Paw Mountains.

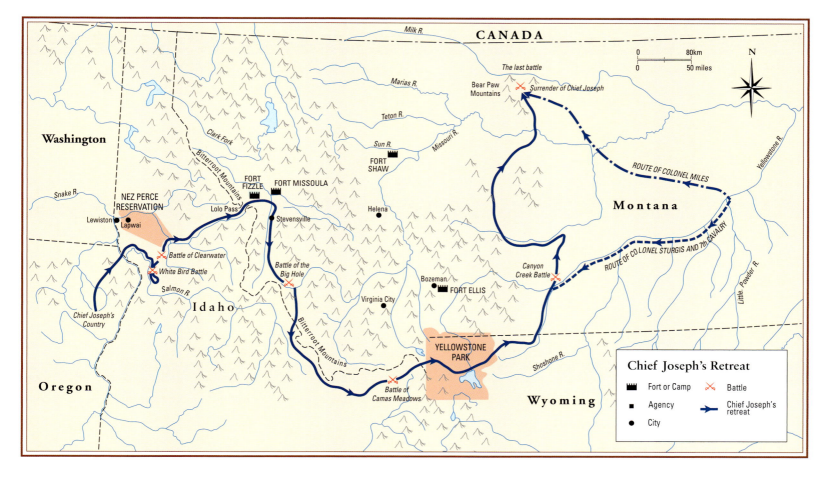

IMPRISONING THE WEST

TO PROTECT WHITE SETTLEMENTS, INTERESTS, AND OVERLAND TRAILS FROM INDIAN ATTACKS, THE U.S. ARMY BUILT A NETWORK OF FORTS ALONG THE FRONTIER.

The United States' peace policy attempted to place all Native Americans on reservations, to separate them geographically from white settlements, trails, and railroad construction. The reservations would be the forum for a white civilizing mission of the Indians. During and after the Civil War, every military campaign in the West and Southwest forced the Indians onto reservations, or made them return there if they fled. Reasons for restricting Indian movement included stimulating the expansion of trade, along the Santa Fé Trail for example, and protecting the immigrants who flooded into Kansas and the West after 1854. Tribal lands were being crossed increasingly by stage and mail routes, and by railroad crews laying track. To pursue all these policies, a network of forts was built along the frontier, moving ever westward as more Indian lands were acquired.

Another major problem facing the West was the vast number of miners chasing new mineral finds. In 1858, there was the Pike's Peak Gold Rush, while in 1875, prospectors discovered gold in the Black Hills. Between 1859 and 1860, about 40,000 miners and squatters encroached upon territory occupied by the Arapaho and Cheyenne, who numbered only 5,000. Such incursions into lands considered inviolate by treaty, and the consequent extra pressure on game supplies, led to violence and war. The 1858 gold rush caused the hostilities that culminated in the Sand Creek Massacre, while the 1875 incident led to the Battle of the Little Bighorn. Elsewhere, in 1866, the Fetterman Massacre resulted from the U.S. government's attempt to defend the Bozeman Trail between Fort Laramie and Bozeman so that Montana miners could be supplied. The construction of Forts C.F. Smith, Philip Kearny, and Reno provoked Red Cloud's War.

Constant hostility led to the construction of many forts for a variety of reasons. Fort Leavenworth, in Kansas, was built to protect the Santa Fé and Oregon trails, and later the Kansas Pacific Railroad. It was also where the African-American 10th Cavalry was raised. Fort Riley on the Smoky Hill Trail, in northeast Kansas, was used as a staging post to protect the frontier, while Fort Larned on the Santa Fé Trail acted as an Indian Bureau agency, and provided escorts for mail coaches and wagon trains. Fort Hays, in western Kansas, on the railroad between Kansas City and Denver, Colorado, protected rail gangs on both the Kansas Pacific and Union Pacific railroads. Fort Dodge was a camping ground and supply depot for wagon trains, and Fort Harker, in central Kansas, was a major distribution depot for the southwestern forts in Colorado, Arizona, and northern Texas. It also protected the Butterfield Overland Despatch Company routes.

Fort Benton, Montana, exemplifies the activities of many forts. Established on the upper Missouri River, it was intended to implement the 1855 Lame Bull's Treaty. The terms of this treaty restricted the Blackfeet to lands around the Hellgate, Musselshell, and Milk rivers in return for $20,000 worth annually of useful goods and services, plus another $15,000 annually to promote Christianization and civilization through instructional farms, schools, and farming equipment. The fort became an agency distributing these goods and services, which the Indians often possessed already, or were disliked by them, such as coffee and rice. As buffalo numbers dwindled, however, the Blackfeet became increasingly dependent upon the fort for government supplies. Fort Benton not only became a distribution point for supplies, but also served as a focal point of the Missouri route to the Columbia River and Pacific Northwest by the Mullen Road. In addition, the agency was a staging post for wolf hunters, prospectors, merchants, whisky traders, and migrant settlers.

A second fort, Shaw, was built on the Sun River, northwest Montana, in 1867 to assuage white fears of the Blackfeet, who were beset by cattle ranchers. In 1873 and 1874, President Grant had the reservation's southern border moved to the north of the Missouri and Marias rivers, and Birch Creek without federal payment. Tensions grew and culminated in an unfortunate attack on the friendly Blackfeet camp of Chief Heavy Runner in 1870. Known as the Baker Massacre, after Major Eugene Baker who led the cavalry detachment involved in the dawn assault, this fight led to the death of 173 Indians, while 140 women and children were abandoned on the prairie to fend for themselves in the Montana winter.

As the nineteenth century progressed, the number and range of the buffalo contracted. Indiscriminate killing by white hunters played a major part in this, but the Indians themselves contributed to the decline. One result was that Indians became more reliant on supplies provided by the government, tying them to the agencies.

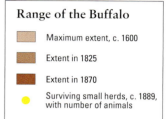

Range of the Buffalo

- Maximum extent, c. 1600
- Extent in 1825
- Extent in 1870
- ● Surviving small herds, c. 1889, with number of animals

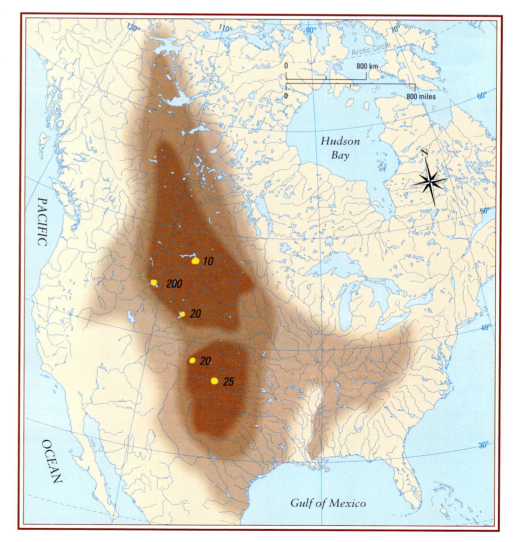

RESERVATIONS

FOR THE UNITED STATES GOVERNMENT, CONFINING NATIVE AMERICANS TO RESERVATIONS SOLVED TWO PROBLEMS: IT KEPT THEM UNDER CONTROL AND ALLOWED THEIR LANDS TO BE OPENED UP TO SETTLEMENT.

Chief Chariot and family on the Flathead Reservation, Montana.

On September 8, 1886, Geronimo, Natchez and their band of Chiricahua Apaches surrendered to end the Apache War. They were transported east across the Arizona desert, eventually arriving in Florida. Apart from Wounded Knee, the wars of the U.S. government's peace policy were over. All tribes were located on reservations or in isolated villages, islands of Indian occupied land administered by white agents of the Indian Office. The original notion of a large western Indian Territory, with one protected border, was abandoned in favor of the demands of settlers, miners, and traders. The Indians had been pressured to cede massive amounts of territory through some 370 treaties.

The reservation system allowed millions of acres of ceded lands to be opened up to migrant settlers. The policy made Native Americans increasingly dependent upon the reservations, especially with the decline of the buffalo. The system could also be used as the foundation stone for a policy of forced assimilation, by which Indians would be Christianized and retrained as farmers. Thus, it attacked traditional tribal authority patterns, and caused social, economic, and psychological disintegration, which helped fuel tribal fragmentation and factionalism as Americanization and white acculturation took hold. The only major region where reservations were created around existing communities was the Southwest, which had the huge Navajo reservation, together with others for Apaches, Pueblos, and other local tribes.

During the 1880s, the Indians were forced to give up more territory. Lumber and railroad interests in the Great Lakes region wanted more land, and the Ojibwa were coerced into accepting 80–acre (32-hectare) individual allotments. After this allocation, the remaining land (around 50 percent of the reservation) was sold off to white settlers and business interests.

On the Pacific Coast, salmon fisheries were farmed commercially by white Americans, and the Indians could not compete; the Colville and Coeur d'Alene lands were sold off. The Klamaths were forced into selling 87,000 acres (35,000 hectares) of ponderosa pine forest to the California and Oregon Land Company.

Nevertheless, Canadian Indians facing similar conditions, and the Yankton Sioux in South Dakota, turned to wheat and corn farming; cash crops were substituted for hunting. Overall, however, new capitalist methods damaged Indian economic interests. The Five Civilized Tribes of Oklahoma, like the Pacific Coast Indians, could not compete with industrial interests and the powerful cattle ranchers. Few Californian Indians lived on reservations, and thousands were dispossessed. In 1903, for example, Cupeño, San Luiseño, and Kumeyay Indians were thrown out of their villages in the San Jose Valley by a wealthy landowner and moved onto a reservation in the Pala Valley by the Army. They were forced to abandon their ancestral home, their churches, and their graveyards.

In an attempt to resocialize Native Americans, between 1880 and 1895, the U.S. Office of Indian Affairs created twenty off-reservation boarding schools, and opened or developed day schools at every agency. The industrial training school at Carlisle, Pennsylvania, was especially well known; it produced a clutch of graduates, who became academics and Native American leaders, an unintentional outcome. The Canadians copied the system. Whatever the aims of Christian-run boarding schools, the reservations provided little sanctuary for Native Americans, instead becoming segregated areas of poverty, unhappiness, and neglect for their 250,000 inhabitants.

When the 1887 Dawes Act turned reservations into individual allotments, new land losses occurred. Tribal holdings dropped from 136 million acres (55 million hectares) in that year to approximately 48 million acres (19.5 million hectares) in 1934, when the policy was abandoned. In reality, Native Americans were the victims of a federal policy that attempted to eradicate tribal land holdings, political organizations, communal customs, and trust status. At the termination of the trust period, a twenty-five-year program was established to facilitate Indian "competency" to grant citizenship. In 1924, Congress enacted the Citizenship Act, giving all Indians citizenship. Even so, some states did not allow Indians to vote; New Mexico, Arizona, and Maine did not grant the franchise until after World War II, despite Indian military service during both world wars.

Native American pupils at the Carlisle Indian Industrial School, Pennsylvania, c. 1900. The school was founded by Captain Richard Henry Pratt in 1879 in an attempt to assimilate Indian children into the culture of the United States. Many children ran away from the school's brutal regime; some later became Indian rights activists.

Cheyenne: From Farms to Reservations

WHEN THE CHEYENNE FINALLY RESISTED THE EVER-GROWING INCURSIONS OF SETTLERS AND MINERS, THEY WERE CRUSHED BY THE ARMY AND SENT TO OVERCROWDED RESERVATIONS.

Originally, the Cheyenne had lived in central Minnesota, where they had farmed, lived in earth lodges, hunted, gathered wild rice, and made ceramics. After 1700, they were expelled from the area by the Lakota and Ojibwa. They migrated gradually westward, establishing an earth-lodge village on the Cheyenne River in North Dakota. The horse probably reached them at this time, and the Cheyenne began to hunt buffalo. However, the Ojibwa destroyed their village in about 1770, and the Cheyenne moved to South Dakota, settling near present-day Bear Butte.

With the horse, the Cheyenne developed a nomadic lifestyle, living in tepees. When nearby Mandan and Arikara were hit by smallpox and attacked by the Lakota, the Cheyenne moved on to the Black Hills. One of their rituals was the Sun Dance. In this, warriors "danced" while suspended from a pole by ropes attached to wooden skewers pushed under their chest muscles. During the nineteenth century, the Cheyenne migrated to the headwaters of the Platte River, and by 1832, a large group had split off to camp along the Arkansas River. These Northern and Southern Cheyenne were so designated by the 1851 Fort Laramie Treaty. The Cheyenne constantly fought the Kiowa until 1840, when the two tribes made enduring peace.

Stump Horn and his family of the Northern Cheyenne pose for the camera outside their simple home. The travois was a common means of transport for nomadic Plains Indians.

In general, the Cheyenne acted peaceably toward encroaching American settlers. However, a massive incursion by prospectors during the Pike's Peak gold rush established the boomtown of Denver, Colorado, and from 1858 to 1879, the Cheyenne raided wagon trains, settlements, and military outposts. This violence resulted in Chivington's massacre of Black Kettle's Cheyennes at Sand Creek in 1864. Three years later, under the terms of the Medicine Lodge Creek Treaty, the Southern Cheyenne and their Arapaho allies moved to a reservation in Indian Territory. Then, in 1868, Black Kettle's village on the Washita River was destroyed by Custer and the 7th Cavalry. The Cheyenne joined the general Plains uprisings, and in 1876, the Northern Cheyenne were with the Lakota at the Battle of the Little Bighorn. When they surrendered in 1877, after Little Wolf and Dull Knife's village had been destroyed, and hundreds of horses shot, many Cheyennes were deported by train to the Southern Cheyenne reservation in Indian Territory.

The reservation was rife with malaria and malnutrition, however, and the Northern Cheyenne were expected to farm barren land when there was not enough for those already resident. On September 9, 1878, Dull Knife and Little Wolf decided to attempt the 1,500-mile (2,400-kilometer) trek back to their lands on the Tongue River in Wyoming and Montana. Nearly 300 men, women, and children fled through territory dotted with white ranches and farms, and crossed by roads and railroads, while eluding 10,000 pursuing troops and 3,000 civilians. Despite being nearly captured, the Cheyennes avoided severe losses until they reached the Platte River. There, a dispute left the strong, under Little Wolf, continuing on to the Tongue River, while the exhausted decided to head toward Red Cloud's agency at Fort Robinson, Nebraska. This latter group was captured and was refused permission to settle on Red Cloud's new reservation in South Dakota; instead, it was to be sent back to Oklahoma.

The group was held in an unheated room at the fort. Cheyenne woman Iron Teeth said the room was 30 feet (9 meters) square and contained forty-three men, twenty women, and 20–30 children. Most had not eaten for eleven days, nor had they drunk for three. Iron Teeth's son broke a window, and the group escaped. During their flight and subsequent recapture, sixty-four Cheyennes were killed. Iron Teeth recounted how she and one of her daughters had hidden in a cave for seven days and nights, their only sustenance being snow. Eventually, she was caught and reunited with her other daughter: "*After a little while the little girl came to me. I asked her about her brother. It appeared she did not hear me, so I asked again. This time she burst out crying. Then I knew he had been killed ... A few days later we were taken to the Pine Ridge Reservation Agency in South Dakota. Dull Knife, his wife, son, daughter-in-law, grandchild and another boy made it there, too, although his daughter was killed.*"

Meanwhile, Little Wolf and his group wintered on Lost Chokecherry Creek, a tributary of the Niobrara. When the weather improved, they headed north again, but they encountered Lieutenant William Clark and some Cheyenne scouts, who persuaded them to surrender. They were taken to Montana.

Today, some 11,000 Cheyenne live on the Tongue River in southeastern Montana, and in Oklahoma. Cheyennes have served in the U.S. armed forces during both world wars, in Korea, in Vietnam, and in the recent Gulf wars.

Chief of the Northern Cheyenne, Little Wolf (left). With Dull Knife (right), he led an escape from Indian Territory, heading back to their homeland on the Tongue River. They split up and Dull Knife's group was captured, many being killed in a subsequent escape attempt. Little Wolf continued northward, but his group was eventually persuaded to surrender.

THE RIEL REBELLIONS

LOUIS RIEL, OF FRENCH-OJIBWA DESCENT, LED THE MÉTIS (THE DESCENDANTS OF EUROPEAN-NATIVE AMERICAN MARRIAGES) IN TWO UPRISINGS AGAINST THE DOMINION OF CANADA.

Louis Riel, c. 1875. Of French-Ojibwa descent, Riel fought hard for the rights of the Métis in the new Dominion of Canada. Hanged for the execution of Thomas Scott, he has since become a Métis icon and is celebrated in modern Canada.

Formed in 1867, the Dominion of Canada was a confederation of Ontario, Québec, New Brunswick, and Nova Scotia. In 1869, it purchased Rupert's Land from the Hudson's Bay Company and immediately encouraged settlement in the region to counter any threat of encroachment from the United States—some 800,000 American Civil War veterans were unemployed and were hungry for land

Settlers flooded into the Red River area, spearheaded by the Canada Firsters, members of the Protestant Orangemen Canada Party. With a hatred of Roman Catholics, Indians, and the French, this group, led by Dr. John Christian Schultz, posed an immense threat to Métis land rights. Government surveyors were sent in by Prime Minister John Macdonald, with orders to section off square townships of 800 acres (320 hectares) each. However, the Métis had always laid out their land according to criteria established under French rule. Each Red River inhabitant had a strip of land that began on the river bank and extended back through woods to farm fields, and then to communal prairie land for grazing livestock. Thus, the government's intentions would damage and disrupt Métis traditions.

On October 11, 1869, the Montréal-educated Riel, with a small group of supporters, confronted the surveyors and drove them away. An attempt to enter the region by the new territorial governor, William McDougall, was thwarted by Riel, who captured Fort Garry (Winnipeg). Riel's subsequent List of Rights delivered to the government in Ottowa demanded land rights, the right to be heard in the confederation government, and consultation on issues affecting the Red River country. The government sent in militia plus Canada Firsters, but these were interned. The National Committee of Métis proclaimed independence, and on February 9, 1870, Riel was elected president.

One Firster, Thomas Scott, attacked a guard, was tried for attacking the state, and executed. Riel fled from arrest. In 1870, the Manitoba Act granted the Red River region provincial status. However, its terms were ignored by Protestants, who squatted on Métis lands during their seasonal hunts. In response, many of the several thousand Métis migrated westward to the Saskatchewan River.

A contemporary illustration of a lancer of the North West Mounted Police. The force was established in 1873 and soon established a formidable presence in the Dominion of Canada. The Mounties' attempt to eject some Métis from a trading post they had occupied sparked armed conflict in the second Riel rebellion.

The second Riel uprising resulted from Métis and Native American grievances. By 1879, the buffalo were nearly extinct, smallpox had torn through the Plains Indians, the transcontinental Canadian Pacific Railway was bringing in more settlers, and the North West Mounted Police had established a formidable presence. Once more, the Métis faced the end of their traditional landholding customs, and they petitioned Ottawa for surveys to reflect their traditions, but to no avail. The Métis sent for Riel, who had become a U.S. citizen and was working at a mission school, asking him to lead a campaign for Métis rights. Riel formed the Provisional Government of Saskatchewan, and led a sabotage campaign against telegraph lines and government stores; also he took hostages.

Armed conflict ensued when a detachment of Mounties attempted to retake an occupied trading post at Duck Lake. The government forces sustained twenty-four casualties and retreated.

Riel tried to negotiate alliances with several Indian tribes, but only two Cree chiefs, Poundmaker and Big Bear, chose to join him. Hating reservation life, these men campaigned hard. Poundmaker attacked Battleford in a three-week siege, while, 150 miles (240 kilometers) away, Big Bear assaulted the Frog Lake settlement, where nine colonists were killed.

Government troops were brought in by the Canadian Pacific, but attacks on Métis and Indian positions were repelled. Eventually, at the Métis' main stronghold at Batoche, the defenders ran out of ammunition and succumbed to a bayonet charge. Elsewhere, Poundmaker surrendered, while Big Bear

Louis Riel surrounded by members of the Métis Provisional Government of Saskatchewan. Their rebellion would eventually be quelled by government troops.

was attacked at Frenchman's Butte and Loon Lake, eventually giving up at Fort Carlton in July. The two chiefs were imprisoned for two years, but when Riel was captured and tried, he was sentenced to death for the execution of Thomas Scott during the first uprising. He was hanged on November 16, 1885.

Riel has since become a Métis icon. In 1982, the Canadian Constitution included the Métis as one of Canada's three aboriginal peoples, and in 1994, the aboriginal peoples were granted the right to self-government.

GHOST DANCE AND WOUNDED KNEE

BEATEN, RESENTFUL, AND CONFINED TO THEIR RESERVATIONS, THE NORTHERN BANDS OF NATIVE AMERICANS GRASPED AT ONE LAST, FORLORN HOPE OF RETURNING TO THE OLD WAYS.

Wovoka, the Paiute shaman whose revelation gave rise to the Ghost Dance religion.

I n 1889, a part-Christian Paiute mystic, Wovoka, had a revelation while sick with fever. Son of another mystic, Tavibo, Wovoka incorporated his father's teachings with a vision that came to him during an eclipse of the sun, and spread a gospel ultimately known as the Ghost Dance religion. The revelation enabled him to meet his ancestors, and he received instructions from the Great Spirit— he must forget fighting and work for the white man, and dance the traditional Round Dance. The dance and ideas spread rapidly among the Indians of the Plains and Southwest, appealing to the traditional notion of warrior society that the spiritual world would inform the physical world.

One Lakota, Kicking Bear, visited Wovoka in Nevada. Upon returning to his reservation, he ignored Wovoka's teaching that good behavior would be rewarded in the afterlife; he and others thought that the white man could be eliminated because Indians could make special Ghost Dance shirts that would stop bullets. A religious, apocalyptic fervor spread through the Lakota reservations, and white officialdom banned the Ghost Dance in 1890. The fearful U.S. government even sent over half the Army to the reservations.

Eventually, the Ghost Dancers, some 3,000 Lakota, Oglala, and Sicangus from the Rosebud reservation, moved out and made camp in a remote region of the Badlands, in southwest South Dakota. They had chosen a natural fortress known as the Stronghold. Trouble really started when Sitting Bull broke his peace pipe, saying that he would fight and kill all whites. A party of forty Indian police was sent to arrest the chief before he left for the Stronghold, but a bitter fight broke out between them and 160 Ghost Dancers. Eventually, troops of the 8th Cavalry rescued the police, but Sitting Bull had been shot dead

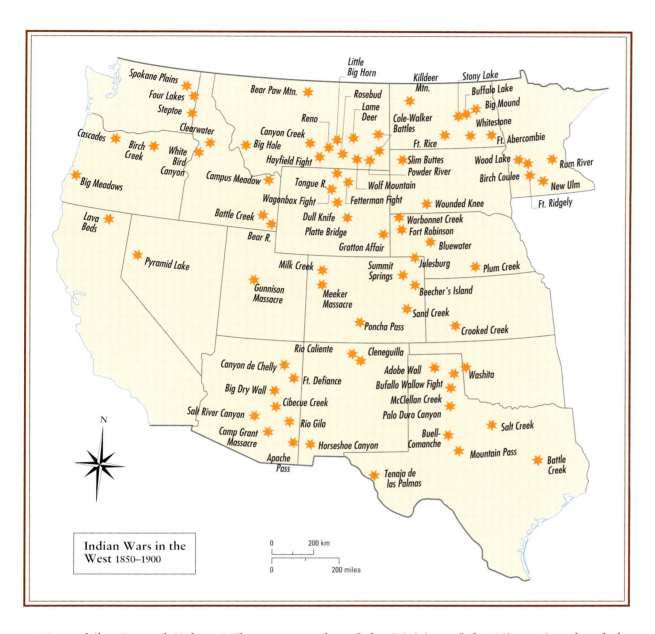

Indian Wars in the
West 1850–1900

0   200 km

0   200 miles

In the second half of the nineteenth century, the West was a tinderbox where armed conflict between the Indians and Army could erupt anywhere and at any time. Pushed around, cheated, and dispossessed, the Indians were fighting desperately against overwhelming odds to retain their homes and their way of life.

Meanwhile, General Nelson Miles, commander of the Division of the Missouri, ordered the arrest of Big Foot, a Miniconjou. Big Foot had already left the Cheyenne River in South Dakota for Pine Ridge in the south. He had been asked there not by Ghost Dancers, but by Red Cloud and other pro-white reservation Indians who wanted peace and stability. Miles dispatched Major S.M. Whitside with the 7th Cavalry to bring in Big Foot, and they found him at Porcupine Creek, some 30 miles (48 kilometers) east of Pine Ridge. No resistance was offered, and the Indians were ordered to make camp 5 miles (8 kilometers) to the west at Wounded Knee Creek. Colonel James Forsyth arrived, took charge, surrounded the camp with his 500 soldiers, and mounted four rapid-fire Hotchkiss machine guns on a bluff overlooking the camp. The Lakota numbered 120 men, and 230 women and children.

On December 29, Forsyth sent soldiers into the camp to disarm the men. Few weapons were offered up, but body searches of men and women revealed guns. In one scuffle, a shot was fired. Shooting began on both sides, the soldiers using their single-shot Springfields, while the Lakota replied with repeating rifles. Some Indians were gunned down, some ran for their families, and

A mass grave dug at Wounded Knee for the Lakota killed during the massacre.

Opposite: Big Foot's Miniconjou band at a Grass Dance on the Cheyenne River in South Dakota. Almost all of the men in this photograph were killed at Wounded Knee.

others broke through the encircling line. The Hotchkiss guns were brought into action, and a massacre resulted. The shrapnel from some American weapons killed U.S. troops. In all, 153 men, women, and children were killed, while thirty-three were wounded. The bodies of women and children were found up to 3 miles (5 kilometers) from the camp, evidence of relentless pursuit and bloodlust. The Army lost twenty-five killed and had thirty-seven wounded. Forsyth was removed from his command, but eventually was reinstated, making major general; eighteen officers and men received the Medal of Honor.

Some Indians were captured on December 30 at White Clay Creek, but fighting continued for two weeks. At one stage, Forsyth and the 7th Cavalry were surrounded and had to be rescued by the all-black 9th Cavalry. About 4,000 Ghost Dancers, among them 1,000 warriors, were found and surrounded by General Miles; they surrendered on January 15, 1891. Kicking Bear personally handed his rifle to Miles. The Wounded Knee Massacre brought an end to the Lakota wars, but not to Indian expressions of anger. In 1897, there was a civil disturbance by the Chippewa, while in 1906, 400 Utes terrorized part of Wyoming.

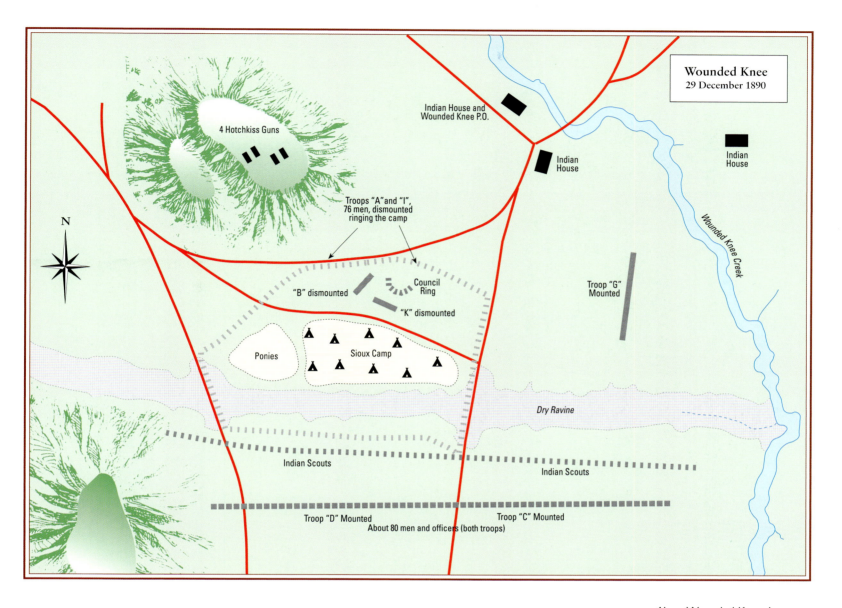

Wounded Knee
29 December 1890

4 Hotchkiss Guns

Indian House and
Wounded Knee P.O.

Indian
House

Indian
House

N

Troops "A" and "I",
76 men, dismounted
ringing the camp

Council
Ring

Troop "G"
Mounted

"B" dismounted

"K" dismounted

Ponies

Sioux Camp

Wounded Knee Creek

Dry Ravine

Indian Scouts

Indian Scouts

Troop "D" Mounted

Troop "C" Mounted

About 80 men and officers (both troops)

Above: Wounded Knee. In December 1890, a group of Lakota led by Big Foot were apprehended by the Army after leaving their reservation on the Cheyenne River and heading for the Pine Ridge reservation. They were ordered to camp by Wounded Knee Creek and surrounded by the 7th Cavalry. During a search for weapons, a shot was fired and shooting broke out on both sides. The troops opened up with rapid-fire Hotchkiss guns and around half of Big Foot's 350 followers were killed. It is possible that many more crawled away to die elsewhere.

THE BIRTH OF OKLAHOMA.

IN 1885, THE NATIVE AMERICANS OCCUPYING INDIAN TERRITORY
THOUGHT THAT THEY WOULD NOT BE REQUIRED TO MOVE
AGAIN. THE UNITED STATES GOVERNMENT HAD OTHER IDEAS.

Groups of white settlers were squatting on Indian reservations, and these "Boomers" prompted commercial interests to pressure the government to allow further development of Indian lands. Congress passed The General Allotment (Dawes) Act in 1887. The legislation proposed that the reservations should be broken up and a 160-acre (65-hectare) holding, or allotment, be given to each Indian head of family. This would turn the Indians into farmers, strip the chiefs of their powers, and finally assimilate the Indians into white culture.

The Act authorized surveys of reservations, the preparation of a tribal consensus, and then division of the land. The Five Civilized Tribes, the Osage in Oklahoma, and the Seneca in New York were exempt. An Indian taking an allotment became a U.S. citizen, but the land was held in trust for twenty-five years, during which time the owner could neither lease, sell, nor will the land. The Dawes Act was modified in 1891, when each adult received an 80-acre (32-hectare) holding, and the Commissioner of Indian Affairs was allowed to lease allotments to white farmers.

In 1889, there were two significant developments. Congress established a separate federal court at Muskogee for the Indian Territory, defining the territory as that land bordered by the states of Kansas, Missouri, Arkansas, Texas, and New Mexico Territory. On April 22, the Unassigned Lands, in the southwestern part of Indian Territory, were opened to settlement by non-Indians, and over 50,000 settlers moved in during a single day. In May 1890, Indian Territory was reduced to the reservations belonging to the Five Civilized Tribes, together with those reservations in the far northeastern portion of the original territory. The remainder, including all the reservations in the Cherokee Outlet, became Oklahoma Territory.

Surplus lands of the Cheyenne and Arapaho were opened to settlement on April 19, 1892. The Cherokee Outlet, and the surplus lands of the Tonkawa and Pawnee reservations were thrown open on September 16, 1893, and those of the Kickapoo on May 25, 1895. The invasion of the Cherokee Outlet saw 100,000 people surrounding the area. There was a 4-mile (6-kilometer) line of people on horseback, in wagons, hacks, and carriages, and on bicycles, all waiting for the signal to homestead. Such wild settler races and scrambles were repeated as the lands were homesteaded in a disorganized fashion. However, disposal of the surplus lands of the Comanche-Kiowa and Wichita-Caddo reservations was accomplished by prior registration, each settler taking part in a land lottery.

The 1898 Curtis Act promoted sweeping changes in Indian Territory. It established tribal courts, and authorized the Dawes Commission to make allotments to the Five Civilized Tribes and eradicate tribal government without tribal consent. In all, 15.79 million acres (6.39 million hectares) were allotted to 101,506 tribal members, including 2,582 whites married to Indians, and 23,405 African-Americans who had been slaves before 1863.

Seeing their land holdings being steadily eroded, the Five Civilized Tribes organized a convention to write a constitution and asked to be allowed into the Union as the state of Sequoyah. This notion was rejected by Congress. The original treaties of removal signed by the Five Civilized Tribes had promised them lands in perpetuity. The Choctaw Treaty stated, *"No part of the land granted them shall ever be embraced in a territory (non-Indian) or state."*

In 1907, Congress approved a law that combined Indian Territory and Oklahoma Territory into the new state of Oklahoma. Legacies of the allotment policy are the checkerboarding of small reservations and many allotments that are too small to be economically viable. Another ironic outcome is that the Osage reservation, which was created in 1866 from a small slice of the large Cherokee Nation, is now the largest in Oklahoma.

Settlers preparing to take part in a land run. These "races" for land were started on the hour that a territory was opened for settlement, and usually the land was allocated on a "first come, first served" basis.

SURVIVAL AND RENAISSANCE, 1900–2002

"... MANY TRIBES ARE WILLING TO ADOPT FOREIGN INFLUENCES AND TO ALLOW THEMSELVES TO MAKE ACCOMMODATIONS TO THE KINDS OF MODELS OF GOVERNANCE THAT OTHER PEOPLES HAVE. SOMETIMES THEY DO THAT IF ONLY TO BE ABLE TO SURVIVE. SOME OF US DO NOT WISH TO DO THAT, AND I THINK YOU WILL SEE THAT MANY OF US WILL NOT OFTENTIMES IN THE FUTURE."

SUZAN HARJO, CHEYENNE, TO THE U.S. CIVIL RIGHTS COMMISSION, 1988.

The film *Windtalkers* focused upon the Navajo code talkers' contribution to U.S. military activities during World War II. Their importance cannot be underestimated, but it is only one example of Native American military service on behalf of the USA. Stockbridge Indians became Minutemen and fought for George Washington, while various units served on both sides during the Civil War. In 1866, the U.S. Army established the Indian Scouts, who went on to take part in campaigns under General John Pershing against Pancho Villa in Mexico in 1916. The Scouts were finally decommissioned in 1947. Oklahoma Indians were recruited by Teddy Roosevelt's Rough Riders and fought in Cuba during the 1898 Spanish-American War. One Indian fighter from Michigan, Jonas Shawandase, was with Roosevelt on San Juan Hill.

Despite some 50 percent of Native Americans not being eligible for the draft in 1917, about 12,000 Indians served in the U.S. military during World War I. An estimated 600 Oklahoma Indians, mainly Choctaw and Cherokee, were sent to the 142nd Infantry of the 36th Texas-Oklahoma National Guard Division. The unit saw action in France, and its soldiers were praised for their military efforts. Of special interest are the eight Choctaw code talkers who were invaluable to the American Expeditionary Force in several important battles in the Meuse-Argonne campaign. The Choctaws were in the same battalion, which was about to be surrounded by Germans. The enemy had broken U.S. radio codes, tapped into telephone lines, and captured some 25 percent of message runners. An officer overheard some soldiers talking in Choctaw, and soon each field company headquarters had been assigned a Choctaw speaker, radio messages and written field orders being expressed in their language. Within 72 hours, the Germans had retreated, having lost their intelligence advantage. Other Choctaws were employed in the same manner, and they were instrumental in the successful 36th Division assault at Foret Ferme in France. Their success encouraged the military to use Comanche, Cheyenne, Cherokee, Osage, and Yankton Sioux as code talkers. The Native American contribution to the war effort was rewarded by blanket citizenship in 1924.

A group of Native Americans in U.S. military service during World War II. Many Indians served in the armed forces during the conflict, some being employed as code talkers to aid secure communications.

During 1940, the U.S. Army realized that it might become embroiled in World War II, because the German Army was conquering much of Europe. Therefore, it recruited Native Americans to create new codes based upon their languages. Such codes were confusing, even to fellow tribal members. This program employed seventeen Chippewas and Oneidas, seventeen Comanches, nineteen Sacs and Foxes (Mesquakie), and, in 1941, eleven Hopi. After the United States entered World War II, many Indians were recruited into the Army. Cherokees, Assiniboines, Choctaws, Kiowas, Lakota and Dakota Sioux, Menominees, Muskogee Creeks, and Seminoles became code talkers. The Army's success was so impressive that the Marines recruited 420 Navajos, who played a vital role in the capture of Iwo Jima.

After World War II came the Cold War, and all code talkers were pledged to secrecy about their previous role. Some served in the Korean War and in Vietnam. The Navajo have received much publicity, but other tribes deserve recognition. Lakota code talkers took part in several Pacific island battles, while Muskogee Creeks were employed in the campaign to regain Attu in the Aleutian Islands, off Alaska.

Comanche code talkers served in the 4th Signal Company Motorized Division in Europe. Seventeen Comanches were trained at Fort Benning, Georgia, and fourteen of them served in Europe. However, after they landed in the second wave on Utah Beach, on D-Day, apparently they remained there laying telephone lines, and were not employed in combat like their fellow Native Americans.

During the Korean War, Native American veterans were joined by recently recruited Indians to fight the North Koreans and Chinese. Between 10,000 and 15,000 Indians saw action in Korea. Over 42,000 Native Americans—90 percent were volunteers—served in Southeast Asia during the Vietnam War. Indians continued to make a military contribution throughout the 1980s and 1990s, taking part in actions in Grenada, Panama, and Somalia, and in the first Gulf War. In 1990, before Operation Desert Storm, there were approximately 24,000 Native American men and women in the military. Some 3,000 served in the Persian Gulf. One 1990s estimate stated that there were 160,000 surviving Native American service veterans. Today, there are 20–30,000 Indians serving in the U.S. military.

On the home front during World War II, Native Americans made outstanding contributions to the war effort. Tribes and individuals bought Treasury Stamps and Bonds, spending some $50 million on these by 1944. They also made significant donations to the Red Cross. Three thousand Indians, especially Navajo, helped build the Fort Wingate Ordnance Depot in New Mexico, while Pueblo Indians did similar work at the Naval Supply Depot in Utah. Women took over many male roles on reservations, becoming mechanics, lumberjacks, farmers, and firefighters. By 1943, the Young Women's Christian Association estimated that 12,000 young Native American women had left reservations to work in defense industries. Many were employed as welders in aircraft plants and shipyards.

Indian men took on a number of occupations. Two thousand Sioux helped construct military depots and flight training facilities. Apaches did maintenance work on the Santa Fé Railroad, while Hopis were employed by the Denver & Rio Grande Railroad in Colorado. By 1943, 46,000 Indians had left reservations and were working in mines, sawmills, canneries, and shipyards. Three hundred Papagos were recruited to work in the Phelps-Dodge Copper Mine at Ajo, Arizona, because white miners had enlisted and production targets had been increased.

The war caused Native Americans some severe problems. Detribalization took place, many Indians deciding to adopt white culture and not return to the reservations. High wages earned during World War II raised expectations, which required fulfilment or abandonment. An important impact of the war was the GI Bill, which provided many Native Americans with the opportunity to enrol as college students, something that had been impossible hitherto. Many of those who graduated remained in the towns and cities to look for jobs; some enjoyed a good life, but others did not. Another problem for the Indians was the reduction in their land holding. The government purchased 300,000 acres (120,000 hectares) on the Pine Ridge Reservation, South Dakota, and leased 100,000 acres (40,000 hectares) to create an aerial gunnery range. Camps for interned Japanese-Americans were constructed on the Colorado and Gila rivers. The federal government seized natural resources like oil, gas, lead, zinc, copper, vanadium, asbestos, and gypsum. The Manhattan Project, in New Mexico, used Navajo helium in the development of the atomic bomb, while Blackfeet oil reserves were severely depleted.

Since then, Native Americans have expressed concern over threats to their resources, land, and environment. The 1908 Winters Doctrine gave tribes "First rights" to any water touching their reservations, but these rights are often ignored. Dams have been built that have flooded Indian land. Among those tribes who have experienced this treatment are the Seneca (the Kinzua Dam) and the Eastern Cherokee (the Tellico Dam). Water rights are vitally important, especially since many Indians inhabit arid western regions. The 1978 American Indian Religious Freedom Act protects Indian cultural and religious practices, and Indians have safeguarded access to sacred nonreservation areas and resources. Thus, dams like those on the Columbia River, which caused the flooding of religious sites and the destruction of fisheries like the Celilo Falls, together with upstream salmon spawning waters, can no longer be built.

Mineral-extraction methods have severely damaged Indian lands ever since oil was found in Osage territory in 1900. Moreover, many tribes have been virtually forced to lease land to mineral companies to reduce poverty among their populations. Such exploitation can be detrimental to the environment and the health of those who live nearby.

The Four Corners region, where Arizona, New Mexico, Colorado, and Utah meet, is the location of the Black Mesa. Beneath the mesa is the richest lode of high-grade, low-sulphur coal in the United

States. The Navajo and Hopi each signed leasing agreements that allowed companies to strip-mine the mesa, and acquiesced in the construction of vast, coal-fired powerplants that generate electricity for Los Angeles, Phoenix, Las Vegas, and Tucson. Strip-mining has created an enormous pit where the topsoil has been removed. Black Mesa coal is transported along a 273-mile (440-kilometer) coal-slurry pipeline, which uses 1.4 billion gallons (5.3 billion liters) of water annually. As a result, the water table has been lowered, springs have dried up, and the Hopi have lost many water sources. Moreover, the underground aquifers are the only sources of water for the Navajo and Hopi. Some 20 billion gallons (76 billion liters) are sucked out annually by the Peabody Coal Company, and water depletion could threaten the cultural survival of local Native Americans. The Navajo Generating Station, near Page, Arizona, uses Black Mesa coal, the burning of which creates a yellow-grey haze that covers more than 10,000 square miles (26,000 square kilometers). Navajos and Hopis have to breathe this miasmic air, which is polluted with lead, mercury, sulphuric acid, and other toxins.

The Black Hills region, covering parts of Montana, Wyoming, and North and South Dakota, is rich in uranium. It is inhabited by the second largest group of Native Americans—the Shoshone, Crow, Arapaho, Sioux, and Northern Cheyenne. By the 1970s, energy companies had extracted so much uranium that part of the Black Hills had become irradiated; also they were covered with the spoil from open-pit mining. The level of contamination was considered to be beyond the safe limit for animals. In this particular case, the Native Americans were not concerned with health issues alone; the Black Hills are a sacred site, *Paha Saha*, the life's blood for the Sioux.

Other dangers from industrial toxins exist in both water and air. In Montana, the leaching of cyanide from a gold mining process is polluting water on the Fort Belknap reservations. Toxic waste from the Hanford nuclear plant, in south-central Washington, has polluted the Columbia River and poisoned the salmon upon which so many Indians depend economically. A nuclear plant has been constructed on the edge of the small reservation on Prairie Island, Minnesota, home of the Mdewakanton Sioux. They fear for their safety, while the Western Shoshone are angered because their land has been used as a nuclear test site. Industrial waste dumps are dangerously close to the St. Regis Mohawk Reservation on the St. Lawrence River in New York.

Native Americans hold a variety of opinions concerning economic development and its dangers. The Standing Rock Sioux and Northern Cheyenne are attempting to enforce federal laws that protect their environment from pollution. Others, however, place economic needs over older cultural requirements. Some tribes welcome the storage of nuclear waste on their reservations, seeing it as an asset that produces dollars. For example, the tribal council of the Mescalero Apache approved a joint venture for building an above-ground storage unit capable of holding 25 percent of all high-level fuels created at nuclear plants in the USA. One Mescalero leader, Fred Peso, argued that storage of nuclear waste provided diversification in the tribe's employment base and helped build economic self-sufficiency.

The debate about environment versus corporations and economic development will continue over health, water, fishing and hunting rights, and government requests for waste storage. More recently, the western Indian nations have attempted to control their own resources, aided by the Council of Energy Resource Tribes (CERT). This shows that Native Americans are beginning to manage their own affairs, and ending dependency and exploitation.

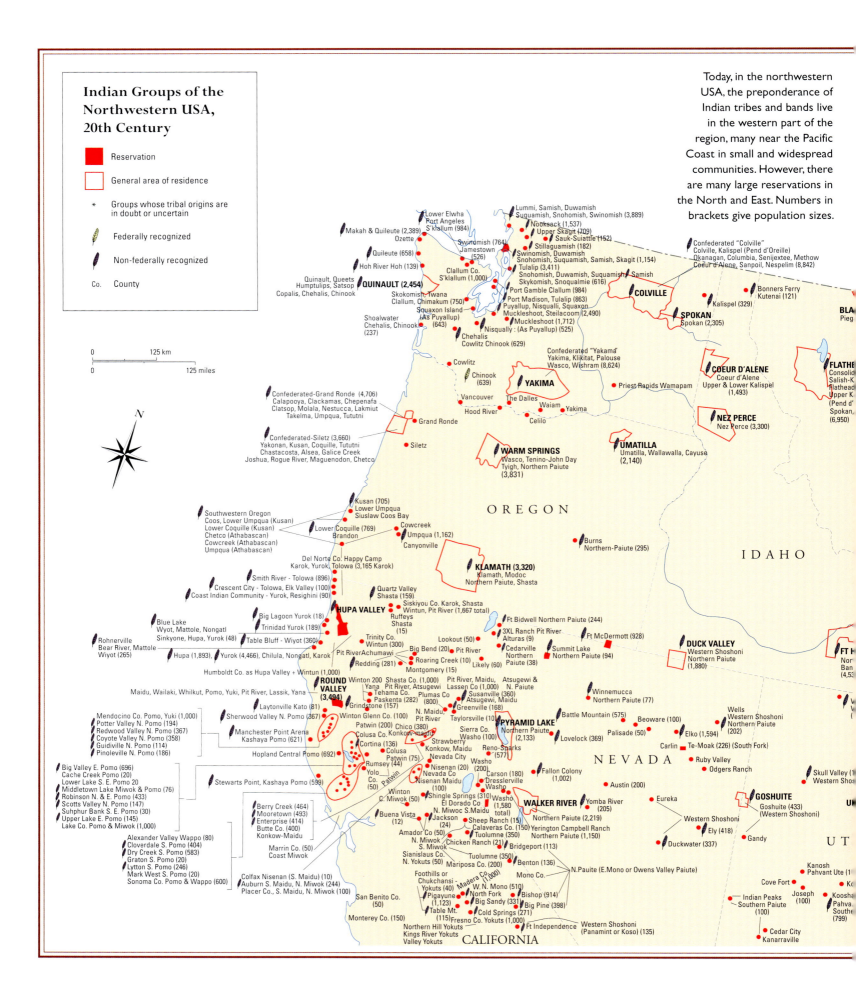

Indian Groups of the Northwestern USA, 20th Century

■ Reservation

□ General area of residence

* Groups whose tribal origins are in doubt or uncertain

🪶 Federally recognized

🪶 Non-federally recognized

Co. County

0 — 125 km
0 — 125 miles

N

Today, in the northwestern USA, the preponderance of Indian tribes and bands live in the western part of the region, many near the Pacific Coast in small and widespread communities. However, there are many large reservations in the North and East. Numbers in brackets give population sizes.

Makah & Quileute (2,389)
Lower Elwha Port Angeles S'klallum (984)
Ozette
Lummi, Samish, Duwamish Suquamish, Snohomish, Swinomish (3,889)
Nooksack (1,537)
Upper Skagit (709)
Sauk-Suiattle (152)
Quileute (658)
Jamestown (526)
Swinomish (764)
Stillaguamish (182)
Hoh River Hoh (139)
Clallam Co. S'klallum
Swinomish, Duwamish Snohomish, Suquamish, Samish, Skagit (1,154)
Tulalip (3,411)
Confederated "Colville" Colville, Kalispel (Pend d'Oreille) Okanagan, Columbia, Senijextee, Methow Coeur d'Alene, Sanpoil, Nespelim (8,842)
Bonners Ferry Kutenai (121)
Quinault, Queets Humptulips, Satsop Copalis, Chehalis, Chinook
QUINAULT (2,454)
Skokomish, Twana Clallum, Chimakum (750)
Clallam Co. S'klallum (1,000)
Snohomish, Duwamish, Suquamish, Samish Skykomish, Snoqualmie (616)
Port Gamble Clallam (984)
Port Madison, Tulalip (863)
Puyallup, Nisqualli, Squaxon Muckleshoot, Steilacoom (2,490)
COLVILLE
Kalispel (329)
SPOKAN Spokan (2,305)
BLA Pieg
Shoalwater Chehalis, Chinook (237)
Squaxon Island (As Puyallup) (643)
Muckleshoot (1,712)
Nisqually : (As Puyallup) (525)
Chehalis Cowlitz Chinook (629)
Confederated "Yakama" Yakima, Klikitat, Palouse Wasco, Wishram (8,624)
COEUR D'ALENE Coeur d'Alene Upper & Lower Kalispel (1,493)
FLATHE Consolid Salish-K Flathead Upper K (Pend d' Spokan, (6,950)
Cowlitz
Chinook (639)
Vancouver
YAKIMA
Priest Rapids Wamapam
Hood River
The Dalles
Waiam
Yakima
Celilo
NEZ PERCE Nez Perce (3,300)
Confederated-Grand Ronde (4,706) Calapooya, Clackamas, Chepenafa Clatsop, Molala, Nestucca, Lakmiut Takelma, Umpqua, Tututni
Grand Ronde
UMATILLA Umatilla, Wallawalla, Cayuse (2,140)
Confederated-Siletz (3,660) Yakonan, Kusan, Coquille, Tututni Chastacosta, Alsea, Galice Creek Joshua, Rogue River, Maguenodon, Chetco
Siletz
WARM SPRINGS Wasco, Tenino-John Day Tyigh, Northern Paiute (3,831)
OREGON
Kusan (705) Lower Umpqua Siuslaw Coos Bay
Southwestern Oregon Coos, Lower Umpqua (Kusan) Lower Coquille (Kusan) Chetco (Athabascan) Cowcreek (Athabascan) Umpqua (Athabascan)
Lower Coquille (769) Brandon
Cowcreek
Umpqua (1,162)
Canyonville
Burns Northern-Paiute (295)
IDAHO
Del Norte Co. Happy Camp Karok, Yurok, Tolowa (3,165 Karok)
KLAMATH (3,320) Klamath, Modoc Northern Paiute, Shasta
Smith River - Tolowa (896)
Crescent City - Tolowa, Elk Valley (100)
Coast Indian Community - Yurok, Resighini (90)
Quartz Valley Shasta (159)
Siskiyou Co. Karok, Shasta Wintun, Pit River (1,667 total)
Blue Lake Wyot, Mattole, Nongatl Sinkyone, Hupa, Yurok (48)
Big Lagoon Yurok (18)
Trinidad Yurok (189)
HUPA VALLEY
Ruffeys Shasta (15)
Ft Bidwell Northern Paiute (244)
3XL RANCH Pit River Alturas (9)
Ft McDermott (928)
DUCK VALLEY Western Shoshoni Northern Paiute (1,880)
FT H Nor Ban (4,53
Rohnerville Bear River, Mattole Wiyot (265)
Table Bluff - Wiyot (360)
Trinity Co. Wintun (300)
Lookout (50)
Cedarville Northern Paiute (38)
Summit Lake Northern Paiute (94)
Hupa (1,893), Yurok (4,466), Chilula, Nongatl, Karok
Pit RiverAchumawi
Big Bend (20)
Pit River
Redding (281)
Roaring Creek (10)
Likely (60)
Humboldt Co. as Hupa Valley + Wintun (1,000)
Montgomery (15)
ROUND VALLEY (3,494)
Winton 200
Shasta Co. (1,000)
Pit River, Maidu, Atsugewi & N. Paiute
Winnemucca Northern Paiute (77)
Wells Western Shoshoni Northern Paiute (202)
Maidu, Wailaki, Whilkut, Pomo, Yuki, Pit River, Lassik, Yana
Yana Pit River, Atsugewi Tehama Co. (800)
Lassen Co (1,000)
Susanville (360)
Battle Mountain (575)
Beoware (100)
Paskenta (282)
Plumas Co
Atsugewi, Maidu
Elko (1,594)
Laytonville Kato (81)
Grindstone (157)
Greenville (168)
Mendocino Co. Pomo, Yuki (1,000) Potter Valley N. Pomo (194) Redwood Valley N. Pomo (367) Coyote Valley N. Pomo (358) Guidiville N. Pomo (114) Pinoleville N. Pomo (186)
Sherwood Valley N. Pomo (367)
Winton Glenn Co. (100)
N. Maidu, Pit River
Taylorsville (10)
PYRAMID LAKE Northern Paiute (2,133)
Palisade (50)
Carlin Te-Moak (226) (South Fork)
Ruby Valley
Odgers Ranch
Skull Valley (Western Shos
Manchester Point Arena Kashaya Pomo (621)
Patwin (200)
Chico (380)
Sierra Co.
Washo (100)
Lovelock (369)
Big Valley E. Pomo (696) Cache Creek Pomo (20) Lower Lake S. E. Pomo 20 Middletown Lake Miwok & Pomo (76) Robinson N. & E. Pomo (433) Scotts Valley N. Pomo (147) Suhphur Bank S. E. Pomo (30) Upper Lake E. Pomo (145) Lake Co. Pomo & Miwok (1,000)
Hopland Central Pomo (692)
Colusa Co. Konkow-maidu
Cortina (136)
Colusa
Strawberry Konkow, Maidu
Reno-Sparks (577)
NEVADA
Rumsey (44)
Patwin
Yolo Co. (50)
Nevada City
Washo (200)
Carson (180)
Dresslerville (200)
Fallon Colony (1,002)
Austin (200)
Eureka
GOSHUITE Goshuite (433) (Western Shoshoni)
Stewarts Point, Kashaya Pomo (599)
Winton C. Miwok (50)
Nisenan (200)
Nisenan Maidu (100)
Washo 1,580 total
WALKER RIVER Northern Paiute (2,219)
Yomba River (205)
Western Shoshoni
Duckwater (337)
UT
Berry Creek (464) Mooretown (493) Enterprise (414) Butte Co. (400) Konkow-Maidu
Shingle Springs (310)
El Dorado Co.
N. Miwoc S.Maidu
Yerington Campbell Ranch Northern Paiute (1,150)
Ely (418)
Gandy
Alexander Valley Wappo (80) Cloverdale S. Pomo (404) Dry Creek S. Pomo (583) Graton S. Pomo (20) Lytton S. Pomo (246) Mark West S. Pomo (20) Sonoma Co. Pomo & Wappo (600)
Marrin Co. (50) Coast Miwok
Buena Vista (12)
Amador Co (50)
Sheep Ranch (15)
Calaveras Co. (150)
Jackson (24)
N. Miwoc
Bridgeport (113)
Benton (136)
Kanosh Pahvant Ute (1
Colfax Nisenan (S. Maidu) (10) Auburn S. Maidu, N. Miwok (244) Placer Co., S. Maidu, N. Miwok (100)
N. Miwok S. Miwok
Chicken Ranch (21)
Tuolumne (350)
Mariposa Co. (200)
Mono Co.
N.Paiute (E.Mono or Owens Valley Paiute)
Cove Fort
Ke
San Benito Co. (50)
Sianislaus Co. N. Yokuts (50)
Foothills or Chukchansi Yokuts (40)
Madera Co. (1,000)
W. N. Mono (510)
Bishop (914)
Indian Peaks Southern Paiute (100)
Joseph (100)
Koosha Pahva Southe (799)
Monterey Co. (150)
Pigayune (1,123)
North Fork
Big Sandy (331)
Big Pine (398)
Table Mt. (115)
Cold Springs (271)
Fresno Co. Yokuts (1,000)
Ft Independence
Western Shoshoni (Panamint or Koso) (135)
Cedar City Kanarraville
Northern Hill Yokuts Kings River Yokuts Valley Yokuts
CALIFORNIA

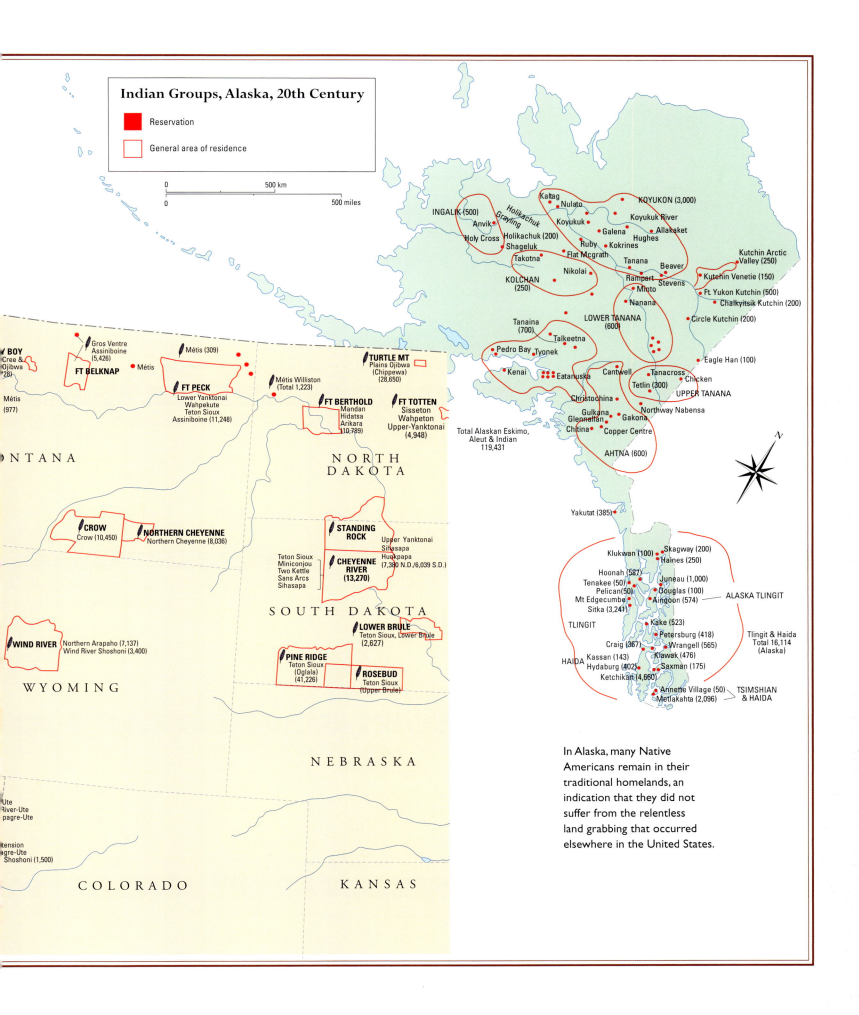

Indian Groups, Alaska, 20th Century

- ■ Reservation
- ▭ General area of residence

0 ——— 500 km
0 ——— 500 miles

Alaska (right map labels):

INGALIK (500)
Holikachuk
Grayling
Anvik
Holy Cross
Shageluk
Holikachuk (200)
Takotna
Kaltag
Nulato
Koyukuk
KOYUKON (3,000)
Koyukuk River
Galena
Hughes
Allakeket
Ruby
Kokrines
Flat Mcgrath
Tanana
Nikolai
KOLCHAN (250)
Beaver
Kutchin Arctic Valley (250)
Rampart
Stevens
Kutchin Venetie (150)
Minto
Ft Yukon Kutchin (500)
Nanana
Chalkyitsik Kutchin (200)
Circle Kutchin (200)
Tanaina (700)
LOWER TANANA (600)
Talkeetna
Eagle Han (100)
Pedro Bay
Tyonek
Kenai
Eatanuska
Cantwell
Tanacross
Tetlin (300)
Chicken
UPPER TANANA
Christochina
Gulkana
Northway Nabensa
Glennallan
Gakona
Chitina
Copper Centre
AHTNA (600)

Total Alaskan Eskimo, Aleut & Indian 119,431

Yakutat (385)

Klukwan (100)
Skagway (200)
Haines (250)
Hoonah (587)
Tenakee (50)
Juneau (1,000)
Pelican (50)
Douglas (100)
Mt Edgecumbe
Aingoon (574)
ALASKA TLINGIT
Sitka (3,241)
TLINGIT
Kake (523)
Petersburg (418)
Tlingit & Haida Total 16,114 (Alaska)
Craig (367)
Wrangell (565)
Kassan (143)
Klawak (476)
HAIDA
Hydaburg (402)
Saxman (175)
Ketchikan (4,660)
Annette Village (50)
TSIMSHIAN & HAIDA
Metlakahta (2,096)

Left map labels:

BOY
Cree & Ojibwa (28)
Métis (977)
Gros Ventre Assiniboine (5,426)
FT BELKNAP
Métis
Métis (309)
FT PECK
Lower Yanktonai Wahpekute Teton Sioux Assiniboine (11,248)
Métis Williston (Total 1,223)

TURTLE MT
Plains Ojibwa (Chippewa) (28,650)
FT BERTHOLD
Mandan Hidatsa Arikara (10,789)
FT TOTTEN
Sisseton Wahpeton Upper-Yanktonai (4,948)

MONTANA

NORTH DAKOTA

CROW
Crow (10,450)
NORTHERN CHEYENNE
Northern Cheyenne (8,036)

STANDING ROCK
Upper Yanktonai Sihasapa Hunkpapa (7,380 N.D./6,039 S.D.)
Teton Sioux Miniconjou Two Kettle Sans Arcs Sihasapa
CHEYENNE RIVER (13,270)

SOUTH DAKOTA

WIND RIVER
Northern Arapaho (7,137) Wind River Shoshoni (3,400)

LOWER BRULE
Teton Sioux, Lower Brule (2,627)
PINE RIDGE
Teton Sioux (Oglala) (41,226)
ROSEBUD
Teton Sioux (Upper Brule)

WYOMING

NEBRASKA

Ute River-Ute pagre-Ute
tension agre-Ute Shoshoni (1,500)

COLORADO

KANSAS

In Alaska, many Native Americans remain in their traditional homelands, an indication that they did not suffer from the relentless land grabbing that occurred elsewhere in the United States.

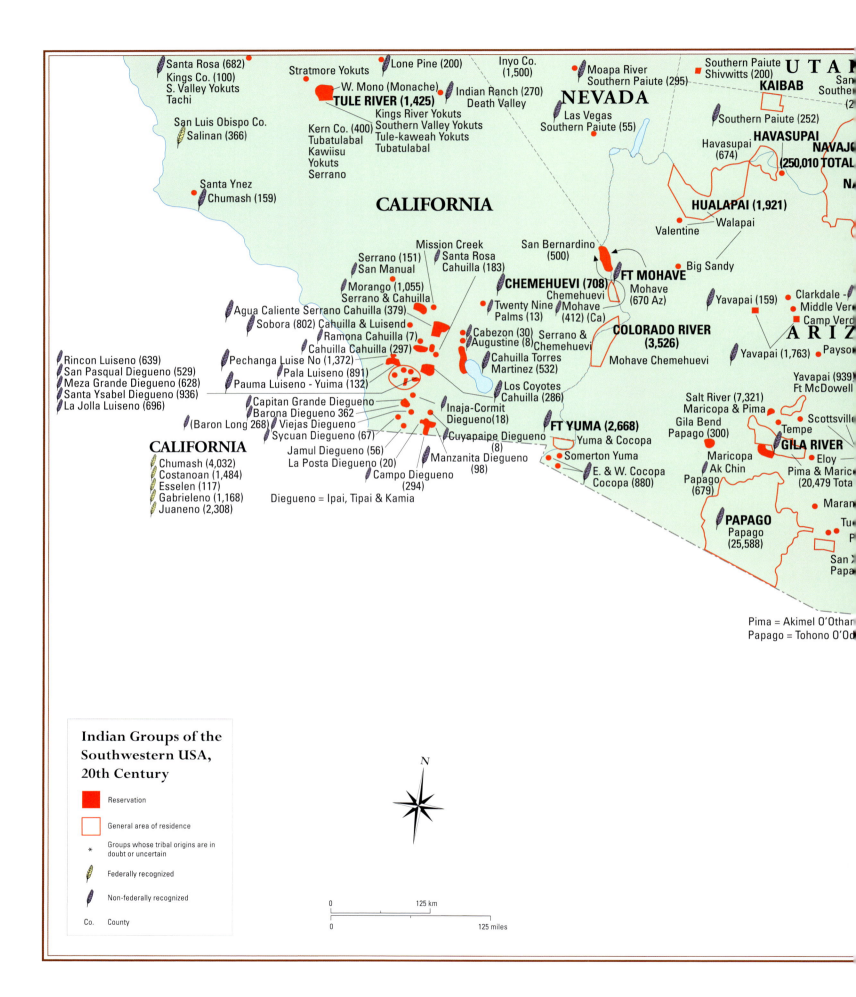

Santa Rosa (682)
Kings Co. (100)
S. Valley Yokuts
Tachi

Stratmore Yokuts

Lone Pine (200)

Inyo Co.
(1,500)

Moapa River
Southern Paiute (295)

Southern Paiute
Shivwitts (200)

UTAH

KAIBAB

San
Souther

W. Mono (Monache)
TULE RIVER (1,425)

Indian Ranch (270)
Death Valley

NEVADA

Southern Paiute (252)

San Luis Obispo Co.
Salinan (366)

Kern Co. (400)
Tubatulabal
Kawiisu
Yokuts
Serrano

Kings River Yokuts
Southern Valley Yokuts
Tule-kaweah Yokuts
Tubatulabal

Las Vegas
Southern Paiute (55)

Havasupai
(674)

HAVASUPAI

NAVAJO
(250,010 TOTAL

Santa Ynez
Chumash (159)

CALIFORNIA

HUALAPAI (1,921)

Valentine

Walapai

NA

Mission Creek

San Bernardino
(500)

Big Sandy

Serrano (151)
San Manual

Santa Rosa
Cahuilla (183)

CHEMEHUEVI (708)

FT MOHAVE

Mohave
(670 Az)

Clarkdale –
Middle Ver

Morango (1,055)
Serrano & Cahuilla

Chemehuevi

Twenty Nine
Palms (13)

Mohave
(412) (Ca)

Yavapai (159)

Camp Verc

Agua Caliente Serrano Cahuilla (379)
Sobora (802) Cahuilla & Luisend
Ramona Cahuilla (7)
Cahuilla Cahuilla (297)

Cabezon (30)
Augustine (8)

Serrano &
Chemehuevi

COLORADO RIVER
(3,526)

ARIZ

Yavapai (1,763)

Payson

Mohave Chemehuevi

Rincon Luiseno (639)
San Pasqual Diegueno (529)
Meza Grande Diegueno (628)
Santa Ysabel Diegueno (936)
La Jolla Luiseno (696)

Pechanga Luise No (1,372)
Pala Luiseno (891)
Pauma Luiseno - Yuima (132)

Cahuilla Torres
Martinez (532)

Los Coyotes
Cahuilla (286)

Salt River (7,321)
Maricopa & Pima

Yavapai (939)
Ft McDowell

Capitan Grande Diegueno
Barona Diegueno 362
(Baron Long 268) Viejas Diegueno
Sycuan Diegueno (67)

Inaja-Cormit
Diegueno(18)

FT YUMA (2,668)

Gila Bend
Papago (300)

Tempe

Scottsville

GILA RIVER

Eloy

CALIFORNIA

Jamul Diegueno (56)
La Posta Diegueno (20)

Cuyapaipe Diegueno
(8)

Manzanita Diegueno
(98)

Yuma & Cocopa
Somerton Yuma

Maricopa
Ak Chin

Pima & Maric
(20,479 Tota

Chumash (4,032)
Costanoan (1,484)
Esselen (117)
Gabrieleno (1,168)
Juaneno (2,308)

Campo Diegueno
(294)

Diegueno = Ipai, Tipai & Kamia

E. & W. Cocopa
Cocopa (880)

Papago
(679)

Maran

PAPAGO
Papago
(25,588)

Tu
P

San X
Papa

Pima = Akimel O'Othan
Papago = Tohono O'Od

N

0   125 km
0   125 miles

ng Allen
n Ute (50)

Wiminuche-Ute **SOUTHERN UTE**
(2,012)   Southern-Ute
(1,375)

Paiute

UTE MT.

● Sanford Catawba

K A N S A S

C O L O R A D O

O K L A H O M A

Navajo Former
Joint Use Area

opi & Tewa (11,267)

Zuni
(8,790)

ZUNI

Ramah
Navajo
(2,463)

Keres
(6,344)

ACOMA

White Mountain
& Cibecue Apache
(12,900)

San Carlos
Apache (11,916)

qui
I Total)

JICARILLA
Jicarilla-Apache (3,403)

Santa Clara-Tawa
(2,800)

San Ildefonso-Tewa (628)
Jemez Pecos-Tewa (3,486)
Keres-Zia (773)
Laguna
Keres(7,825)

Taos-Tiwa (2,443)
Picurus-Tiwa (324)
San Juan-Tewa (324)
Pojoaque-Tewa (2,723)
Nambe-Tewa (327)
Tesuque-Tewa (404)
Cochiti-Keres (1,189)
Santo Domingo-Keres (4,492)
San Felipe-Keres (3,131)
Santa Ana-Keres (716)
Sandia-Tiwi (485)
Isleta-Tiwa (4,441)

Canoncita
Navajo (1,500)

Alamo Navajo
(Puertocito 700)

**N E W
M E X I C O**

MESCALERO
Mescalero-Apache
Chiricahua-Apache
Lipan-Apache
(3,979)

Caddo-Anadarko (3,261)
Wichita-Tawakoni (2,174))

Southern Cheyenne
and Arapaho
(11,459 Combined)

CHEYENNE

ARAPAHO

KIOWA

COMANCHE

T E X A S

Ysleta-Tigua (Southern Tiwa)
El Paso Co.
Seneco ●   Pueblo (1,270)
● Secorro

Kickapoo (880)
Eagle Pass
Seminole-Negro

In the Southwest, California has
the largest population of Native
Americans in the United States;
Arizona has the third largest
population, and New Mexico
the fifth largest. Large tracts of
land in the last two states were
used to create reservations.

Walhalla
Métis

FORT TOTTEN
Sisseton
Wahpeton
Upper-Yanktonai
(4,948)

RED LAKE
Chippewa
(9,610)

Deer Creek

NETT LAKE
Chippewa
(2,857 - Bois Forte Total)

VERMILLON LAKE
Chippewa
(200)

Isle Royal

Scattered Chippewa
Ottawa
Potawatomi
(5,000)

Chippewa = Ojibwa

GRAND PORTAGE
Chippewa
(1,089)

Keweenaw Bay
Community (2,000)
Chippewa (3,120)

ONTONAGON
Chippewa

**NORTH
DAKOTA**

WHITE EARTH
Chippewa
(20,820)

LEECH LAKE
Chippewa
(8,294)

FOND DU LAC
Chippewa
(3,905)

Apostle Is.

RED CLIFF
Chippewa
(4,064)

BAD RIVER
Chippewa
(6,292)

Lac Vieux Desert
Chippewa (442)

L'ANSE
Chippewa

Brimley

Sugar Island

Sault St.
Band (3

BAY MILLS
(1,462)
Chippewa

M I C H I G

MINNESOTA

MILLE LACS
Chippewa
(3,292)

Danbury

**LAC COURTE
OREILLES**
Chippewa
(2,000)

ST CROIX
Chippewa
(500)

LAC DU FLAMBEAU
Chippewa (3,143)

Pearson
Chippewa
(300)

Mole Lake
Sokaogon
(1,163)

Forest Co.
Wabend
Stonelake

Potawatomi
(1,186)

Nahma

Drummond
Burt Lake (60)
Cross Village
Little Traverse Ba
Petoskey

Hannahville, Harris & Wilson
Potawatomi (692)

Peshabestown

Ottawa &
Chippewa

Os

LAKE TRAVERSE
Sisseton
Wahpeton
(Santee-Sioux)
(10,759)

Santee
Browns Valley
(50)

Upper Sioux,
Santee-Sioux
(404)

STOCKBRIDGE
Stockbridge & Munsee
(1,531)

Arpin

MENOMINI
Menomini
(8,074)

Grand Traverse
Band (3,792)

Traverse City

**SOUTH
DAKOTA**

Lower Sioux
Morton
Santee-Sioux
(820)

Prior lake
Santee-Sioux
(820)
(Mdewakanton)

Prairie Island
Santee-Sioux
(622)

WINNEBAGO
Jackson Co.
Black River Falls
Winnebago
(6,145)
(Ho-Chunk)

Potawatomi
(500)

ONEIDA
Oneida
(14,745)

Brotherton
(622)

Manistee &
Mason Cos.
Little River Band
(2,738)

Ba

ISABELLA
Chippewa
(2,921)

Sa

CROW CREEK
Lower Yanktonai
(3,507)

FLANDREAU
Wahpeton
Mdewakanton -
Santee-Sioux
(716)

Pipestone
Santee-Sioux (622)

Waupun

Grand River
Band

Grand Rapids Ottawa
Potawatomi
Match-E-Be-Nash-She-Wish
(276)

YANKTON
Yankton
(7,570)

PONCA
Ponca (2,095)

SANTEE

Mdewakanton
Wahpeton
(Santee-Sioux)
(2,662)

Calhoun Co.
Potawatomi of
Huron (428)

WINNEBAGO
Winnebago
(4,033)

OMAHA
Omaha (5,427)

IOWA

TAMA
Mesquakie
Sac & Fox
(1,260)

Cass Co.
Pokagon
Potawatomi
(2,730)

WISCONSIN

Peru Miami Co.

Miami
(557)

*Hardin C

INDIANA

*Darke
(200)
Piqua
Shawn

*Marion Co.
Kiscopo Shawnee

SAC-FOX
Sac & Fox
(433)

IOWA
Iowa (2,897)

KICKAPOO
Kickapoo
(1,605)

ILLINOIS

POTAWATOMI
Potawatomi
(4,870)

MISSOURI

Wyandot (100)
Wyandot Co.

*Centralia

KANSAS

Munsee-Delaware Chippewa
Franklin Co.
(200)

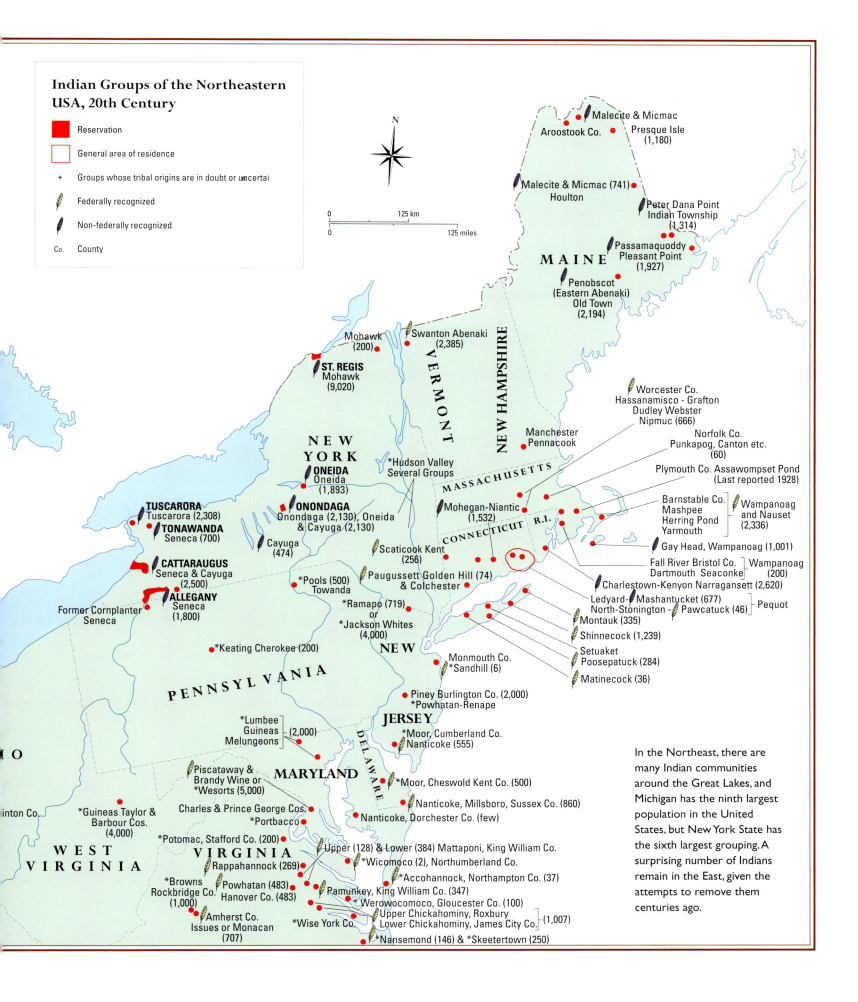

Indian Groups of the Northeastern USA, 20th Century

■ Reservation

□ General area of residence

* Groups whose tribal origins are in doubt or uncertain

🪶 Federally recognized

🪶 Non-federally recognized

Co. County

N

0 — 125 km
0 — 125 miles

MAINE

Malecite & Micmac
Aroostook Co.
Presque Isle (1,180)

Malecite & Micmac (741)
Houlton

Peter Dana Point
Indian Township (1,314)

Passamaquoddy
Pleasant Point (1,927)

Penobscot
(Eastern Abenaki)
Old Town (2,194)

VERMONT

NEW HAMPSHIRE

Mohawk (200)

Swanton Abenaki (2,385)

ST. REGIS
Mohawk (9,020)

Worcester Co.
Hassanamisco - Grafton
Dudley Webster
Nipmuc (666)

Manchester
Pennacook

Norfolk Co.
Punkapog, Canton etc. (60)

NEW YORK

ONEIDA
Oneida (1,893)

ONONDAGA
Onondaga (2,130), Oneida & Cayuga (2,130)

*Hudson Valley
Several Groups

MASSACHUSETTS

Plymouth Co. Assawompset Pond (Last reported 1928)

Barnstable Co.
Mashpee
Herring Pond
Yarmouth

Wampanoag and Nauset (2,336)

TUSCARORA
Tuscarora (2,308)
TONAWANDA
Seneca (700)

Cayuga (474)

Mohegan-Niantic (1,532)

CONNECTICUT R.I.

Gay Head, Wampanoag (1,001)

CATTARAUGUS
Seneca & Cayuga (2,500)

Scaticook Kent (256)

Paugussett Golden Hill (74)
& Colchester

Fall River Bristol Co. Wampanoag
Dartmouth Seaconke (200)

ALLEGANY
Seneca (1,800)

*Pools (500)
Towanda

Charlestown-Kenyon Narragansett (2,620)

Ledyard- Mashantucket (677)
North-Stonington - Pawcatuck (46) Pequot

Former Cornplanter
Seneca

*Ramapo (719)
or
*Jackson Whites (4,000)

Montauk (335)

Shinnecock (1,239)

*Keating Cherokee (200)

NEW

Setuaket
Poosepatuck (284)

Matinecock (36)

Monmouth Co.
*Sandhill (6)

PENNSYLVANIA

Piney Burlington Co. (2,000)
*Powhatan-Renape

JERSEY

*Moor, Cumberland Co.
Nanticoke (555)

DELAWARE

*Lumbee
Guineas (2,000)
Melungeons

Piscataway &
Brandy Wine or
*Wesorts (5,000)

MARYLAND

*Moor, Cheswold Kent Co. (500)

Nanticoke, Millsboro, Sussex Co. (860)

*Guineas Taylor &
Barbour Cos. (4,000)

Charles & Prince George Cos.
*Portbacco

Nanticoke, Dorchester Co. (few)

inton Co.

*Potomac, Stafford Co. (200)

WEST VIRGINIA

VIRGINIA
Rappahannock (269)

Upper (128) & Lower (384) Mattaponi, King William Co.

*Wicomoco (2), Northumberland Co.

*Browns
Rockbridge Co. (1,000)

Powhatan (483)
Hanover Co. (483)

Pamunkey, King William Co. (347)

*Accohannock, Northampton Co. (37)

Amherst Co.
Issues or Monacan (707)

*Wise York Co.

Werowocomoco, Gloucester Co. (100)

Upper Chickahominy, Roxbury
Lower Chickahominy, James City Co. (1,007)

*Nansemond (146) & *Skeetertown (250)

In the Northeast, there are many Indian communities around the Great Lakes, and Michigan has the ninth largest population in the United States, but New York State has the sixth largest grouping. A surprising number of Indians remain in the East, given the attempts to remove them centuries ago.

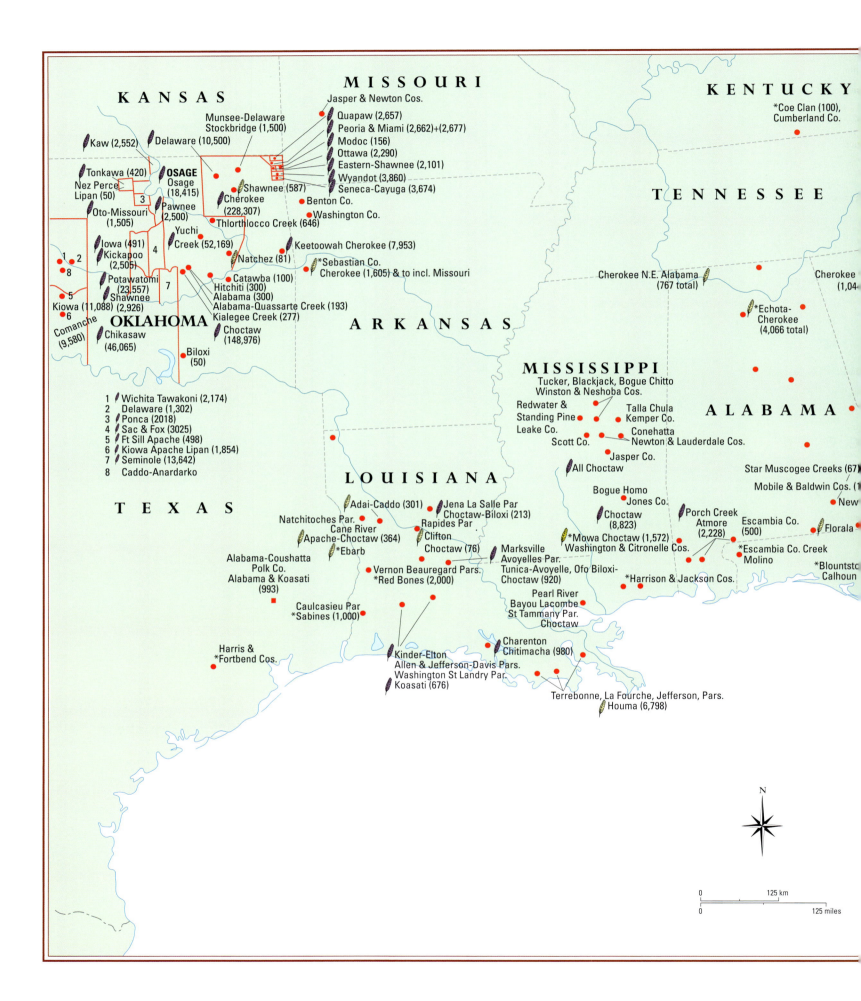

KANSAS

MISSOURI

KENTUCKY

*Coe Clan (100),
Cumberland Co.

Munsee-Delaware
Stockbridge (1,500)
Delaware (10,500)
Kaw (2,552)
Tonkawa (420)
Nez Perce
Lipan (50)
OSAGE
Osage
(18,415)

Jasper & Newton Cos.
Quapaw (2,657)
Peoria & Miami (2,662)+(2,677)
Modoc (156)
Ottawa (2,290)
Eastern-Shawnee (2,101)
Wyandot (3,860)
Seneca-Cayuga (3,674)

TENNESSEE

Oto-Missouri
(1,505)
Pawnee
2,500
Shawnee (587)
Cherokee
(228,307)
Benton Co.
Washington Co.
Thlorthlocco Creek (646)

1 2
8
Iowa (491)
Kickapoo
(2,505)
Yuchi
Creek (52,169)
Keetoowah Cherokee (7,953)
Natchez (81)
*Sebastian Co.
Cherokee (1,605) & to incl. Missouri

Cherokee N.E. Alabama
(767 total)
Cherokee
(1,04

5
Potawatomi
(23,557)
7
Shawnee
(2,926)
Catawba (100)
Hitchiti (300)
Alabama (300)
Alabama-Quassarte Creek (193)
Kialegee Creek (277)

ARKANSAS

*Echota-
Cherokee
(4,066 total)

Kiowa (11,088)
6
OKLAHOMA
Chikasaw
(46,065)
Choctaw
(148,976)

MISSISSIPPI

ALABAMA

Comanche
(9,580)

Biloxi
(50)

Tucker, Blackjack, Bogue Chitto
Winston & Neshoba Cos.
Redwater &
Standing Pine
Leake Co.
Scott Co.
Talla Chula
Kemper Co.
Conehatta
Newton & Lauderdale Cos.
Jasper Co.
All Choctaw

1 ⸙ Wichita Tawakoni (2,174)
2   Delaware (1,302)
3   Ponca (2018)
4 ⸙ Sac & Fox (3025)
5 ⸙ Ft Sill Apache (498)
6 ⸙ Kiowa Apache Lipan (1,854)
7 ⸙ Seminole (13,642)
8   Caddo-Anardarko

TEXAS

LOUISIANA

Bogue Homo
Jones Co.
Choctaw
(8,823)
Porch Creek
Atmore
(2,228)

Star Muscogee Creeks (67
Mobile & Baldwin Cos. (1
New

Adai-Caddo (301)
Natchitoches Par.
Cane River
Apache-Choctaw (364)
*Ebarb
Jena La Salle Par
Choctaw-Biloxi (213)
Rapides Par.
Clifton
Choctaw (76)
Marksville
Avoyelles Par.
Tunica-Avoyelle, Ofo Biloxi-
Choctaw (920)
*Mowa Choctaw (1,572)
Washington & Citronelle Cos.
Escambia Co.
(500)
*Escambia Co. Creek
Molino

Florala

Alabama-Coushatta
Polk Co.
Alabama & Koasati
(993)
Vernon Beauregard Pars.
*Red Bones (2,000)
Pearl River
Bayou Lacombe
St Tammany Par.
Choctaw

*Harrison & Jackson Cos.

*Blountsto
Calhoun

Caulcasieu Par
*Sabines (1,000)

Harris &
*Fortbend Cos.

Kinder-Elton
Allen & Jefferson-Davis Pars.
Washington St Landry Par.
Koasati (676)

Charenton
Chitimacha (980)

Terrebonne, La Fourche, Jefferson, Pars.
Houma (6,798)

N

0 ___ 125 km
0 ___ 125 miles

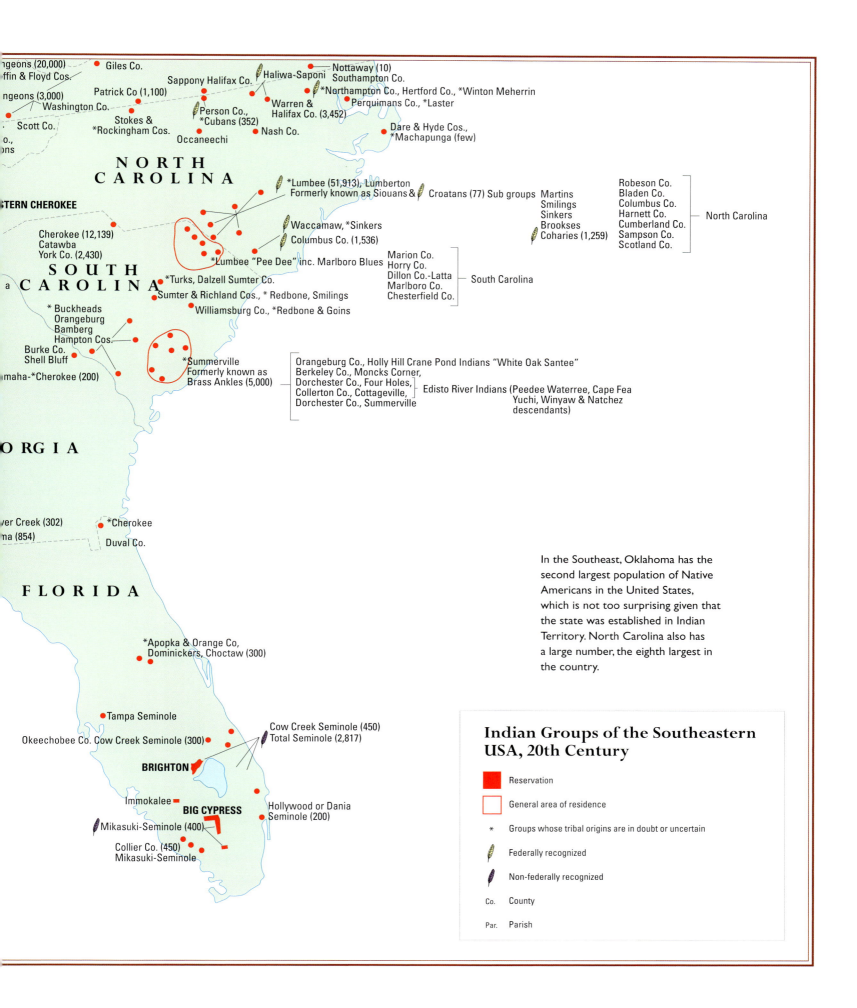

ngeons (20,000)
ffin & Floyd Cos.
ngeons (3,000)
Washington Co.
Scott Co.

• Giles Co.
Sappony Halifax Co.
Patrick Co (1,100)
Stokes &
*Rockingham Cos.
Occaneechi

Haliwa-Saponi
Nottaway (10)
Southampton Co.
*Northampton Co., Hertford Co., *Winton Meherrin
Warren &   Perquimans Co., *Laster
Halifax Co. (3,452)
Person Co.,
*Cubans (352)
Nash Co.
Dare & Hyde Cos.,
*Machapunga (few)

N O R T H
C A R O L I N A

TERN CHEROKEE

*Lumbee (51,913), Lumberton
Formerly known as Siouans &   Croatans (77) Sub groups

Cherokee (12,139)
Catawba
York Co. (2,430)

S O U T H
a C A R O L I N A

Waccamaw, *Sinkers
Columbus Co. (1,536)

*Lumbee "Pee Dee" inc. Marlboro Blues

*Turks, Dalzell Sumter Co.
Sumter & Richland Cos., * Redbone, Smilings
Williamsburg Co., *Redbone & Goins

* Buckheads
Orangeburg
Bamberg
Hampton Cos.
Burke Co.
Shell Bluff
maha-*Cherokee (200)

*Summerville
Formerly known as
Brass Ankles (5,000)

Martins
Smilings
Sinkers
Brookses
Coharies (1,259)

Robeson Co.
Bladen Co.
Columbus Co.
Harnett Co.   North Carolina
Cumberland Co.
Sampson Co.
Scotland Co.

Marion Co.
Horry Co.
Dillon Co.-Latta
Marlboro Co.   South Carolina
Chesterfield Co.

Orangeburg Co., Holly Hill Crane Pond Indians "White Oak Santee"
Berkeley Co., Moncks Corner,
Dorchester Co., Four Holes,   Edisto River Indians (Peedee Waterree, Cape Fea
Collerton Co., Cottageville,   Yuchi, Winyaw & Natchez
Dorchester Co., Summerville   descendants)

RG I A

ver Creek (302)
ma (854)

*Cherokee
Duval Co.

F L O R I D A

*Apopka & Orange Co,
Dominickers, Choctaw (300)

•Tampa Seminole

Okeechobee Co. Cow Creek Seminole (300)

BRIGHTON

Immokalee

BIG CYPRESS

*Mikasuki-Seminole (400)

Collier Co. (450)
Mikasuki-Seminole

Cow Creek Seminole (450)
Total Seminole (2,817)

Hollywood or Dania
Seminole (200)

In the Southeast, Oklahoma has the
second largest population of Native
Americans in the United States,
which is not too surprising given that
the state was established in Indian
Territory. North Carolina also has
a large number, the eighth largest in
the country.

Indian Groups of the Southeastern USA, 20th Century

◼ Reservation

◻ General area of residence

* Groups whose tribal origins are in doubt or uncertain

🪶 Federally recognized

🪶 Non-federally recognized

Co. County

Par. Parish

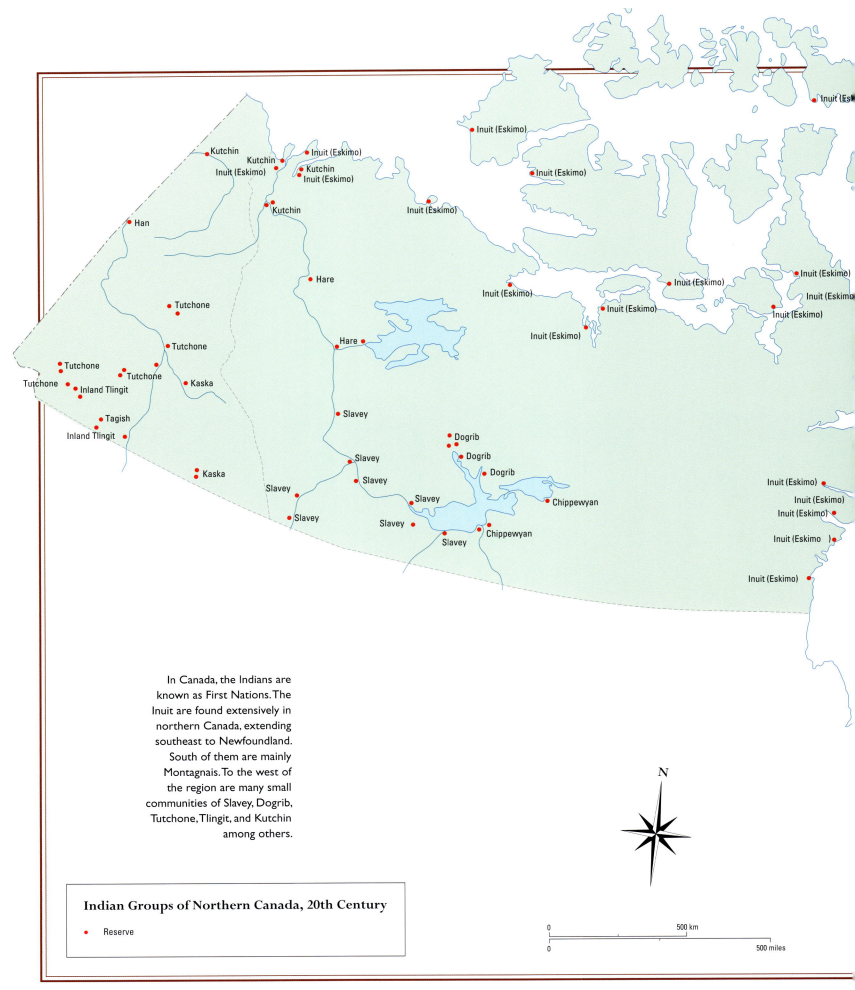

Kutchin

Kutchin
Inuit (Eskimo)

Inuit (Eskimo)

Inuit (Eskimo)

Kutchin
Inuit (Eskimo)

Inuit (Eskimo)

Inuit (Eskimo)

Kutchin

Han

Inuit (Eskimo)

Inuit (Eskimo)

Hare

Tutchone

Inuit (Eskimo)

Inuit (Eskimo)

Inuit (Eskimo)

Tutchone

Hare

Inuit (Eskimo)

Tutchone

Tutchone

Tutchone

Kaska

Tutchone

Inland Tlingit

Slavey

Tagish

Dogrib

Inuit (Eskimo)

Inland Tlingit

Dogrib

Dogrib

Kaska

Slavey

Dogrib

Inuit (Eskimo)

Slavey

Chippewyan

Inuit (Eskimo)

Slavey

Slavey

Inuit (Eskimo)

Slavey

Chippewyan

Inuit (Eskimo)

Slavey

Slavey

Inuit (Eskimo)

In Canada, the Indians are
known as First Nations. The
Inuit are found extensively in
northern Canada, extending
southeast to Newfoundland.
South of them are mainly
Montagnais. To the west of
the region are many small
communities of Slavey, Dogrib,
Tutchone, Tlingit, and Kutchin
among others.

N

Indian Groups of Northern Canada, 20th Century

• Reserve

0   500 km

0   500 miles

Inuit (Eskimo)

Inuit (Eskimo)

Inuit (Eskimo)

Inuit (Eskimo)

Inuit (Eskimo)

Inuit (Eskimo)

Inuit (Eskimo)

Inuit (Eskimo)

Inuit (Eskimo)

Inuit (Eskimo)

Inuit (Eskimo)

Inuit (Eskimo)

Inuit (Eskimo)

Inuit (Eskimo)

Inuit (Eskimo)

Inuit (Eskimo)

Inuit (Eskimo)

Inuit (Eskimo)

Inuit (Eskimo)

Inuit (Eskimo)

Inuit (Eskimo)

Naskapi

Naskapi

Naskapi

**NEWFOUNDLAND
(LABRADOR)**

Montagnais

Montagnais

Montagnais

Montagnais

Micmac

Inuit (Eskimo)

Inuit (Eskimo)

Montagnais

Montagnais

Montagnais

Montagnais (Cree)

Montagnais

Montagnais

Montagnais

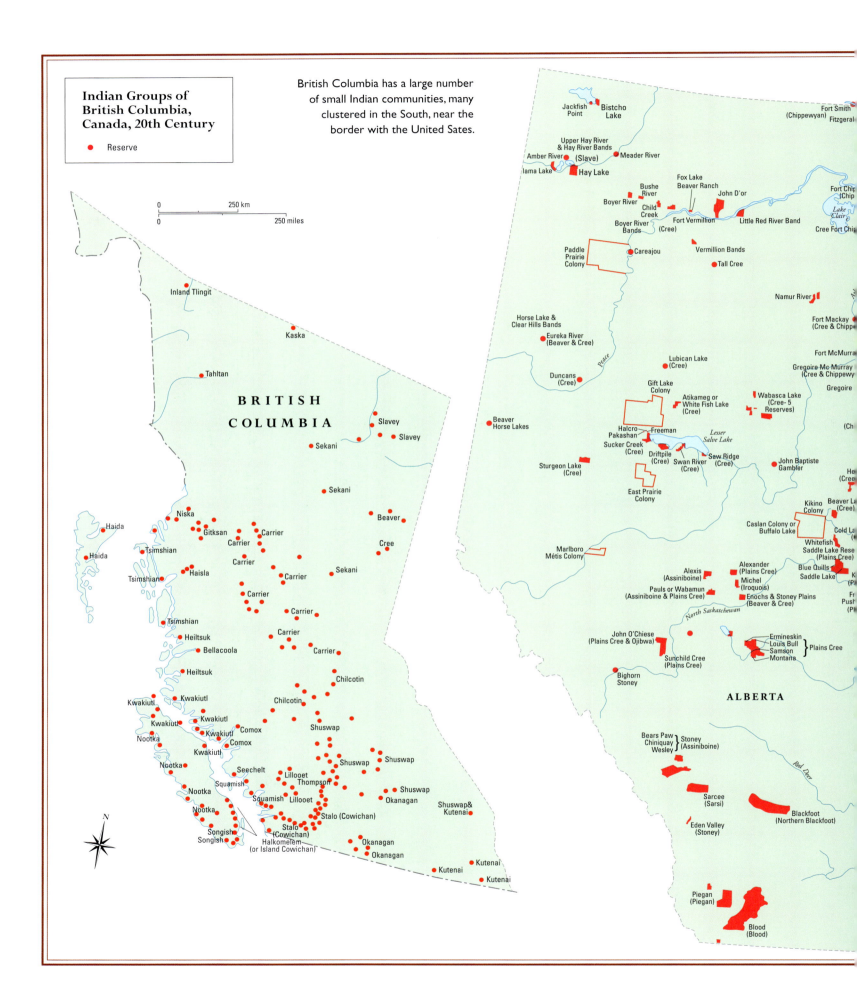

Indian Groups of British Columbia, Canada, 20th Century

● Reserve

British Columbia has a large number of small Indian communities, many clustered in the South, near the border with the United Sates.

0 _____ 250 km
0 _____ 250 miles

BRITISH COLUMBIA

Inland Tlingit

Kaska

Tahltan

Slavey
Slavey

Sekani

Sekani

Beaver

Cree

Niska

Haida

Gitksan   Carrier
Carrier

Tsimshian

Sekani

Haisla   Carrier
Tsimshian

Carrier

Carrier

Carrier

Tsimshian

Heiltsuk   Carrier

Bellacoola   Carrier

Heiltsuk

Chilcotin

Kwakiutl

Kwakiutl   Chilcotin

Kwakiutl

Kwakiutl   Shuswap
Kwakiutl   Comox

Nootka   Kwakiutl   Comox

Kwakiutl

Seechelt   Shuswap   Shuswap
Nootka   Lillooet
Squamish   Thompson

Nootka   Squamish   Lillooet   Shuswap
Okanagan
Nootka   Stalo (Cowichan)   Shuswap &
Kutenai

Songish   Stalo
Songish   (Cowichan)   Okanagan
Halkomelem
(or Island Cowichan)   Okanagan

Kutenai   Kutenai

Kutenai

Jackfish Point   Bistcho Lake   Fort Smith
(Chippewyan)
Fitzgeral

Upper Hay River
& Hay River Bands
Amber River   (Slave)   Meader River
llama Lake   Hay Lake

Fox Lake   Fort Chip
Bushe   Beaver Ranch   (Chip
River   John D'or
Boyer River   Child
Creek   Lake
Boyer River   Fort Vermillion   Little Red River Band   Clair
Bands   (Cree)   Cree Fort Chip

Paddle
Prairie   Careajou   Vermillion Bands
Colony   Tall Cree

Namur River   Fort Mackay
(Cree & Chippe

Horse Lake &
Clear Hills Bands   Fort McMurra
Eureka River   Lubican Lake   Gregoire Mc Murray
(Beaver & Cree)   (Cree)   (Cree & Chippewy

Duncans   Gift Lake   Gregoire
(Cree)   Colony
Atikameg or   Wabasca Lake
White Fish Lake   (Cree-5   (Ch
(Cree)   Reserves)

Beaver   Halcro
Horse Lakes   Pakashan   Freeman   Lesser
Sucker Creek   Salve Lake   John Baptiste
(Cree)   Driftpile   Saw Ridge   Gambler
Sturgeon Lake   (Cree)   Swan River   (Cree)
(Cree)   (Cree)   He
East Prairie   (Cree
Colony

Kikino   Beaver L
Colony   (Cree

Caslan Colony or   Cold La
Buffalo Lake   (

Marlboro   Whitefish
Métis Colony   Saddle Lake Rese
(Plains Cree)

Alexis   Alexander   Blue Quills   K
(Assiniboine)   (Plains Cree)   Saddle Lake   (Pl
Michel
Pauls or Wabamun   (Iroquois)   Fr
(Assiniboine & Plains Cree)   Enochs & Stoney Plains   Push
(Beaver & Cree)   (Pl

North Saskatchewan

John O'Chiese   Ermineskin
(Plains Cree & Ojibwa)   Louis Bull
Samson   Plains Cree
Sunchild Cree   Montana
(Plains Cree)

Bighorn
Stoney

ALBERTA

Bears Paw
Chiniquay   Stoney
Wesley   (Assiniboine)

Sarcee
(Sarsi)   Blackfoot
(Northern Blackfoot)
Eden Valley
(Stoney)

Piegan
(Piegan)

Blood
(Blood)

N

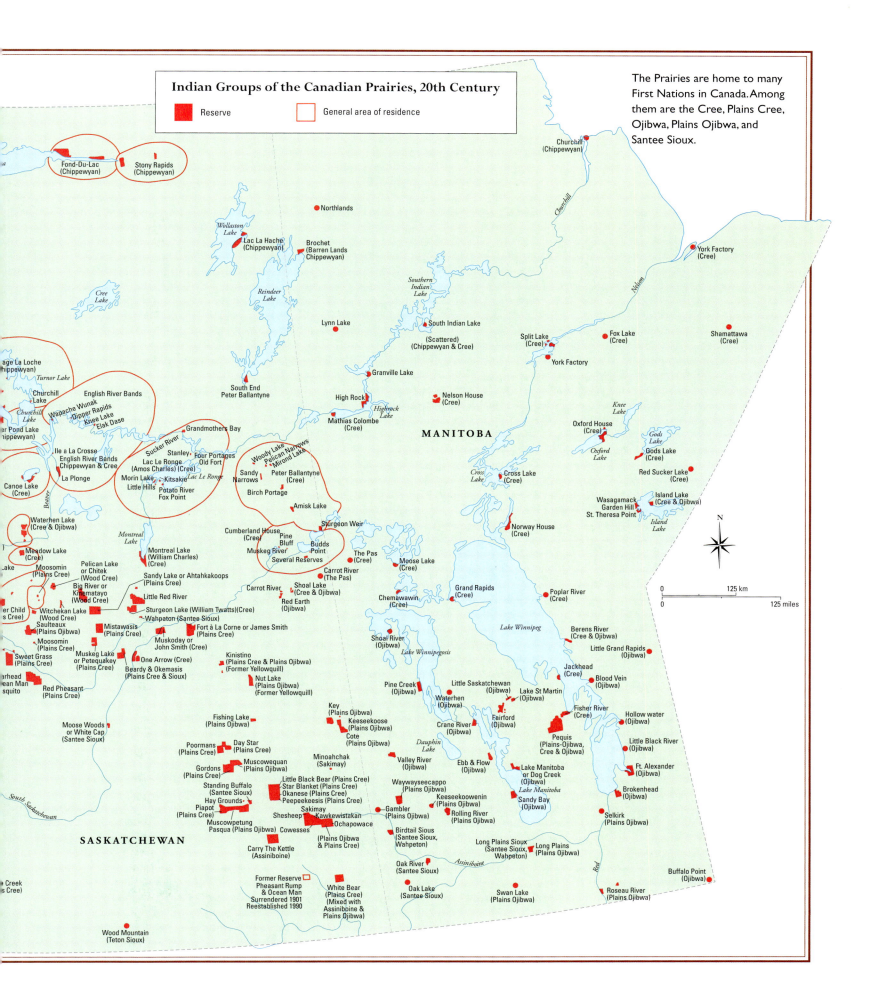

Indian Groups of the Canadian Prairies, 20th Century

■ Reserve ▢ General area of residence

The Prairies are home to many First Nations in Canada. Among them are the Cree, Plains Cree, Ojibwa, Plains Ojibwa, and Santee Sioux.

Fond-Du-Lac (Chippewyan)
Stony Rapids (Chippewyan)
Churchill (Chippewyan)
York Factory (Cree)

Northlands
Wollaston Lake
Lac La Hache (Chippewyan)
Brochet (Barren Lands Chippewyan)

Reindeer Lake
Cree Lake

Lynn Lake
South Indian Lake
(Scattered) (Chippewyan & Cree)
Split Lake (Cree)
Fox Lake (Cree)
Shamattawa (Cree)
York Factory

ge La Loche (hippewyan)
Turnor Lake
Granville Lake
Nelson House (Cree)
Knee Lake
Oxford House (Cree)
Gods Lake (Cree)

Churchill Lake
English River Bands
South End Peter Ballantyne
High Rock
Highrock Lake
Mathias Colombe (Cree)

Churchill Lake
Wapache Wunak
Dipper Rapids
Knee Lake
Elak Dase
MANITOBA
Oxford Lake
Gods Lake
Red Sucker Lake (Cree)

r Pond Lake hippewyan)
Ile a La Crosse English River Bands Chippewyan & Cree
La Plonge
Grandmothers Bay
Sucker River
Stanley
Four Portages Old Fort
Woody Lake
Pelican Narrows
Mirond Lake
Cross Lake
Cross Lake (Cree)
Island Lake (Cree & Ojibwa)
Wasagamack Garden Hill St. Theresa Point
Island Lake

Canoe Lake (Cree)
Lac Le Ronge (Amos Charles) (Cree)
Morin Lake
Kitsakie
Little Hills
Potato River
Fox Point
Sandy Narrows
Peter Ballantyne (Cree)
Birch Portage
Amisk Lake
Norway House (Cree)

Waterhen Lake (Cree & Ojibwa)
Montreal Lake
Cumberland House (Cree)
Pine Bluff
Budds Point
Several Reserves
Sturgeon Weir
Cross Lake

Meadow Lake (Cree)
Montreal Lake (William Charles) (Cree)
Muskeg River
The Pas (Cree)
Moose Lake (Cree)
Grand Rapids (Cree)
Poplar River (Cree)

Moosomin (Plains Cree)
Pelican Lake or Chitek (Wood Cree)
Sandy Lake or Ahtahkakoops (Plains Cree)
Carrot River (The Pas)
Chemawawin

Big River or Kinematayo (Wood Cree)
Little Red River
Carrot River
Shoal Lake (Cree & Ojibwa)
Red Earth (Ojibwa)

r Child s Cree)
Witchekan Lake (Wood Cree)
Sturgeon Lake (William Twatts) (Cree)
Wahpaton (Santee Sioux)
Shoal River (Ojibwa)
Berens River (Cree & Ojibwa)

Saulteaux (Plains Ojibwa)
Mistawasis (Plains Cree)
Fort à La Corne or James Smith (Plains Cree)
Lake Winnipegosis
Lake Winnipeg
Little Grand Rapids (Ojibwa)

Moosomin (Plains Cree)
Muskeg Lake or Petequakey (Plains Cree)
Muskoday or John Smith (Cree)
Jackhead (Cree)
Blood Vein (Ojibwa)

Sweet Grass (Plains Cree)
One Arrow (Cree)
Kinistino (Plains Cree & Plains Ojibwa) (Former Yellowquill)
Little Saskatchewan (Ojibwa)
Lake St Martin (Ojibwa)
Fisher River (Cree)
Hollow water (Ojibwa)

arhead ean Man squito
Red Pheasant (Plains Cree)
Beardy & Okemasis (Plains Cree & Sioux)
Nut Lake (Plains Ojibwa) (Former Yellowquill)
Waterhen (Ojibwa)
Crane River (Ojibwa)
Fairford (Ojibwa)
Pequis (Plains-Ojibwa, Cree & Ojibwa)
Little Black River (Ojibwa)

Moose Woods or White Cap (Santee Sioux)
Fishing Lake (Plains Ojibwa)
Key (Plains Ojibwa)
Keeseekoose (Plains Ojibwa)
Cote (Plains Ojibwa)
Ebb & Flow (Ojibwa)
Ft. Alexander (Ojibwa)

Poormans (Plains Cree)
Day Star (Plains Cree)
Minoahchak (Sakimay)
Valley River (Ojibwa)
Dauphin Lake
Lake Manitoba or Dog Creek (Ojibwa)
Brokenhead (Ojibwa)

Gordons (Plains Cree)
Muscowequan (Plains Ojibwa)
Little Black Bear (Plains Cree)
Star Blanket (Plains Cree)
Okanese (Plains Cree)
Peepeekeesis (Plains Cree)
Waywayseecappo (Plains Ojibwa)
Keeseekoowenin (Plains Ojibwa)
Rolling River (Plains Ojibwa)
Sandy Bay (Ojibwa)
Selkirk (Plains Ojibwa)

Standing Buffalo (Santee Sioux)
Hay Grounds
Piapot (Plains Cree)
Sakimay
Kawkewistakan
Gambler (Plains Ojibwa)
Birdtail Sious (Santee Sioux, Wahpeton)

Muscowpetung
Pasqua (Plains Ojibwa)
Cowesses
Shesheep
Ochapowace
(Plains Ojibwa & Plains Cree)
Oak River (Santee Sioux)
Long Plains Sioux (Santee Sioux, Wahpeton)
Long Plains (Plains Ojibwa)
Buffalo Point (Ojibwa)

SASKATCHEWAN
Carry The Kettle (Assiniboine)
Former Reserve Pheasant Rump & Ocean Man Surrendered 1901 Reestablished 1990
White Bear (Plains Cree) (Mixed with Assinibboine & Plains Ojibwa)
Oak Lake (Santee Sioux)
Swan Lake (Plains Ojibwa)
Roseau River (Plains Ojibwa)

Wood Mountain (Teton Sioux)

0   125 km
0   125 miles

N

Poplarhill • Pikangikum - Ojibwa

• Cat Lake - Ojibwa

Central Patricia • Pickle Crow

Slate Falls • • Pickle Lake - Ojibwa

■ Ft. Hope - Ojibwa

Martin
- Ojit

• Red Lake

• Osnaburg House - Ojibwa

Ontario

Oneman Lake &
Islington Ojibwa

Wabauskang - Ojibwa

Grassy Narrows or
English River Ojibwa

Lac Seul - Ojibwa

Frenchmans Head
Ignace

Allen
Water   Collins   Mud
River   Whitesand - Ojibwa

Dalles - Ojibwa

Armstrong   • Auden   Aroland - Ojibwa
Whitesand - Ojibwa

Shoal Lake Ojibwa

Rat Portage - Ojibwa

Sioux
Lookout   Ghost
River   Savant
Lake

Ferland

N.W.A.33 - Ojibwa

N.W.A.37 - Ojibwa

Eagle Lake - Ojibwa

Jackfish - Ojibwa

Lake
Nipigon

Long La
- Ojibw

Wabigoon - Ojibwa

Gull Bay - Ojibwa

Big Island Ojibwa 200

Whitefish Bay - Ojibwa

N.W.A. 33 - Ojibwa

Rocky Bay - Ojibwa

Sabaskong Bay Ojibwa

Rainy River - Ojibwa

Big Grassy
Ojibwa   Naicatchewenin

Seine River - Ojibwa

Manitou Rapids - Ojibwa

Nickickousemenecaning
(Seine River) Ojibwa

Red Rock - Ojibwa

Pays Plat - Ojibwa

Coughiching   Stangecoming - Ojibwa

Lac Des Mille Lacs - Ojibwa

Pic Mober

Pic Her
Bay Oji

Fort William - Ojibwa

Lake Superior

Michipicot

In the Great Lakes region of Canada, there are
many Ojibwa reserves, evidence of the wide spread
of the tribe. In the northeast of the region can be
found Cree, while to the east are Algonkin and
some Iroquois.

N

**Indian Groups, Great Lakes Region,
Canada, 20th Century**

■ Reserve

0   125 km
0   125 miles

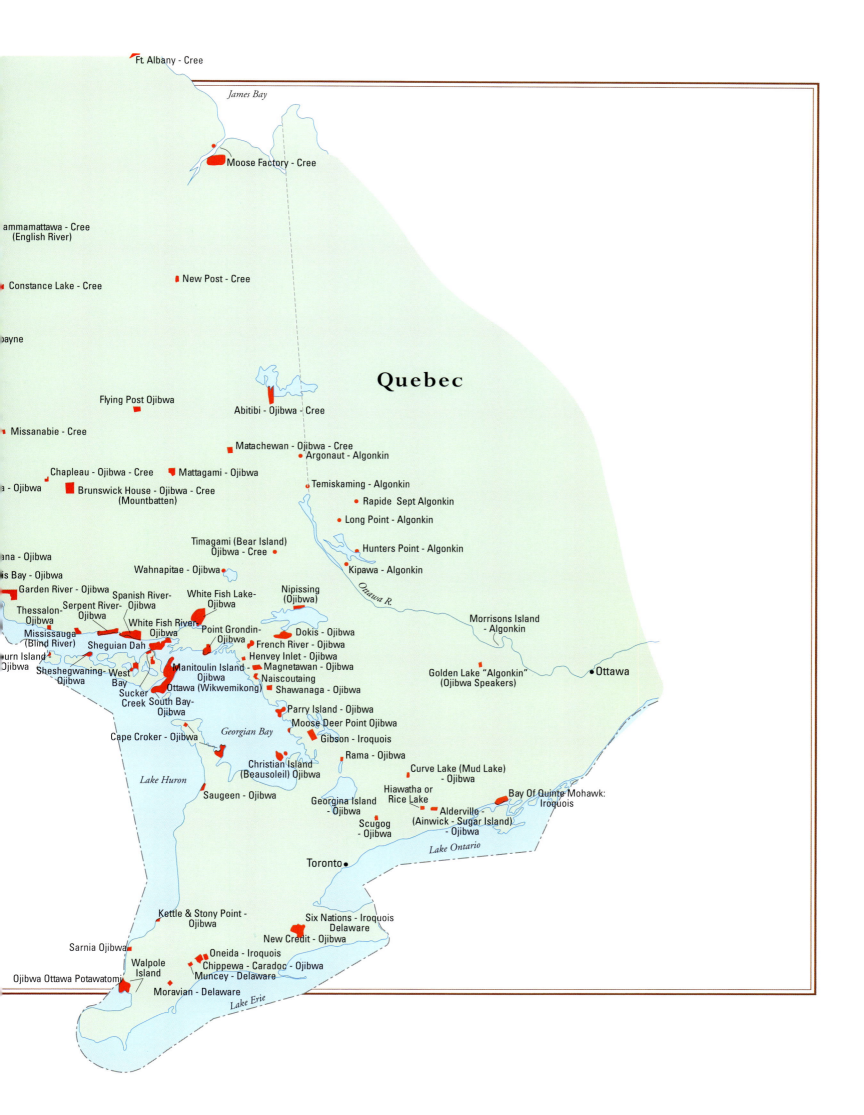

Ft. Albany - Cree

James Bay

Moose Factory - Cree

ammamattawa - Cree
(English River)

New Post - Cree

Constance Lake - Cree

payne

Quebec

Flying Post Ojibwa

Abitibi - Ojibwa - Cree

Missanabie - Cree

Matachewan - Ojibwa - Cree

Argonaut - Algonkin

Chapleau - Ojibwa - Cree   Mattagami - Ojibwa

Temiskaming - Algonkin

- Ojibwa

Brunswick House - Ojibwa - Cree
(Mountbatten)

Rapide Sept Algonkin

Long Point - Algonkin

Timagami (Bear Island)
Ojibwa - Cree

Hunters Point - Algonkin

ana - Ojibwa

Wahnapitae - Ojibwa

Kipawa - Algonkin

s Bay - Ojibwa

Garden River - Ojibwa   White Fish Lake-
                           Ojibwa   Nipissing
Thessalon-   Spanish River-   (Ojibwa)
Ojibwa   Ojibwa
         Serpent River-
         Ojibwa   Morrisons Island
Mississauga   White Fish River-   Point Grondin-   - Algonkin
(Blind River)   Ojibwa   Ojibwa
                                Dokis - Ojibwa
         Sheguian Dah
urn Island   French River - Ojibwa
- Ojibwa   Manitoulin Island- Henvey Inlet - Ojibwa
         Sheshegwaning- West   Ojibwa   Magnetawan - Ojibwa
         Ojibwa   Bay   Golden Lake "Algonkin"
                    Sucker Ottawa (Wikwemikong) Naiscoutaing   (Ojibwa Speakers)   •Ottawa
                    Creek South Bay-   Shawanaga - Ojibwa
                           Ojibwa
                                   Parry Island - Ojibwa
         Cape Croker - Ojibwa   Moose Deer Point Ojibwa
                    Georgian Bay   Gibson - Iroquois
                           Christian Island   Rama - Ojibwa
                           (Beausoleil) Ojibwa
         Lake Huron   Curve Lake (Mud Lake)
                                                - Ojibwa
                    Saugeen - Ojibwa   Hiawatha or
                                       Rice Lake   Bay Of Quinte Mohawk:
                    Georgina Island   Iroquois
                    - Ojibwa   Alderville
                            (Ainwick - Sugar Island)
                    Scugog   - Ojibwa
                    - Ojibwa
                                   Lake Ontario

Toronto•

Kettle & Stony Point -
Ojibwa   Six Nations - Iroquois
                       Delaware
         New Credit - Ojibwa

Sarnia Ojibwa   Oneida - Iroquois
Walpole   Chippewa - Caradoc - Ojibwa
Ojibwa   Muncey - Delaware
Ojibwa Ottawa Potawatomi
         Moravian - Delaware   *Lake Erie*

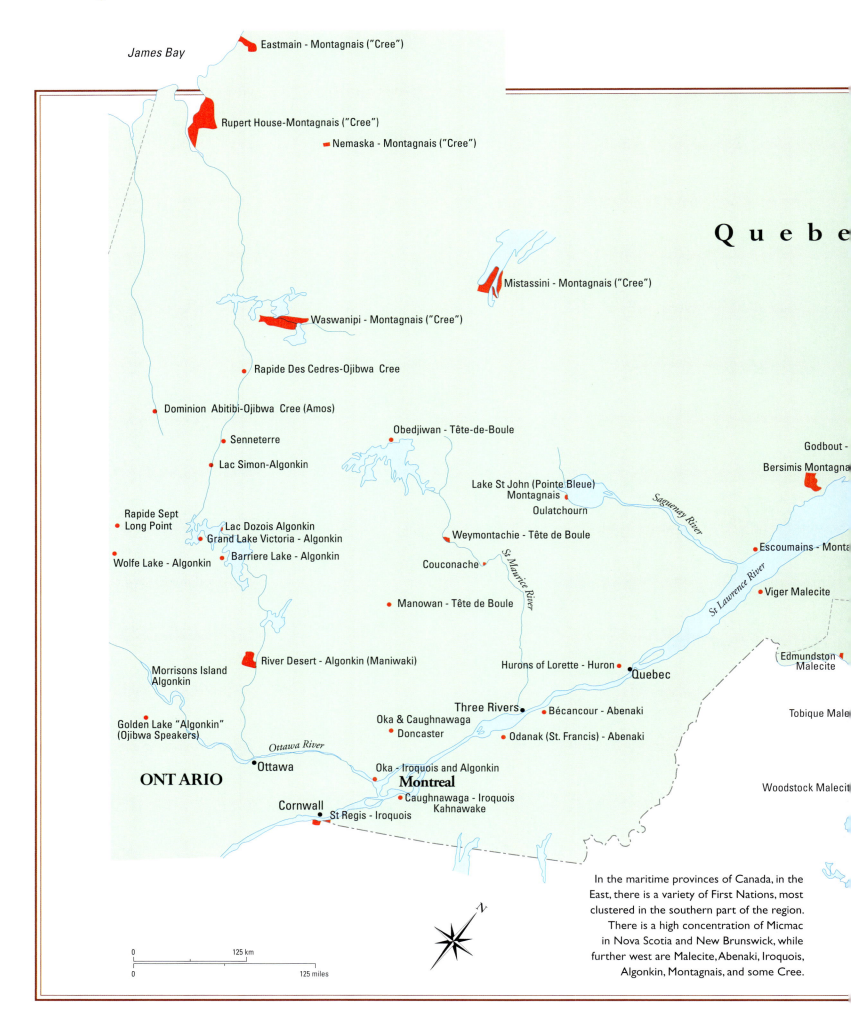

James Bay

Eastmain - Montagnais ("Cree")

Rupert House-Montagnais ("Cree")

Nemaska - Montagnais ("Cree")

Q u e b e

Mistassini - Montagnais ("Cree")

Waswanipi - Montagnais ("Cree")

Rapide Des Cedres-Ojibwa Cree

Dominion Abitibi-Ojibwa Cree (Amos)

Obedjiwan - Tête-de-Boule

Senneterre

Godbout -

Lac Simon-Algonkin

Bersimis Montagna

Lake St John (Pointe Bleue)
Montagnais

Saguenay River

Oulatchourn

Rapide Sept
Long Point

Lac Dozois Algonkin

Grand Lake Victoria - Algonkin

Weymontachie - Tête de Boule

Escoumains - Monta

Barriere Lake - Algonkin

Couconache

Wolfe Lake - Algonkin

St Lawrence River

St Maurice River

Viger Malecite

Manowan - Tête de Boule

River Desert - Algonkin (Maniwaki)

Edmundston
Malecite

Morrisons Island
Algonkin

Hurons of Lorette - Huron

Quebec

Golden Lake "Algonkin"
(Ojibwa Speakers)

Three Rivers

Bécancour - Abenaki

Tobique Male

Ottawa River

Oka & Caughnawaga

Doncaster

Odanak (St. Francis) - Abenaki

Ottawa

Oka - Iroquois and Algonkin

Woodstock Malecit

ONTARIO

Montreal

Caughnawaga - Iroquois
Kahnawake

Cornwall

St Regis - Iroquois

In the maritime provinces of Canada, in the
East, there is a variety of First Nations, most
clustered in the southern part of the region.
There is a high concentration of Micmac
in Nova Scotia and New Brunswick, while
further west are Malecite, Abenaki, Iroquois,
Algonkin, Montagnais, and some Cree.

N

| 0 | 125 km |
| 0 | 125 miles |

St Augustin Montagnais

Sept - Îles Montagnais

Mingan Montagnais

Natashquan Montagnais

Romaine Montagnais

Anticost Island

Gulf of St Lawrence

Newfoundland

Gaspe Micmac

Perce Micmac

gouche
cmac

Maria Micmac

ver Micmac

Miscou Micmac

Conne River Micmac

Bathurst
and
bineau Micmac

Pokemouche Micmac

Tabusintac Micmac

Eel Ground
Micmac

Burnt Church Micmac

d Bank
icmac

Newcastle Micmac

Prince Edward Island

Indian Island Micmac
Big Cove Micmac

Lennox Island
Micmac

Buctouche Micmac

Abegweit or
Scotchfort Micmac
Morell Micmac

*Cape Breton
Island*

Wagmatcook or
Middle River
Micmac

w Brunswick

ary's Malecite

Ft Folly Micmac

Rocky Point
Micmac

Sydney Micmac
(Membertou)

omocto
alecite

Eskasoni Micmac

Whycocomagh
Micmac

Malagawatch

Franklin Manor
Micmac

Pictou
Landing Micmac
(Band)

Fishers Grant
Merigomish Harbour

Chapel Island Micmac

Amalecite

t

Truro Micmac or
Millbrooko

Antigonish

Afton
Pomuet
Micmac
(Band)

Cambridge Horton

Annapolis Valley Micmac

Shubenacadie Micmac

St Croix Micmac

Beaver Lake Micmac

New Ross

Grand Lake Micmac

Bear River Micmac

Shubenacadie Band

va Scotia

Gold River

Halifax

Wildcat Micmac

Acadia
Band

Ponhook Micmac

armouth

**Indian Groups of the
Maritime Provinces of
Canada, 20th Century**

Reserve

Boarding Schools

DURING THE LATE NINETEENTH CENTURY, THE UNITED STATES GOVERNMENT ADOPTED AN EDUCATION POLICY DESIGNED TO ASSIMILATE NATIVE AMERICANS BY "KILLING THE INDIAN AND SAVING THE MAN."

The techniques used by Major Richard H. Pratt in reeducating seventy-two male prisoners of war, mostly Cheyenne, at Fort Marion, St. Augustine, Florida, were applied to an Indian boarding school he founded in 1879, at an abandoned military post in Carlisle, Pennsylvania. There, he enroled 169 students recruited from the High Plains Sioux. Pratt's educational philosophy was laid down in his book, *Battlefield and Classroom: Four Decades with the American Indian, 1864–1904*. Twenty-five such schools followed, handling 20,000 Indian male and female children from dozens of tribes. In its final year, 1917, Carlisle had students from fifty-eight tribes.

The U.S. government thought that Indian children could be saved and become a ready source of labor, a vital commodity for the spreading industrial society. Little or no understanding of indigenous educational methods was sought by white people. Among Native Americans, play, experience, and the example of elders comprised the normal teaching environment. However, the boarding schools cut off Indians' hair, gave them white people's clothes and names, and ordered the daily routine via the bell. Only English could be spoken. Strict discipline, military drill, poor-quality staff, violence, and verbal abuse were common. The culture shock sometimes broke minds, leading to alcoholism or suicide. Humiliation and degradation killed self-respect, dignity, and the human spirit.

The notion of removing Indian children from tribal contamination is ironic, considering the diseases encountered at school. Tuberculosis, measles, and influenza killed many, and trachoma spread rapidly in the early twentieth century. Some schools maintained their own cemeteries. Overwork, malnutrition, cruel punishments, poor training, and insufficient clothing permeated these Dickensian institutions. Sometimes, when sickness broke out, pupils were sent home, where they infected their brothers and sisters.

However, the portrayal of all boarding schools as inhuman hellholes would be incorrect. Some students overcame all difficulties, flourishing in an environment that they were determined to face bravely and use to the best effect. Children from different nations forged bonds in adversity, despite the variety of languages, cultures, and geographical origins. Later, some married. Cross-cultural exchanges facilitated the growth of a united Native American consciousness, and the realization that new methods were required to keep their sovereignty when confronting American domination and cultural imperialism.

One student, Luther Standing Bear (c. 1868–1939), a Brulé Sioux, returned to his reservation, where he assisted at the government school. He held a number of jobs, wrote essays and articles, and contributed four significant books with the aid of a niece. His novels were not just autobiographical, but also a method of confronting the prejudicial stereotype of the Indian as being a savage who needed to be assimilated into white society. His books are far more important than his roles in films, for example, *The Santa Fé Trail* (1930). He advocated Indian rights and urged America to see the Native American world as a human world.

Another success story is that of Wa Tha Huch, Bright Path, otherwise known as Jim Thorpe (1887–1953). Of mixed ancestry (Sauk and Fox, Potawatomi, Kickapoo, Menominee, Irish, and French), Thorpe always considered himself an Indian at Carlisle. He was a brilliant football player, and he won two gold medals for the decathlon and pentathlon at the 1912 Olympic Games in Sweden. In 1913, he signed a contract to play as a professional for the New York Giants baseball team, later moving to the Boston Braves. He also played professional football in Ohio. For fifteen years, he played baseball in the spring and football in fall.

Some Native Americans rejected the enforced education. Sometimes the Hopi hid their children from government agents, soldiers, and missionaries. In 1895, Chief Lomahongewa and eighteen Hopi men chose imprisonment at Alcatraz rather than give up their children.

A variety of problems were generated by the schools. Phoenix Indian School (built 1892) failed to develop industrial skills among its students. Instead, the school channeled its charges into menial, unskilled jobs on local farms; the school authorities often forced local Indian children to attend the school to ensure a pool of cheap labor. Changes did not occur until 1935. Buffalo Woman, a Hidatsa woman, maintained that, within the tribe, girls were carefully monitored by their mothers and did not become pregnant before marriage. When the reservation schools began, so did unmarried pregnancies.

Generally speaking, Native Americans feared that their children would acquire new values of materialism and lose their culture. Moreover, parents missed their children. Interestingly, the boarding schools contributed to the creation of Pan-Indianism, a number of boarding-school graduates becoming militants in the 1960s.

A group of Native American children at a government boarding school. The aim of such schools was to "kill the Indian and save the man". Often, that meant preparing the children to be a source of cheap labor for menial work.

THE SOCIETY OF AMERICAN INDIANS

FORMED BY A GROUP OF INDIAN ACADEMICS IN 1911, THE SOCIETY OF AMERICAN INDIANS HAD THE AIM OF EDUCATING THE PUBLIC ABOUT THE ACHIEVEMENTS OF NATIVE AMERICANS.

Charles A. Eastman was active in matters dealing with Indian rights. In 1903, President Theodore Roosevelt assigned Eastman the responsibility for revising the allotment method of dividing tribal lands. This was to become an internal problem for The Society of American Indians.

The Society of American Indians came into being after much discussion among a group of Indian academics. Led by Fayette Avery McKenzie, an Ohio State University sociologist, these notable Native Americans included Carlos Montezuma (Yavapai), Charles A. Eastman (Santee), Sherman Coolidge (Arapaho), Charles E. Daganett (Peoria), Minnine Kellogg (Oneida), Arthur Parker (Seneca), and Gertrude Simmons Bonnin (Yankton). These people organized the first national Indian conference in the fall of 1911.

Some members of the society believed that strengthening tribal values was vital, but most of them favored complete assimilation. Historian Arthur Parker urged Native Americans *"to strike out into duties of modern life and find every right that has escaped them before."*

The society allowed individual, not tribal, membership, and offered associate membership to non-tribal people. By 1913, enrolments had reached 619, with some 400 associates. Many tribes were represented, the majority of members emanating from the Plains and the Great Lakes-New York region. This fact is probably explained by the society holding its conferences in the Midwest. Western support developed over the next few years. The society was committed to the notion of collective tribal action and became a vehicle for the demand of U.S.

citizenship for Native Americans.

Those who held office in the society were generally assimilationists. Many had been educated at the Carlisle Indian Industrial School, designed to wean its students from Indian culture. Especially significant were the high-powered Native American women, who had strong personal agendas and radical approaches. Bonnin (Zitkala Sa) edited the society's *American Indian* magazine, and fought against peyote and for citizenship. She also criticized white civilization and wanted reservations with self-sustaining communities; she broke with the society in 1912. Kellogg was strongly opposed to the Bureau of Indian Affairs' economic and educational policies, unlike her colleagues. Other important women were Emma D. Johnson Goulette, Marie L.B. Baldwin, and Rose B. LaFlesche.

The task of the society was to educate the public about the achievements and hopes of Native Americans, and its publications were sent to universities and libraries throughout the United States. The national conferences commissioned reports, but the numbers attending gradually declined, from around 200 to a handful in the 1920s. One of the major problems faced by the society was the difference of opinion held by members with such strong personalities, notably over U.S. intervention in World War I. In this respect, divisions between traditionalists, progressives, and the undecided were made manifest.

The society was pulled in various directions, but it had strong relations with the Bureau of Indian Affairs, which resulted in criticism that it was the BIA's stalking horse. Many BIA Indian employees were members. Into these divisions were thrown American objectives in World War I, as proclaimed by President Woodrow Wilson. One of these was "the self-determination of subject peoples." Many Indians hoped that this principle would lead to a relaxation of BIA policies, but opinions differed on how to approach the war. Some Native Americans volunteered for combat, considering that this action would progress assimilation and win U.S. citizenship. Other Indians claimed that the lack of citizenship negated wartime obligations, and they resisted the war, either actively or passively. Arthur Parker and Carlos Montezuma exemplified these respective reactions. Parker tried to ensure draft registration of New York Indians, while Montezuma attempted to persuade tribal leaders to ignore the draft.

The citizenship question became crucial, and the society promoted a campaign for universal Native American citizenship, which finally was granted by the 1924 Indian Citizenship Act. When this was passed by Congress, it was hailed as a victory by all of the society's factions, but the organization virtually collapsed after achieving its goal. However, the society provided valuable experience for the Indian urban middle class, which supplied members to succeeding pan-Indian organizations. Other inter-tribal groups were formed, such as the All Pueblo Council (1922), which successfully opposed the Bursum Bill giving rights to squatters on the Rio Grande. The Grand Council Fire of Native Americans was founded in 1923, the Indian Association of America in 1932, and the Indian Confederation of America in 1933. This tradition of activism eventually resulted in the National Congress of American Indians (1944) and the later, more youthful, Red Power Movement.

Gertrude Simmons Bonnin was the editor of the society's *American Indian* magazine. She helped organize the first national Indian conference in the fall of 1911.

TRIBAL ENTERPRISES

WHILE AGRICULTURE HAS BEEN THE TRADITIONAL ACTIVITY
OF NATIVE AMERICANS, MANY TRIBES HAVE TURNED TO MORE
RELIABLE AND LUCRATIVE MEANS OF BOOSTING INCOME.

Despite many tribes owning gaming halls, today most remain in a cycle of poverty. Indeed, many nations are paying off debts incurred in establishing casinos. Thus, many tribes and bands have attempted economic diversification. Agriculture has been a mainstay of Indian life, but finances are required for irrigation, and capital investment and farm incomes have dropped. Moreover, there is not enough tribally owned land for a thriving, independent, agricultural economy. Therefore, such tribes as the Northern Cheyenne lease out land for grazing and farming.

Major economic resources are minerals and oil under tribal lands, but much oil was stolen during early exploitation, as the 1981 Linowes Commission discovered. Coal mining has damaged tribal lands and water resources; the Northern Cheyenne have refused access to their estimated 23 billion tons of coal, in case their culture and values are destroyed. Some tribes established the Council of Energy Resource Tribes (CERT) to gain real control over their resources, managing them in the face of capitalist greed. The Jicarilla Apache, and the Fort Peck Assiniboine and Sioux tribes have drilled independently and successfully for oil. Meanwhile, the Navajo have a joint arrangement with private industry to operate a Dineh powerplant.

The Apache have been particularly successful in their economic ventures. The Naishan and Chiricahua depend on grazing and agriculture, while other bands run lumber and recreational industries. The Northern Paiute rely on agriculture, and some who inhabit the Warm Springs Reservation, living with Sahaptin and Chinook speakers, used the reservation corporation to establish fishing and plywood industries. The corporation was financed by compensation monies for the flooded Celilo Falls fishery. Now, these confederated tribes own an electricity producing dam, the Kah-Nee-Ta resort complex, and

Opposite: A Navajo woman at work on a loom. The Navajo are renowned for their weaving skills, among several other crafts.

two radio stations. Fishing is important to all tribes around Puget Sound, and Washington State has twenty-eight tribally owned fish hatcheries; the Muckleshoot, with 1,000 enrolled members, own two, at Keta Creek and the White River.

The Colorado River tribes, mainly Mojave, are financed by riverfront property rentals, the recreational Aha Quin Park, and over 90,000 acres (36,000 hectares) farmed for cotton, alfalfa, wheat, lettuce, and melons. Other notable tribal industries are run by the Pima, who have three industrial parks for the production of aluminum, concrete, and telecommunications equipment. They also run the Gila River Arts and Craft Center, commercial recreational facilities, and the Firebird International Raceway Park dragstrip. In addition, the Pima own a 120-acre (49-hectare) boat racing lake. In Oklahoma, the Miami run a trucking line for transporting their oil and fuel throughout the United States. The Hopi rely on arts and crafts, especially silverwork, textiles, and kachina dolls. They also run gas stations. The Lakota own the Lake Traverse plastic-bag plant, and a factory at Devil's Lake manufactures military camouflage material.

The Inupiat of Alaska still go whaling, but are subject to International Whaling Commission quotas. The communal participation in whaling and its rituals forms the bedrock of Inupiat society and culture, without which the people would lose their character. A spectacular aspect of the development of tribal income are the 7,500 or so Native American ironworkers in Canada and the United States. Among these are Akwesasne Mohawks from the New York State St. Regis Reservation and Caughnawaga Mohawks from the Kahnawake Reservation in Ontario. Working as steel erectors for bridge and skyscraper construction, these "skywalkers" helped build Toronto's CN Tower, the Golden Gate Bridge in San Francisco, and the New York World Trade Center.

Despite some economic improvements, Native Americans remain the poorest ethnic group in the United States, with a high unemployment rate on reservations; the 1990 census showed 30.9 percent as living in poverty, that is individuals earning less than $6,300 annually. Only gaming is likely to improve conditions. For example, Foxwoods, in Connecticut, plans to support 20,000 jobs with an annual payroll of $480 million. Adding indirect employment to the total, Foxwoods will probably underpin $6 billion of jobs in the early twenty-first century.

Legalized gambling on reservations began with a 1976 court case, in which the U.S. Supreme Court ruled that states do not have regulatory jurisdiction over Native American tribes. Other court rulings said that states could not prevent tribes from pursuing gaming activities. In 1988, the Indian Gaming Regulatory Act was passed into law, legalizing gambling for profit by Native American tribes on their self-governing lands. Today, the tribally owned casinos are flourishing.

Native Americans run some 100 high-stake bingo operations and over sixty casinos in more than twenty states. About 180 tribes own bingo halls, and 20–25 tribes run high-stake bingo operations producing from $100,000 to $1 million each month. By 1993, over sixty-three tribes were running high-stake casino establishments. Gaming revenue will probably be used by more tribes as they build new facilities. The highest concentrations of gaming activities are in Arizona, New Mexico, California, Wisconsin, and Minnesota. The first really big operation to open was Foxwoods in Ledyard, owned by the Mashantucket Pequot in southeast Connecticut. They began with high-stakes bingo on the reservation, then opened a casino in 1992. Built with a $55 million loan, the casino repaid the debt within seven months of opening and now produces $3 million daily. Today, the Foxwoods Resort comprises five casinos with over 300,000 square feet (28,000 square meters) for gaming, a 3,000-seat bingo hall, the 1,450-seat Fox Theater, thirty restaurants, and three hotels. The casino pays 20 percent of its slot-machine profits to the state of Connecticut.

The range of tribes involved in gaming is extraordinary: the Apache, Cherokee, Chinook, Coeur d'Alene, Coleville, Kickapoo, Standing Rock Sioux, Cheyenne-Arapaho, Coquille, Pechanga, Oglala Sioux, San Manuel, Seminole, Turtle Mountain Band of Chippewa, and Oneida are all represented. The Apache Gold Casino Resort operates 500-plus slot machines, and offers bingo, keno, and racebook. There is a championship golf course, a hotel, a covered rodeo pavilion, an RV park, restaurants, a convention center, cabaret, gift shops, a convenience store, and a BMX track. In contrast, facilities are more limited at the Oglala owned Prairie Wind Casino on the Pine Ridge Reservation in South Dakota. The casino operates a variety of slot machines, while table games include three-card poker and blackjack.

The development of gaming has generated much needed revenue to provide loans for other tribal businesses, to fund tribal land purchases, to give full medical and dental coverage to tribal members, and to finance scholarships and education. The Cabazon Band of Mission Indians in California uses gaming revenue to develop employment opportunities, as well as for welfare, housing, and educational purposes. In addition, the band has built a biomass-fueled electricity generating plant and a 950-unit housing development. Furthermore, reservation gaming boosts economic development by providing jobs for non-Indians and helps boost tourism.

The downside of gambling is that occasionally it provokes conflict within tribes, between modernizers and traditionalists.

A sign in front of the Apache Gold Casino and Resort, located in San Carlos, Arizona. The Casino is owned and run by the local Apache tribe, and includes gaming, restaurants, and a hotel.

In 1990, for example, violence broke out in the St. Regis Akwesasne Reservation in upstate New York. The Mohawk Warrior Society saw gaming as a means of increasing economic independence and obtaining sovereignty from white society, while traditionalists and tribal officials opposed it. On the Oneida reservation in New York State, a bingo hall was destroyed in a disagreement between tribal factions. Disputes with state governments have been rife. Some states fear that competition from Indian gaming will have an adverse effect on non-Indian casinos and lead to a decline in state tax revenues. Court cases have ensued, but states argue that the 11th Amendment bars tribes from suing them.

THE INDIAN NEW DEAL

THE 1930S SAW THE IMPLEMENTATION OF THE INDIAN
REORGANIZATION ACT, WHICH SECURED A NUMBER OF RIGHTS
FOR NATIVE AMERICANS. THESE INCLUDED THE RIGHT TO TRIBAL
SELF-GOVERNMENT.

By 1933, during the Great Depression, large areas of Native American tribal lands had become privately owned, as a consequence of the Dawes Act and similar legislation. When President Roosevelt was elected, he was determined to end his country's economic crisis and began introducing legislation to this end. He was unaware of Indian issues, but trusted his Indian Commissioner, John Collier, who served from 1933 to 1945. New Deal laws were passed for the United States and the Indians.

In 1934, Collier put forward the Indian Reorganization Act (IRA), otherwise known as the Wheeler-Howard Act, which sought to reverse the Dawes Act. The bill was too radical for Congress, but certain elements of it were enacted. First, tribal governments could be created, but with limited powers, and tribes could accept or reject the IRA by a referendum. The land provisions of the Dawes Act were abolished, but the Indians of Oklahoma were outside the provisions of the new Act. An unfortunate feature was that Alaskan Indians could not have access to credit loan funds. Financial appropriations were considerably increased for Native American education, as were loans to tribal corporations for economic development, although these monies were intended to help assimilate Indians into white society, rather than stimulate and preserve Indian society. Thus, overall, the IRA was a compromise between encouraging Indian independence and assimilation.

The next stage in the IRA's life was for each reservation to accept or reject it. The plebiscite resulted in 174 Native American bands or tribes (some 129,750 people) accepting, while seventy-eight tribes (approximately 86,365 people) rejected its application to their reservations. Important tribes like the Crow, Navajo, Assiniboine, Fort Peck Lakota, Klamath, Crow Creek Lakota, and the Wyoming Arapaho voted against the IRA. The unfortunate outcome of this decision was that they now had no right to adopt a tribal constitution under an IRA protectorate, nor did they qualify for land-purchase and economic-development loans. One estimate suggests that ultimately only one third of those eligible for IRA benefits actually qualified for them.

Collier persevered in his attempts to spread the benefits of the IRA. In 1936, he managed to get passed the Alaska Reorganization Act and the Oklahoma Indian Welfare Act, which ensured that the most important IRA provisions were extended to Indians of those regions.

Another success was the 1935 Indian Arts and Crafts Act, which promoted artists and craftsmen to such an extent that two major exhibitions were held, one at the 1939 World's Fair in San Francisco, the other at the Museum of Modern Art in New York in 1941. Two key figures involved in the Indian Arts and Crafts Board, established under the Act, were Rene d'Harnoncourt, chairman until 1961, and the Cherokee Lloyd Kiva New, who became chairman in 1972. Both were prominent in promoting Indian controlled cultural institutions.

Also established was the Indian Civilian Conservation Corps (CCC), which has helped preserve forested regions and worked to upgrade ranges in the northern Plains, the Great Basin, and the Southwest.

Two groups of Native Americans were vociferous in their antagonism toward the IRA. One, the Five Civilized Tribes of Oklahoma, tended to favor integration into white society. The other group was the Navajo, who were forced to cull their sheep under a conservation program aimed at protecting ranges and pastures. Those Navajos with small flocks were wiped out economically, while all were forced to witness rotting sheep carcases because no programs existed to sell the meat. On the other hand, the Mescalero Apache established a business committee that canceled grazing leases so that they could run their own cattle on the reservation; the Mescaleros' yearly income grew from $18,000 to $101,000 in three depression years. In 1963, the business committee borrowed finance from New Mexico banks to buy the Sierra Blanca ski resort. They also built a fish hatchery, a resort hotel, golf courses, and an industrial park. The Jicarilla Apache benefited from oil company exploration fees, while the tribal council published newspapers and ran an alcoholism program.

When John Collier proposed the Indian Reorganization Act in 1934, many Indians, like this Chippewa in Wisconsin, were struggling to survive through farming. Although agriculture is still a mainstay of Indian life, the Act made it possible for the tribes to exploit many resources previously denied them.

Native Americans in World War II

Large numbers of Native Americans served in the U.S. military during World War II, making a great, and at times unique, contribution to the country's war effort.

Native Americans saw action in all branches of the U.S. armed forces during World War II, but those who served in the Marines, some of them Navajo code talkers, have received the most publicity. However, the 45th (Thunderbird) Infantry Division had the highest proportion of Indian soldiers of any division. It was involved in amphibious landings on Sicily, at Salerno and Anzio, and in southern France. Indians also served with distinction in the 4th and 88th Divisions, the 19th and 180th Infantry Regiments, the 147th Field Artillery, and various Oklahoma National Guard units.

Several traditions imbued Native Americans as warriors. Mental and spiritual strength, the ability to ignore thirst, and enthusiasm for battle have made Indians formidable fighters throughout history. Warriors also attained status within their families and communities. Moreover, military service provides education and decent pay, and can satisfy the spirit of adventure. Reputedly, Indians excelled at bayonet fighting, marksmanship, and scouting. Indeed, one Lakota soldier, Kenneth Scisson, a member of an American commando unit, killed ten Germans on one patrol.

The scale of Native American enlistment during World War II was greater as a percentage of their total number than any other ethnic group. Of 350,000 Native Americans, 44,000 saw military service. The Pueblos provided 213 men, 10 percent of their 2,205 population; nearly all able-bodied Ojibwa at the Grand Portage Reservation enlisted, while the Navajo contributed 3,600 men. One quarter of the New Mexico Mescalero Apache enlisted, rather than wait for their draft cards. Several hundred Indian women also served as WACs, WAVEs, and Army Medical Corps nurses. Native Americans in the Army often hit the headlines, but three times as many served in the Navy, and one, Oklahoma Cherokee

Joseph (Jocko) Clark, an Annapolis graduate, made the rank of admiral. The Air Corps generally took Indians from the more assimilated tribes in Oklahoma, Texas, and Wisconsin. In addition, over 40,000 Indian men and women left their lands to take up war related work.

An all-Navajo Marine Corps signal unit encoded messages in their own language, evolving translations of military and naval terms. Orders could be transmitted over the radio by voice, and the Japanese never cracked the code. For example, the code for "Saipan" was "dibeh (sheep) wo-la-chee (ant) tkin (ice) bi-so-dih (pig) wo-la-chee (ant) nesh-chee (nut)." Code talkers chose alternative

A group of Comanche code talkers of the 4th Signal Company, U.S. Army during World War II. Indians from many tribes made this special contribution to the war effort, helping to ensure secure communications.

Navajo words for the most common used letters in English—E, T, A, O, I, and N. Thus, the letter "A" could be represented by be-la-sana (apple). Military terms included "dive-bomber" (gini, chicken hawk), "submarine" (besh-lo, iron fish), "cruiser" (lo-tso-yazzie, small whale), and "brigadier general" (so-a-la-ih, one star).

By the end of the war, over 400 Navajos had become code talkers. They were used first in 1942 on Guadalcanal, but were especially effective on Iwo Jima. There, six Navajo radio nets sent and received over 800 messages during the first forty-eight hours of the assault. When the Marines raised the Stars and Stripes on Mount Suribachi, the Navajo relayed the message, "Suribachi" (sheep, uncle, ram, ice, bear, ant, cat, horse, itch). The next day, the small American flag was replaced by a large one for the benefit of photographer Joe Rosenthal, whose image became an icon of the war. Among the five men shown raising the flag was Ira Hayes, a Pima, born on the Gila Reservation in Arizona.

The Navajo Code was kept secret until the 1969 reunion of the 4th Marine Division Association in Chicago. The code talkers are now honored by a sculpture in Phoenix Plaza, Phoenix, Arizona.

Combat honors can be a measure of extraordinary bravery in the face of the enemy, especially the award of the Medal of Honor. One Indian recipient of this award was First Lieutenant Jack Montgomery, a Cherokee, who was with the Thunderbirds near Padiglione, Italy. Alone, he attacked three enemy positions that had pinned down his platoon. He mopped up the enemy and took prisoners. Another Medal of Honor winner was Van Barfoot, a Choctaw and second lieutenant in the Thunderbirds, who was at Anzio during the breakout to Rome. On May 23, 1944, he wiped out two machine-gun nests and captured seventeen German soldiers. Later that day, he repelled a German tank assault, destroyed a German artillery piece, and carried two wounded commanders to safety.

THE NATIVE AMERICAN CHURCH

"THE WHITE MAN GOES INTO HIS CHURCH AND TALKS ABOUT JESUS. THE INDIAN GOES INTO HIS TEPEE AND TALKS WITH JESUS."

QUANAH PARKER, COMANCHE CHIEF,

FOUNDER OF THE NATIVE AMERICAN CHURCH.

Since the European colonization of North America, Native Americans have produced many prophets, and religious prophecy has been associated with resistance to white imperialism. Pontiac, Tecumseh, and Black Hawk worked with Delaware, Shawnee, and Winnebago prophets respectively. Other religious leaders have sought to ease the Indian transition from the traditional way of life to the new, white world. Handsome Lake's 1799 Longhouse religion and the Wanapam Dreamer faith of Smoholla paved the way for Wovoka's Ghost Dance religion. Then, a Comanche chief, Quanah Parker, and a Caddo-Delaware, John Wilson (Nishkuntu), established a liturgy and a peyote sacrament, blending Christianity and Native American ancient religious traditions in the Native American Church.

Peyote is a form of small cactus that grows in northern Mexico and the Rio Grande Valley. The rounded, spineless body of the plant can be cut off and dried to form a peyote button. Chewing the button can induce vomiting, followed by a feeling of euphoria. Mexican tribes and nomadic Apaches used peyote for sacred and recreational purposes. Apache and Comanche raiders carried it northward onto the Great Plains, but peyote was also spread by the Caddo, Karankawa, and Tonkawa tribes of southern Texas and New Mexico, From 1875, the peyote ceremonies began taking place in Oklahoma, where the ritual was first described by anthropologist James Mooney in 1890, after witnessing its use by Oklahoma Kiowa. The failure of the Ghost Dance movement and the confinement of reservation life helped spread the ritual to the Kiowa-Apache, Wichita, Delaware, Southern Cheyenne, Southern

Arapaho, Osage, Quapaw, Seneca, Ponca, Kaw, Oto, Pawnee, Sauk and Fox, Iowa, Kickapoo, and Shawnee in Oklahoma. Peyote use then reached the Winnebago, Omaha, Prairie Potawatomi, Menominee, Ojibwa, Lakota, Northern Cheyenne, Crow, Northern Arapaho, Shoshone, and Ute.

The ceremony that uses this non-addictive hallucinogenic includes singing, the playing of drums and rattles, praying, and chewing the buttons. After midnight, there is a ritual of taking water and food, such as parched corn, sweetened meat, and fruit. Most Native American churches use either the Quanah Parker tradition, the Half Moon Way, or the Nishkuntu, the Cross Fire Way. Church ministers who officiate at prayer meetings are known as road men, and they are aided by fire men, drummers. Services accompany weddings, funerals, Thanksgiving, and curing and healing ceremonies.

Opposition to the Native American Church came from Christian missionaries, federal Indian agents, and the Oklahoma Territorial Legislature, which adopted a law banning peyote, although it was repealed in 1908. Native Americans responded by incorporating the Church in Oklahoma in 1918, its charter being amended in 1944, 1950, and 1955. The amendments reflected the expansion of the Church from Oklahoma to the Midwest, Great Plains, Southwest, and Canada. Furthermore, the Texas Department of Public Safety allows peyote to be gathered for Church purposes. Texas is the only state where. the cactus grows. It is also recognized that members of the Native American Church are forbidden alcohol; thus, peyotism helps prevent alcoholism.

In 1962, three Navajos were arrested in California for distributing peyote and were convicted. In 1964, however, the California Supreme Court stated that prohibiting the use of peyote was an infringement of religious freedom under the Constitution's First Amendment. To protect the Indian religion, the 1978 Native American Religious Freedom Act stated that Native Americans should enjoy the exercise of religious freedom, but sometimes this conflicted with state laws. In 1994, Congress amended the law to state that *"the use, possession, or transportation of peyote, by an Indian who uses peyote in a traditional manner for bone fide ceremonial purposes in conjunction with the practice of a traditional Indian religion is lawful and shall not be prohibited by the United States or any State."*

The various branches of the Church have formed a national council, and owing to the illegal harvesting of peyote, this is attempting to legalize its importation from Mexico and its cultivation. Estimates of Church membership suggest that 200,000 observe Chief Peyote sharing the place of honor on the altar with the Bible.

Quanah Parker, a chief of the Comanche, was instrumental in founding the Native American Church, a blend of Christianity and Native American religious traditions.

The Fate of the Inuit

With their way of life and environment under attack, the Inuit peoples of the far north have had to band together to make their voices heard.

On April 18, 2002, four Canadian soldiers were killed in Afghanistan by "friendly" fire. To commemorate these men, and those injured by the incident, Canadian soldiers built an *inuksuk* (a stone marker). The *inuksuk* is traditionally used by Inuit hunters to help them find their way. The national Inuit organization in Canada, the Inuit Tapiriit Kanatami, stated that, when considering a new logo, it looked at many designs, including the maple leaf, but that the *inuksuk* had become a national soldiers' symbol. The organization's president, Jose Kusugak, said, "I think we're on the same wavelength." Were Inuit-white relations always so cooperative in the twentieth century?

Traditionally, Eskimos (Inuit, Inupiat, and Yup'ik) pursued a program of annual subsistence activities, generally fixed to animals' seasonal migrations. Their customs have been assailed by state educational policies, however, the Christian mission schools and boarding high schools having taught Inuits alien concepts, such as individuality, which opposes their essential cooperative community spirit. Other aspects of the white world that have damaged the Arctic peoples' way of life include gold mining, alcoholism, the International Whaling Commission, and the dumping of 15,000 pounds (7,000 kilograms) of radioactive material from Nevada. Ecological issues affecting the Inuit include mercury pollution on the Labrador and Québec coasts, and at Giaque Lake. Arsenic leaching has been discovered at Yellowknife, while caribou migration has been disrupted by the Dempster Lateral Pipeline. Further ecological damage has been caused by the Alaska Highway Pipeline. In addition, Alaska faces many problems caused by the oil industry.

In partial retaliation, the eight Alaskan Inuit whaling communities formed the Alaskan Eskimo Whaling Commission in an attempt to obtain an increase in their harvest quota from the International

Whaling Commission, with considerable success. Similar associations deal with the hunting of the walrus, sea otter, porcupine, and caribou. The Inuit have also developed cooperative agreements across state and national borders to monitor pollutants, and to manage and protect shared animal populations, such as water fowl, the polar bear, and walrus. Pressure-group activity, such as the Arctic Slope Native Association and the Northwest Alaska Native Association (formed in 1963 by Willie Hensley, later a senator), pushed for the Alaska Native Claims Settlement Act (ANCSA) of 1971. Indians, Aleuts, and Inuit received title to 40 million acres (16 million hectares) of land, a billion dollars in compensation, and mineral rights plus eventual shareholdings in mineral companies. The legislators assumed that the Native Americans were in a period of transition from subsistence to a modern lifestyle, however, and removed all hunting and fishing rights outside protected lands around villages. Thus, attacks on traditions still occur. Ironically, the Iglulik Inuit prefer all-terrain vehicles to dog sleds for traveling and hunting.

In 1977, the Inuit Circumpolar Conference (ICC) was established by Eben Hopson because he had been unsuccessful in convincing U.S. policy makers of the need to involve the Inuit in decisions affecting them. The ICC's first meeting took place in June of that year, bringing together, for the first time, Inuit from Alaska, Canada, and Greenland. In 1989, the Russian Inuit sent a delegation, and they became full members in 1992.

The ICC's aims are to strengthen Inuit regional unity, protect their culture and environment, and be an active partner in decision making in respect of the circumpolar region. In 1983, the ICC achieved non-governmental organization status with a formal voice at the United Nations. It works with the UN Working Group on Indigenous Peoples, and thereby helps monitor the status and conditions of similar peoples throughout the world. The ICC made an important contribution to the 1989 revision of the International Labor Organization Indigenous and Tribal Peoples' Convention. The institution has helped develop an Inuit Regional Conservation Strategy; shares in the Arctic Monitoring and Assessment Program initiated by the Finnish government in 1989; promotes and spreads the traditional knowledge of Inuit peoples, such as soapstone carving and beliefs in the spirituality of the natural world; and protects traditional economies based on whaling, seal hunting, fishing, and similar activities.

An Inuit hunting caribou. The traditional Eskimo lifestyle relied heavily on the annual migration pattern of such creatures, but increasingly this is being disrupted by industrial processes.

Urbanization of Native Americans

DURING THE TWENTIETH CENTURY, THERE WAS A STEADY MIGRATION OF INDIANS FROM RESERVATIONS TO THE TOWNS AND CITIES, WHERE THERE WERE GREATER EMPLOYMENT OPPORTUNITIES.

Large numbers of Native Americans have inhabited urban areas for thousands of years. At the time of European contact, Tenochtitlan may have contained between 150,000 and 300,000 people. In North America, Cahokia housed up to 40,000, while other Indian cities, such as Moundville in Alabama and Pueblo Bonita, New Mexico, also had significant populations. Later, Indians began living in East Coast colonial cities, Californian towns, and urban centers in east Oklahoma Indian Territory, Arizona, and New Mexico. Since World War II, the urbanization of Native Americans has accelerated, kickstarted by influxes during the two world wars as Indians aided the war effort. This exposed them to urban American culture, industrial society, and leisure opportunities; reservation life was starkly different.

World War II generated the GI Bill, which provided Native American servicemen with the opportunity of obtaining a college education. University and community college graduates, together with boarding-school survivors, sought urban employment, as did many involved in government relocation programs. The better educated formed the nucleus of an emergent Native American middle class, many becoming educators. Typically, this class lives in mainly white neighborhoods. Various studies show the economic upside and downside of relocation; many Indians move from reservation to urban environment, and back again. This two-way movement is often prompted by the desire for better health care through the Indian Health Service on reservations, urban medicine providing nothing specific for Native Americans.

Another class of Indian is that of skilled laborers and artisans, who populate the outskirts of cities, many residing in small urban centers. Today, major Native American populations can be found in New York City, Oklahoma City, Phoenix, Tulsa, Los Angeles, Minneapolis-St. Paul, Anchorage, and Albuquerque.

Urbanized Native Americans are thought to experience white acculturation and loss of tribal lifeways. A key factor lies in inter-marriage. A majority of the over 50 percent of Indians residing in towns and cities have inter-married. Therefore, certification is often required as proof of Indianness. Also, the new Native Americans who changed self-definition in Census 2000 are more likely to be inter-married.

Another issue is that Indians living in an urban environment are less likely to use their native language, since English dominates in the assimilation process. Nevertheless, social scientists have observed how Native Americans can alter their urban environment to engender opportunities for cultural expression. Arizona State University's Professor Donald Fixico (of Sauk and Fox, Shawnee, Creek, and Seminole blood) argues that most Native Americans keep a link with their reservation origins and maintain their cultures in urban environments. In many major cities there are Indian centers that provide help with employment, job counseling, drug rehabilitation, and other personal issues. They also host language classes, dances, powwows, arts and craft shows, and sports, especially basketball. Urban Indian churches replicate reservation missions. Because a city is likely to contain members of many tribes, Indian centers tend to be informal tribal institutions or develop into pan-Indian organizations.

This pan-Indianism creates a supra-tribal identity and ideology, generated by an urbanization outside the social, economic, and political goals of particular tribes. This unifying force has given birth to political activism, represented by such organizations as Women of All Red Nations (WARN), the National Indian Youth Council (NIYC), and the American Indian Movement (AIM). In some cases, one tribal group may be more prevalent than others, owing to its reservations being near the city, such as the Ojibwa in Minneapolis, and the Iroquois nations in Buffalo.

The urbanization process can benefit Native American traditions. For example, Mohawk men can demonstrate qualities of courage by working on the high steel frameworks of modern buildings. Thus,

Native American health workers demonstrate for labor recognition, Oakland, California, 1980.

prestige can be carried home to their families and communities in a modern analogue to tradition. On the downside, urban life has led to the continuation of alcoholism, suicide, and death by homicide. Towns and cities adjacent to reservations have been the scenes of numerous murders and suspicious accidental deaths. Police in Minneapolis, Los Angeles, and Chicago have been accused of excessive abuse of Indians. Moreover, there have been reports of white youths saturating Indians with gasoline prior to torching them. Murder charges have been reduced to manslaughter, virtually sanctioning racist atrocities. As Native Americans uphold their sovereignty and civil rights, with the use of casino wealth, attacks increase, but they never deter Indian resistance.

TRIBALLY CHARTERED SCHOOLS AND COLLEGES

MANY NATIVE AMERICAN TRIBES HAVE ESTABLISHED THEIR OWN SCHOOLS AND COLLEGES, ENSURING THAT THEIR VALUES, TRADITIONS, AND CULTURE ARE NOT LOST IN THE EDUCATION OF THEIR CHILDREN.

Educational opportunities for Native Americans were poor during the 1950s and 1960s. Movements for Native American self-determination argued the need for Indian controlled institutions so that Indian values could imbue all subjects taught. The Navajo created their own school at Rough Rock, Arizona, followed by the Viejas Indian School in California. In Minneapolis, urban Indians founded the Heart of Earth School, while others established the Red School House in St. Paul.

In 1968, the first tribally chartered college was established on the Navajo reservation. This community college opened at Many Farms before moving to Tsaile, Arizona. The main campus offers a broad curriculum, including Native American history, literature, arts, language, and government. The program was designed to facilitate the continuation of schooling at university or the acquisition of vocational skills. In 1971, Congress passed the Navajo Community College Act, which provided funding, and accreditation was received from the North Central Association of Colleges. Subsequently, the college was named Diné College. All students are urged to preserve their tribal culture and language, and to pursue aspects of Navajo studies.

The Navajo owned and operated institution became a beacon for other Native American educational visionaries, and many new community colleges sprang up. These included Nebraska Indian Community College, serving the Omaha and Santee Sioux; Lac Courte Oreilles Ojibwa Community College, Wisconsin; Little Big Horn College for the Crow; Oglala Lakota College, South Dakota; Fort

Belknap College for the Gros Ventre and Assiniboine in Montana; and D-Q University, California. Many others exist. The virtue of tribal colleges lies in providing education in a friendly, culturally supportive, and more financially viable environment compared with off-reservation facilities. Despite variations in size, poverty of accommodation, and funding problems, the colleges constantly increase their enrolments, and growing numbers of Native Americans are attaining bachelor's degrees, master's degrees, and doctorates. As the number of Native American graduates and academics increases, so they will be able to improve the tribal college system.

The colleges help preserve tribal cultures, languages, traditions, and values. Training is offered for tribal needs, and courses can be customized for those students unwilling to leave the reservations. An added benefit is that unemployment rates among tribal college graduates are around a quarter of normal reservation rates. Colleges also sponsor research and development programs for the wider reservation community. For example, Little Hoop Community College, Fort Totten, North Dakota, works closely with a tribal factory producing bullet-resistant materials for the U.S. military. Other colleges support general literacy and health-awareness programs to combat alcoholism and other health risks, such as heart disease and diabetes.

The Navajo Community College Act generates money according to the college's need. Other tribal colleges are funded by the Tribally Controlled Community Colleges Act, however, which allocates monies according to enrolments. Thus, the allocation can fluctuate annually, and funds seldom reach the authorized per capita level, sometimes being less than half the amount specified by the Act. Nevertheless, Native American college students have flourished. Some have become political activists, demanding that mainstream universities transform their Native American studies programs into something other than an orientalist vision of the savage, noble or otherwise.

As an academic discipline, Native American studies encompass such aspects as history, modern literature, oral histories and narratives, community development, government, federal policy, and regional affairs. Language courses have been developed, as have academic journals covering the discipline, while universities publish works by Native Americans. The ranks of Native American academics swell constantly, and they provide valuable role models, teaching self-worth and aiding self-empowerment by demonstrating that the achievements of Native Americans go beyond those of the Navajo code talkers. Native American experts exist in all academic disciplines; also there are poets, sculptors, painters, and people in the professions. Native American creation stories are reaching a wider audience too, sometimes being studied in multicultural curricula in mainstream primary education.

A particularly interesting example of educational excellence has been achieved by the Lumbee of North Carolina, once known as the Croatans. In 1887, the Croatan Normal School was founded as part of the Robson County school system; there was one school for white children, one for African-Americans, and one for Indians. However, Indian schools were community based, and thus enhanced community and tribal identities. Between 1940 and 1953, the school was known as Pembroke State College for Indians, the only U.S. state supported, four-year college for Native Americans. Subsequently, it became Pembroke State University, one of the constituent campuses of the University of North Carolina, and today it is the University of North Carolina at Pembroke.

NATIVE AMERICAN WOMEN

THROUGHOUT HISTORY, WOMEN HAVE PLAYED A MAJOR ROLE IN NATIVE AMERICAN CULTURE AND SOCIETY. SOME HAVE EVEN FOUGHT AS WARRIORS.

Maria Montoya Martinez (1887–1980) was renowned for her pottery, the sales of which generated employment and provided financial support for her village.

Native American women have suffered from being ignored after their first encounters with Europeans. White males carried their prejudicial culture to the Americas, and contemporary reports were paternalistic and male centered. Few Europeans understood the many roles and activities played by women in Indian society. The facts that descent was matrilineal in many communities, such as the Cherokee, and that women, under their clan mother, would select Iroquois chiefs did not receive mention. Normally, male and female roles were complementary, and male and female work was egalitarian. The diplomatic functions instigated by women between Native Americans and whites are either buried deep in history or have been fantasized, such as the Pocahontas story. Creek Mary Musgrove, Mohawk Molly Brant, and Modoc Winema are largely ignored, together with their roles as intermediaries. Similarly, women who adopted the role of warrior are shunted into darkness. Chiricahua Apache women Lozen and Dahtaste fought against U.S. and Mexican troops. Lozen rode with with her brother, Victorio. Unmarried and with no children, she was regarded as a holy woman and treated as such. After the Chiricahua were rounded up and sent to Florida, and then to Alabama, Lozen died of tuberculosis.

Traditionally, Native American women have been primary child carers, passing on cultural knowledge and language. They have been instrumental in preserving tribal traditions and identities. In recent years, educated Native American women have played an important role in maintaining values and easing the path into the white world. Many women have achieved much success in all walks of life. Brenda Schad, born of a Cherokee father and Choctaw mother, became a supermodel and featured in the Wonderbra campaign. She supports the rainforest and helps a Native American Children's fund in Oklahoma. The actress Helen Locklear is a Lumbee Indian, as is the musician Jana of the funk group Pace N'Love.

Native American female artists are grounded in ancient traditions, but just as older generations absorbed ideas from other tribes, so modem artists have been influenced by European and African artistic traditions. Artwork includes basket weaving, carving, painting, textiles, musical instrument making, photography, and older traditions, such as making wampum, porcupine quillwork, and rawhide parfleche containers. Lakota doll artist Rhonda Holy Bear makes not only ordinary dolls, but also "war honor dresses," small replicas of dresses sewn in the 1890s. In those days, Sioux women would cut up tepee linings that had been painted with male battle exploits, making them into dresses to honor their sons and husbands.

Three other exemplary Native American women are Maria Montoya Martinez, Joy Halo, and Suzan Shown Harjo. Martinez was born in 1887 in the Tewa San Ildefonso Pueblo, in New Mexico, and eventually became an important potter, marketing her wares to non-Indians. She became well known for creating old-style, thinly-constructed pots with a dark, shiny, gray surface decorated with fine black lines. She gained a national reputation and passed on her skills to family members. The minor industrial scale of her pottery production led to the employment of many, helping to finance village life. She died in 1980.

Joy Halo, a Muskogee Creek and graduate of the University of New Mexico (1976), is a noted poetess, like Roberta Hill Whiteman, Linda Hogan, and Wendy Rose. This group writes about the conflict of self-identity in contemporary society, striving for a balance between modern life and ancient tribal values. Halo's major works include *She Had Some Horses*, *The Last Song*, and *The Woman Who Fell From the Sky*. Her poetry is important, if only because non-Indian readers become aware and gain an understanding of the power of memory associated with Indian culture.

Suzan Harjo, of Cheyenne and Hodulgee Muskogee Creek blood, is a poetess, writer, lecturer, and curator. She was instrumental in helping Indians recover more than a million acres (400,000 hectares) of land, which included sacred sites. She has cooperated in developing federal law, including the 1978 American Religious Freedom Act, the 1989 Native American Graves Protection and Repatriation Act, and the 1996 Executive Order on Indian Sacred Sites. Suzan presides over The Morning Star Institute, which promotes national Indian rights. This organization fueled the case against Pro-Football, Inc., regarding the name of Washington's professional football team, the Redskins.

Sarah Winnemucca (1841–81), a Paiute, was the first Native American woman to obtain a copyright and publish a book in the English language: *Life Among the Paiutes: Their Wrongs and Claims*. Sarah was employed by the U.S. Army as a translator during the Bannock War and later took to lecturing on the plight of her people.

CHOCTAW JOURNEY

FROM MISSISSIPPI TO CALIFORNIA, OVER THE COURSE OF
FIFTY YEARS, THE JOURNEY OF ONE CHOCTAW WOMAN AND
HER FAMILY IS A TALE FULL OF HARDSHIP, HEARTACHE, AND
INDOMITABLE SPIRIT.

The Treaty of Dancing Rabbit Creek allowed some Choctaw to remain in Mississippi and register for an allotment after the removal of most of the tribe in 1831–32. Few received title to the land, however, and they were reduced to sharecroppers and wage laborers. One descendant of the Mississippi Choctaw was Lesa Phillip, who was born in February 1890, in Cushtusa, Nashoba County. In the early 1890s, the Phillip family moved to a home near the Roman Catholic Holy Rosary Mission at Tucker. Lesa attended school for one year, but returned after her father died. In 1901, Lesa, her mother Lucie, and her sister were enrolled as eligible Mississippi Choctaws. In 1903, the Dawes Commission persuaded the Choctaw to move to Oklahoma; some 300 made the journey, but about 1,000 remained. The Phillip family moved to Meridian, Mississippi. Then, in August 1903, after selling up, they traveled by train to Dallas, Texas. The journey continued to Atoka in Oklahoma, from where the Phillips and other Choctaws were taken to Smallwood's Switch. On September 29, the family moved to Bennington, Bryan County, where Lucie was given a homestead.

The Bennington years were tragic for Lesa, who married four times, her first three husbands dying quickly. At the age of seventeen, in 1907, she married Daniel Williams. He was followed, in 1911, by Charles Billey, and in 1916 by Dawson Billey. Finally, in 1919, she wed Jesse Roberts, who died in 1934. During these years, Lesa gave birth to several children, although some died. Despite their deaths, and that of her mother in 1916, Lesa achieved a stable marriage and life. The Roberts built a house on 40 acres (16 hectares) of land near Chish Oktok, the location of their Presbyterian church, which became a focal point of life, the services being in Choctaw. Between 1919 and 1926, Lesa gave birth to four children: Pearl (1920), William (1922), Juanita (1924), and Gladys (1926).

The Roberts farm produced corn, cotton, oats, sorghum, and peanuts. The Great Depression proved a disaster for the family, however, and the debts began to pile up. Then Jesse died of tuberculosis. Lesa's earlier children, Carl and Nellie, married white people, which caused some consternation. Meanwhile, Lesa found it difficult to hold the farm together. In 1943, Carl migrated to Richmond, California; Nellie and her family followed, but unlike Carl, her husband did not work in the shipyards. He found dairy work at Madera in the San Joaquin Valley.

Lesa missed all the family being together, so decided to join her children in California. Although Carl sent her some money, there was not enough for the whole family to make the trip. So, to increase her income, Lesa moved with her other children to Benham, Texas, to work in the cotton fields. By June 1944, they had made sufficient money for the journey, and the move began. Joining a train at Durant, the family traveled to Kansas City, and then on to Richmond. Because of the war, there was plenty of work in the shipyards, and Pearl became a welder on a segregated night shift staffed entirely by Indians.

A life of hardship and heartache: a Choctaw woman pounds corn using a hollowed tree stump. Taken in Louisiana in 1930, this photograph shows that for most Indians life was a struggle during the first half of the twentieth century.

Lesa lived with Carl, although his apartment was crowded. She looked after the grandchildren and did the shopping. She always spoke Choctaw, passed on her culture, and became the focal point for handling family problems. The family itself found it difficult to adjust to their new, bustling lifestyle of high wages, movie theaters, and bars. After the war, jobs became difficult to keep as industries were downsized.

In 1945, the family began working in orchards in Santa Paula and a cannery in Sunnyvale. In September of that year, they moved to Madera County, where they occupied tar-paper shacks at Berenda Slough, 8 miles (13 kilometers) from Chowchilla. Subsequently, they became migrant workers within the county, pursuing an insecure lifestyle. In December 1950, Lesa moved to Chowchilla, where she remained. Links with Oklahoma gradually faded after her sister died. Then Pearl died, aged twenty-eight years, in 1948; Nellie died in 1972. All the family members are buried in Chowchilla cemetery. Eventually, Lesa had fourteen grandchildren (nine born in California), thirty-two great-grandchildren, and nine great-great-grandchildren. Today, most live near Chowchilla, but some have moved to Sacramento, while others are in Florida and Alaska. A relative documented this account when Lesa was ninety-eight.

Modern Arts

MUSIC, PAINTING, SCULPTURE, AND OTHER ARTS ARE HELPING NATIVE AMERICAN CULTURES TO SURVIVE AND ADAPT IN THE FACE OF A CHANGING CONTEMPORARY WORLD.

The last fifty years have seen a growth in Native American arts, such as pottery, painting, sculpture and carving, jewelry, quilling, basketry, and ribbonwork, not to mention music, whether it be rock, rap, or protest songs. Artisans have continued traditions, eradicated stylized romanticism, often demanded originally by white purchasers and patrons, and experimented in the use of materials and abstraction. Native American artists argue that their work is not about being Indian, but is the result of their own experiences, as articulated by Chiricahua Apache sculptor Allan Houser, although his son claimed to be a Native American artist. Whatever the attitude about Indianness, Native Americans draw inspiration from their past, and ideas from other tribes and the contemporary world.

Chanagmiut Inuit sculptor Lawrence Beck employed materials found in junkyards, industrial waste facilities, and dumpsters, much like his ancestors used driftwood and material from shipwrecks. He was fascinated by Inuit masks, worn to honor the spirits of the animals they depict. Beck used car rearview mirrors, dental mirrors, and kitchen utensils, welding them together and decorating them to create masks representing walruses, polar bears, and mosquitoes. One work, *Inukshuk*, a steel sculpture, is located outside the arrivals building at King's County International Airport in Washington.

Carving wooden masks is an important art among the tribes of the Pacific Northwest Coast, and is exemplified in the work of Kwakiutl carver James Matthew and Tsimshian Andrew Morrison. Basket weaving has been carried on for over 7,000 years, especially among the southern Cherokee, Choctaw, Chickasaw, Muskogee Creek, and the Indians of the Great Basin, eastern California, and Pacific Coast— Shoshone, Ute, Palouse, and Cayuse among others. Particularly notable is the work of Cherokee Eva

Wolfe of the Eastern Band. In the late 1950s, she realized that there were only two older women who could make double-weave baskets. Using river-cane, she learned the technique of weaving one basket inside another, *"in order that it might be retained for future generations of Cherokee craft workers."*

Indian painters are many in number, thanks to the tuition provided by Bacone College, Muskogee, Oklahoma, and the Santa Fé Institute of American Indian Arts (IAIA), and the support of organizations like the Indian Arts and Crafts Board. Among the key artists are Chippewa George Morrison and Navajo Carl Gorman. San Ildefonso Pueblo polychrome pottery is well known, the work of Maria Martinez and Nampeyo of the Hopi realizing five-figure sums at auction. What is less well known is the Native American contribution to music.

Song and music are highly important in Native American rituals, for example when planting. Stomp dances are common in the Southeast, and there are gourd, peyote, love, first food, and Sun Dance songs. Cherokee Litefoot, the first Native American rapper, started his own label, Red Vinyl Records, to distribute Indian lyrics after RCA said that Indians did not buy tapes, they bought alcohol.

Buffy Sainte-Marie, a Cree, has a PhD in fine arts from the University of Massachusetts, and has written protest songs and film scores, including the famous *Up Where We Belong* from the movie, *An Officer and a Gentleman*. She spent many years in the cast of Sesame Street. Her rationale for this project: *"I had one reason and that was to let little kids and their caretakers know that Indians exist and that we are not all dead and stuffed in museums."*

A well-known rock band, Red Thunder, has a mix of Apache, Pueblo, and Mayan members. The amusingly named jazz/reggae band Poetic Justice was created by Muskogee Creek poetess Joy Harjo, who wanted to blend music and poetry, since in Native American terms they complement each other, rather than being separate, as normally is the case in their mainstream forms. Having since split, the band had Harjo on saxophone, lawyer Susan Williams (Sisseton-Wahpeton Sioux) on drums, tribal judge Willie Bluehouse Johnson (Isleta Pueblo and Navajo) on guitar, John Williams (Susan's brother) on bass, and Frank Poocha (Hopi-Pima) on keyboards.

The most popular venues for song and dance are the powwow gatherings held througout the Native American world. Competitions are held in a drug- and alcohol-free environment. Attending the celebrations will be sellers offering ribbon shirts, shawls, drums, paintings, jewelry, leatherware, T-shirts, beadwork, books, rattles, and dresses. In addition to powwows, individual Indian nations hold their own annual ceremonies, clan gatherings, and dances.

Night Chant Ceremonial Hunt, a watercolor by renowned, award-winning Navajo artist Harrison Begay. Born in 1917, Begay studied art at the Santa Fé Indian School, then went on to study architecture at Black Mountain College in North Carolina. His work is sought after internationally.

Tribal Museums and Cultural Centers

TOWARD THE END OF THE TWENTIETH CENTURY, THE NUMBER OF TRIBAL MUSEUMS GREW AS NATIVE AMERICANS SOUGHT TO DEFINE THEIR IDENTITY AND CULTURE.

The character of museums displaying Native American artifacts and lifeways has changed over time. Thousands of museums collected Indian objects, together with the skeletal remains of many individuals. Before 1900, these were in non-Indian hands. After World War II, the U.S. government recognized that many sacred objects should be returned to tribal possession, like the Zuni war gods from the Denver Art Museum. The desire to allow Native Americans access to religious objects and sites was highlighted in the 1978 American Indian Religious Freedom Act. Legislation has encouraged the protection of historic sites, and the 1990 Native American Graves Protection and Repatriation Act requires federal institutions to return Native American human remains and artifacts to their respective peoples. This does not apply to the Smithsonian, however, although that institution has repatriated some 18,500 skeletal remains, including 756 to Alaska. The Smithsonian has also returned remains to the South Dakota Sisseton-Wahpeton Sioux, and may do the same for other tribes. Wampum belts have been sent to the Iroquois, while medicine bundles have been returned to the Navajo, Hopi, and Mohawk, as has a sacred pole to the Omaha. Other institutions, such as the University of Nebraska, have repatriated museum materials.

This more sensitive approach to Native American culture, religion, and lifestyles has been negotiated by non-Indian museums with Indians, who are now consulted about displays and museum aims. An even more significant outcome is the mushrooming number of Native American

An exhibition of Native American artifacts discovered by the Oxbow Archaelogists at the Chippewa Nature Center..

and Alaskan Native museums in the United States and Canada, from about forty in the 1980s to over 175 by 1992.

Tribally operated museums have two basic rationales. They allow groups to define their own identity and culture, and they meet the government's obligation to identify and preserve culture. Tribal museums help conserve historical sites and channel tourism, which aids the commercial development of archaeological sites. An example of this is the Makah Cultural and Research Center at Neah Bay, Washington, which has recreated Ozette Village.

The repatriation process requires a means of preserving and storing archaeological remains, which has prompted the establishment of more tribal museums. Such museums can also rekindle traditional skills, and promote old ways of passing on history and systems of belief. Museums have been helped by the Department of Commerce Economic Development Administration, which supports the construction costs of projects that focus on tourism, such as the Gila River Indian Arts and Crafts Center in Arizona. Native Americans realize that for them to control their destiny, the continuation and transfer of tribal knowledge is essential. Thus, managing culture, artifacts, archives and libraries, language, historical sites, and rituals and ceremonies is paramount.

Four basic types of museum exist. The first are tribally operated museums on reservations. These may be managed by tribal governments or advisory committees made up of community delegates. Second, there are some urban cultural and recreational centers that cover a variety of tribes. These give tourists a Native

Native Americans clothing displayed at the Hoard Historical Museum, Fort Atkinson, Wisconsin.

American perspective of history, and provide a showcase for Indian arts and crafts. The Daybreak Star Arts Center in Seattle exemplifies this type of not-for-profit, tax-exempt enterprise. A third type is a Native American controlled department located within another institution, such as the Southeast Alaska Indian Cultural Center in the U.S. National Park Service building in Sitka. Finally, a family or individually owned museum might be located on a tribal reservation. One such non-profit organization is the Lenni Lenape Historical Society in Pennsylvania.

Typically, tribal museums display prehistoric artifacts, tools, clothing, weapons, household goods, transport items, musical instruments, and ceremonial articles. Photographs and oral history recordings preserve a community's heritage, while opportunities are provided to research the museum's archives, genealogy, and linguistics. Exhibitions concerning creation myths, pre-European-contact lifestyles, art, and inter-tribal relationships are common. The wealthy Mashantucket Pequots in Connecticut will eventually possess the largest tribally owned museum in the United States, which will incorporate extensive exhibit galleries, a significant library, and archives.

Native Americans in the 21st Century

WHILE THE RECORDED POPULATION OF NATIVE AMERICANS HAS JUMPED IN RECENT YEARS, AND LIFE HAS IMPROVED FOR MANY, THERE ARE STILL ISSUES TO BE RESOLVED, NOT LEAST HEALTH AND POVERTY.

Successive U.S. census figures have differed in the ways in which they distinguish Native Americans. Since 1960, the Census Bureau has relied on self-identification to ascertain a person's race. Thus, the recorded Indian population increased from 523,591 in 1960 to 1.9 million (including Inuit and Aleut) in 1990 as more people identified themselves as Native Americans. Often, a stigma was associated with Indian racial identity, but ethnic-pride movements have helped change attitudes. In the early 1980s, the members of the 300 U.S. recognized tribes numbered approximately 900,000, so many of the people identifying themselves as Indians were not enroled in federally recognized tribes. In 1990, 53 percent of the 1.9 million were not enroled..

Indians face a problem too, in that some tribes in the United States are still seeking federal recognition, and this number may increase in the future. The Bureau of Indian Affairs normally requires a one-fourth degree of Native American blood for recognition as a tribal member. However, some tribes require a half, while others specify only a thirty-second blood quantity. Therefore, the federal government and some Indian nations differ over ethnicity.

Census 2000 showed that the U.S. population on April 1, 2000, was 281.4 million, of which 1.5 percent reported "American Indian" or "Alaska Native" as their race. Those terms refer to individuals possessing origins in any of the native peoples of North, South, or Central America, who keep their tribal affiliation or community attachment.

Another issue associated with Census 2000 was a change in the race question. Respondents were asked to report one or more races they considered themselves, or their households, to be. Thus, the data showed the race-alone population, which only acknowledged one race, and race in combination, such as American Indian and White, or Black, or Asian, etc. This meant that people could identify themselves as entirely or partially Native American. Now, 2.5 million people, or 0.9 percent of the total, reported only American Indian, but an additional 1.6 million specified American Indian plus one other race. So, 4.1 million of the U.S. population reported American Indian alone or in combination with one or more races. Comparing the Indian-alone population of 2000 with 1990, this group increased by 516,722, or 26 percent, during the decade. If the second definition is used, an increase of 2.2 million, or 11 percent, is demonstrated. Thus, between 1990 and 2000, the Native American population increase ranged from 26 to 110 percent in comparison with the rest of the United States population, which expanded by 13 percent.

The census showed 43 percent of Indians living in the West, 31 percent in the South, 17 percent in the Midwest, and 9 percent in the Northeast. The ten states with the largest Native American populations were, in order, California, Oklahoma, Arizona, Texas, New Mexico, New York, Washington, North Carolina, Michigan, and Alaska. These states included 62 percent of the total Indian population, while California and Oklahoma were home to 25 percent.

The largest Native American tribal groupings are the Cherokee, Navajo, Latin American Indian, Choctaw, Sioux, and Chippewa (Ojibwa). In Census 2000, 281,069 respondents reported Cherokee alone, while an additional 448,464 indicated Cherokee with at least one other race. Interestingly, there are many Cherokees who are not enroled in one of the three bands, which raises another issue—those who claim Native American blood, as opposed to tribally enroled Native Americans.

In Alaska, the largest tribal groupings comprise the Eskimo (Inuit), Tlingit, Haida, Alaska Athabaskan, and Aleut.

Indians have always been affected by health issues. Intestinal parasites developed with weaning caused diarrhea, dehydration, and a high child mortality rate. When Native Americans abandoned the hunter-gatherer lifestyle for agriculture, the population increased, but so did anemia because the proportion of iron in their diet diminished. Another illness was arthritis, while serious diseases included tuberculosis, syphilis, yaws, and pinta. Fever, famine, nutritional deficiencies, parasites, dysentery, and warfare also contributed to a short life expectancy. European contact caused epidemics because Native Americans possessed no resistance to the new diseases, such as measles and smallpox.

A powwow in Washington, D.C., in 1976. Such Native American cultural events are organized throughout North America, helping to maintain traditional values and educate the wider public about Indian affairs.

When forced onto crowded reservations, Indians faced new health problems, such as influenza, cholera, and meningitis. The major killer on reservations was tuberculosis, however, the main sufferers being young people between the ages of fifteen and thirty. Health suffered as wildlife was hunted out, and ranchers and farmers depleted natural food resources. Reservation populations became dependent upon government rations, which often were of poor quality. Moreover, changes in diet contributed to late-onset, or Type 2, diabetes with associated heart disease, high blood pressure, renal disease, and amputations. In addition, Native Americans had no knowledge of how to contain bacteria, how to maintain hygienic conditions, or how to isolate patients.

In World War II, some 25,000 Native American men joined the armed forces, while tens of thousands of men and women worked off-reservation to support the war effort. In the white man's environment, Indians changed their diet, while higher incomes encouraged the purchase of processed food with all its health risks. The lack of natural foods forced bodies to adapt and adjust to a potentially dangerous health situation. Diabetes increased further, with many instances of retinopathy, as did cancerous tumors and heart disease.

More recently, HIV and AIDs have contributed to death rates, while alcoholism has always stalked the unfortunate. In 1993, the Indian Health Service reported that tuberculosis mortality among Indians was 700 times greater than among the general population. Illness of spirit has resulted in a high suicide rate, especially among the Yakama.

Health-care programs are tackling the diabetes problem, and gastrointestinal diseases are decreasing, but they remain disproportionately high. The Indian Health Service has instituted sanitation and health programs on reservations, but water and sewage systems are still inadequate in many cases. The service has proven success rates in reducing diabetes and fetal alcohol syndrome, and in improving maternal and child care; community health programs tackle injuries and alcoholism while respecting cultural differences and traditions. Native Americans have developed the National Native American AIDs Prevention Center, and there are independent Indian AIDs programs. Also, funding has been made available under the 1976 Indian Health Care Improvement Act, which encourages tribes to contract with the government to generate and run their own health-care programs.

Today, the Native American population appears to be recovering. A lower mortality rate and a rise in life expectancy have augmented numbers, but death rates for some diseases remain higher than in the mass of the population. Fertility has increased too, rates being higher than in the general U.S. population. Native American women who marry other races have higher fertility rates than whites, but lower rates than those who marry Native Americans.

Native Americans are the poorest group in American society. Successive U.S. government attempts to turn reservation Indians into farmers failed. The allotment program damaged communal agricultural systems, such as irrigation, while small farms have steadily declined for all Americans during economic downturns. Thus, few Indians are employed in agriculture; instead, men tend to have manual occupations as skilled workers, or as semi-skilled industrial or unskilled labor. Indian women normally find jobs in technical fields, service, administrative support, retail sales, nursing, and teaching. Few Native Americans have joined the middle-class professions or gone into business. The income gap between Indian and white households has grown steadily, being over 40 percent less. Greater employment participation notwithstanding, Native American economic deprivation is greater than that of African-Americans. The federal government shows little concern for improving Indian living standards. Education, job experience, and skill acquisition are all essential for urban employment, and reservations need to build sustainable economic projects to generate work and incomes for residents. Unemployment is high.

A major issue facing Indians is how to apply pressure to the federal government to change the law so that long-term leases for extracting reservation resources in oil, natural gas, coal, and uranium can be renegotiated. The Organization of Petroleum Exporting Countries (OPEC), influenced by Libya's Colonel Quaddafi, quadrupled the price of oil in 1974, making Native American resources more valuable. In 1975, the Council of Energy Resource Tribes (CERT) was established to protect tribal interests. CERT helps tribes renegotiate leases, as in 1982, when the Supreme Court ruled that the New Mexico-based Jicarilla Apaches had the right to levy severance taxes on corporations extracting oil and natural gas from their reservation.

Another problem is the lack of payment of trust funds, the federal government being accused of violating its trust responsibilities. The Bureau of Indian Affairs' records are in chaos, and no one knows how much money is owed (estimated at $40 billion) to some half-million Indian trust beneficiaries. In the early part of the twenty-first century, beset by the cost of wars in Afghanistan and Iraq, the Bush adminstration appeared hell-bent on denying Native Americans an accounting of the funds that belong to them, such that many Republican and Democrat senators, and House members accused the administration of acting unconstitutionally. Some economic difficulties have been ameliorated by self-determined economic developments. Under the 1975 Indian Self-Determination and Education Assistance Act, tribal governments can augment their power by implementing strategies to develop reservation economies.

Improvements come from a variety of sources. The Maine Passamaquoddy regained lands and financial compensation in 1980, using the money to purchase trust lands. Today, the tribe is federally recognized and is a municipality in its own right. The Passamaquoddy operate blueberry farms, a casino, two radio stations, and other businesses. Tribal members receive quarterly payments (approximately $250 each) from trust-fund interest and investment dividends, and are offered jobs, new housing, free health care, and education opportunities.

In Washington State, the Yakama own the largest commercial forest in the United States, which provides 90 percent of tribal income. Profits have been poured into a furniture factory and irrigation works in the Wapato Project. Seasonal agriculture and fishing supplement incomes. Even so, depression in the lumber industry can increase unemployment and diminish economic gains. Education is provided by the Stanley Smartlowit Education Center in Toppenish. There is a tribal cultural center and a radio station, while the Yakama are proud of their bi-weekly newspaper, *The Yakama Nation Review*.

The Yakama experience has preserved the tribal language and tribal values, while the education system has helped several Yakama gain advanced degrees. The Tribal Council, made up of men and women, helps preserve traditions and old wedding rites, while Christianity coexists peacefully with the Longhouse religion.

BIBLIOGRAPHY

Berlo, Janet C., and Phillips, Ruth B., *Native North American Art*, Oxford University Press, Oxford, 1998.

Bierhorst, J., *Myths and Tales of the American Indians*, Indian Head Books, New York, 1992.

Billington, Ray Allen, *Westward Expansion: A History of the American Frontier*, Macmillan, New York, 1974.

Black, J., *War for America: The Fight for Independence, 1775–1783*, Alan Sutton, Gloucester, 1991.

Blanco, R.L., *The American Revolution, 1775–1783: An Encyclopedia* (2 volumes), Garland Publishing, Inc., New York, 1993.

Blevins, W. (ed.), *The Wordsworth Dictionary of the American West*, Wordsworth Editions, Ware, 1995.

Brine, L., *Ancient Earthworks and Temples of the American Indians*, Oracle Publishing, London, 1996.

Brown, D., *Bury My Heart at Wounded Knee*, Picador, London, 1971.

Brown, R.D., *Major Problems in the Era of the American Revolution, 1760–91*, D.C. Heath & Co., Lexington, 1992.

Burland, C., *North American Indian Mythology*, Paul Hamlyn Ltd., London, 1965.

Burland, C.A., *Peru under the Incas*, George Rainbird Ltd., London, 1967.

Caldwell, E.K., *Dreaming the Dawn: Conversations with Native Artists and Activists*, University of Nebraska, Lincoln, 1999.

Calloway, C.G., *New Worlds for All: Indians, Europeans and the Remaking of Early America*, The John Hopkins University Press, Baltimore, 1997.

Calloway, C.G., *Our Hearts Fell to the Ground: Plains Indian Views of How the West was Lost*, Bedford Books of St. Martin's Press, New York, 1996.

Calloway, C.G., *The World Turned Upside Down: Indian Voices from Early America*, Bedford Books of St. Martin's Press, New York, 1994.

Catlin, G., *Letters and Notes on the North American Indians* (M.M. Mooney, ed.), Gramercy Books, New York, 1975.

Chant, C., *The Indian Wars*, Tiger Books International, London, 1992.

Children's Atlas of Native Americans: Native Cultures of North and South America, Rand MacNally & Co., Chicago, 1992.

Coe, M., Snow. D., & Benson, E., *Atlas of Ancient America*, Facts on File, Inc., New York, 1986.

Davies, P., *The History Atlas of North America*, Macmillan, Basingstoke, 1998.

Davies, P.K., *Encyclopedia of Invasions and Conquests from Ancient Times to the Present*, ABC-Clio, Santa Barbara, 1996.

Davis, M.B. (ed.), *Native America in the Twentieth Century: An Encyclopedia*, Garland Publishing Inc., New York, 1996.

Dillon, R.H., *North American Indian Wars*, Brompton Books Corp., for Bramley Books, Greenwich, 1997.

Eyewitness Guides, *North American Indians*, Dorling Kindersley, London, 1995.

Gallay, A. (ed.), *Colonial Wars of North America, 1512–1763:*

An Encyclopedia, Garland Publishing, Inc., New York, 1996.

Galloway, P., *Choctaw Genesis: 1500–1700*, University of Nebraska Press, Lincoln, 1995.

Gilbert, M., *American History Atlas*, Weidenfeld & Nicolson, London, 1985.

Greene, J.P. & Pole, J.R. (eds.), *The Blackwell Encyclopedia of the American Revolution*, Blackwell, Oxford, 1994.

Hatley, Allen G., *The Indian Wars in Stephen F. Austin's Texas Colony, 1822–1835*, Eakin Press, Austin, 2001.

Hauptman, Laurence M., *Between Two Fires: American Indians in the Civil War*, The Free Press, New York, 1995.

Hirschfelder, A., *Artists and Craftspeople*, Facts on File, Inc., New York, 1994.

Homberger, E., *The Penguin Atlas of North America*, Penguin, New York, 1995.

Hoxie, F.E., *Encyclopedia of North American Indians*, Houghton Mifflin Co., New York, 1996.

Hurtado, A.L. & Iverson, P., *Major Problems in American Indian History*, D.C. Heath & Co., Lexington, 1994.

Johansen, B.E., *The Native Peoples of North America: A History*, Rutgers University Press, London, 2005.

Josephy, A.M., Jr., *500 Nations: An Illustrated History of North American Indians*, Alfred A. Knopf, New York, 1994.

Josephy, A.M., Jr., *Red Power: The American Indians' Fight for Freedom*, University of Nebraska Press, Lincoln, 1971.

Keegan, John, *Warpaths: Fields of Battle in Canada and America*, Vintage Canada Edition, Random House, Toronto, 1996.

Keenan, J., *Encyclopedia of American Indian Wars, 1492–1890*, ABC-Clio, Santa Barbara, 1998.

Krech III, S., *The Ecological Indian: Myth and History*, W.W. Norton, New York, 2000.

Krupat, A. (ed.), *Native American Autobiography: An Anthology*, The University of Wisconsin Press, Madison, 1994.

Kupperman, K.O., *Major Problems in American Colonial History*, D.C. Heath & Co., Lexington, 1993.

McEwan, C., Barreto, C., & Neves, E., *Unknown Amazon*, The Trustees of the British Museum, London, 2001.

McMaster, G., and Trafzer, C.E. (eds.), *Native Universe: Voices of Indian America*, National Museum of the American Indian, Smithsonian Institution, Washington, D.C., 2004.

McNaught, K., *The Penguin History of Canada*, Penguin, New York, 1988.

Magnusson, M., & Palsson, H. (eds.), *The Vinland Sagas: The Norse Discovery of America*, Penguin, New York, 1965.

Miller, M.E., *The Art of Mesoamerica from Olmec to Aztec*, Thames & Hudson, London, 1986.

Moctezuma, E.M., *The Aztecs*, Rizzoli International Publications, Inc., New York, 1989.

Nabakov, P. (ed.), *Native American Testimony: A Chronicle of Indian-White Relations from Prophecy to the Present, 1492–1992*, Penguin, New York, 1991.

Namias, J., *White Captives: Gender and Ethnicity on the American Frontier*, The University of North Carolina Press, Chapel Hill, 1993.

Parchemin, R., *The Life and History of North America's Indian Reservations*, PRC Publishing for Select Books Ltd., London, 1998.

Perdue, T., *Native Carolinians: The Indians of North Carolina*, North Carolina Department of Cultural Resources, Raleigh, 1985.

Perdue, T. (ed.), *Sifters: Native American Women's Lives*, Oxford University Press, Oxford, 2001.

Rawls, J.J., *Chief Red Fox is Dead: A History of Native Americans since 1945*, Harcourt Brace College Publishers, Fort Worth, 1996.

Rogin, M.P., *Fathers and Children: Andrew Jackson and the Subjugation of the American Indian*, Transations Publishers, New Jersey, 1991.

Starkey, A., *European and Native American Warfare, 1675–1815*, UCL Press, London, 1998.

Stierlin, H., *The Art of the Maya*, Macmillan, Basingstoke, 1981.

Tanner, H.H., *Atlas of Great Lakes Indian History*, University of Oklahoma Press, Norman, 1987.

Tanner, H.H (ed.), *The Settling of North America*, Macmillan, Basingstoke, 1995.

Taylor, C., *North American Indians*, Paragon, London, 1997.

Thomas, D.H., *Exploring Ancient Native America: An Archaeological Guide*, Routledge, Abingdon, 1999.

Thomas, D.H., *Skull Wars: Kennewick Man, Archaeology, and the Battle for Native American Identity*, Basic Books, New York, 2000.

VanDerBeets, R. (ed.), *Held Captive by Indians: Selected Narratives, 1642–1836*, The University of Tennessee, Knoxville, 1994.

Versluis, A., *Native American Traditions*, Element Books, Inc., Rockport, 1994.

Viola, H.J. (ed.), *After Columbus: The Smithsonian Chronicle of the North American Indians*, Smithsonian Institution, Washington, D.C., 1990.

Waldman, C., *Atlas of the North American Indian*, Facts on File, Inc., New York, 1985.

Wallace, A.J.C., *Jefferson and the Indians: The Tragic Fate of the First Americans*, The Belknap Press of Harvard UP, Cambridge, 1999.

Ward, G.C., *The West: An Illustrated History*, The West Book Project Inc., Boston, 1996.

Warner, J.A., *The Life and Art of the North American Indian*, Chancellor Press, London, 1997.

Wearne, P., *Return of the Indian: Conquest and Revival in the Americas*, Cassell, London, 1996.

Weber, D.J., *New Spain's Far Northern Frontier: Essays on Spain in the American West, 1540–1821*, University of New Mexico Press, Albuquerque, 1979.

Wyatt, G., *Spirit Faces: Contemporary Native American Masks from the Northwest Coast*, Thames & Hudson, London, 1994.

INDEX

Figures shown in **bold** type signify maps. Figures in *italics* refer to photographs or illustrations.

ACKNOWLEDGMENTS

For Cartographic Press
Design, Maps and Typesetting: Jeanne Radford, Malcolm Swanston and Jonathan Young

The publishers would like to thank the following picture libraries for their kind permission to use their pictures and illustrations:

Corbis   10, 13, 14, 15, 21, 23, 26, 44, 46/47, 48, 50, 51, 53, 55, 56, 59 (top), 67 (left), 67 (right), 69, 104, 109, 110, 112, 114, 115, 117, 120, 124, 134, 140, 143, 145, 148 (large), 159, 173, 179, 196, 198, 200, 221, 241, 245, 253, 256, 266, 272, 274, 275, 281, 282, 287, 294, 320 (top), 322, 328, 335 (bottom), 351, 365, 371.
Photowest   11, 54, 292, 318, 320 (bottom).
Private and On-Line sources   22, 39, 40, 42, 43, 58, 59 (bottom), 62, 63, 66, 87, 88, 89 (top), 89 (side), 90, 93, 96, 97 (top), 97 (bottom), 99 (top), 99 (bottom), 100, 102, 105, 116, 129, 130, 131, 132, 136, 138, 146, 148 (top), 154, 160 (top), 160 (bottom), 163, 167, 168, 169, 176, 178 (top), 178 (bottom), 181, 183, 184, 185, 187, 202, 208, 210, 214, 215, 224/225, 228, 230, 233, 244, 248, 257, 258, 260, 276, 277, 278 (bottom), 284, 286, 288, 302, 303, 304, 305, 306, 309, 312, 313, 316, 327, 329, 330, 331 (top), 331 (bottom), 332, 335 (top), 337, 339, 345, 347, 365, 374, 382.
Rochester Museum and Science Center, Rochester, New York   31.
Library of Congress   33, 83, 216, 217, 259, 262, 265, 289, 300, 301, 310, 315, 326, 363.
Bildersburg, Hamburg   77.
Indiana University   79.
National Archive of Canada   85.
Getty Images   103, 234, 236, 267, 278 (top).
Bibliotheque des Arts, Paris   128.
Nacket Visitors Center   167.
Smithsonian Institute   175, 296, 307, 317, 346, 377.
Tippecaneo County Historical Association, Laffayette, Indiana   190.
Yale University   205.
Collection of Glenn and Lorraine Myers   212.
Washington University Art Gallery   222.
Denver Public Library   298, 299, 311.
Colorado Historical Society   299 (top).
National Archives and Records Administration (USA)   321, 359,
Nevada Historical Society   375.
Philbrook Museum of Art, Tulsa, Oklahoma   381.
Hoard Historical Museum, Fort Atkinson Historical Society, Wisconsin   383.
Christian F. Feest, Allenstadt, Germany   387.

Every effort had been made to contact the copyright holders for images reproduced in this book.
Any omissions are entirely unintentional, and the details should be addressed to Quantum Publishing.